Lecture Notes in Computer Science 11975

Founding Editors

Gerhard Goos
Karlsruhe Institute of Technology, Karlsruhe, Germany
Juris Hartmanis
Cornell University, Ithaca, NY, USA

Editorial Board Members

Elisa Bertino
Purdue University, West Lafayette, IN, USA
Wen Gao
Peking University, Beijing, China
Bernhard Steffen⬤
TU Dortmund University, Dortmund, Germany
Gerhard Woeginger⬤
RWTH Aachen, Aachen, Germany
Moti Yung
Columbia University, New York, NY, USA

More information about this series at http://www.springer.com/series/7410

Jae Hong Seo (Ed.)

Information Security and Cryptology – ICISC 2019

22nd International Conference
Seoul, South Korea, December 4–6, 2019
Revised Selected Papers

 Springer

Editor
Jae Hong Seo
Hanyang University
Seoul, Korea (Republic of)

ISSN 0302-9743 ISSN 1611-3349 (electronic)
Lecture Notes in Computer Science
ISBN 978-3-030-40920-3 ISBN 978-3-030-40921-0 (eBook)
https://doi.org/10.1007/978-3-030-40921-0

LNCS Sublibrary: SL4 – Security and Cryptology

This Springer imprint is published by the registered company Springer Nature Switzerland AG
The registered company address is: Gewerbestrasse 11, 6330 Cham, Switzerland

Preface

The 22nd International Conference on Information Security and Cryptology (ICISC 2019) was held in Seoul, South Korea, during December 4–6, 2019. This year's conference was hosted by the KIISC (Korea Institute of Information Security and Cryptology).

The aim of this conference was to provide an international forum for the latest results of research, development, and applications within the field of information security and cryptology. This year, we received 43 submissions and were able to accept 19 papers, including 1 merged paper, resulting in 18 presentations at the conference. The challenging review and selection processes were successfully conducted by Program Committee (PC) members and external reviewers via the EasyChair review system. For transparency, it is worth noting that each paper underwent a blind review by at least three PC members, in most cases, and at least four PC members for cases in which a PC member co-authored. Furthermore, for resolving conflicts concerning the reviewer's decisions, individual review reports were open to all PC members, followed by detailed interactive discussions on each paper. For the LNCS post-proceedings, the authors of selected papers had a few weeks to prepare their final versions, based on the comments received from the reviewers.

The conference featured four invited talks: "Information Security in Quantum Time" by Lily Chen, "Practical Applications of Homomorphic Encryption" by Miran Kim, "Lattice-Based Zero-Knowledge Proofs: Shorter and Faster Constructions and Applications" by Ron Steinfeld, and "Secure and Verifiable Computation" by Huaxiong Wang. We thank the invited speakers for their kind acceptances and respectable presentations. We would like to thank all authors who submitted their papers to ICISC 2019, as well as all PC members. It was a truly wonderful experience to work with such talented and hard-working researchers. We also appreciate the external reviewers for assisting the PC members.

Finally, we would like to thank all attendees for their active participation and the organizing members who successfully managed this conference.

December 2019   Jae Hong Seo

Organization

General Chairs

Hyun sook Cho   National Security Research Institute, South Korea
Kyung-Hyune Rhee   Pukyoung National University, South Korea

Organizing Chair

Changhoon Lee   Seoul National University of Science and Technology, South Korea

Organizing Committee

Jin Kwak	Ajou University, South Korea
Taekyoung Kwon	Yonsei University, South Korea
Young-Gab Kim	Sejong University, South Korea
Woo Hwan Kim	NSR, South Korea
Howon Kim	Pusan National University, South Korea
HeeSeok Kim	Korea University, South Korea
Ki Hyo Nam	UMLogics Ltd., South Korea
Haeryong Park	KISA, South Korea
Seog Chung Seo	Kookmin University, South Korea
Seung-Hyun Seo	Hanyang University, South Korea
Hwajeong Seo	Hansung University, South Korea
Mun Kyu Lee	Inha University, South Korea
Jeong Hyeon Lee	Soongsil University, South Korea
Jong-Hyouk Lee	Sangmyung University, South Korea
Dooho Choi	ETRI, South Korea
Seokhie Hong	Korea University, South Korea
Junbeom Hur	Korea University, South Korea

Program Committee Chair

Jae Hong Seo   Hanyang University, South Korea

Program Committee

Joonsang Baek	University of Wollongong, Australia
Olivier Blazy	Université de Limoges, France
Jonathan Bootle	IBM Research Zürich, Switzerland
Donghoon Chang	IIIT Delhi, India

Keita Emura	National Institute of Information and Communications Technology, Japan
Deukjo Hong	Chonbuk National University, South Korea
Dong-Chan Kim	Kookmin University, South Korea
Dongseong Kim	The University of Queensland, Australia
Huy Kang Kim	Korea University, South Korea
Jihye Kim	Kookmin University, South Korea
Myungsun Kim	The University of Suwon, South Korea
Taechan Kim	NTT, Japan
Taekyoung Kwon	Yonsei University, South Korea
Pascal Lafourcade	University Clermont Auvergne, France
Hyang-Sook Lee	Ewha Womans University, South Korea
Jooyoung Lee	Korea Advanced Institute of Science and Technology, South Korea
Iraklis Leontiadis	Inpher, Switzerland
Khoa Nguyen	Nanyang Technological University, Singapore
Daehun Nyang	Inha University, South Korea
Jong Hwan Park	Sangmyung University, South Korea
Josef Pieprzyk	CSIRO/Data61, Australia
Kui Ren	University at Buffalo, State University of New York, USA
Hwajeong Seo	Hansung University, South Korea
Daniel Slamanig	Austrian Institute of Technology (AIT), Austria
Shi-Feng Sun	Monash University, Australia
Qiang Tang	New Jersey Institute of Technology, USA
Wenling Wu	Chinese Academy of Sciences, China
Toshihiro Yamauchi	Okayama University, Japan
Dae Hyun Yum	Myongji University, South Korea
Aaram Yun	Ewha Womans University, South Korea

Additional Reviewers

Chen, Long	Pang, Bo
Chung, Heewon	Park, Jeongeun
Gerault, David	Perez, Octavio
Hasan, Munawar	Ramacher, Sebastian
Haslhofer, Bernhard	Sarkar, Santanu
Jati, Arpan	Song, Kyunghwan
Kim, Jeongsu	Sui, Han
Kim, Taechan	Xue, Haiyang
Koscina, Mirko	Yamada, Shota
Lee, Jiwon	Zhang, Kai
Lee, Seungwha	Zhang, Lei
Mollimard, Victor	Zheng, Yafei
Önen, Melek	

Contents

Revised Version of Block Cipher CHAM

Dongyoung Roh[⊠], Bonwook Koo, Younghoon Jung, Il Woong Jeong,
Dong-Geon Lee, Daesung Kwon, and Woo-Hwan Kim

The Affiliated Institute of ETRI, Daejeon, Republic of Korea
{dyroh,bwkoo,sky1236,iw98jeong,guneez,ds_kwon,whkim5}@nsr.re.kr

Abstract. CHAM is a family of lightweight block ciphers published in
2017 [22]. The CHAM family consists of three ciphers, CHAM-64/128,
CHAM-128/128, and CHAM-128/256. CHAM can be implemented with
a remarkably low area in hardware compared to other lightweight block
ciphers, and it also performs well on software. We found new (related-
key) differential characteristics and differentials of CHAM using a SAT
solver. Although attacks using the new characteristics are limited to the
reduced rounds of CHAM, it is preferable to increase the number of
rounds to ensure a sufficient security margin. The numbers of rounds of
CHAM-64/128, CHAM-128/128, and CHAM-128/256 are increased from
80 to 88, 80 to 112, and 96 to 120, respectively. We provide strong evidence that CHAM with these new numbers of rounds is secure enough
against (related-key) differential cryptanalysis. Because increasing the
number of rounds does not affect the area in low-area hardware implementations, the revised CHAM is still excellent in lightweight hardware
implementations. In software, the revised CHAM is still comparable to
SPECK, one of the top-ranked algorithms in software.

Keywords: Lightweight block cipher · CHAM · (Related-key)
Differential cryptanalysis · SAT solver

1 Introduction

Designing a secure cryptographic algorithm that can operate efficiently on small
computing devices is a very challenging problem in cryptography. In particular,
many block ciphers have been proposed in the area of symmetric-key cryptography to solve this problem: PRESENT [10], CLEFIA [30], KATAN/KTANTAN
[12], PRINTCIPHER [21], LED [18], PRINCE [11], SIMON/ SPECK [4], LEA
[20], MIDORI [2], SPARX [15], SKINNY [7], GIFT [3], CHAM [22], etc.

Of these block ciphers, CHAM, a family of lightweight block ciphers designed
in 2017, has realized a remarkably low hardware area implementation. The family
consists of three variants, CHAM-64/128, CHAM-128/128, and CHAM-128/256.
Specifically, CHAM-64/128 can be implemented using 665 GE on the IBM 130 nm
library, which is much lower than the implementation area of SIMON, one of
the lowest area block ciphers in hardware. The family also shows competitive

© Springer Nature Switzerland AG 2020
J. H. Seo (Ed.): ICISC 2019, LNCS 11975, pp. 1–19, 2020.
https://doi.org/10.1007/978-3-030-40921-0_1

efficiency in terms of software implementation. It has performance comparable to that of SPECK, one of the best-performing lightweight block ciphers in software.

Our Contribution. The contributions of this paper are twofold. First, new (related-key) differential attacks on the round-reduced CHAM are presented. Secondly, we propose a revisison of CHAM with new numbers of rounds to ensure a sufficient security margin and evaluate its performance on both hardware and software.

First, we find (related-key) differential characteristics using the framework of Mouha et al. [27]. We convert the problem of finding them into a Boolean satisfiability problem and then solve this problem using a SAT solver, finding 39- and 62-round differential characteristics of CHAM-64/128 and CHAM-128/k, respectively. We also found 47-round related-key differential characteristics of all variants of CHAM. Next, we find differentials using multiple differential characteristics with the same input and output differences. In this case, we found 44- and 67-round differentials of CHAM-64/128 and CHAM-128/k, respectively. Note that we could not find any related-key differentials longer than 47 rounds. Finally, (related-key) differential attacks on CHAM using the newly found differentials and (related-key) differential characteristics are presented.[1] Specifically, there are (related-key) differential attacks on 56, 72, and 78 rounds of CHAM-64/128, CHAM-128/128, and CHAM-128/256, respectively. All of our results are listed in Tables 1 and 2.

Table 1. (Related-key) Differential characteristics and differentials of CHAM

Variant	Class	Round	Prob.	Reference
CHAM-64/128	Differential characteristic	36	2^{-63}	[22]
	Differential characteristic	39	2^{-63}	This paper
	Differential[a]	44	$2^{-62.19}$	This paper
	RK differential characteristic	34	2^{-61}	[22]
	RK differential characteristic	47	2^{-57}	This paper
CHAM-128/k	Differential characteristic	45	2^{-125}	[22]
	Differential characteristic	62	2^{-126}	This paper
	Differential[a]	67	$2^{-125.54}$	This paper
CHAM-128/128	RK differential characteristic	33	2^{-125}	[22]
	RK differential characteristic	47	2^{-120}	This paper
CHAM-128/256	RK differential characteristic	40	2^{-127}	[22]
	RK differential characteristic	47	2^{-121}	This paper

[a]Differential that starts from the odd round

---

[1] The detailed description of the attacks are omitted due to the page limit. Note that the attacks are designed from the designer's point of view, not from the attacker's point of view. Thus there is room for disagreement as to the feasibility of the attacks, since the situation has been set in favor of the attacker.

Table 2. (Related-key) Differential cryptanalysis on CHAM

Cipher	Attack type	Attacked rounds
CHAM-64/128	Related-key differential cryptanalysis	56
CHAM-128/128	Differential cryptanalysis	72
CHAM-128/256	Differential cryptanalysis	78

Next, we provide new numbers of rounds of CHAM considering the newly found (related-key) differential attacks (see Table 3). We provide strong evidence that the revised CHAM provides a sufficient security margin against (related-key) differential attacks.

Table 3. Numbers of rounds of CHAM

Block/key sizes	64/128	128/128	128/256
Original CHAM	80	80	96
Revised CHAM	88	112	120

Finally, the implementation results of the revised CHAM are given. On hardware, the area-optimized implementation results are given in Table 4. There is almost no change between the area of the original CHAM and the revised CHAM. Specifically, the revised CHAM-64/128 can be implemented in less than 70% of the area of SIMON-64/128. Table 5 outlines the software implementation results. The revised CHAM still outperforms SIMON and is comparable to SPECK.

Table 4. Area-optimized hardware implementation results - GE (IBM 130 nm)

Cipher	64/128	128/128	128/256	Reference
Revised CHAM	665	1,057	1,179	This paper
Original CHAM	665	1,057	1,180	[22]
SIMON	958	1,234	1,782	[4]
SPECK	996	1,280	1,840	[4]

Related Work. To mount a differential cryptanalysis [8] on block ciphers, it is necessary to find a good differential characteristic. There are two notable methods by which to find the differential characteristics of ARX ciphers, [9] and [27]. Biryukov and Velichkov extended Matsui's branch-and-bound algorithm [25], originally proposed for DES-like ciphers, to the class of ARX ciphers by introducing the concept of a partial difference distribution table (pDDT) [9]. Their approach was successfully applied to the block ciphers TEA [33], XTEA [28], SPECK [4], and RAIDEN [29]. Meanwhile, Mouha and Preneel used a SAT solver to find the optimal differential characteristics for ARX ciphers [27].

Table 5. Software efficiency comparison - *rank* metric [5] (Larger is better)

Scenario	Cipher	Atmega128	MSP430	Reference
Fixed key [5]	Revised CHAM-64/128	25.4	45.1	This paper
	Original CHAM-64/128	28.0	49.3	[22]
	SPECK-64/128	29.8	50.0	[4]
	SIMON-64/128	13.6	20.2	[4]
	Revised CHAM-128/128	12.4	18.1	This paper
	Original CHAM-128/128	17.1	25.0	[22]
	SPECK-128/128	12.7	21.7	[4]
	SIMON-128/128	3.5	3.4	[4]
Communication [13, 14] (without decryption)	Revised CHAM-64/128	6.6	10.3	This paper
	Original CHAM-64/128	7.2	11.1	[22]
	SPECK-64/128	6.3	9.7	FELICS website
	SIMON-64/128	3.0	4.7	FELICS website

Once a good differential is found, it becomes necessary to mount a key-recovery attack using the differential. Traditional key-recovery techniques (called counting techniques) were introduced with the development of differential cryptanalysis [8]; these represent the most widely used techniques. Meanwhile, Dinur improved differential attacks on SPECK using a non-traditional key-recovery technique [16]. It was based on an enumeration framework that tests suggestions for the key that are calculated by a sub-cipher attack, generalizing an earlier algebraic-based framework [1]. Recently, Song et al. [31] demonstrated differential attacks on SPECK and LEA by combining two earlier techniques [16, 27].

Notation. We will denote by $x \oplus y$ the bit-wise exclusive OR (XOR) of bit strings x and y. Let $x \boxplus y$ denote the addition of a word x and a word y modulo 2^w, and let $x \lll i$ denote the rotation of a w-bit word x to the left by i bits.

Paper Organization. The outline of the paper is as follows. We provide a brief description of CHAM and present the corresponding new numbers of rounds in Sect. 2. Section 3 describes the manner by which the (related-key) differential characteristics and differentials of CHAM are found. In Sect. 4, we analyze the security of the revised CHAM and show that it provides a sufficient security margin. Section 5 provides details about the hardware and software implementation results. Finally, Sect. 6 concludes the paper.

2   Revised Version of CHAM

In this section, we give a short description of CHAM and define the corresponding new numbers of rounds. CHAM is a family of block ciphers with a 4-branch generalized Feistel structure. Each cipher is denoted by CHAM-n/k, where n and k are the block size and key size, respectively. Table 6 shows the list of ciphers in the family and their parameters. Here, w denotes the bit length of a branch (word), and r_{old} and r represent the original number of rounds and the new number of rounds, respectively.

Table 6. List of CHAM ciphers and their parameters

Cipher	n	k	w	r_{old}	r
CHAM-64/128	64	128	16	80	88
CHAM-128/128	128	128	32	80	112
CHAM-128/256	128	256	32	96	120

By applying r iterations of the key-dependent round function, CHAM-n/k encrypts a plaintext of four w-bit words (x_0, y_0, z_0, w_0) to a ciphertext of four w-bit words (x_r, y_r, z_r, w_r). For $0 \le i < r$, the i-th round outputs

$$(x_{i+1}, y_{i+1}, z_{i+1}, w_{i+1})$$
$$\longleftarrow \left(y_i, z_i, w_i, \left((x_i \oplus i) \boxplus \left((y_i \lll \alpha_i) \oplus rk_{i \bmod 2k/w}\right)\right) \lll \beta_i\right),$$

where $\alpha_i = 1$ and $\beta_i = 8$ when i is even and $\alpha_i = 8$ and $\beta_i = 1$ when i is odd and $rk_{i \bmod 2k/w}$ is the round key.

The key schedule of CHAM-n/k takes a secret key of k/w w-bit words $K[0]$, $K[1]$, $\cdots$, $K[k/w - 1]$ and generates $2k/w$ w-bit round keys rk_0, rk_1, $\cdots$, $rk_{2k/w-1}$. The round keys are generated as follows:

$$rk_i \longleftarrow K[i] \oplus (K[i] \lll 1) \oplus (K[i] \lll 8),$$
$$rk_{(i+k/w)\oplus 1} \longleftarrow K[i] \oplus (K[i] \lll 1) \oplus (K[i] \lll 11),$$

where $0 \le i < k/w$.

The structure of the round function of CHAM is depicted in Fig. 1.

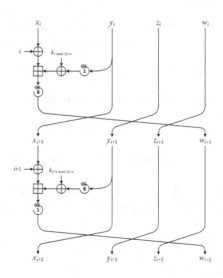

Fig. 1. Two consecutive rounds beginning with the even i-th round

3   Search for (Related-Key) Differential Characteristics and Differentials

This section presents the method by which we search for the (related-key) differential characteristics and differentials of CHAM. We convert the problem of finding them to Boolean satisfiability problems assuming all the operations in the cipher are independent, after which we solve the Boolean satisfiability problems using a SAT solver.

Note that because the SAT problem is NP-complete, only algorithms with exponential worst-case complexity are known in this case. Nevertheless, efficient and scalable algorithms solving the SAT problem are developed continuously. Typical examples are MiniSAT [17], ManySAT [19], and CryptoMiniSat [32]. Among these solvers, we use CryptoMiniSat because multi-threaded operations are possible, XOR clauses are supported, and multiple solutions to a given SAT problem can be obtained.

3.1   Search for Differential Characteristics

Here, we describe how to convert the problem of finding differential characteristics for CHAM to a Boolean satisfiability problem.

It is enough to show how to convert the problem of calculating differential probability of an addition modulo 2^w to a Boolean satisfiability problem, since addition is the only non-linear operations for CHAM. Let $\mathrm{xdp}^+(\alpha, \beta \to \gamma)$ be the XOR-differential probability of addition modulo 2^w, with input differences α and β and an output difference γ. In [24], it is proved that the differential $(\alpha, \beta \to \gamma)$ is valid if and only if

$$\mathsf{eq}(\alpha \ll 1, \beta \ll 1, \gamma \ll 1) \wedge (\alpha \oplus \beta \oplus \gamma \oplus (\beta \ll 1)) = 0, \qquad (1)$$

where $\mathsf{eq}(x, y, z) := (\neg x \oplus y) \wedge (\neg x \oplus z)$. For every valid differential $(\alpha, \beta \to \gamma)$, we define the weight $w(\alpha, \beta \to \gamma)$ of the differential as follows:

$$w(\alpha, \beta \to \gamma) := -\log_2\left(\mathrm{xdp}^+(\alpha, \beta \to \gamma)\right).$$

The weight of a valid differential can then be calculated as:

$$w(\alpha, \beta \to \gamma) = h^*\left(\neg\mathsf{eq}\left(\alpha, \beta, \gamma\right)\right),$$

where $h^*(x)$ denotes the number of non-zero bits in x not containing the most significant bit.

First, we convert the bitwise conditional equation of (1) into a Boolean satisfiability problem to obtain a valid differential (see [23]). Then we calculate the probability of the valid differential. We need to count the number of non-zero bits in a certain word, not containing the most significant bit of it, to calculate the differential probability of a round. Then, it is necessary to sum the log value of differential probability of each round to obtain the differential probability of a differential characteristic.[2] To do this, we have to convert a normal addition operation to a Boolean satisfiability problem. This can be efficiently achieved using a full adder, where $[s, o] = \text{FullAdder}(x, y, i)$ with

$$s = x \oplus y \oplus i \quad \text{and} \quad o = (x \wedge y) \vee (x \wedge i) \vee (y \wedge i).$$

In addition, the following conditions are added to ensure an efficient search for differential characteristics. Suppose that we want to find an i-round differential characteristic of CHAM with probability 2^{-p}. Additionally, assume that the best j-round differential characteristic is 2^{-p_j} for every $1 \leq j < i$. This means that there are no j-round differential characteristics with a probability greater than 2^{-p_j}. First, we added CNF formulas such that the sum of the log values of differential probabilities from the first round to the j-th round is less than or equal to $-p_j$ for every $1 \leq j < i$. And the sum of the log values of differential probabilities from the first round to the $2j$-th round should be greater than or equal to $-p + p_{i-2j}$ for every $1 < 2j < i$ due to the repeating structure arising for every two rounds of CHAM. CNF formulas that represent the conditions above are also added.

At this point, we can convert an equation to find a differential characteristic into a CNF similar to an earlier framework [27]. We then invoke a SAT solver, CryptoMiniSat, to solve the CNF.

Using this framework, we found a 39-round differential characteristic with a probability of 2^{-63} of CHAM-64/128 and a 62-round differential characteristic with a probability of 2^{-126} of CHAM-128/k. We also found a 47-round related-key differential characteristic on each case of CHAM-64/128, CHAM-128/128, and CHAM-128/256. The search results of the differential characteristics and the related-key differential characteristics of CHAM are summarized in Tables 7 and 8, respectively.

3.2 Search for Differentials

When mounting a differential attack on a block cipher, only the input and output differences of a differential are needed, meaning that the internal differences after each round of the differential are not. To compute the differential probability more accurately, it is necessary to find more characteristics with the same input and output differences. Once a good differential characteristic is obtained, we fix the input and output differences and search for characteristics with probabilities less than or equal to that of the differential characteristic obtained. We then sum the probabilities of all of these characteristics to obtain the differential probability of the differential.

For CHAM-64/128, from a 44-round differential characteristic with a probability of 2^{-73}, we obtain the corresponding differential with a probability greater than $2^{-62.19}$. For CHAM-128/k, from a 67-round differential characteristic with a

---

[2] Since we have assumed that all additions in the block cipher are independent of each other with regard to the XOR-difference, we multiply the differential probabilities of all additions to compute the differential probability of a differential characteristic.

Table 7. Differential characteristics and differentials of the revised CHAM

n/k	Type	Rounds	Input difference
		Prob.	Output difference
64/128	DC^a	39	(0102 0280 0000 0400)
		2^{-63}	(0100 0281 0002 0000)
	D^{b,c}	44	(4000 8040 00A0 0000)
		$2^{-62.19}$	(0001 8100 0001 0200)
128/k	DC^a	62	(08000000 04000000 000C0800 00020008)
		2^{-126}	(04000002 00040001 00000800 00000400)
	D^{b,c}	67	(0001000C 08000000 04000000 000C0800)
		$2^{-125.54}$	(08000004 00180002 00000000 00000010)

^{a} Differential characteristic
^{b} Differential
^{c} Differential that starts from the odd round

Table 8. Related-key differential characteristics of the revised CHAM

n/k	Rounds	Key difference
	Prob.	Input difference
		Output difference
64/128	47	(0000 0000 3251 A938 0000 0000 100F A463)
	2^{-57}	(0000 0000 0000 83E0)
		(F8C3 0000 0000 0000)
128/128	47	(00000000 00000000 24924925 24924925)
	2^{-120}	(00000000 00000000 00000000 FFFFFF25)
		(FFFFF925 00000000 00000000 00000000)
128/256	47	(00000000 00000000 5BEE1236 00800000 00000000 00000000 B5DC246C 6AB848D9)
	2^{-121}	(00000000 00000000 00000000 81100000)
		(3EC7091F 00000000 00000000 00000000)

probability of 2^{-138}, we obtain the corresponding differential with a probability greater than $2^{-125.54}$. The probability calculations of the differentials are shown in Figs. 2 and 3. The search results of the differentials of CHAM are summarized in Table 7.

However, for a given related-key differential characteristic, there are few other related-key differential characteristics that have an identical key difference, input difference, and output difference. Therefore, it appears to be impossible to find a related-key differential longer than the related-key differential characteristics previously found.

4   Security Analysis

In this section, we analyze the security of CHAM and show that the revised CHAM provides a sufficient security margin. Essentially, we follow an earlier

Weight	# sols	$\log_2 \Pr$	$\log_2 \sum_{acc}$
73	1	-73.00	-73.00
74	3	-72.42	-71.68
75	14	-71.20	-70.42
76	62	-70.05	-69.22
77	191	-69.43	-68.32
78	666	-68.63	-67.47
79	2,021	-68.02	-66.72
80	5,906	-67.48	-66.05
81	16,754	-66.97	-65.44
82	44,796	-66.55	-64.89
83	118,204	-66.15	-64.39
84	298,296	-65.82	-63.93
85	734,542	-65.52	-63.52
86	1,769,672	-65.25	-63.14
87	4,139,425	-65.02	-62.79
88	9,502,181	-64.83	-62.48
89	21,358,296	-64.66	-62.19

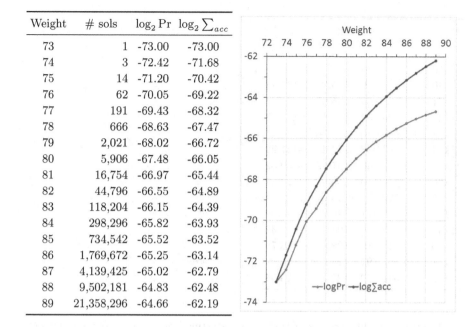

Fig. 2. A 44-round differential of CHAM-64/128 starting from the odd round, $(4000\ 8040\ 00A0\ 0000)_x \longrightarrow (0001\ 8100\ 0001\ 0200)_x$

analysis [22] except for the attacks related to (related-key) differential characteristics.

Table 9 shows the maximum numbers of rounds of characteristics for each attack that was found. Only the numbers of rounds of characteristics for some attacks using (related-key) differential characteristics have changed, while all the others are identical to those in the aforementioned study [22]. The (related-key) differential characteristics can be found in Sect. 3 and the features of the related-key boomerang characteristics and the (related-key) differential-linear approximations can be found in Appendix B.

Tables 10 and 11 depict the maximum probabilities of the differential characteristics and related-key differential characteristics for various rounds, respectively. For example, the maximum probability of a 39-round differential characteristic of CHAM-64/128 is 2^{-63}. This means that there is a 39-round differential characteristic with a probability of 2^{-63}, while there are no 39-round differential characteristics with a probability greater than 2^{-63} under the assumption that every operation in CHAM is independent of each other. This is apparent considering that the CNF formula to find a 39-round differential characteristic with a probability greater than 2^{-63} is unsatisfiable.

Table 10 indicates that there are no 40-round differential characteristics of CHAM-64/128 with a probability greater than 2^{-64}. When we examine the decreasing trend of the differential probability according to the number of rounds

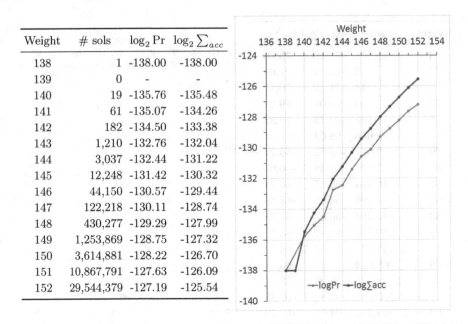

Weight	# sols	$\log_2 \Pr$	$\log_2 \sum_{acc}$
138	1	-138.00	-138.00
139	0	-	-
140	19	-135.76	-135.48
141	61	-135.07	-134.26
142	182	-134.50	-133.38
143	1,210	-132.76	-132.04
144	3,037	-132.44	-131.22
145	12,248	-131.42	-130.32
146	44,150	-130.57	-129.44
147	122,218	-130.11	-128.74
148	430,277	-129.29	-127.99
149	1,253,869	-128.75	-127.32
150	3,614,881	-128.22	-126.70
151	10,867,791	-127.63	-126.09
152	29,544,379	-127.19	-125.54

Fig. 3. A 67-round differential of CHAM-128/k starting from the odd round, $(0001000C$ $08000000\ 04000000\ 000C0800)_x \longrightarrow (08000004\ 00180002\ 00000000\ 00000010)_x$

of CHAM-128/k, it can be strongly contended that there are no 34-round differential characteristics with probabilities greater than 2^{-64}. Hence, there appears to be no 68-round differential characteristics with a probability greater than 2^{-128}. Furthermore, when we examine the trend of the differential probability and that of related-key differential probability of CHAM-128/k, it appears that there are no 68-round related-key differential characteristics with a probability greater than 2^{-128}.

Considering not only existing attacks but also unknown attacks that may exist, we set the numbers of rounds of the revised CHAM conservatively, as follows.

– CHAM-64/128: We know that there are no 40-round differential characteristics and there is a 47-round related-key differential characteristic. Moreover, it appears to be impossible to obtain a related-key differential longer than 47 rounds using the probability gathering technique. In the key-recovery phase of an attack, one can mount at most 16 more rounds than the differential due to the order of round keys in the key schedule.[3] Therefore, it is expected that one cannot mount an attack on more than 63 rounds of CHAM-64/128. Note that the best attack found here is a 56-round related-key differential attack.

---

[3] The value 16 is obtained by considering only the structure of the key schedule, but not the complexity of an attack. However, considering the complexity of the attack, the 16-round key-recovery attack appears to be impossible.

Table 9. Numbers of rounds of the best discovered characteristics for each cipher and cryptanalysis

n/k	DC	RDC	LC	BC	RBC	IDC	ZCLC	DLC	RDLC	IC	RXDC
64/128	39	**47**	34	35	41	18	21	35	36	16	16
128/128	**62**	47	40	47	46	15	18	45	43	16	23
128/256	**62**	47	40	47	42	15	18	45	45	16	23

- (R)DC: (Related-key) Differential Cryptanalysis
- LC: Linear Cryptanalysis
- (R)BC: (Related-key) Boomerang Cryptanalysis
- IDC: Impossible Differential Cryptanalysis
- ZCLC: Zero-Correlation Linear Cryptanalysis
- (R)DLC: (Related-key) Differential-Linear Cryptanalysis
- IC: Integral Cryptanalysis
- RXDC: Rotational-XOR-Differential Cryptanalysis

Table 10. Maximum probabilities of differential characteristics of CHAM for various rounds

Rounds	1	2	3	4	5	6	7	8	9	10
CHAM-64/128	1	1	1	1	2^{-1}	2^{-1}	2^{-2}	2^{-3}	2^{-4}	2^{-5}
CHAM-128/k	1	1	1	2^{-1}	2^{-1}	2^{-2}	2^{-2}	2^{-3}	2^{-4}	2^{-5}
Rounds	**11**	**12**	**13**	**14**	**15**	**16**	**17**	**18**	**19**	**20**
CHAM-64/128	2^{-6}	2^{-7}	2^{-8}	2^{-9}	2^{-11}	2^{-14}	2^{-15}	2^{-16}	2^{-19}	2^{-21}
CHAM-128/k	2^{-7}	2^{-8}	2^{-9}	2^{-11}	2^{-13}	2^{-15}	2^{-17}	2^{-18}	2^{-21}	2^{-24}
Rounds	**21**	**22**	**23**	**24**	**25**	**26**	**27**	**28**	**29**	**30**
CHAM-64/128	2^{-23}	2^{-25}	2^{-28}	2^{-30}	2^{-32}	2^{-34}	2^{-38}	2^{-39}	2^{-41}	2^{-43}
CHAM-128/k	2^{-25}	2^{-28}	2^{-30}	2^{-33}	2^{-35}	2^{-39}	2^{-43}	2^{-46}	2^{-48}	2^{-53}
Rounds	**31**	**32**	**33**	**34**	**35**	**36**	**37**	**38**	**39**	**40**
CHAM-64/128	2^{-46}	2^{-48}	2^{-49}	2^{-51}	2^{-55}	2^{-56}	2^{-58}	2^{-60}	2^{-63}	$< 2^{-63}$
CHAM-128/k	2^{-57}									

- CHAM-128/128: We know that there is a 62-round differential characteristic and a 67-round differential. On the other hand, there appears to be no 68-round (related-key) differential characteristics, as noted earlier. It appears that the probability gathering technique results in a longer differential by approximately five rounds compared to the longest differential characteristic. In the key-recovery phase of an attack, one can mount at most eight more rounds than the differential due to the order of round keys in the key schedule. Therefore, it is likely that one cannot mount an attack on more than 80 rounds of CHAM-128/128. Note that the best attack found here is a 72-round differential attack.

Table 11. Maximum probabilities of related-key differential characteristics of CHAM for various rounds

Rounds	1	2	3	4	5	6	7	8	9	10
CHAM-64/128	1	1	1	1	1	1	1	1	1	1
CHAM-128/128	1	1	1	1	1	1	2^{-1}	2^{-3}	2^{-4}	2^{-5}
CHAM-128/256	1	1	1	1	1	1	1	1	1	1
Rounds	11	12	13	14	15	16	17	18	19	20
CHAM-64/128	2^{-1}	2^{-1}	2^{-2}	2^{-2}	2^{-4}	2^{-7}	2^{-9}	2^{-11}	2^{-13}	2^{-15}
CHAM-128/128	2^{-6}	2^{-7}	2^{-8}	2^{-9}	2^{-11}	2^{-13}	2^{-14}	2^{-17}	2^{-20}	2^{-23}
CHAM-128/256	2^{-1}	2^{-1}	2^{-2}	2^{-3}	2^{-5}	2^{-9}	2^{-11}	2^{-13}	2^{-17}	2^{-19}
Rounds	21	22	23							
CHAM-64/128	2^{-17}	2^{-19}	2^{-23}							
CHAM-128/128	2^{-25}	2^{-28}	2^{-31}							

- CHAM-128/256: The analysis for CHAM-128/256 is very similar to that for CHAM-128/128. The only difference is that one can mount at most 12 more rounds than the differential in the key-recovery phase of an attack. Therefore, it appears that one cannot mount an attack on more than 88 rounds on CHAM-128/256. Note that the best attack found in this case is a 78-round differential attack.

Based on the above arguments, the numbers of rounds of the revised CHAM-64/128, CHAM-128/128, and CHAM-128/256 are set to 88, 112, and 120, respectively, resulting in a security margin of approximately 30%.

5   Hardware and Software Implementations

In this section, we present the hardware and software implementation results of the revised CHAM.

5.1   Hardware Implementation

We use the same hardware architectures and the same environment used in the earlier work [22], except for the numbers of rounds. The implementation results show that the change in the hardware area is negligible and that only the throughput becomes slightly slower due to the increased numbers of rounds. Table 12 shows the hardware implementation results of CHAM and several other ciphers. On average, the revised CHAM can be implemented with an area amounting to 75% of that of SIMON.

Table 12. Hardware implementations results

n/k	Cipher	Bit-serial		Round-based		Tech.	Ref.
		Area[a]	Tput.[b]	Area[b]	Tput.[b]		
64/128	Revised CHAM	665	4.5	852	72.7	IBM130	This paper
	Original CHAM	665	5.0	852	80.0	IBM130	[22]
	Revised CHAM	728	4.5	985	72.7	UMC90	This paper
	Revised CHAM	859	4.5	1,110	72.7	UMC180	This paper
	SIMON	944	4.2	1,403	133.3	IBM130[c]	[34]
	SIMON	958	4.2	1,417	133.3	IBM130	[4]
	SPECK	996	3.4	1,658	206.5	IBM130	[4]
128/128	Revised CHAM	1,057	3.6	1,499	114.3	IBM130	This paper
	Original CHAM	1,057	5.0	1,499	160.0	IBM130	[22]
	Revised CHAM	1,086	3.6	1,691	114.3	UMC90	This paper
	SIMON	1,234	2.9	2,090	182.9	IBM130	[4]
	SPECK	1,280	3.0	2,727	376.5	IBM130	[4]
	Revised CHAM	1,295	3.6	1,899	114.3	UMC180	This paper
	LEA	2,302	4.2	3,826	76.2	UMC130	[20]
	AES	-	-	2,400	57.0	UMC180	[26]
128/256	Revised CHAM	1,179	3.3	1,622	106.7	IBM130	This paper
	Original CHAM	1,180	4.2	1,622	133.3	IBM130	[22]
	Revised CHAM	1,260	3.3	1,864	106.7	UMC90	This paper
	Revised CHAM	1,481	3.3	2,086	106.7	UMC180	This paper
	SIMON	1,782	2.6	2,776	168.4	IBM130	[4]
	SPECK	1,840	2.8	3,284	336.8	IBM130	[4]

[a] Area in gate equivalent
[b] Throughput in Kbps @ 100 KHz
[c] Not exactly same to the non-marked IBM130

5.2   Software Implementation

We compare the software performance of the revised CHAM and other ciphers via the same method used in the aforementioned study [22]. The implementation method is also identical to that in the earlier work [22] except for the numbers of rounds.

Table 13 presents the results of a performance comparison on the AVR and MSP platforms using the rank metric for a fixed-key scenario. Table 14 shows the performances based on the rank metric under a one-way communication scenario. And Table 15 shows a performance comparison based on the FOM metric under the communication scenario.[4]

---

[4] The performance data of SIMON-64/128 and SPECK-64/128 are derived from the FELICS project [13] website. On the other hand, the performance data of SIMON-128/128, SIMON-128/256, SPECK-128/128, and SPECK-128/256 are not yet reported.

Table 13. Performance comparison using the rank metric on AVR and MSP under the fixed-key scenario

n/k	Cipher	AVR				MSP			
		ROM	RAM	cpb	Rank	ROM	RAM	cpb	Rank
64/128	SPECK [6]	218	0	154	29.8	204	0	98	50.0
	Original CHAM [22]	202	3	172	28.0	156	8	118	49.3
	Revised CHAM	202	3	188	25.4	156	8	128	45.1
	SIMON [6]	290	0	253	13.6	280	0	177	20.2
128/128	Original CHAM [22]	362	16	148	17.1	280	20	125	25.0
	SPECK [6]	460	0	171	12.7	438	0	105	21.7
	Revised CHAM	362	16	203	12.4	280	20	172	18.1
	AES [6]	970	18	146	6.8	-	-	-	-
	LEA	754	17	203	6.3	646	24	147	9.8
	SIMON [6]	760	0	379	3.5	754	0	389	3.4
128/256	Original CHAM [22]	396	16	177	13.2	312	20	148	19.2
	SPECK [5]	476	0	181	11.6	-	-	-	-
	Revised CHAM	396	16	219	10.7	312	20	183	15.4
	AES [5]	1,034	18	204	4.7	-	-	-	-
	SIMON [5]	792	0	401	3.1	-	-	-	-

Table 14. Performance comparison using the rank metric in the one-way communication scenario

Platform	Cipher	ROM		RAM		Cycles		cpb	Rank
		EKS[a]	Enc[b]	Stack	Data	EKS	Enc		
AVR	Original CHAM-64/128	72	280	11	184	309	23,664	187	7.2
	Revised CHAM-64/128	72	280	11	184	309	25,792	203	6.6
	SPECK-64/128	178	240	12	260	1,401	19,888	166	6.3
	SIMON-64/128	254	328	16	328	2,911	31,024	265	3.0
MSP	Original CHAM-64/128	66	210	16	184	275	16,715	132	11.1
	Revised CHAM-64/128	66	210	16	194	275	18,123	143	10.3
	SPECK-64/128	126	180	16	260	1,242	14,155	120	9.7
	SIMON-64/128	174	248	24	328	2,002	22,171	188	4.7
ARM	SPECK-64/128	52	164	36	260	516	6,323	53	23.2
	Original CHAM-128/128	44	210	48	192	95	8,846	69	19.5
	Revised CHAM-128/128	44	210	48	192	95	11,150	87	15.5
	SIMON-64/128	112	192	40	328	1,113	10,485	90	10.6
	Original CHAM-64/128	64	256	40	184	192	19,485	153	8.5
	Revised CHAM-64/128	64	256	40	184	192	21,101	166	7.8

[a] Key schedule
[b] Encryption

Table 15. Performance comparison using the FOM metric in the communication scenario

Cipher	AVR				MSP				ARM			
	ROM	RAM	cpb	FOM	ROM	RAM	cpb	FOM	ROM	RAM	cpb	FOM
SPECK-64/128	874	302	350	4.8	572	296	252	4.8	444	308	128	5.8
Original CHAM-128/128	1,230	262	336	4.9	926	258	298	5.6	528	272	144	6.3
Revised CHAM-128/128	1,230	262	449	5.6	926	258	394	6.5	528	272	183	7.2
Original CHAM-64/128	844	225	393	4.6	578	220	290	4.7	640	244	318	10.7
Revised CHAM-64/128	844	225	428	4.8	578	220	312	4.9	640	244	345	11.3
SIMON-64/128	1,122	375	520	6.5	760	372	389	6.7	560	392	186	7.9

Although overall the revised CHAM shows slightly worse software performance than the original CHAM due to the increased numbers of rounds, it nonetheless shows excellent software performance. Specifically, its performance is similar to that of SPECK, while it outperforms the other ciphers.

6   Conclusion

In this paper, we present new results on a (related-key) differential cryptanalysis on CHAM and propose a revised version of CHAM with the numbers of rounds increased in order to ensure a sufficient security margin. First, we presented new (related-key) differential characteristics and differentials which were found using a SAT solver. We demonstrated how to convert the problem of finding a (related-key) differential characteristic and a differential into a CNF formula to invoke a SAT solver. Considering the new cryptanalytic results, the revised CHAM is suggested. The numbers of rounds of CHAM-64/128, CHAM-128/128, and CHAM-128/256 are raised from 80 to 88, 80 to 112, and 96 to 120, respectively. We showed that the revised CHAM provides a sufficient security margin against newly found attacks. Finally, implementation results on both hardware and software are presented. The revised CHAM continued to show very good performance. Specifically, on average CHAM can be implemented using 25% less area than SIMON on hardware. On software, it is still comparable to SPECK.

Acknowledgement. We are grateful to the anonymous reviewers for their help in improving the quality of the paper. This work was supported by Institute for Information & Communications Technology Planning & Evaluation (IITP) grant funded by the Korean government (MSIT) (No.2017-0-00267).

A   Test Vectors

Test vectors are represented in hexadecimal with the prefix '0x'.

CHAM-64/128

```
secret Key : 0x0100 0x0302 0x0504 0x0706 0x0908 0x0b0a 0x0d0c 0x0f0e
plaintext  : 0x1100 0x3322 0x5544 0x7766
ciphertext : 0x6579 0x1204 0x123f 0xe5a9
```

CHAM-128/128
```
secret Key : 0x03020100 0x07060504 0x0b0a0908 0x0f0e0d0c
plaintext  : 0x33221100 0x77665544 0xbbaa9988 0xffeeddcc
ciphertext : 0xd05419ee 0x9f118f4c 0x99e36469 0x1c885ec1
```

CHAM-128/256
```
secret Key : 0x03020100 0x07060504 0x0b0a0908 0x0f0e0d0c
             0xf3f2f1f0 0xf7f6f5f4 0xfbfaf9f8 0xfffefdfc
plaintext  : 0x33221100 0x77665544 0xbbaa9988 0xffeeddcc
ciphertext : 0x027377dc 0x120b5651 0x8f839b95 0x5e5ec075
```

B   Other Characteristics

Table 16 shows a 46-round related-key boomerang characteristic of CHAM-128/128. It is constructed by attaching a 23-round related-key differential characteristic with probability 2^{-31} twice. Note that prior to this, only a 36-round related-key boomerang characteristic was known.

Table 16. Related-key boomerang characteristics of CHAM-128/128

Round Prob.	Key difference Input difference Output difference	Reference
23 2^{-31}	(FFFFFFFF FFFFFFFF 00000000 00000000) (02080001 7FFBFFFE 00000400 00000200) (08080000 04040400 FFFFFFD9 10000000)	This paper

Table 17 shows the features of (related-key) differential-linear approximations of CHAM. Note that prior to this, only a 34-round differential-linear approximation of CHAM-64/128 and a 39-round related-key differential-linear approximation of CHAM-128/128 were known.

Table 17. Features of (related-key) differential-linear approximations

Model	n/k	(RK) diff.-lin. app.		ϕ		ψ		Reference
		Round	pc^2	Round	p	Round	c^2	
Single-key	64/128	35	2^{-31}	21	2^{-23}	14	2^{-8}	This paper
Related-key	128/128	44	2^{-62}	22	2^{-28}	22	2^{-34}	This paper

References

1. Albrecht, M., Cid, C.: Algebraic techniques in differential cryptanalysis. In: Dunkelman, O. (ed.) FSE 2009. LNCS, vol. 5665, pp. 193–208. Springer, Heidelberg (2009). https://doi.org/10.1007/978-3-642-03317-9_12
2. Banik, S., et al.: Midori: a block cipher for low energy. In: Iwata, T., Cheon, J.H. (eds.) ASIACRYPT 2015, Part II. LNCS, vol. 9453, pp. 411–436. Springer, Heidelberg (2015). https://doi.org/10.1007/978-3-662-48800-3_17
3. Banik, S., Pandey, S.K., Peyrin, T., Sasaki, Y., Sim, S.M., Todo, Y.: GIFT: a small present. In: Fischer, W., Homma, N. (eds.) CHES 2017. LNCS, vol. 10529, pp. 321–345. Springer, Cham (2017). https://doi.org/10.1007/978-3-319-66787-4_16
4. Beaulieu, R., Shors, D., Smith, J., Treatman-Clark, S., Weeks, B., Wingers, L.: The SIMON and SPECK families of lightweight block ciphers. Cryptology ePrint Archive, Report 2013/404 (2013). https://eprint.iacr.org/2013/404
5. Beaulieu, R., Shors, D., Smith, J., Treatman-Clark, S., Weeks, B., Wingers, L.: The SIMON and SPECK block ciphers on AVR 8-bit microcontrollers. In: Eisenbarth, T., Öztürk, E. (eds.) LightSec 2014. LNCS, vol. 8898, pp. 3–20. Springer, Cham (2015). https://doi.org/10.1007/978-3-319-16363-5_1
6. Beaulieu, R., Shors, D., Smith, J., Treatman-Clark, S., Weeks, B., Wingers, L.: SIMON and SPECK: block ciphers for the internet of things. IACR Cryptol. ePrint Arch. **2015**, 585 (2015)
7. Beierle, C., et al.: The SKINNY family of block ciphers and its low-latency variant MANTIS. In: Robshaw, M., Katz, J. (eds.) CRYPTO 2016, Part II. LNCS, vol. 9815, pp. 123–153. Springer, Heidelberg (2016). https://doi.org/10.1007/978-3-662-53008-5_5
8. Biham, E., Shamir, A.: Differential cryptanalysis of DES-like cryptosystems. J. Cryptol. **4**(1), 3–72 (1991)
9. Biryukov, A., Velichkov, V.: Automatic search for differential trails in ARX ciphers. In: Benaloh, J. (ed.) CT-RSA 2014. LNCS, vol. 8366, pp. 227–250. Springer, Cham (2014). https://doi.org/10.1007/978-3-319-04852-9_12
10. Bogdanov, A., et al.: PRESENT: an ultra-lightweight block cipher. In: Paillier, P., Verbauwhede, I. (eds.) CHES 2007. LNCS, vol. 4727, pp. 450–466. Springer, Heidelberg (2007). https://doi.org/10.1007/978-3-540-74735-2_31
11. Borghoff, J., et al.: PRINCE – a low-latency block cipher for pervasive computing applications. In: Wang, X., Sako, K. (eds.) ASIACRYPT 2012. LNCS, vol. 7658, pp. 208–225. Springer, Heidelberg (2012). https://doi.org/10.1007/978-3-642-34961-4_14
12. De Cannière, C., Dunkelman, O., Knežević, M.: KATAN and KTANTAN — a family of small and efficient hardware-oriented block ciphers. In: Clavier, C., Gaj, K. (eds.) CHES 2009. LNCS, vol. 5747, pp. 272–288. Springer, Heidelberg (2009). https://doi.org/10.1007/978-3-642-04138-9_20
13. Dinu, D., Biryukov, A., Großschädl, J., Khovratovich, D., Le Corre, Y., Perrin, L.: FELICS-fair evaluation of lightweight cryptographic systems. In: NIST Workshop on Lightweight Cryptography (2015)
14. Dinu, D., Le Corre, Y., Khovratovich, D., Perrin, L., Großschädl, J., Biryukov, A.: Triathlon of lightweight block ciphers for the internet of things. J. Cryptogr. Eng. **9**(3), 283–302 (2019)
15. Dinu, D., Perrin, L., Udovenko, A., Velichkov, V., Großschädl, J., Biryukov, A.: Design strategies for ARX with provable bounds: SPARX and LAX. In: Cheon, J.H., Takagi, T. (eds.) ASIACRYPT 2016. LNCS, vol. 10031, pp. 484–513. Springer, Heidelberg (2016). https://doi.org/10.1007/978-3-662-53887-6_18

16. Dinur, I.: Improved differential cryptanalysis of round-reduced speck. In: Joux, A., Youssef, A. (eds.) SAC 2014. LNCS, vol. 8781, pp. 147–164. Springer, Cham (2014). https://doi.org/10.1007/978-3-319-13051-4_9

17. Eén, N., Sörensson, N.: An extensible SAT-solver. In: Giunchiglia, E., Tacchella, A. (eds.) SAT 2003. LNCS, vol. 2919, pp. 502–518. Springer, Heidelberg (2004). https://doi.org/10.1007/978-3-540-24605-3_37

18. Guo, J., Peyrin, T., Poschmann, A., Robshaw, M.: The LED block cipher. In: Preneel, B., Takagi, T. (eds.) CHES 2011. LNCS, vol. 6917, pp. 326–341. Springer, Heidelberg (2011). https://doi.org/10.1007/978-3-642-23951-9_22

19. Hamadi, Y., Jabbour, S., Sais, L.: ManySAT: a parallel SAT solver. J. Satisf. Boolean Model. Comput. **6**, 245–262 (2008)

20. Hong, D., Lee, J.-K., Kim, D.-C., Kwon, D., Ryu, K.H., Lee, D.-G.: LEA: a 128-bit block cipher for fast encryption on common processors. In: Kim, Y., Lee, H., Perrig, A. (eds.) WISA 2013. LNCS, vol. 8267, pp. 3–27. Springer, Cham (2014). https://doi.org/10.1007/978-3-319-05149-9_1

21. Knudsen, L., Leander, G., Poschmann, A., Robshaw, M.J.B.: PRINTCIPHER: a block cipher for IC-printing. In: Mangard, S., Standaert, F.-X. (eds.) CHES 2010. LNCS, vol. 6225, pp. 16–32. Springer, Heidelberg (2010). https://doi.org/10.1007/978-3-642-15031-9_2

22. Koo, B., Roh, D., Kim, H., Jung, Y., Lee, D.-G., Kwon, D.: CHAM: a family of lightweight block ciphers for resource-constrained devices. In: Kim, H., Kim, D.-C. (eds.) ICISC 2017. LNCS, vol. 10779, pp. 3–25. Springer, Cham (2018). https://doi.org/10.1007/978-3-319-78556-1_1

23. Lee, H., Kim, S., Kang, H., Hong, D., Sung, J., Hong, S.: Calculating the approximate probability of differentials for arx-based cipher using sat solver. J. Korea Inst. Inf. Secur. Cryptol. **28**(1), 15–24 (2018)

24. Lipmaa, H., Moriai, S.: Efficient algorithms for computing differential properties of addition. In: Matsui, M. (ed.) FSE 2001. LNCS, vol. 2355, pp. 336–350. Springer, Heidelberg (2002). https://doi.org/10.1007/3-540-45473-X_28

25. Matsui, M.: On correlation between the order of S-boxes and the strength of DES. In: De Santis, A. (ed.) EUROCRYPT 1994. LNCS, vol. 950, pp. 366–375. Springer, Heidelberg (1995). https://doi.org/10.1007/BFb0053451

26. Moradi, A., Poschmann, A., Ling, S., Paar, C., Wang, H.: Pushing the limits: a very compact and a threshold implementation of AES. In: Paterson, K.G. (ed.) EUROCRYPT 2011. LNCS, vol. 6632, pp. 69–88. Springer, Heidelberg (2011). https://doi.org/10.1007/978-3-642-20465-4_6

27. Mouha, N., Preneel, B.: Towards finding optimal differential characteristics for ARX: application to Salsa20 (2013)

28. Needham, R.M., Wheeler, D.J.: TEA extensions. Report, Cambridge University, Cambridge, UK, October 1997

29. Polimón, J., Hernández-Castro, J.C., Estévez-Tapiador, J.M., Ribagorda, A.: Automated design of a lightweight block cipher with genetic programming. Int. J. Knowl. Based Intell. Eng. Syst. **12**(1), 3–14 (2008)

30. Shirai, T., Shibutani, K., Akishita, T., Moriai, S., Iwata, T.: The 128-bit blockcipher CLEFIA (extended abstract). In: Biryukov, A. (ed.) FSE 2007. LNCS, vol. 4593, pp. 181–195. Springer, Heidelberg (2007). https://doi.org/10.1007/978-3-540-74619-5_12

31. Song, L., Huang, Z., Yang, Q.: Automatic differential analysis of ARX block ciphers with application to SPECK and LEA. In: Liu, J.K., Steinfeld, R. (eds.) ACISP 2016, Part II. LNCS, vol. 9723, pp. 379–394. Springer, Cham (2016). https://doi.org/10.1007/978-3-319-40367-0_24

32. Soos, M., Nohl, K., Castelluccia, C.: Extending SAT solvers to cryptographic problems. In: Kullmann, O. (ed.) SAT 2009. LNCS, vol. 5584, pp. 244–257. Springer, Heidelberg (2009). https://doi.org/10.1007/978-3-642-02777-2_24
33. Wheeler, D.J., Needham, R.M.: TEA, a tiny encryption algorithm. In: Preneel, B. (ed.) FSE 1994. LNCS, vol. 1008, pp. 363–366. Springer, Heidelberg (1995). https://doi.org/10.1007/3-540-60590-8_29
34. Yang, G., Zhu, B., Suder, V., Aagaard, M.D., Gong, G.: The Simeck family of lightweight block ciphers. In: Güneysu, T., Handschuh, H. (eds.) CHES 2015. LNCS, vol. 9293, pp. 307–329. Springer, Heidelberg (2015). https://doi.org/10.1007/978-3-662-48324-4_16

Systematic Construction of Nonlinear Product Attacks on Block Ciphers

Nicolas T. Courtois[1(✉)], Matteo Abbondati[2(✉)], Hamy Ratoanina[1], and Marek Grajek[3]

[1] University College London, Gower Street, London, UK
n.courtois@ucl.ac.uk, hamy.ratoanina@telecom-paris.fr
[2] Independent Maths Teacher, London, UK
matteo.abbondati@mail.uk
[3] Independent Crypto History Expert, Grodzisk Mazowiecki, Poland
mjg@interia.eu

Abstract. A major open problem in block cipher cryptanalysis is discovery of new invariant properties of complex type. Recent papers show that this can be achieved for SCREAM, Midori64, MANTIS-4, T-310 or for DES with modified S-boxes. Until now such attacks are hard to find and seem to happen by some sort of incredible coincidence. In this paper we abstract the attack from any particular block cipher. We study these attacks in terms of transformations on multivariate polynomials. We shall demonstrate how numerous variables including key variables may sometimes be eliminated and at the end two very complex Boolean polynomials will become equal. We present a general construction of an attack where multiply all the polynomials lying on one or several cycles. Then under suitable conditions the non-linear functions involved will be eliminated totally. We obtain a periodic invariant property holding for any number of rounds. A major difficulty with invariant attacks is that they typically work only for some keys. In T-310 our attack works for any key and also in spite of the presence of round constants.

Keywords: Block ciphers · Boolean functions · Feistel ciphers · Weak keys · DES · Generalized linear cryptanalysis · Polynomial invariants · Multivariate polynomials · Annihilator space · Algebraic cryptanalysis · Polynomial rings · Invariant theory

1 Introduction

Block ciphers are widely used and studied since the 1970s. Their periodic structure is prone to round invariant attacks, for example in Linear Cryptanalysis (LC). A natural generalisation is Generalised Linear Cryptanalysis (GLC), first proposed at Eurocrypt'95 [29]. The space for possible attacks grows double-exponentially, and until 2018 extremely few such attacks [4,17,19,30,37] have been found. We call a "product attack" an attack, where an invariant, being a product of simpler polynomials, remains unchanged after some number of $k \geq 1$

© Springer Nature Switzerland AG 2020
J. H. Seo (Ed.): ICISC 2019, LNCS 11975, pp. 20–51, 2020.
https://doi.org/10.1007/978-3-030-40921-0_2

rounds. A key point is that in the ring of Boolean polynomials the factorization is not unique. This has important consequences. Numerous specific events without unique factorisation occur inside many invariant attacks, cf. [11], making the job of the attacker easier. Then, imagine that a researcher finds a new invariant attack which works for a block cipher. It could be very difficult to know if this attack can or not be constructed by multiplying some well chosen polynomials as in our general "product" attack framework which we introduce in this paper.

An essential question is whether invariant attacks do exist at all for any given cipher. This question is currently considered very difficult [1,3,4,6]. For many ciphers we can neither say if it is broken by our attack, nor we can be assured that it is secure and invariant attacks do not exist. Numerous positive examples of working attacks are known for the Cold War cipher T-310 [25,35]. There exist also some basic examples for DES [18,19] which we will revisit here. Then we have results on SCREAM, iSCREAM, Midori64 and MANTIS-4 cf. [4,37]. Most previous non-linear attacks exploited polynomials of degree 2 or 3 [17,19,37] and only sometimes of higher degree [17,18], or the invariants are only correct with a low probability. In this paper we construct invariants of arbitrarily high degree and working with probability 1, in a systematic deterministic way.

This paper is organised as follows. In Sect. 2 we explain what are non-linear invariant attacks and key features of our approach. In Sect. 3 we explain the idea of "closed loop" connection. In Sect. 4 we describe the main idea of cycles with transitions between polynomials. In Sect. 5 we discuss the question of attacks working with strong rather than weak Boolean functions. In Sect. 6 we present a simple attack at degree 4. In Sect. 7 we present our general framework theorem. In Sect. 8 we apply it to construct a stronger attack of with a cycle of length 8. In Sect. 9 we apply our construction to DES with 3 cycles of length 8. In Appendix A we give two different mathematical proofs that our complex attack on DES actually works. In Sect. 10 we provide a better attack at degree 5. In Appendix B we consider DES with original S-boxes.

2 Our Methodology, Scope, Applicability, Features

We call $\mathcal{P}$ a polynomial invariant if the value of $\mathcal{P}$ is preserved after one round of encryption, i.e. if $\mathcal{P}(\text{Inputs}) = \mathcal{P}(\text{Outputs})$. This concept can be applied to any block cipher except that such attacks are quite hard to find, cf. [3].

In this paper we introduce a general method for constructing polynomial invariants of high degree designed to work on more than just one well chosen cipher configuration. Moreover our attacks do NOT seem[1] to require that a block cipher has any special property or weakness. We only use properties, which are very common and which essentially any block cipher ever made has. We assume that our cipher includes a sequence of applications of non-linear functions which transforms the state bit by bit, and different polynomials on the state are constructed step by step, without the necessity of knowing how the whole state is computed. Moreover we relax these transitions in the strongest possible way:

---

[1] Except maybe some combinatorial or probability questions for certain special events.

some transitions assume that they actually do not hold at all, or more precisely their difference is assumed to be an arbitrary non-linear function of the cipher state (which we will later try to eliminate algebraically).

Many research papers in symmetric cryptanalysis spend a lot of time studying the specification of a given block cipher. In this paper we emphasise the idea that it is not necessary to know the full specs of a cipher in order to find an invariant attack. For T-310 we make an essential and deliberate choice of not providing the full specs which are excessively complex, cf. [23]. For DES we assume that the reader is familiar with the basic description of DES. The purpose of this is threefold. First, we want to demonstrate that by their very nature our attacks represent self-contained mathematical results about polynomials involving very few variables, which are **able to eliminate** everything else. Secondly, and as such, our attacks will apply to potentially any cipher, which after renaming the variables satisfies the same basic set of polynomial relations, which will be organised in order to form short cycles, as we will see later. Finally, we want to emphasise the fact, that our attack depends only on a tiny fragment[2] of the cipher's computational circuit. Many traditional attacks depend on probabilistic events on the cipher state. Therefore by their very nature they require to know the full specs of the cipher, in order to know if they work as expected. Sometimes they don't work as predicted, because certain events are biased or not independent. Here polynomial attacks are different: they are theorems on combinations of Boolean polynomials and on relations between different bits holding always, with probability 1, under the conditions specified, for any cipher input. There is no need to be able to compute the cipher circuit in its entirety in order to validate them. For T-310 there are simply no special cases where our attacks would not work as predicted.

For DES we formulate our results in such a way, that the key bits are included inside the S-box specification. Our results, such as later Theorem 10.1, do not make an apparent reference to the secret key. Or rather this question needs to be studied separately[3] when our invariant would be applied inside some attack, cf. Section 9 in [18] and Section 6 in [13]. In general our attacks are meant to be existential over the secret key: work for a fraction of key space which should be as large[4] as possible.

2.1   Limitations and Vulnerability

Some polynomial invariant attacks work for a fraction of keys, other for all possible keys. According to [17, 18, 26], using longer keys in each round could be a good reason, why many ciphers are likely to be secure against non-linear

---

[2] Involving a handful of bits, and only some of the non-linear function(s), and only some key bits. Moreover inside the Boolean functions and S-boxes, we aim at constructing attacks which require only that a certain a small fraction of entries in the truth tables of these functions (at suitable positions) are at zero.

[3] For DES S-boxes, we require that some Boolean function are annihilated by products of simple linear polynomials. Such annihilation remain frequently true, when we transform an S-box by a secret key, added at the input, cf. Remark 2 in page 22.

[4] In T-310 (but not with DES) our attacks work for any key and also in presence of round constants, e.g. in Theorem 6.2 and numerous others examples in [17, 18].

attacks. However even when many key bits are used in each round, cf. [25], it is hard to be sure that a cipher is not vulnerable to the same type of attack. The crucial notion here is the diffusion and the combinatorial problem of the existence of "closed-loop" sub-circuits which was emphasised recently in [38]. This type of property was already studied long time ago, cf. for example Fig. 3–5 in [22], Section 9 in [14] and Fig. 10 in page 21. The philosophy is that our attack is facilitated, if some subset of bits depend "mostly" on themselves, and only "weakly" on other bits inside one round of the cipher. More precisely all the other bits need to be eliminated by polynomial algebra. In this paper we will take this idea to a new level, cf. Sect. 3, and allow linear combinations of bits.

2.2   What Is New - On Existence of Cycles on Basic Polynomials

Can we do better than current (heuristic) approaches? This paper introduces a substantially and **strictly more general** paradigm, which increases the number of possibilities for the attacker. This hopefully leads to more (or better) attacks on block ciphers. Instead of looking at bits, and how they depend on other bits, we will actually ignore individual bits and considerably restrict the set of values which we actually need to study. We consider ONLY a certain (small) set of "basic" polynomials Q_i involving these bits. Then we consider cycles built from such linear/affine [or more generally non-linear] polynomials. Is this possible? Cipher designers have 50+ years of experience in designing complex ciphers aiming at avoiding such attacks. We expect that in most cases no cycles whatsoever involving polynomials of "tractable" size will be found.

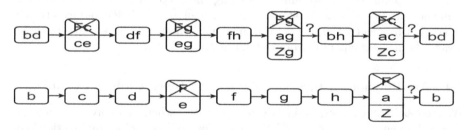

Fig. 1. Example showing how simple polynomials, e.g. bd, are transformed and maybe eventually form cycles in T-310, cf. Section 7.4. in [17]. Terms with crosses in blue such as Fc appear an even number of times and are eliminated mod 2. Terms and transitions with Z in red work, if certain conditions on the Boolean function Z hold. This paper is about how such examples can be constructed from scratch in a systematic way. (Color figure online)

Therefore it is crucial to be able to enhance this basic approach in order to increase the number of possibilities for the attacker. We make the "impossible" question of the existence of short cycles eventually possible. In order to achieve this we cheat in some way and study **imperfect** transitions, cf. also later Sects. 4 and 3. Certain arbitrary non-linear functions Z_i are added on the way. Then eventually we eliminate these extra functions Z_i algebraically [annihilation of polynomials], which is the main idea which eventually makes our attacks work.

2.3   Related Research, Product and Multiple Product Attacks

In recent research there are two major types of invariant attacks: linear or affine sub-space invariants [3,6,31], and more generally, arbitrary non-linear polynomial invariants [17,37]. Several authors [3,4,6,17] study both topics which are closely related. In some cases both paradigms are simply equivalent. For example we consider the concept of the so called "product attack" of [18]. It is easy to see that any affine vector sub-space of $\{0,1\}^n$ can be also described as a set of points, where a product of some affine polynomials $\mathcal{Q}_i$ is at 1. Likewise every set of points in $\{0,1\}^n$ where $\prod \mathcal{Q}_i = 1$ is an affine subspace. Then, linear spaces can be characterised by restricting to the case of linear polynomials $\mathcal{Q}_i$.

In this paper we aim at improving and generalizing such "product" attacks. It is important to see that an attack with a sum of several products will be more general. A somewhat misleading example can be found in Appendix A.2. of [18]: it is a sum of two products however a close examination would show it can also be written as a single product (!). A better example can be found in Section 10.6 of [17], where the invariant is of type $AC + BD$ where A, B, C, D are linear polynomials and $AC + BD$ is irreducible. Different attacks are related to each other, and the exact invariant of type $AC + BD$ in Section 10.6 of [17], hides the existence of a "product" attack for 2 rounds of type $AC \rightarrow BD \rightarrow AC$. This demonstrates that the product attack is NOT necessarily the most general attack. In general it is easy to show that the set of all possible invariants is a polynomial ring; both addition and multiplication are allowed (!). Then the construction of this paper, which emphasises the multiplication, is just the first step. This paper essentially aims at solving the problem of the invariant ring being not empty [existence of at least one invariant attack]. Then, our experience shows that frequently the ring of invariants, will contain additional[5] lower degree invariants, not anticipated[6] from the initial product attack.

2.4   Are Polynomial Invariant Attacks on Block Ciphers Possible?

We are looking for a polynomial which is preserved when we apply one round of encryption, i.e. if $\mathcal{P}(\text{Inputs}) = \mathcal{P}(\text{Outputs})$. Now in finite fields any function is a polynomial and the outputs are also polynomials in the inputs. If we substitute these inside $\mathcal{P}$, we obtain another polynomial, initially very complex, however if $\mathcal{P}$ is well chosen, it will be simpler than expected. In particular the key bits can be eliminated and after this, in our you polynomial was an invariant, we get a situation where, two polynomials[7] will be simply equal. We get a formal equality on two complex polynomials, holding under certain constraints on the key or/and cipher wiring. Interestingly, if $\mathcal{P}$ is a product it is easy to see, that

---

[5] For example, we have generated many concrete examples of S-boxes, for the attack of degree 8 on DES of Sect. 8. In some cases additional invariants of degree 2,4,6 or 7 are also found, cf. [11,12] and our Sect. 8. Or we constructed an attack of degree 10 in Sect. 9 and for some S-boxes we will also have an attack of degree 5 in Theorem 10.1.

[6] Some of these attacks are obtained by the so called "decimated" attack cf. Sect. 4.3.

[7] The original one and the transformed one.

both polynomials are products of many terms. It appears that when two products of polynomials are equal, this does not happen by accident. The ring of Boolean polynomials does not have unique factorisation, and we observe specific types of events: annihilation events, absorption events, etc, cf. [11]. In this paper, for the first time ever, we are going to abstract the non-linear invariant attacks from any block cipher in particular. We are going to formulate our attacks in such a way, that they do not depend on features of any particular block cipher. What we do amounts to doing a "clever" polynomial algebraic combination of a few equations, which are basic facts about how some polynomials are transformed by our cipher.

2.5   Related Work: Linearization, XL, Algebraic Cryptanalysis

Our new attack could be called "Product Cycling Linearization Attack" on block ciphers and is vaguely related to other works which use the word "Linearization" cf. [9,32]. The main idea with linearization (in all cases) is to add new variables so that everything becomes linear and then try to eliminate these new variables. In XL and old "Linearization" [9] we multiplied complex non-linear equations by various variables. In algebraic attacks on stream ciphers [15] we multiply them by well chosen non-linear polynomials. In this paper we multiply non-linear functions by well chosen polynomials which are products of linear factors.

3   Closed Loop Configurations Revisited

In recent research [17,18,21,22,38] it turns out that each time an "interesting" non-linear invariant attack was found, it comes together with a configuration where some set of bits and S-boxes are primarily connected to each other in a "closed-loop" cf. [38]. This idea is not new, for instance for T-310 it was studied

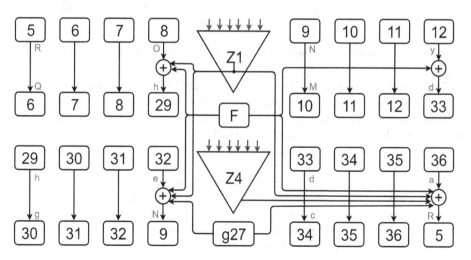

Fig. 2. A complex closed loop configuration for T-310 with 16 active bits.

in Sections 7.4, 8.2, 9.1. and 9.2. and 10.6 and 10.7. in [17]. Such configurations occur in almost every attack previously studied. For example we may look at Fig. 8 in [17] which is reproduced below as Fig. 2. Likewise Fig. 7 in [17] is reproduced in page 8 as Fig. 4. We can also mention Fig. 9, 10, 11, 12 in [17].

For GOST this type of configuration was already studied in Fig. 3–5 in [22] and GOST is known to be a particularly weak cipher in this aspect which is closely related to vulnerability of GOST to truncated differential attacks cf. [10, 21, 22, 31].

Closed loop configurations can be of any size. On Fig. 10 page 21 we show how this works with DES S-boxes 2, 3, 7 and a well chosen set of inputs and outputs of these bits. A larger configuration with five S-boxes is shown in Fig. 3.

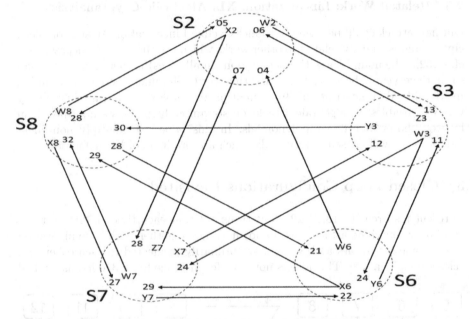

Fig. 3. Closed-loop connection between S-boxes S2,S3,S6,S7,S8 in DES.

This configuration is one of the best possible in DES, it maximises the number of bits active across all possible subsets of 5 S-boxes. Intuitively, the more bits depend only on themselves, in terms of a ratio (or probability) of re-entry, the more we can hope to find an invariant attack.

In this paper we take this idea to a new level: we consider not bits, but rather their linear [and also non-linear] combinations. Intuitively, it seems unthinkable that any block cipher can be cryptanalyzed by showing that it acts in a simple way while acting on some small set of "simple" polynomials and that we can ever obtain short cycles in this way, cf. also Sect. 2.2. For this reason, our cycles are going to be **imperfect** in the following sense: we allow **addition** of several arbitrarily complex non-linear functions which are later eliminated. This is expected to increase the number of possibilities for the attacker.

4   Constructing Cycles on Polynomials

Only those who attempt the absurd will achieve the impossible.
– Maurits Cornelis Escher

We are now going to imagine a larger enhanced graph, where edges represent some polynomials Q_i, and transitions correspond to how these polynomials might be transformed by one round of encryption, if certain conditions are true. Let $A, B, \ldots$ be some linear combinations of input bits for one round. By convention we say that $A \rightarrow B$ if $A(\text{Inputs}) = B(\text{Outputs})$ each time we look at one encryption round. If this happens for every key and for every input we say that $A \rightarrow B$ holds without any condition. More generally in our construction we will have basic Q_i being affine combinations of $A, B, \ldots$, which in turn are well-chosen polynomials. These basic polynomials Q_i and $A, B, \ldots$ are usually linear or affine. For example $Q_1 = A+C+1$, where A and C are two affine expressions[8] in cipher state input variables, and addition is done modulo 2. In general they are meant to form short cycles holding under certain technical conditions.

For example in a hypothetical attack we could have a cycle, such as say $A \rightarrow B \rightarrow C \rightarrow D \rightarrow A$, which does NOT work as such. Initially some transitions are just impossible, in particular $D \rightarrow A$ does not work. Interestingly, we can apply the following idea borrowed from [12] and Section 5 of [17]. Let $Z_i = 0$ be a transition polynomial. Informally, the transition polynomial $Z_i = 0$ characterises exactly the cases where this transition actually works[9].

Here is another example, where we attempt to construct a cycle of length 4 which is illustrated in Fig. 4. We could for example have $D = x_{32} + x_{36}$ and

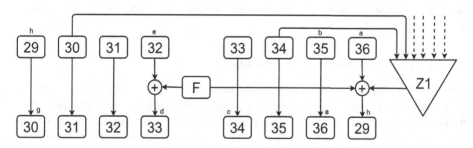

Fig. 4. Transitions inside one simple invariant attack on T-310, cf. [17].

---

[8] This example occurs in our later attack on DES, and we can rewrite $Q_1 = A+C+1 = R05 + R28$, where $R05$ is the 5-th bit in the right branch of a DES plaintext, and A, C are defined in later Fig. 12 page 28.

[9] Informally it is a polynomial such that we actually have $D \rightarrow A$ when $Z_i = 0$. Moreover we mandate that this polynomial Z_i uses the same set of input-side variables which are also the inputs of D. Then we always have $D(\text{Inputs}) = A(\text{Outputs})$ when $Z_i(\text{Inputs}) = 0$. This does not say what happens when $Z_i = 1$, and in this paper the converse will also hold systematically. More precise statements which make sense in all cases will be provided later, cf. Theorem 7.1 page 16.

$A = x_{29} + x_{33}$, $B = x_{30} + x_{34}$ and $C = x_{31} + x_{35}$, where x_i are inputs of one round of encryption, and $Z1(x_1, \dots)$ is some specific non-linear function. Then we imagine that the round constant F is[10] eliminated but the output of $Z1()$ is not eliminated and we have $D \to A$ only when $Z1(\text{Inputs}) = 0$. Importantly we are not going to assume that $Z1()$ will be equal to 0 for every input. We expect that the Boolean function $Z1$ is quite strong.

We will denote each such transition polynomial by $\mathcal{Z}_i$ pertaining to a transition number i. It generalizes the concept of Fundamental Equation (FE) of [17] to arbitrary[11] transitions[12]. The main idea in this paper is that following [12] in many cases this polynomial is not going to be zero. However some multiple of this polynomial is more likely to be zero.

We aim at constructing a configuration with one or several cycles, which can be seen as walks in some graph where our block cipher is acting in a non-deterministic way on a set of our basic polynomials. In addition in some cycles, non-linear polynomials $\mathcal{Z}_i$ are added on the way, in the same way as $Z1()$ in Fig. 4 above, or with $Z \cdot g$ term in earlier Fig. 1. These transition polynomials, initially seem to be a huge obstacle in constructing our attack. Eventually we will show that under suitable annihilation events, $\mathcal{P} = \prod \mathcal{Q}_i$ is an invariant for our cipher, cf. our Theorem 7.1 page 16.

4.1   Non Deterministic Walks on Cycles

We operate by "walks", advancing by one position on a given cycle on polynomials $\mathcal{Q}_i$. This process is not deterministic and the path is not unique. The same polynomial $\mathcal{Q}_i$ could potentially appear on several cycles. This is due to some freedom[13] of choice for the $\mathcal{Z}_i$. This greatly increases the number of possibilities for the attacker. In this paper, for the sake of simplicity, all cycle walks are deterministic.

4.2   Discussion, Success Probability

The attacker works with arbitrary sets of well-chosen cycles. In the basic version of our attack, we simply multiply all the $\mathcal{Q}_i$, and we expect to get a non-zero polynomial invariant, which can[14] then be used in cryptanalysis. Can this be made to work? One factor which increases the chance of success is the size of our configuration with all the $\{\mathcal{Q}_i; \mathcal{Z}_i\}$. The more polynomials we multiply, the

---

[10]   In T-310 cipher F is derived from the public IV used in each encryption, cf. [23].

[11]   This type of equation was previously studied under the name of a *Transition Equation* or (TE) in Section 5 of [17].

[12]   Here transitions are no longer invariants but rather of type $\mathcal{P} \to \mathcal{P}'$ with $\mathcal{P} \neq \mathcal{P}'$.

[13]   It is easy to see that there is no reason why transition should be deterministic. For example we could have $\mathcal{Z}_1 = Z(a, b, c) = abc + ac$ and $\mathcal{Z}_3 = Z(a, b, c) + b = abc + ac + b$ which inevitably lead to two different transitions if starting form the same polynomial assuming $\mathcal{Q}_1 = \mathcal{Q}_3$, and we have simultaneously $Z(b+1)(a+1) = 0$ and $(Z + b)(b + 1)(a + 1) = 0$.

[14]   We refer to Section 9 in [18] and Section 6 in [13] to see how.

more likely it happens that all our polynomials $\mathcal{Z}_i$ are annihilated by some product of the $\mathcal{Q}_i$. It is easy to see that if a [Boolean] polynomial g is a product then for a Boolean function f to be annihilated by this polynomial, i.e. $fg = 0$ for every input, we just need to look at values of f at points where $g = 1$. This will concern only a fraction of the truth table of f, and therefore is more likely to happen. Specific examples are provided later. In Sect. 6.3, g is linear, which makes the attack very weak, cf. later Theorem 6.4. Then in an improved attack in Theorem 8.1 in Sect. 8 every g has 2 factors. Similarly for DES, in [18] some g are linear, then in Theorem 9.1 in Sect. 9 each of five polynomials g has two factors. Our attacks work only for as long as $\mathcal{P} = \prod \mathcal{Q}_i$ remains not zero itself, which strongly limits what we can achieve.

4.3   Additional Attacks with Decimation and Sub-cycles

Decimated variants based on sub-cycles can also be constructed. The main idea is that we can advance by more than 1 step in a cycle. This happens for example in T-310, under certain (more stringent) technical conditions we can have an attack with period of 2 rounds[15] of type $AC \rightarrow BD \rightarrow AC$ cf. [12], which uses the same cycle of period 4, which will also be used in our attack in Fig. 7. For DES we provide in Sect. 10 an example of type $\mathcal{P} \rightarrow \mathcal{P}' \rightarrow \mathcal{P}$, where the degree of $\mathcal{P}$ and $\mathcal{P}'$ is 5. Then it is easy to see that $AC + BD$ and $\mathcal{P} + \mathcal{P}'$ are invariants holding for[16] 1 round.

5   Limitations vs. Vulnerable Boolean Functions

Main limitations of our attacks are that the degree of $\mathcal{P}$ in the attack must increase[17] substantially in order to work with some non-trivial (e.g. highly non-linear) Boolean functions or S-boxes. Then potentially some attacks at lower degree can be also constructed as shown in Sect. 10. However, typically there is a price to pay for such improved attacks to work at a lower degree[18]. For example, our advanced degree 5 result of Theorem 10.1 has a serious drawback. It forces the attacker to use some annihilator g, which is linear, making that this second attack works in extremely few cases, cf. Theorem 6.4. The same problem occurs in the attack on Section 11.7 in [18].

---

[15] Examples of non-linear invariants with a period of 4 rounds can be found in Appendix B.2. in [17].

[16] In contrast, due to the lack on unique factorisation in product attacks, it is not clear if or how our attack of degree 5 in Sect. 10 can be obtained, with or without decimation, from cycles following our general framework.

[17] This is related to the question of biases inside the block cipher induced by polynomial invariants, cf. Section 9 in [18] and Section 6 in [13].

[18] Rather than when we simply multiply all the polynomials.

5.1   On Annihilation Vulnerability and Worst-Case Normality

The primary aim of this paper is to have an even more general attack framework, leading to annihilation assumptions which are more likely to work also when Boolean functions are strong. Our long term goal is to find attacks such as in [18], which operate under weaker and fully realistic assumptions. For example such that every annihilator g is a product of three affine factors, e.g. with $Z(a + b)c(1 + e) = 0$. One question is if there exist non-linear attacks using such properties at degree 3. For example following [17,18] for DES this is already quite difficult to achieve[19] A second question is how many boolean function are vulnerable. There are very few examples in real-life encryption systems, where Boolean functions would have annihilators of degree 2. In contrast properties with degree 3 annihilators can very hardly be avoided in general, which we are going to show now.

One recent and surprising result is that the probability that for example $Z(a + b)(c + d)(e + f) = 0$ is typically quite high, cf. [18]. Accordingly if this property does not hold for the original Boolean function of T-310, this is maybe just accidental rather than deliberate. For example $Z(a + b)c(1 + e) = 0$ holds for the original Boolean function designed in the 1970s, cf. Appendix I.19 in [23]. For general cubic annihilators the Thm 6.0.1 in [15] says that for every Boolean function Z we have either Z or $Z + 1$ which has an annihilator of degree 3. Then Thm. 6.3. and Thm. 6.4. in [18] deals with special cases which split into some specific affine factors.

This property is very highly relevant to our general framework and all attacks studied in this paper. It is not immediately apparent but it turns out, that this type of events were already studied by Dobbertin at FSE'94 under the name of normality [28]. A more general notion called k-normality was introduced and studied by Charpin cf. [8]. Here we discover that a stronger result than Thm 6.0.1 in [15] holds: for every Boolean function on 6 variables either Z or $Z + 1$ is annihilated by a product of 3 affine functions:

Theorem 5.2 (All Boolean functions in 6 variables are 3-normal). Given a Boolean function Z in 6 variables chosen uniformly at random the probability that it is 2-normal i.e. it has an annihilation of type

$$Z \cdot f \cdot g = 0 \text{ or } (Z + 1) \cdot f \cdot g = 0$$

with two arbitrary affine factors f, g is equal to $2^{-1.66}$. Furthermore the probability that it is 3-normal i.e. it has an annihilation of type

$$Z \cdot f \cdot g \cdot h = 0 \text{ or } (Z + 1) \cdot f \cdot g \cdot h = 0$$

with three arbitrary affine factors f, g, h is equal to exactly 1.

Proof. Our property in invariant w.r.t. ordinary affine equivalence of Boolean functions w.r.t arbitrary invertible affine transformations on the 6 variables. We

---

[19] The best example known to us so far requires $\mathcal{P}$ of degree 20.

have examined all the 150357 classes of Boolean functions with 6 variables cf. [7], and found that 47446 classes are 2-normal and all 150357 classes are 3-normal.

6   A Simple Impossible Transition Attack of Degree 4

We first show a simple attack, which demonstrates why it is interesting to have a cycle on four polynomials $\mathcal{Q}_i$. We will then show how to annihilate one non-linear polynomial which will be sufficient to obtain an attack which works. This attack is designed for T-310 cipher, however we do NOT need to know the full specs of this block cipher. Our attack is a formal result on Boolean polynomials. In order to show it all we will need to know are two exact formulas (two Boolean polynomials) by which just **two** output bits 21 and 29 are computed in one round of encryption. In this form, the same attack could be potentially applied to any block cipher if only after renaming variables it would satisfy the same four transitions, three of which are trivial and which are shown on Fig. 7 below.

DES is a Feistel cipher operating on two branches of 32 bits each. T-310 has 4 branches with 9 bits each and bits are numbered 1..36, cf. Fig. 5. In one round of encryption, cf. Fig. 6, all bits numbered $1 \leq k \leq 36$ with $k \neq 0 \mod 4$ are shifted to position $k + 1$, and bits of type $4k + 1$ are those freshly created. By convention $P(i) = j$ if round input vi cf. Fig. 6 is connected to bit number j in the input of the round. Similarly $D(5) = j$ means that wire $D5$ is connected to input j, except when $j = 0$ which would mean that a key bit used instead (left of Fig. 6).

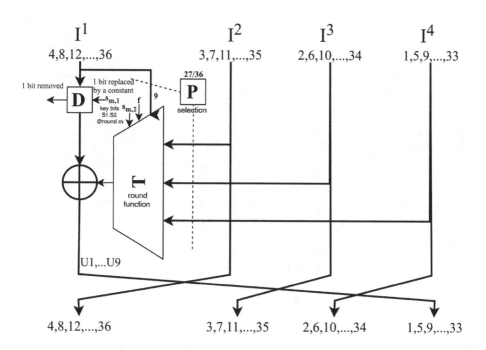

Fig. 5. T-310: a peculiar sort of compressing unbalanced Feistel scheme.

6.1   A Basic Nonlinear Invariant Attack of Degree 4

We will now describe an attack where the value $\in \{0,1\}$ of a certain polynomial $\mathcal{P}$, involving only 8 bits out of 36 in each round, will be shown to be invariant after one round of T-310 block cipher.

Theorem 6.2 (Simple Invariant Attack of Degree 4). For each cipher wiring for T-310 s.t. $D(8) = P(6)$, $D(6) = 32$ and $P(10) = 30$, $P(11) = 22$ and $P(12) = 24$, if the Boolean function is such that $(Y + f)(d + e) = 0$, and for any short term key of 240 bits, and for any IV, and for any initial state on 36 bits, given the sums of 2 variables A, B, C, D defined in Fig. 7, the non-linear invariant $\mathcal{P} = ABCD$, holds with probability 1 for any number of rounds.

Proof. We verify on Fig. 6, that the XOR of two output bits $y_{29} + y_{21}$, is equal to a sum of 4 bits. This is exactly, following explicit general round ANF formulas given in [24, 35], equal to:

$$y_{29} + y_{21} = F + Z(...) + x_{D(8)} + F + Z(...) + x_{P(6)} + Y\left(x_{P(7)}, \ldots, x_{P(12)}\right) + x_{D(6)}$$

Following [23] cipher state variables 1–36 can also be represented as letters with a backwards numbering convention, for instance a is the same x_{36}, up to z which denotes bit x_{11}, and bits 1–10 are named by capital letters M through V. As we study 1-round invariants we need to distinguish between variables and polynomials on the input and output sides. By convention, if a represents a variable, we write a^i if it is on the input side, and a^o on the output side. Then

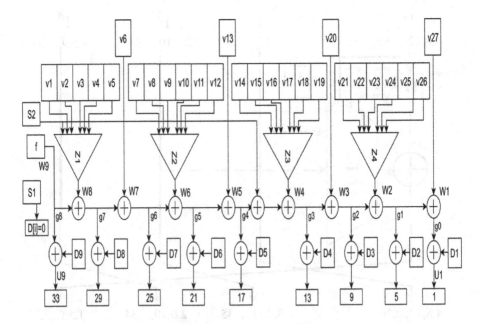

Fig. 6. The internal structure of one round of T-310 block cipher.

if $D = h + p$ is a polynomial and sum of two variables, where h is also variable number 29 and p is the variable number 21, we have by definition:

$$D^i = h^i + p^i = x_{21} + x_{29}$$

where addition is modulo 2 and x_i are inputs of one round numbered from 1 to 36. In the same way if y_i are outputs of the analyzed round, by definition:

$$D^o = h^o + p^o = y_{21} + y_{29}$$

We can now plug-in the only formula (above), which comes from the specs of the cipher getting:

$$D^o = x_{D(8)} + x_{P(6)} + Y() + x_{D(6)}$$

Now we use our assumptions $D(8) = P(6)$, and $P(12) = 24$ and we get:

$$D^o = Y\left(x_{P(7)}, \ldots, x_{P(12)}\right) + x_{D(6)}$$

Now given that $D(6) = 32$ and $A^i = x_{24} + x_{32}$ we have:

$$D^o = Y\left(x_{P(7)}, \ldots, x_{P(12)}\right) + x_{24} + A^i$$

where x_{24} is the same as last input f of this Boolean function $Y()$, which is due to $P(12) = 24$. If for simplicity we denote by $(Y + f)$ a modified Boolean function with addition of the last input, we obtain:

$$D^o = (Y + f)\left(x_{P(7)}, \ldots, x_{P(12)}\right) + A^i$$

In addition we have the trivial transitions

$$C^o = y_{30} + y_{22} = x_{29} + x_{21} = D^i$$

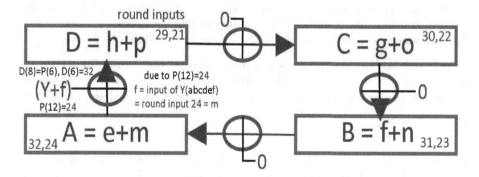

Fig. 7. A cycle and sequence of 4 polynomial transitions for 4 rounds which leads to a non-linear invariant attack with $\mathcal{P} = ABCD$, which is an invariant for 1 round. (Color figure online)

and similarly $B^o = C^i$ and $A^o = B^i$, which comes from bit k becoming $k+1$ in the next round for all k not being a multiple of 4, cf. [24,35]. Here we will see why forming **a cycle** with A, B, C, D matters.

In order to show that $ABCD$ is an invariant we need to show that:

$$\mathcal{P}^o = A^o B^o C^o D^o = A^i B^i C^i D^i = \mathcal{P}^i$$

and we have several immediate trivial transitions:

$$\mathcal{P}^o = A^o B^o C^o D^o = B^i C^i D^i D^o =$$

$$B^i C^i D^i \left((Y+f)\left(x_{P(7)}, \ldots, x_{P(12)}\right) + A^i\right) \overset{?}{=} A^i B^i C^i D^i = \mathcal{P}^i$$

All we need to do now is to show that:

$$B^i C^i D^i \left((Y+f)\left(x_{P(7)}, \ldots, x_{P(12)}\right)\right) = 0$$

Finally we also check that $(Y + x_{24})C^i = 0$ is the same as $(Z + f)(d+e) = 0$ due to $C^i = x_{30} + x_{22}$ and $P(10) = 30$, $P(11) = 22$ and $P(12) = 24$.   □

6.3   Why Current Attack Is Unsatisfactory

It is easy to note that in the last example we have NOT used the full power of the attack. We have requested that $(Y + f)C = 0$ in order to make sure that $(Y + f)BCD = 0$, in other words we must make sure that $Y + f$ is equal to zero in 2^5 points, while we would only need $Y = f$ at 2^3 entries in the truth table. This is due to the fact, that the wiring of the cipher satisfies an extremely complex set of technical requirements known under the name of KT1 specification cf. [24,35]. These requirements seems to prevent our attack in some way. It is clearly meant to prevent attacks where several linear polynomials B, C, D would simultaneously be composed of too many inputs of the same Boolean function Y. We discover that the cryptologists in the former Eastern Bloc have somewhat managed to make our attack harder to apply.

In addition, it is difficult to hope that $(Y + f)C = 0$ could be true for any Boolean function resembling those found in real-life ciphers. Extremely few Boolean functions have linear annihilators. One basic result is as follows:

Theorem 6.4 (Impossibility for Balanced-ness and Non-Linearity). It is not possible to find a Boolean function Z required by our degree 4 attack of Theorem 6.2 in such a way, that $Y + f$ is simultaneously balanced and non-linear.

Proof. Let:

$$g(a, b, c, d, e, f) * Z(a, b, c, d, e, f) = 0$$

where $g()$ is an affine function. Since g is balanced for some 2^{6-1} inputs we have $g = 1$ and for all those we must have $Z = 0$. Now since Z is balanced it must be $Z = 1$ on all the remaining 2^{6-1} inputs and our function is now completely determined and we have $Z = g + 1$ for any input. Finally since g is linear Z also must be linear. This contradiction ends our proof.   □

Observations. With this result, in theory $Y + f$ would not be balanced but Y could after all be balanced. However most ciphers not only use balanced Boolean functions, but also avoid many other correlations carefully, and most modified functions such as $Y + f$ should be balanced or very close to balanced.

6.5   Discussion and Way Forward

We would like to be able design better invariant attacks which operate under weaker assumptions, such as for example $Z(a + b)c(1 + e) = 0$. This sort of annihilation properties with products of 3 affine functions do happen for real-life cryptographic Boolean functions and we have already seen cf. Theorem 5.2 that annihilations with 3 linear factors are in general totally impossible to avoid.

Until now polynomial invariant attacks seem to occur by some sort of coincidence. For example in one very special setting known in [18] as LZS 265 we require that our Boolean function satisfies $Z(a + b)(c + d)(e + f) = 0$, which was not[20] the case for the original Boolean function. We are looking towards constructing a broader family of attacks, which require a larger variety of annihilation conditions. In this paper we show how to construct such attacks in general and potentially for any block cipher. We start by stating our general construction which clearly generalizes the current attack and then we will apply it to construct a new attack on T-310 of degree 8. Moreover it should be obvious that more and better attacks can be obtained at higher degrees.

7   Our General Framework Theorem and Construction

Here is our general attack where we multiply polynomials over one or several cycles. It is possible to distinguish two sorts of transitions in our directed graphs. Simple transitions, where the difference is zero[21] and the input polynomial Q_i will be called a "transformable"[22] polynomial. Then we have the "impossible transitions", where the difference is a sum of complex non-linear polynomials[23].

Theorem 7.1 (General Cycling Product Invariant Attack). We consider a set of basic polynomials Q_j organised in one or several closed loops (directed cycles). Let $\pi(j)$ be the next point on any given cycle where $\pi()$ is an arbitrary permutation (which acts on a union of one or several directed cycles and advances one step forward). We assume that for any j we have (due to internal connections inside the cipher) the following simple transition with a XOR with a non-linear function:

$$Q^o_{\pi(j)} = Q^i_j + Z_j()$$

---

[20] However it is sufficient to modify just the last linear term in order to make the attack work in T-310, cf. Section 7.2. in [18].

[21] We have 0 in red which is XORed at three places in Fig. 7.

[22] This name means that our block cipher transforms it into another polynomial Q_j included in our set.

[23] For example $Z_1 = Y + f$ is XORed at one place in Fig. 7 where Y is a polynomial with 6 inputs.

where $\mathcal{Z}_j()$ are some arbitrary non-linear polynomials[24] using arbitrary variables (which represent some bits inside the cipher). Then we assume that at least **one** of these polynomials is equal to 0, i.e. we have just one trivial transition without any extra non-linear terms. Among all these polynomials those $\mathcal{Q}_j$ inside "simple" transitions as defined above, i.e. exactly those where $\mathcal{Z}_j() = 0$, are called "transformable" polynomials[25]. Other polynomials $\mathcal{Z}_i$ are non-zero[26] and they use the same set of input-side variables as $\mathcal{Q}_i$. Moreover we assume that for every $\mathcal{Z}_j()$ this Boolean function is annihilated by product of (up to) all "transformable" polynomials $\mathcal{Q}_k$, or more precisely that:

$$\forall_j \quad \prod_{\substack{k \\ \text{transformable}}} \mathcal{Q}_k() \cdot \mathcal{Z}_j() = 0$$

for any input. Then

$$\mathcal{P} = \prod_j \mathcal{Q}_j$$

is an invariant for our cipher holding with probability 1, for any secret key, for any initial state on n bits, and for any number of rounds.

Remark. Our attack is non-trivial, if this final product $\mathcal{P} \neq 0$. This needs to be checked in each case, and when $\mathcal{P} = 0$ our attack fails.

Proof. This theorem is formulated in such a way, that the proof is extremely simple. We have

$$\mathcal{P}^o = \prod_j \mathcal{Q}_j^o = \prod_j \mathcal{Q}_{\pi(j)}^o = \prod_j \left(\mathcal{Q}_j^i + \mathcal{Z}_j() \right) =$$

and now the product of all transformable polynomials can be put aside as a factor:

$$= \prod_{\substack{j \\ \text{transformable}}} \mathcal{Q}_j^i() \cdot \prod_{\substack{j \text{ not} \\ \text{transformable}}} \left(\mathcal{Q}_j^i + \mathcal{Z}_j() \right) =$$

and here each and every non-zero $\mathcal{Z}_j()$ is annihilated because the product of all transformable polynomials is a factor, and because our theorem assumes these annihilations. We get:

$$= \prod_j \mathcal{Q}_j^i = \mathcal{P}^i$$

$\square$

---

[24] These polynomials appear in red on our pictures for example $(Y + e)$ where Y is an arbitrary polynomial and e is an additional variable.

[25] Typically about half of all polynomials are "transformable" in all known applications of this theorem.

[26] These polynomials are exactly the same as the notion of *Transition Equation* or *(TE)* which was introduced in Sect. 5 of [17] to extend the concept of Fundamental Equation *(FE)* of [17] to arbitrary transitions of type $\mathcal{P} \rightarrow \mathcal{Q}$ when $\mathcal{P} \neq \mathcal{Q}$.

Observations. This theorem somewhat implicitly assumes quite a few polynomials $\mathcal{Z}_j()$ are equal to zero, which increases the number of "transformable" factors and thus in turn increases the chances for different non-zero polynomials $\mathcal{Z}_j()$ to be annihilated. It is easy to see that older Theorem 6.2. is a direct application of new Theorem 7.1, where all of the B, C, D are transformable polynomials, one of which was actually used to annihilate $Y + f$. We claim (and intend to show) that this theorem can be used to construct a large variety of attacks on block ciphers and that results compare favourably to other known attacks. This is due to the fact (as explained in Sect. 4.2) that the more polynomials we multiply, the easier it is to obtain the annihilations we need. In addition we enjoy a substantial freedom in the choice of these polynomials for any given block cipher. The attacker is happy to observe that there exist vast number of possible choices of the $\{Q_i; \mathcal{Z}_i\}$ some of which might lead to a working attack.

8   Application to T-310: A Better Cycling Attack

We present an improved attack on T-310 which is of degree 8 and[27] is a direct application of Theorem 7.1. The application is shown on Fig. 8 below, the Q_i are 8 polynomials on the edges of our cycle, out of which D, C, B, H, G, F are "transformable" polynomials which we are allowed to use in our annihilation attempts and there are two non-zero polynomials to annihilate $W() + e$ and $Y() + e$. Given the fact that both Boolean $W()$ and $Y()$ are by definition identical, these two polynomials are annihilated in exactly the same way, modulo renaming their 6 inputs.

Theorem 8.1 (An Invariant Attack of Degree 8). With polynomials $A-H$ defined as on Fig. 8, for each cipher wiring for T-310 s.t. $D(5) = 8, P(13) = 16, D(7) = P(11), D(2) = 20, P(20) = 28, D(4) = P(25)$, if the Boolean function (used twice as W and as Y for different sets of inputs) is such that

$$(Z + e)(a + b)(c + d) = 0$$

and if the first 4 inputs of W are in order bits 14, 6, 15, 7, and the first 4 inputs of Y are in order bits 18, 26, 19, 27 also[28], then and for any short term key of 240 bits, and for any initial state on 36 bits, we have the non-linear invariant

$$\mathcal{P} = ABCDEFGH$$

holding with probability 1.0 for any number of rounds.

---

[27] A simpler example of a cycle of length 8 in T-310 is shown on Fig. 4 however the actual invariant studied was of degree 2, cf. Section 7.4 in [17].

[28] These 8 conditions are simply 8 additional conditions on $P()$ e.g. $P(22) = 14$ etc.

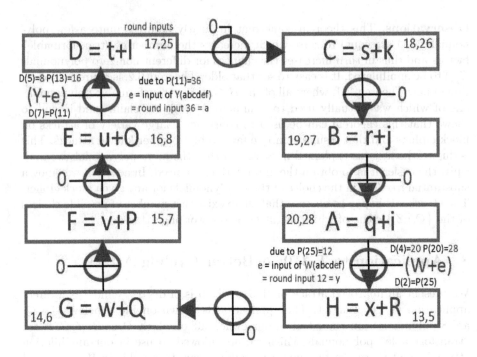

Fig. 8. An attack using a cycle on 8 with $\mathcal{P} = ABCDEFGH$.

Note: This is for example achieved for the following full cipher wiring:

444: P = 17,1,33,2,10,3,18,26,19,27,36,5,16,32,21,34,8,
25,13,28,14,6,15,7,12,23,30 D=24,20,4,12,8,32,36,16,28

and with a Boolean function being for example:

$$Z = fedcb + fedca + fedc + fecba + fecb + feca + fec + feba + feb + fea + fe$$
$$+ fdb + fd + fcb + fc + fb + f + edcb + ed + ec + dcb + dca + da + d + cb + a + 1$$

Proof. The proof is the same as before and both follow the same principle as in Theorem 7.1 We compute

$$\mathcal{P}^o - \mathcal{P}^i =$$

and obtain the following difference, where B, C, D, F, G, H are all transformable polynomials cf. Fig. 8:

$$BCDFGH \cdot ((E + a + Y)(A + y + W) + AE)$$

A quick analysis discarding factors such as D which have variables not used as inputs of out Boolean functions W, Y and renaming variables shows that we need that $FG(y + W) = 0$ and $BC(Y + a) = 0$. Each of 2 terms is cancelled through two identical annihilation requirements of type exactly:

$$(Z + e)(a + b)(c + d) = 0$$

which is exactly our assumption.   □

Remark. With invariants of degree 8 one can do better than $(Z + e)(a + b)(c + d) = 0$. In [18] we discover that it is possible to design a similar attack with a weaker assumption $Z(a + b)(c + d)(e + f) = 0$ which makes that the attack is substantially more likely to work, when the Boolean function is chosen at random. Equivalently, our attack should require to check or modify only a small number of values inside the truth table of this Boolean function Z.

9   On Existence of Polynomial Invariants in DES

DES is one of the most widely used cryptographic algorithms of all times and there exists numerous modified versions of DES [26,33,34]. There are strong connections between various Feistel ciphers used in government communications during the Cold War cf. [10,26]. In Eastern Germany DES was implemented inside a portable electronic cipher machine T-316 [26]. Our methodology and notations emphasise similarities between different ciphers, and we do not believe that a cipher must necessarily be special or weak, in order to exhibit a large variety of polynomial invariants. We will now show that our attack and our systematic construction applies to DES, and allows one to build invariants true with probability 1 for a fraction of the key space. This was never done before and should be seen as improved bi-linear attack on DES of Crypto 2004, cf. [19]. A key observation is that we have phase transition: if we increase the degree of our invariant polynomial, the probabilities that our invariant works can be improved very substantially. Again, we formulate the attack in such a way that the full description of DES is not needed. We just need to see that DES happens to satisfy a number of internal wiring conditions (full detailed wiring is shown later in Fig. 11 28) which after renaming variables could hold for any other cipher. By convention we assume that the secret key of DES is part of the S-box, or is added inside each S-box, i.e. we consider each S-box as a function of variables named $abcdef$ and not those named $ABCDEF$ cf. Fig. 9. This, as we will see later, allows our invariant attacks to be formulated in a surprisingly simple and compact way without reference to the secret key, which will be dealt with later, when we want to apply such results in cryptanalysis, cf. Remark 2 in page 22. Our specific attack below is not meant to work for real-life DES S-boxes. It will work only if the S-boxes (including the key) satisfy some specific annihilation conditions. These are stronger than in any previous non-linear invariant attack on DES [18,19]. In Appendix B we tentatively consider what happens with real-life S-boxes.

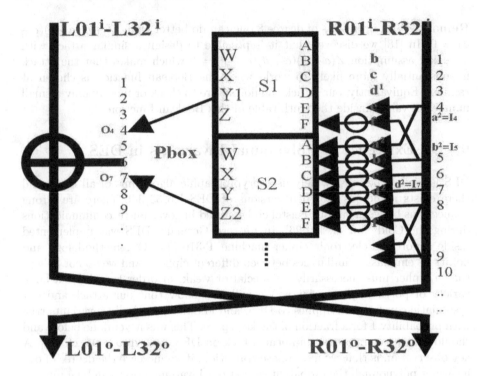

Fig. 9. One round of DES with specific notations we use in this paper.

Notation: We denote by (L01,..., L32; R01,..., R32) the inputs of one rounds of DES. The same notations will be also used for the outputs and when it is needed to distinguish between different instances of the same variable we will use exponents, for example $L05^i$ will be the 5-th input in one round and $L05^o$ will be the 5-th output bit. Now we define the following polynomials:

$$\begin{cases} A = R05 \in \{\text{Input bits of } \mathbf{S2}\} \\ B = R07 \in \{\text{Input bits of } \mathbf{S2}\} \\ C = R28 + 1 \in \{\text{Input bits of } \mathbf{S7}\} \cap \{\text{Input bits of } \mathbf{S8}\} \\ D = R27 + 1 \in \{\text{Input bits of } \mathbf{S7}\} \\ E = R32 \in \{\text{Input bits of } \mathbf{S8.}\} \end{cases}$$

Moreover we also define

$$\begin{cases} A' = L05, & B' = L07 & C' = L28 + 1 \\ D' = L27 + 1 & E' = L32 \end{cases}$$

We will then write that

$$(a + e) * (e) * W8 == 0$$

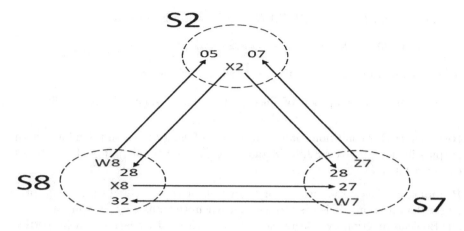

Fig. 10. Closed-loop connection between S-boxes S2, S7, S8 in DES.

if and when the polynomial $(a + e) * (e)$ annihilates the 1st output W of the eighth S-box $S8$, where $a - f$ are inputs of that same respective S-box. By annihilation we mean that the product is zero for any input on 6 bits, i.e. $==$ is formal equality of two polynomials. At other places it there is no ambiguity we will write simply $=$ instead of $==$. We now apply our framework of Theorem 7.1 and construct our attack on DES. Our Q_i will be some well chosen polynomials such as C or E defined above , with for example:

$$W8 * C * E = 0$$

Theorem 9.1 (A Simple Degree 10 Attack On DES). We assume that:

$$\begin{cases} (a + e) * (e) * W8 == 0 \\ (a + e) * (e) * X8 == 0 \\ (d + 1) * (e + 1) * (Z7 + d) == 0 \\ (d + 1) * (e + 1) * (W7 + e) == 0 \\ bd * (X2 + b + d) == 0 \end{cases}$$

We also assume[29] the following connections inside the P-Box of DES, cf. Fig. 11:

$$\begin{cases} P(5) = 29 = W8 \\ P(7) = 28 = Z7 \\ P(28) = 6 = X2 \\ P(27) = 30 = X8 \\ P(32) = 25 = W7 \end{cases}$$

---

[29] By convention we work backwards from output to input side, cf. Fig. 11, and $P(5) = 29$ means that the output 29 of 8 S-boxes connected to round output 5, where numbering goes from 1 to 32. These connections are true for DES, and our attack works also for DES with any modified P-box for as long as it satisfies these conditions.

Then the product $\mathcal{P} = ABCDEA'B'C'D'E'$ which is equal to

$$\mathcal{P} = R05 * R07 * (R28 + 1) * (R27 + 1) * R32 * L05 * L07 * (L28 + 1) * (L27 + 1) * L32$$

is a one-round invariant for DES for a fraction of key space.

Proof We provide two proofs of Theorem 9.1 which are given in Appendix A.

Remark 1: Our conditions only concern $1/4$ of values in truth table for certain outputs in three S-boxes S2,S7,S8 and the content of the remaining five S-boxes can be arbitrary.

Remark 2: This attack works for a fraction of key space which is frequently larger than it seems. It is easy to see that when we translate the input of any of our Boolean function by a secret key (by a bitwise XOR), each of our properties such as $(a + e)(e) * W8 == 0$, still holds with probability being at least 2^{-2}. This is because each annihilating product such as $(a + e)(e)$ is itself not changed (!), with a large probability, when we modify the secret key inside the S-box.

Remark 3: As the degree of our polynomials increases, we can apply our framework and search for better attacks, such that all annihilations required have 3 affine terms. This increases the success probability that the attack works for some S-boxes. At the same time the number of active S-boxes increases. The conclusion is that there exist an optimal size where the attack is the strongest possible. Interestingly there is also a question of optimal size in truncated differential attacks [10] and both questions are related, cf. Sect. 3.

10   An Attack on DES with a Lower Degree of 5

We now show that the degree in our attack of Theorem 9.1 can be reduced from 10 to 5. This attack requires a stronger set of annihilations as shown below.

Theorem 10.1 (2-R invariant of degree 5 derived from degree 10 invariant). If we have the following annihilation conditions:

$$\begin{cases} Z7 * (e + 1) = 0, & W7 * (e + 1) = 0, \\ X8 * (a + 1) = 0, & W8 * e = 0, \\ X2 * d = 0 \end{cases}$$

then the polynomial

$$\mathcal{P} = R05 * L07 * (R28 + 1) * (L27 + 1) * L32$$

is an invariant after two rounds of encryption for DES.

Proof. All we need to do is to show that $\mathcal{P}^\phi = \mathcal{P}^{\phi^{-1}}$. We have:

$$\mathcal{P}^\phi = (\text{L05}+ \overbrace{\text{W8}_{\text{R28=R32,R01}}}^{W8*R32=0}) * \text{R07} * (\text{L28}+ \overbrace{\text{X2}_{\text{R04=R09}}}^{X2*R07=0} +1) * (\text{R27} + 1) * \text{R32}$$
$$= \text{L05} * \text{R07} * (\text{L28} + 1) * (\text{R27} + 1) * \text{R32}$$

where the annihilations occur in the first round and R32 and R07 are inputs of the first round. For the second round we have:

$$\mathcal{P}^{\phi^{-1}} = \text{L05} * (\text{R07}+ \overbrace{\text{Z7}_{\text{L24=L29}}}^{Z7*(L28+1)=0}) * (\text{L28} + 1)*$$
$$(\text{R27}+ \overbrace{\text{X8}_{\text{L28=L32,L01}}}^{X8*(L28+1)=0} +1) * (\text{R32}+ \overbrace{\text{W7}_{\text{L24=L29}}}^{W7*(L28+1)=0})$$
$$= \text{L05} * \text{R07} * (\text{L28} + 1) * (\text{R27} + 1) * \text{R32}$$

Here the annihilations occur in the second round and if R28 is taken at the output of the second round, this variable is in fact equal to L28, or e, when seen as input of the second round S-box S7.   □

Remark 1. It may seem that this proves that the invariant attack works also for 1 round, but it doesn't. After 1 round the two sides L, R are SWAPPED[30].

Remark 2. If we denote by $\mathcal{P}'$ the symmetric version of $\mathcal{P}$ above, then it is easy to see that $\mathcal{P} + \mathcal{P}'$ is an invariant of degree 5 for 1 round, cf. Sect. 4.3.

Remark 3. It is an open problem if a second proof of Theorem 10.1 can at all be obtained from our general framework construction of Theorem 7.1.

11   Conclusion

Non-linear attacks on block ciphers are about two very complex polynomials being equal and as such so far, they were considered to happen by some extraordinary coincidence. In this paper we introduced a method for constructing non-linear attacks on block ciphers in a systematic way. It explains **why** some previously studied attacks work, and we can construct a large variety of new attacks of higher degree. We generalize the concept of closed-loop configuration cf. [38], and extend it to cycles involving arbitrary polynomials $\mathcal{Q}_i$ which cycles initially are rather impossible and are made possible by considering addition of some well chosen non-linear polynomials $\mathcal{Z}_i$. Then we eliminate all the $\mathcal{Z}_i$ algebraically. We obtain a large family of new attacks, which can now be studied.

Our general attack is formulated in such a way, that after renaming the variables it could apply to any block cipher; cf. our framework Theorem 7.1

---

[30] This is closely related to the question of reflection attacks in GOST, cf. [27].

and all our application results. The attack is built on premises that the cipher satisfies a small number of initial assumptions, which concern a tiny fraction of the specification of the cipher. This should be compared to certain results on worst-case algebraic attacks on stream ciphers. All these attacks are about how eliminating a large number of internal variables and many attacks on stream ciphers are also based on polynomial annihilation events [15]. At ICISC 2004, [16], we discover that some stream ciphers can be broken no matter what: for any Boolean function or S-box. Similarly here we observe, that as the number of polynomials in our cycles increases, our annihilation conditions with more linear factors become totally impossible to avoid, cf. Theorem 5.2. This enables us to construct attacks which work, provided that an (increasingly small) fraction of the truth table of our Boolean functions are such as requested. Overall our attacks become increasingly hard to prevent and are not necessarily avoided by standard non-linearity requirements studied in cryptography cf. [2]. We claim that our attacks are not[31] in general prevented with traditional block cipher design methodology [5,20,33,34], cf. Theorem 5.2. A serious limitation however is that for DES our attack only works for a fraction of the key space and not quite for the original S-boxes, cf. Appendix B. For T-310 attacks are substantially stronger and work for 100 % of keys and with arbitrary round constants.

The present work is not exhaustive and does NOT cover all possible invariant attacks, which in the general case form a polynomial ring with sums and products. The main contribution of this paper is to show how to construct attacks with one product, where this ring is not trivial and not empty: existence of at least one invariant attack. Experience shows that then other better attacks with lower degree and more products may also exist, cf. Sect. 2.3 and [11,12,17]. For example we found that with a small modification in Theorem 8.1 we can obtain a larger invariant ring with dimension up to 9, containing further invariants of degree 2, 4 and 6. We demonstrate this for DES in Sect. 10: we show that the degree of the invariant property in Theorem 9.1 can be reduced from 10 to 5. In general it is not easy to know if any given non-linear attack can be constructed using our general framework of Theorem 7.1.

A   Two Proofs of Theorem 9.1

We provide two proofs of Theorem 9.1. First proof just shows that the attack works directly step by step without revealing that it might be an application of Theorem 7.1. Second proof follows our framework based on three cycles, cf. Figs. 12, 13 and 14. Both proofs are about rewriting everything with input variables only.

First Proof of Theorem 9.1: We rewrite our annihilation conditions using $A, B, \ldots$ at input side, for every input:

---

[31] Except in more recent works specifically aiming at thwarting invariant attacks [3,6].

$$\begin{cases} W8 * C * E = X8 * C * E = 0 \\ Z7 * C * D = W7 * C * D = 0 \\ X2 * A * B = 0 \end{cases}$$

Using Fig. 11 we see that on the output side after one round ϕ of encryption:

$$\mathcal{P}^o = \mathcal{P}^\phi = (L05 + P5) * (L07 + P7) * (L28 + P28 + 1) * (L27 + P27 + 1) * (L32 + P32)$$
$$* R05 * R07 * (R28 + 1) * (R27 + 1) * R32 = (L05 + W8) * (L07 + Z7) * (L28 + X2 + 1) *$$
$$(L27 + X8 + 1) * (L32 + W7) * R05 * R07 * (R28 + 1) * (R27 + 1) * R32$$

$$= (L05 + \overbrace{W8}^{C*E*W8=0}) * (L07 + \overbrace{Z7}^{C*D*Z7=0}) * (L28 + \overbrace{X2}^{A*B*X2=0} + 1) * (L27 + \overbrace{X8}^{C*E*X8=0} + 1)$$

$$* (L32 + \overbrace{W7}^{C*D*W7=0}) * A * B * C * D * E = \mathcal{P}^i, \text{ i.e. exactly our input polynomial.}$$

□

Second Proof of Theorem 9.1: We show how our attack follows from Theorem 7.1 and 3 cycles in Figs. 12, 13 and 14. Each output-side polynomial $\mathcal{Q}_{j'}$ is equal to the sum of the input-side polynomial $\mathcal{Q}_j$ and the $\mathcal{Z}_j$ polynomial e.g. $(Z7 + d)$ or 0, added at this step. First we check the cycle on Fig. 12. First transition from R07 to L07 is trivial. In second transition we check that d for $S7$ is the same as $R27^i$ and:

$$(B')^i = (L07)^i = (R07)^o + (Z7 + d) + (R27)^i = (R07 + L27)^o + (Z7 + d) = (B + D' + 1)^o$$

In the same way we carefully check all 24 transitions on all 3 cycles. Each time an input of a Boolean function $a, \ldots, f$ is used we check which input number R01 ... R32 it is, cf. Fig. 11. For example d^7 denotes 4-th input of $S7$ which is $R28^i$. We show how round outputs $5, 7, 27, 28, 32$ are transformed in DES:

$$\begin{cases} L05^i = R05^o + W8(.) & \text{due to } P(5) = W8 \\ L07^i = R05^o + Z7(.) & \text{due to } P(7) = Z7 \\ L28^i = R28^o + X2(.) & \text{due to } P(28) = X2 \\ L27^i = R27^o + X8(.) & \text{due to } P(27) = X8 \\ L32^i = R32^o + W7(.) & \text{due to } P(32) = W7. \end{cases}$$

We recall that "transformable" polynomials are all $\mathcal{Q}_j$ which are transformed into another polynomial $\mathcal{Q}'_j$ included, i.e. all those with 0 added, and exactly those made from $A, B, C, \ldots$ only and not any of $A', B', C', \ldots$, and also those using R01-R32 and without any of L01-L32, which are:

$$\begin{cases} B = R07 \in \{\text{Fig. 12}\} & B + C + 1 = R07 + R28 \in \{\text{Fig. 12}\} \\ A + D + 1 = R05 + R27 \in \{\text{Fig. 13}\} & B + D + 1 = R07 + R27 \in \{\text{Fig. 13}\} \\ E = R32 \in \{\text{Fig. 14}\} & C + E + 1 = R28 + R32 \in \{\text{Fig. 14}\} \end{cases}$$

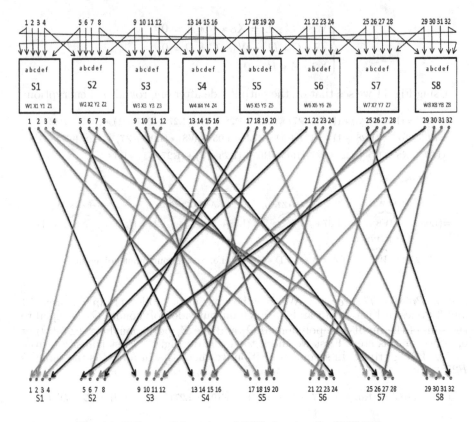

Fig. 11. Full round function of DES showing the DES P-box.

Then we show that the product of 24=8+8+8 polynomials is the same as our intended invariant $\mathcal{P}$ of degree $5 + 5$. We multiply all 6 transformable polynomials:

$$B(B + C + 1)(A + D + 1)(B + D + 1)E(C + E + 1) =$$
$$BC(A + D + 1)DE(C + E + 1) = ABCDE(C + E + 1) = ABCDE$$

Accordingly the identity above proves that the product of exactly **all** "transformable" polynomials on both cycles is simply equal to $ABCDE$ which fact we will use below. This product is of degree 5 in cipher state variables. Similarly we have: $B'(B' + C' + 1)(A' + D' + 1)(B' + D' + 1)E'(C' + E' + 1) = A'B'C'D'E'$. We have now multiplied 12 polynomials out of 24 on our 3 cycles and the result is our exact polynomial invariant as expected $\mathcal{P} = ABCDEA'B'C'D'E'$.

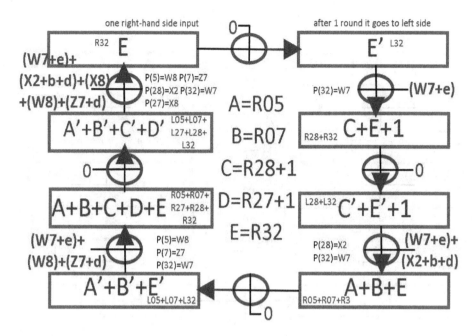

Fig. 12. First of three cycles leading to our invariant attack on DES in Theorem 9.1.

It remains to show that all the remaining 24-12=12 polynomials on the 3 cycles which were not multiplied yet, will be absorbed by $\mathcal{P}$. In other words the result $\mathcal{P}$ does not change if we multiply by these extra 12 factors. This is shown in 3 stages for each cycles in order, and the key observation is that $AB(B + A + 1) = AB$ and $ABC(B + A + C) = ABC$. Thus we have

$$ABCDEA'B'C'D'E'(B + D' + 1)(B' + C' + D) = ABCDEA'B'C'D'E'$$

We observe that all the 24 points at our cycles are such that the parity is odd, i.e. all 24 terms on 3 cycles will become zero if we assign all the 20 variables to 1. Therefore we can apply the rules $AB(B + A + 1) = AB$ and $ABC(B + A + C) = ABC$ for each new term.

Now we need to check that all the $\mathcal{Z}_j$ vanish when multiplied by exactly $ABCDE$ = product of all "transformable" polynomials. All the $\mathcal{Z}_j$ will be annihilated if we annihilate the 5 components $(W7+e), (X2+b+d), (X8), (W8), (Z7+d)$. We will need to check that each is annihilated by the product of all "transformable" polynomials = $ABCDE$.

For this we rewrite our assumptions with additional derived facts using rules $L_1L_2W = L_1L_2(W + L_1 + 1)$ and $L_1L_2W = L_1L_2(W + L_1 + L_2)$. For example $(a + e)e$ is the same as $CE = (R28 + 1)R32 = (R28 + R32)R32$. Likewise $(d + 1)(e + 1) = (R27 + 1)(R28 + 1) = CD$ for W7 and X7, and $bd = A * B$ for X2. We annihilated all 5 terms $(W7 + e), (X2 + b + d), (X8), (W8), (Z7 + d)$:

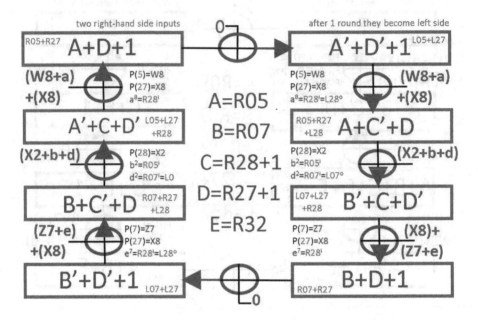

Fig. 13. Second cycle leading to invariant of degree 10 on DES in Theorem 9.1.

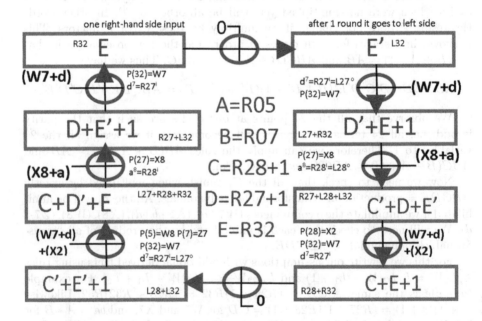

Fig. 14. Third cycle which is combined with other inside our proof of Theorem 9.1.

$$\left\{ \begin{aligned} C * E * \mathrm{W8} &= 0 & C * E * (\mathrm{W8} + \mathrm{a}) &= 0 \\ C * E * \mathrm{X8} &= 0 & C * E * (\mathrm{X8} + \mathrm{a}) &= 0 \\ C * D * (\mathrm{Z7} + d) &= 0 & C * D * (\mathrm{Z7} + e) &= 0 \\ C * D * (\mathrm{W7} + d) &= 0 & C * D * (\mathrm{W7} + e) &= 0 \\ A * B * (\mathrm{X2} + b + d) &= 0 & A * B * (\mathrm{X2}) &= 0 \end{aligned} \right.$$

□

B   Original DES Boxes: Shamir 1985 Paper Revisited

In 1985 Shamir observed that for **every** DES S-box, if we fix the second input variable to 1, the sum of all outputs is very strongly biased [36]. This has important consequences for our attacks. For **every** strongly biased Boolean function either Z or $Z + 1$ has unusually many annihilators, cf. Thm. B.2. in [18]. In particular we have some unusually simple annihilators with only 2 linear factors, e.g. the following property holds with probability 1 for the DES S-box S5:

$$R17(R16 + R20) * (W5 + X5 + Y5 + Z5) = 0.$$

We are not or **not yet** using the full power of Theorem 7.1 which allows the additions of affine terms. By doing we have a simpler linear annihilator:

$$(1 + R16 + R17 + R20) * (W5 + X5 + Y5 + Z5 + 1 + R17) = 0.$$

Here we can annihilate a non-linear function with just **one** transformable polynomial $(1 + R16 + R17 + R20)$ which corresponds to 1-weak-normality in [8]. It is an open problem to discover a full optimised attack using such annihilations.

References

1. Bannier, A., Bodin, N., Filiol, E.: Partition-Based Trapdoor Ciphers. https://ia. cr/2016/493
2. Boyar, J., Find, M., Peralta, R.: Four measures of nonlinearity. In: Spirakis, P.G., Serna, M. (eds.) CIAC 2013. LNCS, vol. 7878, pp. 61–72. Springer, Heidelberg (2013). https://doi.org/10.1007/978-3-642-38233-8_6
3. Beierle, C., Canteaut, A., Leander, G., Rotella, Y.: Proving resistance against invariant attacks: how to choose the round constants. In: Katz, J., Shacham, H. (eds.) CRYPTO 2017. LNCS, vol. 10402, pp. 647–678. Springer, Cham (2017). https://doi.org/10.1007/978-3-319-63715-0_22
4. Beyne, T.: Block cipher invariants as eigenvectors of correlation matrices. In: Peyrin, T., Galbraith, S. (eds.) ASIACRYPT 2018. LNCS, vol. 11272, pp. 3–31. Springer, Cham (2018). https://doi.org/10.1007/978-3-030-03326-2_1
5. Coppersmith, D.: The development of DES, Invited Talk, Crypto 2000, August 2000
6. Calderini, M.: A note on some algebraic trapdoors for block ciphers. https://arxiv. org/abs/1705.08151. Accessed 17 May 2018

7. Calik, C., Sonmez Turan, M., Peralta, R.: The multiplicative complexity of 6-variable Boolean functions. Cryptogr. Commun. **11**, 93–107 (2019). https://ia.cr/2018/002.pdf

8. Charpin, P.: Normal Boolean functions. J. Complex. **20**(2–3), 245–265 (2004)

9. Courtois, N., Klimov, A., Patarin, J., Shamir, A.: Efficient algorithms for solving overdefined systems of multivariate polynomial equations. In: Preneel, B. (ed.) EUROCRYPT 2000. LNCS, vol. 1807, pp. 392–407. Springer, Heidelberg (2000). https://doi.org/10.1007/3-540-45539-6_27

10. Courtois, N., Mourouzis, T., Grocholewska-Czurylo, A., Quisquater, J.-J.: On optimal size in truncated differential attacks. In: CECC 2014, Post-Proceedings in Studia Scientiarum Mathematicarum Hungarica, vol. 52, no. 2, pp. 246–254 (2015)

11. Courtois, N.T., Patrick, A.: Lack of unique factorization as a tool in block cipher cryptanalysis, Preprint, 12 May 2019. https://arxiv.org/abs/1905.04684

12. Courtois, N.T.: Invariant Hopping Attacks on Block Ciphers, accepted at WCC 2019, Abbaye de Saint-Jacut de la Mer, France, 31 March–5 April 2019

13. Courtois, N.T., Georgiou, M.: Variable elimination strategies and construction of nonlinear polynomial invariant attacks on T-310. Cryptologia (2019). https://doi.org/10.1080/01611194.2019.1650845

14. Courtois, N.T., Georgiou, M.: Constructive non-linear polynomial cryptanalysis of a historical block cipher. http://arxiv.org/abs/1902.02748

15. Courtois, N.T., Meier, W.: Algebraic attacks on stream ciphers with linear feedback. In: Biham, E. (ed.) EUROCRYPT 2003. LNCS, vol. 2656, pp. 345–359. Springer, Heidelberg (2003). https://doi.org/10.1007/3-540-39200-9_21

16. Courtois, N.T.: Algebraic attacks on combiners with memory and several outputs. In: Park, C., Chee, S. (eds.) ICISC 2004. LNCS, vol. 3506, pp. 3–20. Springer, Heidelberg (2005). https://doi.org/10.1007/11496618_3. Extended version available on https://ia.cr/2003/125/

17. Courtois, N.T.: On the existence of non-linear invariants and algebraic polynomial constructive approach to backdoors in block ciphers. https://ia.cr/2018/807. Accessed 27 Mar 2019

18. Courtois, N.T.: Structural nonlinear invariant attacks on T-310: attacking arbitrary boolean functions, https://ia.cr/2018/1242. Accessed 12 Sept 2019

19. Courtois, N.T.: Feistel schemes and bi-linear cryptanalysis. In: Franklin, M. (ed.) CRYPTO 2004. LNCS, vol. 3152, pp. 23–40. Springer, Heidelberg (2004). https://doi.org/10.1007/978-3-540-28628-8_2

20. Courtois, N.T., Castagnos, G., Goubin, L.: What do DES S-boxes say to each other? (2003). https://ia.cr/2003/184/

21. Courtois, N.T.: An improved differential attack on full GOST. In: Ryan, P.Y.A., Naccache, D., Quisquater, J.-J. (eds.) The New Codebreakers. LNCS, vol. 9100, pp. 282–303. Springer, Heidelberg (2016). https://doi.org/10.1007/978-3-662-49301-4_18

22. Courtois, N.: An improved differential attack on full GOST. Cryptology ePrint Archive, Report 2012/138, 15 March 2012, December 2015. https://ia.cr/2012/138

23. Courtois, N.T., et al.: Cryptographic security analysis of T-310, monography study on the T-310 block cipher, 132 p., 20 May 2017. https://ia.cr/2017/440.pdf. Accessed 29 June 2018

24. Courtois, N.T., Oprisanu, M.-B.: Ciphertext-only attacks and weak long-term keys in T-310. Cryptologia **42**(4), 316–336 (2018). http://www.tandfonline.com/doi/full/10.1080/01611194.2017.1362065

25. Courtois, N.T., Oprisanu, M.-B., Schmeh, K.: Linear cryptanalysis and block cipher design in East Germany in the 1970s. Cryptologia (2018). https://www.tandfonline.com/doi/abs/10.1080/01611194.2018.1483981

26. Courtois, N., Drobick, J., Schmeh, K.: Feistel ciphers in East Germany in the communist era. Cryptologia **42**(6), 427–444 (2018)

27. Courtois, N.: Algebraic complexity reduction and cryptanalysis of GOST. Monograph study on GOST cipher, 2010–2014, 224 p. https://ia.cr/2011/626

28. Dobbertin, H.: Construction of bent functions and balanced Boolean functions with high nonlinearity. In: Preneel, B. (ed.) FSE 1994. LNCS, vol. 1008, pp. 61–74. Springer, Heidelberg (1995). https://doi.org/10.1007/3-540-60590-8_5

29. Harpes, C., Kramer, G.G., Massey, J.L.: A generalization of linear cryptanalysis and the applicability of Matsui's piling-up lemma. In: Guillou, L.C., Quisquater, J.-J. (eds.) EUROCRYPT 1995. LNCS, vol. 921, pp. 24–38. Springer, Heidelberg (1995). https://doi.org/10.1007/3-540-49264-X_3

30. Knudsen, L.R., Robshaw, M.J.B.: Non-linear approximations in linear cryptanalysis. In: Maurer, U. (ed.) EUROCRYPT 1996. LNCS, vol. 1070, pp. 224–236. Springer, Heidelberg (1996). https://doi.org/10.1007/3-540-68339-9_20

31. Leander, G., Abdelraheem, M.A., AlKhzaimi, H., Zenner, E.: A cryptanalysis of PRINTCIPHER: the invariant subspace attack. In: Rogaway, P. (ed.) CRYPTO 2011. LNCS, vol. 6841, pp. 206–221. Springer, Heidelberg (2011). https://doi.org/10.1007/978-3-642-22792-9_12

32. Lipton, R.J., Regan, K.W.: Nicolas Courtois: the linearization method. In: People, Problems, and Proofs, pp. 259–262. Springer, Heidelberg (2013). https://doi.org/10.1007/978-3-642-41422-0_50

33. De Meyer, L., Vaudenay, S.: DES S-box generator. Cryptologia **41**(2), 153–171 (2017). https://www.tandfonline.com/doi/full/10.1080/01611194.2016.1169456

34. Kim, K., Lee, S., Park, S., Lee, D.: Securing DES S-boxes against three robust cryptanalysis. In: SAC 1995, vol. 2595, pp. 145–157 (1995)

35. Schmeh, K.: The East German encryption machine T-310 and the algorithm it used. Cryptologia **30**(3), 251–257 (2006)

36. Shamir, A.: On the security of DES. In: Williams, H.C. (ed.) CRYPTO 1985. LNCS, vol. 218, pp. 280–281. Springer, Heidelberg (1986). https://doi.org/10.1007/3-540-39799-X_22

37. Todo, Y., Leander, G., Sasaki, Y.: Nonlinear invariant attack: practical attack on full SCREAM, iSCREAM and Midori 64. J. Cryptol. **32**, 1–40 (2018)

38. Wei, Y., Ye, T., Wenling, W., Pasalic, E.: Generalized nonlinear invariant attack and a new design criterion for round constants. IACR Trans. Symmetric Cryptol. **4**, 62–79 (2018). https://tosc.iacr.org/index.php/ToSC/article/view/7361/6531

Authenticated Encryption Based on Lesamnta-LW Hashing Mode

Shoichi Hirose[1]([envelope]) [iD], Hidenori Kuwakado[2], and Hirotaka Yoshida[3] [iD]

[1] University of Fukui, Fukui, Japan
hrs_shch@u-fukui.ac.jp
[2] Kansai University, Osaka, Japan
kuwakado@kansai-u.ac.jp
[3] National Institute of Advanced Industrial Science and Technology, Tokyo, Japan
hirotaka.yoshida@aist.go.jp

Abstract. Authenticated encryption refers to symmetric cryptography providing both privacy and authenticity. It is most common to construct it as a block-cipher mode of operation. Another promising approach is to construct it based on cryptographic hashing. This paper proposes a nonce-based authenticated encryption scheme based on the Lesamnta-LW hashing mode. Lesamnta-LW is a block-cipher-based iterated hash function, which is specified in the ISO/IEC 29192-5 lightweight hash-function standard. This paper also shows that the proposed scheme is secure if the underlying block cipher is a pseudorandom permutation. Both of the other ISO/IEC 29192-5 mechanisms, PHOTON and SPONGENT, are hardware-oriented sponge-based hash functions, and nonce-based authenticated encryption schemes can also be constructed based on them. On the other hand, Lesamnta-LW is a software-oriented Merkle-Damgård hash function. Thus, the proposed scheme is a new option for authenticated encryption based on lightweight cryptographic hashing.

Keywords: Authenticated encryption · Hash function · Lesamnta-LW · Pseudorandom function

1 Introduction

Background. Authenticated encryption (AE) refers to symmetric cryptography providing both privacy and authenticity at the same time. Informally, privacy is confidentiality of plaintexts and authenticity is integrity of ciphertexts. AE schemes often take additional input called associated data which only require authenticity. Such AE schemes are referred to as authenticated encryption with associated data (AEAD).

There are some kinds of approaches for AEAD construction. Among them, one of the most common approaches is to construct it as a mode of operation of a block cipher such as AES [15]. The other is to construct it based on the sponge construction [8]. The sponge construction [6] was invented originally for cryptographic hash functions as well as for MAC functions and stream ciphers. The

© Springer Nature Switzerland AG 2020
J. H. Seo (Ed.): ICISC 2019, LNCS 11975, pp. 52–69, 2020.
https://doi.org/10.1007/978-3-030-40921-0_3

sponge-based hash function Keccak [7] was selected for the SHA-3 standard [16]. The sponge construction is also popular for lightweight hashing.

The ISO/IEC 29192-5 lightweight hash function standard [24] was released in 2016, which specifies three lightweight cryptographic hash functions: PHO-TON [20], SPONGENT [9], and Lesamnta-LW [21]. PHOTON and SPONGENT follow the sponge construction, and the sponge-based AEAD mode can be applied to them. On the other hand, Lesamnta-LW is a Merkle-Damgård [12,27] hash function using a dedicated block cipher whose key size is half the block size as a compression function. In addition, Lesamnta-LW is optimized for software implementation, while both PHOTON and SPONGENT are optimized for hardware implementation. In fact, a software result [21] shows that Lesmanta-LW provides 120-bit collision resistance with 54 bytes of RAM, achieving 20% faster short-message performance over SHA-256, while hardware results show that SPONGENT provides 80-bit collision resistance with 1329 GE and PHO-TON provides the same security level with 1396 GE. Thus, the design and security analysis of AEAD based on Lesamnta-LW seems an interesting challenge and it would be an efficient option for lightweight authenticated encryption on low-cost 8-bit microcontrollers where RAM requirement is critical for cryptographic functionality.

Our Contribution. This paper proposes a nonce-based AEAD scheme based on the Lesamnta-LW hashing mode. The proposed scheme follows the common syntax of nonce-based AEAD. The encryption function, which is depicted in Fig. 3, takes as input a secret key K, a nonce N, associated data A, and a plaintext M and produces a ciphertext C and a tag T. The tag is produced for integrity of both the ciphertext and the associated data. The length of the ciphertext is equal to that of the plaintext. The proposed scheme is online, that is, a given plaintext is encrypted block-by-block, and a new block of the ciphertext depends only on the blocks of the plaintext so far as well as the nonce and the associated data.

The proposed scheme is key-evolving: Each call to the underlying block cipher requires a key-schedule for a new key. It is actually a disadvantage for efficiency. On the other hand, it is an advantage for resistance to side channel attacks. An interesting methodology called leveled implementations (implementations in the leveled leakage setting) [18,31] was proposed against side channel attacks. Strongly protected implementations to reduce leakages through side channels need huge overhead costs in general. The methodology aims at trying to minimize the use of strongly protected implementations and use weakly protected implementations for the bulk of computation. In the encryption of the proposed AEAD scheme, first an ephemeral key is generated with the nonce. Thus, if the nonce is respected, then the encryption is resistant to side channel attacks by generating an ephemeral key using a strongly protected implementation. It is effective for applications which, for example, perform decryption only by central servers free from side channel attacks.

This paper also shows that the proposed scheme is secure in the standard model. The security properties, privacy and authenticity, are reduced to the pseudorandom permutation property of the block cipher underlying the Lesamnta-LW hashing mode. The proof is based on the all-in-one definition of security given in [34]. The proof heavily uses the hybrid argument originated from [17].

Finally, this paper discusses the security of the proposed scheme under misuses. It considers the two typical misuses: nonce repetition (NR) and releasing unverified plaintexts (RUP). It confirms that the proposed scheme satisfies authenticity under the misuses.

The proposed AEAD scheme based on Lesamnta-LW has an advantage over lightweight AEAD schemes based on PHOTON and SPONGENT in provable security. The proposed scheme is shown to be secure in the standard model, while the sponge-based schemes are shown to be secure in the ideal permutation model which assumes that the underlying permutation is chosen uniformly at random.

Related Work. Authenticated encryption received the first formal treatments from Katz and Yung [26] and Bellare and Namprempre [2], which are followed by Jutla [25].

There are many block-cipher modes of operation for AEAD. Only a few examples are mentioned here, however, since it is not the main topic of the paper. OCB [33] is one of the earliest but most efficient modes, and it is inspired by IAPM [25]. CCM [29] and GCM [30] are specified by NIST and ISO/IEC 19772 [23].

As far as we know, there is only one proposal for AEAD based on cryptographic hashing except for the sponge-based proposals. It is OMD (Offset Merkle-Damgård) by Cogliani et al. [11], which is a mode of operation of a compression function for the Merkle-Damgård hashing such as SHA-2 [14].

Nonce-based symmetric encryption was introduced with its formalization by Rogaway [32]. The generic composition of nonce-based AEAD was discussed by Namprempre et al. [28].

For misuse resistance of authenticated encryption, security under nonce-repetition (NR) was formalized by Rogaway and Shrimpton [34]. Security under releasing unverified plaintexts (RUP) was formalized by Andreeva et al. [1]. Robust authenticated encryption was introduced and formalized by Hoang et al. [22], which is secure under NR and RUP. Robust authenticated encryption schemes are inefficient for long plaintexts in terms of memory since the required amount of memory is at least as much as the given plaintext to save it or intermediate states during encryption.

Pereira et al. presented the idea of leveled implementations and proposed a leakage-resilient MAC function and a leakage-resilient encryption scheme based on it [31]. A series of work has been done for leakage-resilient AEAD [3–5,18], which has proposed schemes using (tweakable) block ciphers and cryptographic hash functions. Leakage-resilient AEAD schemes have also been proposed based on sponge construction [13,19].

Organization. Notations and definitions used in the remaining parts are given in Sect. 2. Syntax and security are formalized for AEAD in Sect. 3. The nonce-based

AEAD scheme Lae0 is proposed in Sect. 4, which is based on the Lesamnta-LW hashing mode. The provable security of Lae0 in the standard model is confirmed in Sect. 5. The authenticity of Lae0 under misuses is also confirmed in the provable security setting in Sect. 6. A brief concluding remark is given in Sect. 7.

2 Preliminaries

2.1 Notations and Definitions

Let $\Sigma = \{0, 1\}$. For any integer $l \geq 0$, let Σ^l be identified with the set of all Σ-sequences of length l. $\Sigma^0 = \{\varepsilon\}$, where ε is the empty sequence. $\Sigma^1 = \Sigma$. Let $(\Sigma^l)^* = \bigcup_{i \geq 0} (\Sigma^l)^i$ and $(\Sigma^l)^+ = \bigcup_{i \geq 1} (\Sigma^l)^i$. For non-negative integers $k_1 \leq k_2$, let $(\Sigma^l)^{[k_1, k_2]} = \bigcup_{i=k_1}^{k_2} (\Sigma^l)^i$.

For $x \in \Sigma^*$, the length of x is denoted by $|x|$. For $x_1, x_2 \in \Sigma^*$, $x_1 \| x_2$ represents their concatenation. For $x \in \Sigma^*$ and an integer $0 \leq l \leq |x|$, $\mathsf{msb}_l(x)$ represents the most significant l bits of x, and $\mathsf{lsb}_l(x)$ represents the least significant l bits of x.

Selecting an element s from a set $\mathcal{S}$ uniformly at random is denoted by $s \twoheadleftarrow \mathcal{S}$.

A function $f : \mathcal{K} \times \mathcal{X} \to \mathcal{Y}$ can be regarded as a set of functions with a domain $\mathcal{X}$ and a range $\mathcal{Y}$ indexed by keys in $\mathcal{K}$. $f(K, \cdot)$ is often denoted by $f_K(\cdot)$.

The set of all functions from $\mathcal{X}$ to $\mathcal{Y}$ is denoted by $\mathcal{F}(\mathcal{X}, \mathcal{Y})$. The set of all permutations on $\mathcal{X}$ is denoted by $\mathcal{P}(\mathcal{X})$. ι represents an identity permutation. The set of all block ciphers with a key size κ and a block size n is denoted by $\mathcal{B}(\kappa, n)$. A block cipher in $\mathcal{B}(\kappa, n)$ is called a (κ, n) block cipher.

Let $\Pi \subset \mathcal{P}(\mathcal{X})$. We say that Π is pairwise everywhere distinct if, for every $\pi, \pi' \in \Pi$ such that $\pi \neq \pi'$, $\pi(x) \neq \pi'(x)$ for every $x \in \mathcal{X}$.

2.2 Pseudorandom Functions and Permutations

Let $f : \mathcal{K} \times \mathcal{X} \to \mathcal{Y}$ and let $\mathbf{A}$ be an adversary against it. The goal of $\mathbf{A}$ is to distinguish between f_K and function ρ, where K and ρ are chosen uniformly at random from $\mathcal{K}$ and $\mathcal{F}(\mathcal{X}, \mathcal{Y})$, respectively. $\mathbf{A}$ is given either f_K or ρ as an oracle and makes adaptive queries in $\mathcal{X}$ to the oracle which returns the corresponding outputs. Finally, $\mathbf{A}$ outputs 0 or 1. The prf-advantage of $\mathbf{A}$ against f is defined as

$$\mathrm{Adv}_f^{\mathrm{prf}}(\mathbf{A}) = \left| \Pr\left[\mathbf{A}^{f_K} = 1\right] - \Pr\left[\mathbf{A}^\rho = 1\right] \right|,$$

where $K \twoheadleftarrow \mathcal{K}$ and $\rho \twoheadleftarrow \mathcal{F}(\mathcal{X}, \mathcal{Y})$. The prp-advantage of $\mathbf{A}$ against f is defined similarly as

$$\mathrm{Adv}_f^{\mathrm{prp}}(\mathbf{A}) = \left| \Pr\left[\mathbf{A}^{f_K} = 1\right] - \Pr\left[\mathbf{A}^\rho = 1\right] \right|,$$

where $K \twoheadleftarrow \mathcal{K}$ and $\rho \twoheadleftarrow \mathcal{P}(\mathcal{X})$. In the definitions above, adversary $\mathbf{A}$ is regarded as a random variable which takes values in $\{0, 1\}$.

Informally, f is called a pseudorandom function (permutation), or PRF (PRP) in short, if no efficient adversary $\mathbf{A}$ can have any significant prf-advantage (prp-advantage) against f.

The prf-advantage can be extended straightforwardly to adversaries with multiple oracles. The prf-advantage of adversary $\mathbf{A}$ with access to p oracles is defined as

$$\mathrm{Adv}_f^{p\text{-prf}}(\mathbf{A}) = \left| \Pr[\mathbf{A}^{F_{K_1}, F_{K_2}, \ldots, F_{K_p}} = 1] - \Pr[\mathbf{A}^{\rho_1, \rho_2, \ldots, \rho_p} = 1] \right|,$$

where $K_i \leftarrow \mathcal{K}$ and $\rho_i \leftarrow \mathcal{F}(\mathcal{X}, \mathcal{Y})$ for $i = 1, 2, \ldots, p$. $\mathrm{Adv}_f^{p\text{-prp}}$ can be defined similarly. To simplify the notation, the following types of notations are often used in the remaining parts: For $\boldsymbol{K} = (K_1, K_2, \ldots, K_p)$, $\mathbf{A}^{F_{\boldsymbol{K}}}$ represents $\mathbf{A}^{F_{K_1}, F_{K_2}, \ldots, F_{K_p}}$, and, for $\boldsymbol{\rho} = (\rho_1, \rho_2, \ldots, \rho_p)$, $\mathbf{A}^{\boldsymbol{\rho}}$ represents $\mathbf{A}^{\rho_1, \rho_2, \ldots, \rho_p}$.

The following lemma is a kind of PRP/PRF switching lemma for the prf-advantage with multiple oracles.

Lemma 1 (Lemma 3 of [21]). *Let $\mathbf{A}$ be any adversary with p oracles against E running in time at most t, and making at most q_i queries to its i-th oracle for $1 \leq i \leq p$. Let $q = q_1 + \cdots + q_p$. Then, there exists an adversary $\mathbf{B}$ against E such that*

$$\mathrm{Adv}_E^{p\text{-prf}}(\mathbf{A}) \leq p \cdot \mathrm{Adv}_E^{\mathrm{prp}}(\mathbf{B}) + q^2/2^{n+1}$$

and $\mathbf{B}$ runs in time at most $t + O(qT_E)$ and makes at most $\max\{q_1, q_2, \ldots, q_p\}$ queries, where T_E represents the time required to compute E.

2.3 Indistinguishability Between Sets of Functions

Let $\mathcal{G}_0$ and $\mathcal{G}_1$ be finite sets of functions such that $\mathcal{G}_i \subset \mathcal{F}(\mathcal{X}, \mathcal{Y})$ for $i = 0, 1$. Suppose that some probability distributions are defined over $\mathcal{G}_0$ and $\mathcal{G}_1$. Let $\mathbf{A}$ be an adversary against a pair of $\mathcal{G}_0$ and $\mathcal{G}_1$. The goal of $\mathbf{A}$ is to distinguish between $\mathcal{G}_0$ and $\mathcal{G}_1$, that is, between g_0 and g_1, where g_i is sampled from $\mathcal{G}_i$ according to the probability distribution over $\mathcal{G}_i$ for $i = 0, 1$. $\mathbf{A}$ is given g_i as an oracle and makes adaptive queries in $\mathcal{X}$ to the oracle which returns the corresponding outputs. Finally, $\mathbf{A}$ outputs 0 or 1. The ind-advantage of $\mathbf{A}$ against $(\mathcal{G}_0, \mathcal{G}_1)$ is defined as

$$\mathrm{Adv}_{\mathcal{G}_0, \mathcal{G}_1}^{\mathrm{ind}}(\mathbf{A}) = \left| \Pr[\mathbf{A}^{g_0} = 1] - \Pr[\mathbf{A}^{g_1} = 1] \right|,$$

where g_0 and g_1 are sampled from $\mathcal{G}_0$ and $\mathcal{G}_1$, respectively, according to the corresponding probability distributions.

Informally, it is said that $\mathcal{G}_0$ and $\mathcal{G}_1$, or g_0 and g_1, are indistinguishable if the ind-advantage is negligible for any efficient adversary. The PRF notion of $f : \mathcal{K} \times \mathcal{X} \to \mathcal{Y}$ is the indistinguishability between $\{f(K, \cdot) \mid K \in \mathcal{K}\}$ with the probability distribution induced by the uniform distribution over $\mathcal{K}$ and $\mathcal{F}(\mathcal{X}, \mathcal{Y})$ with the uniform distribution.

Similar to the prf-advantage, the ind-advantage can also be extended to adversaries with multiple oracles. The ind-advantage of adversary $\mathbf{A}$ against $(\mathcal{G}_0, \mathcal{G}_1)$ with access to p oracles is denoted by $\mathrm{Adv}_{\mathcal{G}_0, \mathcal{G}_1}^{p\text{-ind}}(\mathbf{A})$.

2.4   The Hashing Mode of Lesamnta-LW

The hashing mode of Lesamnta-LW [21] is the plain Merkle-Damgård iteration of a block cipher E in $\mathcal{B}(n/2, n)$, where n is a positive even integer. E works as a compression function with domain $\Sigma^{3n/2}$ and range Σ^n. It is depicted in Fig. 1. $IV_0 \| IV_1 \in \Sigma^n$ is an initialization vector, where $|IV_0| = |IV_1| = n/2$. $M_1, M_2, \ldots, M_m$ are message blocks, where $M_i \in \Sigma^{n/2}$ for $i = 1, 2, \ldots, m$.

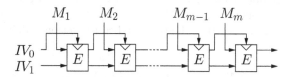

Fig. 1. The hashing mode of Lesamnta-LW. The input of the block cipher E from the top is its key input.

3   Authenticated Encryption with Associated Data

Syntax. A nonce-based scheme of authenticated encryption with associated data (AEAD) consists of a pair of functions for encryption and decryption. The encryption function is $\mathsf{Enc} : \mathcal{K} \times \mathcal{N} \times \mathcal{A} \times \mathcal{M} \to \mathcal{C} \times \mathcal{T}$ and the decryption function is $\mathsf{Dec} : \mathcal{K} \times \mathcal{N} \times \mathcal{A} \times \mathcal{C} \times \mathcal{T} \to \mathcal{M} \cup \{\bot\}$, where $\mathcal{K}$ is a key space, $\mathcal{N}$ is a nonce space, $\mathcal{A}$ is an associated-data space, $\mathcal{M}$ is a message space, $\mathcal{C}$ is a ciphertext space, and $\mathcal{T}$ is a tag space. $\mathcal{M} \subset \Sigma^*$, $\bot \notin \mathcal{M}$ and $\mathcal{A} \subset \Sigma^*$. If $M \in \mathcal{M}$, then $\Sigma^{|M|} \subset \mathcal{M}$. For any $K \in \mathcal{K}$, if $(C, T) \leftarrow \mathsf{Enc}_K(N, A, M)$ for some $(N, A, M) \in \mathcal{N} \times \mathcal{A} \times \mathcal{M}$, then $M \leftarrow \mathsf{Dec}_K(N, A, C, T)$. Otherwise, $\bot \leftarrow \mathsf{Dec}_K(N, A, C, T)$, which means that (N, A, C, T) is invalid with respect to $K \in \mathcal{K}$.

Security. The security requirements for AEAD are privacy and authenticity. Informally, privacy is confidentiality of encrypted messages, and authenticity is integrity of ciphertexts and associated data. Here, they are formalized in the all-in-one manner [34]. Let \$ be a random function taking $(N, A, M) \in \mathcal{N} \times \mathcal{A} \times \mathcal{M}$ as input and returning a binary sequence of length $|\mathsf{Enc}_K(N, A, M)|$, which is chosen uniformly at random if (N, A, M) is new. Let $\bot$ be a function taking (N, A, C, T) as input and always returning $\bot$. The security of an AEAD scheme $(\mathsf{Enc}, \mathsf{Dec})$ is defined by the indistinguishability between $(\mathsf{Enc}_K, \mathsf{Dec}_K)$ and $(\$, \bot)$ and denoted by

$$\mathrm{Adv}^{\mathrm{aead}}_{(\mathsf{Enc}, \mathsf{Dec})}(\mathbf{A}) = \left| \Pr\left[\mathbf{A}^{\mathsf{Enc}_K, \mathsf{Dec}_K} = 1\right] - \Pr\left[\mathbf{A}^{\$, \bot} = 1\right] \right|,$$

where $K \xleftarrow{} \mathcal{K}$. Here, adversary $\mathbf{A}$ makes encryption queries to either Enc_K or \$ and decryption queries to either Dec_K or $\bot$. $\mathbf{A}$ is not allowed to make multiple encryption queries with the same nonce. **A** is not allowed to make a trivial decryption query, either. Namely, if **A** gets (C, T) as an answer to some encryption query (N, A, M), then it is not allowed to ask (N, A, C, T) as a decryption query.

4   The Proposed Scheme: Lae0

Let E be a block cipher in $\mathcal{B}(n/2, n)$, where n is an even integer. Hereafter, let $n/2 = w$ just for simplicity.

The padding function used in the proposed construction is defined as follows: For any $X \in \Sigma^*$,

$$\mathsf{pad}(X) = \begin{cases} X & \text{if } |X| > 0 \text{ and } |X| \equiv 0 \pmod{w} \\ X\|10^t & \text{if } |X| = 0 \text{ or } |X| \not\equiv 0 \pmod{w}, \end{cases}$$

where t is the minimum non-negative integer such that $|X| + 1 + t \equiv 0 \pmod{w}$. pad is not injective since, for example, $\mathsf{pad}(\varepsilon) = \mathsf{pad}(10^{w-1}) = 10^{w-1}$. For any $X \in \Sigma^*$, $|\mathsf{pad}(X)|$ is the minimum positive multiple of w, which is greater than or equal to $|X|$.

Let $\mathsf{pad}(X) = \bar{X} = \bar{X}_1\|\bar{X}_2\|\cdots\|\bar{X}_x$, where $|\bar{X}_i| = w$ for every i such that $1 \le i \le x$. $x = 1$ if $|X| = 0$, and $x = \lceil |X|/w \rceil$ if $|X| > 0$. $\bar{X}_i$ is called the i-th block of $\mathsf{pad}(X)$.

For $E \in \mathcal{B}(w, n)$ and $\pi_0, \pi_1 \in \mathcal{P}(\Sigma^w)$, a function $\mathsf{J}^{E,\{\pi_0,\pi_1\}} : \Sigma^n \times \Sigma^* \to (\Sigma^w)^+$ is defined as follows: $\mathsf{J}^{E,\{\pi_0,\pi_1\}}(Y_0, X) = Y_{0,1}\|Y_{1,1}\|\cdots\|Y_{x-1,1}\|Y_x$ such that $\bar{X} = \mathsf{pad}(X)$,

$$Y_i \leftarrow E_{Y_{i-1,0}}(\bar{X}_i\|Y_{i-1,1})$$

for $1 \le i \le x - 1$, and

$$Y_x \leftarrow \begin{cases} E_{Y_{x-1,0}}(\bar{X}_x\|\pi_0(Y_{x-1,1})) & \text{if } |X| > 0 \text{ and } |X| \equiv 0 \pmod{w} \\ E_{Y_{x-1,0}}(\bar{X}_x\|\pi_1(Y_{x-1,1})) & \text{if } |X| = 0 \text{ or } |X| \not\equiv 0 \pmod{w}, \end{cases}$$

where $Y_j = Y_{j,0}\|Y_{j,1} \in \Sigma^n$ and $|Y_{j,0}| = |Y_{j,1}| = w$ for $0 \le j \le x$. It is also depicted in Fig. 2.

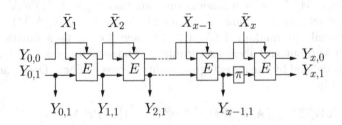

Fig. 2. $\mathsf{J}^{E,\{\pi_0,\pi_1\}}(Y_0, X)$, where $\mathsf{pad}(X) = \bar{X}_1\|\cdots\|\bar{X}_x$

To describe the proposed nonce-based AEAD scheme Lae0, two keyed functions $\mathsf{aJ}^{E,\{\pi_0,\pi_1\}}$ and $\mathsf{mJ}^{E,\{\pi_0,\pi_1\}}$ are defined using $\mathsf{J}^{E,\{\pi_0,\pi_1\}}$.

$\mathsf{aJ}^{E,\{\pi_0,\pi_1\}} : \Sigma^n \times \Sigma^* \to \Sigma^n$ is a keyed function with its key space Σ^n such that

$$\mathsf{aJ}^{E,\{\pi_0,\pi_1\}}(S,A) = \mathsf{lsb}_n(\mathsf{J}^{E,\{\pi_0,\pi_1\}}(S,A)).$$

Let parse be a function taking $X \in \Sigma^*$ as input such that $\mathsf{parse}(X) = (X_1, X_2, \ldots, X_x)$, where $x \geq 1$, $X = X_1 \| X_2 \| \cdots \| X_x$, $|X_i| = w$ for $1 \leq i \leq x-1$, $0 \leq |X_x| \leq w$, and $|X_x| = 0$ only if $X = \varepsilon$.

$\mathsf{mJ}^{E,\{\pi_0,\pi_1\}} : \Sigma^n \times \Sigma^* \times \{\mathsf{e},\mathsf{d}\} \to \Sigma^n$ is a keyed function with its key space Σ^n such that

$$\mathsf{mJ}^{E,\{\pi_0,\pi_1\}}(S,M,\mathsf{e}) = \mathsf{J}^{E,\{\pi_0,\pi_1\}}(S,M)$$

and $\mathsf{mJ}^{E,\{\pi_0,\pi_1\}}(\cdot,\cdot,\mathsf{d})$ is given by Algorithm 1.

Algorithm 1. The function $\mathsf{mJ}^{E,\{\pi_0,\pi_1\}}(\cdot,\cdot,\mathsf{d})$

---

function $\mathsf{mJ}^{E,\{\pi_0,\pi_1\}}(S,C,\mathsf{d})$
    $(C_1, C_2, \ldots, C_m) \leftarrow \mathsf{parse}(C)$
    $Y_0 \leftarrow S$
    for $i = 1$ **to** $m-1$ **do** $\triangleright$ $Y_{i-1} = Y_{i-1,0} \| Y_{i-1,1}$ and $|Y_{i-1,0}| = |Y_{i-1,1}|$
        $M_i \leftarrow C_i \oplus Y_{i-1,1};\ Y_i \leftarrow E_{Y_{i-1,0}}(M_i \| Y_{i-1,1})$
    end for
    $M_m \leftarrow C_m \oplus \mathsf{msb}_{|C_m|}(Y_{m-1,1})$
    return $\mathsf{J}^{E,\{\pi_0,\pi_1\}}(S, M_1 \| M_2 \| \cdots \| M_m)$
end function

The proposed nonce-based AEAD scheme Lae0 is presented by Algorithm 2. The encryption function E0 of Lae0 is also depicted in Fig. 3. For Lae0, the key space is Σ^w, the nonce space is Σ^n, and the tag space is Σ^τ, where $0 < \tau \leq n$. The associated-data space, the message space and the ciphertext space are Σ^*. If $(C,T) \leftarrow \mathsf{E0}_K(N,A,M)$, then the length of C equals the length of M.

Algorithm 2. Encryption E0 and decryption D0 of AEAD Lae0

---

function $\mathsf{E0}_K(N,A,M)$
    $S \leftarrow \mathsf{aJ}^{E,\{\pi_0,\pi_1\}}(E_K(N),A)$
    $V \leftarrow \mathsf{mJ}^{E,\{\pi_0,\pi_1\}}(S,M,\mathsf{e})$
    $C \leftarrow M \oplus \mathsf{msb}_{|M|}(V)$
    $T \leftarrow \mathsf{lsb}_\tau(V)$
    return C,T
end function

function $\mathsf{D0}_K(N,A,C,T)$
    $S \leftarrow \mathsf{aJ}^{E,\{\pi_0,\pi_1\}}(E_K(N),A)$
    $V \leftarrow \mathsf{mJ}^{E,\{\pi_0,\pi_1\}}(S,C,\mathsf{d})$
    if $T = \mathsf{lsb}_\tau(V)$ **then**
        return $C \oplus \mathsf{msb}_{|C|}(V)$
    else
        return $\perp$
    end if
end function

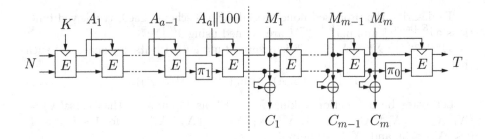

Fig. 3. The encryption function E0 of the nonce-based AEAD scheme Lae0. $(C,T) \leftarrow$ $\mathsf{E0}_K(N, A, M)$, where $\mathsf{parse}(A) = (A_1, A_2, \ldots, A_a)$, $\mathsf{parse}(M) = (M_1, M_2, \ldots, M_m)$, and $C = C_1\|C_2\|\cdots\|C_m$. This figure assumes that $|A_a| = w - 3$, $|M_m| = w$ and $\tau = n$.

5   Security of Lae0

The following theorem states that Lae0 is secure, that is, satisfies both privacy and authenticity, if the underlying block cipher E is a PRP and the underlying non-cryptographic permutations π_0 and π_1 are pairwise everywhere distinct together with the identity permutation.

Theorem 1. *For permutations π_0 and π_1 on Σ^w used in Lae0, suppose that $\{\pi_0, \pi_1, \iota\}$ is pairwise everywhere distinct. Let $\mathbf{A}$ be any adversary against Lae0 running in time at most t and making at most q_e and q_d queries to the encryption and decryption oracles, respectively. Let $q = q_\mathsf{e} + q_\mathsf{d}$. Suppose that the length of a message or a ciphertext in each query is at most $\ell_\mathsf{m} w$. Suppose that the length of associated data in each query is at most $\ell_\mathsf{a} w$. Let $\ell = \ell_\mathsf{m} + \ell_\mathsf{a}$. Then, there exists an adversary $\mathbf{B}$ against E such that*

$$\mathrm{Adv}^{\mathsf{aead}}_{\mathsf{Lae0}}(\mathbf{A}) \leq (\ell+1)q\, \mathrm{Adv}^{\mathsf{prp}}_{E}(\mathbf{B}) + (\ell+1)q^2/2^{n+1} + q_\mathsf{d}/2^{\tau},$$

and $\mathbf{B}$ runs in time at most $t + O(\ell q T_E)$ and makes at most q queries, where T_E is the time required to compute E.

Remark 1. Let $\pi_i(x) = x \oplus c_i$ for $i = 0, 1$, where c_0 and c_1 are non-zero distinct constants in Σ^w. Then, $\{\pi_0, \pi_1, \iota\}$ is pairwise everywhere distinct.

To prove Theorem 1, we will show that $\mathsf{aJ}^{E,\{\pi_0,\pi_1\}}$ is a PRF and $\mathsf{mJ}^{E,\{\pi_0,\pi_1\}}$ is indistinguishable from a random function specified below if E is a PRP and $\{\pi_0, \pi_1, \iota\}$ is pairwise everywhere distinct.

5.1   The PRF-Property of $\mathsf{aJ}^{E,\{\pi_0,\pi_1\}}$

$\mathsf{aJ}^{E,\{\pi_0,\pi_1\}}$ is shown to be a PRF if E is a PRP and $\{\pi_0, \pi_1, \iota\}$ is pairwise everywhere distinct:

Theorem 2. *For permutations π_0 and π_1 on Σ^w, suppose that $\{\pi_0, \pi_1, \iota\}$ is pairwise everywhere distinct. Let $\mathbf{A}$ be any adversary with p oracles against $\mathrm{aJ}^{E,\{\pi_0,\pi_1\}}$ running in time at most t and making at most q queries. Suppose that the length of the associated data in each query is at most ℓw. Then, there exists an adversary $\mathbf{B}$ against E such that*

$$\mathrm{Adv}^{p\text{-prf}}_{\mathrm{aJ}^{E,\{\pi_0,\pi_1\}}}(\mathbf{A}) \leq \ell q\, \mathrm{Adv}^{\mathrm{prp}}_E(\mathbf{B}) + \ell q^2/2^{n+1}$$

and $\mathbf{B}$ runs in time at most $t + O(\ell q T_E)$ and makes at most q queries, where T_E is the time required to compute E.

The proof of Theorem 2 is omitted since it is similar to and easier than that of Theorem 3, which is given later.

5.2   The Indistinguishability of $\mathrm{mJ}^{E,\{\pi_0,\pi_1\}}$

Here, it is shown to be difficult to distinguish between $\mathrm{mJ}^{E,\{\pi_0,\pi_1\}}_S$ with $S \twoheadleftarrow \Sigma^n$ and a random function from a set of functions $\mathcal{Q}$ specified below.

For $M \in \Sigma^*$, let $\mathsf{parse}(M) = (M_1, M_2, \ldots, M_m)$, where $m = |\mathsf{pad}(M)|/w \geq 1$. For $1 \leq i_1 \leq i_2 \leq m$, let $M_{[i_1,i_2]} = M_{i_1}\|M_{i_1+1}\|\cdots\|M_{i_2}$. $M_{[1,0]} = \varepsilon$. Let $\mathcal{R}$ be the set of functions below:

$$\left\{ R \,\middle|\, \begin{array}{l} R(M) = R_0(\varepsilon)\|R_1(M_1)\|R_2(M_{[1,2]})\|\cdots\|R_{m-1}(M_{[1,m-1]})\|R_*(M), \\ \text{where } R_i \in \mathcal{F}((\Sigma^w)^i, \Sigma^w) \text{ for } 0 \leq i \leq m-1 \text{ and } R_* \in \mathcal{F}(\Sigma^*, \Sigma^n) \end{array} \right\}.$$

Notice that $\mathrm{J}^{E,\{\pi_0,\pi_1\}}(S,\cdot) \in \mathcal{R}$.

If the input length is assumed to be bounded from above by ℓw, then the uniform random sampling from $\mathcal{R}$ is implemented by the uniform random sampling from $\mathcal{F}((\Sigma^w)^0, \Sigma^w) \times \mathcal{F}((\Sigma^w)^1, \Sigma^w) \times \cdots \times \mathcal{F}((\Sigma^w)^{\ell-1}, \Sigma^w) \times \mathcal{F}(\Sigma^{[0,\ell w]}, \Sigma^n)$.

Let $\mathcal{Q}$ be the set of functions defined with $\mathcal{R}$ as follows. A function $Q \in \mathcal{Q}$ takes as input $(Z, h) \in \Sigma^* \times \{\mathsf{e}, \mathsf{d}\}$. $Q(\cdot, \mathsf{e}) \in \mathcal{R}$. Let

$$Q(M, \mathsf{e}) = R(M) = R_0(\varepsilon)\|R_1(M_1)\|R_2(M_{[1,2]})\|\cdots\|R_{m-1}(M_{[1,m-1]})\|R_*(M)$$

for some $R \in \mathcal{R}$. Then, $Q(\cdot, \mathsf{d})$ is defined similarly to $\mathrm{mJ}^{E,\{\pi_0,\pi_1\}}(S,\cdot,\mathsf{d})$ as follows: For $C \in \Sigma^*$, $Q(C, \mathsf{d}) = Q(M_1\|M_2\|\cdots\|M_m, \mathsf{e})$, where $(C_1, C_2, \ldots, C_m) \leftarrow \mathsf{parse}(C)$, $M_i \leftarrow C_i \oplus R_{i-1}(M_{[1,i-1]})$ for $1 \leq i \leq m-1$, and $M_m \leftarrow C_m \oplus \mathsf{msb}_{|C_m|}(R_{m-1}(M_{[1,m-1]}))$.

The uniform random sampling from $\mathcal{Q}$ is defined naturally by the uniform random sampling from $\mathcal{R}$ if the input length is bounded from above.

The following theorem states that the function $\mathrm{mJ}^{E,\{\pi_0,\pi_1\}}_S$ with S chosen uniformly at random from Σ^n is indistinguishable from a function chosen uniformly at random from $\mathcal{Q}$ if E is a PRP and $\{\pi_0, \pi_1, \iota\}$ is pairwise everywhere distinct.

Theorem 3. *For permutations π_0 and π_1 on Σ^w, suppose that $\{\pi_0, \pi_1, \iota\}$ is pairwise everywhere distinct. Let $\mathbf{A}$ be any adversary with p oracles against*

$mJ^{E,\{\pi_0,\pi_1\}}$ *running in time at most t and making at most q queries in total. Suppose that the length of each query is at most ℓw. Then, there exists an adversary* **B** *against E such that*

$$\mathrm{Adv}^{p\text{-ind}}_{mJ^{E,\{\pi_0,\pi_1\}},\mathcal{Q}}(\mathbf{A}) \leq \ell q \cdot \mathrm{Adv}^{\mathrm{prp}}_E(\mathbf{B}) + \ell q^2/2^{n+1}$$

and **B** *runs in time at most $t + O(\ell q T_E)$, and makes at most q queries, where T_E is the time required to compute E.*

Theorem 3 immediately follows from Lemma 1 and the following lemma.

Lemma 2. *For permutations π_0 and π_1 on Σ^w, suppose that $\{\pi_0, \pi_1, \iota\}$ is pairwise everywhere distinct. Let* **A** *be any adversary with access to p oracles against* $mJ^{E,\{\pi_0,\pi_1\}}$ *running in time at most t and making at most q queries in total. Suppose that the length of each query is at most ℓw. Then, there exists an adversary* **B** *against E with access to q oracles such that*

$$\mathrm{Adv}^{p\text{-ind}}_{mJ^{E,\{\pi_0,\pi_1\}},\mathcal{Q}}(\mathbf{A}) \leq \ell \cdot \mathrm{Adv}^{q\text{-prf}}_E(\mathbf{B})$$

and **B** *runs in time at most $t + O(\ell q T_E)$, and makes at most q queries, where T_E is the time required to compute E.*

Proof. Let $\Pi = \{\pi_0, \pi_1\}$. First, suppose that $p = 1$.

For $l \in \{0, 1, \ldots, \ell\}$ and functions $\mu_i : (\Sigma^w)^i \to \Sigma^w$ for $0 \leq i \leq l$, $\nu : \Sigma^{[0,lw]} \to \Sigma^n$ and $\xi : (\Sigma^w)^l \to \Sigma^w$, let $Q[l]^{E,\Pi}_{\mu,\nu,\xi} : \Sigma^* \times \{\mathsf{e}, \mathsf{d}\} \to \Sigma^n$ be a function defined as follows. For M such that $\mathsf{parse}(M) = (M_1, M_2, \ldots, M_m)$,

$$Q[l]^{E,\Pi}_{\mu,\nu,\xi}(M, \mathsf{e}) =$$
$$\begin{cases} \mu(M_{[1,m-1]}) \| \nu(M) & \text{if } m \leq l, \\ \mu(M_{[1,l-1]}) \| J^{E,\Pi}(\xi(M_{[1,l]}) \| \mu_l(M_{[1,l]}), \mathsf{lsb}_{|M|-lw}(M)) & \text{if } m \geq l + 1, \end{cases}$$

where $\mu(M_{[1,j]}) = \mu_0(\varepsilon) \| \mu_1(M_1) \| \mu_2(M_{[1,2]}) \| \cdots \| \mu_j(M_{[1,j]})$ and $\mu(M_{[1,-1]}) = \varepsilon$. For C such that $\mathsf{parse}(C) = (C_1, C_2, \ldots, C_m)$,

$$Q[l]^{E,\Pi}_{\mu,\nu,\xi}(C, \mathsf{d}) = Q[l]^{E,\Pi}_{\mu,\nu,\xi}(M_1 \| M_2 \| \cdots \| M_m, \mathsf{e}),$$

where

- for $1 \leq i \leq l$, $M_i \leftarrow C_i \oplus \mathsf{msb}_{|C_i|}(\mu_{i-1}(M_{[1,i-1]}))$, and
- for $i \geq l + 1$, $M_i \leftarrow C_i \oplus \mathsf{msb}_{|C_i|}(Y_{i-1,1})$, where $Y_{l,0} = \xi(M_{[1,l]})$, $Y_{l,1} = \mu_l(M_{[1,l]})$, and $Y_i \leftarrow E_{Y_{i-1,0}}(M_i \| Y_{i-1,1})$.

Let $P_l = \Pr[\mathbf{A}^{Q[l]^{E,\Pi}_{\mu,\nu,\xi}} = 1]$, where $\mu_i \twoheadleftarrow \mathcal{F}((\Sigma^w)^i, \Sigma^w)$ for $0 \leq i \leq l$, $\nu \twoheadleftarrow \mathcal{F}(\Sigma^{[0,lw]}, \Sigma^n)$ and $\xi \twoheadleftarrow \mathcal{F}((\Sigma^w)^l, \Sigma^w)$. Then, the advantage of **A** is

$$\mathrm{Adv}^{\mathrm{ind}}_{mJ^{E,\Pi},\mathcal{Q}}(\mathbf{A}) = |P_0 - P_\ell|.$$

Let **B** be an adversary against E with access to q oracles $(g_1, g_2, \ldots, g_q)$, which are either $(E_{K_1}, E_{K_2}, \ldots, E_{K_q})$ or $(\rho_1, \rho_2, \ldots, \rho_q)$, where $K_i \twoheadleftarrow \Sigma^w$ and $\rho_i \twoheadleftarrow \mathcal{F}(\Sigma^n, \Sigma^n)$ for $1 \leq i \leq q$. **B** works as follows:

1. **B** selects r from $\{1, \ldots, \ell\}$ uniformly at random.
2. For $0 \leq i \leq r - 1$, **B** selects μ_i from $\mathcal{F}((\Sigma^w)^i, \Sigma^w)$ uniformly at random. If $r \geq 2$, then **B** also selects $\tilde{\nu}$ from $\mathcal{F}(\Sigma^{[0,(r-1)w]}, \Sigma^n)$ uniformly at random. Actually, **B** simulates $\mu_0, \ldots, \mu_{r-1}$ and $\tilde{\nu}$ with lazy evaluation.
3. **B** runs **A** and outputs the same value as **A**.

For $1 \leq k \leq q$, let (Z, h) be the k-th query made by **A**, which is either (M, e) or (C, d). Let $\mathsf{parse}(Z) = (Z_1, Z_2, \ldots, Z_z)$ and

$$
\mathsf{P}(Z) = \begin{cases} 0 & \text{if } |Z| > 0 \text{ and } |Z| \equiv 0 \pmod{w}, \\ 1 & \text{if } |Z| = 0 \text{ or } |Z| \not\equiv 0 \pmod{w}. \end{cases}
$$

If $z \geq r$, then **B** makes a query to the $d(k)$-th oracle $g_{d(k)}$, where $d : \{1, \ldots, q\} \to \{1, \ldots, q\}$ is a function defined as follows:

- Suppose that $(Z, h) = (C, \mathsf{d})$. Then, let $M_i \leftarrow C_i \oplus \mathsf{msb}_{|C_i|}(\mu_{i-1}(M_{[1,i-1]}))$ for $1 \leq i \leq r$.
- If $r = 1$, then $d(k) \leftarrow 1$ for $1 \leq k \leq q$.
- If $r \geq 2$, then
  - $d(k) \leftarrow d(k')$ if there exists a previous k'-th query $(k' < k)$ with the corresponding M' such that $|\mathsf{pad}(M')|/w \geq r$ and $M'_{[1,r-1]} = M_{[1,r-1]}$, and
  - $d(k) \leftarrow k$ otherwise.

If $z = r$, then the query made by **B** is $M_r \| \pi_{\mathsf{P}(Z)}(\mu_{r-1}(M_{[1,r-1]}))$. If $z \geq r+1$, then it is $M_r \| \mu_{r-1}(M_{[1,r-1]})$. The answer of **B** to (Z, h) is

$$
\begin{cases} \mu(M_{[1,z-1]}) \| \tilde{\nu}(M) & \text{if } z \leq r - 1, \\ \mu(M_{[1,r-1]}) \| g_{d(k)}(M_r \| \pi_{\mathsf{P}(Z)}(\mu_{r-1}(M_{[1,r-1]}))) & \text{if } z = r, \\ \mu(M_{[1,r-1]}) \| \mathsf{mJ}^{E,\Pi}(g_{d(k)}(M_r \| \mu_{r-1}(M_{[1,r-1]})), \mathsf{lsb}_{|Z|-rw}(Z), h) & \text{if } z \geq r + 1. \end{cases}
$$

Now, suppose that **B** is given $(E_{K_1}, \ldots, E_{K_q})$ as oracles, that is, $g_{d(k)} = E_{K_{d(k)}}$. From the description of d, $K_{d(k)}$ can be regarded as an output of a function chosen uniformly at random from $\mathcal{F}((\Sigma^w)^{r-1}, \Sigma^w)$. Thus, **B** provides **A** with the oracle $\mathsf{Q}[r-1]_{\mu,\nu,\xi}^{E,\Pi}$, and

$$
\Pr[\mathbf{B}^{E_{K_1}, \ldots, E_{K_q}} = 1] = \sum_{u=1}^{\ell} \Pr[r = u \wedge \mathbf{B}^{E_{K_1}, \ldots, E_{K_q}} = 1]
$$

$$
= \frac{1}{\ell} \sum_{u=1}^{\ell} \Pr[\mathbf{B}^{E_{K_1}, \ldots, E_{K_q}} = 1 \mid r = u] = \frac{1}{\ell} \sum_{u=1}^{\ell} \Pr[\mathbf{A}^{\mathsf{Q}[u-1]_{\mu,\nu,\xi}^{E,\Pi}} = 1]
$$

$$
= \frac{1}{\ell} \sum_{u=1}^{\ell} P_{u-1}.
$$

On the other hand, suppose that **B** is given oracles $(\rho_1, \ldots, \rho_q)$, that is, $g_{d(k)} = \rho_{d(k)}$. Since $\{\pi_0, \pi_1, \iota\}$ is pairwise everywhere distinct, $\mu_{r-1}(M_{[1,r-1]})$,

$\pi_0(\mu_{r-1}(M_{[1,r-1]}))$ and $\pi_1(\mu_{r-1}(M_{[1,r-1]}))$ are not equal to each other. Thus, $\mathbf{B}$ provides $\mathbf{A}$ with the oracle $Q[r]_{\mu,\nu,\xi}^{E,\Pi}$, and

$$\Pr[\mathbf{B}^{\rho_1,\dots,\rho_q} = 1] = \frac{1}{\ell}\sum_{i=1}^{\ell} P_i.$$

Thus,

$$\begin{aligned}
\mathrm{Adv}_E^{q\text{-prf}}(\mathbf{B}) &= \left|\Pr[\mathbf{B}^{E_{K_1},\dots,E_{K_q}} = 1] - \Pr[\mathbf{B}^{\rho_1,\dots,\rho_q} = 1]\right| \\
&= \left|\frac{1}{\ell}\sum_{i=1}^{\ell} P_{i-1} - \frac{1}{\ell}\sum_{i=1}^{\ell} P_i\right| = \frac{|P_0 - P_\ell|}{\ell} \\
&= \frac{1}{\ell}\,\mathrm{Adv}_{\mathsf{mJ}^{E,\Pi},\mathcal{Q}}^{\mathrm{ind}}(\mathbf{A}).
\end{aligned}$$

There may exist an adversary with the same amounts of resources as $\mathbf{B}$ and larger advantage. Let us call it $\mathbf{B}$ again. This completes the proof for $p = 1$.

For $p \geq 2$, prepare p instances of $Q[l]_{\mu,\nu,\xi}^{E,\Pi}$ and modify the function $d : \{1,2,\dots,q\} \to \{1,2,\dots,q\}$ accordingly. □

5.3   The Proof of Theorem 1

Let $\mathbf{B}_0$ be an adversary against E with oracle access to a function $f \in \mathcal{F}(\Sigma^n, \Sigma^n)$, which is either E_K with $K \twoheadleftarrow \Sigma^w$ or $\varpi \twoheadleftarrow \mathcal{F}(\Sigma^n, \Sigma^n)$. Let $\mathsf{E0}^f$ and $\mathsf{D0}^f$ be functions obtained from $\mathsf{E0}_K$ and $\mathsf{D0}_K$ in Algorithm 2 simply by replacing the calls to $E_K(N)$ with $f(N)$, respectively. $\mathbf{B}_0$ runs $\mathbf{A}$. For each encryption query (N, A, M) made by $\mathbf{A}$, $\mathbf{B}_0$ computes $\mathsf{E0}^f(N, A, M)$ with oracle access to f and returns it to $\mathbf{A}$. For each decryption query (N, A, C, T) made by $\mathbf{A}$, $\mathbf{B}_0$ computes $\mathsf{D0}^f(N, A, C, T)$ with oracle access to f and returns it to $\mathbf{A}$. Finally, $\mathbf{B}_0$ produces the same output as $\mathbf{A}$. Then,

$$\mathrm{Adv}_E^{\mathrm{prf}}(\mathbf{B}_0) = \left|\Pr[\mathbf{A}^{\mathsf{E0}^{E_K},\mathsf{D0}^{E_K}} = 1] - \Pr[\mathbf{A}^{\mathsf{E0}^\varpi,\mathsf{D0}^\varpi} = 1]\right|,$$

where $\mathsf{E0}^{E_K}$ and $\mathsf{D0}^{E_K}$ are identical to $\mathsf{E0}_K$ and $\mathsf{D0}_K$, respectively. $\mathbf{B}_0$ makes at most q queries to its oracle. The run time of $\mathbf{B}_0$ is at most $t + O(\ell q T_E)$.

Let $\Pi = \{\pi_0, \pi_1\}$. Let $\mathbf{B}_1$ be an adversary against $\mathsf{aJ}^{E,\Pi}$ with oracle access to q functions $\boldsymbol{f} = (f_1, \dots, f_q)$, which are either $\left(\mathsf{aJ}_{K_1}^{E,\Pi}, \dots, \mathsf{aJ}_{K_q}^{E,\Pi}\right)$ with $\boldsymbol{K} = (K_1, \dots, K_q) \twoheadleftarrow (\Sigma^n)^q$ or $\boldsymbol{\rho} = (\rho_1, \dots, \rho_q) \twoheadleftarrow (\mathcal{F}(\Sigma^*, \Sigma^n))^q$. $\mathbf{B}_1$ runs $\mathbf{A}$. For the k-th query involving (N, A) made by $\mathbf{A}$ with $1 \leq k \leq q$, $\mathbf{B}_1$ simulates $\mathsf{E0}_K$ or $\mathsf{D0}_K$ using $\tilde{S} \leftarrow f_{d_a(k)}(A)$ instead of S in Algorithm 2, where $d_a : \{1, \dots, q\} \to \{1, \dots, q\}$ is a function defined as follows: $d_a(k) \leftarrow d_a(k')$ if there exists a previous k'-th query involving (N', A') such that $N = N'$, and $d_a(k) \leftarrow k$ otherwise. Finally, $\mathbf{B}_1$ produces the same output as $\mathbf{A}$. Let $\mathsf{E0}^f$ and $\mathsf{D0}^f$ be the oracles of $\mathbf{A}$ simulated by $\mathbf{B}_1$ as described above. Then,

$$\mathrm{Adv}_{\mathsf{aJ}^{E,\Pi}}^{q\text{-prf}}(\mathbf{B}_1) = \left|\Pr[\mathbf{A}^{\mathsf{E0}^{\mathsf{aJ}_K^{E,\Pi}},\mathsf{D0}^{\mathsf{aJ}_K^{E,\Pi}}} = 1] - \Pr[\mathbf{A}^{\mathsf{E0}^\rho,\mathsf{D0}^\rho} = 1]\right|,$$

where $\mathsf{E0}^{\mathsf{aJ}_K^{E,\Pi}}$ and $\mathsf{D0}^{\mathsf{aJ}_K^{E,\Pi}}$ are identical to $\mathsf{E0}^{\varpi}$ and $\mathsf{D0}^{\varpi}$, respectively. $\mathbf{B}_1$ runs in time at most $t + O(\ell q T_E)$ and makes at most q queries in total. The length of each query is at most $\ell_a w$.

Let $\mathbf{B}_2$ be an adversary against $\mathsf{mJ}^{E,\Pi}$ with oracle access to q functions $\boldsymbol{g} = (g_1, \ldots, g_q)$, which are either $(\mathsf{mJ}_{S_1}^{E,\Pi}, \ldots, \mathsf{mJ}_{S_q}^{E,\Pi})$ with $\boldsymbol{S} = (S_1, \ldots, S_q)$ $\leftarrow (\Sigma^w)^q$ or $\boldsymbol{Q} = (Q_1, Q_2, \ldots, Q_q) \leftarrow \mathcal{Q}^q$. $\mathbf{B}_2$ runs $\mathbf{A}$. For the k-th query involving (N, A) made by $\mathbf{A}$ with $1 \leq k \leq q$, $\mathbf{B}_2$ simulates $\mathsf{E0}_K$ or $\mathsf{D0}_K$ using $\tilde{V} \leftarrow g_{d_m(k)}(M, \mathsf{e})$ or $\tilde{V} \leftarrow g_{d_m(k)}(C, \mathsf{d})$, respectively, where $d_m : \{1, \ldots, q\} \rightarrow \{1, \ldots, q\}$ is a function defined as follows: $d_m(k) \leftarrow d_m(k')$ if there exists a previous k'-th query involving (N', A') such that $(N, A) = (N', A')$, and $d_m(k) \leftarrow k$ otherwise. Finally, $\mathbf{B}_2$ produces the same output as $\mathbf{A}$. Let $\mathsf{E0}^{\boldsymbol{g}}$ and $\mathsf{D0}^{\boldsymbol{g}}$ be the oracles of $\mathbf{A}$ simulated by $\mathbf{B}_2$ as described above. Then,

$$\mathrm{Adv}_{\mathsf{mJ}^{E,\Pi},\mathcal{Q}}^{q\text{-ind}}(\mathbf{B}_2) = \left| \Pr\left[\mathbf{A}^{\mathsf{E0}^{\mathsf{mJ}_S^{E,\Pi}},\mathsf{D0}^{\mathsf{mJ}_S^{E,\Pi}}} = 1\right] - \Pr\left[\mathbf{A}^{\mathsf{E0}^Q,\mathsf{D0}^Q} = 1\right] \right|,$$

where $\mathsf{E0}^{\mathsf{mJ}_S^{E,\Pi}}$ and $\mathsf{D0}^{\mathsf{mJ}_S^{E,\Pi}}$ are identical to $\mathsf{E0}^{\rho}$ and $\mathsf{D0}^{\rho}$, respectively. $\mathbf{B}_2$ runs in time at most $t + O(\ell w)$ and makes at most q queries in total. The length of each query is at most $\ell_m w$.

Now, let us consider $\mathbf{B}_2^{\mathcal{Q}}$. For a decryption query (N, A, C, T) made by $\mathbf{A}$, if (N, A) is new, then $\mathsf{lsb}_n(\tilde{V})$ is chosen uniformly at random. On the other hand, suppose that (N, A) is not new and C is new. Let (N, A, C', T') be a quadruple corresponding to a previous query. Since $C \neq C'$, M corresponding to C is not equal to M' corresponding to C'. Thus, $\mathsf{lsb}_n(\tilde{V})$ is also chosen uniformly at random. Let $\mathbf{B}_3$ be an adversary identical to $\mathbf{B}_2$ except that, for every decryption query, $\mathbf{B}_3$ does nothing but returns $\perp$. Then, $\Pr[\mathbf{B}_2^{\mathcal{Q}} = 1] \leq \Pr[\mathbf{B}_3^{\mathcal{Q}} = 1] + q_d/2^\tau$.

Since $\mathbf{A}$ is nonce-respecting with respect to encryption, an answer (C, T) returned by $\mathbf{B}_3^{\mathcal{Q}}$ for every encryption query made by $\mathbf{A}$ are a pair of sequences chosen uniformly at random. Thus, $\Pr[\mathbf{B}_3^{\mathcal{Q}} = 1] = \Pr[\mathbf{A}^{\$,\perp} = 1]$.

Consequently,

$$\mathrm{Adv}_{\mathsf{Lae0}}^{\mathrm{aead}}(\mathbf{A}) = \left| \Pr[\mathbf{A}^{\mathsf{E0}_K,\mathsf{D0}_K} = 1] - \Pr[\mathbf{A}^{\$,\perp} = 1] \right|$$
$$\leq \mathrm{Adv}_E^{\mathrm{prf}}(\mathbf{B}_0) + \mathrm{Adv}_{\mathsf{aJ}^{E,\Pi}}^{q\text{-prf}}(\mathbf{B}_1) + \mathrm{Adv}_{\mathsf{mJ}^{E,\Pi},\mathcal{Q}}^{q\text{-ind}}(\mathbf{B}_2) + q_d/2^\tau.$$

This completes the proof with Theorems 2 and 3.

6   Authenticity of Lae0 Under Misuses

The security of Lae0 under misuses is discussed. The misuses considered here are nonce repetition (NR) and releasing unverified plaintexts (RUP). For NR, adversaries are not assumed to be nonce-respecting with respect to encryption. For RUP, the decrypt-anyway function $\widetilde{\mathsf{D0}}$ presented in Algorithm 3 is used instead of $\mathsf{D0}$ in Algorithm 2. For given (N, A, C, T), $\widetilde{\mathsf{D0}}_K$ returns a message $\tilde{M}$ recovered anyway as well as whether the input is valid ($\top$) or invalid ($\perp$).

Algorithm 3. Decryption of LaeO under RUP

---

function $\widetilde{\mathsf{DO}}_K(N, A, C, T)$
  $S \leftarrow \mathsf{aJ}^{E, \{\pi_0, \pi_1\}}(E_K(N), A)$
  $V \leftarrow \mathsf{mJ}^{E, \{\pi_0, \pi_1\}}(S, C, \mathsf{d})$
  $\tilde{M} \leftarrow C \oplus \mathsf{msb}_{|C|}(V)$
  if $T = \mathsf{lsb}_\tau(V)$ **then**
      return $\tilde{M}, \top$
  else
      return $\tilde{M}, \bot$
  end if
end function

To confirm the authenticity of LaeO under the misuses, it is shown that $(\mathsf{EO}_K, \widetilde{\mathsf{DO}}_K)$ is indistinguishable from $(\widehat{\mathsf{EO}}^{\boldsymbol{Q}}, \widehat{\mathsf{DO}}^{\boldsymbol{Q}})$, which is presented in Algorithm 4, where $\boldsymbol{Q} = (Q_1, Q_2, \ldots, Q_q)$. For $1 \leq i \leq q$, Q_i is sampled from $\mathcal{Q}$ according to the specified probability distribution. q is the total number of the encryption or decryption queries. For the k-th query, $\widehat{\mathsf{EO}}$ or $\widehat{\mathsf{DO}}$ use $Q_{d_{\mathrm{m}}(k)}$, which depends on the value of the pair (N, A). Namely, the function $d_{\mathrm{m}} : \{1, 2, \ldots, q\} \rightarrow \{1, 2, \ldots, q\}$ is defined as follows. For the k-th query (N, A, M) or (N, A, C, T), if there exists some previous k'-th query with the same value of (N, A), then $d_{\mathrm{m}}(k) \leftarrow d_{\mathrm{m}}(k')$. Otherwise, $d_{\mathrm{m}}(k) \leftarrow k$. Different from $\widetilde{\mathsf{DO}}$, $\widehat{\mathsf{DO}}$ always returns $\bot$ together with a message recovered anyway.

Algorithm 4. Ideal encryption $\widehat{\mathsf{EO}}$ and decryption $\widehat{\mathsf{DO}}$ under NR and RUP

---

function $\widehat{\mathsf{EO}}^{Q_1, Q_2, \ldots, Q_q}(N, A, M)$
  ▷ Let (N, A, M) be the k-th query
  $V \leftarrow Q_{d_{\mathrm{m}}(k)}(M, \mathsf{e})$
  $C \leftarrow M \oplus \mathsf{msb}_{|M|}(V)$
  $T \leftarrow \mathsf{lsb}_\tau(V)$
  return C, T
end function

function $\widehat{\mathsf{DO}}^{Q_1, Q_2, \ldots, Q_q}(N, A, C, T)$
  ▷ Let (N, A, C, T) be the k-th query
  $V \leftarrow Q_{d_{\mathrm{m}}(k)}(C, \mathsf{d})$
  $\tilde{M} \leftarrow C \oplus \mathsf{msb}_{|C|}(V)$
  return $\tilde{M}, \bot$
end function

The following theorem states that $(\mathsf{EO}_K, \widetilde{\mathsf{DO}}_K)$ and $(\widehat{\mathsf{EO}}^{\boldsymbol{Q}}, \widehat{\mathsf{DO}}^{\boldsymbol{Q}})$ are indistinguishable if the underlying block cipher E is a PRP and $\{\pi_0, \pi_1, \iota\}$ is pairwise everywhere distinct. The proof is similar to that of Theorem 1 and omitted due to the page limit. The theorem implies that LaeO satisfies authenticity under the misuses. Actually, the indistinguishability between $(\mathsf{EO}_K, \widetilde{\mathsf{DO}}_K)$ and $(\widehat{\mathsf{EO}}^{\boldsymbol{Q}}, \widehat{\mathsf{DO}}^{\boldsymbol{Q}})$ implies INT-RUP [1] of LaeO.

Theorem 4. *For permutations π_0 and π_1 on Σ^w used in LaeO, suppose that $\{\pi_0, \pi_1, \iota\}$ is pairwise everywhere distinct. Let $\mathbf{A}$ be any adversary against LaeO under misuses running in time at most t and making at most q_{e} and q_{d} queries to the encryption and decryption oracles, respectively. Let $q = q_{\mathrm{e}} + q_{\mathrm{d}}$. Suppose that* *the length of a message or a ciphertext in each query is at most $\ell_m w$. Suppose that the length of associated data in each query is at most $\ell_a w$. Let $\ell = \ell_m + \ell_a$. Then, there exists an adversary* **B** *against E such that*

$$\mathrm{Adv}^{\mathrm{ind}}_{(\mathrm{E0},\widetilde{\mathrm{D0}}),(\widehat{\mathrm{E0}},\widehat{\mathrm{D0}})}(\mathbf{A}) \leq (\ell + 1)q\,\mathrm{Adv}^{\mathrm{prp}}_E(\mathbf{B}) + (\ell + 1)q^2/2^{n+1} + q_d/2^\tau$$

and **B** *runs in time at most $t + O(\ell q T_E)$ and makes at most q queries, where T_E is the time required to compute E.*

7   Conclusion

A nonce-based AEAD scheme Lae0 has been proposed in this paper. It is based on the hashing mode of Lesamnta-LW, which is specified by the ISO/IEC 29192-5 standard. It is shown to be secure in the standard model. It is also shown to satisfy authenticity under the misuses of nonce repetition and releasing unverified plaintexts. Future work is to improve the efficiency of Lae0.

Acknowledgements. The first author was supported in part by JSPS KAKENHI Grant Number JP18H05289.

References

1. Andreeva, E., Bogdanov, A., Luykx, A., Mennink, B., Mouha, N., Yasuda, K.: How to securely release unverified plaintext in authenticated encryption. In: Sarkar, P., Iwata, T. (eds.) ASIACRYPT 2014. LNCS, vol. 8873, pp. 105–125. Springer, Heidelberg (2014). https://doi.org/10.1007/978-3-662-45611-8_6
2. Bellare, M., Namprempre, C.: Authenticated encryption: relations among notions and analysis of the generic composition paradigm. In: Okamoto, T. (ed.) ASIACRYPT 2000. LNCS, vol. 1976, pp. 531–545. Springer, Heidelberg (2000). https://doi.org/10.1007/3-540-44448-3_41
3. Berti, F., Guo, C., Pereira, O., Peters, T., Standaert, F.X.: TEDT, a leakage-resilient AEAD mode for high (physical) security applications. Cryptology ePrint Archive, Report 2019/137 (2019). https://eprint.iacr.org/2019/137
4. Berti, F., Pereira, O., Peters, T., Standaert, F.: On leakage-resilient authenticated encryption with decryption leakages. IACR Trans. Symmetric Cryptol. **2017**(3), 271–293 (2017). https://doi.org/10.13154/tosc.v2017.i3.271-293
5. Berti, F., Pereira, O., Standaert, F.-X.: Reducing the cost of authenticity with leakages: a CIML2-secure AE scheme with one call to a strongly protected tweakable block cipher. In: Buchmann, J., Nitaj, A., Rachidi, T. (eds.) AFRICACRYPT 2019. LNCS, vol. 11627, pp. 229–249. Springer, Cham (2019). https://doi.org/10.1007/978-3-030-23696-0_12
6. Bertoni, G., Daemen, J., Peeters, M., Van Assche, G.: Sponge functions. In: ECRYPT Hash Workshop (2007)
7. Bertoni, G., Daemen, J., Peeters, M., Van Assche, G.: The KECCAK sponge function family (2008). http://keccak.noekeon.org
8. Bertoni, G., Daemen, J., Peeters, M., Van Assche, G.: Duplexing the sponge: single-pass authenticated encryption and other applications. In: Miri, A., Vaudenay, S. (eds.) SAC 2011. LNCS, vol. 7118, pp. 320–337. Springer, Heidelberg (2012). https://doi.org/10.1007/978-3-642-28496-0_19

9. Bogdanov, A., Knežević, M., Leander, G., Toz, D., Varıcı, K., Verbauwhede, I.: SPONGENT: a lightweight hash function. In: Preneel, B., Takagi, T. (eds.) CHES 2011. LNCS, vol. 6917, pp. 312–325. Springer, Heidelberg (2011). https://doi.org/10.1007/978-3-642-23951-9_21

10. Brassard, G. (ed.): CRYPTO 1989. LNCS, vol. 435. Springer, New York (1990). https://doi.org/10.1007/0-387-34805-0

11. Cogliani, S., et al.: OMD: a compression function mode of operation for authenticated encryption. In: Joux, A., Youssef, A. (eds.) SAC 2014. LNCS, vol. 8781, pp. 112–128. Springer, Cham (2014). https://doi.org/10.1007/978-3-319-13051-4_7

12. Damgård, I.: A design principle for hash functions. In: Brassard [10], pp. 416–427

13. Dobraunig, C., Eichlseder, M., Mangard, S., Mendel, F., Unterluggauer, T.: ISAP - towards side-channel secure authenticated encryption. IACR Trans. Symmetric Cryptol. **2017**(1), 80–105 (2017). https://doi.org/10.13154/tosc.v2017.i1.80-105

14. FIPS PUB 180-4: Secure hash standard (SHS), August 2015

15. FIPS PUB 197: Advanced encryption standard (AES) (2001)

16. FIPS PUB 202: SHA-3 standard: Permutation-based hash and extendable-output functions (2015)

17. Goldwasser, S., Micali, S.: Probabilistic encryption. J. Comput. Syst. Sci. **28**(2), 270–299 (1984)

18. Guo, C., Pereira, O., Peters, T., Standaert, F.X.: Authenticated encryption with nonce misuse and physical leakages: definitions, separation results, and leveled constructions. Cryptology ePrint Archive, Report 2018/484 (2018). https://eprint.iacr.org/2018/484

19. Guo, C., Pereira, O., Peters, T., Standaert, F.X.: Towards low-energy leakage-resistant authenticated encryption from the duplex sponge construction. Cryptology ePrint Archive, Report 2019/193 (2019). https://eprint.iacr.org/2019/193

20. Guo, J., Peyrin, T., Poschmann, A.: The PHOTON family of lightweight hash functions. In: Rogaway, P. (ed.) CRYPTO 2011. LNCS, vol. 6841, pp. 222–239. Springer, Heidelberg (2011). https://doi.org/10.1007/978-3-642-22792-9_13

21. Hirose, S., Ideguchi, K., Kuwakado, H., Owada, T., Preneel, B., Yoshida, H.: An AES based 256-bit hash function for lightweight applications: Lesamnta-LW. IEICE Trans. Fundam. **E95−A**(1), 89–99 (2012)

22. Hoang, V.T., Krovetz, T., Rogaway, P.: Robust authenticated-encryption AEZ and the problem that it solves. In: Oswald, E., Fischlin, M. (eds.) EUROCRYPT 2015. LNCS, vol. 9056, pp. 15–44. Springer, Heidelberg (2015). https://doi.org/10.1007/978-3-662-46800-5_2

23. ISO/IEC 19772: Information technology – security techniques – authenticated encryption (2009)

24. ISO/IEC 29192-5: Information technology – security techniques – lightweight cryptography – part 5: Hash-functions (2016)

25. Jutla, C.S.: Encryption modes with almost free message integrity. In: Pfitzmann, B. (ed.) EUROCRYPT 2001. LNCS, vol. 2045, pp. 529–544. Springer, Heidelberg (2001). https://doi.org/10.1007/3-540-44987-6_32

26. Katz, J., Yung, M.: Complete characterization of security notions for probabilistic private-key encryption. In: Proceedings of the Thirty-Second Annual ACM Symposium on Theory of Computing, pp. 245–254 (2000)

27. Merkle, R.C.: One way hash functions and DES. In: Brassard [10], pp. 428–446

28. Namprempre, C., Rogaway, P., Shrimpton, T.: Reconsidering generic composition. In: Nguyen, P.Q., Oswald, E. (eds.) EUROCRYPT 2014. LNCS, vol. 8441, pp. 257–274. Springer, Heidelberg (2014). https://doi.org/10.1007/978-3-642-55220-5_15

29. NIST Special Publication 800-38C: Recommendation for block cipher modes of operation: The CCM mode for authentication and confidentiality (2004)
30. NIST Special Publication 800-38D: Recommendation for block cipher modes of operation: Galois/counter mode (GCM) and GMAC (2007)
31. Pereira, O., Standaert, F., Vivek, S.: Leakage-resilient authentication and encryption from symmetric cryptographic primitives. In: Ray, I., Li, N., Kruegel, C. (eds.) Proceedings of the 22nd ACM SIGSAC Conference on Computer and Communications Security, Denver, CO, USA, 12–16 October 2015, pp. 96–108. ACM (2015). https://doi.org/10.1145/2810103.2813626
32. Rogaway, P.: Nonce-based symmetric encryption. In: Roy, B., Meier, W. (eds.) FSE 2004. LNCS, vol. 3017, pp. 348–358. Springer, Heidelberg (2004). https://doi.org/10.1007/978-3-540-25937-4_22
33. Rogaway, P., Bellare, M., Black, J., Krovetz, T.: OCB: a block-cipher mode of operation for efficient authenticated encryption. In: ACM Conference on Computer and Communications Security, pp. 196–205 (2001)
34. Rogaway, P., Shrimpton, T.: A provable-security treatment of the key-wrap problem. In: Vaudenay, S. (ed.) EUROCRYPT 2006. LNCS, vol. 4004, pp. 373–390. Springer, Heidelberg (2006). https://doi.org/10.1007/11761679_23

All the HIGHT You Need on Cortex–M4

Hwajeong Seo[1(✉)] and Zhe Liu[2]

[1] Division of IT Convergence Engineering, Hansung University, Seoul, South Korea
hwajeong84@gmail.com
[2] College of Computer Science and Technology, Nanjing University of Aeronautics
and Astronautics, Nanjing, China
sduliuzhe@gmail.com

Abstract. In this paper, we present high-speed and secure implementations of HIGHT block cipher on 32-bit ARM Cortex-M4 microcontrollers. We utilized both data parallelism and task parallelism to reduce the execution timing. In particular, we used the 32-bit wise ARM–SIMD instruction sets to perform the parallel computations in efficient way. Since the HIGHT block cipher is constructed upon 8-bit word, four 8-bit operations are performed in the 32-bit wise ARM–SIMD instruction of ARM Cortex-M4 microcontrollers. We also presented a novel countermeasure against fault attack on target microcontrollers. The method achieved the fault attack resistance with intra-instruction redundancy feature with reasonable performance. Finally, the proposed HIGHT implementation achieved much better performance and security level than previous works.

Keywords: HIGHT block cipher · ARM Cortex-M4 · Parallel implementation · Software implementation · Fault attack resistance

1 Introduction

Internet of Things (IoT) applications become feasible services as the technology of embedded processors are developed. In order to provide fully customized services, the IoT applications need to analyze and process big data and the data should be securely encrypted before packet transmission. However, the data encryption is high computation overheads for the low-end IoT devices with limited computation frequency, energy, and storage. For this reason, lightweight block cipher algorithms should be implemented in efficient manner to fit into the certain requirements of applications. In order to evaluate the efficiency of block cipher algorithms in objective manner, Fair Evaluation of Lightweight Cryptographic Systems (FELICS) evaluated the implementations of block ciphers on low-end IoT devices [3]. FELICS framework fairly evaluated the all block ciphers, including Addition, Rotation, and bitwise eXclusive-or (ARX) and Substitution-Permutation Network (SPN) based block ciphers, on low-end IoT devices, including 8-bit AVR, 16-bit MSP, and 32-bit ARM Cortex-M3 microcontrollers. The evaluation metric is execution time, code size, and RAM. However, they didn't consider the recent ARM microcontroller, namely Cortex-M4.

© Springer Nature Switzerland AG 2020
J. H. Seo (Ed.): ICISC 2019, LNCS 11975, pp. 70–83, 2020.
https://doi.org/10.1007/978-3-030-40921-0_4

In this paper, we introduce the optimization techniques for HIGHT block cipher on 32-bit ARM Cortex-M4 microcontrollers. We utilized both data parallelism and task parallelism to reduce the execution timing. In particular, we used the ARM–SIMD instruction sets to perform the parallel computations in efficient way. Since the HIGHT block cipher has 8-bit word, four 8-bit operations can be efficiently performed in a ARM–SIMD instruction of ARM Cortex-M4 microcontrollers. To get compact results, we used platform-specific assembly-level optimizations for HIGHT block ciphers since the features of IoT platforms vary (e.g. word size, number of registers, and instruction set). We also presented a novel countermeasure against fault attack on target microcontrollers. The method achieved the fault attack resistance with intra-instruction redundancy feature. Finally, high-speed and secure HIGHT implementation achieved much better performance and security than previous works. The proposed implementation methods for HIGHT block cipher can be used for other ARX based block ciphers, such as SPECK and SIMON, straightforwardly.

Summary of Research Contributions

The contributions of our work are summarized as follows.

1. *Optimized task and data parallel implementation of HIGHT.* A modern 32-bit ARM processor provides a byte-wise SIMD feature, which performs four bytes addition or subtraction operation without overflow or underflow problem. This SIMD instruction is used to perform the parallel computations for HIGHT block cipher. The specialized rotation routines are also used to optimize the F0 and F1 functions of HIGHT block cipher.
2. *Fault attack resistance techniques for HIGHT.* We introduced the new approach to resist the fault attack for HIGHT block cipher on the 32-bit ARM Cortex-M4 microcontrollers. We used intra-instruction redundant implementation and randomly shuffle the data to increase the randomness of data location. All routines are finely optimized on the target microcontrollers.
3. *HIGHT implementations on 32-bit ARM Cortex-M4 in open source.* We share all HIGHT implementations for reproduction of results. The following link provides the source codes: https://bit.ly/2ZogBRI.

The remainder of this paper is organized as follows. In Sect. 2, we overview HIGHT block cipher, FELICS framework and previous block cipher implementations on the 32-bit ARM Cortex-M microcontrollers. In Sect. 3, we introduce compact and secure implementations of HIGHT block cipher for the 32-bit ARM Cortex-M4 microcontrollers. In Sect. 4, we summarize our experimental results and compare the results with the state-of-the-art works. In Sect. 5, we conclude the paper.

2 Related Works

2.1 HIGHT Block Cipher

In CHES'06, lightweight block cipher HIGHT, was introduced by Korea, and it was enacted as ISO/IEC 18033-3 international block cryptographic algorithm standard [9]. Since the HIGHT has lightweight features, this is suitable for the low-end IoT applications. The block size is 64-bit and key size is 128-bit. HIGHT block cipher performs 8-bit wise ARX operations. The encryption or decryption operation requires 32 round functions. In each round function, a 64-bit round key is required. In total, 2,048-bit of round keys are needed to process a 64-bit plaintext during the encryption routine (Fig. 1).

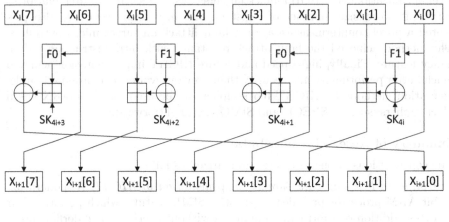

$$FO(X) = X^{<<<1} \oplus X^{<<<2} \oplus X^{<<<7}$$

$$F1(X) = X^{<<<3} \oplus X^{<<<4} \oplus X^{<<<6}$$

Fig. 1. One round of HIGHT encryption; X and SK represent input data and session key

2.2 FELICS

In 2015, a benchmarking framework of software based block cipher implementations named Fair Evaluation of Lightweight Cryptographic Systems (FELICS) was held by Luxembourg University. The FELICS benchmarking framework only targets the low-end embedded devices, including 8-bit AVR ATmega128, 16-bit MSP430, and 32-bit ARM Cortex-M3. The FELICS framework provides unified methods for measuring the performance of block ciphers in terms of code size, RAM, and execution timing under the same compiler specifications and target platform. The implementations were evaluated in three scenarios, including cipher operation, communication protocol, and challenge-handshake authentication protocol. By using the framework, the lightweight block cipher competition (i.e. FELICS Triathlon) was held by Luxembourg University. In the competition, more than one hundred block cipher implementations on low-end IoT devices were submitted by world-wide cryptographic engineers. After competition, they reported the most optimized results and HIGHT implementation won the second round. This result shows that HIGHT block cipher has the one of the most reasonable lightweight block cipher. For this reason, we decide to investigate the optimized HIGHT implementations in modern low-end microcontrollers (i.e. 32-bit ARM Cortex-M4 microcontrollers) in this paper.

2.3   Previous Block Cipher Implementations on IoT Devices

Several works have investigated the implementation of block ciphers on IoT embedded processors. In the past, 8-bit AVR and 16-bit MSP microcontrollers were representative low-end target processors. Many works reported the optimized block cipher implementations on 8-bit AVR and 16-bit MSP microcontrollers [2,4,6,7,12]. In recent works, they consider the advanced 32-bit ARM microcontrollers as the reasonable low-end microcontrollers in terms of computation power and energy consumption. In order to fully utilize the 32-bit word size of ARM processors, LEA block cipher selected the 32-bit wise Addition, Rotation, and eXclusive-or (ARX) operations. For this reason, LEA implementation on ARM microcontroller (i.e. ARM926EJ-S) shows higher performance than previous AES implementations [8]. In [15], the LEA implementations through on-the-fly method over ARM Cortex-M3 processors were proposed. They utilized the available registers to retain many parameters as possible and optimized the rotation operation with the barrel-shifter techniques. In [10], the lightweight block cipher CHAM was implemented on ARM Cortex-M3 microcontrollers. Compared with the SPECK block cipher, the CHAM block cipher shows better performance. In [14], highly-optimized AES-CTR assembly implementations for the ARM Cortex-M3 and M4 microcontrollers were introduced. The implementations are about twice as fast as existing implementations. The implementations include an architecture-specific instruction scheduler and register allocator. In [16], LEA and HIGHT block ciphers are evaluated on ARM Cortex-M3 microcontrollers. In particular, pseudo-SIMD technique is used for HIGHT implementation on ARM Cortex-M3. This technique can perform two encryption operations at once on a 32-bit ARM processor. In this paper, we further improve the performance of HIGHT block cipher on ARM Cortex-M4 microcontrollers by using SIMD instruction and parallelism. Furthermore, the secure design against fault attack is also introduced.

2.4   ARM Cortex-M Microcontrollers

The ARM Cortex-M is a family of 32-bit processors for use in embedded microcontrollers. The microcontrollers are designed to be energy efficient, while being fast enough to provide high performance in applications.

ARM Cortex-M4. ARM Cortex-M4 is a 32-bit microcontroller based on ARMv7-M architecture developed by ARM Holdings. ARM Cortex-M4 was announced in 2010. Cortex-M4 has 32-bit registers and a Thumb/Thumb-2 instruction set that supports both 16-bit and 32-bit operations. Arithmetic instructions take one cycle but memory access instructions take more cycles. The microcontrollers supports barrel-shifter, which performs rotated or shifted registers without additional costs. In particular, the Cortex-M4 supports additional instructions for digital signal processing than Cortex-M3. In this paper, We used the MK20DX256VLH7 development board. This equips 256 KB of flash memory, 64 KB of RAM, and 2 KB of EEPROM. In can run at up-to 72 MHz. The detailed instructions for ARM Cortex-M4 are given in Table 1. In particular, UADD8 and USUB8 instructions perform four byte-wise SIMD operations. This is very efficient to handle carry-less addition and borrow-less subtraction operations.

Table 1. Instruction set summary for 32-bit ARM Cortex-M4

Mnemonics	Operands	Description	Operation	#Clock
ADD	C, A, B	Add word without Carry	C ← A+B	1
EOR	C, A, B	Exclusive OR	C ← A⊕B	1
AND	C, A, B	Bitwise-AND	C ← A&B	1
ORR	C, A, B	Bitwise-OR	C ← A|B	1
LSL	C, A, B	Shift Left	C ← A<<B	1
ROR	C, A, B	Rotate Right	C ← A>>>B	1
MOV	C, A	Move	C ← A	1
PUSH	A	Push word	STACK ← A	2
POP	A	Pop word	STACK → A	2
UADD8	C, A, B	Add bytes without Carry	C ← A+B	1
USUB8	C, A, B	Sub bytes without Carry	C ← A-B	1

3   Proposed Methods

The block cipher encryption usually performed in either sequential or parallel way. The sequential implementation can only compute single block at once, while the parallel implementation utilizes the multiple computing units (e.g. multiple cores) or SIMD instruction sets (e.g. ARM-SIMD, NEON, and AVX2) to perform multiple blocks at once. The parallel computations ideally result in a speed-up of n over sequential execution, where n is the number of parallel computation units. For this reason, the parallel implementation is usually considered to achieve the fast and efficient computations than serial implementations. In this paper, we focused on the parallel computation of lightweight block cipher (i.e. HIGHT) on low-end microcontrollers (i.e. 32-bit ARM Cortex-M4). Furthermore, we improve the security against the fault attack by using parallel implementation.

There are largely two ways of parallelism techniques, including data parallelism and task parallelism. First, the data parallelism is running the same task on different components of data. Second, the task parallelism, also known as function parallelism or control parallelism, runs many different tasks at the same time on the same data. In this paper, we target both task and data parallel HIGHT implementations on 32-bit ARM Cortex-M4 microcontrollers.

3.1 Key Scheduling

Round key generation requires byte-wise addition operations and byte-wise rotation operations. The byte-wise rotation operations are performed with barrel-shifter and masked approach. The four byte-wise addition is easily performed with UADD8 instruction at once. Among 14 general purpose registers (R0~R12, R14), we utilized 13 registers for key scheduling of HIGHT block cipher as described in Table 2. For the task parallel encryption, only one round key is stored in the word by two bytes. The round key format is $\{??, SK_{4i+2}, ??, SK_{4i+0}\}$ or $\{??, SK_{4i+3}, ??, SK_{4i+1}\}$, where SK and $??$ represent the round keys and byte padding, respectively.

For the data parallel encryption, the same round key is duplicated to remaining part (i.e. two bytes out of four bytes) of registers and the word is fully used (i.e. $\{SK_{4i+2}, SK_{4i+2}, SK_{4i+0}, SK_{4i+0}\}$ or $\{SK_{4i+3}, SK_{4i+3}, SK_{4i+1}, SK_{4i+1}\}$).

Table 2. Register utilization for key scheduling on ARM Cortex-M4.

Register	Utilization
R0	Master key pointer → delta pointer
R1	Round key pointer
R2~R5	Delta variables
R6	Loop counter
R7~R8	Temporal variables
R9~R12	Round keys

3.2 Encryption and Decryption

In this section, we introduce two encryption modes, including task parallelism and data parallelism, for HIGHT block cipher. The task parallel implementation performs one encryption block in parallel way, while the data parallel implementation performs two or more encryption blocks at once. The detailed register utilization is available in Table 3. The decryption can be implemented with same techniques used for encryption.

Table 3. Register utilization for task-parallel, data-parallel and fault-resistance encryption on ARM Cortex-M4.

Register	Task-parallel	Data-parallel	Fault resistance
R0	Plaintext pointer	Plaintext pointer	Plaintext pointer → random number
R1	Round key pointer	Round key pointer	Round key pointer
R2~R5	Plaintext	Plaintext	Plaintext
R6	Mask	Mask	Mask
R7	Loop counter	Temporal variable	Temporal variable
R8~R9	Round key	Round key	Round key
R10~R12	Temporal variables	Temporal variables	Temporal variables
R14	–	Loop counter	Loop counter

Task Parallelism. In order to perform task parallel HIGHT computation, two bytes are paired (i.e. $\{??, X_i[4], ??, X_i[0]\}$, $\{??, X_i[5], ??, X_i[1]\}$, $\{??, X_i[6], ??, X_i[2]\}$, and $\{??, X_i[7], ??, X_i[3]\}$, where X and ?? represent the plaintext and byte padding, respectively.). The F0 and F1 functions are performed with masked rotation and exclusive-or, which is proposed in [16]. For the two computations (i.e. XOR after ADD and ADD after XOR), the computations are getting much simpler with UADD8 (SIMD) instruction than previous masked approach. The comparison between with and without SIMD instruction sets is given in Table 4.

Table 4. Comparison between w/o and w/SIMD instruction sets for HIGHT computations.

Computations	w/o SIMD	w/SIMD
XOR after ADD	ADD → EOR → AND	UADD8 → EOR
ADD after XOR	EOR → ADD → AND	EOR → UADD8

Data Parallelism. The data parallel HIGHT implementation performs two encryption blocks at once. Each encryption is performed in task parallel and two task parallel blocks are combined and performed in data parallel approach. For the data parallel implementation, four bytes are paired and two bytes are duplicated (i.e. $\{X_i[4], X_i[4], X_i[0], X_i[0]\}$, $\{X_i[5], X_i[5], X_i[1], X_i[1]\}$, $\{X_i[6], X_i[6], X_i[2], X_i[2]\}$, and $\{X_i[7], X_i[7], X_i[3], X_i[3]\}$, where X represents the plaintext.). The XOR after ADD and ADD after XOR operations are performed with the technique described in Table 4.

The both F0 and F1 functions require rotation operation. In the task parallel implementation, the data is stored with padding blocks. This prevents the data overflow between bytes. However, the data parallel implementation fully utilizes

---

Algorithm 1. F0 function for data parallel implementation.

Input: R2, temporal variables (R10 and
    R11)
Output: R6
1: AND R11,R2, #0x00FF00FF
2: LSL R10, R11,#1
3: EOR R10, R10, R11, LSR #7
4: EOR R10, R10, R11, LSL #2
5: EOR R10, R10, R11, LSR #6
6: EOR R10, R10, R11, LSL #7
7: EOR R10, R10, R11, LSR #1
8: AND R6, R10, #0x00FF00FF

9: AND R11,R2, #0xFF00FF00
10: LSL R10, R11, #1
11: EOR R10, R10, R11, LSR #7
12: EOR R10, R10, R11, LSL #2
13: EOR R10, R10, R11, LSR #6
14: EOR R10, R10, R11, LSL #7
15: EOR R10, R10, R11, LSR #1
16: AND R10, R10, #0xFF00FF00

17: ORR R6, R6, R10

---

the block, which means no padding or margin. In order to prevent the data overflow, the format is converted to the padded version, whenever the rotation operation is performed. The detailed descriptions are given in Algorithm 1. In Step 1–8, the half word is extracted from the word (R2) and F0 function is performed with half word. From Step 9 to 16, the remaining half word of R2 is performed. Finally, the Step 17 merges the two results.

Fault Attack Resistance. The high-speed implementation is not enough for real world cryptography implementations. For this reason, we need to provide the sufficient security against physical attack (e.g. fault attack). In this section, we cover the new HIGHT design to prevent the fault attack.

The fault model performs the fault injection on a cryptography implementation and manipulates the instruction opcodes (i.e. instruction faults) or data (i.e. computation faults). The fault attack is under very strong assumption but it is possible by a certain attacker with sophisticated equipment and sufficient funding (e.g. government agency). In this paper, we used the identical fault models used in previous works to evaluate our secure implementations [13,17]. The detailed descriptions of four computational fault models are as follows.

- **Random Word:** The adversary can target a specific word in a program and change its value into a random value unknown to the adversary.
- **Random Byte:** The adversary can target a specific word in a program and change a single byte of it into a random value unknown to the adversary.
- **Random Bit:** The adversary can target a specific word in a program and change a single bit of it into a random value unknown to the adversary.
- **Chosen Bit Pair:** The adversary can target a chosen bit pair of a specific word in a program, and change it into a random value unknown to the adversary.

Second, the instruction faults can change the program flow (the opcode of an instruction) by fault injection. The well-known approach is replace the operation into no-operation (nop) instruction.

Fault attack detection in software is proposed in [1]. They perform the duplicate encryption, which is based on the time redundancy of encryption. When the instruction duplication and triplication are performed, the performance is degraded by a factor of 3.4 and 10.6, respectively. Furthermore, the sophisticated fault injection may break the duplicate encryption. Second approach is an information redundancy based encryption. This approach evaluates the additional check variables or parity bits for fault detection. However, this approach also cannot figure out the instruction set level fault attack.

In SAC'16, the intra-instruction redundancy based fault attack countermeasure is suggested [13]. The method implemented the redundant bit-slicing and provides the ability to detect both instruction faults and computation faults. However, the bit-slicing implementation is only efficient over certain computers with a number of general purpose registers for block ciphers without linear operations. In [11], they evaluated the block cipher PRIDE and TRIVIUM on the Cortex-M3/M4 microcontrollers. They utilized the intra-instruction redundancy. Based on previous intra-instruction redundancy technique, in FDSC'17, they introduce the automatic vectorization compiler to mitigate the fault attack [5]. In WISA'17, the intra-instruction redundancy based fault attack countermeasure on NEON instruction (i.e. SIMD instruction set of 32-bit ARM Cortex-A) is introduced [17]. The implementation shuffles the variables each time to make attack difficult. The shuffling is based on random numbers and the random numbers are also generated in each encryption, simultaneously. Finally, they applied to the LEA encryption to achieve high security against fault attacks. However, there is no practical fault detection on low-end devices with random shuffling method.

In this paper, we utilized the intra-instruction redundancy based fault attack countermeasure for HIGHT block cipher on the low-end Cortex-M4 microcontrollers. In order to mitigate the fault attack, the data is formatted in intra-instruction redundancy and shuffled in each round. In order to efficiently handle the random shuffling, we suggested the novel shuffling technique. Proposed model is based on the combination of data and task parallelism. The overall procedures of secure HIGHT implementation are as follows:

```
Message Loading →                      Message Duplication →
Message / Round Key Shuffling #1 →     Round Function #1 →
...

Message / Round Key Shuffling #32 →    Round Function #32 →
Last Message Shuffling →               Last Round Function →
Fault Attack Check →                   Message Storing
```

The message duplication is easily implemented with barrel-shifter and bit-wise or operations. When the registers (R2, R3, R4, R5) are formatted in paired two bytes (i.e. $\{??, X_i[4], ??, X_i[0]\}$, $\{??, X_i[5], ??, X_i[1]\}$, $\{??, X_i[6], ??, X_i[2]\}$, and $\{??, X_i[7], ??, X_i[3]\}$), the duplication is performed as follows:

Algorithm 2. Message and Round Key Shuffling.

Input: message variables (R2~R5), round key variables (R8 and R9), temporal variables (R10 and R11) random number (R0)

Output: shuffled message variables (R2~R5), shuffled round key variables (R8 and R9)

1: AND R10, R0, #1
2: LSL R10, R10, #4
3: ROR R0, R0, #1

4: ROR R2, R2, R10
5: ROR R3, R3, R10
6: ROR R4, R4, R10
7: ROR R5, R5, R10

8: POP {R11}
9: EOR R10, R10, R11
10: PUSH {R10}

11: ROR R8, R8, R10
12: ROR R9, R9, R10

ORR R2, R2, R2, LSL#8 → ORR R3, R3, R3, LSL#8 →
ORR R4, R4, R4, LSL#8 → ORR R5, R5, R5, LSL#8

Afterward, in each round, we perform 16-bit wise swap shuffling, which exchanges lower 16-bit and higher 16-bit, when the random bit is set to 1. The HIGHT block cipher consists of 32 rounds. For the full round shuffling, we need 32-bit random numbers. The Cortex-M4 microcontroller has 32-bit wise word and one random word can retain 32-bit random numbers. Another consideration is shuffling condition. The shuffling on the message is accumulated but the new round key is shuffled in each time per round. For this reason, we maintain the accumulated shuffling conditions. Due to lack of register, the accumulated shuffling condition is stored in the STACK. The detailed descriptions are given in Algorithm 2. In Step 1–3, 1-bit random is extracted from R0. When the random bit is set, the offset register (R10) is set to 16. Otherwise, the offset register is set to 0. From Step 4–7, the message variables are shuffled depending on the offset register. From Step 8–10, the accumulated offset is loaded from STACK and the current offset is accumulated and stored again into the STACK. Finally, the accumulated shuffling offset is used for round key shuffling in Step 11–12.

After full round functions, we need to check the fault attack by comparing the duplicated data. The detailed descriptions are given in Algorithm 3. In Step 1–8, the four bytes pair is divided into two groups. In Step 9–12, we check whether both results output identical or not. In Step 13–15, we accumulated all different bits. Finally, we return the check word (R0).

4   Evaluation

In this section, we evaluate the proposed implementation on 32-bit ARM Cortex-M4 microcontrollers. The detailed comparison is available in Table 5. Since this is the first HIGHT implementation on 32-bit ARM Cortex-M4, we only report the previous works on 32-bit ARM Cortex-M3 as a reference. The comparison

Algorithm 3. Fault Attack Check.

Input: message variables (R2~R5),
    temporal variables (R6~R12 and R14),
Output: check word (R0)

```
1: AND R6, R2, #0xFF00FF00          8: AND R5, R5, #0x00FF00FF
2: AND R7, R3, #0xFF00FF00          9: EOR R10, R6, R2, LSL #8
3: AND R8, R4, #0xFF00FF00         10: EOR R11, R7, R3, LSL #8
4: AND R9, R5, #0xFF00FF00         11: EOR R12, R8, R4, LSL #8
                                   12: EOR R14, R9, R5, LSL #8
5: AND R2, R2, #0x00FF00FF
6: AND R3, R3, #0x00FF00FF         13: ORR R10, R10, R11
7: AND R4, R4, #0x00FF00FF         14: ORR R12, R12, R14
                                   15: ORR R0, R10, R12
```

between task parallel and data parallel implementations shows that the data parallel is faster than task parallel in key scheduling by 62%, because data parallel needs to perform key duplication for two block encryption. The encryption and decryption operations of data parallel shows better performance than task parallel by 25% and 22%, respectively. The data parallel performs two plaintext at once while the task parallel only performs a plaintext. The code size of data parallel is almost twice larger than task since data parallel needs to perform two plaintext, which requires additional routines. The fault resistance version is similar size of data parallel implementation. The execution time is slower than others since the fault resistance version only perform one encryption and the shuffling operation consumes additional clock cycles. One nice property is that the proposed fault approach is only 2x slower than task parallel implementation.

In terms of security model, we tested several different fault attack scenario studied in previous works as follows [13].

Table 5. Comparison of HIGHT block cipher results on 32-bit ARM in terms of code size (byte), RAM (byte), and execution time (clock cycle)

Impl.	Code size (bytes)				RAM (bytes)			Execution time (cycles per byte)		
	EKS	ENC	DEC	SUM	EKS	ENC	DEC	EKS	ENC	DEC
32-bit ARM Cortex-M3										
w/ LUT [16]	316	860	896	1,560	324	704	704	34	269	298
w/o LUT [16]	316	344	384	1,044	324	180	180	37	258	287
32-bit ARM Cortex-M4										
Task parallel	116	348	332	796	316	180	180	18	76	71
Task/Data parallel	160	592	544	1,296	316	188	188	49	56	55
Fault resistance	160	536	520	1,216	316	188	188	49	143	143

- **Random Word:** The adversary has no control on the number of faulty bits. The adversary can only create random faults in the target word (32-bit).
- **Random Byte:** The adversary can tune the fault injection to randomly affect a single byte of the 32-bit data.
- **Random Bit:** The fault injection can be tuned to affect single bit of the target word.
- **Chosen Bit Pair:** The adversary can inject faults into two chosen, adjacent bits of the target word.

The security comparison of proposed method is given in Table 6. In the unprotected HIGHT implementation, any computation or instruction fault injection attacks are easily exploited by the adversaries because the unprotected implementation doesn't include fault detection mechanism. The bitslicing approach by [13] is not working for HIGHT since HIGHT consists of some non-linear operations such as addition and subtraction. The previous SIMD implementation by [17] is efficient and secure but it is only working on the high-end processors. Unlike previous work, we targeted low-end processors. We used the data parallel implementation and random shuffling feature. This design efficient prevents several fault attack models based on random byte, random bit, and chosen bit pair. However, we can partly prevent the random word attack. Since the ARM word contains original data and duplicated data, the random word can influence both original data and duplicated data. When the same bit position is selected, the attack succeeds but it is very low possibility. The instruction skip attack is trade-off with other security. If we use the known answer data for fault attack detection, we can check the skip attack but we cannot figure out other attacks. This is limitation of low-end microcontroller. We will extend this method to high-end processors to cover all attack surfaces.

Table 6. Security comparison of proposed method for HIGHT block cipher on 32-bit ARM Cortex-M4, where Rand: Random shuffling, RW: random word, RB: random byte, Rb: random bit, CbP: chosen bit pair, IS: instruction skip.

Method	Instruction	Rand	RW	RB	Rb	CbP	IS
Seo et al. [16]	ARM	–	–	–	–	–	–
Proposed Method	SIMD	√	√	√	√	√	–

5 Conclusion

In this paper, we presented new compact and secure fault attack countermeasures for HIGHT block cipher algorithm on representative low-end microcontrollers, namely 32-bit ARM Cortex-M4. We firstly optimize the HIGHT block cipher, in terms of task parallelism and data parallelism. For the secure implementation, we proposed the intra-instruction redundancy by using optimized data parallel implementation. This new technique successfully prevent several fault attack models that is infeasible in previous HIGHT implementations on low-end devices.

The proposed methods improved the performance and security of HIGHT implementations. For this reason, there are many future works remained. First, we can directly apply the fault attack countermeasures to the other ARX block ciphers, such as SPECK and SIMON. Recent works on 32-bit ARM Cortex-M do not consider the any secure measures proposed in this paper. We can enhance the security by applying the proposed method, straightforwardly. Second, we only explore the 32-bit ARM Cortex-M4 platform in this paper. However, there are many low-end microcontrollers, such as 8-bit AVR and 16-bit MSP micro-controllers. We will explore the new block cipher implementation techniques for these low-end devices.

Acknowledgement. This work was supported as part of Military Crypto Research Center (UD170109ED) funded by Defense Acquisition Program Administration (DAPA) and Agency for Defense Development (ADD).

References

1. Barenghi, A., Breveglieri, L., Koren, I., Pelosi, G., Regazzoni, F.: Countermeasures against fault attacks on software implemented AES: effectiveness and cost. In: Proceedings of the 5th Workshop on Embedded Systems Security, p. 7. ACM (2010)
2. Beaulieu, R., Shors, D., Smith, J., Treatman-Clark, S., Weeks, B., Wingers, L.: The SIMON and SPECK block ciphers on AVR 8-bit microcontrollers. In: Eisenbarth, T., Öztürk, E. (eds.) LightSec 2014. LNCS, vol. 8898, pp. 3–20. Springer, Cham (2015). https://doi.org/10.1007/978-3-319-16363-5_1
3. Biryukov, A., et al.: FELICS - fair evalutation of lightweight cryptographic systems. In: NIST Workshop on Lightweight Cryptography (2015). https://www.cryptolux. org/index.php/FELICS
4. Buhrow, B., Riemer, P., Shea, M., Gilbert, B., Daniel, E.: Block cipher speed and energy efficiency records on the MSP430: system design trade-offs for 16-bit embedded applications. In: Aranha, D.F., Menezes, A. (eds.) LATINCRYPT 2014. LNCS, vol. 8895, pp. 104–123. Springer, Cham (2015). https://doi.org/10.1007/ 978-3-319-16295-9_6
5. Chen, Z., Shen, J., Nicolau, A., Veidenbaum, A., Ghalaty, N.F., Cammarota, R.: CAMFAS: a compiler approach to mitigate fault attacks via enhanced SIMDiza-tion. In: 2017 Workshop on Fault Diagnosis and Tolerance in Cryptography (FDTC), pp. 57–64. IEEE (2017)
6. Eisenbarth, T., et al.: Compact implementation and performance evaluation of block ciphers in ATtiny devices. In: Mitrokotsa, A., Vaudenay, S. (eds.) AFRICACRYPT 2012. LNCS, vol. 7374, pp. 172–187. Springer, Heidelberg (2012). https://doi.org/10.1007/978-3-642-31410-0_11
7. Eisenbarth, T., Kumar, S., Paar, C., Poschmann, A., Uhsadel, L.: A survey of lightweight-cryptography implementations. IEEE Des. Test Comput. 24(6), 522–533 (2007)
8. Hong, D., Lee, J.-K., Kim, D.-C., Kwon, D., Ryu, K.H., Lee, D.-G.: LEA: a 128-bit block cipher for fast encryption on common processors. In: Kim, Y., Lee, H., Perrig, A. (eds.) WISA 2013. LNCS, vol. 8267, pp. 3–27. Springer, Cham (2014). https://doi.org/10.1007/978-3-319-05149-9_1

9. Hong, D., et al.: HIGHT: a new block cipher suitable for low-resource device. In: Goubin, L., Matsui, M. (eds.) CHES 2006. LNCS, vol. 4249, pp. 46–59. Springer, Heidelberg (2006). https://doi.org/10.1007/11894063_4

10. Koo, B., Roh, D., Kim, H., Jung, Y., Lee, D.-G., Kwon, D.: CHAM: a family of lightweight block ciphers for resource-constrained devices. In: Kim, H., Kim, D.-C. (eds.) ICISC 2017. LNCS, vol. 10779, pp. 3–25. Springer, Cham (2018). https://doi.org/10.1007/978-3-319-78556-1_1

11. Lac, B., Canteaut, A., Fournier, J.J., Sirdey, R.: Thwarting fault attacks using the internal redundancy countermeasure (IRC). IACR Cryptology ePrint Archive 2017:910 (2017)

12. Osvik, D.A., Bos, J.W., Stefan, D., Canright, D.: Fast software AES encryption. In: Hong, S., Iwata, T. (eds.) FSE 2010. LNCS, vol. 6147, pp. 75–93. Springer, Heidelberg (2010). https://doi.org/10.1007/978-3-642-13858-4_5

13. Patrick, C., Yuce, B., Ghalaty, N.F., Schaumont, P.: Lightweight fault attack resistance in software using intra-instruction redundancy (2016)

14. Schwabe, P., Stoffelen, K.: All the AES you need on Cortex-M3 and M4. In: Avanzi, R., Heys, H. (eds.) SAC 2016. LNCS, vol. 10532, pp. 180–194. Springer, Cham (2017). https://doi.org/10.1007/978-3-319-69453-5_10

15. Seo, H.: High speed implementation of LEA on ARM Cortex-M3 processor. J. Korea Inst. Inf. Commun. Eng. **22**(8), 1133–1138 (2018)

16. Seo, H., Jeong, I., Lee, J., Kim, W.: Compact implementations of ARX-based block ciphers on IoT processors. ACM Trans. Embed. Comput. Syst. (TECS) **17**(3), 60 (2018)

17. Seo, H., Park, T., Ji, J., Kim, H.: Lightweight fault attack resistance in software using intra-instruction redundancy, revisited. In: Kang, B.B.H., Kim, T. (eds.) WISA 2017. LNCS, vol. 10763, pp. 3–15. Springer, Cham (2018). https://doi.org/10.1007/978-3-319-93563-8_1

Fast AES Implementation Using ARMv8 ASIMD Without Cryptography Extension

Hayato Fujii[✉][iD], Félix Carvalho Rodrigues[iD], and Julio López

Institute of Computing, University of Campinas (Unicamp), Campinas, SP, Brazil
{hayato.fujii,felix.rodrigues,jlopez}@ic.unicamp.br

Abstract. While the ARMv8-A ISA allows for hardware accelerated cryptographic instructions, such extension is not available for every device, being added at the discretion of the CPU manufacturer. Prime examples of ARMv8 devices without this support are the low cost Raspberry Pi 3B/3B+/4 single board computers. This work presents an optimized AES implementation targeting CPUs without Cryptography Extension instructions, relying only on ASIMD operations. We show a new implementation that processes four blocks at the same time, which requires block permutations and modified versions of the main layers. In particular, we provide a new efficient formula for computing the MixColumns layer. The time performance our AES implementation outperforms the current ASIMD implementation found in the Linux Kernel by about 5%.

Keywords: AES · ARMv8 · ASIMD · Linux cryptography API

1 Introduction

The introduction of the ARMv8 architecture brought, in addition to the native AArch64 instruction set operating on 64-bit registers, the optional *Cryptography Extension* instructions. Those instructions provide hardware-accelerated operations used in the Advanced Encryption Standard (AES) in both encryption and decryption operations and some hashing algorithms in the Secure Hash Algorithm (SHA) family, such as SHA-1, SHA-224 and SHA-256 hash functions. Although specified in the ARMv8.2 revision, the Cryptography Extension is optionally added into a CPU core at the sole discretion of its manufacturer. More recent mobile devices are usually equipped with both 64-bit support and cryptographic instructions, but devices in other categories, such as televisions and set-up boxes, may not support the latter causing market fragmentation. The need of supporting multiple hardware capabilities makes software development convoluted, as more code has to be (re)written for different hardware.

The authors gracefully acknowledge financial support from the São Paulo Research Foundation (FAPESP), under the "Segurança e Confiabilidade da Informação: Teoria e Aplicações" Thematic Project no. 2013/25.977-7.

© Springer Nature Switzerland AG 2020
J. H. Seo (Ed.): ICISC 2019, LNCS 11975, pp. 84–101, 2020.
https://doi.org/10.1007/978-3-030-40921-0_5

The Raspberry Pi single board computers, designed to encourage Computer Science teaching in schools[1], costing USD 35, is a prominent example of hardware lacking cryptographic hardware support. The 3A/3B/3B+ models are all equipped with a quad-core Cortex-A53 implementing the ARMv8.2 ISA without the Cryptography Extension. On the newer Raspberry Pi 4 model, a quad-core Cortex-A72 CPU is employed, yet without the hardware cryptographic extension. However, as specified in the ARMv8.2-A architecture, the CPUs used in the Raspberry Pi models 3A onwards are equipped with the Advanced Single Instruction-Multiple Data (ASIMD) units, allowing 128-bit processing capabilities. On the earlier ARMv7 ISA, ASIMD was commonly referred as the NEON instruction set. This allows faster and efficient implementations in comparison to native, 64-bit, AArch64 implementations. Other examples of ARMv8 CPUs without the Cryptography Extension are the Qualcomm's Snapdragon 410, which powers various low-end mobile devices, and the Amlogic S905, equipping the Odroid C2 single board computer, among various set-up TV boxes.

The Linux Kernel Cryptography API implements multiple cryptographic algorithms, ranging from the CRC32 hash algorithm to modern stream ciphers such as Salsa20 proposal [1]. As part of the operating system, multiple hardware platform support is a major goal. In the ARMv8 scenario, we find several implementations of the AES algorithm, such as a generic (portable) code, and hardware-backed (using Cryptography Extension instructions) versions, in which availability is defined by the underlying platform.

Related Work. Hamburg [10] discusses AES implementations using vector permute instructions using x86 SIMD and in PowerPC AltiVec instructions. The usage of those is inspired by the need of computing on-the-fly the S-box substitutions, as the usage of lookup tables may expose timing data, making side-channel attacks practical [15].

There are AES implementations for ARM processors protected against cache-timing side-channel attacks without relying on hardware cryptographic instructions with an acceptable level of performance [2]. Bit slicing initiatives for the AES block cipher, also inspired by the need of eliminating table lookups and thus safeguarding against timing attacks, were implemented on Intel platforms [11], being further ported to ARM hardware and merged into the Linux Kernel Cryptography API [3].

Various ciphers employ a multiplication step to provide diffusion on the state. One example is the θ transformation present on the SPNbox family of ciphers [5]. In this sense, Rodrigues et al. [16] presents an optimized implementation of such operation, similar to the formulation presented in this work.

Authenticated encryption modes of operation were also implemented on the ARM scenario [12]. Relying on the Cryptography Extension and the carry-less multiplication instructions, Gouvêa and López [9] implemented the Galois/Counter Mode (GCM) mode of operation using the 32-bit processing capabilities of the ARMv8 architecture, dubbed AArch32, presenting timings for an AES implementation with hardware support.

---

[1] See: https://www.bbc.co.uk/blogs/thereporters/rorycellanjones/2011/05/a_15_computer_to_inspire_young.html.

Efficient ciphers not relying on cryptographic hardware support are now widely used on entry-level Android devices, particularly for storage encryption. In this sense, the Adiantum proposal [7] fills this gap, being 75% faster than AES in these kinds of devices.

Contributions. This work presents a modified implementation of AES algorithm using ASIMD instructions. We explore a modification on how the AES state is organized, impacting on each AES layer. Specifically, we propose an optimized algorithm for processing four blocks, which involves an improved formula for the `MixColumns` step and an algorithm for the key expansion using ASIMD instructions. The timing results of our AES implementation shows an improvement of about 5% compared to the ASIMD based Linux Kernel implementation.

Paper Organization. In Sect. 2, we introduce the AES block cipher algorithm, and its composing layers. We detail the implementation aspects in Sect. 3, briefly presenting some of the relevant instructions in the ARMv8 architecture, and describing different implementation strategies for each step of the AES algorithm. The experimental performance results are presented in Sect. 4, followed by a comparison with other implementations. Our final remarks are shown in Sect. 5.

2   The Advanced Encryption Standard

The Advanced Encryption Standard (AES) [14] is the current standard for encryption of digital data established by the *U.S. National Institute of Standards and Technology* (NIST). It supports three security levels (key sizes): 128-bits, 192-bits and 256-bits, and, for each level, the corresponding cipher uses 10, 12 or 14 rounds, respectively. For each round, a subkey is specified from the secret key. Each round modifies a 16-byte state, represented by the array of bytes $state = [state_{i,j}]_{0 \leq i,j \leq 3}$. We may also refer the bytes of $state$ as $[a_{i,j}]_{0 \leq i,j \leq 3}$. When the encryption process starts, the state is initialized with a 128-bit block of plaintext; by the last round, the state contains the ciphertext.

Each AES round has the following operations:

SubBytes: applies the AES S-box, a non-linear bijective mapping from 8 bits to 8 bits, to every byte in the state. The mapping relies on the inversion operation in the finite field $GF(2^8)$ with irreducible polynomial $P(x) = x^8 + x^4 + x^3 + x + 1$. This operation was designed to add confusion to the encryption process [8].

ShiftRows: applies a rotation to the left by i byte positions to each row i of the state array:

$$
\begin{bmatrix}
a_{0,0} & a_{0,1} & a_{0,2} & a_{0,3} \\
a_{1,0} & a_{1,1} & a_{1,2} & a_{1,3} \\
a_{2,0} & a_{2,1} & a_{2,2} & a_{2,3} \\
a_{3,0} & a_{3,1} & a_{3,2} & a_{3,3}
\end{bmatrix}
\xrightarrow{\text{ShiftRows}}
\begin{bmatrix}
a_{0,0} & a_{0,1} & a_{0,2} & a_{0,3} \\
a_{1,1} & a_{1,2} & a_{1,3} & a_{1,0} \\
a_{2,2} & a_{2,3} & a_{2,0} & a_{2,1} \\
a_{3,3} & a_{3,0} & a_{3,1} & a_{3,2}
\end{bmatrix} ,
$$

where $0 \leq i \leq 3$. Note that the row $i = 0$ remains unchanged.

MixColumns: is a linear operation in which the state is updated by interpreting each column j as a 4×1 vector over $GF(2^8)$ multiplied by the polynomial $c(x) = 3x^3 + x^2 + x + 2$ and reduced by the polynomial $l(x) = x^4 + 1$. This operation can be interpreted as the multiplication of the column j of the AES state by the MC matrix, both defined in $GF(2^8)$:

$$A' = \begin{bmatrix} a'_{0,j} \\ a'_{1,j} \\ a'_{2,j} \\ a'_{3,j} \end{bmatrix} = MC \times \begin{bmatrix} a_{0,j} \\ a_{1,j} \\ a_{2,j} \\ a_{3,j} \end{bmatrix} \text{ with } MC = \begin{bmatrix} 02 & 03 & 01 & 01 \\ 01 & 02 & 03 & 01 \\ 01 & 01 & 02 & 03 \\ 03 & 01 & 01 & 02 \end{bmatrix}, \tag{1}$$

for $j = 0, 1, 2, 3$. Diffusion is added to the state through the combination of the ShiftRows and the MixColumns operations.

AddRoundKey: adds the round's key $k^{(r)}, (1 \le r \le R + 1)$ bitwise modulo two (i.e., a XOR operation) to the AES state.

A description of a full AES-128 encryption is presented in Algorithm 1; refer to FIPS 197 [14] for more details.

2.1 The AES Key Expansion

The AES Key Expansion takes the cipher key to generate the key schedule. When used on the AES128 cipher, this algorithm generates a total of eleven 128-bit subkeys, in which the first subkey is the cipher key. Each subsequent key i is calculated in a serial manner, as shown in Algorithm 2.

Algorithm 1. AES128 Encryption

Input: A 128-bit block of plaintext, 128-bit cipher key $k^{(0)}$, and 128-bit round keys $k^{(r)}$, $r \in \{1, \dots, 10\}$

Output: The 128-bit encrypted block (ciphertext).

---

state $\leftarrow$ plaintext
state $\leftarrow$ AddRoundKey(state, $k^{(0)}$)
for $r = 1$ to 9 **do**
   state $\leftarrow$ SubBytes(state)
   state $\leftarrow$ ShiftRows(state)
   state $\leftarrow$ MixColumns(state)
   state $\leftarrow$ AddRoundKey(state, $k^{(r)}$)
end for
state $\leftarrow$ SubBytes(state)
state $\leftarrow$ ShiftRows(state)
state $\leftarrow$ AddRoundKey(state, $k^{(10)}$)
return state

Algorithm 2. AES128 Key Expansion

Input: 128-bit cipher key
$K_0 = \{k_{0,0}, k_{0,1}, k_{0,2}, k_{0,3}\}$
Output: Ten 128-bit round keys
$K_i = \{k_{i,0}, k_{i,1}, k_{i,2}, k_{i,3}\}$, $i \in \{1, \dots, 10\}$

---

for $i = 1$ to 10 **do**
   $k_{i,0} \leftarrow k_{(i-1),3}$
   $k_{i,0} \leftarrow$ SubBytes($k_{i,0}$)
   $k_{i,0} \leftarrow$ RotLeft($k_{i,0}$)
   $k_{i,0} \leftarrow k_{i_0} \oplus rcon_{(i-1)}$
   $k_{i_0} \leftarrow k_{i_0} \oplus k_{(i-1),0}$
   for $j = 1$ to 3 **do**
      $k_{i_j} \leftarrow k_{i,(j-1)} \oplus k_{(i-1),j}$
   end for
   $K_i = \{k_{i,0}, k_{i,1}, k_{i,2}, k_{i,3}\}$
end for
return K_i, $i = 1$ to 10

The RotLeft permutation is defined as $RotLeft(X) = (x_1, x_2, x_3, x_0)$ where $X = (x_0, x_1, x_2, x_3)$ is a vector composed of bytes $x_n, 0 \leq n \leq 3$. Note that, throughout this paper, we use the notation $F^2(x)$ as the composition $F(F(x))$.

3 Implementation

In this section, we present a quick overview of the ARMv8 architecture and some of its instructions, followed by a description of the AES implementation present on the Linux Kernel geared towards the ARMv8 architecture without support of hardware-assisted cryptographic acceleration, but with ASIMD capabilities. We show our "transposed" AES implementation proposal, alongside the required modifications for each layer. Finally, we note how the AES key expansion may be implemented without relying on the last 32-bit word of each computed key every time.

3.1 ARMv8-A Architecture

The ARMv8 architecture is a reduced instruction set computer (RISC) employing a load-store architecture. Specifically, the ARMv8-A architecture profile is targeted towards complex computer application areas such as servers, mobile and infotainment devices.

The ARMv8-A profile introduces, in comparison to the older ARMv7-A architecture profile, 64-bit processing capabilities. CPUs based on this profile are equipped with a bank of 31 general purpose registers (x0 to x30) in addition to the dedicated stack pointer (sp) and zero (zr) registers, while all of those are 64-bit wide. In addition, the ARMv8-A profile also specifies that the Advanced Single Instruction-Multiple Data (ASIMD) unit, also commonly known as NEON, must be present, providing scalar/vector instructions and registers. This engine is designed towards multimedia applications but also useful in scientific and high performance computing. In this unit, a separate set of 32 registers, each one 128-bit wide, can be used.

The NEON unit has special instructions to support permutations and byte substitutions, common operations in a block cipher:

Table Lookup and Table Lookup Extended (tbl/tbx). This instruction builds a new vector based on an index vector, looking up a table residing in one up to four registers, effectively being a bytewise table lookup. The tbl instruction can be repurposed to work as an arbitrary byte permutation if a single source vector is used as a table, at the cost of setting up the permutation index.

Vector Extract (ext). Extracts bytes from a pair of source vectors. The resulting vector combines the most significant bytes from the first operand and least significant bytes of the second. This instruction can also be used to compute byte rotations on a 128-bit vector, as well as to execute left and right byte shifts, by using the same input vectors on the first case or using a zero-filled vector on the second.

Interleaved Load (ld*n*). The memory load unit of the ASIMD pipeline can fill different registers with memory values in an interleaved fashion depending on the *n* argument. For example, the ld2 instruction can fill a vn register with bytes at even addresses, while the vm register is filled with bytes located at odd addresses.

Cryptography Extension. CPU manufacturers may also include a Cryptograpy Extension directly on the CPU cores, without relying to proprietary external engines usually employed as a co-processor. This extension adds new instructions to the ASIMD unit, making it capable of hardware-accelerated operations such as one used in the AES algorithm (both encryption and decryption operations) and the hash functions SHA-1, SHA-224 and SHA-256. Of interest, we note that the instructions aese and aesmc can be used together to perform a full round of the AES cipher.

The table lookup instructions (tbl and tbx) are powerful since they allow the computation of arbitrary byte permutations, but are quite expensive in terms of CPU cycles in comparison to special instructions such as Reverse (rev) or Vector Extract (ext). The latency of both tbl and tbx is $3 \times n + 3$ cycles, where n is the number of registers required to store the lookup table input. In addition, two instructions per clock can be issued.

3.2 Linux Kernel Implementation

The Linux Kernel provides a range of implementations of cryptographic algorithms to support various uses, such as to secure wireless connections and remote access. This subsection focus on detailing the AES implementation present within the Cryptography API (shortned to CryptoAPI).

SubBytes and ShiftRows. The AES implementation in the Linux Kernel (since version 4.11) uses the tbl/tbx instructions to execute the SubBytes layers.

In order to compute the substitution, we first use the tbl instruction with a 16-byte input block as a lookup index and the first quarter of the AES S-box lookup table stored in four 128-bit registers, since the instruction accepts up to four 128-bit registers for this operand. This first operation effectively substitutes bytes in the 0x00 to 0x3F range of the 16-byte input; if a byte is outside of this span, its respective output is set to 0x00. To substitute bytes outside of the first quarter, it is necessary to subtract every input byte by 64 (0x40), then use it as a lookup index for the tbx instruction, in addition of using the second quarter of the S-box as the lookup table. This operation substitutes the original input bytes in the 0x40 to 0x7F range without changing the execution of the earlier tbl instruction; differently from tbl, the tbx instruction does not clear bytes of the output if the lookup index is out of range.

To complete the substitution process, two more iterations of the subtraction and the substitution process must be done, covering the third and fourth quarters of the S-box in each iteration. Listing 1 shows a code for implementing the AES S-box using tbl/tbx instructions.

```
sub v7.16b, v1.16b, v15.16b
tbl v1.16b, { v16.16b - v19.16b }, v1.16b
sub v6.16b, v7.16b, v15.16b
tbx v1.16b, { v20.16b - v23.16b }, v7.16b
sub v5.16b, v6.16b, v15.16b
tbx v1.16b, { v24.16b - v27.16b }, v6.16b
tbx v1.16b, { v28.16b - v31.16b }, v5.16b
```

Listing 1: Using `tbl` and `tbx` instructions to substitute 16 bytes in register `v1` using a 256-byte table stored in registers `v16-v31`. Register `v15` contains the `0x40` value repeated 16 times.

By setting a permutation vector in a setup phase, the `ShiftRows` step is also done using a single `tbl` instruction, as explained in Sect. 3.1.

MixColumns Formulation. To compute the `MixColumns` step on each 32-bit column from a single AES state, Biesheuvel [3] reorganizes Eq. (1) as follows:

$$
A' = \begin{bmatrix} a'_{0,j} \\ a'_{1,j} \\ a'_{2,j} \\ a'_{3,j} \end{bmatrix} = \begin{bmatrix} 02\ 03\ 01\ 01 \\ 01\ 02\ 03\ 01 \\ 01\ 01\ 02\ 03 \\ 03\ 01\ 01\ 02 \end{bmatrix} \begin{bmatrix} a_{0,j} \\ a_{1,j} \\ a_{2,j} \\ a_{3,j} \end{bmatrix} = \begin{bmatrix} a_{0,j}\ a_{3,j}\ a_{2,j}\ a_{1,j} \\ a_{1,j}\ a_{0,j}\ a_{3,j}\ a_{2,j} \\ a_{2,j}\ a_{1,j}\ a_{0,j}\ a_{3,j} \\ a_{3,j}\ a_{2,j}\ a_{1,j}\ a_{0,j} \end{bmatrix} \begin{bmatrix} 02 \\ 01 \\ 01 \\ 03 \end{bmatrix} =
$$

$$
= 2\begin{bmatrix} a_{0,j} \\ a_{1,j} \\ a_{2,j} \\ a_{3,j} \end{bmatrix} + \begin{bmatrix} a_{3,j} \\ a_{0,j} \\ a_{1,j} \\ a_{2,j} \end{bmatrix} + \begin{bmatrix} a_{2,j} \\ a_{3,j} \\ a_{0,j} \\ a_{1,j} \end{bmatrix} + 3\begin{bmatrix} a_{1,j} \\ a_{2,j} \\ a_{3,j} \\ a_{0,j} \end{bmatrix}. \tag{2}
$$

Hence, the `MixColumns` step can be calculated by

$$
A' = (2A + \texttt{RotLeft}^2(A)) + \texttt{RotLeft}((2A + \texttt{RotLeft}^2(A)) + A), \tag{3}
$$

where $A = \begin{bmatrix} a_{0,j} \\ a_{1,j} \\ a_{2,j} \\ a_{3,j} \end{bmatrix}$ and $\texttt{RotLeft}(A) = \begin{bmatrix} a_{1,j} \\ a_{2,j} \\ a_{3,j} \\ a_{0,j} \end{bmatrix}$.

In terms of 32-bit operations, two rotations, one multiplication by x in $GF(2^8)$ and three bitwise exclusive or (XORs) are needed to compute the `MixColumns` step for each of the j columns of the AES state; considering byte operations, 16 XORs and 8 multiplications by x are required.

128-bit `MixColumns` Implementation. Equation (2) shows how to compute partial results of the `MixColumns` operation. This formulation reveals that byte permutations on every 32 bits word X composed of 4 bytes $x_i, 0 \le i \le 3$ must be performed before multiplying by x or $x + 1$ in $GF(2^8)$. Given a 32-bit word $A = (a_0, a_1, a_2, a_3)$, we use the notation:

$$\texttt{RotLeft}(A) = (a_1, a_2, a_3, a_0), \qquad \texttt{Rev32}(A) = (a_2, a_3, a_0, a_1),$$
$$\texttt{RotRight}(A) = (a_3, a_0, a_1, a_2).$$

Note that $\mathtt{RotLeft}^2(X) = \mathtt{Rev32}(X)$ and $\mathtt{RotRight}(X) = \mathtt{Rev32}(\mathtt{RotLeft}(X))$.

The AES state can be seen as a composition of four 32-bit words $[A, B, C, D]$. In order to compute $\mathtt{MixColumns}$ for this composition, we replicate Eq. (3) for each of the 32-bit words:

$$
\begin{aligned}
A' &= (2A + \mathtt{RotLeft}^2(A)) + \mathtt{RotLeft}((2A + \mathtt{RotLeft}^2(A)) + A) \\
B' &= (2B + \mathtt{RotLeft}^2(B)) + \mathtt{RotLeft}((2B + \mathtt{RotLeft}^2(B)) + B) \\
C' &= (2C + \mathtt{RotLeft}^2(C)) + \mathtt{RotLeft}((2C + \mathtt{RotLeft}^2(C)) + C) \\
D' &= (2D + \mathtt{RotLeft}^2(D)) + \mathtt{RotLeft}((2D + \mathtt{RotLeft}^2(D)) + D)
\end{aligned}
\tag{4}
$$

Given $S = [A, B, C, D]$, a 128-bit value, we use the notation:

$$
\begin{aligned}
\mathtt{RotLeft\_128}(S) &= [\mathtt{RotLeft}(A), \mathtt{RotLeft}(B), \mathtt{RotLeft}(C), \mathtt{RotLeft}(D)], \\
\mathtt{Rev32\_128}(S) &= [\mathtt{Rev32}(A), \mathtt{Rev32}(B), \mathtt{Rev32}(C), \mathtt{Rev32}(D)], \\
\mathtt{RotRight\_128}(S) &= [\mathtt{RotRight}(A), \mathtt{RotRight}(B), \mathtt{RotRight}(C), \mathtt{RotRight}(D)], \\
2S &= [2A, 2B, 2C, 2D].
\end{aligned}
$$

If $S = [A, B, C, D]$ represents an AES state stored in a 128-bit register, we can compute the $\mathtt{MixColumns}$ step on S using the following formula:

$$
\begin{aligned}
\mathtt{MixColumns}(S) = {}&(2S + \mathtt{RotLeft\_128}^2(S)) \\
&+ \mathtt{RotLeft\_128}((2S + \mathtt{RotLeft\_128}^2(S)) + S).
\end{aligned}
\tag{5}
$$

To implement Eq. (5), 128-bit ASIMD instructions can be used, affecting the four 32-bit words composing the AES state. For example, $\mathtt{Rev32\_128}$ can be implemented using a single $\mathtt{rev32}$ ($\mathtt{vrev32q\_u16}$) instruction:

$$
\text{S} = [\; a_{0,0}\; a_{0,1}\; a_{0,2}\; a_{0,3}\; a_{1,0}\; a_{1,1}\; a_{1,2}\; a_{1,3}\; a_{2,0}\; a_{2,1}\; a_{2,2}\; a_{2,3}\; a_{3,0}\; a_{3,1}\; a_{3,2}\; a_{3,3}\;]
$$

$\downarrow \text{S}' = \mathtt{vrev32q\_u16}(\text{A})$

$$
\text{S}' = [\; a_{0,2}\; a_{0,3}\; a_{0,0}\; a_{0,1}\; a_{1,2}\; a_{1,3}\; a_{1,2}\; a_{1,1}\; a_{2,2}\; a_{2,3}\; a_{2,0}\; a_{2,1}\; a_{3,2}\; a_{3,3}\; a_{3,0}\; a_{3,1}\;].
$$

Analogously, the $\mathtt{RotLeft\_128}$ permutation affecting four 32-bit words can be computed using two ASIMD instructions:

$$
\text{S} = [\; a_{0,0}\; a_{0,1}\; a_{0,2}\; a_{0,3}\; a_{1,0}\; a_{1,1}\; a_{1,2}\; a_{1,3}\; a_{2,0}\; a_{2,1}\; a_{2,2}\; a_{2,3}\; a_{3,0}\; a_{3,1}\; a_{3,2}\; a_{3,3}\;]
$$

$$
\begin{aligned}
&\text{T} = \mathtt{vrev32q\_u8}(\text{S}) \\
&\text{S}' = \mathtt{vtrn2q\_u8}(\text{S}, \text{T})
\end{aligned}
$$

$$
\text{S}' = [\; a_{0,1}\; a_{0,2}\; a_{0,3}\; a_{0,0}\; a_{1,1}\; a_{1,2}\; a_{1,3}\; a_{1,0}\; a_{2,1}\; a_{2,2}\; a_{2,3}\; a_{2,0}\; a_{3,1}\; a_{3,2}\; a_{3,3}\; a_{3,0}\;].
$$

To multiply each byte of a 16-byte register by x in $GF(2^8)$, each byte is shifted left by 1 bit and reduced modulo $P(x)$. Given a 16-byte register v0, Listing 2 shows how to multiply each byte of v0 by x in $GF(2^8)$ using ASIMD instructions.

```
sshr  v8.16b,  v0.16b,  #7
 shl  v4.16b,  v0.16b,  #1
 and  v8.16b,  v8.16b,  v13.16b
 eor  v4.16b,  v4.16b,   v8.16b
```

Listing 2: Multiplying each byte of v0 (a 16-byte register) by x in $GF(2^8)$ using the irreducible polynomial $P(x) = x^8 + x^4 + x^3 + x + 1$. Register v13 holds the value 0x1B, which represents $P(x)$ in its hexadecimal form, repeated 16 times. The output is stored in register v4.

Performance Notes. The biggest performance cost comes from the usage of tbl and tbx instructions. While in 32-bit execution mode, the Cortex-A53 cores can issue two of these instructions in a parallel way to the execution pipeline. Then, the output is written by the third cycle after the issue. However, due to architectural changes, execution of both instructions in 64-bit mode are more expensive, depending on the number of the input registers representing the substitution values. This effect is further exacerbated in Cortex-A57 based CPUs, as the changes led to the need of more microoperations emitted per tbl/tbx instruction [4].

Processing Multiple Blocks. As shown before, the Kernel Linux implementation strategy uses ASIMD instructions to apply transformations over a single AES state stored in a 128-bit register. Same treatment can be applied to multiple blocks stored over various ASIMD registers, as implemented for processing 2 or 4 blocks in an interleaved way [3].

Applying the algorithm in a single block can cause data dependencies between adjacent instructions dealing with the same arguments, causing degraded performance. When multiple blocks are being processed, this penalty is mitigated as dependencies are diminished, and similar and adjacent instructions may be executed in a pipelined fashion.

3.3   A MixColumns Formulation for an AES Block

Breaking down Eq. (2), for each j column of a single AES state, the MixColumns multiplication can be rewritten by joining up common terms and, using the fact that a subtraction is the same as a addition in $GF(2^8)$:

$$A' = \begin{bmatrix} a'_{0,j} \\ a'_{1,j} \\ a'_{2,j} \\ a'_{3,j} \end{bmatrix} = \begin{bmatrix} 02 & 03 & 01 & 01 \\ 01 & 02 & 03 & 01 \\ 01 & 03 & 02 & 03 \\ 03 & 01 & 01 & 02 \end{bmatrix} \begin{bmatrix} a_{0,j} \\ a_{1,j} \\ a_{2,j} \\ a_{3,j} \end{bmatrix} = \begin{bmatrix} 2(a_{0,j} + a_{1,j}) + a_{1,j} + (a_{2,j} + a_{3,j}) \\ 2(a_{1,j} + a_{2,j}) + a_{0,j} + (a_{2,j} + a_{3,j}) \\ 2(a_{2,j} + a_{3,j}) + a_{3,j} + (a_{0,j} + a_{1,j}) \\ 2(a_{3,j} + a_{0,j}) + a_{2,j} + (a_{0,j} + a_{1,j}) \end{bmatrix}.$$

$$(6)$$

Equation (6), in terms of 8-bit operations, requires 13 XORs and four multiplications by 2 (multiplication by x in $GF(2^8)$). From there, one can derive the following properties:

$$a_{0,j} + a_{1,j} + a_{2,j} + a_{3,j} = a'_{0,j} + a'_{1,j} + a'_{2,j} + a'_{3,j}$$
$$a'_{0,j} + a'_{1,j} = 2(a_{0,j} + a_{2,j}) + a_{0,j} + a_{1,j}$$
$$a'_{2,j} + a'_{3,j} = 2(a_{0,j} + a_{2,j}) + a_{2,j} + a_{3,j}.$$

Based on these properties, a more compact representation of Eq. (6) can be written with a computational cost of 11 XORs and 3 multiplications by x:

$$\begin{aligned} a'_{0,j} &= 2(a_{0,j} + a_{1,j}) + a_{1,j} + (a_{2,j} + a_{3,j}) \\ a'_{1,j} &= 2(a_{0,j} + a_{2,j}) + \mathbf{a'_{0,j}} + (a_{0,j} + a_{1,j}) \\ a'_{2,j} &= 2(a_{2,j} + a_{3,j}) + a_{3,j} + (a_{0,j} + a_{1,j}) \\ a'_{3,j} &= 2(a_{0,j} + a_{2,j}) + \mathbf{a'_{2,j}} + (a_{2,j} + a_{3,j}) \end{aligned} \tag{7}$$

Maximov [13] reports that a circuit to compute MixColumns takes 92 gates, based on the fact that a multiplication by x in $GF(2^8)$ can be implemented using three 2-input XOR gates. Analogously, a hardware implementation of Eq. (7) takes 8×11 XORs, as well as three multiplications by x, each one taking 3 XORs, summing up to 97 gates.

3.4   Transposed AES Implementation for Four Blocks

In this section we describe an implementation of AES that processes four blocks in each iteration and uses Eq. (6) for the MixColumns step. This method does not require permutations on the inputs.

A "transposition" operation simply rearranges bytes in the AES state A:

$$A = \begin{bmatrix} a_{0,0} & a_{0,1} & a_{0,2} & a_{0,3} \\ a_{1,0} & a_{1,1} & a_{1,2} & a_{1,3} \\ a_{2,0} & a_{2,1} & a_{2,2} & a_{2,3} \\ a_{3,0} & a_{3,1} & a_{3,2} & a_{3,3} \end{bmatrix} \xrightarrow{\text{Transposition}} A' = \begin{bmatrix} a_{0,0} & a_{1,0} & a_{2,0} & a_{3,0} \\ a_{0,1} & a_{1,1} & a_{2,1} & a_{3,1} \\ a_{0,2} & a_{1,2} & a_{2,2} & a_{3,2} \\ a_{0,3} & a_{1,3} & a_{2,3} & a_{3,3} \end{bmatrix}.$$

Let $X = [X_0, X_1, X_2, X_3]$ be four consecutive 128-bit AES states $X_i, 0 \le i \le 3$, i.e., If X is saved in four registers, transposing X groups bytes from each column j of each of the four states in each j register:

$$X = \begin{bmatrix} X_0 \\ X_1 \\ X_2 \\ X_3 \end{bmatrix} = \begin{bmatrix} a_{0,0} & a_{0,1} & a_{0,2} & a_{0,3} & a_{1,0} & a_{1,1} & a_{1,2} & a_{1,3} & a_{2,0} & a_{2,1} & a_{2,2} & a_{2,3} & a_{3,0} & a_{3,1} & a_{3,2} & a_{3,3} \\ b_{0,0} & b_{0,1} & b_{0,2} & b_{0,3} & b_{1,0} & b_{1,1} & b_{1,2} & b_{1,3} & b_{2,0} & b_{2,1} & b_{2,2} & b_{2,3} & b_{3,0} & b_{3,1} & b_{3,2} & b_{3,3} \\ c_{0,0} & c_{0,1} & c_{0,2} & c_{0,3} & c_{1,0} & c_{1,1} & c_{1,2} & c_{1,3} & c_{2,0} & c_{2,1} & c_{2,2} & c_{2,3} & c_{3,0} & c_{3,1} & c_{3,2} & c_{3,3} \\ d_{0,0} & d_{0,1} & d_{0,2} & d_{0,3} & d_{1,0} & d_{1,1} & d_{1,2} & d_{1,3} & d_{2,0} & d_{2,1} & d_{2,2} & d_{2,3} & d_{3,0} & d_{3,1} & d_{3,2} & d_{3,3} \end{bmatrix}$$

$\downarrow$ Transposition

$$X_P = \begin{bmatrix} X'_0 \\ X'_1 \\ X'_2 \\ X'_3 \end{bmatrix} = \begin{bmatrix} a_{0,0} & a_{1,0} & a_{2,0} & a_{3,0} & b_{0,0} & b_{1,0} & b_{2,0} & b_{3,0} & c_{0,0} & c_{1,0} & c_{2,0} & c_{3,0} & d_{0,0} & d_{1,0} & d_{2,0} & d_{3,0} \\ a_{0,1} & a_{1,1} & a_{2,1} & a_{3,1} & b_{0,1} & b_{1,1} & b_{2,1} & b_{3,1} & c_{0,1} & c_{1,1} & c_{2,1} & c_{3,1} & d_{0,1} & d_{1,1} & d_{2,1} & d_{3,1} \\ a_{0,2} & a_{1,2} & a_{2,2} & a_{3,2} & b_{0,2} & b_{1,2} & b_{2,2} & b_{3,2} & c_{0,2} & c_{1,2} & c_{2,2} & c_{3,2} & d_{0,2} & d_{1,2} & d_{2,2} & d_{3,2} \\ a_{0,3} & a_{1,3} & a_{2,3} & a_{3,3} & b_{0,3} & b_{1,3} & b_{2,3} & b_{3,3} & c_{0,3} & c_{1,3} & c_{2,3} & c_{3,3} & d_{0,3} & d_{1,3} & d_{2,3} & d_{3,3} \end{bmatrix}.$$

Implementing the Transposition. When input bytes are already in 128-bit ARMv8 ASIMD registers, the transposition operation can be implemented using a sequence of 16 `trn1`/`trn2` instructions. As an alternative, those 64 bytes may be saved back to memory and reread using a single `ld4` instruction, in which transposition is already done by it. Note that, on ARMv8 CPUs, issuing four 128-bit stores then reading 64 bytes back using the interleaved load is usually faster then issuing 16 transposition instructions. To reverse the interleave pattern, the `st4` instruction can be used over those four registers, saving them into memory in a contiguous fashion.

Transposed `MixColumns`. The non-transposed 128-bit implementation of Eq. (3) as in the Linux Kernel can be applied to each state $X_i \in X$ as in Algorithm 3.

While $\texttt{RotLeft}(X_i)$ applies a bytewise rotation over four 32-bit words X_i, its 512-bit analogous $\texttt{RotLeft}_P(X_P)$ is a rearrangement of 128-bit vectors: given $X_P = [X_0', X_1', X_2', X_3']$, then $\texttt{RotLeft}_P(X_P) = [X_1', X_2', X_3', X_0']$. Note that byte rotations (or permutation) are not required to compute $\texttt{RotLeft}_P(X_P)$, since it simply is an rearrange of the its representation.

Based on Eq. (3), the `MixColumns` step can be computed for four blocks $X_P = [X_0', X_1', X_2', X_3']$ as follows:

$$
\begin{aligned}
X_P' &= \texttt{MixColumns}(X_P) = T_0 + T_1 \\
T_0 &= 2X_P + \texttt{RotLeft}_P^2(X_P) \\
&= [2X_0', 2X_1', 2X_2', 2X_3'] + [X_2', X_3', X_0', X_1'] \\
&= [2X_0' + X_2', 2X_1' + X_3', 2X_2' + X_0', 2X_3' + X_1'] \\
T_1 &= \texttt{RotLeft}_P(T_0 + X_P) \\
&= \texttt{RotLeft}_P([2X_0' + X_2', 2X_1' + X_3', 2X_2' + X_0', 2X_3' + X_1'] \\
&\quad + [X_0', X_1', X_2', X_3']) \\
&= \texttt{RotLeft}_P([3X_0' + X_2', 3X_1' + X_3', 3X_2' + X_0', 3X_3' + X_1']) \\
&= [3X_1' + X_3', 3X_2' + X_0', 3X_3' + X_1', 3X_0' + X_2'] \\
X_P' &= [2X_0' + X_2', 2X_1' + X_3', 2X_2' + X_0', 2X_3' + X_1'] \\
&\quad + [3X_1' + X_3', 3X_2' + X_0', 3X_3' + X_1', 3X_0' + X_2'] \\
X_P' &= [2X_0' + 3X_1' + X_2' + X_3', X_0' + 2X_1' + 3X_2' + X_3', \\
&\quad X_0' + X_1' + 2X_2' + 3X_3', 3X_0' + X_1' + X_2' + 2X_3'] \\
&= [2(X_0' + X_1') + X_1' + (X_2' + X_3'), \ 2(X_1' + X_2') + X_0' + (X_2' + X_3'), \\
&\quad 2(X_2' + X_3') + X_3' + (X_0' + X_1'), \ 2(X_3' + X_0') + X_2' + (X_0' + X_1')].
\end{aligned}
\tag{8}
$$

Algorithm 3. 4-way `MixColumns`

Input: 128-bit AES states $X_i, 0 \le i \le 3$.
Output: 128-bit AES states processed with `MixColumns` $X_i', 0 \le i \le 3$.
1: **for** $i = 0$ to 3 **do**
2:     $T \leftarrow 2X_i + \texttt{RotLeft}^2(X_i)$
3:     $X_i' \leftarrow T + \texttt{RotLeft}(T + X_i)$
4: **end for**
5: **return** $X_i', 0 \le i \le 3$

Now, by using Eq. (7), Algorithm 4 shows how to compute X'_P in terms of 128-bits operations.

Algorithm 4. 4-way Transposed MixColumns

Input: 128-bit transposed AES states $X'_i, 0 \leq i \leq 3$.
Output: 128-bit transposed AES states processed with MixColumns $X''_i, 0 \leq i \leq 3$.
1: $T0 \leftarrow X'_0 \oplus X'_1$
2: $T1 \leftarrow X'_2 \oplus X'_3$
3: $T2 \leftarrow X'_0 \oplus X'_2$
4: $T3 \leftarrow 2 \cdot T0$ {a multiplication by x in $GF(2^8)$}
5: $T4 \leftarrow 2 \cdot T1$
6: $T5 \leftarrow 2 \cdot T2$
7: $X''_0 \leftarrow T1 \oplus (X'_1 \oplus T3)$
8: $X''_1 \leftarrow T0 \oplus (X''_0 \oplus T5)$
9: $X''_2 \leftarrow T0 \oplus (X'_3 \oplus T4)$
10: $X''_3 \leftarrow T1 \oplus (X''_2 \oplus T5)$
11: **return** $X''_i, 0 \leq i \leq 3$

Transposed AddRoundKey and Modified Key Expansion. To process four transposed AES states in parallel, the round key addition must be done on each input block, and, for each one, also in a transposed way. To that, the key expansion has to be slightly modified to store four copies of each key in a transposed way. Each in-register round key is saved four times into main memory. Then, leveraging the ld4 instruction, four registers are filled with the key duplicates in an already transposed fashion. Finally, a single store instruction writes out the replicates, ready to be used by the transposed cipher.

Note that, instead of the usual output of 10 round keys totaling 160 bytes, a total of $11 \times 16 \times 4$ bytes are written as result, as the first key must be processed to fit the proposed format. For each key, three more 128 bits saves to main memory, one transposed load of 64 bytes and a final 64-byte writeout to memory are needed. Those operations make the transposed key expansion to use about 758 CPU cycles on a Raspberry Pi 3B.

Transposed ShiftRows. As in Sect. 2, the original ShiftRows operation rotates the i-th row of the AES state i bytes to the left. For a single AES state represented in a 128-bit register in a column-after-column style, this operation is effectively a permutation. In a AArch64 scenario, implementing this permutation requires the usage of the tbl instruction to reorder the bytes.

On the transposed situation, the ShiftRows operation must now operate over columns, instead of lines. In addition, as result of the reorganization, bytes of a line are grouped in a single register, transforming the ShiftRows operation into a sequence of byte rotations over 32-bit words for each *register*:

$$\begin{bmatrix} X_0 \\ X_1 \\ X_2 \\ X_3 \end{bmatrix} = \begin{bmatrix} a_{0,0}\ a_{1,0}\ a_{2,0}\ a_{3,0}\ b_{0,0}\ b_{1,0}\ b_{2,0}\ b_{3,0}\ c_{0,0}\ c_{1,0}\ c_{2,0}\ c_{3,0}\ d_{0,0}\ d_{1,0}\ d_{2,0}\ d_{3,0} \\ a_{0,1}\ a_{1,1}\ a_{2,1}\ a_{3,1}\ b_{0,1}\ b_{1,1}\ b_{2,1}\ b_{3,1}\ c_{0,1}\ c_{1,1}\ c_{2,1}\ c_{3,1}\ d_{0,1}\ d_{1,1}\ d_{2,1}\ d_{3,1} \\ a_{0,2}\ a_{1,2}\ a_{2,2}\ a_{3,2}\ b_{0,2}\ b_{1,2}\ b_{2,2}\ b_{3,2}\ c_{0,2}\ c_{1,2}\ c_{2,2}\ c_{3,2}\ d_{0,2}\ d_{1,2}\ d_{2,2}\ d_{3,2} \\ a_{0,3}\ a_{1,3}\ a_{2,3}\ a_{3,3}\ b_{0,3}\ b_{1,3}\ b_{2,3}\ b_{3,3}\ c_{0,3}\ c_{1,3}\ c_{2,3}\ c_{3,3}\ d_{0,3}\ d_{1,3}\ d_{2,3}\ d_{3,3} \end{bmatrix}$$

$$\left\lfloor \begin{array}{l} X_0' = X_0 \\ X_1' = \texttt{RotLeft\_128}(X_1) \\ X_2' = \texttt{Rev32\_128}(X_2) \\ X_3' = \texttt{RotRight\_128}(X_3) \end{array} \right.$$

$$\begin{bmatrix} X_0' \\ X_1' \\ X_2' \\ X_3' \end{bmatrix} = \begin{bmatrix} a_{0,0}\ a_{1,0}\ a_{2,0}\ a_{3,0}\ b_{0,0}\ b_{1,0}\ b_{2,0}\ b_{3,0}\ c_{0,0}\ c_{1,0}\ c_{2,0}\ c_{3,0}\ d_{0,0}\ d_{1,0}\ d_{2,0}\ d_{3,0} \\ a_{1,1}\ a_{2,1}\ a_{3,1}\ a_{0,1}\ b_{1,1}\ b_{2,1}\ b_{3,1}\ b_{0,1}\ c_{1,1}\ c_{2,1}\ c_{3,1}\ c_{0,1}\ d_{1,1}\ d_{2,1}\ d_{3,1}\ d_{0,1} \\ a_{2,2}\ a_{3,2}\ a_{0,2}\ a_{1,2}\ b_{2,2}\ b_{3,2}\ b_{0,2}\ b_{1,2}\ c_{2,2}\ c_{3,2}\ c_{0,2}\ c_{1,2}\ d_{2,2}\ d_{3,2}\ d_{0,2}\ d_{1,2} \\ a_{3,3}\ a_{0,3}\ a_{1,3}\ a_{2,3}\ b_{3,3}\ b_{0,3}\ b_{1,3}\ b_{2,3}\ c_{3,3}\ c_{0,3}\ c_{1,3}\ c_{2,3}\ d_{3,3}\ d_{0,3}\ d_{1,3}\ d_{2,3} \end{bmatrix}.$$

All those operations can be implemented using one or two ASIMD instructions, as in Sect. 3.2.

3.5   A New AES Key Schedule Implementation

As shown in Sect. 2.1, the key expansion is mostly a serial algorithm, depending on 32-bit words of each key. This dependency can be eliminated by computing the entire subkey using ASIMD instructions, rather by computing each 32-bit parts of the subsequent key.

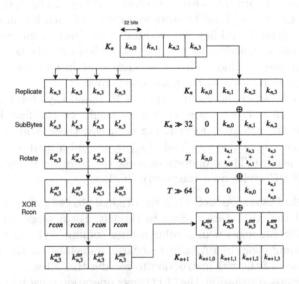

Fig. 1. One round of the proposed AES key expansion using 128-bit words.

Instead of extracting the last 32-bit word of the last key, we start by replicating the last 32-bit word four times, resulting in a 128-bit value. Then, instead of operating over a single 32-bit word, the SubBytes, RotLeft_128 and the round constant addition steps operate on the 128-bit register. The `SubBytes` transformation and the `RotLeft_128` permutation are done in the same way as the Linux Kernel AES implementation shown in Sect. 3.2.

To eliminate the 32-bit word dependency, the series of additions over $GF(2^8)$ are done while shifting by 32-bit the *entire* previous key using the `vext` instruction, as illustrated in Fig. 1.

4 Experimental Results

In this section, we present the performance measurements of our AES implementations, compared to the widely used implementation present in the Linux Kernel[2].

4.1 Setup

Performance measurements of the proposed AES implementations were taken using hardware cycle counters present on the Performance Monitoring Unit (PMU) of each CPU, as an integral part of an ARMv8-A compliant CPU.

Hardware wise, a Raspberry Pi 3B was used, running Linux Kernel 5.2. This board is equipped with a Broadcom BCM2837 CPU, with four Cortex-A53 cores without the Cryptography Extension. For reproducibility purposes, frequency scaling and CPU shutdown features were disabled. CPU was clocked at their maximum supported frequency (1.2GHz), by setting the scaling governor to `performance`. For completude, the `aarch64-linux-gnu-gcc` version 8.3 was choosen as toolchain, but since assembly language was used to implement our versions, no compiler influence is expected.

4.2 Performance Comparison

The performance test was done using ECB and CTR modes of operation to encrypt messages of size 4KiB for 2^{15} iterations, in which each test takes as input the output of the previous one; the first message was sampled from `/dev/urandom`. Results are shown in Fig. 2.

Our implementations are pipelined-optimized versions (n-way), in which $n = 4$ blocks are processed in an interleaved fashion. This eliminates data hazards between adjacent instructions, thus avoiding pineline stalls and lowering the instruction per cycle count. The "transposed" experiments follows the proposal as in Sect. 3.4. In addition, the "PreGen" experiment refers to a version in which the input counter is incremented and written on a temporary buffer, then encrypted four blocks at the same time. This implementation frees up scratch registers, thus avoiding slower memory usage.

For comparison purposes, performance of AES implementations of the Cryptography API ("CryptoAPI") within the Linux Kernel were also evaluated. The

---

[2] See: https://git.kernel.org/pub/scm/linux/kernel/git/torvalds/linux.git/tree/arch/arm64/crypto/aes-neon.S.

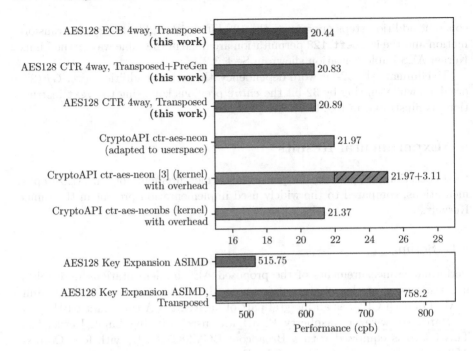

Fig. 2. Comparison of different AES implementations in cycles per byte (cpb) for messages of 4 KiB on a Raspberry Pi 3B. Experiments using Kernel calls are subject to overhead: for example, CryptoAPI ctr-aes-neon (kernel) call has a 3.11 cpb overhead.

ctr-aes-neon experiment uses the AES implementation of Cryptography API relying only on ASIMD instructions, while ctr-aes-neonbs experiment does the same but using a bitsliced strategy [3,11]. On these experiments, some call overhead may be expected, since the Cryptography API must be called through a Netlink interface. The libkcapi library, used in these experiments, allows userspace calls from that interface. To provide a more direct comparison of our implementation and the one used in the Linux Kernel, a userspace version of ctr-aes-neon was also implemented, replacing all macro calls present in the Kernel code and compiled in the same manner as with our own implementations. The usage of this version avoids delays associated to inter-process communication between kernel and userspace, revealing a 3.11 cycles per byte call overhead for the experimented parameters.

Performance results of the AES Key Expansion (as in Sect. 3.5) are also shown in Fig. 2. While the Linux Kernel also implements this algorithm, this is done in a generic way, compliant to the cryptographic framework, to support other AES variants and ciphers. Therefore, no direct comparison can be drawn, as this setup operation takes more than 4000 cycles to complete.

Discussion. As expected, the usage of implementations embedded within the Linux Kernel has a significant overhead if compared when a similar userspace implementation is used. Within the first scope, the bitsliced version in the CryptoAPI outperforms the ASIMD CryptoAPI implementation, considering that both are subject to call overheads. To properly explore the speed up of our proposal, further experiments were run in which each AES layer was disabled, turning them into "partial" ciphers. These numbers are shown in Fig. 3.

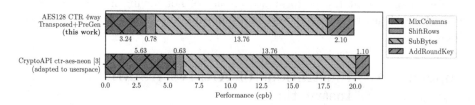

Fig. 3. Breakdown of cycles per byte (cpb) cost of each AES step in a standard and transposed implementations. The cpb sum of each implementation does not represent the totality of the cipher, as reading the input, output writeout and other necessary operations costs are not included.

Due to the heavy use of the `tbl/tbx` instructions, added to their inefficiency on processing 128-bit data, almost 66% of the AES computation is spent on the `SubBytes` parts. Removing the need of the permutation steps and the use of a faster formula in the `MixColumns` step impacted in a 42.47% speedup on this layer, compared to the same one in the Cryptography API's implementation. However, the need of loading the replicated and transposed round keys brings a 90% slowdown on each `AddRoundKey` step. As for the `ShiftRows` changes, the usage of the `rev` and `trn` instead of the `tbl` instructions brought in a 25% slowdown locally. It should be noted that this step amounts for less than 5% of AES computation of either implementation, lowering the impact of the performance prejudice.

Replicating and transposing keys on the Key Expansion procedure amounts in a 31.98% slowdown in comparison to a key scheduling implementation outputting 10×16 bytes. Some of the key preprocessing could be done on-the-fly during the ciphering data, making the `AddRoundKey` step to be more expensive in terms of CPU cycles. We choose to implement this setup in the expansion phase since this cost is amortized over large messages.

5   Final Remarks

In this work we presented an optimized AES implementation in which four blocks are processed at the same time. In particular, we show a new formulation for the `MixColumn` layer, reducing the number of operations required to process it. While the representation of the four AES blocks is changed, requiring modifications of other AES layers, no negative impacts can be seen overall; in fact, a 5% speed up is shown in our experiments.

As a final note, modern ARMv8-A processors, specially those tailored for use in mobile phones at different price points, are being designed with the Cryptography Extension in mind, given the relevance of the AES cipher. Due to the fact that further new ciphers proposals (such as the WEM algorithm [6], tailored towards white-box cryptography) use parts (or the entire) AES algorithm, we also imagine that the performance impact of not having in-hardware AES support on cheaper devices should be diminished on implementations of new ciphers.

Appendix A: Illustrations of ARMv8 ASIMD Instructions

Figures 4 and 5 in this appendix presents illustrations of some ARMv8 ASIMD instructions summarized in Sect. 3.1.

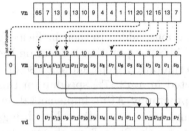

(a) `tbl vd, {vm}, vn`. Lookup table is stored in `vm`.

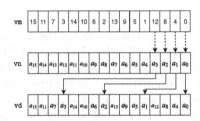

(b) `tbl vd, {vn}, vm`. The permutation pattern is held in `vm`.

Fig. 4. Usage of the `tbl` instruction to substitute or permute the input vector `vn`. Results written on register `vd`.

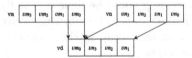

(a) `ext vd, vn, vm, #1`. Note that by zero filling `vm` and reordering arguments, shift left and rights can be done.

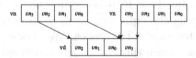

(b) `ext vd, vn, vn, #3`. Rotations in either direction can be made by changing the last argument.

Fig. 5. Usage of the `ext` instruction to extract words or execute rotations a 128-bit word.

References

1. Bernstein, D.J.: The Salsa20 family of stream ciphers. In: Robshaw, M., Billet, O. (eds.) New Stream Cipher Designs. LNCS, vol. 4986, pp. 84–97. Springer, Heidelberg (2008). https://doi.org/10.1007/978-3-540-68351-3_8
2. Bernstein, D.J., Schwabe, P.: NEON crypto. In: Prouff, E., Schaumont, P. (eds.) CHES 2012. LNCS, vol. 7428, pp. 320–339. Springer, Heidelberg (2012). https://doi.org/10.1007/978-3-642-33027-8_19
3. Biesheuvel, A.: Accelerated AES for the Arm64 Linux kernel, January 2017. https://www.linaro.org/blog/accelerated-aes-for-the-arm64-linux-kernel/
4. blu: How ARM Nerfed NEON Permute Instructions in ARMv8, August 2017. https://www.cnx-software.com/2017/08/07/how-arm-nerfed-neon-permute-instructions-in-armv8/
5. Bogdanov, A., Isobe, T., Tischhauser, E.: Towards practical whitebox cryptography: optimizing efficiency and space hardness. In: Cheon, J.H., Takagi, T. (eds.) ASIACRYPT 2016. LNCS, vol. 10031, pp. 126–158. Springer, Heidelberg (2016). https://doi.org/10.1007/978-3-662-53887-6_5
6. Cho, J., Choi, K.Y., Dinur, I., Dunkelman, O., Keller, N., Moon, D., Veidberg, A.: WEM: a new family of white-box block ciphers based on the even-mansour construction. In: Handschuh, H. (ed.) CT-RSA 2017. LNCS, vol. 10159, pp. 293–308. Springer, Cham (2017). https://doi.org/10.1007/978-3-319-52153-4_17
7. Crowley, P., Biggers, E.: Adiantum: length-preserving encryption for entry-level processors. IACR Trans. Symmetric Cryptol. **2018**(4), 39–61 (2018)
8. Daemen, J., Rijmen, V.: The Design of Rijndael. Springer, Heidelberg (2002). https://doi.org/10.1007/978-3-662-04722-4
9. Gouvêa, C.P.L., López, J.: Implementing GCM on ARMv8. In: Nyberg, K. (ed.) CT-RSA 2015. LNCS, vol. 9048, pp. 167–180. Springer, Cham (2015). https://doi.org/10.1007/978-3-319-16715-2_9
10. Hamburg, M.: Accelerating AES with vector permute instructions. In: Clavier, C., Gaj, K. (eds.) CHES 2009. LNCS, vol. 5747, pp. 18–32. Springer, Heidelberg (2009). https://doi.org/10.1007/978-3-642-04138-9_2
11. Käsper, E., Schwabe, P.: Faster and timing-attack resistant AES-GCM. In: Clavier, C., Gaj, K. (eds.) CHES 2009. LNCS, vol. 5747, pp. 1–17. Springer, Heidelberg (2009). https://doi.org/10.1007/978-3-642-04138-9_1
12. Krovetz, T., Rogaway, P.: The software performance of authenticated-encryption modes. In: Joux, A. (ed.) FSE 2011. LNCS, vol. 6733, pp. 306–327. Springer, Heidelberg (2011). https://doi.org/10.1007/978-3-642-21702-9_18
13. Maximov, A.: AES MixColumn with 92 XOR gates. Cryptology ePrint Archive, Report 2019/833 (2019). https://eprint.iacr.org/2019/833
14. NIST: Announcing the Advanced Encryption Standard (AES). U.S. Department of Commerce/National Institute of Standards and Technology (2001). Federal Information Processing Standards Publication 197. http://csrc.nist.gov/publications/fips/fips197/fips-197.pdf
15. Osvik, D.A., Shamir, A., Tromer, E.: Cache attacks and countermeasures: the case of AES. In: Pointcheval, D. (ed.) CT-RSA 2006. LNCS, vol. 3860, pp. 1–20. Springer, Heidelberg (2006). https://doi.org/10.1007/11605805_1
16. Rodrigues, F.C., Fujii, H., Zoppi Serpa, A.C., Sider, G., Dahab, R., López, J.: Fast white-box implementations of dedicated ciphers on the ARMv8 architecture. In: Schwabe, P., Thériault, N. (eds.) LATINCRYPT 2019. LNCS, vol. 11774, pp. 341–363. Springer, Cham (2019). https://doi.org/10.1007/978-3-030-30530-7_17

FACE–LIGHT: Fast AES–CTR Mode Encryption for Low-End Microcontrollers

Kyungho Kim[1], Seungju Choi[1], Hyeokdong Kwon[1], Zhe Liu[2],
and Hwajeong Seo[1(✉)]

[1] Division of IT Convergence Engineering, Hansung University, Seoul, South Korea
pgm.kkh@gmail.com, bookingstore3@gmail.com, korlethean@gmail.com,
hwajeong84@gmail.com
[2] Aeronautics and Astronautics, Nanjing University, Nanjing, Jiangsu, China
sduliuzhe@gmail.com

Abstract. In this paper, we revisited the previous Fast AES–CTR mode Encryption (FACE) method for high-end processors and tailored the method to the microcontrollers, namely FACE–LIGHT. We targeted the 32-bit counter mode of operation for AES in constant timing. This optimized technique pre-computes the 2 Add-RoundKey, 2 Sub-Bytes, 2 Shift-Rows and 1 Mix-Columns operations. The FACE–LIGHT is implemented on the representative low-end microcontrollers (e.g. 8-bit AVR). The execution timing of AES–CTR algorithm for 128-bit and 256-bit security levels achieved the 2,218 and 3,184 clock cycles, respectively. This is faster than previous works by 22 % for 128-bit security level. The FACE–LIGHT can be used to extend the FACE to round 3. The AES is also implemented to be secure against the CPA (Correlation Power Analysis).

Keywords: AES · Software implementation · Counter mode · Microcontroller · Correlation Power Analysis

1 Introduction

Low-end IoT (Internet of Things) platforms are resource constrained devices, which have limited memory size and low computing power. In order to apply the cryptography protocols, the research on lightweight cryptography, which is relatively simple and has short computation time, has been actively conducted. Typical lightweight encryption algorithms include LEA, HIGHT, SIMON, SPECK, and CHAM [1–4]. However, most of these lightweight cipher algorithms adopt the ARX (Addition, Rotation, and XOR) structure, which has the disadvantage that it takes much additional time when applying the masking operation to prevent the side channel attack [5].

Even though the AES encryption algorithm is not considered as a lightweight encryption due to its relatively long computation time than other lightweight block ciphers, AES has been the world's most used encryption algorithm for a

© Springer Nature Switzerland AG 2020
J. H. Seo (Ed.): ICISC 2019, LNCS 11975, pp. 102–114, 2020.
https://doi.org/10.1007/978-3-030-40921-0_6

long period of time, and is an international standard encryption algorithm with high security and generality [6]. In addition, AES adopts the SPN (Substitution-Permutation-Network) structure, which requires relatively less time for masking computation than the ARX structure. If the AES can be optimized and implemented on a low-end processor, it can be used as a lightweight cipher with high security and generality. In contrast to most of previous AES-CTR implementations, which focused mostly on the high-end processors, this paper concretes on low-end microcontrollers. We revisited the previous works and tailored the method to fit into the low-end environments.

This paper is organized as follows. Section 2 discusses the previous AES implementations and Fast AES CTR mode Encryption (FACE) technique, which is the fastest AES-CTR implementation method. In Sect. 3, we introduce FACE–LIGHT method for microcontrollers. In Sect. 4, we evaluate the performance of the proposed implementation. Section 5 concludes this paper.

2   FACE: Fast AES CTR Mode Encryption

In CHES'18, the efficient AES-CTR implementation (i.e. FACE) for high-end processor was suggested [7]. The FACE method utilizes the value of IV depending only on the change of counter values. Since the IV value, except for the counter value, remains the same as the following blocks, an identical pattern is repeated in specific part of the encrypted value until the Round 2 of AES. By utilizing this feature, repeated values can be stored in the cache table and used, which minimizes the encryption operation of subsequent blocks during the encryption operation, thereby effectively reducing the encryption operation time.

The first step is the $FACE_{rd0}$. In this step the FACE utilizes the fact that in Round 0, only the Add-RoundKey operation is performed. In the case of Add-RoundKey operation, a byte calculation is not affected by other bytes since it is a XOR operation which only deals with single bytes independently. The only byte difference between the first IV block and the second IV block is the last byte that is used as a counter. The Add-RoundKey operation can be minimized by storing the previous 12 bytes out of 16 bytes in the precomputed table. The table is only replaced after a 2^{32-1} block operation where all unused 4 bytes are 0xFFFFFFFF. This approach requires only one cache update while processing 65.5 GB of plaintext. The description of the step is shown in Fig. 1 and the Add-RoundKey result values, the State, can be seen stored in the cache. The cache consists of 4×4 bytes in total. Among the cache, only the values in the 0, 1, and 2 columns are reused. The values in the third column are not reused to minimize the cache update.

The second step is $FACE_{rd1}$. The State value from Round 0 is used as the input value of Round 1, where $FACE_{rd1}$ reuses some of the values stored in the cache. In Fig. 2, it is shown that after the Round 1, the value of $S[15]$, which was the only different byte from previous block, affects the whole first column through the Mix-Columns operation. The remaining columns except the first can be reused since they are not affected by $S[15]$. The reusable column values

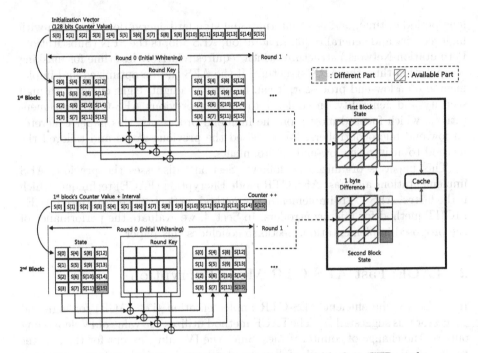

Fig. 1. Initial whitening of the first and the second block in CTR mode

can be used until the value of $S[15]$ exceeds 0xFF and affects $S[14]$, which can be used up to 256 times.

The third step is FACE$_{rd1+}$. In this step, it is suggested that the value of the first column, which gets changed in the step FACE$_{rd1}$, be created as a cache table through a precomputation. The value in the first column consists of $S[0]$, $S[5]$, $S[10]$ and $S[15]$, which get affected by $S[15]$ in the Mix-Columns operation. Therefore, 1 KB (256×4) of cache can be generated through a pre-calculation based on the $S[15]$ value that changes according to the counter value. The cache table can be created beforehand based on $S[15]$ since the value of $S[10]$, the high byte of $S[15]$, is not affected until a total of 0xFFFFFFFFFF blocks are initialized from $S[15]$ to $S[11]$, the 1,099,511,627,776-th block (16 TB), is calculated.

The forth step is FACE$_{rd2}$. This step deals with Round 2 which utilizes the output of the Round 1. Through Round 1 operation, the value of the first column of Round 2 is affected by the changes of the counter value. Figure 3 shows the Round 2 process of the first and second blocks. $S[0], S[1], S[2]$ and $S[3]$, which are affected by the counter value, are spread to other columns by the Sub-Bytes operation. The values affect all 16 Bytes through Mix-Columns operation. In conclusion, the whole byte is affected by the counter value. However, during the Mix-Columns operation, some of the values can be reused. Shown in Fig. 3, operation values except $S[0]$ can be reused such as $S[5], S[10], S[15]$ and round

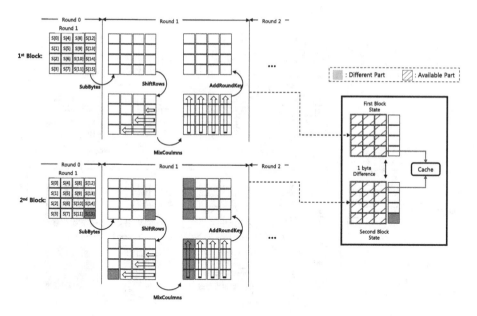

Fig. 2. Round 1 and the difference between the first and the second block

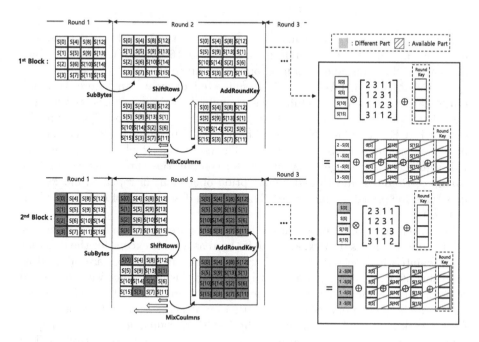

Fig. 3. Round 2 and the difference between the first and the second block

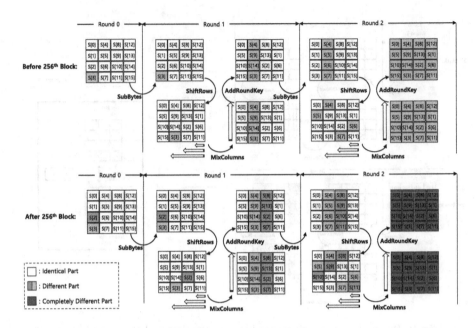

Fig. 4. Overview of FACE

key. These values will not change and repeat until the IV $S[14]$ is not affected by the counter increment. Therefore, making these 16 Bytes of unaffected values into cache table, can be used during operation up to the 256th block.

In the final step, $FACE_{rd2+}$, it is suggested to create and store 4 KBytes (16×256) table which contains the changing operation values which were excluded from $FACE_{rd2}$ and involves around $S[0], S[1], S[2]$ and $S[3]$. As in the case of $FACE_{rd1+}$, while calculating the 1,099,511,627,776-th block (16 TB), a previously calculated table can be used. The use of these lookup tables can provide significant advantages in cryptographic computation time, since it minimize Round 0, Round 1 and Round 2 encryption operations in repeated blocks and uses the same pre-computed values. The detailed descriptions of FACE are given in Fig. 4.

However, this work is only efficient for 8-bit counter mode. In Fig. 4, if the last 8-bit counter value is 0 to 0xFF, it can be used as a table except for the different parts painted in black. However, after 256 blocks, more values are affected as the value of $S[14]$ is changed as shown below. In this case, since we can not use pre-stored table, we need to update the cache table in each 256 times encryption. Since this frequent updates can be abused by attacker as an attack point (i.e. fault attack), we need to implement the FACE in regular form. In this paper, we revisit the FACE and optimize the method for low-end microcontrollers. The proposed FACE–LIGHT is regular fashion and we don't need to update the cache table throughout the whole AES-CTR life-cycle.

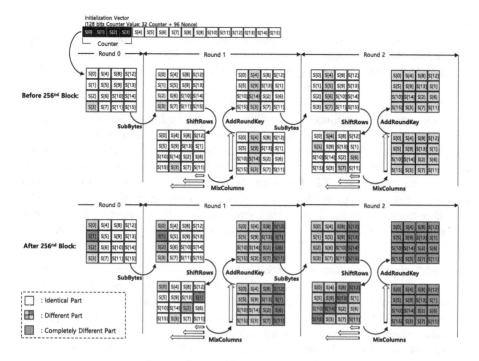

Fig. 5. Overview of FACE–LIGHT

3   FACE-LIGHT

In this section, we introduce the new implementation techniques for AES-CTR mode. Compared with previous work (i.e. FACE), we optimized the method for low-end microcontrollers and evaluated the masked implementation as well. The CTR mode consists of nonce and counter values. For the general setting, nonce and counter are set to 96-bit and 32-bit, respectively. The nonce is not changed throughout the whole sessions but the counter is changed in each transaction. Previous work focused on the low 8-bit and this needs to update the cache table in 256-times of encryption. In proposed work, we consider the 32-bit counter. We only need to set the pre-computed table in the initialization stage and it is not changed during the whole sessions. The detailed descriptions are given in Fig. 5. The above figure indicates first block and the below figure indicates n-th block. Each square contains 8-bit data and the white and black colors represent identical and different parts, respectively.

Round 0. In Round 0, the only computation is Add-RoundKey. The plaintext and round key is xored. The only difference between two blocks is 4 bytes.

Round 1. In Round 1, Sub-Bytes, Shift-Rows, Mix-Columns, and Add-RoundKey operations are performed in order. The Sub-Bytes operation only changes the 8-bit input into the 8-bit output. This does not spread the values to the adjacent squares. The Shift-Rows tries to shift the square by certain offsets. In the Mix-Columns, the 8-bit data is mixed with 32-bit column. Finally, the Add-RoundKey adds the round keys to each square. Between first and N-th blocks, there is no common values. However, the both results are originated from IV. In particular, the low 32-bit value, namely counter value (i.e. $S[0], S[1], S[2]$, and $S[3]$), mainly contributes to the differences. In the Mix-Columns, $S[0]$ square influences to the first column (i.e. $S[5], S[10]$, and $S[15]$). For this reason, each column (i.e. 32-bit) depends on the 8-bit square. Similarly, other columns are also based on the squares (i.e. $S[1], S[2]$, and $S[3]$). This means each 32-bit column has only 256 cases. The following Add-RoundKey only applied to the each square so the pre-computation complexity is not changed. For this stage, the FACE performs in round 2 since they concern the 8-bit counter case with table update, while FACE–LIGHT is 32-bit counter case without table update.

Round 2. In the previous stage, each column is based on the 8-bit square value. This is still maintained in Sub-Bytes operation which is only based on the each square value and the value is determined by 8-bit square of previous round. Since the Shift-Rows operation does not perform any mixing and changing on the value, the pre-computation is still working. For pre-computation, we need to keep 4 look-up tables. The input values are $S[0], S[1], S[2]$, and $S[3]$ in 8-bit wise. The length of output value is 32-bit wise. The total size for look-up table is 4 KB. In Fig. 6, pre-computed table for FACE–LIGHT is described. In each table, we only receive the 8-bit input value and the value goes through the Mix-Columns, Add-RoundKey, and Sub-Bytes in this order. The Shift-Rows operation is not combined in the pre-computed table. It is optimized away by directly assigning the results to the specific squares.

Extended Round for FACE. The FACE–LIGHT is applied to the Round 2. This can be utilized for the FACE Round 3 since the different value is same with Round 2 of FACE–LIGHT. By using this technique, the Sub-Bytes and Add-RoundKey of Round 3 can be also cached. The detailed extended round for FACE are given in Fig. 7. We used FACE Round 1 method for AES Round 1. From Round 2 to 3, we used the FACE-LIGHT strategy to extend the 1 round more than FACE method.

Optimized Implementation. The pre-computed table is stored before encryption operation. The 8-bit AVR microcontroller has very limited SRAM. For storing huge pre-computed table, we used the PROGRAM MEMORY. In each look-up table access, 32-bit results are extracted. For this reason, 8-bit input offset is extended to the 32-bit input offset by using quadrupling on the offset. Afterward, the input offset is added to the based address of each look-up table.

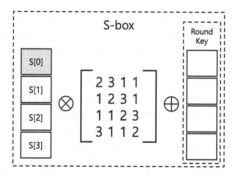

Fig. 6. Pre-computation for FACE–LIGHT

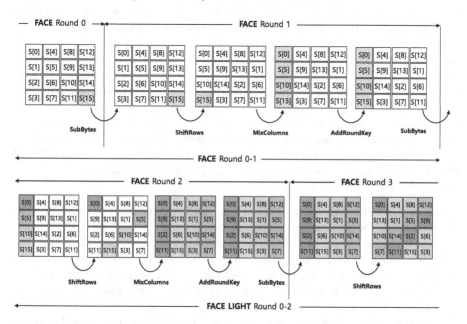

Fig. 7. Extended round for FACE round 3

In AES algorithm, a substitution operation is performed during Sub-Bytes operation. During the operation, value of 256 Bytes to be substituted is stored in memory as a table called SBOX in advance to shorten the computation time. In Sub-Bytes operation, the values which to be substituted are loaded based on the input ciphertext. Therefore, when the value stored in the SBOX is loaded using the Z pointer (R30, R31), the lower memory address and the upper memory address of the SBOX are loaded in R30 and R31, respectively, and the ciphertext value to be used as the index value should be added to R30 to match the index. In this process, a carry might occur at the lower address of the SBOX memory loaded in R30, so that the value of R31 might needs to be increased by one.

Therefore, if the ciphertext value is added to R30, the lower address of SBOX memory, to refer to the SBOX memory, the ADC operation which performs carry operation, must be performed on R31, which stores the upper address of SBOX memory.

However, if the carry does not occur, the ADC is not only a meaningless operation, but it cause a big overhead since two operations (ADD, ADC) is performed for each Sub-Bytes operation for the index operation. To solve this problem, we utilize the memory size of the SBOX, 256 Bytes. If the lower address of memory is set to 0x00, the carry value does not occur when indexing for memory access with the last index value of 0xFF. Therefore, the ADC operation on R31, including the carry value can be omitted and the ciphertext can be loaded directly without performing the ADD operation on R30. In the same way, the computation time when storing or loading values in the Masked–SBOX table, a table created for masking, can also be reduced using the same address sorting method.

LD and ST instructions are used to load or store the key and the round key values stored in consecutive memory. In the case of the AVR, 16-bit addresses are accessed using the X(R26, R27), Y(R28, R29) and Z(R30, R31) pointers. Therefore, when accessing the repetitive memory or the peripheral memory, the memory address to be accessed should be set by using the ADD and ADC operators in the register that constitutes the pointer. In this case, carry value operation should be included as described above which causes a large overhead. Therefore, the address access without additional operator was performed by using LDD and STD or memory address post incremental instruction provided by AVR.

Optimization for Masking Operation. Masking operations aim to prevent the attacker from accurately measuring power usage by adding useless operations without affecting the encryption operations themselves. Therefore, the clock cycle is inevitably longer than the conventional encryption operation. In this paper, in order to minimize this disadvantage, we propose two methods.

The first method is as follows. Before performing encryption operation, 10 sets of round keys, from Round 0 to Round 9, pre-computed by fixed key encryption, should perform XOR operation with the value M0. Then carry out XOR operation on the first row with M6, the second row with M7, the third row with M8 and the last row with M9. In the case of Round 10, the last round, does not include M6, M7, M8 and M9 operations, but XORs the M1 value to all of the key values. If the corresponding operation is performed in advance, the XOR operation repeated in each round is minimized, and the memory in which the masking value is stored does not have to be loaded in each round. It can be observed in Algorithm 1 that M0 is XORed with M6, M7, M8, M9 in line 4. At label 1, M6, M7, M8 and M9 are XORed row by row for a total of 10 key sets from Round 0 to Round 9. By XORing M0 value to each mask value in advance, 160 XOR operations can be reduced. It is also shown in label 2, M1 XORs with the last round key.

The second method is as follows. Sub-Bytes operation is a relatively clock cycle consuming since it needs to access SBOX memory stored as a table. In

Algorithm 1. Masking operation optimization

```
 1: mov HI, ROUND         15: ld r0, Z
 2: lsl HI                16: eor r0, MASK8        28: ld r0, Z
 3: lsl HI                17: st Z+, r0            29: eor r0, MASK1
                                                  30: st Z+, r0
 4: eor MASK6, MASK0      18: ld r0, Z
 5: eor MASK7, MASK0      19: eor r0, MASK9        31: ld r0, Z
 6: eor MASK8, MASK0      20: st Z+, r0            32: eor r0, MASK1
 7: eor MASK9, MASK0                               33: st Z+, r0
                          21: dec HI
 8: 1:                    22: brne 1b             34: ld r0, Z
 9: ld r0, Z                                      35: eor r0, MASK1
10: eor r0, MASK6         23: ldi HI, 4           36: st Z+, r0
11: st Z+, r0
                          24: 2:                  37: dec HI
12: ld r0, Z              25: ld r0, Z            38: brne 2b
13: eor r0, MASK7         26: eor r0, MASK1
14: st Z+, r0             27: st Z+, r0
```

Algorithm 2. Generating Masked SBOX

```
 1: ldi r31, hi8(MSBOX)    6: ld r26, Y           10: st Z, r26
 2: ldi r29, hi8(SBOX)     7: eor r26, T1
 3: ldi xREDUCER, 0x1b                            11: inc r0
                           8: mov r30, r0         12: brne 1b
 4: 1:                     9: eor r30, T0
 5: mov r28, r0
```

addition, after performing Sub-Bytes operation, the masked value, M0, needs to be replaced with M1. Therefore, overhead occurs when executing the memory load operation and XOR operation every round. In order to minimize the overhead, Masked-SBOX table should have been precomputed and be referenced in the Sub-Bytes operation. The detailed descriptions of the implementation are given in Algorithm 2.

4   Evaluation

In this paper, we utilized the 8-bit AVR microcontroller. In particular, we used the Arduino UNO platform, which equips the ATmega328 processor. The hardware follows the Harvard architecture and the working frequency is 16 MHz. It contains 32 8-bit general purpose registers and has a total of 131 instruction sets. Flash memory is 32 KB in size, with 1 KB of EEPROM and 2 KB of internal SRAM. We compile the code in -OS option and the performance is compared in terms of clock cycles. For performance measurement, the software was developed with

Table 1. Comparison of AES implementations on 8-bit AVR, in terms of clock cycles.

Security level	Dinu et al. [8]	Otte et al. [9]	FACE–LIGHT (this work)	Extended FACE (this work)
AES-128	2,835	2,507	**2,218**	**1,967**
AES-192	N/A	2,991	**2,702**	**2,449**
AES-256	N/A	3,473	**3,184**	**2,931**

Table 2. Comparison of FACE and FACE–LIGHT.

	FACE [7]	FACE–LIGHT (This work)
Table update	√	–
Constant timing	–	√
Target processor	32-bit or above	8-bit or above
Expandable Round	Round 2	Round 3

Arduino IDE and Atmel Studio 7 on an Arduino UNO board with Atmega328p. All the functions in the program were implemented in Assembly except the loop function. The Arduino UNO board's frequency was 16 MHz and the results were obtained using the Arduino IDE and Atmel Studio 7 for accurate performance measurements. In addition, in order to confirm that the proposed AES is safe against power analysis attack, the power consumption during encryption operation is measured by Chipwhisperer-Lite (CW1173). In addition, CPA was performed by collecting 5,000 waveforms in the third round with the output value of the Sub-Bytes operation as the middle value.

Table 1 shows the comparison of the clock cycles of four AES. Previous AES implementations are under ECB mode. The proposed method is CTR mode by using FACE–LIGHT method and extended FACE which FACE–LIGHT is applied. The main differences are mode of operation and their input values. For more details, Dinu et al. [8] is the result of code size software optimization and Otte et al. [9] is the result of clock cycle software optimization. In our setting, we used some special cases as mentioned in Chap. 3. For this reason, FACE–LIGHT is faster than previous state-of-art by 617 clock cycles and Extended FACE is faster by 868 clock cycles. The proposed method efficiently passes the certain routines with pre-computed tables.

In Table 2, the comparison results between FACE and FACE–LIGHT are given. The FACE–LIGHT does not require table update during computations. This means the encryption timing is always regular fashion. The timing information indicates the order of messages. By measuring the timing, we can get these information and this can be linked to the privacy issue. The target processor varies in each method. The FACE is for 32-bit processor while the FACE–LIGHT is for 8-bit microcontrollers. In addition, the FACE can be expanded till Round 2 while our work, FACE–LIGHT, can be expanded to the Round 3.

Existing lightweight ciphers have also been studied for the implementation of additional masking techniques to cope with side channel attacks. However,

Table 3. Comparison of LEA and optimized masked AES implementations on 8-bit AVR microcontroller, in terms of clock cycles.

LEA-128 [10]	Masked LEA-128 [11]	Masked AES-128 (this work)
2,688	36,589	**6,219**

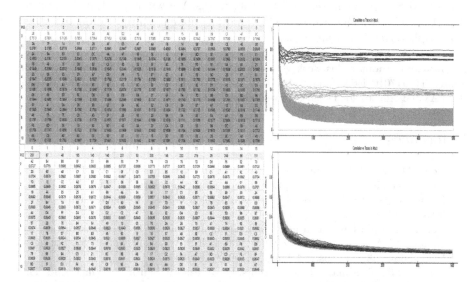

Fig. 8. Comparison of non-masked AES and masked FACE–LIGHT on CPA attack (top left) table of analyzed key value via CPA attack on non-masking AES (top right) correlation graph of key values through CPA attack on non-masking AES (bottom left) table of analyzed key value via CPA attack on masking AES (bottom right) correlation graph of key values through CPA attack on masking AES

most lightweight ciphers with ARX structures have significant overhead since the ciphers must undergo Arithmetic-to-Boolean operation during masking operations. On the other hand, the SPN structure, AES, has a relatively short operation time. Therefore it has an advantage over other lightweight ciphers in the masking operation, which is a side channel countermeasure.

Table 3 shows the clock cycles of none masked LEA, masked LEA and AES encryption algorithm with masking operation. In the case of masked LEA–128, the encryption operation time increases rapidly when masking is applied to LEA. However, it can be observed that the proposed AES has robustness against power consumption analysis attack while having less computation time.

Figure 8 shows a graph of key value and correlation coefficient estimated by performing CPA on AES without mask and AES presented in this paper. In case of the AES without masking operation, the correlation coefficient of all key values is significantly higher than other values. However, in the case of the AES proposed in this paper, the attacker cannot guess the key value since all of the key values have equal correlation coefficients.

5   Conclusion

In this paper, we demonstrate the implementation of AES–CTR encryption on 8-bit AVR microcontrollers. The proposed FACE–LIGHT efficiently improves the performance. Furthermore, we investigated the extended round method and masked AES implementations. For future works, We will apply this method to the AES–GCM, which consists of CTR and polynomial multiplication and other block ciphers/mode of operations.

Acknowledgement. This work was supported as part of Military Crypto Research Center (UD170109ED) funded by Defense Acquisition Program Administration (DAPA) and Agency for Defense Development (ADD).

References

1. Hong, D., Lee, J.-K., Kim, D.-C., Kwon, D., Ryu, K.H., Lee, D.-G.: LEA: a 128-bit block cipher for fast encryption on common processors. In: Kim, Y., Lee, H., Perrig, A. (eds.) WISA 2013. LNCS, vol. 8267, pp. 3–27. Springer, Cham (2014). https://doi.org/10.1007/978-3-319-05149-9_1
2. Hong, D., et al.: HIGHT: a new block cipher suitable for low-resource device. In: Goubin, L., Matsui, M. (eds.) CHES 2006. LNCS, vol. 4249, pp. 46–59. Springer, Heidelberg (2006). https://doi.org/10.1007/11894063_4
3. Beaulieu, R., Treatman-Clark, S., Shors, D., Weeks, B., Smith, J., Wingers, L.: The SIMON and SPECK lightweight block ciphers. In: 2015 52nd ACM/EDAC/IEEE Design Automation Conference (DAC), pp. 1–6. IEEE (2015)
4. Koo, B., Roh, D., Kim, H., Jung, Y., Lee, D.-G., Kwon, D.: CHAM: a family of lightweight block ciphers for resource-constrained devices. In: Kim, H., Kim, D.-C. (eds.) ICISC 2017. LNCS, vol. 10779, pp. 3–25. Springer, Cham (2018). https://doi.org/10.1007/978-3-319-78556-1_1
5. Goubin, L.: A sound method for switching between boolean and arithmetic masking. In: Koç, Ç.K., Naccache, D., Paar, C. (eds.) CHES 2001. LNCS, vol. 2162, pp. 3–15. Springer, Heidelberg (2001). https://doi.org/10.1007/3-540-44709-1_2
6. Standard, N.-F.: Announcing the advanced encryption standard (AES). In: Federal Information Processing Standards Publication, vol. 197, no. 1–51, p. 3 (2001)
7. Park, J.H., Lee, D.H.: FACE: fast AES CTR mode encryption techniques based on the reuse of repetitive data. IACR Trans. Cryptogr. Hardw. Embed. Syst. **2018**(3), 469–499 (2018)
8. Dinu, D., Biryukov, A., Großschädl, J., Khovratovich, D., Le Corre, Y., Perrin, L.: FELICS-fair evaluation of lightweight cryptographic systems. In: NIST Workshop on Lightweight Cryptography, vol. 128 (2015)
9. Otte, D., et al.: AVR-crypto-lib (2009). http://www.das-labor.org/wiki/AVR-Crypto-Lib/en
10. Seo, H., Jeong, I., Lee, J., Kim, W.: Compact implementations of ARX-based block ciphers on IoT processors. ACM Trans. Embed. Comput. Syst. (TECS) **17**(3), 60 (2018)
11. Park, E., Oh, S., Ha, J.: Masking-based block cipher LEA resistant to side channel attacks. J. Korea Inst. Inf. Secur. Cryptol. **27**(5), 1023–1032 (2017)

Sum It Up: Verifiable Additive Homomorphic Secret Sharing

Georgia Tsaloli$^{(\boxtimes)}$ and Aikaterini Mitrokotsa

Chalmers University of Technology, Gothenburg, Sweden
{tsaloli,aikmitr}@chalmers.se

Abstract. In many situations, clients (*e.g.*, researchers, companies, hospitals) need to outsource joint computations based on joint inputs to external cloud servers in order to provide useful results. Often clients want to guarantee that the results are *correct* and thus, an output that can be *publicly* verified is required. However, important security and privacy challenges are raised, since clients may hold sensitive information and the cloud servers can be untrusted. Our goal is to allow the clients to protect their secret data, while providing *public verifiability i.e.,* everyone should be able to verify the correctness of the computed result.

In this paper, we propose three concrete constructions of *verifiable additive homomorphic secret sharing* (VAHSS) to solve this problem. Our instantiations combine an *additive homomorphic secret sharing* (HSS) scheme, which relies on Shamir's secret sharing scheme over a finite field $\mathbb{F}$, for computing the sum of the clients' secret inputs, and three different methods for achieving *public verifiability*. More precisely, we employ: *(i)* homomorphic collision-resistant hash functions; *(ii)* linear homomorphic signatures; as well as *(iii)* a threshold RSA signature scheme. In all three cases we provide a detailed correctness, security and verifiability analysis and discuss their efficiency.

Keywords: Function secret sharing · Homomorphic secret sharing · Verifiable computation · Public verifiability

1 Introduction

The emergence of communication technologies is changing the way data are stored, processed and used. Data collected from multiple, often resource-constrained devices are stored and processed by remote, untrusted (cloud) servers and subsequently, used by third parties (*e.g.*, electricity companies, doctors, researchers). Furthermore, many applications involve joint computations on data collected from multiple clients (*e.g.*, compute statistics on electricity consumption via smart metering, measure emissions via environmental sensors or even e-voting systems). To avoid single points of failure, multiple servers can be recruited to perform joint computations for multiple clients. Although this distributed cloud-assisted environment is very attractive and has tremendous advantages, it is accompanied by serious *security* and *privacy* challenges.

© Springer Nature Switzerland AG 2020
J. H. Seo (Ed.): ICISC 2019, LNCS 11975, pp. 115–132, 2020.
https://doi.org/10.1007/978-3-030-40921-0_7

In such settings, it is often desirable to solve the cloud-assisted computing problem described by the following constraints: *(i)* n clients want to outsource their joint computations on their joint inputs to multiple servers; *(ii)* the clients want to keep their individual values secret; *(iii)* the servers are untrusted; *(iv)* the clients cannot communicate with each other; and *(v)* everyone should be able to verify the correctness of the computed result (*i.e., public verifiability*). Let us consider that n clients (as depicted in Fig. 1), with n individual secret inputs $x_1, x_2, \ldots x_n$, want to outsource the joint computation of a function on their joint inputs $f(x_1, x_2, \ldots, x_n)$. Tsaloli *et al.* [16] addressed the problem of computing the joint multiplications of n inputs corresponding to n clients and introduced the concept of *verifiable homomorphic secret sharing* (VHSS). More precisely, VHSS allows to split n secret inputs into m shares and perform the joint computation of a function $f(x_1, x_2, \ldots, x_n) = y$, without any communication between the clients; while also providing a proof π that allows the *public verification* of the computed result, *i.e.*, having access to the pair (y, π) *anyone* can verify that the computed result is correct. However, the possibility to achieve verifiable homomorphic secret sharing for other functions has been left open.

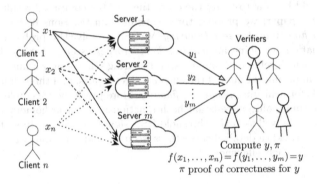

Fig. 1. n clients outsourcing the joint computation of their joint inputs to m servers.

In this paper, we revisit the concept of *verifiable homomorphic secret sharing* (VHSS) and we investigate whether it is possible to achieve *verifiable additive homomorphic secret sharing*. The answer is affirmative and we introduce three constructions that can be employed in order to compute securely and privately the joint addition of n inputs from n clients by employing m servers, while also providing *public verifiability*. These constructions can be useful, for instance, when statistics need to be computed about electricity consumption with data collected from multiple users, or when collecting data for remote monitoring and diagnosis from multiple patients, as well as when data from environmental sensors (*e.g.*, temperature, humidity) are collected from multiple sensors.

Our Contributions. We focus on the problem of outsourcing joint *additions*, while providing strong security and privacy guarantees when: *(i)* multiple clients outsource joint additions on their joint secret inputs; *(ii)* multiple untrusted servers are employed for the computation; and *(iii)* anyone can verify that the output of the computation is correct. We propose for the first time three different instantiations of *verifiable additive homomorphic secret sharing* (VAHSS).

We discriminate three different cases of VAHSS depending on the employed primitive (homomorphic hash functions, linearly homomorphic signatures and threshold signatures) as well as whether the partial proofs (used in order to check the correctness of the computed result) are computed by either the clients or the servers. Furthermore, we have modified the original VHSS definition in order to capture the different cases regarding the generation of the proofs; thus, allowing the employment of VHSS in multiple application settings.

Our constructions rely on casting Shamir's secret sharing scheme over a finite field $\mathbb{F}$ as an n-client, m-server, t-perfectly secure additive *homomorphic secret sharing* (HSS) for the function that sums n field elements. Such an additive HSS exists, if and only if $m > n \cdot t$. By employing the additive HSS in combination with homomorphic collision-resistant hash functions [13,17], we provide an instantiation, where the partial proofs are computed by the servers. Subsequently, we combine the additive HSS with a linearly homomorphic signature scheme [10], or a threshold RSA signature scheme [8] to obtain two different instantiations of VAHSS depending on whether the partial proofs are computed by the clients or by a subset of the servers correspondingly. In all three cases, we provide a detailed correctness, security and verifiability analysis.

1.1   Related Work

Homomorphic Secret Sharing. In threshold secret sharing schemes [15] a secret x is split into multiple shares (*e.g.*, $x_1, x_2, \ldots, x_m$) in such a way that by combining some subsets of the shares, it is possible to reconstruct the secret, while from smaller subsets of the shares, it is not possible to recover any information related to the secret. *Homomorphic secret sharing* (HSS) [7] can be seen as the secret sharing analogue of homomorphic encryption. More precisely, HSS allows the local evaluation of functions on shares on one or more secret inputs by relying on local computations on the shares of the secrets; while at the same time guaranteeing that the shares of the output are short. The first instance of additive HSS considered in the literature [3] is computed in some finite Abelian group. However, HSS does not provide any verifiability guarantees about the computed result.

Verifiable Function Secret Sharing. *Function secret sharing* (FSS) [5] can be seen as a natural generalization of distributed point functions (DPF) and provides a method for additively secret sharing a function f from a given function family $\mathcal{F}$. In FSS a function f is split into m functions $f_1, \ldots, f_m$, described by the corresponding keys $k_1, \ldots, k_m$ such that for any input x it holds $f(x) = f_1(x) + \ldots + f_m(x)$. Boyle *et al.* introduced the concept of *verifiable* FSS (VFSS) [6], which provides interactive protocols to verify that keys $(k_1^*, \ldots, k_m^*)$, obtained from a potentially malicious user, are consistent with some $f \in \mathcal{F}$. However, Boyle *et al.*'s VFSS applies in the setting of one client and multiple servers. On the contrary, VHSS can be applied when multiple clients (multi-input) outsource the joint computation to multiple servers. In addition, VFSS focuses on verifying that the shares $f_1, \ldots, f_m$ are consistent with f; while VHSS generates a proof that guarantees that the final result is correct.

Publicly Auditable Secure Multi-party Computation. Outsourcing computations is inherently connected to secure multi-party computation (MPC) protocols. In MPC [4,11,12], the public verifiability is traditionally achieved by employing non-interactive zero-knowledge (NIZK) proofs. Baum *et al.* [1] introduced the notion of *publicly auditable* MPC protocols that are suitable for the multi-client and multi-server setting. Publicly auditable MPC can be seen as an extension of the classic formalization of secure function evaluation; it relies on the SPDZ protocol [11,12] and NIZK proofs, while it enhances each shared input x with a Pedersen commitment. Baum *et al.* [1] require correctness and privacy, when there is at least one honest party, while everyone having access to the transcript of the protocol (published in a bulletin board) can verify the correctness of the computed result. We should note that *publicly auditable* MPC protocols are very expressive regarding the class of functions being computed, but often require heavy computations. To formalize auditable MPC an extra *non-corruptible* party is introduced in the standard MPC model, namely the *auditor*. On the contrary, in VAHSS, no additional non-corruptible party is required, while we avoid the employment of expensive cryptographic operations and primitives such as NIZK.

Organization. The paper is organized as follows. In Sect. 2, we provide the modified definition of verifiable homomorphic secret sharing (VHSS). In Sect. 3, we introduce three verifiable additive homomorphic secret sharing (VAHSS) constructions using homomorphic hash functions, linearly homomorphic signatures and a threshold signature scheme respectively. In all three proposed instantiations, we provide the corresponding correctness, security and verifiability proofs. Finally, Sect. 4 summarizes the paper.

2   Preliminaries

Our concrete instantiations for the additive VHSS problem are based on the VHSS definition proposed in [16]. However, we propose a slightly modified version of the VHSS definition to capture cases when partial proofs (used to verify the correctness of the final result) are computed either from the clients or the servers. We added the **Setup** algorithm to allow the generation of keys and we modified the **PartialProof** algorithm accordingly to allow the different scenarios.

Definition 1 (Verifiable Homomorphic Secret Sharing (VHSS)). *An n-client, m-server, t-secure verifiable homomorphic secret sharing scheme for a* *function* $f : \mathcal{X} \mapsto \mathcal{Y}$, *is a 7-tuple of PPT algorithms (**Setup, ShareSecret, PartialEval, PartialProof, FinalEval, FinalProof, Verify**) which are defined as follows:*

- $(pp, sk) \leftarrow$ ***Setup**(1^λ): On input 1^λ, where λ is the security parameter, the algorithm outputs a secret key sk and some public parameters pp.*
- $(\mathsf{share}_{i1}, \ldots, \mathsf{share}_{im}, \tau_i) \leftarrow$ ***ShareSecret**$(1^\lambda, i, \boldsymbol{x}_i)$: The algorithm takes as input 1^λ, $i \in \{1, \ldots, n\}$ which is the index for the client c_i and $\boldsymbol{x}_i$ which denotes a vector of one (i.e., $x_i \in \mathcal{X}$) or more secret values that belong to each client and should be split into shares. The algorithm outputs m shares share_{ij} (denoted also by $x_{ij} \in \mathcal{X}$ when $\boldsymbol{x}_i = x_i$) for each server s_j, as well as, if necessary, a publicly available value $\tau_i{}^1$ related to the secret x_i.*
- $y_j \leftarrow$ ***PartialEval**$(j, (x_{1j}, x_{2j}, \ldots, x_{nj}))$: On input $j \in \{1, \ldots, m\}$ which denotes the index of the server s_j, and $x_{1j}, x_{2j}, \ldots, x_{nj}$ which are the shares of the n secret inputs $x_1, \ldots, x_n$ that the server s_j has, the algorithm **PartialEval** outputs $y_j \in \mathcal{Y}$.*
- $\sigma_k \leftarrow$ ***PartialProof**$(sk, pp, secret_{values}, k)$: On input the secret key sk, public parameters pp, secret values (based on which the partial proofs are generated), denoted by $secret_{values}$; and the corresponding index k (where k is either i or j), a partial proof σ_k is computed.*
- $y \leftarrow$ ***FinalEval**$(y_1, y_2, \ldots, y_m)$: On input $y_1, y_2, \ldots, y_m$ which are the shares of $f(x_1, x_2, \ldots, x_n)$ that the m servers compute, the algorithm **FinalEval** outputs y, the final result for $f(x_1, x_2, \ldots, x_n)$.*
- $\sigma \leftarrow$ ***FinalProof**$(pp, \sigma_1, \ldots, \sigma_{|k|})$: On input public parameters pp and the partial proofs $\sigma_1, \sigma_2, \ldots, \sigma_{|k|}$, the algorithm **FinalProof** outputs σ which is the proof that y is the correct value.*
- $0/1 \leftarrow$ ***Verify**(pp, σ, y): On input the final result y, the proof σ, and, when needed, public parameters pp, the algorithm **Verify** outputs either 0 or 1.*

Correctness, Security, Verifiability. The algorithms (**Setup, ShareSecret, PartialEval, PartialProof, FinalEval, FinalProof, Verify**) should satisfy the following correctness, verifiability and security requirements:

- **Correctness:** For any secret input $x_1, \ldots, x_n$, for all m-tuples in the set $\{(\mathsf{share}_{i1}, \ldots, \mathsf{share}_{im}), \tau_i\}_{i=1}^n$ coming from **ShareSecret**, for all $y_1, \ldots, y_m$ computed by **PartialEval**, $\sigma_1, \ldots, \sigma_{|k|}$ computed from **PartialProof**, and for y and σ generated by **FinalEval** and **FinalProof** respectively, the scheme should satisfy the following correctness requirement:

$$\Pr\left[\mathbf{Verify}(pp, \sigma, y) = 1 \right] = 1.$$

- **Verifiability:** Let T be the set of corrupted servers with $|T| \leqslant m$. Denote by $\mathcal{A}$ any PPT adversary and consider n secret inputs $x_1, \ldots, x_n \in \mathbb{F}$. Any PPT adversary $\mathcal{A}$ who controls the shares of the secret inputs for any j such that $s_j \in T$, can cause a wrong value to be accepted as $f(x_1, x_2, \ldots, x_n)$ with negligible probability. We define the following experiment $\mathbf{Exp}_{\mathrm{VHSS}}^{\mathrm{Verif.}}(x_1, \ldots, x_n, T, \mathcal{A})$:

---

1 τ_i, when computed, can be included in the list of public parameters pp.

1. For all $i \in \{1, \ldots, n\}$, generate $(\text{share}_{i1}, \ldots, \text{share}_{im}, \tau_i) \leftarrow$ **ShareSecret**$(1^\lambda, i, x_i)$ and publish τ_i.

2. For all j such that $s_j \in T$, give $\begin{pmatrix} \text{share}_{1j} \\ \text{share}_{2j} \\ \vdots \\ \text{share}_{nj} \end{pmatrix}$ to the adversary.

3. For the corrupted servers $s_j \in T$, the adversary $\mathcal{A}$ outputs modified shares y_j' and σ_k'. Then, for j such that $s_j \notin T$, we set $y_j' = $ **PartialEval**$(j, (x_{1j}, \ldots, x_{nj}))$ and $\sigma_k' = $ **PartialProof**$(sk, pp, \text{secret}_{\text{values}}, k)$. Note that we consider modified σ_k' only when computed by the servers.

4. Compute the modified final value $y' = $ **FinalEval**$(y_1', y_2', \ldots, y_m')$ and the modified final proof $\sigma' = $ **FinalProof**$(pp, \sigma_1', \ldots, \sigma_{|k|}')$.

5. If $y' \neq f(x_1, x_2, \ldots, x_n)$ and **Verify**$(pp, \sigma', y') = 1$, then output 1 else 0.

We require that for any n secret inputs $x_1, x_2, \ldots, x_n \in \mathbb{F}$, any set T of corrupted servers and any PPT adversary $\mathcal{A}$ it holds:

$$\Pr[\mathbf{Exp}_{\text{VHSS}}^{\text{Verif.}}(x_1, x_2, \ldots, x_n, T, \mathcal{A}) = 1] \leq \varepsilon, \text{for some negligible } \varepsilon.$$

- **Security:** Let T be the set of the corrupted servers with $|T| < m$. Consider the following semantic security challenge experiment:

  1. The adversary $\mathcal{A}_1$ gives $(i, x_i, x_i') \leftarrow \mathcal{A}_1(1^\lambda)$ to the challenger, where $i \in [n]$, $x_i \neq x_i'$ and $|x_i| = |x_i'|$.

  2. The challenger picks a bit $b \in \{0, 1\}$ uniformly at random and computes $(\widehat{\text{share}}_{i1}, \ldots, \widehat{\text{share}}_{im}, \widehat{\tau}_i) \leftarrow$ **ShareSecret**$(1^\lambda, i, \hat{x}_i)$ where the secret input $\hat{x}_i = \begin{cases} x_i, \text{if } b = 0 \\ x_i', \text{otherwise} \end{cases}$.

  3. Given the shares from the corrupted servers T and $\widehat{\tau}_i$, the adversary distinguisher outputs a guess $b' \leftarrow \mathcal{D}((\widehat{\text{share}}_{ij})_{j|s_j \in T}, \widehat{\tau}_i)$.

  Let $\text{Adv}(1^\lambda, \mathcal{A}, T) := \Pr[b = b'] - 1/2$ be the advantage of $\mathcal{A} = \{\mathcal{A}_1, \mathcal{D}\}$ in guessing b in the above experiment, where the probability is taken over the randomness of the challenger and of $\mathcal{A}$. A VHSS scheme is t-secure if for all $T \subset \{s_1, \ldots, s_m\}$ with $|T| \leq t$, and all PPT adversaries $\mathcal{A}$, it holds that $\text{Adv}(1^\lambda, \mathcal{A}, T) \leq \varepsilon(\lambda)$ for some negligible $\varepsilon(\lambda)$.

In our solution, we employ a simple variant of the (Strong) RSA based signature introduced by Catalano *et al.* [9], which can be seen as a linearly homomorphic signature scheme on $\mathbb{Z}_N$.

Definition 2 (Linearly Homomorphic Signature [10]). *A linearly homomorphic signature scheme is a tuple of PPT algorithms (**HKeyGen, HSign, HVerify, HEval**) defined as follows:*

- *HKeyGen$(1^\lambda, k)$ takes as input the security parameter λ and an upper bound k for the number of messages that can be signed in each dataset. It outputs a secret signing key sk and a public key vk. The public key defines a message space M, a signature space S, and a set $\mathcal{F}$ of admissible linear functions such that any $f : M^n \mapsto M$ is linear.*

- **HSign**(sk, fid, m_i, i) algorithm takes as input the secret key sk, a dataset identifier fid, and the i-th message m_i to be signed, and outputs a signature σ_i.
- **HVerify**(vk, fid, m, σ, f) algorithm takes as input the verification key vk, a dataset identifier fid, a message m, a signature σ and a function f. It outputs either 1 if the signature corresponds to the message m or 0 otherwise.
- **HEval**$(vk, fid, f, \sigma_1, \ldots, \sigma_n)$ algorithm takes as input the verification key vk, a dataset identifier fid, a function $f \in \mathcal{F}$, and a tuple of signatures $\sigma_1, \ldots, \sigma_n$. It outputs a new signature σ.

We use homomorphic hash functions in order to achieve verifiability. Below, we provide the definition of such a function. More precisely, we employ a homomorphic hash function satisfying additive homomorphism [13].

Definition 3 (Homomorphic Hash Function [17]). *A homomorphic hash function* $h : \mathbb{F}_N \mapsto \mathbb{G}_q$, *where* $\mathbb{F}$ *is a finite field and* $\mathbb{G}$ *is a multiplicative group of prime order* q, *is defined as a collision-resistant hash function satisfying the homomorphism in addition to the properties of a universal hash function* $uh : (0, 1)^* \mapsto (0, 1)^l$.

1. *One-way: It is computationally hard to compute* $h^{-1}(x)$.
2. *Collision-free: It is computationally hard to find* $x, y \in \mathbb{F}^N (x \neq y)$ *such that* $h(x) = h(y)$.
3. *Homomorphism: For any* $x, y \in \mathbb{F}^N$, *it holds* $h(x \circ y) = h(x) \circ h(y)$ *where* "$\circ$" *is either* "+" *or* "·".

For completeness, we also provide the definition of a secure pseudorandom function PRF.

Definition 4 (Pseudorandom Function (PRF)). *Let* S *be a distribution over* $\{0, 1\}^\ell$ *and* $F_s : \{0, 1\}^m \to \{0, 1\}^n$ *be a family of functions indexed by strings* s *in the support of* S. *We say* $\{F_s\}$ *is a pseudorandom function family if for every PPT adversary* D, *there exists a negligible function* ϵ *such that:*

$$|\Pr[D^{F_s}(\cdot) = 1] - \Pr[D^R(\cdot) = 1]| \leq \epsilon,$$

where s *is distributed according to* S, *and* R *is a function sampled uniformly at random from the set of all functions from* $\{0, 1\}^m$ *to* $\{0, 1\}^n$.

3   Verifiable Additive Homomorphic Secret Sharing

In this section, we present three different instantiations to achieve *verifiable additive homomorphic secret sharing* (VAHSS). More precisely, we consider n clients with their secret values $x_1, \ldots, x_n$ respectively, and m servers $s_1, \ldots, s_m$ that perform computations on shares of these secret values. Firstly, the clients split their secret values into shares, that reveal nothing about the secret value itself and then, they distribute the shares to each of the m servers. Each server performs some calculations in order to publish a value, which is related to the final result $f(x_1, \ldots, x_n) = x_1 + \ldots + x_n$. Then, depending on the instantiation proposed, partial proofs are generated in a different way. The partial proofs are values such that their combination results in a final proof, which confirms the correctness of the final computed value $f(x_1, \ldots, x_n)$.

3.1 Construction of VAHSS Using Homomorphic Hash Functions

In this section, we aim to compute the function value y, which corresponds to $f(x_1, \ldots, x_n) = x_1 + \ldots + x_n$ as well as a proof σ that y is correct. We combine an additive HSS for the algorithms related to the value y and hash functions for the generation of the proof σ. Let $c_1, \ldots, c_n$ denote n clients and $x_1, \ldots, x_n$ their corresponding secret inputs. Let, for any $\{i\}_{i=1,\ldots,n}$, $\theta_{i1}, \ldots, \theta_{im}$ be distinct non-zero field elements and $\lambda_{i1}, \ldots, \lambda_{im}$ be field elements ("Lagrange coefficients") such that for any univariate polynomial p_i of degree t over a finite field $\mathbb{F} = \mathbb{F}_N$ we have:

$$p_i(0) = \sum_{j=1}^{m} \lambda_{ij} p_i(\theta_{ij}) \tag{1}$$

Each client c_i generates shares of the secret x_i, denoted by $x_{i1}, \ldots, x_{im}$ respectively, and gives the share x_{ij} to each server s_j. The servers, in turn, compute a partial sum, denoted by y_j, and publish it. Anyone can then compute $y = y_1 + \ldots + y_m$, which corresponds to the function value $y = f(x_1, \ldots, x_n) = x_1 + \ldots + x_n$. We suggest that every client c_i uses a homomorphic collision-resistant function $H : x \mapsto g^x$ proposed by Krohn et al. [13] to generate a public value τ_i which reveals nothing about x_i (under the discrete logarithm assumption). Then, the servers compute values $\sigma_1, \ldots, \sigma_m$ which will be appropriately combined so that they give the proof σ that we are interested in. The value y comes from the combination of partial values y_j, which are computed by the m servers. More precisely, our solution is composed of the following algorithms:

1. **ShareSecret**$(1^\lambda, i, x_i, file_i)$: For elements $\{a_i\}_{i \in \{1,\ldots,t\}} \in \mathbb{F}$ selected uniformly at random, pick a t-degree polynomial p_i of the form $p_i(X) = x_i + a_1 X + a_2 X^2 + \ldots + a_t X^t$ with $t \cdot n < m$. Notice that the free coefficient of p_i is the secret input x_i. Let $H : x \mapsto g^x$ (with g a generator of the multiplicative group of $\mathbb{F}$) be a collision-resistant homomorphic hash function [17]. Let R_i be the output of a pseudorandom function (PRF) $F : \{0,1\}^{l_1} \times \{0,1\}^{l_2} \mapsto \mathbb{F}$ where $R_i = F_k(i, file_i)$ for a key $k \in \{0,1\}^{l_1}$ given to the clients and an input $file_i$ associated with client i such that $(i, file_i) \in \{0,1\}^{l_2}$. For $i = n$ we require $\mathbb{F} \ni R_n = \phi(N) \lceil \frac{\sum_{i=1}^{n-1} R_i}{\phi(N)} \rceil - \sum_{i=1}^{n-1} R_i$. Then, compute $\tau_i = H(x_i + R_i)$, define $x_{ij} = \lambda_{ij} p_i(\theta_{ij})$ (given thanks to the Eq. (1)) and output $(x_{i1}, x_{i2}, \ldots, x_{im}, \tau_i) = (\lambda_{i1} \cdot p_i(\theta_{i1}), \ldots, \lambda_{im} \cdot p_i(\theta_{im}), H(x_i + R_i))$.

2. **PartialEval**$(j, (x_{1j}, x_{2j}, \ldots, x_{nj}))$: Given the j-th shares of the secret inputs, compute the sum of all $x_{ij} = \lambda_{ij} \cdot p_i(\theta_{ij})$ for the given j and $i \in [n]$. Output y_j with $y_j = \lambda_{1j} \cdot p_1(\theta_{1j}) + \ldots + \lambda_{nj} \cdot p_n(\theta_{nj}) = \sum_{i=1}^{n} \lambda_{ij} \cdot p_i(\theta_{ij})$.

3. **PartialProof**$(j, (x_{1j}, x_{2j}, \ldots, x_{nj}))$: Given the j-th shares of the secret inputs, compute and output the partial proof $\sigma_j = g^{\sum_{i=1}^{n} x_{ij}} = g^{y_j} = H(y_j)$.
4. **FinalEval**$(y_1, y_2, \ldots, y_m)$: Add the partial sums $y_1, \ldots, y_m$ together and output y (where $y = y_1 + \ldots + y_m$).
5. **FinalProof**$(\sigma_1, \ldots, \sigma_m)$: Given the partial proofs $\sigma_1, \sigma_2, \ldots, \sigma_m$, compute the final proof $\sigma = \prod_{j=1}^{m} \sigma_j$. Output σ.
6. **Verify**$(\tau_1, \ldots, \tau_n, \sigma, y)$: Check whether $\sigma = \prod_{i=1}^{n} \tau_i \wedge \prod_{i=1}^{n} \tau_i = H(y)$ holds. Output 1 if the check is satisfied or 0 otherwise.

Each client runs the **ShareSecret** algorithm to compute and distribute the shares of x_i to each of the m servers and a public value τ_i, which is needed for the verification. Then, each server s_j has the shares given from the n clients and runs the **PartialEval** algorithm to output the public values y_j related to the final function value. Furthermore, each server runs the **PartialProof** algorithm and produces the value σ_j. Finally, any user or verifier is able to run the **FinalEval** algorithm to get y and the **FinalProof** algorithm to get the proof σ. Lastly, **Verify** algorithm ensures that y and σ match and thus, $y = f(x_1, \ldots, x_n)$ is correct. Our construction is illustrated in the Table 1.

Table 1. VAHSS using homomorphic hash functions

Secret inputs (held by the clients)	Servers				Public values
	s_1	s_2	$\cdots$	s_m	
x_1	x_{11}	x_{12}	$\cdots$	x_{1m}	τ_1
x_2	x_{21}	x_{22}	$\cdots$	x_{2m}	τ_2
$\vdots$	$\vdots$	$\vdots$	$\vdots$	$\vdots$	$\vdots$
x_n	x_{n1}	x_{n2}	$\cdots$	x_{nm}	τ_n
Partial sums	y_1	y_2	$\cdots$	y_m	Total Sum: y
Partial proofs	σ_1	σ_2	$\cdots$	σ_m	Final Proof: σ

- **Correctness:** To prove the correctness of this construction, we need to prove that $\Pr\left[\mathbf{Verify}(\tau_1, \ldots, \tau_n, \sigma, y) = 1\right] = 1$. By construction it holds that:

$$y = \sum_{j=1}^{m} y_j = \sum_{j=1}^{m} \sum_{i=1}^{n} \lambda_{ij} \cdot p_i(\theta_{ij}) = \sum_{i=1}^{n} \sum_{j=1}^{m} \lambda_{ij} \cdot p_i(\theta_{ij}) = \sum_{i=1}^{n} p_i(0) = \sum_{i=1}^{n} x_i \tag{2}$$

Additionally, by construction, we have:

$$\sigma = \prod_{j=1}^{m} \sigma_j = \prod_{j=1}^{m} H(y_j) = \prod_{j=1}^{m} g^{y_j} = g^{\sum_{j=1}^{m} y_j} = g^y = H(y)$$

$$\text{and} \quad \prod_{i=1}^{n} \tau_i = \prod_{i=1}^{n} g^{x_i + R_i} = g^{\sum_{i=1}^{n} x_i} g^{\sum_{i=1}^{n} R_i} = g^{\sum_{i=1}^{n} x_i} g^{\sum_{i=1}^{n-1} R_i + R_n}$$

$$= g^{\sum_{i=1}^{n} x_i} g^{\phi(N) \lceil \frac{\sum_{i=1}^{n-1} R_i}{\phi(N)} \rceil} = g^{\sum_{i=1}^{n} x_i} = g^{x_1 + \dots + x_n} \tag{3}$$

$$\stackrel{see \ eq.(2)}{=} g^y = H(y)$$

Combining the last two results we get that $\sigma = \prod_{i=1}^{n} \tau_i \wedge \prod_{i=1}^{n} \tau_i = H(y)$ holds. Therefore, the algorithm **Verify** outputs 1 with probability 1.

- **Security:** See [2] for a proof that the selected hash function H of our construction is a secure collision-resistant hash function under the discrete logarithm assumption.
  We will now prove that $\text{Adv}(1^\lambda, \mathcal{A}, T) \leq \varepsilon(\lambda)$ for some negligible $\varepsilon(\lambda)$.

Proof. **Game 0:** Consider $m - 1$ corrupted servers. Then, $|T| = m - 1$. Without loss of generality, let the first $m - 1$ servers be the corrupted ones. Therefore, the adversary $\mathcal{A}$ has $(m - 1)n$ shares from the corrupted servers and no additional information.

For any fixed i with $i \in \{1, \dots, n\}$, it holds that $\sum_{j=1}^{m} \widehat{\text{share}}_{ij} = \hat{x}_i$ and hence:

$$\sum_{j=1}^{m-1} \widehat{\text{share}}_{ij} + \widehat{\text{share}}_{im} = \hat{x}_i \iff \widehat{\text{share}}_{im} = \hat{x}_i - \sum_{j=1}^{m-1} \widehat{\text{share}}_{ij}$$

The adversary holds $\sum_{j=1}^{m-1} \widehat{\text{share}}_{ij}$. Furthermore, the adversary holds the public value $\hat{\tau}_i = g^{\hat{x}_i + R_i}$. Since R_i is the output of a PRF then $\hat{\tau}_i$ is also a pseudorandom value.

Game 1: Consider that the adversary holds the same shares $\sum_{j=1}^{m-1} \widehat{\text{share}}_{ij}$ and $\hat{\tau}_i$ is now a truly random value.

Firstly, $\widehat{\text{share}}_{im} \in \mathcal{Y}$ is just a value, which implies nothing to the adversary regarding whether it is related to x_i or x_i'. Moreover, **Game 0** and **Game 1** are computationally indistinguishable due to the security of the PRF. Thus, any PPT adversary has probability $1/2$ to decide whether $\hat{x}_i$ is x_i or x_i' and so, $\text{Adv}(1^\lambda, \mathcal{A}, T) \leq \varepsilon(\lambda)$ for some negligible $\varepsilon(\lambda)$.

- **Verifiability:** In this construction, for $y = x_1 + x_2 + \dots + x_n$, if $y' \neq x_1 + \dots + x_n$ and **Verify**$(\tau_1, \dots, \tau_n, \sigma', y') = 1$, then the verifiability follows:

$$\textbf{Verify}(\tau_1, \dots, \tau_n, \sigma', y') = 1 \Rightarrow \sigma' = \prod_{i=1}^{n} \tau_i \wedge \prod_{i=1}^{n} \tau_i = H(y')$$

$$\Rightarrow \prod_{i=1}^{n} \tau_i = H(y') \quad (\text{see Eq. 3}) \Rightarrow H(y) = H(y')$$

which is a contradiction since $y \neq y'$ and H is collision-resistant. Therefore,

$$\Pr[\textbf{Exp}_{\text{VHSS}}^{\text{Verif.}}(x_1, \dots, x_n, T, \mathcal{A}) = 1] \leq \varepsilon, \text{ as desired.}$$

3.2   Construction of VAHSS with Linear Homomorphic Signatures

Our goal is always to compute $f(x_1, \ldots, x_n) = x_1 + \ldots + x_n = y$ as well as a proof σ that y is correct. We compute y using additive HSS and we employ a linearly homomorphic signature scheme, presented in [10] as a simple variant of Catalano et al.'s [9] signature scheme, for the generation of the proof. All clients hold the same signing and verification key. This could be the case if the clients are sensors of a company collecting information (e.g., temperature, humidity) useful for some calculations. Since the sensors/clients belong to the same company, sharing the same key might be necessary to facilitate configuration. In applications scenarios where clients should be set up with different keys, a multi-key scheme [14] could be used. However, in our construction, the clients can use the same signing key to sign their own secret value. In fact, they sign $x_{i,R}$ where $x_{i,R} = x_i + R_i$ with R_i chosen from each client as described in the Sect. 3.1. The signatures, denoted by $\sigma_1, \ldots, \sigma_n$ are public and combined they form a final signature σ, which verifies the correctness of y. Our instantiation constitutes of the following algorithms:

1. **Setup**$(1^k, N)$: Let N be the product of two safe primes each one of length $k'/2$. This algorithm chooses two random (safe) primes $\hat{p}, \hat{q}$ each one of length $k/2$ such that $\gcd(N, \phi(\hat{N})) = 1$ with $\hat{N} = \hat{p} \cdot \hat{q}$. Subsequently, the algorithm chooses $g, g_1, h_1, \ldots, h_n$ in $\mathbb{Z}_{\hat{N}}^*$ at random. Then, it chooses some (efficiently computable) injective function $H : \{0,1\}^* \mapsto \{0,1\}^l$ with $l < k'/2$. It outputs the public key $vk = (N, H, \hat{N}, g, g_1, h_1, \ldots, h_n)$ to be used by any verifier; and the secret key $sk = (\hat{p}, \hat{q})$ to be used for signing the secret values.

2. **ShareSecret**$(1^\lambda, i, x_i)$: For elements $\{a_i\}_{i \in \{1, \ldots, t\}} \in \mathbb{F}$ selected uniformly at random, pick a t-degree polynomial p_i of the form $p_i(X) = x_i + a_1 X + a_2 X^2 + \ldots + a_t X^t$ with $t \cdot n < m$. Notice that the free coefficient of p_i is the secret input x_i. Then, define $x_{ij} = \lambda_{ij} p_i(\theta_{ij})$ (given using the equation (1)) and output $(x_{i1}, x_{i2}, \ldots, x_{im}) = \lambda_{i1} \cdot p_i(\theta_{i1}), \lambda_{i2} \cdot p_i(\theta_{i2}), \ldots, \lambda_{im} \cdot p_i(\theta_{im}))$.

3. **PartialEval**$(j, (x_{1j}, x_{2j}, \ldots, x_{nj}))$: Given the j-th shares of the secret inputs, compute the sum of all $x_{ij} = \lambda_{ij} \cdot p_i(\theta_{ij})$ for the given j and $i \in [n]$. Output y_j with $y_j = \lambda_{1j} \cdot p_1(\theta_{1j}) + \ldots + \lambda_{nj} \cdot p_n(\theta_{nj}) = \sum_{i=1}^n \lambda_{ij} \cdot p_i(\theta_{ij})$.

4. **PartialProof**$(sk, vk, fid, x_{i,R}, i)$: Parse the verification key vk to get N, H, $\hat{N}, g, g_1$ and $h_1, \ldots, h_n$. For the (efficiently computable) injective function H that is chosen from **Setup**, map fid to a prime: $H(fid) \mapsto e$. We denote the i-th vector of the canonical basis on $\mathbb{Z}^n$ by e_i. Choose random elements s_i and solve, using the knowledge for $\hat{p}$ and $\hat{q}$, the equation: $x^{eN} = g^{s_i} \prod_{j=1}^n h_j^{f_j^{(i)}} g_1^{x_{i,R}} \mod \hat{N}$ where $f_j^{(i)}$ denotes the j-th coordinate of the vector $f^{(i)}$. Notice that for our function e_i, the equation becomes $x^{eN} = g^{s_i} h_i g_1^{x_{i,R}} \mod \hat{N}$. Set $\tilde{x}_i = x$. Output σ_i, where $\sigma_i = (e, s_i, fid, \tilde{x}_i)$ is the signature for x_i w.r.t. the function $f^{(i)} = e_i$.

5. **FinalEval**$(y_1, y_2, \ldots, y_m)$: Add the partial sums $y_1, \ldots, y_m$ together and output y (where $y = y_1 + \ldots + y_m$).

6. **FinalProof**$(vk, \hat{f}, \sigma_1, \sigma_2, \ldots, \sigma_n)$: Given the public verification key vk, the signatures $\sigma_1, \ldots, \sigma_n$, let $\hat{f} = (\alpha_1, \ldots, \alpha_n)$. Define $f' = (\sum_{i=1}^n \alpha_i f^{(i)} - f)/eN$ where $f = \sum_{i=1}^n \alpha_i f^{(i)} \mod eN$. Set $s = \sum_{i=1}^n \alpha_i s_i \mod eN$,

$s' = (\sum_{i=1}^{n} \alpha_i s_i - s)/eN$ and $\widetilde{x} = \frac{\prod_{i=1}^{n} \widetilde{x}_i^{\alpha_i}}{g^{s'} \prod_{j=1}^{n} h_j^{f_j'}}$ mod $\hat{N}$. For $\hat{f} = (1, \ldots, 1)$,

compute $\widetilde{x} = \frac{\prod_{i=1}^{n} \widetilde{x}_i}{g^{s'} \prod_{j=1}^{n} h_j^{f_j'}}$ mod $\hat{N}$. Output σ where $\sigma = (e, s, fid, \widetilde{x})$.

7. **Verify**(vk, f, σ, y): Compute $e = H(fid)$. Check that $y, s \in \mathbb{Z}_{eN}$ and $\widetilde{x}^{eN} = g^s \prod_{j=1}^{n} h_j^{f_j f_j} g_1^y$ holds. Output: 1 if all checks are satisfied or 0 otherwise.

All n clients get the secret key sk from **Setup** and hold their secret value $x_1, \ldots, x_n$ respectively. Each client runs **ShareSecret** to split its secret value x_i into m shares and **PartialProof** to produce the partial signature (for the secret x_i) σ_i. The values σ_i's are not generated by the servers; since in that case, malicious compromised servers would not be detected. Then, each client distributes the shares to each of the m servers and publishes σ_i. Each server s_j computes and publishes the partial function value y_j by running **PartialEval**. Any verifier is able to get the function value $y = f(x_1, \ldots, x_n)$ from the **FinalEval** and the proof σ from the **FinalProof**. The **Verify** algorithm outputs 1 if and only if $y = x_1 + \ldots + x_n$. An illustration of our solution is reported in the Table 2.

Table 2. VAHSS using linear homomorphic signatures

Secret inputs (held by the clients)	Servers				Public values
	s_1	s_2	$\cdots$	s_m	vk
x_1, sk	x_{11}	x_{12}	$\cdots$	x_{1m}	σ_1
x_2, sk	x_{21}	x_{22}	$\cdots$	x_{2m}	σ_2
$\vdots$	$\vdots$	$\vdots$	$\vdots$	$\vdots$	$\vdots$
x_n, sk	x_{n1}	x_{n2}	$\cdots$	x_{nm}	σ_n
Partial sums (public)	y_1	y_2	$\cdots$	y_m	Final proof (public)
Total sum (public)	y				σ

- **Correctness:** To prove the correctness of our construction we need to prove that $\Pr\left[\textbf{Verify}(vk, f, \sigma, y) = 1\right] = 1$. It holds that:

$$\widetilde{x}^{eN} = \left(\frac{\prod_{i=1}^{n} \widetilde{x}_i}{g^{s'} \prod_{j=1}^{n} h_j^{f_j'}}\right)^{eN} = \frac{\prod_{i=1}^{n} \widetilde{x}_i^{eN}}{g^{s'eN} \prod_{i=1}^{n} h_j^{f_j'eN}} = \frac{\prod_{i=1}^{n} (g^{s_i} \prod_{j=1}^{n} h_j^{f_j^{(i)}} g_1^{x_{i,R}})}{g^{s'eN} \prod_{i=1}^{n} h_j^{f_j'eN}}$$

$$= \frac{g^{\sum_{i=1}^{n} s_i}}{g^{s'eN}} \cdot \frac{\prod_{i=1}^{n} \prod_{j=1}^{n} h_j^{f_j^{(i)}}}{\prod_{i=1}^{n} h_j^{f_j'eN}} \cdot g_1^{\sum_{i=1}^{n} x_{i,R}}$$

$$= \frac{g^{\sum_{i=1}^{n} s_i}}{g^{s'eN}} \cdot \frac{\prod_{i=1}^{n} \prod_{j=1}^{n} h_j^{f_j^{(i)}}}{\prod_{i=1}^{n} h_j^{f_j'eN}} \cdot g_1^{\sum_{i=1}^{n} x_i} \cdot g_1^{\sum_{i=1}^{n} R_i}$$

$$\stackrel{see \ eq.(3)}{=} g^{\sum_{i=1}^{n} s_i - s'eN} \prod_{j=1}^{n} h_j^{\sum_{i=1}^{n} f_j^{(i)} - f_j'eN} g_1^{\sum_{i=1}^{n} x_i} = g^s \prod_{j=1}^{n} h_j^{f_j} g_1^{\sum_{i=1}^{n} x_i}$$

(4)

Thanks to the equation (2), it also holds that $y = \sum_{i=1}^{n} x_i$. Then $\tilde{x}^{eN} = g^s \cdot \prod_{j=1}^{n} h_j{}^{f_j} \cdot g_1{}^y$ and thus, **Verify**$(vk, \sigma, y, f) = 1$ with probability 1.

- **Security:** The security of the signatures results easily from the original signature scheme proposed by Catalano et al. [9]. Moreover, $\mathrm{Adv}(1^\lambda, \mathcal{A}, T) \le \varepsilon(\lambda)$ for some negligible $\varepsilon(\lambda)$ as we have proven in the Sect. 3.1. We should note that, since in this construction no τ_i values are incorporated, the arguments related to the pseudorandomness of τ_i are not necessary.

- **Verifiability:** Verifiability is by construction straightforward since the final signature $\sigma \leftarrow$ **FinalProof**$(vk, \hat{f}, \sigma_1, \ldots, \sigma_n)$ is obtained using the correctly computed (by the clients) $\sigma_1, \ldots, \sigma_n$ and thus, $\sigma' = \sigma$ in this case. Therefore, if $y' \ne x_1 + \ldots + x_n$ while $y = x_1 + \ldots + x_n$ and **Verify**$(vk, \sigma', y', f) = 1$ then:

$$\textbf{Verify}(vk, \sigma', y', f) = 1 \Rightarrow \textbf{Verify}(vk, \sigma, y', f) = 1$$

$$\Rightarrow \tilde{x}^{eN} = g^s \prod_{j=1}^{n} h_j{}^{f_j} g_1{}^{y'} \text{ (see equation (4))}$$

$$\Rightarrow g^s \prod_{j=1}^{n} h_j{}^{f_j} g_1{}^{\sum_{i=1}^{n} x_i} = g^s \prod_{j=1}^{n} h_j{}^{f_j} g_1{}^{y'} \Rightarrow \sum_{i=1}^{n} x_i = y'$$

which is a contradiction!

Therefore, $\Pr[\textbf{Exp}_{\text{VHSS}}^{\text{Verif.}}(x_1, \ldots, x_n, T, \mathcal{A}) = 1] \le \varepsilon$.

3.3 Construction of VAHSS with Threshold Signature Sharing

We propose a scheme where the clients generate and distribute shares of their secret values to the m servers and the servers mutually produce shares of the final value y similarly to the previous constructions. However, in order to generate the proof σ that confirms the correctness of y, our scheme employs the (t, n)-threshold RSA signature scheme proposed in [8] so that a signature σ is successfully generated even if $t - 1$ servers are corrupted. Our proposed scheme (illustrated in the Table 3) acts in accordance with the following algorithms:

1. **Setup** $(1^k, N)$: Let $N = p \cdot q$ be the RSA modulus such that $p = 2p' + 1$ and $q = q' + 1$, where p', q' are large primes. Choose the public RSA key e_i such that $e_i \gg \binom{n}{t}$ and then, pick the private RSA key d_i so that $e_i d_i \equiv 1$ mod $(p'q')$. Output the public key e_i and the private key d_i.

2. **ShareSecret**$(1^\lambda, i, x_i, d_i, file_i)$: For elements $\{a_i\}_{i \in \{1, \ldots, t\}} \in \mathbb{F}$ selected uniformly at random, pick a t-degree polynomial p_i of the form $p_i(X) = x_i + a_1 X + a_2 X^2 + \ldots + a_t X^t$ with $t \cdot n < m$. Notice that the free coefficient of p_i is the secret input x_i. Then, define $x_{ij} = \lambda_{ij} p_i(\theta_{ij})$ (given thanks to the Eq. (1)). Let $\mathcal{A}_i$ be an $m \times t$ full-rank public matrix with elements from $\mathbb{F} = \mathbb{Z}_r{}^*$ for a prime r. Let $\boldsymbol{d} = (d_i, r_2, \ldots, r_t)^\mathsf{T}$ be a secret vector from $\mathbb{F}^t$, where d_i is the private RSA key and $r_2, \ldots, r_t \in \mathbb{F}$ are randomly chosen. Let a_{ij} be the entry at the i-th row and j-th column of the matrix $\mathcal{A}_i$. For all $j \in [m]$, set $\omega_{ij} = a_{j1} d_i + a_{j2} r_2 + \ldots + a_{jt} r_t \in \mathbb{F}$ to be the share generated from the client c_i for the server s_j. It is now formed an $m \times t$ system $\mathcal{A}_i \boldsymbol{d} = \boldsymbol{\omega}_i$.

Let $H : x_i \mapsto g^{x_i}$ (with g a generator of the multiplicative group of $\mathbb{F}$) be a collision-resistant homomorphic hash function [17]. Let R_i be randomly selected values as described in the Sect. 3.1. Output the public matrix $\mathcal{A}_i$, the (x_i's) shares $(x_{i1}, x_{i2}, \ldots, x_{im}) = \lambda_{i1} \cdot p_i(\theta_{i1}), \lambda_{i2} \cdot p_i(\theta_{i2}), \ldots, \lambda_{im} \cdot p_i(\theta_{im}))$, the shares of the private key $\omega_i = (\omega_{i1}, \ldots, \omega_{im})$ and $H(x_i + R_i)$.

3. **PartialEval**$(j, (x_{1j}, x_{2j}, \ldots, x_{nj}))$: Given the j-th shares of the secret inputs, compute the sum of all $x_{ij} = \lambda_{ij} \cdot p_i(\theta_{ij})$ for the given j and $i \in [n]$. Output y_j with $y_j = \lambda_{1j} \cdot p_1(\theta_{1j}) + \ldots + \lambda_{nj} \cdot p_n(\theta_{nj}) = \sum_{i=1}^{n} \lambda_{ij} \cdot p_i(\theta_{ij})$.

4. **PartialProof**$(\omega_1, \ldots, \omega_n, H(x_1 + R_1), \ldots, H(x_n + R_n), \mathcal{A}_1, \ldots, \mathcal{A}_n, N)$: For all $i \in [n]$ run the algorithm **PartialProof**$_i(\omega_i, H(x_i + R_i), \mathcal{A}_i, i, N)$ where:

   PartialProof$_i(\omega_i, H(x_i + R_i), \mathcal{A}_i, i, N)$: Let $S = \{s_1, s_2, \ldots, s_t\}$ be the coalition of t servers ($t < m$) (w.l.o.g. take the first t), forming the system $\mathcal{A}_{iS} d = \omega_{iS}$. Let the $t \times t$ adjugate matrix of $\mathcal{A}_{iS}$ be:

$$\mathcal{C}_{iS} = \begin{bmatrix} c_{11} & c_{21} & \cdots & c_{t1} \\ \vdots & \vdots & \ddots & \vdots \\ c_{1t} & c_{2t} & \cdots & c_{tt} \end{bmatrix}$$

   Denote the determinant of $\mathcal{A}_{iS}$ by Δ_{iS}. It holds that:

$$\mathcal{A}_{iS}\mathcal{C}_{iS} = \mathcal{C}_{iS}\mathcal{A}_{iS} = \Delta_{iS}\mathbb{I}_t \tag{5}$$

   where $\mathbb{I}_t$ stands for the $t \times t$ identity matrix. Compute the partial signature of x_i: $\sigma_{ij} = H(x_i + R_i)^{2c_{j1}\omega_{ij}} \mod N$. Output $\sigma_i = (\sigma_{i1}, \ldots, \sigma_{it})$.

   PartialProof outputs $\sigma_1, \ldots, \sigma_n$.

5. **FinalEval**$(y_1, y_2, \ldots, y_m)$: Add the partial sums $y_1, \ldots, y_m$ together and output y (where $y = y_1 + \ldots + y_m$).

6. **FinalProof**$(e_1, \ldots, e_n, H(x_1 + R_1), \ldots, H(x_n + R_n), \sigma_1, \ldots, \sigma_n, N)$: For all $i \in \{1, \ldots, n\}$ run the algorithm **FinalProof**$_i(e_i, H(x_i + R_i), \sigma_i, N)$ where:

   FinalProof$_i(e_i, H(x_i + R_i), \sigma_i, N)$: Combine the partial signatures by computing $\overline{\sigma}_i = \prod_{j \in S} \sigma_{ij} \mod N$. Compute $\sigma_i = \overline{\sigma}_i^{\alpha_i} H(x_i + R_i)^{\beta_i} \mod N$ with α_i, β_i integers such that

$$2\Delta_{iS}\alpha_i + e_i\beta_i = 1. \tag{6}$$

   Output σ_i, i.e., the signature that corresponds to the secret x_i.
   FinalProof outputs $\sigma = \prod_{i=1}^{n} \sigma_i^{e_i}$.

7. **Verify**$(H(x_1 + R_1), \ldots, H(x_n + R_n), \sigma, y)$: Check if $\sigma = \prod_{i=1}^{n} H(x_i + R_i) \wedge H(y) = \prod_{i=1}^{n} H(x_i + R_i)$ holds. Output 1 if the check is satisfied or 0 otherwise.

After the initialization with the **Setup**, each client c_i gets its public and private RSA keys, e_i and d_i respectively. Then, each c_i runs **ShareSecret** to compute and distribute the shares of x_i to each of the m servers, and form a public matrix

$\mathcal{A}_i$, shares of the private key $(\omega_{i1}, \ldots, \omega_{im})$ and the hash of the secret input and a randomly chosen value, $H(x_i + R_i)$, to be used for the signatures' generation. $H(x_i + R_i)$ is a publicly available value. Subsequently, each server runs **PartialEval** to generate public values y_j related to the final function value. A set of a coalition of the servers runs **PartialProof** and get the partial signatures. For instance, σ_1 is the vector that contains the partial signatures of x_1, σ_2 is the vector that contains the partial signatures of x_2 and so on. Anyone is able to run **FinalEval** to get y and **FinalProof** to get σ, which is the final signature that corresponds to the secret inputs $x_1, \ldots, x_n$. Finally, the **Verify** algorithm succeeds if and only if the final value y is correct.

Table 3. VAHSS with threshold signature sharing

Secret inputs (held by the clients)	Public values	Servers				
		s_1	s_2	$\cdots$	s_m	$\{s_{j_1}, \ldots, s_{j_t}\}$
x_1, d_1	$H(x_1 + R_1), e_1, \mathcal{A}_1$	x_{11}, ω_{11}	x_{12}, ω_{12}	$\cdots$	x_{1m}, ω_{1m}	σ_1
x_2, d_2	$H(x_2 + R_2), e_2, \mathcal{A}_2$	x_{21}, ω_{21}	x_{22}, ω_{22}	$\cdots$	x_{2m}, ω_{2m}	σ_2
$\vdots$	$\vdots$	$\vdots$	$\vdots$	$\vdots$	$\vdots$	$\vdots$
x_n, d_n	$H(x_n + R_n), e_n, \mathcal{A}_n$	x_{n1}, ω_{n1}	x_{n2}, ω_{n2}	$\cdots$	x_{nm}, ω_{nm}	σ_n
Partial sums (public)		y_1	y_2	$\cdots$	y_m	Final proof (public)
Total sum (public)		y				σ

- **Correctness:** To prove the correctness of our construction we need to prove that $\Pr\left[\textbf{Verify}(H(x_1 + R_1), \ldots, H(x_n + R_n), \sigma, y) = 1\right] = 1$. For convenience, here, denote $H(x_i + R_i)$ by H_i. By construction:

$$\sigma = \prod_{i=1}^{n} \sigma_i{}^{e_i} = \prod_{i=1}^{n} (\overline{\sigma_i}^{\alpha_i} H_i^{\beta_i})^{e_i} = \prod_{i=1}^{n} \left(\prod_{j \in S} \sigma_{ij}^{\alpha_i} H_i^{\beta_i}\right)^{e_i}$$

$$= \prod_{i=1}^{n} (H_i^{\beta_i} \prod_{j \in S} H_i^{2c_{j1}\omega_{ij}\alpha_i})^{e_i} = \prod_{i=1}^{n} H_i^{\beta_i e_i} H_i^{\sum_{j \in S} 2c_{j1}\omega_{ij}\alpha_i e_i}$$

$$\overset{see\ eq.(5)}{=} \prod_{i=1}^{n} H_i^{\beta_i e_i} H_i^{2\Delta_{iS} d_i \alpha_i e_i} = \prod_{i=1}^{n} H_i^{2\Delta_{iS}\alpha_i + \beta_i e_i} (\mod N)$$

$$\overset{see\ eq.(6)}{=} \prod_{i=1}^{n} H_i = \prod_{i=1}^{n} H(x_i + R_i) \text{ and also,}$$

$$\prod_{i=1}^{n} H(x_i + R_i) = \prod_{i=1}^{n} g^{x_i + R_i} \overset{see\ eq.(3)}{=} H(y) \qquad (7)$$

Therefore, **Verify**$(H(x_1 + R_1), \ldots, H(x_n + R_n), \sigma, y) = 1$ with probability 1, as desired.

- **Security:** The security of the signatures follows from the fact that the threshold signature scheme, which is employed in our construction, is secure, for $|T| \leq t - 1$, under the static adversary model given that the standard RSA signature scheme is secure [8]. Additionally, for $|T| \leq m - 1$, $\mathrm{Adv}(1^\lambda, \mathcal{A}, T) \leq \varepsilon(\lambda)$ for some negligible $\varepsilon(\lambda)$ as we have proven in the Sect. 3.1. Therefore, our construction is secure for $|T| \leq \min\{t - 1, m - 1\}$.

- **Verifiability:** For $\mathbf{Verify}(H(x_1 + R_1), \ldots, H(x_n + R_n), \sigma', y') = 1$ and $y' \neq y$ we have:

$$\mathbf{Verify}(H(x_1 + R_1), \ldots, H(x_n + R_n)), \sigma', y') = 1$$

$$\Rightarrow \sigma' = \prod_{i=1}^{n} H(x_i + R_i) \wedge H(y') = \prod_{i=1}^{n} H(x_i + R_i)$$

$$\Rightarrow H(y') = \prod_{i=1}^{n} H(x_i + R_i)(\text{see equation (7)}) \Rightarrow H(y') = H(y)$$

which is a contradiction! Thus,

$$\Pr[\mathbf{Exp}_{\mathrm{VHSS}}^{\mathrm{Verif.}}(x_1, \ldots, x_n, T, \mathcal{A}) = 1] \leq \varepsilon.$$

Table 4. Summary and comparison between the VAHSS proposed constructions.

Proposed construction	Cooperation between servers	Computations on client*
VAHSS with homomorphic hash functions	No	$(+)^{**} : 2m^2 + 3m + 1$, $(\times) : 2m^2 + 2m$ (Exp.): 1
VAHSS with linear homomorphic signatures	No	$(+)^{**} : 2m^2 + 3m + 1$, $(\times) : 2m^2 + 2m + 2$ (Exp.): 3
VAHSS with threshold signature sharing	Yes	$(+)^{**} : 2m^2 + 2m + mt + 1$, $(\times) : 2m^2 + 2m + mt$ (Exp.): 1

*(+), ($\times$), (Exp.) denote the number of additions, multiplications and exponentiations corresp.
**client n needs to perform $n - 1$ additional additions

4　Conclusion

In this paper, we addressed the problem of outsourcing joint additions, such that multiple clients give shares of their secret inputs to multiple untrusted servers. The latter perform the computations and then, anyone is able to ensure that the final output is correct (*i.e., public verifiability*). We instantiated three concrete constructions for the *verifiable additive homomorphic secret sharing* (VAHSS) problem by employing different cryptographic primitives and allowing the generation of the partial proofs by either the clients or the servers. In all three constructions, we achieved the property of public verifiability *i.e.,* anyone is able to confirm that the final result y is indeed the sum of the n secret inputs. In

Table 4, we provide a comparison of the proposed VAHSS constructions in terms of the employed primitives, the need for collaboration between the servers as well as the computation requirements on the client side. In all cases the computational cost required on the client side is rather similar *i.e.*, the computational complexity in all cases is $O(m^2)$ (where m denotes the number of servers) similarly to the complexity of a simple secret sharing scheme, while the one based on homomorphic hash functions seems to be slightly more lightweight. Our work is complementary to the multiplicative VHSS solution proposed by Tsaloli *et al.* [16]. The technique introduced in our constructions in order to randomize the τ_i values can also be incorporated in the multiplicative VHSS construction and, thus, provide better security guarantees.

Acknowledgement. This work was partially supported by the Wallenberg AI, Autonomous Systems and Software Program (WASP) funded by the Knut and Alice Wallenberg Foundation. We would also like to thank Daniel Slamanig and Bei Liang for the helpful comments and discussions.

References

1. Baum, C., Damgård, I., Orlandi, C.: Publicly auditable secure multi-party computation. In: Abdalla, M., De Prisco, R. (eds.) SCN 2014. LNCS, vol. 8642, pp. 175–196. Springer, Cham (2014). https://doi.org/10.1007/978-3-319-10879-7_11
2. Bellare, M., Goldreich, O., Goldwasser, S.: Incremental cryptography: the case of hashing and signing. In: Desmedt, Y.G. (ed.) CRYPTO 1994. LNCS, vol. 839, pp. 216–233. Springer, Heidelberg (1994). https://doi.org/10.1007/3-540-48658-5_22
3. Benaloh, J.C.: Secret sharing homomorphisms: keeping shares of a secret secret (extended abstract). In: Odlyzko, A.M. (ed.) CRYPTO 1986. LNCS, vol. 263, pp. 251–260. Springer, Heidelberg (1987). https://doi.org/10.1007/3-540-47721-7_19
4. Boyle, E., Garg, S., Jain, A., Kalai, Y.T., Sahai, A.: Secure computation against adaptive auxiliary information. In: Canetti, R., Garay, J.A. (eds.) CRYPTO 2013. LNCS, vol. 8042, pp. 316–334. Springer, Heidelberg (2013). https://doi.org/10.1007/978-3-642-40041-4_18
5. Boyle, E., Gilboa, N., Ishai, Y.: Function secret sharing. In: Oswald, E., Fischlin, M. (eds.) EUROCRYPT 2015. LNCS, vol. 9057, pp. 337–367. Springer, Heidelberg (2015). https://doi.org/10.1007/978-3-662-46803-6_12
6. Boyle, E., Gilboa, N., Ishai, Y.: Function secret sharing: improvements and extensions. In: Proceedings of the 2016 ACM SIGSAC Conference on Computer and Communications Security, pp. 1292–1303. ACM (2016)
7. Boyle, E., Gilboa, N., Ishai, Y.: Group-based secure computation: optimizing rounds, communication, and computation. In: Coron, J.-S., Nielsen, J.B. (eds.) EUROCRYPT 2017. LNCS, vol. 10211, pp. 163–193. Springer, Cham (2017). https://doi.org/10.1007/978-3-319-56614-6_6
8. Bozkurt, İ.N., Kaya, K., Selçuk, A.A.: Practical threshold signatures with linear secret sharing schemes. In: Preneel, B. (ed.) AFRICACRYPT 2009. LNCS, vol. 5580, pp. 167–178. Springer, Heidelberg (2009). https://doi.org/10.1007/978-3-642-02384-2_11
9. Catalano, D., Fiore, D., Warinschi, B.: Efficient network coding signatures in the standard model. In: Fischlin, M., Buchmann, J., Manulis, M. (eds.) PKC 2012.

LNCS, vol. 7293, pp. 680–696. Springer, Heidelberg (2012). https://doi.org/10.1007/978-3-642-30057-8_40

10. Catalano, D., Marcedone, A., Puglisi, O.: Authenticating computation on groups: new homomorphic primitives and applications. In: Sarkar, P., Iwata, T. (eds.) ASIACRYPT 2014. LNCS, vol. 8874, pp. 193–212. Springer, Heidelberg (2014). https://doi.org/10.1007/978-3-662-45608-8_11

11. Damgård, I., Keller, M., Larraia, E., Pastro, V., Scholl, P., Smart, N.P.: Practical covertly secure MPC for dishonest majority – or: breaking the SPDZ limits. In: Crampton, J., Jajodia, S., Mayes, K. (eds.) ESORICS 2013. LNCS, vol. 8134, pp. 1–18. Springer, Heidelberg (2013). https://doi.org/10.1007/978-3-642-40203-6_1

12. Damgård, I., Pastro, V., Smart, N., Zakarias, S.: Multiparty computation from somewhat homomorphic encryption. In: Safavi-Naini, R., Canetti, R. (eds.) CRYPTO 2012. LNCS, vol. 7417, pp. 643–662. Springer, Heidelberg (2012). https://doi.org/10.1007/978-3-642-32009-5_38

13. Krohn, M., Freedman, M., Mazieres, D.: On-the-fly verification of rateless erasure codes for efficient content distribution. In: 2004 Proceedings of the IEEE Symposium on Security and Privacy, Berkeley, CA, USA, pp. 226–240 (2004)

14. Schabhüser, L., Butin, D., Buchmann, J.: Context hiding multi-key linearly homomorphic authenticators. In: Matsui, M. (ed.) CT-RSA 2019. LNCS, vol. 11405, pp. 493–513. Springer, Cham (2019). https://doi.org/10.1007/978-3-030-12612-4_25

15. Shamir, A.: How to share a secret. Commun. ACM **22**(11), 612–613 (1979)

16. Tsaloli, G., Liang, B., Mitrokotsa, A.: Verifiable homomorphic secret sharing. In: Baek, J., Susilo, W., Kim, J. (eds.) ProvSec 2018. LNCS, vol. 11192, pp. 40–55. Springer, Cham (2018). https://doi.org/10.1007/978-3-030-01446-9_3

17. Yao, H., Wang, C., Hai, B., Zhu, S.: Homomorphic hash and blockchain based authentication key exchange protocol for strangers. In: International Conference on Advanced Cloud and Big Data (CBD), Lanzhou, pp. 243–248 (2018)

There Is Always an Exception: Controlling Partial Information Leakage in Secure Computation

Máté Horváth$^{(\boxtimes)}$, Levente Buttyán, Gábor Székely, and Dóra Neubrandt

Laboratory of Cryptography and Systems Security (CrySyS),
Department of Networked Systems and Services,
Budapest University of Technology and Economics, Budapest, Hungary
{mhorvath,buttyan,gszekely,dneubrandt}@crysys.hu

Abstract. Private Function Evaluation (PFE) enables two parties to jointly execute a computation such that one of them provides the input while the other chooses the function to compute. According to the traditional security requirements, a PFE protocol should leak no more information, neither about the function nor the input, than what is revealed by the output of the computation. Existing PFE protocols inherently restrict the scope of computable functions to a certain function class with given output size, thus ruling out the direct evaluation of such problematic functions as the identity map, which would entirely undermine the input privacy requirement. We observe that when not only the input x is confidential but certain partial information $g(x)$ of it as well, standard PFE fails to provide meaningful input privacy if g and the function f to be computed fall into the same function class.

Our work investigates the question whether it is possible to achieve a reasonable level of input and function privacy simultaneously even in the above cases. We propose the notion of Controlled PFE (CPFE) with different flavours of security and answer the question affirmatively by showing simple, generic realizations of the new notions. Our main construction, based on functional encryption (FE), also enjoys strong reusability properties enabling, e.g. fast computation of the same function on different inputs. To demonstrate the applicability of our approach, we show a concrete instantiation of the FE-based protocol for inner product computation that enables secure statistical analysis (and more) under the standard Decisional Diffie–Hellman assumption.

Keywords: Cryptographic protocols · Private function evaluation · Functional encryption · Oblivious transfer · Secure data markets

This work was partially performed in the frames of the projects no. FIEK_16-1-2016-0007 and no. 2017-1.3.1-VKE-2017-00042, implemented with the support provided from the National Research, Development and Innovation Fund of Hungary, financed under the FIEK_16 and the 2017-1.3. funding schemes, and it was also partially supported by the National Research, Development and Innovation Office NKFIH, under grant contract no. 116675 (K). The first author was also supported by the Sándor Csibi Grant.

© Springer Nature Switzerland AG 2020
J. H. Seo (Ed.): ICISC 2019, LNCS 11975, pp. 133–149, 2020.
https://doi.org/10.1007/978-3-030-40921-0_8

1   Introduction

Secure two-party computation (2PC) a.k.a. secure function evaluation (SFE) protocols enable two parties, Alice and Bob, to compute a function of their choice on their private inputs without disclosing their secrets to each other or anyone else (see Fig. 1a). In real life, however, the participants not necessarily have interchangeable roles. We call private function evaluation (PFE) a protocol if one party can alone choose the function to evaluate, while the other provides the input to it (see Fig. 1b) while both of them intends to hide their contribution. PFE can be realized by invoking 2PC after the function was turned into data. A universal function [23] is a "programmable function" that can implement *any* computation up to a given complexity. It takes two inputs, the description of the function to be computed and the input to it. By evaluating a public universal function using 2PC, all feasibility results extend from 2PC to PFE. Improving efficiency turns out to be more challenging. Indeed, universal functions cause significant – for complex computations even prohibitive – overhead, and the elimination of this limitation was the primary focus of PFE research [16,18].

In this work, we initiate the study of a security issue that – to the best of our knowledge – received no attention earlier. More concretely, we focus on the opportunities of the input provider to control the information leakage of her input. As PFE guarantees Bob that his function is hidden from Alice, he can learn some information about the input of Alice such that it remains hidden what was exactly revealed. Disclosing the entire input by evaluating the identity function is typically ruled out by the restriction that the computable function class has shorter output length than input length. At the same time, the following question arises: is it really possible to determine the computable function class so that no function is included which could reveal sensitive information about the input? We argue that most often exceptions occur in every function class, so measures are required to also protect such partial information besides the protection of the input as a whole. As intentional partial information recovery does not cause anomalies when only the function provider, Bob receives the function's output, later on we consider this scenario.

For a simple and illustrative example, let us recall one of the most popular motivating applications for PFE. In privacy-preserving credit checking [20, §7], Alice feeds her private data to a Boolean function of her bank (or another service provider) that decides whether she is eligible for credit or not. Using PFE for such computation allows Alice to keep her data secret and the bank to hide its crediting policy. Notice that the function provider can extract *any binary information* about the input and use it, e.g. to discriminate clients. The leaked partial information can be, e.g. gender or the actual value of any indicator variable about the data that should not be necessary to reveal for credit checking. Our goal is to enable Alice to rule out the leakage of specific sensitive information in PFE without exposing what partial information she wants to hide.

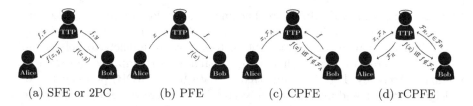

(a) SFE or 2PC   (b) PFE   (c) CPFE   (d) rCPFE

Fig. 1. Comparison of the *ideal functionality* of different concepts for secure function evaluation, realized with the help of a trusted third party (TTP). The key difference lies in which information Alice and Bob can or cannot have access to.

1.1 Our Contributions

Our contributions can be summarized as follows.

- We initiate the study of partial information protection in the context of private function evaluation.
- To take the first step, we put forward the notion of Controlled PFE (CPFE) and formally define its security (see Fig. 1c for its ideal functionality). We also devise a relaxed definition, called rCPFE (see Fig. 1d) that guarantees weaker (but still reasonable) k-anonymity style function privacy leading to a trade-off between security and efficiency.
- Then we show conceptually simple, generic realizations of both CPFE and rCPFE. In the latter case, we utilize the modified function privacy guarantee (through using functional encryption) to enable the reusability of the protocol messages in case of multiple function evaluations. As a result, in our rCPFE when evaluating the same function(s) on multiple, say d inputs, the communication and online computation overhead only increases with an additive factor proportional to d instead of a multiplicative factor as in ordinary PFE.
- To demonstrate the practicality of the rCPFE approach, we instantiate our generic protocol for the inner product functionality enabling secure statistical analysis in a controlled manner under the standard Decisional Diffie–Hellman (DDH) assumption. Our proof of concept implementation shows that the reusability property indeed results in a significant performance improvement over the state of the art secure inner product evaluation method [8].

1.2 Applications

We believe that in most PFE applications, the evaluated function class also permits the leakage of potentially sensitive partial information about the input as our above example demonstrates this even for very restricted Boolean functions. To motivate our inner product rCPFE, we mention two of its possible application scenarios.

Logistic Regression Evaluation. The linear part of logistic regression computation is an inner product of the input and weight vectors. Our inner product rCPFE can help to rule out weight vectors that are unlikely to belong to a model but are base vectors that could reveal a sensitive input vector element.

Location Privacy. Let us assume that a "data broker" (DB) periodically collects location-based information in vector form, where vector elements correspond to information related to specific positions. Such data can be important for service providers (SP), offering location-based services, without the proper infrastructure to collect the necessary data. During their interaction that can be an inner product computation,[1] the SP should hide the location of its users, while the DB may want to protect the exact information in specific locations or to adjust higher price if specific measurements are used. These can be achieved by having control over the possible queries of SP.

1.3 Related Work

Some PFE variants share ideas with our concepts. Semi-private function evaluation (semi-PFE) [15,20] for instance, also relaxes the function privacy requirement of PFE by revealing the topology of the function being evaluated. While this relaxation also leads to a useful trade-off between function privacy and efficiency, unfortunately, the available extra information about the function does not necessarily allow Alice to rule out the evaluation of functions that are against her interest.

Selective private function evaluation (SPFE) [6] deals with a problem that is orthogonal to the one considered in this paper. Namely, SPFE also aims to conceal information that is leaked in PFE. However, instead of protecting Alice (the data owner), it intends to increase the security of Bob by hiding from Alice the location of the function's input in her database via using private information retrieval (PIR).

Leaving the field of PFE and comparing our work to related problems in secure computation, we find that hiding the computed function raises similar issues in other contexts. [4] put forth the notion of verifiable obfuscation that is motivated by the natural fear for executing unknown programs. The goal here is similar than in our setting: some assurance is required that the hidden functionality cannot be arbitrary. However, the fundamental difference between our CPFE and the verifiable obfuscation and verifiable FE of [4] is that while the latter ones enforce correctness when an obfuscator or authority may be dishonest, CPFE tries to disable semi-honest parties to evaluate specific functions (i.e. to handle exceptions in PFE).

Our rCPFE is built upon functional encryption (FE) in a black-box manner. This generalization of traditional encryption was first formalized by [5]. While general-purpose FE candidates [10,11] currently rely on untested assumptions

---

[1] E.g. multiplying the data vector with a position vector (that is non-zero in all positions representing locations close to the user – possibly containing weights depending on the distance – and zero otherwise) can give useful information.

The functionality is parametrized by two integers $k < n$, and two parties: a sender S and a receiver R.

FUNCTIONALITY:

On input $m_1, \ldots, m_n$ messages from S and an index set $\{i_1, \ldots, i_k\} \subset [n]$ from R
- S obtains no output,
- R receives $m_{i_1}, \ldots, m_{i_k}$ but nothing else.

Fig. 2. Ideal functionality $\mathcal{F}_{OT_k^n}$ of k out of n OT.

like the existence of indistinguishability obfuscation or multilinear maps, our application does not require such heavy hammers of cryptography (see details in Sect. 2.2). In the context of FE, [19] raised the question of controllability of function evaluation. The essential difference, compared to our goals, is that they want to limit repeated evaluations of the *same* function[2] that they solve with the involvement of a third party.

Finally, we sum up the state of the art of private inner product evaluation. The provably secure solutions are built either on partially homomorphic encryption schemes [9,12] or 2PC protocols [8] but public-key inner product FE [1] is also capable of the same task. At the same time, several ad-hoc protocols achieve better performance in exchange for some information leakage (see, e.g. [24] and the references therein), but these constructions lack any formal security argument.

2 Preliminaries

In this section, we briefly summarize the relevant background for the rest of the paper. We will always assume that the participants of the considered protocols are semi-honest, i.e. while following the protocol honestly, they try to recover as much information from the interactions as they can. We also use the OT-hybrid model that assumes that the parties have access to an ideal process that securely realizes oblivious transfer, which we discuss in more detail in Sect. 2.1.

2.1 Oblivious Transfer

Oblivious transfer (OT) is one of the most fundamental primitives in cryptography and a cornerstone of secure computation. It enables transferring data between two parties, the sender (S) and the receiver (R, a.k.a. chooser), in a way that protects both of them. S can be sure that R only obtains a subset of the sent messages, while R is assured that S does not know which messages he selected to reveal. In Fig. 2 the ideal functionality of k out of n OT [7] is represented that we are also going to rely on.

---

[2] In FE schemes, the control over the computable functions is in the hand of the master secret key holder, so this is not an issue unlike in PFE.

While being a public-key primitive, so-called OT-extension protocols enable rather efficient OT evaluation. To do so, the participants first pre-compute a limited number of "base-OTs" with certain inputs that are independent of their real inputs. Then using the obtained values, they can evaluate a much larger number of OTs by executing more efficient symmetric-key operations only. This kind of efficiency improvement automatically applies to our protocols after substituting plain OT, with OT-extension with the same functionality [17,21].

2.2 Functional Encryption

As we already introduced, FE is a generalized encryption scheme that enables certain computations on hidden data for authorized parties. Both public- and secret-key variants are known, but here we limit ourselves to the secret-key setting that suffices for our purposes. An sk-FE scheme consists of the following four algorithms.

FE.Setup(λ) $\rightarrow$ ($\mathsf{msk_{FE}}$, $\mathsf{pp_{FE}}$) Upon receiving a security parameter λ it produces the public system parameters $\mathsf{pp_{FE}}$ and the master secret key $\mathsf{msk_{FE}}$.

FE.Enc($\mathsf{msk_{FE}}, x$) $\rightarrow$ ct The encryption algorithm takes the master secret key $\mathsf{msk_{FE}}$ and a message x and outputs a ciphertext ct.

FE.KeyGen($\mathsf{msk_{FE}}, f$) $\rightarrow$ fsk_f The key generation algorithm can be used to generate a functional secret key fsk_f for a function f with the help of the $\mathsf{msk_{FE}}$.

FE.Dec($\mathsf{ct}, \mathsf{fsk}_f$) $\rightarrow$ y Having a functional secret key fsk_f (for function f) and a ciphertext ct (corresponding to x), the decryption outputs the value y.

The correctness of FE requires that if fsk_f and ct were indeed generated with the corresponding algorithms using inputs f and x respectively, then $y = f(x)$ must hold. Regarding security, in this work we are going to use the non-adaptive simulation-based security definition of FE [13], which we recall in Appendix A. We note that while the SIM security of FE is impossible to realize in general [5], for several restricted – yet important – cases it is still achievable, e.g. when the number of functional keys are a priori bounded [13], or when the computable function class is restricted [2]. As our applications also use these restrictions, known FE impossibility results do not affect the way we use FE.

3 General Approaches for Securing Partial Input Information in PFE

In this part, we introduce the notion of controlled PFE and in Sect. 3.1 formally define its security in different flavours. Next, in Sects. 3.2 and 3.3, we propose two general protocols satisfying these security requirements.

PARAMETERS: participants P_1, P_2, a class $\mathcal{F} = \{f : \mathcal{X} \to \mathcal{Y}\}$ of deterministic functions *[and an integer $\kappa > k$]*

FUNCTIONALITY:
On inputs $x_1, \ldots, x_d \in \mathcal{X}$ and $\mathcal{F}_A \subset \mathcal{F}$ from P_1; and $\mathcal{F}_B = \{f_1, \ldots, f_k\} \subset \mathcal{F}$ from P_2
 - P_1 receives no output, *[or P_1 receives $\mathcal{F}_R$ s.t. $\mathcal{F}_B \subset \mathcal{F}_R \subset \mathcal{F}$ and $|\mathcal{F}_R| = \kappa$]*
 - P_2 obtains $\{y'_{i,j} = f'_j(x_i)\}_{i \in [d], j \in [k]} \subset \mathcal{Y} \cup \{\bot\}$ for

$$f'_j(x_i) = \begin{cases} f_j(x_i) & \text{if } f_j \notin \mathcal{F}_A \\ \bot & \text{otherwise.} \end{cases}$$

Fig. 3. Ideal functionalities for $\mathcal{F}_{\text{CPFE}}$ and $\mathcal{F}_{\text{rCPFE}}$ (see the extensions in brackets) formulated generally for multiple inputs and multiple functions.

3.1 Definitional Framework

Our first security definition for controlled PFE captures the intuitive goal of extending the PFE functionality with a blind function verification step by P_1 to prevent unwanted information leakage. See the corresponding ideal functionality $\mathcal{F}_{\text{CPFE}}$ in Fig. 3 that we call controlled PFE, and the security definition below. For the ease of exposition, later on we denote the inputs of the participants as $\text{inp} = (\{x_i\}_{i \in [d]}, \mathcal{F}_A, \{f_j\}_{j \in [k]})$ with the corresponding parameters.

Definition 1 (SIM Security of CPFE wrt. Semi-honest Adversaries).
Let Π denote a Controlled PFE (CPFE) protocol for a function class $\mathcal{F}$ with functionality $\mathcal{F}_{\text{CPFE}}$ (according to Fig. 3). We say that Π achieves SIM security against semi-honest adversaries, if the following criteria hold.

 - Correctness: *the output computed by Π is the required output, i.e.*

$$\Pr[\text{output}^{\Pi}(1^\lambda, \text{inp}) \neq \mathcal{F}_{\text{CPFE}}(\text{inp})] \leq \text{negl}(\lambda).$$

 - Function Privacy: *there exists a probabilistic polynomial time (PPT) simulator $\mathcal{S}_{P_1}$, s.t.*

$$\{\mathcal{S}_{P_1}(1^\lambda, \{x_i\}_{i \in [d]}, \mathcal{F}_A)\}_{\lambda, x_i, \mathcal{F}_A} \overset{c}{\approx} \{\text{view}_{P_1}^{\Pi}(1^\lambda, \text{inp})\}_{\lambda, x_i, f_j, \mathcal{F}_A}.$$

 - Data Privacy: *there exists a PPT simulator $\mathcal{S}_{P_2}$, s.t.*

$$\{\mathcal{S}_{P_2}(1^\lambda, \{f_j\}_{j \in [k]}, \{y'_{i,j}\}_{i \in [d], j \in [k]})\}_{\lambda, f_j} \overset{c}{\approx} \{\text{view}_{P_2}^{\Pi}(1^\lambda, \text{inp})\}_{\lambda, x_i, f_j, \mathcal{F}_A}$$

where $\text{inp} = (\{x_i\}_{i \in [d]}, \mathcal{F}_A, \{f_j\}_{j \in [k]}), f_j \in \mathcal{F}, \mathcal{F}_A \subset \mathcal{F}, x_i \in \mathcal{X}, y'_{i,j} \in \mathcal{Y} \cup \{\bot\},$ *and* $\lambda \in \mathbb{N}$.

We also propose a relaxation of Definition 1, which on the one hand gives up perfect function privacy but on the other, allows us to construct efficient protocols while still maintaining a k-anonymity style guarantee for function privacy. As SIM security alone cannot measure how much information is leaked by a set of functions, we formulate an additional requirement to precisely characterise function privacy.

Definition 2 (SIM Security of Relaxed CPFE wrt. Semi-honest Adversaries). *Let Π denote a relaxed CPFE (rCPFE) protocol for a function class $\mathcal{F}$ with functionality $\mathcal{F}_{rCPFE}$ (according to Fig. 3). We say that Π achieves SIM security against semi-honest adversaries, if the following criteria hold.*

– Correctness: *the output computed by Π is the required output, i.e.*

$$\Pr[\text{output}^{\Pi}(\lambda, \kappa, \text{inp}) \neq \mathcal{F}_{rCPFE}(\kappa, \text{inp})] \leq \text{negl}(\lambda).$$

– Function Privacy: *is defined in two flavours:*
  • *κ-relaxed function privacy holds, if $\exists\, \mathcal{S}_{P_1}$, a PPT simulator, s.t.*

$$\{\mathcal{S}_{P_1}(1^\lambda, \kappa, \{x_i\}_{i \in [d]}, \mathcal{F}_A)\}_{\lambda, \kappa, x_i, \mathcal{F}_A} \overset{c}{\approx} \{\text{view}_{P_1}^{\Pi}(1^\lambda, \kappa, \text{inp})\}_{\lambda, \kappa, x_i, f_j, \mathcal{F}_A}.$$

  • *Strong κ-relaxed function privacy holds if besides the existence of the above $\mathcal{S}_{P_1}$, it also holds that for any PPT $\mathcal{A}$:*

$$\left| \Pr[\mathcal{A}(\text{aux}, \mathcal{F}_R) \in \mathcal{F}_B] - \frac{k}{\kappa} \right| \leq \text{negl}(\lambda)$$

  where aux $\in \{0,1\}^*$ denotes some a priori known auxiliary information about $\mathcal{F}_B$.

– Data Privacy: *there exists a PPT simulator $\mathcal{S}_{P_2}$, s.t.*

$$\{\mathcal{S}_{P_2}(\lambda, \kappa, \{f_j\}_{j \in [k]}, \{y'_{i,j}\}_{i \in [d], j \in [k]})\}_{\lambda, \kappa, f_j} \overset{c}{\approx} \{\text{view}_{P_2}^{\Pi}(\lambda, \kappa, \text{inp})\}_{\lambda, \kappa, x_i, f_j, \mathcal{F}_A}$$

where inp $= (\{x_i\}_{i \in [d]}, \mathcal{F}_A, \{f_j\}_{j \in [k]}), f_j \in \mathcal{F}, \mathcal{F}_A \subset \mathcal{F}, x_i \in \mathcal{X}, y'_{i,j} \in \mathcal{Y} \cup \{\bot\},$ *and* $\lambda, \kappa \in \mathbb{N}$.

3.2 Universal Circuit-Based CPFE

The natural approach for realizing CPFE comes from the traditional way of combining universal circuits and SFE to obtain PFE. Figure 4 shows how the same idea with conditional evaluation leads to CPFE in the single input, single function setting. The following theorem is a straightforward consequence of the security of SFE.

Theorem 1. *The CPFE protocol of Fig. 4 is secure according to Definition 1, if the used SFE protocol is SIM secure in the semi-honest model.*

The main drawback of this approach is that when extending the protocol to handle multiple inputs or functions, its complexity will multiplicatively depend on the number of inputs or functions because of the single-use nature of 2PC.

Protocol $\Pi_{\mathcal{F}}^{\mathrm{CPFE}}$

PARAMETERS: λ parametrizing security, a function class $\mathcal{F} = \{f : \mathcal{X} \to \mathcal{Y}\}$, and a universal circuit UC for the function class $\mathcal{F}$

INPUTS:

  - P_1: $x, \mathcal{F}_A \subset \mathcal{F}$
  - P_2: $f \in \mathcal{F}$

PROTOCOL:

Using a secure two-party computation protocol, P_1 and P_2 executes the following computation on their inputs:

  - If $f \in \mathcal{F}_A$, return $\perp$ to both P_1 and P_2.
  - Otherwise compute the universal circuit $UC(f, x) = f(x) \in \mathcal{Y}$ outputting $\perp$ to P_1 and $f(x)$ to P_2.

Fig. 4. General 2PC-based CPFE

3.3   Reusable Relaxed CPFE from FE

We observe that the notion of rCPFE not only allows the input provider to verify the functions to be evaluated but also opens the door for making parts of the protocol messages reusable multiple times, thus leading to significant efficiency improvements.

A naive first attempt to realize rCPFE is to execute the computation on the side of P_1. Upon receiving a κ function descriptions (including both the intended and dummy functions) P_1 can easily verify the request and evaluate the allowed ones on her input. The results then can be shared with P_2, using an OT scheme achieving both the required data and function privacy level. Unfortunately, the κ function evaluations lead to scalability issues. The subsequent natural idea is to shift the task of function evaluation to P_2, to eliminate the unnecessary computations and to hide the output from P_1 entirely. Since at this point P_1 has both the inputs and the functions to evaluate, the task resembles secure outsourcing of computation where function evaluation must be under the strict control of P_1. These observations lead us to the usage of FE and the protocol in Fig. 5 in which both ciphertext and functional keys can be reused in multiple computations. When instantiated with the FE scheme of [13], $\Pi_{\mathcal{F}}^{\mathrm{rCPFE}}$ can be used for all polynomial sized functions in theory (in practice verifying the circuits would be a bottleneck).

Theorem 2. *The protocol of Fig. 5 is SIM secure according to Definition 2 achieving κ-relaxed function privacy for k function queries by P_2, if the underlying FE scheme is k-query non-adaptive SIM secure (k-NA-SIM) for a single message and the used OT protocol is SIM secure against semi-honest adversaries.*

The proof of the theorem is postponed to Appendix B.

Protocol $\Pi_{\mathcal{F}}^{\text{rCPFE}}$

PARAMETERS: κ, λ parametrizing security and function class $\mathcal{F} = \{f : \mathcal{X} \to \mathcal{Y}\}$

INPUTS:

- P_1: $x_1, \ldots, x_d \in \mathcal{X}, \mathcal{F}_A \subset \mathcal{F}$
- P_2: $\mathcal{F}_B = \{f_1, \ldots, f_k\} \subset \mathcal{F}$

PROTOCOL:

ONLINE PHASE

Step I. To initiate the evaluation of functions in $\mathcal{F}_B$, P_2

    (1) samples $\kappa - k$ functions randomly: $\{f_i \leftarrow_\$ \mathcal{F}\}_{k < i \leq \kappa}$,

    (2) takes a random permutation on κ elements to set $\mathcal{F}_R := (\hat{f}_1, \ldots, \hat{f}_\kappa)$, where $\hat{f}_i = f_{\sigma^{-1}(i)}$ so that each f_i ends up at position $\sigma(i)$ in the sequence,

    (3) finally, sends $\mathcal{F}_R$ to P_1.

Step II. Upon receiving a function request $\mathcal{F}_R$, P_1

    (1) samples $(\text{msk}_{\text{FE}}, \text{pp}_{\text{FE}}) \leftarrow_\$ \text{FE.Setup}(\lambda)$,

    (2) encrypts the input data: $\text{ct}_j \leftarrow_\$ \text{FE.Enc}(\text{pp}_{\text{FE}}, \text{msk}_{\text{FE}}, x_j)$ for all $j \in [d]$,

    (3) determines the index set of allowed functions $I := \{i \mid \hat{f}_i \notin \mathcal{F}_A\}$,

    (4) generate functional keys $\text{fsk}_{\hat{f}_i} \leftarrow_\$ \text{FE.KeyGen}(\text{pp}_{\text{FE}}, \text{msk}_{\text{FE}}, \hat{f}_i)$ for all $i \in I$.

    (5) finally, sends pp_{FE} and $\{\text{ct}_j\}_{j \in [d]}$ to P_2.

Step III. P_1 and P_2 invoke the $\mathcal{F}_{OT_k^n}$-functionality:

    (1) P_1 act as *sender* with κ messages as input: $m_i = \text{fsk}_{\hat{f}_i}$ for $i \in I$ and $m_i = \bot$ for $i \in [\kappa] \setminus I$.

    (2) P_2 act as *receiver* with input $(\sigma(1), \ldots, \sigma(k))$

    (3) P_2 receives $m_{\sigma(1)}, \ldots, m_{\sigma(k)}$ where $m_{\sigma(i)} = \text{fsk}_{f_i}$ or $m_{\sigma(i)} = \bot$ if it was not an allowed function (thus implicitly also obtaining the index set $I \cap [k]$).

OFFLINE PHASE

P_2 can evaluate the allowed functions from $\mathcal{F}_B$ on all input of P_1 by running $\text{FE.Dec}(\text{fsk}_{f_i}, \text{ct}_j) = f_i(x_j)$ for all $i \in I \cap [k]$.

Fig. 5. General rCPFE construction.

Corollary 1. *The protocol of Fig. 5[3] also achieves* strong κ-relaxed function privacy *if in (1) of Step I., all f_i are sampled from the same distribution as the elements of $\mathcal{F}_B$ and* aux $= \bot$.

4   Concrete Instantiation for Inner Products

To demonstrate the practicality of our approach, we instantiate our generic rCPFE protocol (Fig. 5) using the k-NA-SIM secure FE scheme of [2] for the inner product functionality and the semi-honest 1 out of κ OT protocol of [22]. Theorem 2 and the assumptions of [2,22] directly imply the following theorem.

---

[3] Depending on $\mathcal{F}$ and the sampling of the dummy functions, communication cost of transferring the function descriptions can be reduced. In [14] we describe such optimizations for the inner product function class.

Theorem 3. *There is a SIM secure* rCPFE *protocol (according to Definition 2) for inner product computation, achieving κ-relaxed function privacy, if the DDH assumption holds.*

Corollary 2. *The inner product* rCPFE *protocol derived from $\Pi_{\mathcal{F}}^{rCPFE}$ (on Fig. 5) also achieves* strong κ-relaxed function privacy *(as defined in Definition 2) if* aux $= \perp$ *and the dummy function vectors are chosen from the same distribution as the real ones.*

For the detailed description of the inner product rCPFE (or IP-rCPFE for short) we refer to the full version of this paper [14].

4.1 Performance and Possible Optimizations

For our IP-CPFE protocol, we prepared a proof of concept implementation using the Charm framework [3]. To evaluate its performance in two scenarios, we compared its running times and communication costs with that of the state of the art secure arithmetic inner product computation method of the ABY framework [8]. For our experiments we used a commodity laptop with a 2.60GHz Intel® Core™ i7-6700HQ CPU and 4GB of RAM.

Simulating Regression Model Evaluation. In the first use-case, we do not assume that the vectors have a special structure. The vectors to be multiplied can correspond to data and weight vectors of a binary regression model, in which case it is likely that the same model (weight vector) is evaluated over multiple inputs. Figure 6a and 6d depict running times and overall communication costs respectively depending on the number of inputs to the same model. Figure 6c and 6f show the cost of the dummy queries. In the same setting, our experiments show that without optimizations[4] IP-rCPFE reaches the running time of ABY for $\kappa \approx 6200$. For this scenario, we also propose a method (denoted as rCPFE opt) to pre-compute the dummy function queries of Step I. thus reducing both the online communication and computation costs. The key insight of this is that sending a value together with dummy values is essentially the same as hiding the value with a one time pad (OTP) and attaching the OTP key together with dummy keys. The gain comes from the fact that the OTP keys can be computed and sent beforehand, moreover it is enough to transmit the used seeds for a pseudo-random generator instead of the entire keys (see details in [14]). Security is not affected as long as aux $= \perp$.

Sparse Vector Products For Location Privacy. The location privacy scenario of §1.2 implies the usage of sparse query vectors. Figure 6b and 6e show how the number of queries (k) affects running time and message sizes respectively, when roughly 5% of the vector elements are non-zero. We note that as queries are related to real-time user requests, batching these requests, as done in Step I.

---

[4] We note that while our implementation is only a proof of concept without any code level optimization, ABY has a very efficient and parallelizable implementation.

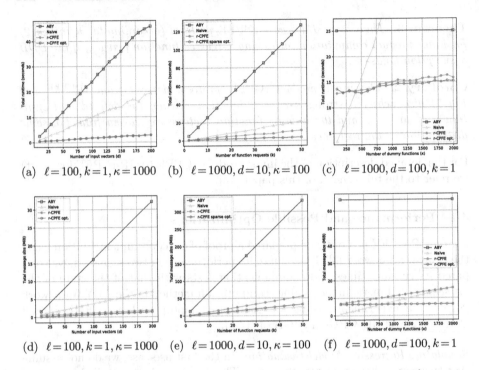

Fig. 6. Comparisons of the overall running times (6a–c) and communication costs (6d–f) of our rCPFE protocols with the ABY framework [8] and the naive OT-based approach for inner product computation (ℓ denotes vector dimension, d and k are the number of input and "function" vectors, while κ is the number of dummy vectors).

of the protocol, can be unrealistic when data vectors are not changing in real time but, e.g. periodically. Because of this, in our implementation, we allowed P_2 to repeat Step I. for a single function and P_1 to answer the queries independently of encrypting the data.[5] While sparsity disables the above optimization, after masking the places of non-zero elements, the above idea can be extended for sparse vectors as long as other structural properties are not known about the vector in form of auxiliary information. For more details on the optimized variants, we refer to [14].

5   Conclusion and Open Directions

In this work, we attempted to draw attention to the problem of possibly sensitive partial information leakage in the context of private function evaluation. We proposed a definitional framework for protocols that aim to prevent such leakage and showed both generic and concrete protocols to solve the problem.

---

[5] It means that (3)–(4) of Step II., and Step III. are repeated until the input data changes at the end of the period.

The main advantage of our FE-based protocol is that it turns the privacy sacrifice required by controllability into performance improvement whenever more function evaluations are necessary.

Our work also leaves open several problems for future work. For instance, it would be important to investigate the effects of having different types of auxiliary information about the evaluated functions. Transmission and verification of dummy functions can be serious bottlenecks in our rCPFE in case of complex functions, making further efficiency improvements desirable. A first step towards this could be to find a way for restricting the set of forbidden functions – as most often very simple functions are the only undesired ones. Finally, looking for different trade-offs between function privacy and efficiency can also be interesting direction for future work.

Appendix

A   Simulation Security of Functional Encryption

For completeness we recall the simulation security of FE as defined in [13].

Definition 3 (q-NA-SIM and q-AD-SIM Security of FE). *Let $\mathcal{FE}$ be a functional encryption scheme for a circuit family $\mathcal{C} = \{\mathcal{C}_\nu : \mathcal{X}_\nu \to \mathcal{Y}_\nu\}_{\nu \in \mathbb{N}}$. For every PPT adversary $\mathcal{A} = (\mathcal{A}_1, \mathcal{A}_2)$ and a PPT simulator $\mathcal{S} = (\mathcal{S}_1, \mathcal{S}_2)$ consider the following two experiments:*

$\mathsf{Exp}^{\mathsf{real}}_{\mathcal{FE},\mathcal{A}}(\lambda)$	$\mathsf{Exp}^{\mathsf{ideal}}_{\mathcal{FE},\mathcal{S}}(\lambda)$

$\mathsf{Exp}^{\mathsf{real}}_{\mathcal{FE},\mathcal{A}}(\lambda)$

1 : $(\mathsf{pp}_{\mathsf{FE}}, \mathsf{msk}_{\mathsf{FE}}) \leftarrow_\$ \mathsf{FE.Setup}(\lambda)$

2 : $(x, \mathsf{st}) \leftarrow_\$ \mathcal{A}_1^{\mathsf{FE.KeyGen}(\mathsf{msk}_{\mathsf{FE}}, \cdot)}(\mathsf{pp}_{\mathsf{FE}})$

3 : $\mathsf{ct} \leftarrow_\$ \mathsf{FE.Enc}(\mathsf{pp}_{\mathsf{FE}}, x)$

4 : $\beta \leftarrow_\$ \mathcal{A}_2^{O(\mathsf{msk}_{\mathsf{FE}}, \cdot)}(\mathsf{pp}_{\mathsf{FE}}, \mathsf{ct}, \mathsf{st})$

5 : $\mathsf{output}(\beta, x)$

$\mathsf{Exp}^{\mathsf{ideal}}_{\mathcal{FE},\mathcal{S}}(\lambda)$

1 : $(\mathsf{pp}_{\mathsf{FE}}, \mathsf{msk}_{\mathsf{FE}}) \leftarrow_\$ \mathsf{FE.Setup}(\lambda)$

2 : $(x, \mathsf{st}) \leftarrow_\$ \mathcal{A}_1^{\mathsf{FE.KeyGen}(\mathsf{msk}_{\mathsf{FE}}, \cdot)}(\mathsf{pp}_{\mathsf{FE}})$

– *Let $(C_1, \ldots, C_q)$ be $\mathcal{A}_1$'s oracle queries*

– *Let fsk_{f_i} be the oracle reply to C_i*

– *Let $\mathcal{V} := \{y_i = C_i(x), C_i, \mathsf{fsk}_{f_i}\}$.*

3 : $(\mathsf{ct}, \mathsf{st}') \leftarrow_\$ \mathcal{S}_1(\mathsf{pp}_{\mathsf{FE}}, \mathcal{V}, \lambda)$

4 : $\beta \leftarrow_\$ \mathcal{A}_2^{O'(\mathsf{msk}_{\mathsf{FE}}, \mathsf{st}', \cdot)}(\mathsf{pp}_{\mathsf{FE}}, \mathsf{ct}, \mathsf{st})$

5 : $\mathsf{output}(\beta, x)$

We distinguish between two cases of the above experiment:

1. *The* adaptive *case, where:*
   – *the oracle $O(\mathsf{msk}_{\mathsf{FE}}, \cdot) = \mathsf{FE.KeyGen}(\mathsf{msk}_{\mathsf{FE}}, \cdot)$ and*
   – *the oracle $O'(\mathsf{msk}_{\mathsf{FE}}, \mathsf{st}', \cdot)$ is the second stage of the simulator, namely $\mathcal{S}_2^{U_x(\cdot)}(\mathsf{msk}_{\mathsf{FE}}, \mathsf{st}', \cdot)$ where $U_x(C) = C(x)$ for any $C \in \mathcal{C}_\nu$.*
   The simulator algorithm $\mathcal{S}_2$ is stateful in that after each invocation, it updates the state st' which is carried over to its next invocation. We call a simulator algorithm $\mathcal{S} = (\mathcal{S}_1, \mathcal{S}_2)$ admissible if, on each input C, $\mathcal{S}_2$ just makes a single query to its oracle $U_x(\cdot)$ on C itself.

The functional encryption scheme $\mathcal{FE}$ is then said to be q-query-simulation-secure for one message against adaptive adversaries (q-AD-SIM secure for short) if there is an admissible PPT simulator $\mathcal{S} = (\mathcal{S}_1, \mathcal{S}_2)$ such that for every PPT adversary $\mathcal{A} = (\mathcal{A}_1, \mathcal{A}_2)$ that makes at most q queries, the following two distributions are computationally indistinguishable:

$$\left\{ \mathsf{Exp}^{\mathsf{real}}_{\mathcal{FE}, \mathcal{A}}(\lambda) \right\}_{\nu \in \mathbb{N}} \overset{c}{\approx} \left\{ \mathsf{Exp}^{\mathsf{ideal}}_{\mathcal{FE}, \mathcal{S}}(\lambda) \right\}_{\nu \in \mathbb{N}}$$

2. *The non-adaptive case, where the oracles $O(\mathsf{msk}_{\mathsf{FE}}, \cdot)$ and $O'(\mathsf{msk}_{\mathsf{FE}}, \mathsf{st}, \cdot)$ are both the "empty oracles" that return nothing: the functional encryption scheme $\mathcal{FE}$ is then said to be q-query-simulation-secure for one message against non-adaptive adversaries (q-NA-SIM secure, for short) if there is a PPT simulator $\mathcal{S} = (\mathcal{S}_1, \bot)$ such that for every PPT adversary $\mathcal{A} = (\mathcal{A}_1, \mathcal{A}_2)$ that makes at most q queries, the two distributions above are computationally indistinguishable.*

As shown by [13, Theorem A.1.], in the non-adaptive setting (that we also use), q-NA-SIM security for one message is equivalent to q-NA-SIM security for many messages.

B   Proof of Theorem 2

We prove Theorem 2, by showing that the protocol of Fig. 5 fulfils the requirements of Definition 2 with the assumption that the underlying FE and OT are SIM secure against semi-honest adversaries. As correctness directly follows from the correctness of the underlying FE and OT, we turn our attention towards the security requirements. We argue input and weak relaxed function privacy by showing that the view of both parties can be simulated (without having access to the inputs of the other party) using the simulators guaranteed by the SIM security of FE and OT.

Corrupted P_1: Weak Relaxed Function Privacy. Besides its input and output, the view of P_1 consists of the received OT messages and the function query $\mathcal{F}_R$. Simulation becomes trivial because of the fact that the output of P_1 also contains $\mathcal{F}_R$. Thus $\mathcal{S}_{P_1}((x_1, \ldots, x_d), \mathcal{F}_R)$ can return $\mathcal{F}_R$ and the output of the sender's simulator $\mathcal{S}^{\mathcal{S}}_{OT}$ guaranteed by the SIM security of OT. The simulated view is clearly indistinguishable from the real one.

Corrupted P_2: Input Privacy. The following simulator $\mathcal{S}_{P_2}$ simulates the view of a corrupt P_2, that consists of its input $(f_1, \ldots, f_k)$, output $\{y'^{*}_{i,j} = f'_i(x_j)\}_{i \in [k], j \in [d]}$, the used randomness and the incoming messages. $\mathcal{S}_{P_2}$ first determines the index set $I^* = \{i \mid \exists j : y'_{i,j} \neq \bot\} \subseteq [k]$. Next, it sets up the parameters of the ideal experiment according to Definition 3. To do so, it samples $(\mathsf{msk}_{\mathsf{FE}}^*, \mathsf{pp}_{\mathsf{FE}}^*) \leftarrow_\$ \mathsf{FE}.\mathsf{Setup}(\lambda)$ and then for all $i \in I^*$ generates keys $\mathsf{fsk}^*_{f_i} \leftarrow_\$ \mathsf{FE}.\mathsf{KeyGen}(\mathsf{pp}_{\mathsf{FE}}^*, \mathsf{msk}_{\mathsf{FE}}^*, f_i)$. For the simulation of the FE ciphertexts (corresponding to unknown messages), we can use the FE simulator $\mathcal{S}_{FE}$ for many messages (implied by one-message q-NA-SIM security [13]). Thus

$\mathcal{S}_{FE}(\mathsf{pp}_{\mathsf{FE}}^*, \{y_{i,j} = f_i(x_j), f_i, \mathsf{fsk}_{f_i}^*\}_{i \in I^*, j \in [d]}, \lambda) = (\mathsf{ct}_1^*, \ldots, \mathsf{ct}_d^*)$ can be appended to the simulated view together with $\mathsf{pp}_{\mathsf{FE}}^*$. The incoming messages of Step III. are simulated using the OT simulator $\mathcal{S}_{OT}^{\mathcal{R}}$ for the receiver. Finally the output of $\mathcal{S}_{OT}^{\mathcal{R}}(\lambda, \{\mathsf{fsk}_{f_i}^*\}_{i \in I^*} \cup \{\perp_i\}_{i \in [k] \setminus I^*})$ is appended to the simulated view.

Now we show the indistinguishability of the real and simulated views. As the inputs and outputs are the same in both cases, we have to compare the randomness and the incoming messages. First notice that $\mathsf{pp}_{\mathsf{FE}}$ and $\mathsf{pp}_{\mathsf{FE}}^*$ are generated with different random choices. At the same time, these cannot be told apart as otherwise the choices were not random. The rest of the incoming messages depend on these parameters. Observe that $I^* = I \cap [k]$. The security of the used FE scheme guarantees that $(\mathsf{ct}_1^*, \ldots, \mathsf{ct}_d^*)$ even together with functional keys $\{\mathsf{fsk}_{f_i}^*\}_{i \in I^*}$ are indistinguishable from $(\mathsf{ct}_1, \ldots, \mathsf{ct}_d)$ with $\{\mathsf{fsk}_{f_i}\}_{i \in I \cap [k]}$. Finally, the security of the OT simulation guarantees that $(\mathsf{msg}_1^{\mathsf{OT}}, \ldots, \mathsf{msg}_\kappa^{\mathsf{OT}})$ and $(\mathsf{msg}_1^{\mathsf{OT}^*}, \ldots, \mathsf{msg}_\kappa^{\mathsf{OT}^*})$ are indistinguishable. This also implies that functional keys for the same functions (with respect to either $\mathsf{pp}_{\mathsf{FE}}$ or $\mathsf{pp}_{\mathsf{FE}}^*$) can be obtained both from the real and simulated OT messages. In other words, FE ciphertexts and functional keys are consistent in both cases (i.e. they allow one to obtain the same decryption outputs) due to the correctness of the FE simulation, which concludes our proof. □

References

1. Abdalla, M., Bourse, F., De Caro, A., Pointcheval, D.: Simple functional encryption schemes for inner products. In: Katz, J. (ed.) PKC 2015. LNCS, vol. 9020, pp. 733–751. Springer, Heidelberg (2015). https://doi.org/10.1007/978-3-662-46447-2_33
2. Agrawal, S., Libert, B., Stehlé, D.: Fully secure functional encryption for inner products, from standard assumptions. In: Robshaw, M., Katz, J. (eds.) CRYPTO 2016. LNCS, vol. 9816, pp. 333–362. Springer, Heidelberg (2016). https://doi.org/10.1007/978-3-662-53015-3_12
3. Akinyele, J.A., et al.: Charm: a framework for rapidly prototyping cryptosystems. J. Cryptogr. Eng. **3**(2), 111–128 (2013). https://doi.org/10.1007/s13389-013-0057-3
4. Badrinarayanan, S., Goyal, V., Jain, A., Sahai, A.: Verifiable functional encryption. In: Cheon, J.H., Takagi, T. (eds.) ASIACRYPT 2016. LNCS, vol. 10032, pp. 557–587. Springer, Heidelberg (2016). https://doi.org/10.1007/978-3-662-53890-6_19
5. Boneh, D., Sahai, A., Waters, B.: Functional encryption: definitions and challenges. In: Ishai, Y. (ed.) TCC 2011. LNCS, vol. 6597, pp. 253–273. Springer, Heidelberg (2011). https://doi.org/10.1007/978-3-642-19571-6_16
6. Canetti, R., Ishai, Y., Kumar, R., Reiter, M.K., Rubinfeld, R., Wright, R.N.: Selective private function evaluation with applications to private statistics. In: Kshemkalyani, A.D., Shavit, N. (eds.) Proceedings of the Twentieth Annual ACM Symposium on Principles of Distributed Computing, PODC 2001, pp. 293–304. ACM (2001). https://doi.org/10.1145/383962.384047
7. Chu, C.-K., Tzeng, W.-G.: Efficient k-out-of-n oblivious transfer schemes with adaptive and non-adaptive queries. In: Vaudenay, S. (ed.) PKC 2005. LNCS, vol. 3386, pp. 172–183. Springer, Heidelberg (2005). https://doi.org/10.1007/978-3-540-30580-4_12

8. Demmler, D., Schneider, T., Zohner, M.: ABY - a framework for efficient mixed-protocol secure two-party computation. In: 22nd Annual Network and Distributed System Security Symposium, NDSS 2015. The Internet Society (2015). https://doi.org/10.14722/ndss.2015.23113

9. Dong, C., Chen, L.: A fast secure dot product protocol with application to privacy preserving association rule mining. In: Tseng, V.S., Ho, T.B., Zhou, Z.-H., Chen, A.L.P., Kao, H.-Y. (eds.) PAKDD 2014. LNCS (LNAI), vol. 8443, pp. 606–617. Springer, Cham (2014). https://doi.org/10.1007/978-3-319-06608-0_50

10. Garg, S., Gentry, C., Halevi, S., Raykova, M., Sahai, A., Waters, B.: Candidate indistinguishability obfuscation and functional encryption for all circuits. In: 54th Annual IEEE Symposium on Foundations of Computer Science, FOCS 2013, pp. 40–49. IEEE Computer Society (2013). https://doi.org/10.1109/FOCS.2013.13

11. Garg, S., Gentry, C., Halevi, S., Zhandry, M.: Functional encryption without obfuscation. In: Kushilevitz, E., Malkin, T. (eds.) TCC 2016. LNCS, vol. 9563, pp. 480–511. Springer, Heidelberg (2016). https://doi.org/10.1007/978-3-662-49099-0_18

12. Goethals, B., Laur, S., Lipmaa, H., Mielikäinen, T.: On private scalar product computation for privacy-preserving data mining. In: Park, C., Chee, S. (eds.) ICISC 2004. LNCS, vol. 3506, pp. 104–120. Springer, Heidelberg (2005). https://doi.org/10.1007/11496618_9

13. Gorbunov, S., Vaikuntanathan, V., Wee, H.: Functional encryption with bounded collusions via multi-party computation. In: Safavi-Naini, R., Canetti, R. (eds.) CRYPTO 2012. LNCS, vol. 7417, pp. 162–179. Springer, Heidelberg (2012). https://doi.org/10.1007/978-3-642-32009-5_11

14. Horváth, M., Buttyán, L., Székely, G., Neubrandt, D.: There is always an exception: controlling partial information leakage in secure computation (full version). Cryptology ePrint Archive, Report 2019/1302 (2019). https://eprint.iacr.org/2019/1302

15. Kennedy, W.S., Kolesnikov, V., Wilfong, G.: Overlaying conditional circuit clauses for secure computation. In: Takagi, T., Peyrin, T. (eds.) ASIACRYPT 2017. LNCS, vol. 10625, pp. 499–528. Springer, Cham (2017). https://doi.org/10.1007/978-3-319-70697-9_18

16. Kiss, Á., Schneider, T.: Valiant's universal circuit is practical. In: Fischlin, M., Coron, J.-S. (eds.) EUROCRYPT 2016. LNCS, vol. 9665, pp. 699–728. Springer, Heidelberg (2016). https://doi.org/10.1007/978-3-662-49890-3_27

17. Kolesnikov, V., Kumaresan, R., Rosulek, M., Trieu, N.: Efficient batched oblivious PRF with applications to private set intersection. In: Weippl, E.R., et al. (eds.) Proceedings of the 2016 ACM SIGSAC Conference on Computer and Communications Security, pp. 818–829. ACM (2016). https://doi.org/10.1145/2976749.2978381

18. Kolesnikov, V., Schneider, T.: A practical universal circuit construction and secure evaluation of private functions. In: Tsudik, G. (ed.) FC 2008. LNCS, vol. 5143, pp. 83–97. Springer, Heidelberg (2008). https://doi.org/10.1007/978-3-540-85230-8_7

19. Naveed, M., et al.: Controlled functional encryption. In: Ahn, G., Yung, M., Li, N. (eds.) Proceedings of the 2014 ACM SIGSAC Conference on Computer and Communications Security, 2014, pp. 1280–1291. ACM (2014). https://doi.org/10.1145/2660267.2660291

20. Paus, A., Sadeghi, A.-R., Schneider, T.: Practical secure evaluation of semi-private functions. In: Abdalla, M., Pointcheval, D., Fouque, P.-A., Vergnaud, D. (eds.) ACNS 2009. LNCS, vol. 5536, pp. 89–106. Springer, Heidelberg (2009). https://doi.org/10.1007/978-3-642-01957-9_6

21. Rindal, P., Rosulek, M.: Improved private set intersection against malicious adversaries. In: Coron, J.-S., Nielsen, J.B. (eds.) EUROCRYPT 2017. LNCS, vol. 10210, pp. 235–259. Springer, Cham (2017). https://doi.org/10.1007/978-3-319-56620-7_9
22. Tzeng, W.: Efficient 1-out-of-n oblivious transfer schemes with universally usable parameters. IEEE Trans. Comput. **53**(2), 232–240 (2004). https://doi.org/10.1109/TC.2004.1261831
23. Valiant, L.G.: Universal circuits (preliminary report). In: Chandra, A.K., Wotschke, D., Friedman, E.P., Harrison, M.A. (eds.) Proceedings of the 8th Annual ACM Symposium on Theory of Computing, pp. 196–203. ACM (1976). https://doi.org/10.1145/800113.803649
24. Zhu, Y., Wang, Z., Hassan, B., Zhang, Y., Wang, J., Qian, C.: Fast secure scalar product protocol with (almost) optimal efficiency. In: Guo, S., Liao, X., Liu, F., Zhu, Y. (eds.) CollaborateCom 2015. LNICST, vol. 163, pp. 234–242. Springer, Cham (2016). https://doi.org/10.1007/978-3-319-28910-6_21

An Automated Security Analysis Framework and Implementation for MTD Techniques on Cloud

Hooman Alavizadeh[1]([✉])[iD], Hootan Alavizadeh[2][iD], Dong Seong Kim[3][iD],
Julian Jang-Jaccard[1][iD], and Masood Niazi Torshiz[4]

[1] School of Natural and Computational Sciences, Massey University,
Auckland, New Zealand
{h.alavizadeh,j.jang-jaccard}@massey.ac.nz
[2] Department of Computer Engineering,
Imam Reza International University, Mashhad, Iran
h.alavizadeh@imamreza.ac.ir
[3] School of Information Technology and Electrical Engineering,
The University of Queensland, Brisbane, Australia
dan.kim@uq.edu.au
[4] Department of Computer Engineering, Mashhad Branch,
Islamic Azad University, Mashhad, Iran
niazi@mshdiau.ac.ir

Abstract. Cloud service providers offer their customers with on-demand and cost-effective services, scalable computing, and network infrastructures. Enterprises migrate their services to the cloud to utilize the benefit of cloud computing such as eliminating the capital expense of their computing need. There are security vulnerabilities and threats in the cloud. Many researches have been proposed to analyze the cloud security using Graphical Security Models (GSMs) and security metrics. In addition, it has been widely researched in finding appropriate defensive strategies for the security of the cloud. Moving Target Defense (MTD) techniques can utilize the cloud elasticity features to change the attack surface and confuse attackers. Most of the previous work incorporating MTDs into the GSMs are theoretical and the performance was evaluated based on the simulation. In this paper, we realized the previous framework and designed, implemented and tested a cloud security assessment tool in a real cloud platform named UniteCloud. Our security solution can (1) monitor cloud computing in real-time, (2) automate the security modeling and analysis and visualize the GSMs using a Graphical User Interface via a web application, and (3) deploy three MTD techniques including Diversity, Redundancy, and Shuffle on the real cloud infrastructure. We analyzed the automation process using the APIs and showed the practicality and feasibility of automation of deploying all the three MTD techniques on the UniteCloud.

Keywords: Cloud computing · Moving Target Defense · Security analysis · Security modeling · Cloud security framework

© Springer Nature Switzerland AG 2020
J. H. Seo (Ed.): ICISC 2019, LNCS 11975, pp. 150–164, 2020.
https://doi.org/10.1007/978-3-030-40921-0_9

1   Introduction

The growth of the cloud computing as a powerful and affordable context for users has caused many business and commerce migrate to this on-demand, scalable, and cost-effective paradigm. The organizations outsource their network infrastructures, computing needs, software and services into the cloud in order to benefit from the cloud's utilities such as economical benefits (cutting off physical resources and damages). However, many organizations and enterprises find this migration undesirable due to cloud security issues [21,23].

Many security mechanisms and defensive strategies have been proposed by researchers both theoretically and practically. In order to improve the security of cloud computing, it is important to evaluate the security posture of cloud. Graphical Security Models (GSMs) (such as Attack Graphs (AGs) [8], Attack Trees (ATs) [15], Attack-defense threes (ADTrees) [16], Hierarchical Attack Representation Model (HARM) [11]) are the widely adopted methods to analyze the security of enterprise networks [14,22]; a GSM can be used to define attack surfaces and summarize the attack scenarios, and compute security metrics to show the cloud security posture. GSMs can also be used to evaluate the effectiveness of defensive techniques such as Moving Target Defense (MTD). MTD techniques are proactive defensive techniques and the primary idea is mainly changing the attack surface in order to introduce confusions to attackers carrying out cyber attackers. Only a few researches have been proposed for the uses of GSM in evaluating MTD techniques for cloud computing. However, most of the previous researches are theoretical and use simulation only [2–5,12] to show the feasibility of their approaches.

To the best of our knowledge, the incorporation of GSMs and MTD techniques together for security analysis and deployment of MTD techniques in the infrastructures of the real clouds has not been proposed. In this paper, we tackle the aforementioned shortcomings by designing and development of a cloud security assessment framework. We focus on the practical side rather theoretical appraisal. We demonstrate the practicality of implementation, feasibility of automation, usability of the project using a real cloud platform named UniteCloud [1]. The main contributions of this paper are as follows:

- *Cloud monitoring*: We developed a cloud security framework which can automate the process of cloud vulnerability scanning to collect the information of the cloud's components and the vulnerabilities of each component.
- *Cloud security evaluation:* Cloud security framework can create the HARM based on the collected information for security analysis and MTD evaluation.
- *MTD Deployment*: Cloud security framework automated the deployment of MTD techniques on the real cloud platform.
- *Automation evaluation*: We investigated on a private cloud platform and uses of OpenStack Application Programming Interfaces (APIs) to analyze the automation process for implementation steps.
- *MTD visualization*: We developed a graphical user interface (GUI) as a web application for interaction between cloud security framework and security experts including both cloud provider view and HARM [12] visualization.

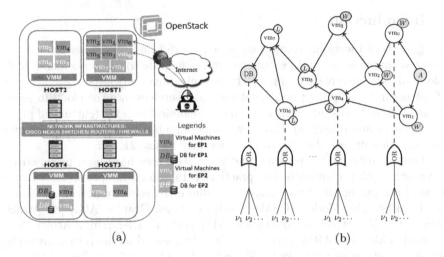

Fig. 1. (a) Running Example and cloud model for two enterprises migrated into the cloud named EP1 and EP2, (b) Two-layer HARM of the EP1 in the Cloud.

- *Security analysis*: We evaluate MTD techniques on the real cloud based on three security metrics: system risk, attack cost, and return on attack.

The rest of the paper is organized as follows. Section 2 defines the proposed approach including a brief explanation on preliminaries, concepts, and definitions. Section 3 presents the design and implementation of our proposed framework. Discussion and limitations of this work are given in Sect. 4. Section 5 summarizes the related work. Finally, we conclude the paper in Sect. 6.

2   Proposed Approach

We design and implement a cloud security assessment framework which is able to monitor the cloud, analyze and deploy the three MTD techniques including Shuffle, Diversity, and Redundancy on the real cloud platform. The main part of this paper is the automation of the cloud assessment framework in the real cloud. The uses of APIs in the implementation and automation of the project are nontrivial. This work includes four main phases elucidated as follows. (1) Information Collection, (2) Cloud Security Modeling using HARM, (3) Security Analysis Engine, (4) Deployment Phase.

2.1   System and Attack Models

Figure 1a shows a running example for the migrations of two independent organizations entitled Enterprise-1 (EP1) and Enterprise-2 (EP2) to a private cloud. Those companies decide to cut off the physical equipment and use a private cloud for accommodating their computing needs. Each organization has launched 8

Virtual Machines (VMs) on the cloud together with a Database (DB) creating a virtual network. We assume that the first four VMs use Windows10 and the rest use Linux Ubuntu. Moreover, the VMs vm_0 and vm_1 for both organizations are connected to the Internet. Later on, we deploy the running example shown in Fig. 1a in a realistic cloud. System constraints are usually defined based on both cloud provider and security experts. For instance, the cloud provider can determine which physical hosts are available for the customers. Moreover, the cloud provider can set the limitations on the physical hosts such as defining the maximum VMs that can be located on each host and so forth. However, the security experts of enterprises migrated into the cloud may have their own security policies like defining firewalls rules and Access Control Lists (ACL). We assume that an attacker can launch the attacks from outside of the cloud using exploiting the software vulnerabilities of the VMs connected to the Internet. Then, the attacker can launch a series of other attacks in order to access the DB along the identified attack paths.

2.2 Security Model for Cloud

In this paper, we use HARM [11,12] for graphical security modeling, analysis and evaluation. HARM consists of two hierarchical layers which use an Attack Graph (AG) in the upper layer and an Attack Tree (AT) in the lower layer. Since multiple independent organizations can reside in the same cloud, we define HARM based on sub-clouds for each independent organization migrated to the cloud as follows. HARM can be modeled as a 3-tuple $H_{sc} = (U_{sc}, L_{sc}, M_{sc})$ where U_{sc} refers to an AG corresponding to a sub-cloud sc_x, and L_{sc} denotes an AT corresponding to a sub-cloud sc_x, and M_{sc} is a one-to-one mapping link from the AG to the corresponding AT, $M_{sc} = U_{sc} \rightarrow L_{sc}$ (the dashed lines in Fig. 1b). The upper layer of HARM captures the connectivities of VMs, and the lower layer captures the vulnerabilities of each VMs $V_{vm_i} = \{\nu_1, \nu_2, \ldots, \nu_m\}$, such that the vulnerabilities make the leaves of three and the root is a logical gate.

Figure 1b represents the two-layered HARM for EP1. Constructing the security model, we can leverage HARM to compute the security metrics and quantify the cloud security. In this paper, we use three security metrics, which are Cloud Risk (Risk), Attack Cost (AC), and Return on Attack (RoA), to evaluate the cloud security posture before and after deploying MTD techniques to find out the most effective defensive strategy. The uses of those metrics for evaluation of cloud are theoretically investigated through simulation in [3]. HARM uses the vulnerability information which can be obtained from National Vulnerability Database (NVD) [19] and generate the lower layer using the vulnerability values such as Impact, Exploitability, Base Score.

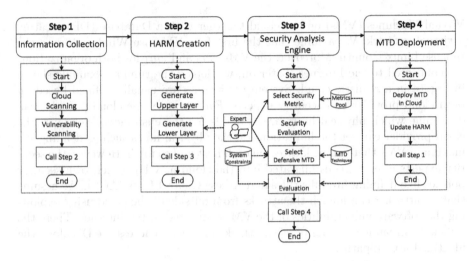

Fig. 2. Security modeling, analysis, and deployment phases

3   Design and Implementation

We investigate the feasibility and practical requirements such as Software tools, packages, programming interfaces, libraries in order to implement and automate the security analysis tool and MTD techniques in the real-world cloud deployment. We develop a framework which can perform security modeling, evaluation, MTD deployment for enterprises migrated to the cloud. The cloud security framework is able to automate information collection: cloud scanning, vulnerability scanning, HARM creation, security evaluation, and MTD deployment on a real cloud infrastructure. To implement the framework we utilize a private cloud named UniteCloud and develop our framework on UniteCloud platform.

3.1   Case Study: UniteCloud Analysis

The UniteCloud uses the OpenStack cloud platform. We set up the project by creating the VMs with different flavors and OS, assigning internal and floating IP addresses, defining firewall rules and ACL, *etc.* However, we first create the cloud example VMs shown in Fig. 1a on the UniteCloud platform. The cloud consisting of 16 physical Hosts (Compute Hosts) is distributed over three availability zones: IBMZone, HPZone, and Nova. We also used four hosts each of which includes different VMs with various flavors. We assign two flavors for the VMs: m1.medium and m1.generic. The specification of the former VM is 2 VCPUs, 4 GB RAM, and 80 GB Disk, and that of the latter is 1 VCPUs, 1 GB RAM, and 20 GB Disk. We assign two floating IP addresses for both VMs vm_0 and vm_1 of two enterprises which are connected to the Internet. Moreover, VMs vm_6 and vm_7 of both enterprises EP1 and EP2 are connected to their own DB.

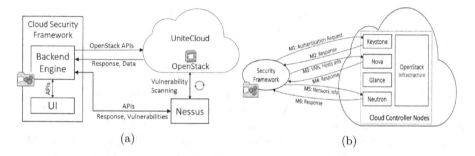

Fig. 3. A Cloud system: (a) Security framework and communication overview. (b) OpenStack API Calls for information collection phase.

3.2   Cloud Security Framework

The security framework consists of a backend engine and user interface (UI). The backend engine is responsible for information collection, security modeling, analysis, and deployment phases which are demonstrated in Fig. 2. The UI is used for interactions between security experts of enterprises and the backend engine for configuration and visualization purposes. The generated graphical security model can be visualized in the UI. Figure 3a shows an overview of the security framework prototype and related tools and communication. The cloud security framework utilizes the following programming languages, tools, and concepts: .NET Core, JSON, JavaScript, jQuery Ajax, Python, Nessus [6], and Data-Driven Documents JavaScript (D3.js). Security modeling is the first phase of the implementation of cloud security framework and consists of two phases: (1) information collection, (2) HARM creation, which are shown as steps 1 and 2 in Fig. 2. Creating the model, we can evaluate the cloud security posture alongside the effectiveness of deployed MTD techniques which are steps 3 and 4 in Fig. 2.

Information Collection Automation. First, the cloud infrastructure should be scanned in order to obtain Hosts, VMs, and reachability information. Then, the vulnerabilities existing on each VM should be obtained using the vulnerability scanning tools such as Nessus [6]. Cloud security framework needs to automatically fetch two information: (1) cloud information such as the number of VMs, the number of physical hosts, the host of each VM, the reachability between the VMs and (2) vulnerability information existing on each VM. We use .NET Core as the backend engine programming language and call APIs in order to access both OpenStack and Nessus automatically and fetch information. Accessing to the UniteCloud OpenStack consists of two parts: OpenStack authentication and fetching information. OpenStack uses Keystone feature for user authentication. Moreover, it uses nove-computes, neutron-networks, Glance-images features for different purposes such as accessing to compute nodes (VMs, Hosts, Zones, *etc*). In order to access to the OpenStack and retrieve the information, we first need to access keystone using APIs for authentication. We utilize

JSON API call for authentication process. Then, OpenStack sends a response including the authentication token (X-Subject-Token), other OpenStack Controllers' address including nova, neutron, glance, cinder, *etc.* which can be used for further API calls. The received message should be first parsed to receive the authentication token together with the nova controller address. Then, the backend engine sends another API call using the authentication token and the nova controller to gather the list of VMs and Hosts. The received message contains unnecessary information including VM status, availability zone, created, *etc.*. It should be parsed to fetch only the required information. Similarly, another API including the authentication token and neutron controller should be called to get network-related information. The received information should be again parsed to obtain VMs' IP addresses and the reachability of VMs. Figure 3b demonstrates the API calls and related responses between the cloud security framework and OpenStack to gain the information. Moreover, cloud security framework needs vulnerability information for each VM on the cloud. We use Nessus to scan the cloud and obtain vulnerabilities. Then, cloud security framework uses a backend engine to access to Nessus and retrieve the vulnerabilities' information. The first API called is used for authentication. Having obtained the response message, the backend engine sends other API calls using the authentication token in order to get the vulnerability information. The extracted information contains useful information related to Vulnerability, possible threats, Base Score [19], and CVE identifier (CVE-ID). However, cloud security framework only need CVE-ID for selected vulnerabilities so that it can obtain the other information such as vulnerability impact and exploitability through National Vulnerability Database (NVD) [19]. Note that cloud scanning using Nessus is a time-consuming process and can be utilized once a while to keep the vulnerabilities updated, or run once a change catches on the VMs such as adding new VM, or changing OS, *etc.*

HARM Creation. The upper layer of HARM can be generated using the VMs and reachability information obtained from the previous step. This information is saved as a key and value dictionary representing the VMs' links as a graph. Thus, the backend engine can generate the AG based on the dictionary. The second part of the information obtained from Nessus scanning is a dictionary of VMs and related vulnerabilities on each VM which can be used to generate the lower layer of HARM. The lower layer of HARM uses the ATs. The backend Engine uses Python programming language to generate HARM. However, other software and tools can also be used like Gephi which is a network analysis and visualization software package. Moreover, we use Python as the security analysis engine to compute security metrics and evaluate MTD techniques.

Security Analysis Engine. Security analysis engine has two main phases: general security evaluation and MTD evaluation. HARM can be adopted to compute the security metrics in the pool. Security analysis engine is implemented on the backend engine using Python. It consists of security evaluation and MTD evaluation subroutine. Security analysis engine uses the generated HARM and the security metrics. In fact, security experts can choose or prioritize various security metrics and add them to the metric pools based on the security requirements such as System Risk, Attack Cost, Return on Attack and so forth. Once the security metrics are selected, security analysis engine uses HARM for security evaluation and computing the selected security metrics. Security analysis framework uses MTD techniques as the main defensive strategies for security the organizations on the cloud. However, deploying MTD techniques could be limited based on system constraints. For instance, VM-LM (Shuffle) might be restricted from one host to another one due to lack of space on the target host, or OS Diversification (Diversity) could be limited to only a few OS instances due to the cost of the license for the cloud provider. Thus, the MTD techniques should be chosen based on the defined system constraints.

MTD Deployment Implementation. The final phase of the cloud security framework is the deployment of selected MTD techniques on the cloud infrastructure. It uses .NET Core and OpenStack APIs to deploy MTD techniques, it utilizes glance for creating and retrieving OS instance images, nova, and network controllers for accessing and manipulating VMs and Network purposes.

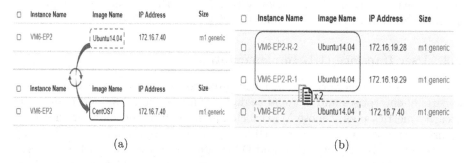

(a)   (b)

Fig. 4. MTD Techniques for (a) OS Diversification: Ubuntu14.04 replaces with CentOS7 for vm_6-EP2, (b) OS Replication: Create 2 replicas for vm_6-EP2.

Diversity: Security analysis framework uses OS diversification technique for deploying Diversity. To deploy Diversity, backend engine uses nova to access the desired VM and update the VM instances with another OS image. Then, the user credential information should be sent to the Keystone controller using JSON API call for authentication. Backend engine omits this phase as the authentication token is already received in information collection phase. Moreover, both nova and glance controllers are fetched from the response message. Before calling API to change the VM instance, we need to fetch the ImageRef by sending an API to glance. Then, the ImageRef associated to the desired VM image can be obtained. Finally, an API is called to pass the authentication token, VM ID, ImageRef to the nova to change the OS variant. Figure 4a shows the results of calling APIs for replacing Ubuntu14.04 with CentOS7 for vm_6-EP2 on the cloud.

Redundancy: Redundancy technique creates different replicas of a VM should so that each replica has the same feature as the main VM. Backend engine is responsible for deploying redundancy. However, the number of replicas for deploying redundancy is chosen by either MTD evaluation part or expert entry using UI. There is no feature on OpenStack to create replication for each VM. Thus, deploying redundancy on OpenStack needs creation r new VMs based on the similar existing instance or copied snapshot. Backend engine can use the same authentication token already obtained from the information collection phase and use nova controller. Thus, the backend engine sends an API to nova controller including the authentication token, ImageRef, FlavorRef, NetworkID together with a max_count which is the number of required replicas (r). Figure 4b demonstrates the results of calling APIs for the creation of two new replicas of vm_6-EP2 with the same OS, links, hosts, flavors.

Shuffle: We utilize VM-LM to deploy Shuffle technique. VM-LM can be deployed on the OpenStack using nova controller. Similar to other MTD techniques, the backend engine omits the authentication API call because the authentication token and nove controllers have already been fetched in the information collection section. The target host can be selected either by MTD evaluation results or security experts. In order to deploy VM-LM, an API including authentication token together with the VM ID and Target Host ID is called.

3.3   User Interface (UI) Implementation

Cloud security framework uses a UI in order to interact between the security experts of enterprises and backend engine. Security experts can add update the security metrics pool, choose MTD techniques, analyze and monitor the cloud security using visualization panel. UI is implemented as a web application using JavaScript, JSON, jQuery Ajax, and D3.js interacting with the backend engine. UI web application includes two different perspectives for visualization. Cloud provider and security model previews. Cloud provider preview illustrates the internal connection of the VMs, routers, subnets, and etc. in the cloud, and security model preview visualizes the generated upper layer of HARM which captures the reachability of VMs based on the firewall rules and possible attack scenarios. UI also shows the vulnerabilities captured for each VM. UI uses internal APIs to communicate with backend engine and update and gain information. Figure 6 demonstrates the UI panel showing two different previous based on the UniteCloud network and HARM view.

4   Results and Discussion

We evaluated the usability of the cloud security framework engine by considering the API calls passing through the backend and two other parties: Nessus vulnerability scanning tool, and OpenStack controllers. The details of API calls like the type of APIs and elapsed times are elucidated in this section.

Cloud security framework uses two types of APIs which can be categorized as *informative calls (ICs)* and *operational calls (OCs)*. The first group can be only used to get the information like getting authentication tokens, list of hosts, VMs, *etc.*, these APIs will not make any changes on the cloud. Unlike the first group, *operational calls* can perform an operation and make the changes on the cloud such as migrating a VM from one host to another one, or changing the VM's instance, *etc.* We measure the informative calls with the response time (T_R). Particularly, T_R is the total time needed for sending a request to the cloud and receiving the required information. For instance, the T_R of a keystone authentication call is the time elapsed between calling API and receiving the response from keystone showing accepted status 202 together with the required information in the body of message. However, *operational calls* consist of: (1) Reaction Time (T_γ) which is the time between calling API and the start time of an operation. Note that the response for an API call may include some acknowledge such as denied, abort, unauthorized, *etc.* which means the operational call was unsuccessful. In this case T_γ includes the response time. (2) Operational Time (T_o) which means the difference between the start of an operation using API calls and the time in which the task is fully done. (3) Completion Time (T_C) which is the total time for completion of an operational call: $T_\gamma + T_o$; for instance, the total time between sending a request for VM-LM process and the end of the process.

Table 1. Benchmark Analysis for MTD API calls.

API calls		VM status	Request numbers (time in Second)										Ave.	Std.
MTD	Time type		1	2	3	4	5	6	7	8	9	10		
S	T_γ	Up	0.65	0.77	0.42	0.43	0.42	0.55	0.45	0.45	0.71	0.43	0.53	0.13
	T_o	Down	10.00	11.00	13.00	12.00	9.00	18.00	11.00	13.00	17.00	11.00	12.50	2.77
	T_C	N/A	10.65	11.77	13.42	12.43	9.42	18.55	11.45	13.45	17.71	11.43	13.03	2.80
D	T_γ	Up	0.56	0.72	0.66	0.44	0.42	0.42	0.70	0.81	0.44	0.68	0.58	0.14
	T_o	Down	18.00	17.00	18.00	20.00	17.00	19.00	16.00	19.00	18.00	18.00	18.00	1.10
	T_C	N/A	18.56	17.72	18.66	20.44	17.42	19.42	16.70	19.81	18.44	18.68	18.58	1.06
R (3-R)	T_γ	Up	0.73	0.73	0.76	0.74	1.08	0.76	0.82	0.75	0.91	1.06	0.83	0.13
	T_o	Up	10.00	10.00	11.00	11.00	12.00	12.00	11.00	12.00	11.00	11.00	11.10	0.70
	T_C	Up	10.73	10.73	11.76	11.74	13.08	12.76	11.82	12.75	11.91	12.06	11.93	0.75

MTD Deployment Measures: We developed the experiments by performing a Benchmark analysis for deploying three Shuffle (S), Diversity (D), and Redundancy (R) MTD techniques on the OpenStack. We evaluated the operational API calls by measuring the T_γ, T_o, and T_C obtained based on a sequence of 10 API requests. We sent these request to the cloud for deploying MTD techniques on

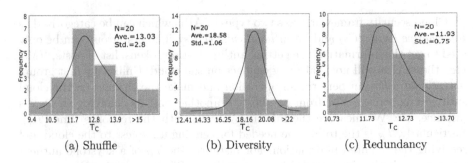

(a) Shuffle   (b) Diversity   (c) Redundancy

Fig. 5. The historgams showing the T_C distributions for MTD deployments.

the VM-6-EP2 which uses Ubuntu14.04 and m1.generic flavor size. For analyzing Shuffle, we send operational API calls to the cloud for randomly migrating vm_6-EP2 to other Hosts and measured the operational times for each request. For Diversity, we repeated the experiments by changing the vm_6-EP2 OS to CentOS and vice versa and measured the time. Finally, we analyze Redundancy by creating three replicas (3-R) for vm_6-EP2 named as vm_6-EP2-R-1, vm_6-EP2-R-2, and vm_6-EP2-R-3. We tabulated the measurements of operational times for all MTD techniques on each request together with the average, and standard deviation values in Table 1. The results show that the average T_C for S, D, and R (3-R) are 13.03, 18.58, and 11.93 s, respectively. Moreover, the results show that the VM is active (Up) during T_γ, while the VM is not accessible (Down) during T_o for both S and D. The VM status is N/A during T_C if there T_γ be in Up and T_o be in Down states. However, the VM status for R is always UP as there are always at least one replication of a VM which can work without the interruption or downtime. We extended our analysis by conducting experiments for a sequence of 20 API requests to measure the operational time for MTD techniques with

Table 2. The results of three security metrics: Risk, AC, and RoA on the cloud resulting from deploying MTD techniques on EP_1 and EP_2.

VM	Shuffle (EP1)			Diversity (EP1)			Shuffle (EP2)			Diversity (EP2)		
	R	AC	RoA	R	AC	RoA	R	AC	RoA	R	AC	RoA
vm_0	34.2	50.5	18.9	48.7	79.2	26.6	47.9	70.9	26.9	65.0	117.9	35.2
vm_1	31.1	45.7	16.9	47.3	87.9	25.1	53.5	79.2	30.3	65.5	115.1	35.8
vm_2	32.1	47.3	17.6	47.8	85.0	25.6	44.7	66.1	24.9	65.0	117.9	35.2
vm_3	45.4	67	25.1	47.8	85.0	25.6	53.3	78.8	29.7	63.7	126.6	33.6
vm_4	34.5	51.2	19.5	47.6	81.2	26.1	56.6	84	32.3	66.4	105.7	37.3
vm_5	30.7	45.5	17.5	45.5	89.0	24.4	63.9	94.8	36.4	65.7	108.3	36.8
vm_6	31.9	47.4	18.2	46.9	83.8	25.5	49.9	74.1	28.3	62.2	121.3	34.0
vm_7	25.4	37.5	14.2	45.5	89.0	24.4	41.4	61.4	23.6	62.9	118.7	34.6

more accuracy. We divided the T_C into different intervals and counted the number of occurrence for each group. Figure 5 demonstrates the histograms for MTD techniques based on the measured times for 20 requests (N = 20). We observe that most Shuffle technique requests can be completed between 11.7 and 12.8 s. Moreover, Diversity can be fully deployed between 18.16 and 20.08 s in most of the cases. Finally, Redundancy API requests for creation of three replicas (3-R) can be fully served between 11.73 and 12.73 s in most of the cases.

Security Metrics Evaluation: We also evaluated the effectiveness of the MTD techniques in terms of system security. We adopted three security metrics Risk, AC, and RoA into the metrics pool and evaluate each MTD technique. Those metrics are useful for evaluation of Shuffle and Diversity and have already been investigated for evaluation of MTD techniques on cloud through simulation [3]. However, more security metrics can be similarly used to evaluate other security aspects of the cloud [22]. Table 2 shows the security metrics resulting from deploying MTD techniques on each VM on the cloud for both EP1 and EP2. Those results can be used by MTD Evaluation phase in the Security Analysis Engine 3a to find and deploy the most effective deployment. Comparing the results for deploying MTD techniques for EP1, we can observe that deploying Shuffle on vm_7 can lead to better result in terms of Risk and RoA metrics which yield 25.4 and 14.2, respectively. Similarly, deploying Diversity on vm_7 yields 45.5, 89, and 24.4 for Risk, AC, and RoA, respectively. Likewise, deploying Shuffle on vm_7 for EP2 cause lower Risk and RoA values and deploying Diversity on vm_6 provides the better results in terms of Risk and RoA which yields 62.9 and 34.6, respectively. However, the best results for AC is deploying Diversity on vm_6 yields 121.3. Ultimately, the results shows that deploying Shuffle yields better results that Diversity in terms of Risk and RoA metrics. Deploying Diversity yields a gentle decrements for Risk and RoA in the best case while those metrics are almost halved after deploying best Shuffle scenario. However, Diversity yields better results for AC and increases AC.

Limitations: The update phase has not been implemented in cloud security framework. This includes running of Nessus scanning and recreation of HARM based on any changes captured in the cloud, such as updating VMs or vulnerabilities. We will further consider the update phase in our future work. The main aim of Redundancy technique is to enhance the service availability in the cloud. Redundancy can be measured with the concepts of system dependability (e.g. reliability and availability) which is out of scope of this paper. We will further consider dependability metrics for evaluating Redundancy on real cloud in our future work.

5   Related Work

The theoretical investigation and evaluation of the security modeling and analysis adopting based on the MTD techniques for cloud computing have been proposed in the work [4, 12]. However, most of the proposed frameworks have focused on the implementations of GSMs on the networks [9, 10, 14, 17]. The security modeling and analysis tools on the literature can be categorized based on the context of implementation test-bed such as cloud computing [7], networks and enterprises [18], or based on GSMs [11], ATs [9], AGs [13], *etc.*, the automation approaches and levels [20], or based on the effectiveness of solution like response time and the probability of success [20]. The work [10] proposed a prototype for 3D graphical visualization of the system, attack, and countermeasure model. In [18], the authors proposed and implemented a fast network security assessment prototype based on the real scenario. However, the work [7] developed a framework named NICE in the virtual network systems which is able to detect possible attacks against the cloud infrastructure. To the best of our knowledge, there is no prior work developing the MTD techniques incorporated with the automated GSMs in a cloud environment. In this paper, we developed an automated cloud security framework able to monitor and detect a private cloud and deploy MTD techniques on the infrastructures of the cloud.

6   Conclusions

In this paper, we have investigated on practicability and usability of incorporating MTD techniques into GSMs as a framework on the real cloud. We have developed a cloud security framework which is able to run on a private cloud platform named UniteCloud. The developed framework can (1) automatically monitor the cloud and collect the information such as hosts, VMs, network, and vulnerabilities existing on each VM using OpenStack APIs, (2) model and evaluate the cloud's security and adopt defensive MTD techniques, (3) automate the deployment of three MTD techniques OS Diversification as the Diversity technique, VM replication as the Redundancy technique, and VM-LM as the shuffle technique on the infrastructures of the UniteCloud using API calls, and (4) use a web application UI for interaction between the security experts and the backend engine of the framework and also visualize the generated security model. Finally, we have evaluated MTD techniques based on real measurements and security metrics and showed that MTD techniques can be adopted in the real cloud infrastructure.

Appendix A

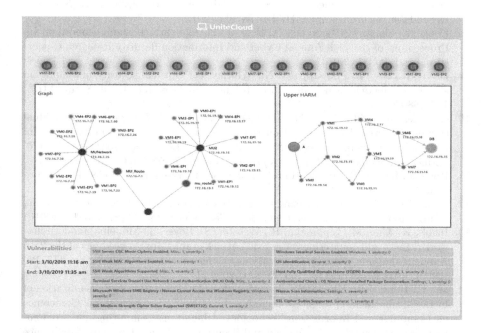

Fig. 6. Cloud security framework UI panel: UniteCloud Graph view and HARM visualization.

References

1. Unitecloud. http://www.unitecloud.net/
2. Alavizadeh, H., Hong, J.B., Jang-Jaccard, J., Kim, D.S.: Comprehensive security assessment of combined MTD techniques for the cloud. In: Proceedings of the 5th ACM Workshop on Moving Target Defense, pp. 11–20. ACM (2018)
3. Alavizadeh, H., Jang-Jaccard, J., Kim, D.S.: Evaluation for combination of shuffle and diversity on moving target defense strategy for cloud computing. In: 2018 17th IEEE International Conference on Trust, Security and Privacy in Computing and Communications/12th IEEE International Conference on Big Data Science and Engineering (TrustCom/BigDataSE), pp. 573–578. IEEE (2018)
4. Alavizadeh, H., Kim, D.S., Hong, J.B., Jang-Jaccard, J.: Effective security analysis for combinations of MTD techniques on cloud computing (Short Paper). In: Liu, J.K., Samarati, P. (eds.) ISPEC 2017. LNCS, vol. 10701, pp. 539–548. Springer, Cham (2017). https://doi.org/10.1007/978-3-319-72359-4_32
5. Alavizadeh, H., Kim, D.S., Jang-Jaccard, J.: Model-based evaluation of combinations of shuffle and diversity MTD techniques on the cloud. Fut. Gener. Comput. Syst. (2019). https://doi.org/10.1016/j.future.2019.10.009

6. Beale, J., Deraison, R., Meer, H., Temmingh, R., Walt, C.: The NESSUS project. Syngress Publishing (2002). http://www.nessus.org
7. Chung, C.J., Khatkar, P., Xing, T., Lee, J., Huang, D.: Nice: Network intrusion detection and countermeasure selection in virtual network systems. IEEE Trans. Dependable Secure Comput. 10(4), 198–211 (2013)
8. Cook, K., Shaw, T., Hawrylak, P., Hale, J.: Scalable attack graph generation. In: Proceedings of the 11th Annual Cyber and Information Security Research Conference, p. 21. ACM (2016)
9. Dewri, R., Ray, I., Poolsappasit, N., Whitley, D.: Optimal security hardening on attack tree models of networks: a cost-benefit analysis. Int. J. Inf. Secur. 11(3), 167–188 (2012)
10. Gonzalez Granadillo, G., Débar, H., Jacob, G., Gaber, C., Achemlal, M.: Individual countermeasure selection based on the return on response investment index. In: Kotenko, I., Skormin, V. (eds.) MMM-ACNS 2012. LNCS, vol. 7531, pp. 156–170. Springer, Heidelberg (2012). https://doi.org/10.1007/978-3-642-33704-8_14
11. Hong, J., Kim, D.S.: Harms: Hierarchical attack representation models for network security analysis (2012)
12. Hong, J.B., Kim, D.S.: Assessing the effectiveness of moving target defenses using security models. IEEE Trans. Dependable Secure Comput. 13(2), 163–177 (2016)
13. Ingols, K., Chu, M., Lippmann, R., Webster, S., Boyer, S.: Modeling modern network attacks and countermeasures using attack graphs. In: Proceedings of the 25th Annual Computer Security Applications Conference (ACSAC 2009), pp. 117–126 (2009). https://doi.org/10.1109/ACSAC.2009.21
14. Jia, F., Hong, J.B., Kim, D.S.: Towards automated generation and visualization of hierarchical attack representation models. In: 2015 IEEE International Conference on Computer and Information Technology; Ubiquitous Computing and Communications; Dependable, Autonomic and Secure Computing; Pervasive Intelligence and Computing, pp. 1689–1696. IEEE (2015)
15. Kordy, B., Pietre-Cambacedes, L., Schweitzer, P.: DAG-Based Attack and Defense Modeling: Don't Miss the Forest for the Attack Trees. CoRR abs/1303.7397 (2013)
16. Kordy, B., Mauw, S., Radomirović, S., Schweitzer, P.: Attack-defense trees. J. Logic Comput. 24(1), 55–87 (2014)
17. Kotenko, I., Chechulin, A.: Computer attack modeling and security evaluation based on attack graphs. In: 2013 IEEE 7th International Conference on Intelligent Data Acquisition and Advanced Computing Systems (IDAACS), vol. 2, pp. 614–619. IEEE (2013)
18. Kotenko, I.V., Doynikova, E.: Evaluation of computer network security based on attack graphs and security event processing. JoWUA 5(3), 14–29 (2014)
19. Mell, P., Scarfone, K., Romanosky, S.: Common vulnerability scoring system. IEEE Secur. Priv. 4(6), 85–89 (2006)
20. Nespoli, P., Papamartzivanos, D., Mármol, F.G., Kambourakis, G.: Optimal countermeasures selection against cyber attacks: a comprehensive survey on reaction frameworks. IEEE Commun. Surv. Tutor. 20(2), 1361–1396 (2018)
21. Sgandurra, D., Lupu, E.: Evolution of attacks, threat models, and solutions for virtualized systems. ACM Comput. Surv. (CSUR) 48(3), 46 (2016)
22. Yusuf, S.E., Ge, M., Hong, J.B., Kim, H.K., Kim, P., Kim, D.S.: Security modelling and analysis of dynamic enterprise networks. In: 2016 IEEE International Conference on Computer and Information Technology (CIT), pp. 249–256. IEEE (2016)
23. Zissis, D., Lekkas, D.: Addressing cloud computing security issues. Future Gener. Comput. Syst. 28(3), 583–592 (2012)

Security Analysis of Group Action Inverse Problem with Auxiliary Inputs with Application to CSIDH Parameters

Taechan Kim[✉]

NTT Secure Platform Laboratories, Tokyo, Japan
taechan.kim.ym@hco.ntt.co.jp

Abstract. In this paper, we consider the security of a problem called *Group Action Inverse Problem with Auxiliary Inputs (GAIPwAI)*. The Group Action Inverse Problem (GAIP) plays an important role in the security of several isogeny-based cryptosystems, such as CSIDH, SeaSign and CSI-FiSh.

Briefly speaking, given two isogenous supersingular curves E and E' over $\mathbb{F}_p$, where E' is defined by an ideal $\mathfrak{a}$ in the $\mathbb{F}_p$-endomorphism ring of E and denoted by $E' = [\mathfrak{a}] * E$, GAIP requires finding $\mathfrak{a} \subset \mathrm{End}_{\mathbb{F}_p}(E)$. Its best classical algorithm is based on the baby-step-giant-step method and it runs in time $O(p^{1/4})$.

In this paper, we show that if E and E' are given together with $[\mathfrak{a}^d] * E$ for a positive divisor d that divides the order of the class group of $\mathbb{Z}[\sqrt{-p}]$, then $\mathfrak{a}$ can be computed in $O\big((p^{1/2}/d)^{1/2} + d^{1/2}\big)$ time complexity. In particular, when $d \approx p^{1/4}$, it can be solved in time $O(p^{1/8})$ which is significantly less than $O(p^{1/4})$.

Applying the idea to CSIDH-512 parameters, we show that, if an additional isogenous curve $[\mathfrak{a}^d] * E$ is given, the security level of this cryptosystem reduces to 68-bit security instead of 128-bit security as originally believed.

Keywords: Isogeny-based cryptography · Cryptanalysis · Post-quantum cryptography · CSIDH · Cheon's algorithm

1 Introduction

In the first proposal, Couveignes [12] and independently Robstovtsev and Stolbunov [18] described a non-interactive key exchange protocol based on the group action of the ideal class group $\mathrm{Cl}(\mathcal{O})$ on the set of $\mathbb{F}_q$-isomorphism classes of ordinary elliptic curves over $\mathbb{F}_q$, where $\mathcal{O}$ is an order in imaginary quadratic field and is isomorphic to the endomorphism ring of the ordinary curve. Since $\mathrm{Cl}(\mathcal{O})$ is commutative, it naturally allows one to construct Diffie-Hellman type key exchange protocol.

Later, however, this commutativity allowed Childs, Jao and Soukharev [11] to obtain a quantum algorithm to break the Couveignes-Robstovtsev-Stolbunov

© Springer Nature Switzerland AG 2020
J. H. Seo (Ed.): ICISC 2019, LNCS 11975, pp. 165–174, 2020.
https://doi.org/10.1007/978-3-030-40921-0_10

scheme in subexponential time complexity $L_q[1/2]$. Since then, cryptographic research mainly concentrated on isogeny problems related to supersingular elliptic curves, where the class group action is not used. A popular scheme in this line of research is SIDH (Supersingular Isogeny Diffie-Hellman).

A rehabilitation of Couveignes-Robstovtsev-Stolbunov scheme is recently carried out by Castryck et al. [6], where they restricted their consideration to the group action on the set of $\mathbb{F}_p$-isomorphism classes of supersingular elliptic curves defined over $\mathbb{F}_p$. In such cases, the $\mathbb{F}_p$-rational endomorphism ring of the supersingular curve is again isomorphic to an order $\mathcal{O}$ in an imaginary quadratic field, thus $\mathrm{Cl}(\mathcal{O})$ becomes commutative. There still remains the issue that this commutativity allows subexponential quantum algorithms for the base problem, but since it is very practical compared to previous schemes, it is considered to be secure although it suffers from a subexponential quantum attack. This proposal is called CSIDH and it is our main concern in this paper. Since the proposal of CSIDH, there have been several attempts to achieve practical isogeny-based signature schemes based on the class group actions. This includes schemes such as SeaSign [13] and CSI-FiSh [1].

An important computational problem in the class group action based cryptosystems is to compute an explicit isogeny between two supersingular curves E and E' over $\mathbb{F}_p$, where E' is a curve isogenous to E defined by an ideal $\mathfrak{a}$ in the $\mathbb{F}_p$-rational endomorphism ring of E, denoted by $\mathcal{O} \cong \mathrm{End}_{\mathbb{F}_p}(E)$. We denote this action of $\mathfrak{a}$ on E by $\mathfrak{a} * E$, i.e. $E' = \mathfrak{a} * E$. This action can be shown to be free and transitive, and it only depends on the class of $\mathfrak{a}$ in $\mathrm{Cl}(\mathcal{O})$, where $\mathrm{Cl}(\mathcal{O})$ denotes the class group of $\mathcal{O}$. Finding an explicit isogeny between E and $\mathfrak{a} * E$ is equivalent to finding the secret ideal $\mathfrak{a}$. This problem is called the *Group Action Inverse Problem (GAIP)*. The GAIP can be considered as a generalization of the notion of the discrete logarithm problem (DLP): given g and $h := g^a$ in a cyclic group G, find $a \in \mathbb{Z}_{\#G}$. As with DLP, a best classical algorithm of solving GAIP is based on the meet-in-the-middle approach, where the time complexity is $O\big(\sqrt{\#\mathrm{Cl}(\mathcal{O})}\big)$.

In the setting of DLP-based cryptography, there have been lots of attempts to use variants of DLP to construct cryptosystems that achieve fruitful functionalities. For instance, many pairing-based cryptography base their security on problems called, to name a few, strong-DH problem, bilinear DH inversion problem, and so on. In general, these variant problems can be considered as particular instances of the problem called DLP with Auxiliary Inputs (DLPwAI), where the problem asks to find the discrete logarithm a for given $g, g^a, g^{a^2}, \ldots, g^{a^d}$. There are several algorithms [8–10,16] that tackle this problem which started from Cheon's algorithm [7,8]. Cheon proposed an efficient algorithm better than the usual baby-step-giant-step algorithm, when d is a divisor of $p \pm 1$ where p is a prime order of the group G.

Recalling the similarities of GAIP and DLP, our motivation in this paper is to answer the following question: if we are given E and $\mathfrak{a} * E$ together with some more informations on the secret $\mathfrak{a} \subset \mathcal{O}$, will there be any efficient algorithm to solve $\mathfrak{a}$ better than time complexity of $O(\sqrt{\#\mathrm{Cl}(\mathcal{O})})$? To answer this question, we generalize the notion of DLPwAI to the setting of GAIP. Then it is not hard to see Cheon's algorithm also applies to our setting.

2   Preliminaries

2.1   Elliptic Curves and Isogenies

Let E be an elliptic curve over a finite field $\mathbb{F}_p$ with p a large prime. The curve E is called supersingular if and only if $\#E(\mathbb{F}_p) = p + 1$, and ordinary otherwise.

Given two elliptic curves E and E', an isogeny $\phi : E \to E'$ is a non-constant rational map which is also a group homomorphism from E to E' over the algebraic closure of $\mathbb{F}_p$. A separable isogeny ϕ is uniquely determined by a subgroup $S \subset E(\mathbb{F}_{p^k})$ with $\ker \phi = S$, i.e. $E' = E/S$. Vélu's algorithm [19] computes an equation for E' and thus enables one to compute the isogeny ϕ. Its computation requires $O(\#S(k \log p)^2)$ operations in $\mathbb{F}_{p^k}$.

For an elliptic curve E over a prime field $\mathbb{F}_p$, we define $\mathrm{End}(E)$ to be the ring of endomorphisms (isogenies from E to itself) of E defined over the algebraic closure of $\mathbb{F}_p$, and $\mathrm{End}_{\mathbb{F}_p}(E)$ to be the ring of endomorphisms of E defined over $\mathbb{F}_p$. Let $\mathcal{O}$ be an order in the imaginary quadratic field $\mathbb{Q}(\sqrt{-p})$. For an ordinary curve E, we have $\mathrm{End}(E) \cong \mathcal{O}$, whereas $\mathrm{End}_{\mathbb{F}_p}(E) \cong \mathcal{O}$ for a supersingular curve E.

The ideal class group of $\mathcal{O}$, denoted by $\mathrm{Cl}(\mathcal{O})$, is the quotient of the group of fractional invertible ideals in $\mathcal{O}$ by the principal fractional invertible ideals. Given an ideal $\mathfrak{a} \subset \mathcal{O}$, one can consider the subgroup $E[\mathfrak{a}] = \{P \in E(\overline{\mathbb{F}}_p) : \alpha(P) = 0, \forall \alpha \in \mathfrak{a}\}$ and this uniquely determines the isogenous curve $E' = E/E[\mathfrak{a}]$ under the isogeny $\phi : E \to E'$ with $\ker \phi = E[\mathfrak{a}]$. This defines the action of $\mathcal{O}$ on E and we denote E' by $\mathfrak{a} * E$. Since $\mathfrak{a} * E$ only depends on the class of $\mathfrak{a}$ in $\mathrm{Cl}(\mathcal{O})$, it again defines an action of $\mathrm{Cl}(\mathcal{O})$ on the set $\mathcal{E}$ of $\mathbb{F}_p$-isomorphism classes of elliptic curves with $\mathbb{F}_p$-rational endomorphism ring $\mathcal{O}$. One can show $\mathrm{Cl}(\mathcal{O})$-action on $\mathcal{E}$ is free and transitive, i.e. $\mathcal{E}$ is a principal homogenous space for $\mathrm{Cl}(\mathcal{O})$ in terms of Couveigne [12].

2.2   CSIDH

For an arbitrary ideal $\mathfrak{a} \subset \mathcal{O}$, the subgroup $E[\mathfrak{a}]$ could be defined over $\mathbb{F}_{p^k}$ for arbitrarily large k. In such a case, the group action $\mathfrak{a} * E$ is unlikely to be computed efficiently. For the $\mathrm{Cl}(\mathcal{O})$-action on $\mathcal{E}$ to be efficiently computable, Castryck et al. [6] suggested using a supersingular curve $E/\mathbb{F}_p$ with a special form of p so that $\#E(\mathbb{F}_p)$ is smooth, i.e. only contains small prime factors. More precisely, let p be a prime of the form $4 \cdot \ell_1 \cdots \ell_n - 1$ with ℓ_i small distinct odd primes. Then we have $\#E(\mathbb{F}_p) = p + 1 = 4 \cdot \ell_1 \cdots \ell_n$. Furthermore, all ℓ_i are Elkies primes, i.e. the principal ideal (ℓ_i) splits as $(\ell_i) = \langle \ell_i, \pi - 1 \rangle \langle \ell_i, \pi + 1 \rangle$ in $\mathcal{O} \cong \mathrm{End}_{\mathbb{F}_p}(E)$, where $\pi = \sqrt{-p}$ represents the $\mathbb{F}_p$-Frobenius endomorphism. As the subgroup $E[\mathfrak{l}_i]$ corresponding to the prime ideal $\mathfrak{l}_i = \langle \ell_i, \pi - 1 \rangle$ is defined over $\mathbb{F}_p$, Vélu's formula can efficiently compute the action of $\mathfrak{l}_i$ which requires $O(\ell_i (\log p)^2)$ operations.

CSIDH [6] performs the Diffie-Hellman key exchange protocol by acting on ideals of the form $\prod_{i=1}^{n} \mathfrak{l}_i^{e_i}$, where the exponents are chosen uniformly from an interval, say, $[-B, B]$. This group action can be computed efficiently as the composition of actions by small prime ideals. In CSIDH, we assume that the ideal $\prod_{i=1}^{n} \mathfrak{l}_i^{e_i}$ is uniformly distributed over $\mathrm{Cl}(\mathcal{O})$. This deliberate choice of ideals is due to the fact that the structure of the class group is unknown, and it seems difficult to represent any random ideal $\mathfrak{a}$ as a factorisation of small prime ideals. As a remark, the class group computation requires subexponential time in $\log(p)$ using classical algorithms [15].

Recently, Beullens et al. [1] succeed in the computing the structure of the class group of an imaginary quadratic field of 154-digit discriminant which is central to the CSIDH-512 cryptosystem. They exploit the structure of this class group to propose an efficient isogeny-based signature scheme called CSI-FiSh.

2.3   Computational Problems

Several isogeny-based cryptosystems based on the class group action, such as CSIDH [6], SeaSign [13] and CSI-FiSh [1], base their security on the hardness of inverting the group action problem. Stolbunov called it *Group Action Inverse Problem (GAIP)* and Couveignes called it *Hard Homogenous Spaces*. Throughout this paper, we shall use Stolbunov's term.

Definition 1 (Group Action Inverse Problem (GAIP)). *Let G be a finite abelian group and X be a set. Denote G-action on X by $* : G \times X \to X$. Assume that $*$ is free and transitive. Given x and x' in X, the group action inverse problem (GAIP) is a problem of recovering $a \in G$ such that $x' = a * x$.*

In class group-based cryptosystems, it translates to finding an ideal $\mathfrak{a} \subset \mathcal{O}$ such that $E' = \mathfrak{a} * E$, given two isogenous curves E and E' with $\mathrm{End}(E) = \mathrm{End}(E') = \mathcal{O}$.

The discrete logarithm problem (DLP) can also be seen as an instance of GAIP with $G = \mathbb{Z}_N$ and X a cyclic group generated by x of order N. In this case, G-action on X is defined as the exponentiation of $x \in X$ by $a \in G$, i.e. x^a, and the DLP is to find $a \in \mathbb{Z}_N$ given x and x^a.

The best classical algorithm to solve the GAIP problem is the baby-step-giant-step approach where its time complexity is $O(\sqrt{\#G})$.

2.4   Discrete Logarithm Problem with Auxiliary Inputs

Several pairing-based cryptosystems [2–4] base their security on variants of DLP such as the strong Diffie-Hellman problem. Cheon [7,8] generalized these variant problems and called it the *discrete logarithm problem with auxiliary inputs* which is stated as follows:

Definition 2 (DLP with Auxiliary Inputs (DLPwAI)). *Let X be a cyclic group generated by x of prime order q. Define $G = \mathbb{Z}_q^\times$, a multiplicative group of integers modulo q. Given $x, x^a, \ldots, x^{a^d}$ for an integer d and $a \in G$, the discrete logarithm problem with auxiliary inputs is solved by finding a.*

Cheon also proposed an efficient algorithm when d is a divisor of $q - 1$. This runs in time complexity $O(\sqrt{p/d} + \sqrt{d})$ which is faster than the baby-step-giant-step algorithm. Essentially, the key observation used by his algorithm is that G has a subgroup H of order d when $d \mid (q - 1)$.

3   Group Action Inverse Problem with Auxiliary Inputs

In this section, we define the group action inverse problem with auxiliary inputs (GAIPwAI). Roughly speaking, it is a problem to find the secret group element $a \in G$, given x and $x' = a * x$ in X together with several elements in X that contain some information on a. It can be seen as a generalization of the notion of DLPwAI. And we show that Cheon's algorithm can easily be adapted to solve this problem.

In the following, we assume that the group G is always a finite abelian group. By the structure theorem for finite abelian groups, we can write G as

$$G \cong \langle g_1 \rangle \times \cdots \times \langle g_n \rangle,$$

where g_i has the order N_i and denote $\#G$ by $N = \prod_{i=1}^{n} N_i$.

We state the definition of GAIPwAI as follows.

Definition 3 (GAIP with Auxiliary Inputs (GAIPwAI)). *Consider a free and transitive G-action on a set X with an operation $*$. For $a \in G$, we write $a = \prod_{i=1}^{n} g_i^{r_i}$, where $0 \leq r_i < N_i$. Let $d := (d_1, \ldots, d_n)$ be n-tuple of positive integers. Define $a^d = a^{(d_1, \ldots, d_n)} := \prod_{i=1}^{n} (g_i^{r_i})^{d_i}$. Given $x, x_1 := a * x$ and $x_d := (a^d) * x$, GAIP with auxiliary inputs is the problem of finding $a \in G$.*

We show the following theorem of which the proof can be seen as a simple generalization of Cheon's algorithm. This algorithm is deterministic, but relatively large storage is required. We shall also describe the low-memory version of this algorithm later which is based on Pollard's lambda approach.

Theorem 1. *Use the same notation as above. Assume that d_i is a divisor of N_i for all $i = 1, \ldots, n$. Given x, x_1 and x_d, one can find $a \in G$ deterministically in time complexity $O\left(\prod_{i=1}^{n} \sqrt{N_i/d_i} + \prod_{i=1}^{n} \sqrt{d_i} \right)$ using the same amount of storage.*

Proof. First, observe that $b := a^d$ is an element in a subgroup $H \subset G$, where

$$H \cong \langle g_1^{d_1} \rangle \times \cdots \times \langle g_n^{d_n} \rangle := \langle h_1 \rangle \times \cdots \times \langle h_n \rangle$$

and h_i is of order N_i/d_i. As a first step, we would like to find out $l_i \in \mathbb{Z}_{N_i/d_i}$ satisfying $b = h_1^{l_1} \cdots h_n^{l_n}$. Write l_i as $l_i = \left\lceil \sqrt{N_i/d_i} \right\rceil u_i + v_i$, where u_i and v_i are integers less than $\sqrt{N_i/d_i}$. Given x_d, one computes the group actions by $\prod_{i=1}^{n} h_i^{-v_i}$ on x_d for all integers v_i less than $\sqrt{N_i/d_i}$ and stores them. It requires

$O(\prod_{i=1}^n \sqrt{N_i/d_i})$ group actions and the same amount of storage. Then one computes $\left(\prod_{i=1}^n h_i^{\lceil \sqrt{N_i/d_i} \rceil \cdot u_i}\right) * x$ using $O(\prod_{i=1}^n \sqrt{N_i/d_i})$ group actions. If we have a tuple $(u_1, \ldots, u_n, v_1, \ldots, v_n)$ such that

$$\left(\prod_{i=1}^n h_i^{-v_i}\right) * x_d = \left(\prod_{i=1}^n h_i^{\lceil \sqrt{N_i/d_i} \rceil \cdot u_i}\right) * x,$$

we recover $(l_1, \ldots, l_n)$ such that $b = h_1^{l_1} \cdots h_n^{l_n}$.

Once we have found such l_i's, then it remains to recover $k_i \in \mathbb{Z}_{d_i}$ such that $r_i = (N_i/d_i)k_i + l_i$, where $a = \prod_{i=1}^n g_i^{r_i}$. In other words, it satisfies that

$$\left(\prod_{i=1}^n g_i^{-l_i}\right) \cdot a = \prod_{i=1}^n g_i^{(N_i/d_i)k_i}.$$

To find such k_i's, similarly as before we first write $k_i = \lceil \sqrt{d_i} \rceil s_i + t_i$, where s_i and t_i are less than $\sqrt{d_i}$. By finding a collision such that

$$\left(\prod_{i=1}^n g_i^{-(N_i/d_i)t_i}\right) * \left(\left(\prod_{i=1}^n g_i^{-l_i}\right) * x_1\right) = \left(\prod_{i=1}^n g_i^{(N_i/d_i)\lceil \sqrt{d_i} \rceil s_i}\right) * x,$$

we deduce the desired value for k_i's. This second step costs $O(\prod_{i=1}^n \sqrt{d_i})$ time complexity and the same amount of memory. $\qquad\square$

From the above proof, one might observe that solving GAIPwAI splits into the following problems: (1) one is to find $(l_1, \ldots, l_n) \in \mathbb{Z}_{N_1/d_1} \times \cdots \times \mathbb{Z}_{N_n/d_n}$ given $x, b * x = (h_1^{l_1} \cdots h_n^{l_n}) * x \in X$ and $h = (h_1, \ldots, h_n) \in G$, and (2) the other is to find $(k_1, \ldots, k_n) \in \mathbb{Z}_{d_1} \times \cdots \times \mathbb{Z}_{d_n}$ given $x, \tilde{b} * x := (\tilde{h}_1^{k_1} \cdots \tilde{h}_n^{k_n}) * x \in X$ and $\tilde{h} = (\tilde{h}_1, \ldots, \tilde{h}_n) \in G$, where we define $\tilde{h}_i := g^{N_i/d_i}$ and $\tilde{b} * x$ is computed as $(g_1^{-l_1} \cdots g_n^{-l_n}) * x_1$.

As mentioned above, GAIP can be considered as a generalization of DLP. In the case of DLP, the G-action on a cyclic group X is given by the exponentiation, i.e. $a * x = x^a$ for $a \in G$ and $x \in X$. Note particularly that G is a cyclic group. Therefore we might consider DLP as a particular instance of GAIP where G is a cyclic group, i.e. $n = 1$, and the group action is defined by the exponentiation. Similarly, our definition of GAIPwAI can be considered as a generalization of DLPwAI. In [17, Section 3.1], Kim called the problem of finding $l \in \mathbb{Z}_L$ for given $x, (g^l) * x \in X$ and $g \in G$ in DLP setting *DLPX* (DLP in the exponent) and showed DLPwAI reduces to solving two instances of DLPX.

On the other hand, the problem of solving $(l_1, \ldots, l_n) \in \mathbb{Z}_{L_1} \times \cdots \times \mathbb{Z}_{L_n}$ given $g_1, \ldots, g_n$ and $h = g_1^{l_1} \cdots g_n^{l_n}$ is called *multi-dimensional DLP* (the term might be found, for instance, in [14]). Combining the above terminology, one might define *multi-dimensional DLP in the group action* as follows.

Definition 4 (Multi-dimensional DLP in the Group Action). *Let $G \cong \langle g_1 \rangle \times \cdots \times \langle g_n \rangle$ be a finite abelian group where g_i is of order N_i. Consider a G-action $*$ on a set X. Given $(g_1, \ldots, g_n) \in G$ and $x, h * x := (g_1^{l_1} \cdots g_n^{l_n}) * x \in X$,* the problem is to find $(l_1, \ldots, l_n) \in \mathbb{Z}_{N_1} \times \cdots \times \mathbb{Z}_{N_n}$. In particular, we say that this problem is defined over $\mathbb{Z}_{N_1} \times \cdots \times \mathbb{Z}_{N_n}$.

With the above definition, the problem of solving GAIPwAI reduces to solving two multi-dimensional DLP in the group action, one is defined over $\mathbb{Z}_{N_1/d_1} \times \cdots \times \mathbb{Z}_{N_n/d_n}$ and the other is defined over $\mathbb{Z}_{d_1} \times \cdots \times \mathbb{Z}_{d_n}$.

As mentioned in [8,17], Pollard's lambda approach gives us a memory-efficient probabilistic algorithm to solve DLPX. Similarly, it is not hard to generalize this algorithm to solve multi-dimensional DLP in the group action with small amount of storage. Thus we can show there exists a probabilistic algorithm for GAIPwAI with constant storage. The technique is rather straightforward, so we omit the proof in this paper.

4 Cryptographic Considerations

4.1 Class Group Action on Supersingular Curves

A main interest of GAIP in cryptographic applications arises from several isogeny-based cryptosystems. Let $E/\mathbb{F}_p$ a supersingular curve with $p = 4\ell_1 \cdots \ell_n - 1$ for small distinct odd primes ℓ_i. Consider the endomorphism ring $\mathrm{End}_{\mathbb{F}_p}(E)$ defined over p which is isomorphic to an order $\mathcal{O}$ in an imaginary quadratic field $\mathbb{Q}(\sqrt{-p})$. As briefly mentioned in Sect. 2, for an ideal $\mathfrak{a} \subset \mathcal{O}$, the class group action of $\mathrm{Cl}(\mathcal{O})$ on the set $\mathcal{E}$ of $\mathbb{F}_p$-isomorphism classes of supersingular curves over $\mathbb{F}_p$ is a well-defined group action and denoted by $E' := [\mathfrak{a}] * E = E/E[\mathfrak{a}]$. The hardness of GAIP with $G = \mathrm{Cl}(\mathcal{O})$ and $X = \mathcal{E}$ is at the core of the security of such cryptosystems.

Consider $\mathrm{Cl}(\mathcal{O}) \cong \langle \mathfrak{g}_1 \rangle \times \cdots \times \langle \mathfrak{g}_n \rangle$ and $\mathfrak{a} = \mathfrak{g}_1^{a_1} \cdots \mathfrak{g}_n^{a_n}$. For $d = (d_1, \ldots, d_n)$, GAIPwAI translates to solve the ideal $\mathfrak{a} \subset \mathcal{O}$ given $E, E_1 := [\mathfrak{a}] * E$ and $E_d := [\mathfrak{a}^d] * E$. However, we note the structure of $\mathrm{Cl}(\mathcal{O})$ is unknown in general, one should compute $\mathrm{Cl}(\mathcal{O})$ in subexponential time using the Hafner-McCurley algorithm before applying the proposed algorithm. The Hafner-McCurley algorithm starts from a generating set $\{\mathfrak{p}_1, \ldots, \mathfrak{p}_k\} \subset \mathrm{Cl}(\mathcal{O})$ which consists of small prime ideals and this generating set might not coincide with the generators $\{\mathfrak{g}_i : i = 1, \ldots, n\}$. For $\mathrm{Cl}(\mathcal{O})$-group action to be efficiently computable, it might be desirable to represent $\mathfrak{g}_i$ with small prime ideals. As mentioned in [5], it can be done by computing a basis of the lattice

$$L = \{(e_1, \ldots, e_k) \in \mathbb{Z}^k : \prod_{i=1}^{k} \mathfrak{p}_i^{e_i} = 1\}$$

and subsequently computing the Smith normal form of the basis. Since it only takes subexponential time in $\log(p)$, the overall complexity of solving GAIPwAI is dominated by $O\left(\prod_i \sqrt{N_i/d_i} + \prod_i \sqrt{d_i}\right)$. The best complexity is attained when N_i has a divisor d_i satisfying $\sqrt{\prod_{i=1}^{n} N_i} \approx \prod_{i=1}^{n} d_i$.

4.2   CSIDH-512 Parameter

Recently, Beullens et al. [1] computed the class group of an imaginary quadratic field having 154-digit discriminant. Based on this computation an efficient isogeny-based signature scheme called CSI-FiSh was proposed, using the CSIDH-512 parameter. As a result, the structure of the class group corresponding to the CSIDH-512 parameters is known: The prime parameter p in CSIDH-512 is chosen to be $p = 4 \cdot \ell_1 \cdots \ell_{73} \cdot 587 - 1$, where ℓ_1 through ℓ_{73} are the smallest 73 odd primes. The ideal class group $G = \mathrm{Cl}\left(\mathbb{Z}[\sqrt{-p}]\right)$ defines an efficient group action on $\mathcal{E}$, where G is cyclic with a generator $\mathfrak{g} = \langle 3, \sqrt{-p} - 1 \rangle$ of order

$$N = \#G = 3 \cdot 37 \cdot 1407181 \cdot 51593604295295867744293584889 \cdot d,$$

where d is 135-bit prime.

Assume that we are given E, $E_1 = [\mathfrak{a}] * E$ and $E_d = [\mathfrak{a}^d] * E$ for a secret ideal $\mathfrak{a} \subset G$. Using our proposed algorithm, $\mathfrak{a}$ can be computed in time complexity $O(\sqrt{N/d} + \sqrt{d}) \approx O(2^{68})$. In other words, if we are *additionally* given E_d, then the security of the GAIP problem in the CSIDH-512 parameter, which was originally believed to be 128-bit secure, decreases to 68-bit security level.

5   Discussions and Open Research

Recently, the GAIP problem has been of particular interest since it supports the security of several isogeny-based cryptosystems. In this paper, we discussed on the security of GAIP problem when some information on the secret value is additionally provided: Let $E/\mathbb{F}_p$ be a supersingular curve with $\mathbb{F}_p$-endomorphism ring $\mathcal{O} = \mathbb{Z}[\sqrt{-p}]$. Note that $\#\mathcal{O} \approx p^{1/2}$. Given E, $[\mathfrak{a}] * E$ and $[\mathfrak{a}^d] * E$ for $\mathfrak{a} \subset \mathcal{O}$, the cost of finding the secret ideal $\mathfrak{a}$ becomes $O(p^{1/8})$ when $d \approx p^{1/4}$ is a divisor of $\#\mathcal{O} \approx p^{1/2}$. It would be comparable to $O(p^{1/4})$, the time complexity of solving GAIP problem without additional informations.

A main motivation of this study is from the DLPwAI problem where a number of pairing-based cryptosystems base their security on DLPwAI. However, in the case of GAIP for class group, it is unknown whether there exist cryptosystems for which the security relies on GAIPwAI problem. We recommend that cryptographers are more careful when they want to construct any cryptosystems based on some variants of GAIP problem because the problems might be instances of the GAIPwAI problem that might yield a security loss compared to the original GAIP problem.

Another intriguing problem is to consider when the class group of $\mathbb{Z}[\sqrt{-p}]$ has an order with a sufficiently large divisor d. If we assume the order of $\mathbb{Z}[\sqrt{-p}]$ behaves as a random integer of size $\approx p^{1/2}$ and d is an integer close to $p^{1/4}$, then the number of integers less than $\approx p^{1/2}$ divisible by d is approximately $p^{1/4}$. However, currently many isogeny-based cryptosystems use a prime p of special form, so the structure of the class group corresponding to such primes p might be far from behaving randomly. Thus, it would be interesting to consider how many families of such special primes exist (or not) such that the corresponding class group has an order divisible by a sufficiently large integer.

References

1. Beullens, W., Kleinjung, T., Vercauteren, F.: CSI-FiSh: efficient isogeny based signatures through class group computations. In: Galbraith, S., Moriai, S. (eds.) ASI-ACRYPT 2019. LNCS, vol. 11921, pp. 227–247. Springer, Cham (2019). https://doi.org/10.1007/978-3-030-34578-5_9
2. Boneh, D., Boyen, X.: Efficient selective-ID secure identity-based encryption without random oracles. In: Cachin, C., Camenisch, J. (eds.) EUROCRYPT 2004. LNCS, vol. 3027, pp. 223–238. Springer, Heidelberg (2004). https://doi.org/10.1007/978-3-540-24676-3_14
3. Boneh, D., Boyen, X.: Short signatures without random oracles. In: Cachin, C., Camenisch, J. (eds.) EUROCRYPT 2004. LNCS, vol. 3027, pp. 56–73. Springer, Heidelberg (2004). https://doi.org/10.1007/978-3-540-24676-3_4
4. Boneh, D., Boyen, X., Goh, E.-J.: Hierarchical identity based encryption with constant size ciphertext. In: Cramer, R. (ed.) EUROCRYPT 2005. LNCS, vol. 3494, pp. 440–456. Springer, Heidelberg (2005). https://doi.org/10.1007/11426639_26
5. Buchmann, J.A., Düllmann, S.: On the computation of discrete logarithms in class groups. In: Menezes, A.J., Vanstone, S.A. (eds.) CRYPTO 1990. LNCS, vol. 537, pp. 134–139. Springer, Heidelberg (1991). https://doi.org/10.1007/3-540-38424-3_9
6. Castryck, W., Lange, T., Martindale, C., Panny, L., Renes, J.: CSIDH: an efficient post-quantum commutative group action. In: Peyrin, T., Galbraith, S. (eds.) ASI-ACRYPT 2018. LNCS, vol. 11274, pp. 395–427. Springer, Cham (2018). https://doi.org/10.1007/978-3-030-03332-3_15
7. Cheon, J.H.: Security analysis of the strong Diffie-Hellman problem. In: Vaudenay, S. (ed.) EUROCRYPT 2006. LNCS, vol. 4004, pp. 1–11. Springer, Heidelberg (2006). https://doi.org/10.1007/11761679_1
8. Cheon, J.H.: Discrete logarithm problems with auxiliary inputs. J. Cryptol. **23**(3), 457–476 (2010)
9. Cheon, J.H., Kim, T.: A new approach to the discrete logarithm problem with auxiliary inputs. LMS J. Comput. Math. **19**(1), 115 (2016)
10. Cheon, J.H., Kim, T., Song, Y.S.: A group action on $\mathbb{Z}_p^\times$ and the generalized DLP with auxiliary inputs. In: Lange, T., Lauter, K., Lisoněk, P. (eds.) SAC 2013. LNCS, vol. 8282, pp. 121–135. Springer, Heidelberg (2014). https://doi.org/10.1007/978-3-662-43414-7_6
11. Childs, A.M., Jao, D., Soukharev, V.: Constructing elliptic curve isogenies in quantum subexponential time. CoRR, abs/1012.4019 (2010)
12. Couveignes, J.M.: Hard homogeneous spaces. IACR Cryptol. ePrint Arch. **2006**, 291 (2006)
13. De Feo, L., Galbraith, S.D.: SeaSign: compact isogeny signatures from class group actions. In: Ishai, Y., Rijmen, V. (eds.) EUROCRYPT 2019. LNCS, vol. 11478, pp. 759–789. Springer, Cham (2019). https://doi.org/10.1007/978-3-030-17659-4_26
14. Galbraith, S.D.: Mathematics of Public Key Cryptography. Cambridge University Press, Cambridge (2012)
15. Hafner, J.L., McCurley, K.S.: A rigorous subexponential algorithm for computation of class groups. J. Am. Math. Soc. **2**(4), 837–850 (1989)
16. Kim, M., Cheon, J.H., Lee, I.: Analysis on a generalized algorithm for the strong discrete logarithm problem with auxiliary inputs. Math. Comput. **83**(288), 1993–2004 (2014)

17. Kim, T.: Extended tower number field sieve: a new complexity for medium prime case. IACR Cryptol. ePrint Arch. **2015**, 1027 (2015)
18. Rostovtsev, A., Stolbunov, A.: Public-key cryptosystem based on isogenies. IACR Cryptol. ePrint Arch. **2006**, 145 (2006)
19. V'elu, J.: Isogénies entre courbes elliptiques. C. R. Acad. Sci. Paris **273**, 238–241 (1971)

Secure Key Encapsulation Mechanism with Compact Ciphertext and Public Key from Generalized Srivastava Code

Jayashree Dey$^{(\boxtimes)}$ and Ratna Dutta

Department of Mathematics, Indian Institute of Technology Kharagpur,
Kharagpur 721302, India
deyjayashree@iitkgp.ac.in, ratna@maths.iitkgp.ernet.in

Abstract. Code-based public key cryptosystems have been found to be an interesting option in the area of Post-Quantum Cryptography. In this work, we present a key encapsulation mechanism (KEM) using a parity check matrix of the Generalized Srivastava code as the public key matrix. Generalized Srivastava codes are privileged with the decoding technique of Alternant codes as they belong to the family of Alternant codes. We exploit the dyadic structure of the parity check matrix to reduce the storage of the public key. Our encapsulation leads to a shorter ciphertext as compared to DAGS proposed by Banegas et al. in Journal of Mathematical Cryptology which also uses Generalized Srivastava code. Our KEM provides IND-CCA security in the random oracle model. Also, our scheme can be shown to achieve post-quantum security in the quantum random oracle model.

Keywords: Key encapsulation mechanism · Generalized Srivastava code · Quasi-dyadic matrix · Alternant decoding

1 Introduction

Cryptography and coding theory are at the core of implementation of telecommunication systems, computational systems and secure networks. Cryptography based on error correcting codes is one of the main approaches to guarantee secure communication in post-quantum world. The security of current widely used classical cryptosystems relies on the difficulty of number theory problems like factorization and the discrete logarithm problem. Shor [21] showed in 1994 that most of these cryptosystems can be broken once sufficiently strong quantum computers become available. Thus, it is necessary to devise alternatives that can survive quantum attacks while offering reasonable performance with solid security guarantees.

Code-based cryptosystems are usually very fast and can be implemented on several platforms, both software and hardware. They do not require special-purpose hardware, specifically no cryptographic co-processors. The security of code based cryptography mainly relies on the following two computational assumptions:

© Springer Nature Switzerland AG 2020
J. H. Seo (Ed.): ICISC 2019, LNCS 11975, pp. 175–193, 2020.
https://doi.org/10.1007/978-3-030-40921-0_11

(i) the hardness of generic decoding [8] which is NP complete and also believed to be hard on average even against quantum adversaries
(ii) the pseudorandomness of the underlying code $\mathcal{C}$ for the construction which states that it is hard to distinguish a random matrix from a generator (or parity check) matrix of $\mathcal{C}$ used as a part of the public key of the system.

Designing practical alternative cryptosystems based on difficulty of decoding unstructured or random codes is currently a major research area. The public key indistinguishability problem strongly depends on the code family. For instance, the McEliece encryption scheme [17] uses binary Goppa codes for which this indistinguishability assumption holds. On the other hand, the assumption does not hold for other families such as Reed Solomon codes, Concatenated codes, Low Density Parity Check (LDPC) codes etc. In [12], Faugere et al. devise a distinguisher for high rate Goppa codes. One of the key challenges in code-based cryptography is to come up with families of codes for which the indistinguishability assumption holds.

Constructing efficient and secure code-based cryptographic scheme is a challenging task. The crucial fact in designing code-based cryptosystems is to use a linear error-correcting code in such a way that the public key is indistinguishable from a random key. A codeword is used as ciphertext of a carefully chosen linear error-correcting code to which random errors are added. The decryptor with the knowledge of a trapdoor can perform fast polynomial time decoding, remove the errors and recover the plaintext. Attackers are reduced to a generic decoding problem and the system remains secure against an adversary equipped with a quantum computer.

Our Contribution. In this paper, we focus on designing an IND-CCA secure efficient code-based KEM that relies on the difficulty of generic decoding problem. Our starting point is the key encapsulation mechanism DAGS [5] that uses the quasi-dyadic structure of Generalized Srivastava (GS) code. Quasi-dyadic structure reduces the public key size remarkably in DAGS while the encapsulation procedure increases the size of ciphertext. We aim to design a KEM with relatively short ciphertext. We deploy the Niederreiter framework to develop our KEM using a syndrome as ciphertext and achieve IND-CCA security in the random oracle model. More precisely, we use the parity check matrix of the Generalized Srivastava code as the public key and utilize its block dyadic structure to reduce the public key size. We consider the syndrome of a vector as the ciphertext header where the vector is formed by parsing two vectors – the first vector is an error vector that is generated by a deterministic error vector generation algorithm and the second vector is constructed from a hash value of a randomly chosen message by the encapsulator. This significantly reduces the ciphertext header size that makes the scheme useful in application with limited communication bandwidth. Also, the use of the parity check matrix directly in computing the ciphertext is more fast and efficient. For decapsulation, we form an equivalent parity check matrix using the secret key to decode the ciphertext header and then proceed to get the decapsulation key. Note that, Generalized Srivastava codes belong to the class of Alternant codes which have benefits of an efficient decoding algorithm. The complexity of decoding is $O(n \log^2 n)$ [20] which is the same as that of Goppa codes where n is the length of the code.

In Table 1, we provide a theoretical comparison of our KEM with other recently proposed code-based KEMs. All the schemes in the table are based on finite fields having characteristic 2. We summarize the following features of our KEM.

- The closest related work to ours is DAGS [5]. Similar to DAGS, we also use quasi-dyadic form of Generalized Srivastava code. However, DAGS uses generator matrix whereas we use parity check matrix. Consequently, in our construction, the ciphertext size is reduced by $k \log_2 q$ bits as compared to DAGS [5] whereas the public key and the secret key sizes remain the same. Furthermore our encapsulation is faster than DAGS.
- The public key sizes in our approach are better than NTS-KEM [2], Classic McEliece [9] and BIG QUAKE [6]. Although the BIKE variants are efficient in terms of key sizes and achieve IND-CCA security, they still suffer from small decoding failure rate. The erlier BIKE variants proposed in [3] have a non-negligible decoding failure rate and only attain IND-CPA security.

Table 1. Summary of IND-CCA secure KEMs using random oracles

Scheme	pk size (in bits)	sk size (in bits)	CT size (in bits)	Code used	Cyclic/Dyadic	Correctness error
NTS-KEM [2]	$(n-k)k$	$2(n-k+r)m+nm+r$	$(n-k+r)$	Binary Goppa code	–	No
BIKE-1 [4]	n	$n+w\cdot\lceil\log_2 k\rceil$	n	MDPC code	Quasi-Cyclic	Yes
BIKE-2 [4]	k	$n+w\cdot\lceil\log_2 k\rceil$	k	MDPC code	Quasi-Cyclic	Yes
BIKE-3 [4]	n	$n+w\cdot\lceil\log_2 k\rceil$	n	MDPC code	Quasi-Cyclic	Yes
Classic McEliece [9]	$k(n-k)$	$n+mt+mn$	$(n-k)+r$	Binary Goppa code	–	No
BIG QUAKE [6]	$\frac{k}{\ell}(n-k)$	$mt+mn$	$(n-k)+2r$	Binary Goppa code	Quasi-Cyclic	No
DAGS [5]	$\frac{k}{s}(n-k)\log_2 q$	$2mn\log_2 q$	$[n+k']\log_2 q$	GS code	Quasi-Dyadic	No
This work	$\frac{k}{s}(n-k)\log_2 q$	$2mn\log_2 q$	$[k'+(n-k)]\log_2 q$	GS code	Quasi-Dyadic	No

pk = Public key, sk = Secret key, CT = Ciphertext, k = dimension of the code, n = length of the code, ℓ = length of each blocks, t = error correcting capacity, $k' < k$, s, r, w, p_1, p_2 are positive integers ($\ell << s$), $s = 2^{p_2}$, $q = 2^{p_1}$, m = the degree of field extension, r = the desired key length, GS = Generalized Srivastava, MDPC = Moderate Density Parity Check

In the comparison table, we mostly highlight the KEMs which rely on the error correcting codes that belong to the class of Alternant codes except BIKE variants which use QC (Quasi-Cyclic)-MDPC codes. We exclude the schemes like LEDAkem, RLCE-KEM, LAKE, Ouroboros-R, LOCKER, QC-MDPC, McNie etc. In fact, the schemes LAKE, Ouroboros-R, LOCKER use rank metric codes (Low Rank Parity Check (LRPC) codes) while RLCE-KEM is based on random linear codes and McNie relies on any error-correcting code, specially QC-LRPC codes. LEDAkem uses QC-LDPC codes and has a small decoding failure rate.

Moreover, it has risks in case of keypair reuse which may cause a reaction attack [11] for some particular instances. The schemes proposed in [1] are also kept out as both HQC and RQC are constructed for any decodable linear code. Also, HQC has a decryption failure and RQC uses rank metric codes. The protocol QC-MDPC may have a high decoding failure rate for some particular parameters which enhances the risk of GJS attack [14]. The scheme CAKE is another important KEM which is merged with another independent construction Ouroboros to obtain BIKE [3].

Organization of the Paper. This rest of the paper is organized as follows. In Sect. 2, we describe necessary background related to our work. We illustrate our approach to design a KEM in Sect. 3 and discuss its security in Sect. 4. Finally, we conclude in Sect. 5.

2   Preliminaries

In this section, we provide mathematical background and preliminaries that are necessary to follow the discussion in the paper.

Notation. We use the notation $x \xleftarrow{U} X$ for choosing a random element from a set or distribution, $\mathsf{wt}(\mathbf{x})$ to denote the weight of a vector $\mathbf{x}$, $(\mathbf{x}||\mathbf{y})$ for the concatenation of the two vectors $\mathbf{x}$ and $\mathbf{y}$. The matrix I_n is the $n \times n$ identity matrix. We let $\mathbb{Z}^+$ to represent the set $\{a \in \mathbb{Z} | a \geq 0\}$ where $\mathbb{Z}$ is the set of integers. We denote the transpose of a matrix A by A^T and concatenation of the two matrices A and B by $[A|B]$. The uniform distribution over $(n-k) \times n$ random q-ary matrices is denoted by $U_{(n-k)\times n}$.

2.1   Hardness Assumptions

Definition 1 ((Decision) (q-ary) Syndrome Decoding (SD) Problem [8]). Given a full-rank matrix $H_{(n-k)\times n}$ over $\mathsf{GF}(q)$, a vector $\mathbf{e} \in (\mathsf{GF}(q))^n$ and a non-negative integer w, is it possible to distinguish between a random syndrome $\mathbf{s}$ and the syndrome $H\mathbf{e}^T$ associated to a w-weight vector $\mathbf{e}$?

Suppose $\mathcal{D}$ is a probabilistic polynomial time algorithm. For every positive integer λ, we define the advantage of $\mathcal{D}$ in solving the decisional SD problem by

$$\mathsf{Adv}^{\mathsf{DEC}}_{\mathcal{D},\mathsf{SD}}(\lambda) = |\Pr[\mathcal{D}(H, H\mathbf{e}^T) = 1 \mid \mathbf{e} \in (\mathsf{GF}(q))^n, H \xleftarrow{U} U_{(n-k)\times n}]$$
$$- \Pr[\mathcal{D}(H, \mathbf{s}) = 1 \mid \mathbf{s} \xleftarrow{U} U_{(n-k)\times 1}, H \xleftarrow{U} U_{(n-k)\times n}]|.$$

Also, we define $\mathsf{Adv}^{\mathsf{DEC}}_{\mathsf{SD}}(\lambda) = \max_{\mathcal{D}}[\mathsf{Adv}^{\mathsf{DEC}}_{\mathcal{D},\mathsf{SD}}(\lambda)]$ where the maximum is taken over all $\mathcal{D}$. The decisional SD problem is said to be hard if $\mathsf{Adv}^{\mathsf{DEC}}_{\mathsf{SD}}(\lambda) < \delta$ where $\delta > 0$ is arbitrarily small.

In addition, some code based schemes require the following computational assumption. Most of the schemes output a public key that is either a generator matrix or a parity check matrix by running key generation algorithm.

Definition 2 (Indistinguishability of public key matrix H [18]). Let $\mathcal{D}$ be a probabilistic polynomial time algorithm and PKE = (Setup, KeyGen, Enc, Dec) be a public key encryption scheme that uses an $(n - k) \times n$ matrix H as a public key over $GF(q)$. For every positive integer λ, we define the advantage of $\mathcal{D}$ in distinguishing the public key matrix H from a random matrix R as $\mathsf{Adv}_{\mathcal{D},H}^{\mathsf{IND}}(\lambda) = \Pr[\mathcal{D}(H) = 1 | (\mathsf{pk} = H, \mathsf{sk}) \longleftarrow \mathsf{PKE.KeyGen}(\mathsf{param}), \mathsf{param} \longleftarrow \mathsf{PKE.Setup}(1^\lambda)] - \Pr[\mathcal{D}(R) = 1 | R \xleftarrow{U} U_{(n-k)\times n}]$.

We define $\mathsf{Adv}_H^{\mathsf{IND}}(\lambda) = \max_{\mathcal{D}}[\mathsf{Adv}_{\mathcal{D},H}^{\mathsf{IND}}(\lambda)]$ where the maximum is over all $\mathcal{D}$. The matrix H is said to be indistinguishable if $\mathsf{Adv}_H^{\mathsf{IND}}(\lambda) < \delta$ where $\delta > 0$ is arbitrarily small.

2.2 Basic Definitions from Coding Theory

Definition 3 (Dyadic Matrix and Quasi-Dyadic Matrix [7]). Given a ring $\mathbf{R}$ and a vector $\mathbf{h} = (h_0, h_1, \ldots, h_{n-1}) \in \mathbf{R}^n$, the *dyadic* matrix $\Delta(\mathbf{h}) \in \mathbf{R}^{n \times n}$ is a symmetric matrix having components $\Delta_{ij} = h_{i \oplus j}$ where $\oplus$ stands for bitwise exclusive-or. The vector $\mathbf{h}$ is called a signature of the dyadic matrix. The signature of a dyadic matrix forms its first row. A matrix is called *quasi-dyadic* if it is a block matrix whose component blocks are $s \times s$ dyadic submatrices. An $s \times s$ dyadic matrix block can be generated from its first row.

Generating the dyadic signature [7]: A valid dyadic signature $\mathbf{h} = (h_0, h_1, \ldots, h_{n-1})$ over $\mathbf{R} = GF(q^m)$ is derived using Algorithm 1.

Definition 4 (The Generalized Srivastava (GS) Code [16]). Let $m, n, s, t \in \mathbb{N}$ and q be a prime power. Let $\alpha_1, \alpha_2, \ldots, \alpha_n, w_1, w_2, \ldots, w_s$ be $n + s$ distinct elements of $GF(q^m)$ and $z_1, z_2, \ldots, z_n$ be nonzero elements of $GF(q^m)$. The Generalized Srivastava (GS) code of length n is a linear code with $st \times n$ parity-check matrix of the form $H = \begin{bmatrix} H_1 & H_2 & \cdots & H_s \end{bmatrix}^T$ where

$$H_i = \begin{bmatrix} \frac{z_1}{\alpha_1 - w_i} & \frac{z_2}{\alpha_2 - w_i} & \cdots & \frac{z_n}{\alpha_n - w_i} \\ \frac{z_1}{(\alpha_1 - w_i)^2} & \frac{z_2}{(\alpha_2 - w_i)^2} & \cdots & \frac{z_n}{(\alpha_n - w_i)^2} \\ \cdots & \cdots & \cdots & \cdots \\ \frac{z_1}{(\alpha_1 - w_i)^t} & \frac{z_2}{(\alpha_2 - w_i)^t} & \cdots & \frac{z_n}{(\alpha_n - w_i)^t} \end{bmatrix}$$

is a $t \times n$ matrix block. The code is of length $n \leq q^m - s$, dimension $k \geq n - mst$ and minimum distance $d \geq st + 1$. It can correct at most $w = \left\lfloor \frac{d-1}{2} \right\rfloor = \frac{st}{2}$ errors and is an Alternant code. In the parity check matrix

$$H = \begin{bmatrix} y_1 g_1(\alpha_1) & y_2 g_1(\alpha_2) & \cdots & y_n g_1(\alpha_n) \\ y_1 g_2(\alpha_1) & y_2 g_2(\alpha_2) & \cdots & y_n g_2(\alpha_n) \\ y_1 g_3(\alpha_1) & y_2 g_3(\alpha_2) & \cdots & y_n g_3(\alpha_n) \\ \cdots & \cdots & \cdots & \cdots \\ y_1 g_r(\alpha_1) & y_2 g_r(\alpha_2) & \cdots & y_n g_r(\alpha_n) \end{bmatrix}$$

Algorithm 1. Constructing a dyadic signature

Input: q, m, s, n.
Output: A dyadic signature $\mathbf{h} = (h_0, h_1, \ldots, h_{n-1})$ over $\mathsf{GF}(q^m)$.
1: **repeat**
2:     $X = \mathsf{GF}(q^m) \setminus \{0\}$; $\widehat{h}_0 \xleftarrow{U} X$; $X = X \setminus \{\widehat{h}_0\}$;
3:     **for** $(l = 0$ to $\lfloor \log q^m \rfloor)$ **do**
4:         $i = 2^l$; $\widehat{h}_i \xleftarrow{U} X$; $X = X \setminus \{\widehat{h}_i\}$;
5:         **for** $(j = 1$ to $i - 1)$ **do**
6:             **if** $(\widehat{h}_i \neq 0 \wedge \widehat{h}_j \neq 0 \wedge \frac{1}{\widehat{h}_i} + \frac{1}{\widehat{h}_j} + \frac{1}{\widehat{h}_0} \neq 0)$ **then**
7:                 $\widehat{h}_{i+j} = 1/(\frac{1}{\widehat{h}_i} + \frac{1}{\widehat{h}_j} + \frac{1}{\widehat{h}_0})$;
8:             **else**
9:                 $\widehat{h}_{i+j} = 0$; // undefined entry
10:            **end if**
11:            $X = X \setminus \{\widehat{h}_{i+j}\}$;
12:         **end for**
13:     **end for**
14:     $c = 0$;
15:     **if** $(0 \notin \{\widehat{h}_0, \widehat{h}_1, \ldots, \widehat{h}_{s-1}\})$ **then**
16:         $b_0 = 0$; $c = 1$; $B_0 = \{\widehat{h}_0, \widehat{h}_1, \ldots, \widehat{h}_{s-1}\}$;
17:         **for** $(j = 1$ to $\lfloor q^m/s \rfloor - 1)$ **do**
18:             **if** $(0 \notin \{\widehat{h}_{js}, \widehat{h}_{js+1}, \ldots, \widehat{h}_{(j+1)s-1}\})$ **then**
19:                 $b_c = j$; $c = c + 1$; $B_c = \{\widehat{h}_{js}, \widehat{h}_{js+1}, \ldots, \widehat{h}_{(j+1)s-1}\}$;
20:             **end if**
21:         **end for**
22:     **end if**
23: **until** $(cs \geq n)$
24: **return** $\mathbf{h} = (h_0, h_1, \ldots, h_{n-1}) = (B_0, B_1, \ldots, B_{c-1})$

---

where $g_i(x) = c_{i1} + c_{i2}x + \cdots + c_{ir}x^{r-1}$, $i = 1, 2, \ldots, r$ is a polynomial of degree $< r$ over $\mathsf{GF}(q^m)$ for the Alternant code $\mathcal{A}(\boldsymbol{\alpha}, \mathbf{y})$, let $r = st$. Also set

$$g_{(l-1)t+k}(x) = \prod_{j=1}^{s} (x - w_j)^t / (x - w_l)^k, \quad l = 1, 2, \ldots, s \text{ and } k = 1, 2, \ldots, t \text{ and}$$

$$y_i = z_i / \prod_{j=1}^{s} (\alpha_i - w_j)^t, \quad i = 1, 2, \ldots, n \text{ so that } y_i g_{(l-1)t+k}(\alpha_i) = z_i/(\alpha_i - w_l)^k.$$

The resulting code will be a Generalized Srivastava code.

3   Our KEM Protocol

We construct a key encapsulation mechanism $\mathsf{KEM} = (\mathsf{Setup}, \mathsf{KeyGen}, \mathsf{Encaps}, \mathsf{Decaps})$ as described below.

- $\mathsf{KEM.Setup}(1^\lambda) \longrightarrow \mathsf{param}$: Taking security parameter λ as input, a trusted authority proceeds as follows to generate the global public parameters param.

  (i) Sample $n_0, p_1, p_2, m \in \mathbb{Z}^+$, set $q = 2^{p_1}$, $s = 2^{p_2}$ and $n = n_0 s < q^m$.
  (ii) Select $t \in \mathbb{Z}^+$ such that $mst < n$. Set $w \leq st/2$ and $k = n - mst$.
  (iii) Sample $k' \in \mathbb{Z}^+$ with $k' < k$.
  (iv) Select three cryptographically secure hash functions $\mathcal{G} : (\mathsf{GF}(q))^{k'} \longrightarrow (\mathsf{GF}(q))^k$, $\mathcal{H} : (\mathsf{GF}(q))^{k'} \longrightarrow (\mathsf{GF}(q))^{k'}$ and $\mathcal{H}' : \{0,1\}^* \longrightarrow \{0,1\}^r$ where $r \in \mathbb{Z}^+$ denotes the desired key length.

(v) Publish the global parameters param $= (n, n_0, k, k', w, q, s, t, r, m, \mathcal{G}, \mathcal{H}, \mathcal{H}')$.

- KEM.KeyGen(param) $\longrightarrow$ (pk, sk) : A user on input param, performs the following steps to generate the public key pk and secret key sk.

(i) Generate dyadic signature $\mathbf{h} = (h_0, h_1, \ldots, h_{n-1})$ using Algorithm 1 where $h_i \in \mathsf{GF}(q^m)$ for $i = 0, 1, \ldots, n-1$.

(ii) Select $\omega \xleftarrow{U} \mathsf{GF}(q^m)$ with $\omega \neq \frac{1}{h_j} + \frac{1}{h_0}$, $j = 0, 1, \ldots, n-1$ and compute $u_i = \frac{1}{h_i} + \omega$, $i = 0, 1, \ldots, s-1$ and $v_j = \frac{1}{h_j} + \frac{1}{h_0} + \omega$, $j = 0, 1, \ldots, n-1$. Set $\mathbf{u} = (u_0, u_1, \ldots, u_{s-1})$ and $\mathbf{v} = (v_0, v_1, \ldots, v_{n-1})$.

(iii) Construct $st \times n$ quasi-dyadic matrix $A = \begin{bmatrix} A_1 & A_2 & \cdots & A_t \end{bmatrix}^T$ where

$A_i =$

$$
\begin{bmatrix}
\frac{1}{(u_0-v_0)^i} & \frac{1}{(u_0-v_1)^i} & \cdots & \frac{1}{(u_0-v_{n-1})^i} \\
\frac{1}{(u_1-v_0)^i} & \frac{1}{(u_1-v_1)^i} & \cdots & \frac{1}{(u_1-v_{n-1})^i} \\
\cdots & \cdots & \cdots & \cdots \\
\frac{1}{(u_{s-1}-v_0)^i} & \frac{1}{(u_{s-1}-v_1)^i} & \cdots & \frac{1}{(u_{s-1}-v_{n-1})^i}
\end{bmatrix}
=
\begin{bmatrix}
\frac{1}{(v_0-u_0)^i} & \frac{1}{(v_1-u_0)^i} & \cdots & \frac{1}{(v_{n-1}-u_0)^i} \\
\frac{1}{(v_0-u_1)^i} & \frac{1}{(v_1-u_1)^i} & \cdots & \frac{1}{(v_{n-1}-u_1)^i} \\
\cdots & \cdots & \cdots & \cdots \\
\frac{1}{(v_0-u_{s-1})^i} & \frac{1}{(v_1-u_{s-1})^i} & \cdots & \frac{1}{(v_{n-1}-u_{s-1})^i}
\end{bmatrix}
$$

is the $s \times n$ matrix block that can be written as $A_i = [\hat{A}_{i_1} | \hat{A}_{i_2} | \cdots | \hat{A}_{i_{n_0}}]$. Each block $\hat{A}_{i_k}$ is an $s \times s$ dyadic matrix for $k = 1, 2, \ldots, n_0$. For instance, take the first block

$$
\hat{A}_{i_1} =
\begin{bmatrix}
\frac{1}{(u_0-v_0)^i} & \frac{1}{(u_0-v_1)^i} & \cdots & \frac{1}{(u_0-v_{s-1})^i} \\
\frac{1}{(u_1-v_0)^i} & \frac{1}{(u_1-v_1)^i} & \cdots & \frac{1}{(u_1-v_{s-1})^i} \\
\cdots & \cdots & \cdots & \cdots \\
\frac{1}{(u_{s-1}-v_0)^i} & \frac{1}{(u_{s-1}-v_1)^i} & \cdots & \frac{1}{(u_{s-1}-v_{s-1})^i}
\end{bmatrix}
$$

which is symmetric as $u_i - v_j = \frac{1}{h_i} + \frac{1}{h_j} + \frac{1}{h_0} = u_j - v_i$ and dyadic of order s as the $s \times s$ matrix

$$
\begin{bmatrix}
\frac{1}{(u_0-v_0)} & \frac{1}{(u_0-v_1)} & \frac{1}{(u_0-v_2)} & \cdots & \frac{1}{(u_0-v_{s-1})} \\
\frac{1}{(u_1-v_0)} & \frac{1}{(u_1-v_1)} & \frac{1}{(u_1-v_2)} & \cdots & \frac{1}{(u_1-v_{s-1})} \\
\cdots & \cdots & \cdots & \cdots & \cdots \\
\frac{1}{(u_{s-1}-v_0)} & \frac{1}{(u_{s-1}-v_1)^i} & \frac{1}{(u_{s-1}-v_2)^i} & \cdots & \frac{1}{(u_{s-1}-v_{s-1})}
\end{bmatrix}
$$

$$
=
\begin{bmatrix}
h_0 & h_1 & h_2 & \cdots & h_{s-1} \\
h_1 & h_0 & h_3 & \cdots & h_{s-2} \\
\cdots & \cdots & \cdots & \cdots \\
h_{s-1} & h_{s-2} & h_{s-3} & \cdots & h_0
\end{bmatrix}
=
\begin{bmatrix}
h_{0 \oplus 0} & h_{0 \oplus 1} & h_{0 \oplus 2} & \cdots & h_{0 \oplus (s-1)} \\
h_{1 \oplus 0} & h_{1 \oplus 1} & h_{1 \oplus 2} & \cdots & h_{1 \oplus (s-1)} \\
\cdots & \cdots & \cdots & \cdots \\
h_{(s-1) \oplus 0} & h_{(s-1) \oplus 1} & h_{(s-1) \oplus 2} & \cdots & h_{(s-1) \oplus (s-1)}
\end{bmatrix}
$$

can be derived from the first row of the block using the relation $\frac{1}{h_{i \oplus j}} = \frac{1}{h_i} + \frac{1}{h_j} + \frac{1}{h_0}$. Since the powering process acts on every single element, $\hat{A}_{i_1}$ preserves its dyadic structure.

(iv) Choose $z_{is} \xleftarrow{U} GF(q^m)$, $i = 0, 1, \ldots, n_0 - 1$ and set $z_{is+p} = z_{is}$, $p = 0, 1, \ldots, s - 1$ where $n = n_0 s$. Also set

$$\mathbf{z} = (z_{0s}, z_{0s+1}, \ldots, z_{0s+s-1}; z_{1s}, z_{1s+1}, \ldots, z_{1s+s-1}; \cdots; z_{(n_0-1)s}, z_{(n_0-1)s+1},$$
$$\ldots, z_{(n_0-1)s+s-1}) = (z_0, z_1, \ldots, z_{n-1}) \in (GF(q^m))^n.$$

(v) Compute $y_j = z_j / \prod_{i=0}^{s-1} (u_i - v_j)^t$ for $j = 0, 1, \ldots, n - 1$ and set $\mathbf{y} = (y_0, y_1, \ldots, y_{n-1}) \in (GF(q^m))^n$.

(vi) Construct $st \times n$ matrix $B = \begin{bmatrix} B_1 & B_2 & \cdots & B_t \end{bmatrix}^T$ where

$$B_i = \begin{bmatrix} \frac{z_0}{(v_0-u_0)^i} & \frac{z_1}{(v_1-u_0)^i} & \cdots & \frac{z_{n-1}}{(v_{n-1}-u_0)^i} \\ \frac{z_0}{(v_0-u_1)^i} & \frac{z_1}{(v_1-u_1)^i} & \cdots & \frac{z_{n-1}}{(v_{n-1}-u_1)^i} \\ \cdots & \cdots & \cdots & \cdots \\ \frac{z_0}{(v_0-u_{s-1})^i} & \frac{z_1}{(v_1-u_{s-1})^i} & \cdots & \frac{z_{n-1}}{(v_{n-1}-u_{s-1})^i} \end{bmatrix}$$

is $s \times n$ matrix block. Sample a permutation matrix P of order st and compute $st \times n$ matrix $\overline{B} = PB$. The matrix $\overline{B}$ is a parity-check matrix of the GS code equivalent to its parity check matrix as in Definition 4, Subsect. 2.2.

(vii) Project $\overline{B}$ onto $GF(q)$ using the co-trace function to form a $mst \times n$ matrix C where co-trace function converts an element of $GF(q^m)$ to an element of $GF(q)$ with respect to a basis of $GF(q^m)$ over $GF(q)$. For $\mathbf{a} \in GF(q^m)$, co-trace$(\mathbf{a}) = (a_0, a_1, \ldots, a_{m-1}) \in (GF(q))^m$ satisfying $< \mathbf{g}, \mathbf{a} > = a_0 + a_1 q + a_2 q^2 + \cdots + a_{m-1} q^{m-1}$ where $a_i \in GF(q)$ and $\mathbf{g} = (1, q, q^2, \ldots, q^{m-1})$ is a basis of $GF(q^m)$ over $GF(q)$. Thus if $\overline{B} = (\overline{b}_{ij})$ where $\overline{b}_{ij} \in GF(q^m)$, then $C = (c_{ij})$ is obtained from $\overline{B}$ by replacing $\overline{b}_{ij}$ by co-trace$(\overline{b}_{ij})$. Write the matrix C in the systematic form $(M | I_{n-k})$ where M is $(n - k) \times k$ matrix with $k = n - mst$. Note that, the z_i are chosen to be equally having s-length block and all the operations during the row reduction are performed block-wise. Consequently, the dyadic structure is maintained in C and in particular in M. Let $M = \begin{bmatrix} M_{0,0} & M_{0,1} & \cdots & M_{0,\frac{k}{s}-1} \\ M_{1,0} & M_{1,1} & \cdots & M_{1,\frac{k}{s}-1} \\ \cdots & \cdots & \cdots & \cdots \\ M_{mt-1,0} & M_{mt-1,1} & \cdots & M_{mt-1,\frac{k}{s}-1} \end{bmatrix}$

where each block matrix $M_{i,j}$ is $s \times s$ dyadic matrix with dyadic signature $\psi_{i,j} \in (GF(q))^s$ which is the first row of $M_{i,j}$, $i = 0, 1, \ldots, mt - 1$, $j = 0, 1, \ldots, \frac{k}{s} - 1$.

(viii) Publish the public key $pk = \{\psi_{i,j} \mid i = 0, 1, \ldots, mt-1, \ j = 0, 1, \ldots, \frac{k}{s}-1\}$ and keep the secret key $sk = (\mathbf{v}, \mathbf{y})$ to itself.

- KEM.Encaps(param, pk) $\longrightarrow$ (CT, K) : Given system parameters param and public key pk, an encapsulator proceeds as follows to generate a ciphertext header CT $\in (GF(q))^{n-k+k'}$ and an encapsulation key $K \in \{0, 1\}^r$.

Algorithm 2. Error vector derivation

Input: q, n, a seed $\bar{\mathbf{s}} = (\bar{s}_0, \bar{s}_1, \ldots, \bar{s}_{k-1}) \in (\mathsf{GF}(q))^k$, a weight w, a function $\mathcal{F} : \mathsf{GF}(q) \longrightarrow \mathbb{Z}^+$.
Output: An error vector $\mathbf{e}$ of length n and weight w.
```
 1: s = (s₀, s₁,…, sₙ₋₁)=Expand(s̄); // Expand is an expansion function
 2: j = 0; temp = 0; d = 0; e = 0; v = 0;
 3: for (i = 0 to n − 1) do
 4:     if (sᵢ mod q ≠ 0) then
 5:         if (j = w) then
 6:             break;
 7:         end if
 8:         temp = F(s_d) mod n; d = d + 1;
 9:         for (ν = 0 to j) do
10:             if (temp = v_ν) then
11:                 goto step 9;
12:             end if
13:         end for
14:         v_j = temp; e_temp = sᵢ  mod q; temp = 0; j = j + 1;
15:     end if
16: end for
17: return e = (e₀, e₁,…, eₙ₋₁)
```

(i) Sample $\mathbf{m} \xleftarrow{U} (\mathsf{GF}(q))^{k'}$ and compute $\mathbf{r} = \mathcal{G}(\mathbf{m}) \in (\mathsf{GF}(q))^k$, $\mathbf{d} = \mathcal{H}(\mathbf{m}) \in (\mathsf{GF}(q))^{k'}$ where $\mathcal{G}$ and $\mathcal{H}$ are the hash functions given in param.

(ii) Parse $\mathbf{r}$ as $\mathbf{r} = (\boldsymbol{\rho}\|\boldsymbol{\sigma})$ where $\boldsymbol{\rho} \in (\mathsf{GF}(q))^{k-k'}$, $\boldsymbol{\sigma} \in (\mathsf{GF}(q))^{k'}$. Set $\boldsymbol{\mu} = (\boldsymbol{\rho}\|\mathbf{m}) \in (\mathsf{GF}(q))^k$.

(iii) Run Algorithm 2 to generate a error vector $\mathbf{e}$ of length $n - k$ and weight $w - \mathsf{wt}(\boldsymbol{\mu})$ using $\boldsymbol{\sigma}$ as a seed. Note that Algorithm 2 uses an expansion function[1]. Set $\mathbf{e}' = (\mathbf{e}\|\boldsymbol{\mu}) \in (\mathsf{GF}(q))^n$.

(iv) Using the public key $\mathsf{pk} = \{\boldsymbol{\psi}_{i,j} \mid i = 0, 1, \ldots, mt - 1, \ j = 0, 1, \ldots, \frac{k}{s} - 1\}$, compute $s \times s$ dyadic matrix $M_{i,j}$ with signature $\boldsymbol{\psi}_{i,j} \in (\mathsf{GF}(q))^s$ and reconstruct the parity check matrix $H = (M|I_{n-k})$ for the the GS code where $n - k = mst$ and

$$M = \begin{bmatrix} M_{0,0} & M_{0,1} & \cdots & M_{0,\frac{k}{s}-1} \\ M_{1,0} & M_{1,1} & \cdots & M_{1,\frac{k}{s}-1} \\ \cdots & \cdots & \cdots & \cdots \\ M_{mt-1,0} & M_{mt-1,1} & \cdots & M_{mt-1,\frac{k}{s}-1} \end{bmatrix}$$

(v) Compute the syndrome $\mathbf{c} = H(\mathbf{e}')^T$ and the encapsulation key $K = \mathcal{H}'(\mathbf{m})$ where $\mathcal{H}'$ is the hash function given in param.

(vi) Publish the ciphertext header $\mathsf{CT} = (\mathbf{c}, \mathbf{d})$ and keep K as secret.

- KEM.Decaps(param, sk, CT) $\longrightarrow K$: On receiving a ciphertext header $\mathsf{CT} = (\mathbf{c}, \mathbf{d})$, a decapsulator executes the following steps using public parameters param and its secret key $\mathsf{sk} = (\mathbf{v}, \mathbf{y})$ where $\mathbf{v} = (v_0, v_1, \ldots, v_{n-1})$ and $\mathbf{y} = (y_0, y_1, \ldots, y_{n-1})$.

(i) First proceed as follows to decode $\mathbf{c}$ and find error vector $\mathbf{e}''$ of length n and weight w:

---

[1] For example, kangaroo twelve function [10] can be used as an expansion function.

184   J. Dey and R. Dutta

(a) Use sk $= (\mathbf{v}, \mathbf{y})$ to construct $st \times n$ matrix H' in the form

$$
\begin{bmatrix}
y_0 & y_1 & \cdots & y_{n-1} \\
v_0 y_0 & v_1 y_1 & \cdots & v_{n-1} y_{n-1} \\
v_0^2 y_0 & v_1^2 y_1 & \cdots & v_{n-1}^2 y_{n-1} \\
\cdots & \cdots & \cdots & \cdots \\
v_0^{st-1} y_0 & v_1^{st-1} y_1 & \cdots & v_{n-1}^{st-1} y_{n-1}
\end{bmatrix}
=
\begin{bmatrix}
1 & 1 & \cdots & 1 \\
v_0 & v_1 & \cdots & v_{n-1} \\
v_0^2 & v_1^2 & \cdots & v_{n-1}^2 \\
\cdots & \cdots & \cdots & \cdots \\
v_0^{st-1} & v_1^{st-1} & \cdots & v_{n-1}^{st-1}
\end{bmatrix}
\begin{bmatrix}
y_0 & 0 & \cdots & 0 \\
0 & y_1 & \cdots & 0 \\
0 & 0 & y_2 & 0 \\
\cdots\cdots\cdots\cdots \\
0 & 0 & \cdots & y_{n-1}
\end{bmatrix}.
$$

Note that, H' is a parity check matrix in alternant form of the GS code over $GF(q^m)$ whereas the matrix $H = [M|I_{(n-k)}]$ constructed during KEM.KeyGen or KEM.Encaps is a parity check matrix in the systematic form of the GS code over $GF(q)$.

(b) As the GS code is an Alternant code, the parity check matrix H' is used to decode $\mathbf{c}$ by first computing the syndrome $S = H'(\mathbf{c}\|\mathbf{0})^T$ where $\mathbf{0}$ represents the vector $(0, 0, \ldots, 0)$ of length k and then by running decoding algorithm for the Alternant code to find the error locator polynomial $\omega(z) = \sum_{\nu=1}^{w} Y_\nu y_{i_\nu} \prod_{\mu=1, \mu\neq\nu}^{w} (1 - X_\mu z)$ and error evaluator polynomial $\sigma(z) = \prod_{i=1}^{w} (1 - X_i z)$. Let $X_1 = v_{i_1}, X_2 = v_{i_2}, \ldots, X_w = v_{i_w}$ be the error locations and $Y_1 = e_{X_1}, Y_2 = e_{X_2}, \ldots, Y_w = e_{X_w}$ be the error values.

(c) Set $\mathbf{e}'' = (e_1, e_2, \ldots, e_n)$ with $e_j = \begin{cases} 0 & \text{if } j \neq X_i, 1 \leq i \leq w \\ Y_i & \text{if } j = X_i, 1 \leq i \leq w \end{cases}$.

(ii) Let $\mathbf{e}'' = (\mathbf{e}_0\|\boldsymbol{\mu}') \in (GF(q))^n$ and $\boldsymbol{\mu}'=(\boldsymbol{\rho}'\|\mathbf{m}') \in (GF(q))^k$ where $\mathbf{e}_0 \in (GF(q))^{n-k}$, $\boldsymbol{\rho}' \in (GF(q))^{k-k'}$, $\mathbf{m}' \in (GF(q))^{k'}$.

(iii) Compute $\mathbf{r}' = \mathcal{G}(\mathbf{m}') \in (GF(q))^k$ and $\mathbf{d}' = \mathcal{H}(\mathbf{m}') \in (GF(q))^{k'}$ where $\mathcal{G}$ and $\mathcal{H}$ are the hash functions given in param.

(iv) Parse $\mathbf{r}'$ as $\mathbf{r}' = (\boldsymbol{\rho}''\|\boldsymbol{\sigma}')$ where $\boldsymbol{\rho}'' \in (GF(q))^{k-k'}$, $\boldsymbol{\sigma}' \in (GF(q))^{k'}$.

(v) Run Algorithm 2 to generate deterministically an error vector $\mathbf{e}_0'$ of length $n - k$ and weight $w - \text{wt}(\boldsymbol{\mu}')$ using $\boldsymbol{\sigma}'$ as seed.

(vi) If $(\mathbf{e}_0 \neq \mathbf{e}_0') \vee (\boldsymbol{\rho}' \neq \boldsymbol{\rho}'') \vee (\mathbf{d} \neq \mathbf{d}')$, output $\perp$ indicating decapsulation failure. Otherwise, compute the encapsulation key $K = \mathcal{H}'(\mathbf{m}')$ where $\mathcal{H}'$ is the hash function given in param.

Correctness: While decoding $\mathbf{c}$, we form an $st \times n$ parity check matrix H' over $GF(q^m)$ using the secret key sk $= (\mathbf{v}, \mathbf{y})$ and find the syndrome $H'(\mathbf{c}\|\mathbf{0})^T$ to estimate the error vector $\mathbf{e}'' \in (GF(q))^n$ with $\text{wt}(\mathbf{e}'') = w$. Note that, the ciphertext component $\mathbf{c} = H(\mathbf{e}')^T$ is the syndrome of $\mathbf{e}'$ where the matrix H is a parity check matrix in the systemetic form over $GF(q)$ which is indistinguishable from a random matrix over $GF(q)$. At the time of decoding $\mathbf{c}$, we need a parity check matrix in alternant form over $GF(q^m)$. The parity check matrix H, a parity check matrix of GS code in the systemetic form derived from the public key pk, does not help to decode $\mathbf{c}$ as the SD problem is hard over $GF(q)$. The decoding algorithm in our decapsulation procedure uses the parity check matrix H' (derived from the secret key sk) which is in alternant form over $GF(q^m)$. This procedure can correct upto $st/2$ errors. In our scheme, the error vector $\mathbf{e}'$

used in the procedure KEM.Encaps satisfies $\text{wt}(e') = w \leq st/2$. Consequently, the decoding procedure will recover the correct e'. We regenerate e_0' and ρ'' and compare it with e_0 and ρ' obtained after decoding. Since the error vector generation uses a deterministic function to get a fixed low weight error vector, $e_0 = e_0'$ and $\rho' = \rho''$ occurs.

4 Security

4.1 Security Notions

Definition 5 (Indistinguishability under Chosen Plaintext Attack (IND-CPA) [13]). The IND-CPA game between a challenger S and a PPT adversary A for a public key encryption scheme PKE=(Setup, KeyGen, Enc, Dec) is described below.

1. The challenger S generates param $\longleftarrow$ PKE.Setup(1^λ), (pk, sk) $\longleftarrow$ PKE.Key-Gen(param) where λ is a security parameter and sends param, pk to A.
2. The adversary A sends a pair of messages $m_0, m_1 \in M$ of the same length to S.
3. The challenger S picks a random bit $b \in \{0, 1\}$, computes a challenge ciphertext CT $\longleftarrow$ PKE.Enc(param, pk, m_b; r_b) and sends it to A.
4. The adversary A outputs a bit b'.

The adversary A wins the game if $b' = b$. We define the advantage of A against the above IND-CPA security game for the PKE scheme as

$$\text{Adv}_{\text{PKE}}^{\text{IND-CPA}}(A) = |\Pr[b' = b] - 1/2|.$$

A PKE scheme is IND-CPA secure if $\text{Adv}_{\text{PKE}}^{\text{IND-CPA}}(A) < \epsilon$ where $\epsilon > 0$ is arbitrarily small.

We also define the following four security notions for PKE scheme that are (i) One-Wayness under Chosen Plaintext Attacks (OW-CPA), (ii) One-Wayness under Plaintext Checking Attacks (OW-PCA), (iii) One-Wayness under Validity Checking Attacks (OW-VA) and (iv) One-Wayness under Plaintext and Validity Checking Attacks (OW-PCVA).

Definition 6 (OW-ATK [15]). For ATK $\in \{$CPA, PCA, VA, PCVA$\}$, the OW-ATK game between a challenger S and a PPT adversary A for a public key encryption scheme PKE $=$ (Setup, KeyGen, Enc, Dec) is outlined below where A can make polynomially many queries to the oracle O_{ATK} given by

$$O_{\text{ATK}} = \begin{cases} - & \text{ATK} = \text{CPA} \\ \text{PCO}(\cdot, \cdot) & \text{ATK} = \text{PCA} \\ \text{CVO}(\cdot) & \text{ATK} = \text{VA} \\ \text{PCO}(\cdot, \cdot), \text{CVO}(\cdot) & \text{ATK} = \text{PCVA} \end{cases}$$

where the oracle PCO($\cdot, \cdot$) takes a message m and a ciphertext CT as input and checks if the message recovered from CT is m or not while the oracle CVO($\cdot$)

takes a ciphertext CT as input distinct from the challenge ciphertext CT^* and checks whether the message recovered from CT belongs to the message space or not.

1. The challenger S generates param $\longleftarrow$ PKE.Setup(1^λ), (pk, sk) $\longleftarrow$ PKE.Key-Gen(param) where λ is a security parameter and sends param, pk to A.
2. The challenger S chooses a message $\mathbf{m}^* \in M$, computes the challenge ciphertext $CT^* \longleftarrow$ PKE.Enc(param, pk, $\mathbf{m}^*; \mathbf{r}^*$) and sends it to A.
3. The adversary A having access to the oracle O_{ATK}, outputs $\mathbf{m}'$.

The adversary A wins the game if $\mathbf{m}' = \mathbf{m}^*$. We define the advantage of A against the above OW-ATK security game for PKE scheme as $\mathsf{Adv}_{PKE}^{OW-ATK}(A) = \Pr[\mathbf{m}' = \mathbf{m}^*]$. The PKE scheme is said to be OW-ATK secure if $\mathsf{Adv}_{PKE}^{OW-ATK}(A) < \epsilon$ for arbitrarily small non zero ϵ.

Definition 7 (Indistinguishability under Chosen Ciphertext Attack (IND-CCA) [19]). The IND-CCA game between a challenger S and a PPT adversary A for a key encapsulation mechanism KEM = (Setup, KeyGen, Encaps, Decaps) is described below.

1. The challenger S generates param $\longleftarrow$ KEM.Setup(1^λ) and (pk, sk) $\longleftarrow$ KEM.KeyGen(param) where λ is a security parameter and sends param, pk to A.
2. The PPT adversary A has access to the decapsulation oracle KEM.Decaps to which A can make polynomially many ciphertext queries CT_i and gets the corresponding key $K_i \in K$ from S.
3. The challenger S picks a random bit b from $\{0, 1\}$, runs KEM.Encaps(param, pk) to generate a ciphertext-key pair (CT^*, K_0^*) with $CT^* \neq CT_i$, selects randomly $K_1^* \in K$ and sends the pair (CT^*, K_b^*) to A.
4. The adversary A having the pair (CT^*, K_b^*) keeps performing polynomially many decapsulation queries on $CT_i \neq CT^*$ and outputs b'.

The adversary succeeds the game if $b' = b$. We define the advantage of A against the above IND-CCA security game for the KEM as

$$\mathsf{Adv}_{KEM}^{IND-CCA}(A) = |\Pr[b' = b] - 1/2|.$$

A KEM is IND-CCA secure if $\mathsf{Adv}_{KEM}^{IND-CCA}(A) < \epsilon$ where $\epsilon > 0$ is arbitrarily small.

4.2 Security Proof

Our KEM provides IND-CCA security in random oracle model by Theorem 1.

Theorem 1. *Assuming the hardness of decisional* SD *problem (Definition 1, Sect. 2.1) and indistinguishability of the public key matrix H (derived from the public key* pk *by running* KEM.KeyGen(param) *where* param $\longleftarrow$ KEM.Setup(1^λ), λ *being the security parameter), our* KEM = (Setup, KeyGen, Encaps, Decaps) *described in Sect. 3 provides* IND-CCA *security (Definition 7, Sect. 4.1) when the hash functions $\mathcal{H}'$ and $\mathcal{G}$ are modeled as random oracles.*

- $PKE_1.Setup(1^\lambda) \longrightarrow param$: A trusted authority runs $KEM.Setup(1^\lambda)$ to get global parameters $param = (n, n_0, k, k', w, q, s, t, r, m, \mathcal{G}, \mathcal{H}, \mathcal{H}')$ taking security parameter λ as input.

- $PKE_1.KeyGen(param) \longrightarrow (pk, sk)$: A user generates public-secret key pair (pk, sk) by running $KEM.KeyGen(param)$ where $pk = \{\psi_{i,j} | i = 0, 1, \ldots, mt-1, \ j = 0, 1, \ldots, \frac{k}{s}-1\}$, $\psi_{i,j} \in (GF(q))^s$ and $sk = (\mathbf{v}, \mathbf{y})$.

- $PKE_1.Enc(param, pk, \mathbf{m}; \mathbf{r}) \longrightarrow CT$: An encryptor encrypts a message $\mathbf{m} \in \mathcal{M} = (GF(q))^{k'}$ and produces a ciphertext CT as follows.

  1. Compute $\mathbf{r} = \mathcal{G}(\mathbf{m}) \in (GF(q))^k$, $\mathbf{d} = \mathcal{H}(\mathbf{m}) \in (GF(q))^{k'}$.
  2. Parse $\mathbf{r} = (\rho || \sigma)$ where $\rho \in (GF(q))^{k-k'}$, $\sigma \in (GF(q))^{k'}$. Set $\mu = (\rho || \mathbf{m}) \in (GF(q))^k$.
  3. Run Algorithm 2 using σ as a seed to obtain an error vector $\mathbf{e}$ of length $n-k$ and weight $w - wt(\mu)$ and set $\mathbf{e}' = (\mathbf{e} || \mu) \in (GF(q))^n$.
  4. Use the public key $pk = \{\psi_{i,j} | i = 0, 1, \ldots, mt-1, \ j = 0, 1, \ldots, \frac{k}{s} - 1\}$ as in $KEM.Encaps(param, pk)$ and construct the matrix $H_{(n-k) \times n} = (M | I_{n-k})$ where $M = (M_{i,j})$, $M_{i,j}$ is a $s \times s$ dyadic matrix with signature $\psi_{i,j}$, $i = 0, 1, \ldots, mt-1$, $j = 0, 1, \ldots, \frac{k}{s} - 1$.
  5. Compute $\mathbf{c} = H(\mathbf{e}')^T$. Return the ciphertext $CT = (\mathbf{c}, \mathbf{d}) \in \mathcal{C} = (GF(q))^{n-k+k'}$.

- $PKE_1.Dec(param, sk, CT) \longrightarrow \mathbf{m}'$: On receiving the ciphertext CT, the decryptor executes the following steps using public parameters $param$ and its secret key $sk = (\mathbf{v}, \mathbf{y})$.

  1. Use the secret key $sk = (\mathbf{v}, \mathbf{y})$ to form a parity check matrix H' as in the procedure $KEM.Decaps(param, sk, CT)$.
  2. To decode $\mathbf{c}$ (extracted from CT), find error $\mathbf{e}''$ of weight w and length n by running the decoding algorithm for Alternant codes with syndrome $H'(\mathbf{c} || \mathbf{0})^T$.
  3. Parse $\mathbf{e}'' = (\mathbf{e_0} || \mu') \in (GF(q))^n$ and $\mu' = (\rho' || \mathbf{m}') \in (GF(q))^k$ where $\mathbf{e_0} \in (GF(q))^{n-k}$, $\rho' \in (GF(q))^{k-k'}$, $\mathbf{m}' \in (GF(q))^{k'}$.
  Compute $\mathbf{r}' = \mathcal{G}(\mathbf{m}') \in (GF(q))^k$ and $\mathbf{d}' = \mathcal{H}(\mathbf{m}') \in (GF(q))^{k'}$.
  4. Parse $\mathbf{r}' = (\rho'' || \sigma')$ where $\rho'' \in (GF(q))^{k-k'}$, $\sigma' \in (GF(q))^{k'}$.
  5. Generate error vector $\mathbf{e}'_0$ of length $n-k$ and weight $w - wt(\mu')$ by running Algorithm 2 with σ' as seed.
  6. If $(\mathbf{e_0} \neq \mathbf{e}'_0) \vee (\rho' \neq \rho'') \vee (\mathbf{d} \neq \mathbf{d}')$, output $\perp$ indicating decryption failure. Otherwise, return $\mathbf{m}'$.

Fig. 1. Scheme $PKE_1 = (Setup, KeyGen, Enc, Dec)$

The proof of the above theorem is the immediate consequence of Theorem 2, Corollary 1 and Theorem 4.

Theorem 2. *If the public key encryption scheme* $PKE_1 = (Setup, KeyGen, Enc, Dec)$ *described in Fig. 1 is* OW-VA *secure (Definition 6, Sect. 4.1) and there exist cryptographically secure hash functions, then the key encapsulation mechanism* KEM $= (Setup, KeyGen, Encaps, Decaps)$ *as described in Sect. 3 achieves* IND-CCA *security (Definition 7, Sect. 4.1) when the hash function* $\mathcal{H}'$ *is modeled as a random oracle.*

Proof. Let $\mathcal{B}$ be a PPT adversary against the IND-CCA security of KEM providing at most n_D queries to KEM.Decaps oracle and at most $n_{\mathcal{H}'}$ queries to the hash oracle $\mathcal{H}'$. We show that $\exists$ a PPT adversary $\mathcal{A}$ against the OW-VA security of the scheme PKE_1. We start with a sequence of games and the view of the adversary $\mathcal{B}$ is shown to be computationally indistinguishable in any of the consecutive games. Finally, we end up in a game that statistically hides the challenge bit as required. All the games are defined in Figs. 2 and 3. Let E_j be the event that $b = b'$ in game $\mathbf{G}_j$, $j = 0, 1, 2, 3$.

- The challenger S generates param $\longleftarrow$ KEM.Setup(1^λ) and (pk, sk) $\longleftarrow$ KEM.KeyGen(param) for a security parameter λ and sends param, pk to B.
- The PPT adversary B has access to the decapsulation oracle KEM.Decaps to which B can make polynomially many ciphertext queries CT_i and gets the corresponding key $K_i \in \mathcal{K} = \{0,1\}^r$ from S.
- The challenger S picks a random bit b from $\{0,1\}$, runs KEM.Encaps(param, pk) to generate a ciphertext-key pair (CT^*, K_0^*) with $CT^* \neq CT_i$, selects randomly $K_1^* \in \mathcal{K}$ and sends the pair (CT^*, K_b^*) to B.
- The adversary B having the pair (CT^*, K_b^*) keeps performing polynomially many decapsulation queries on $CT_i \neq CT^*$ and outputs b'.

Fig. 2. Game G_0 in the proof of Theorem 2

- The challenger S generates param $\longleftarrow$ PKE$_1$.Setup(1^λ), (pk, sk) $\longleftarrow$ PKE$_1$.KeyGen(param) for a security parameter λ and sends param, pk to B.
- The PPT adversary B has access to the decapsulation oracle Decaps (see Figure 4) to which B can make polynomially many ciphertext queries CT_i and gets the corresponding key $K_i \in \mathcal{K}$ from S.
- The challenger S picks a random bit b from $\{0,1\}$, chooses a message $\mathbf{m}^* \xleftarrow{U} \mathcal{M}$, runs PKE$_1$.Enc(param, pk, $\mathbf{m}^*$; $\mathbf{r}^*$) to generate a ciphertext CT^*, computes $K_0^* = \mathcal{H}'(\mathbf{m}^*)$, selects randomly $K_1^* \in \mathcal{K}$ and sends the pair (CT^*, K_b^*) to B.
- The adversary B having the pair (CT^*, K_b^*) keeps performing polynomially many decapsulation queries on $CT_i \neq CT^*$ to Decaps oracle and hash queries on $\mathbf{m}_i$ to hash oracle $\mathcal{H}'$ and outputs b' (see Figure 4 for hash oracle $\mathcal{H}'$ and decapsulation oracle Decaps).

Fig. 3. Sequence of games $G_j, j = 1, 2, 3$ in the proof of Theorem 2

Game G_0: As usual, game G_0 (Fig. 2) is the standard IND-CCA security game (Definition 7, Sect. 4.1) for the KEM and we have $|\Pr[E_0] - 1/2| = \mathsf{Adv}_{\mathsf{KEM}}^{\mathsf{IND\text{-}CCA}}(B)$.
Game G_1: In game G_1, a message $\mathbf{m}^*$ is chosen randomly and the ciphertext CT^* is computed by running PKE$_1$.Enc(param, pk, $\mathbf{m}^*$; $\mathbf{r}^*$). The challenger S maintains a hash list $Q_{\mathcal{H}'}$ (initially empty) and records all entries of the form $(\mathbf{m}, K)$ where hash oracle $\mathcal{H}'$ is queried on some message $\mathbf{m} \in \mathcal{M}$. Note that both games G_0 and G_1 proceed identically and we get $\Pr[E_0] = \Pr[E_1]$.
Game G_2: In game G_2, the hash oracle $\mathcal{H}'$ and the decapsulation oracle Decaps are answered in such a way that they no longer make use of the secret key sk except for testing whether PKE$_1$.Dec(param, sk, CT) $\in \mathcal{M}$ for a given ciphertext CT (line 12 of Decaps oracle in Fig. 4). The hash list $Q_{\mathcal{H}'}$ records all entries of the form $(\mathbf{m}, K)$ where hash oracle $\mathcal{H}'$ is queried on some message $\mathbf{m} \in \mathcal{M}$. Another list Q_D stores entries of the form (CT, K) where either Decaps oracle is queried on some ciphertext CT or the hash oracle $\mathcal{H}'$ is queried on some message $\mathbf{m} \in \mathcal{M}$ satisfying $CT \longleftarrow$ PKE$_1$.Enc(param, pk, $\mathbf{m}$; $\mathbf{r}$) with PKE$_1$.Dec(param, sk, CT) $\longrightarrow \mathbf{m}$.

Let X denotes the event that a correctness error has occurred in the underlying PKE$_1$ scheme. More specifically, X is the event that either the list $Q_{\mathcal{H}'}$ contains an entry $(\mathbf{m}, K)$ with the condition PKE$_1$.Dec(param, sk, PKE$_1$.Enc(param, pk, $\mathbf{m}$; $\mathbf{r}$)) $\neq \mathbf{m}$ or the list Q_D contains an entry (CT, K) with the condition PKE$_1$.Enc(param, pk, PKE$_1$.Dec(param, sk, CT); $\mathbf{r}$) $\neq CT$ or both.
Claim: The view of B is identical in games G_1 and G_2 unless the event X occurs.

$\mathcal{H}'(\mathbf{m})$	Decaps(CT $\neq$ CT*)
1. **for** the game $\mathbf{G}_1, \mathbf{G}_2, \mathbf{G}_3$ **do** 2. **if** $\exists K$ such that $(\mathbf{m}, K) \in Q_{\mathcal{H}'}$ 3. **return** K; 4. **end if** 5. CT $= (\mathbf{c}, \mathbf{d}) \longleftarrow$ PKE$_1$.Enc(param, pk, $\mathbf{m}$; $\mathbf{r}$); 6. $K \xleftarrow{U} \mathcal{K}$; 7. **end for** 8. **for** the game $\mathbf{G}_3$ **do** 9. **if** $\mathbf{m} = \mathbf{m}^*$ and CT* defined 10. $Y =$ true; 11. **abort**; 12. **end if** 13. **end for** 14. **for** the game $\mathbf{G}_2, \mathbf{G}_3$ **do** 15. **if** $\exists K'$ such that $(\text{CT}, K') \in Q_D$ 16. $K = K'$; 17. **else** 18. $Q_D = Q_D \cup \{(\text{CT}, K)\}$; 19. **end if** 20. **end for** 21. **for** the game $\mathbf{G}_1, \mathbf{G}_2, \mathbf{G}_3$ **do** 22. $Q_{\mathcal{H}'} = Q_{\mathcal{H}'} \cup \{(\mathbf{m}, K)\}$; 23. **return** K; 24. **end for**	1. **for** game $\mathbf{G}_1$ **do** 2. $\mathbf{m}' \longleftarrow$ PKE$_1$.Dec(param, sk, CT); 3. **if** $\mathbf{m}' = \perp$ 4. **return** $\perp$; 5. **end if** 6. **return** $K = \mathcal{H}'(\mathbf{m}')$; 7. **end for** 8. **for** games $\mathbf{G}_2, \mathbf{G}_3$ **do** 9. **if** $\exists K$ such that $(\text{CT}, K) \in Q_D$ 10. **return** K; 11. **end if** 12. **if** PKE$_1$.Dec(param, sk, CT) $\notin \mathcal{M}$ 13. **return** $\perp$; 14. **end if** 15. $K \xleftarrow{U} \mathcal{K}$; 16. $Q_D = Q_D \cup \{(\text{CT}, K)\}$; 17. **return** K; 18. **end for**

Fig. 4. The hash oracles $\mathcal{H}'$ and the decapsulation oracle Decaps for games $\mathbf{G}_j, j = 1, 2, 3$ in the proof of Theorem 2

$\mathcal{A}^{\mathsf{CVO}(\cdot)}(\text{param}, \text{pk}, \text{CT}^*)$	Decaps(CT $\neq$ CT*)
1. $K^* \xleftarrow{U} \mathcal{K}$; 2. $b' \longleftarrow \mathcal{B}^{\mathsf{Decaps}(\cdot), \mathcal{H}'(\cdot)}(\text{param}, \text{pk}, \text{CT}^*, K^*)$; 3. **if** $\exists(\mathbf{m}', K') \in Q_{\mathcal{H}'}$ such that PKE$_1$.Enc(param, pk, $\mathbf{m}'$; $\mathbf{r}$) $\longrightarrow$ CT* 4. **return** $\mathbf{m}'$; 5. **else** 6. **abort**; 7. **end if**	1. **if** $\exists K$ such that $(\text{CT}, K) \in Q_D$ 2. **return** K; 3. **end if** 4. **if** CVO(CT) $= 0$ 5. **return** $\perp$; 6. **end if** 7. $K \xleftarrow{U} \mathcal{K}$; 8. $Q_D = Q_D \cup \{(\text{CT}, K)\}$; 9. **return** K;

Fig. 5. Adversary $\mathcal{A}$ against OW-VA security of PKE$_1$

Proof of claim. To prove this, consider a fixed PKE$_1$ ciphertext CT (placed as a Decaps query) with $\mathbf{m} \longleftarrow$ PKE$_1$.Dec(param, sk, CT). Note that when $\mathbf{m} \notin \mathcal{M}$, the decapsulation oracle Decaps(CT) returns $\perp$ in both games $\mathbf{G}_1$ and $\mathbf{G}_2$. Suppose $\mathbf{m} \in \mathcal{M}$. We now show that in game $\mathbf{G}_2$, Decaps(CT) $\longrightarrow \mathcal{H}'(\mathbf{m})$ for the PKE$_1$ ciphertext CT of a message $\mathbf{m} \in \mathcal{M}$ with PKE$_1$.Enc(param, pk, $\mathbf{m}$; $\mathbf{r}$) $\longrightarrow$ CT. We distinguish two cases – $\mathcal{B}$ queries hash oracle $\mathcal{H}'$ on $\mathbf{m}$ before making Decaps oracle on CT, or the other way round.

Case 1: Let the oracle $\mathcal{H}'$ be queried on $\mathbf{m}$ first by $\mathcal{B}$ before decapsulation query on PKE$_1$ ciphertext CT. Since Decaps oracle was not yet queried on CT, no entry of the form (CT, K) exist in the current list Q_D yet. Therefore, besides adding $(\mathbf{m}, K \xleftarrow{U} \mathcal{K})$ to the list $Q_{\mathcal{H}'}$ (line 22 of $\mathcal{H}'$ oracle in Fig. 4), the challenger $\mathcal{S}$

also adds (CT, K) to the list Q_D (line 18 of $\mathcal{H}'$ oracle in Fig. 4), thereby defining $\mathsf{Decaps}(\mathsf{CT}) \longrightarrow K = \mathcal{H}'(\mathbf{m})$.

Case 2: Let the oracle Decaps be queried on PKE_1 ciphertext CT before the hash oracle $\mathcal{H}'$ is queried on $\mathbf{m}$. Then no entry of the form (CT, K) exists in Q_D yet. Otherwise, $\mathcal{H}'$ already was queried on a message $\mathbf{m}'' \neq \mathbf{m}$ (because Decaps oracle is assumed to be queried first on CT and the oracle $\mathcal{H}'$ was not yet queried on $\mathbf{m}$) satisfying $\mathsf{PKE}_1.\mathsf{Enc}(\mathsf{param}, \mathsf{pk}, \mathbf{m}''; \mathbf{r}'') \longrightarrow \mathsf{CT}$ with $\mathsf{PKE}_1.\mathsf{Dec}(\mathsf{param}, \mathsf{sk}, \mathsf{CT}) \longrightarrow \mathbf{m}''$. This is a contradiction to the fact that the same PKE_1 ciphertext CT is generated for two different messages $\mathbf{m}'', \mathbf{m}$ using randomness $\mathbf{r}, \mathbf{r}''$ respectively where $\mathbf{r} = \mathcal{G}(\mathbf{m}) \neq \mathcal{G}(\mathbf{m}'') = \mathbf{r}''$ for a cryptographically secure hash function $\mathcal{G}$. Therefore, Decaps oracle adds $(\mathsf{CT}, K \xleftarrow{U} \mathcal{K})$ to the list Q_D, thereby defining $\mathsf{Decaps}(\mathsf{CT}) \longrightarrow K$. When queried on $\mathbf{m}$ afterwards for hash oracle $\mathcal{H}'$, an entry of the form (CT, K) already exists in the list Q_D (line 15 of $\mathcal{H}'$ oracle in Fig. 4). By adding $(\mathbf{m}, K)$ to the list $Q_{\mathcal{H}'}$ and returning K, the hash oracle $\mathcal{H}'$ defines $\mathcal{H}'(\mathbf{m}) = K \longleftarrow \mathsf{Decaps}(\mathsf{CT})$.

Hence, $\mathcal{B}$'s view is identical in games $\mathbf{G}_1$ and $\mathbf{G}_2$ unless a correctness error X occurs. □ (of Claim)

As $\Pr[X] = 0$ for our KEM, we have $\Pr[E_1] = \Pr[E_2]$.

Game $\mathbf{G}_3$: In game $\mathbf{G}_3$, the challenger $\mathcal{S}$ sets a flag $Y = \mathsf{true}$ and aborts (with uniformly random output) immediately on the event when $\mathcal{B}$ queries the hash oracle $\mathcal{H}'$ on $\mathbf{m}^*$. Hence, $|\Pr[E_2] - \Pr[E_3]| \leq \Pr[Y = \mathsf{true}]$. In game $\mathbf{G}_3$, $\mathcal{H}'(\mathbf{m}^*)$ will never be given to $\mathcal{B}$ neither through a query on hash oracle $\mathcal{H}'$ nor through a query on decapsulation oracle Decaps, meaning bit b is independent from $\mathcal{B}$'s view. Thus, $\Pr[E_3] = 1/2$. To bound $\Pr[Y = \mathsf{true}]$, we construct an adversary $\mathcal{A}$ against the OW-VA security of PKE_1 simulating game $\mathbf{G}_3$ for $\mathcal{B}$ as in Fig. 5. Here $\mathcal{B}$ uses Decaps oracle given in Fig. 5 with the same hash oracle $\mathcal{H}'$ for game $\mathbf{G}_2$ in Fig. 4. Consequently, the simulation is perfect until $Y = \mathsf{true}$ occurs. Furthermore, $Y = \mathsf{true}$ ensures that $\mathcal{B}$ has queried $\mathcal{H}'(\mathbf{m}^*)$, which implies that $(\mathbf{m}^*, K') \in Q_{\mathcal{H}'}$ for some $K' \in \mathcal{K}$ where the list $Q_{\mathcal{H}'}$ is maintained by the adversary $\mathcal{A}$ simulating G_3 for $\mathcal{B}$. In this case, we have $\mathsf{PKE}_1.\mathsf{Enc}(\mathsf{param}, \mathsf{pk}, \mathbf{m}^*; \mathbf{r}^*) \longrightarrow \mathsf{CT}^*$ and hence $\mathcal{A}$ returns $\mathbf{m}^*$. Thus, $\Pr[Y = \mathsf{true}] = \mathsf{Adv}_{\mathsf{PKE}_1}^{\mathsf{OW\text{-}VA}}(\mathcal{A})$. Combining all the probabilities, we get $\mathsf{Adv}_{\mathsf{KEM}}^{\mathsf{IND\text{-}CCA}}(\mathcal{B}) = |\Pr[E_0] - 1/2| = |\Pr[E_1] - 1/2| = |\Pr[E_2] - 1/2| = |\Pr[E_2] - \Pr[E_3]| \leq \Pr[Y = \mathsf{true}] = \mathsf{Adv}_{\mathsf{PKE}_1}^{\mathsf{OW\text{-}VA}}(\mathcal{A})$ which completes our proof. □

Theorem 3. *If the public key encryption scheme* $\mathsf{PKE}_2 = $ (Setup, KeyGen, Enc, Dec) *described in Fig. 6 is* IND-CPA *secure (Definition 5, Sect. 4.1), then the public key encryption scheme* $\mathsf{PKE}_1 = $ (Setup, KeyGen, Enc, Dec) *as described in Fig. 1 provides* OW-PCVA *security (Definition 6, Sect. 4.1) when the hash function* $\mathcal{G}$ *is modeled as a random oracle.*

- PKE$_2$.Setup(1^λ) $\longrightarrow$ param : A trusted authority takes security parameter λ as input and runs PKE$_1$.Setup(1^λ) to get public parameters param $= (n, n_0, k, k', w, q, s, t, r, m, \mathcal{G}, \mathcal{H}, \mathcal{H}')$.

- PKE$_2$.KeyGen(param) $\longrightarrow$ (pk, sk) : A user generates the key pair (pk, sk) by running PKE$_1$.KeyGen(param) where the public key pk $= \{\boldsymbol{\psi}_{i,j} \mid i = 0, 1, \ldots, mt-1, \ j = 0, 1, \ldots, \frac{k}{s} - 1\}$, $\boldsymbol{\psi}_{i,j} \in (\mathsf{GF}(q))^s$ and the secret key sk $= (\mathbf{v}, \mathbf{y})$.

- PKE$_2$.Enc(param, pk, $\mathbf{m}$; $\mathbf{r}$) $\longrightarrow$ $\mathbf{c}$: An encryptor encrypts a message $\mathbf{m} \in \mathcal{M} = (\mathsf{GF}(q))^{k'}$ and produces a ciphertext $\mathbf{c}$ as follows.

  1. Compute $\mathbf{r} = \mathcal{G}(\mathbf{m}) \in (\mathsf{GF}(q))^k$, $\mathbf{d} = \mathcal{H}(\mathbf{m}) \in (\mathsf{GF}(q))^{k'}$.
  2. Parse $\mathbf{r} = (\boldsymbol{\rho}||\boldsymbol{\sigma})$ where $\boldsymbol{\rho} \in (\mathsf{GF}(q))^{k-k'}$, $\boldsymbol{\sigma} \in (\mathsf{GF}(q))^{k'}$. Set $\boldsymbol{\mu} = (\boldsymbol{\rho}||\mathbf{m}) \in (\mathsf{GF}(q))^k$.
  3. Run Algorithm 2 using $\boldsymbol{\sigma}$ as a seed to obtain an error vector $\mathbf{e}$ of length $n - k$ and weight $w - \mathsf{wt}(\boldsymbol{\mu})$ and set $\mathbf{e}' = (\mathbf{e}||\boldsymbol{\mu}) \in (\mathsf{GF}(q))^n$.
  4. Use the public key pk $= \{\boldsymbol{\psi}_{i,j} | i = 0, 1, \ldots, mt - 1, \ j = 0, 1, \ldots, \frac{k}{s} - 1\}$ as in PKE$_1$.Enc(param, pk, $\mathbf{m}$; $\mathbf{r}$) and construct the matrix $H_{(n-k) \times n} = (M|I_{n-k})$ where $M = (M_{i,j})$, $M_{i,j}$ is a $s \times s$ dyadic matrix with signature $\boldsymbol{\psi}_{i,j}$, $i = 0, 1, \ldots, mt - 1$, $j = 0, 1, \ldots, \frac{k}{s} - 1$. Compute $\mathbf{c} = H(\mathbf{e}')^T$.

- PKE$_2$.Dec(param, sk, $\mathbf{c}$) $\longrightarrow$ $\mathbf{m}'$: On receiving the ciphertext $\mathbf{c}$, the decryptor performs the following steps using public parameters param and its secret key sk $= (\mathbf{v}, \mathbf{y})$.

  1. Use the secret key sk $= (\mathbf{v}, \mathbf{y})$ to form a parity check matrix H' as in the procedure PKE$_1$.Dec(param, sk, CT)
  2. To decode $\mathbf{c}$, find error $\mathbf{e}''$ of weight w and length n by running the decoding algorithm for Alternant codes with syndrome $H'(\mathbf{c}||\mathbf{0})^T$.
  3. Parse $\mathbf{e}'' = (\mathbf{e}_0||\boldsymbol{\mu}') \in (\mathsf{GF}(q))^n$ and $\boldsymbol{\mu}' = (\boldsymbol{\rho}'||\mathbf{m}') \in (\mathsf{GF}(q))^k$ where $\mathbf{e}_0 \in (\mathsf{GF}(q))^{n-k}$, $\boldsymbol{\rho}' \in (\mathsf{GF}(q))^{k-k'}$, $\mathbf{m}' \in (\mathsf{GF}(q))^{k'}$. Return $\mathbf{m}'$.

Fig. 6. Scheme PKE$_2$ = (Setup, KeyGen, Enc, Dec)

The OW-PCVA security for a PKE scheme trivially implies the OW-VA security of the PKE scheme considering zero queries to the PCO($\cdot, \cdot$) oracle. Therefore, the following corollary is an immediate consequence of Theorem 3.

Corollary 1. *If the public key encryption scheme* PKE$_2$ *=(Setup, KeyGen, Enc, Dec) described in Fig. 6 is* IND-CPA *secure (Definition 5, Sect. 4.1), then the public key encryption scheme* PKE$_1$ = (Setup, KeyGen, Enc, Dec) *as described in Fig. 1 provides* OW-VA *security (Definition 6, Sect. 4.1) when the hash function $\mathcal{G}$ is modeled as a random oracle.*

Theorem 4. *If the decisional* SD *problem (Definition 1, Sect. 2.1) is hard, the public key matrix H (derived from the public key* pk *which is generated by running* PKE$_2$.KeyGen(param) *where* param $\longleftarrow$ PKE$_2$.Setup(1^λ)) *is indistinguishable (Definition 2, Sect. 2.1) and the hash function $\mathcal{G}$ is modeled as a random oracle, then the public key encryption scheme* PKE$_2$ = (Setup, KeyGen, Enc, Dec) *presented in Fig. 6 is* IND-CPA *secure (Definition 5, Sect. 4.1).*

Due to limited space, proofs of Theorems 3 and 4 will appear in the full version of the paper.

Remark 1. The KEM protocol also can be shown to provide security in quantum random oracle model following the work in [15] and thus we can get Theorem 5.

Theorem 5. *Assuming the hardness of decisional* SD *problem (Definition 1, Sect. 2.1) and indistinguishability of the public key matrix H (derived from the* *public key* pk *by running* KEM.KeyGen(param) *where* param ⟵ KEM.Setup(1^λ), λ *being the security parameter), our* KEM = (Setup, KeyGen, Encaps, Decaps) *described in Sect. 3 provides* IND-CCA *security (Definition 7, Sect. 4.1) when the hash functions* $\mathcal{G}, \mathcal{H}$ *and* $\mathcal{H}'$ *are modeled as quantum random oracles.*

Note that, proof of Theorem 5 follows from Theorems 4, 6 and 7 along with the fact that IND-CPA security implies OW-CPA security.

Theorem 6. *If the public key encryption scheme* PKE_2 = (Setup, KeyGen, Enc, Dec) *described in Fig. 6 is* OW-CPA *secure (Definition 6, Sect. 4.1), then the public key encryption scheme* PKE_1 = (Setup, KeyGen, Enc, Dec) *as described in Fig. 1 provides* OW-PCA *security (Definition 6, Sect. 4.1) when the hash function* $\mathcal{G}$ *is modeled as a quantum random oracle.*

Theorem 7. *If the public key encryption scheme* PKE_1 = (Setup, KeyGen, Enc, Dec) *described in Fig. 1 is* OW-PCA *secure (Definition 6, Sect. 4.1) and there exist cryptographically secure hash functions, then the key encapsulation mechanism* KEM = (Setup, KeyGen, Encaps, Decaps) *as described in Sect. 3 achieves* IND-CCA *security (Definition 7, Sect. 4.1) when the hash functions* $\mathcal{H}$ *and* $\mathcal{H}'$ *are modeled as quantum random oracles.*

5   Conclusion

In this work, we give a proposal to design an IND-CCA secure key encapsulation mechanism based on Generalized Srivastava codes. In terms of storage, our work seems well as compared to some other code-based KEM protocols as shown in Table 1. The scheme instantiated with Generalized Srivastava code does not involve any correctness error like some lattice-based schemes which allows achieving a simpler and tighter security bound for the IND-CCA security. In the upcoming days, it would be desirable to devise more efficient and secure constructions using suitable error-correcting codes.

References

1. Aguilar-Melchor, C., Blazy, O., Deneuville, J.C., Gaborit, P., Zémor, G.: Efficient encryption from random quasi-cyclic codes. IEEE Trans. Inf. Theor. **64**(5), 3927–3943 (2018)
2. Albrecht, M., Cid, C., Paterson, K.G., Tjhai, C.J., Tomlinson, M.: NTS-KEM. NIST Submissions (2019)
3. Aragon, N., et al.: BIKE: bit flipping key encapsulation. NIST Submissions (2017)
4. Aragon, N., et al.: BIKE: bit flipping key encapsulation. NIST Submissions (2019)
5. Banegas, G., et al.: DAGS: key encapsulation using dyadic GS codes. J. Math. Cryptol. **12**(4), 221–239 (2018)
6. Bardet, M., et al.: Big quake. NIST Submissions (2017)
7. Barreto, P.S.L.M., Cayrel, P.-L., Misoczki, R., Niebuhr, R.: Quasi-dyadic CFS signatures. In: Lai, X., Yung, M., Lin, D. (eds.) Inscrypt 2010. LNCS, vol. 6584, pp. 336–349. Springer, Heidelberg (2011). https://doi.org/10.1007/978-3-642-21518-6_23

8. Berlekamp, E., McEliece, R., Van Tilborg, H.: On the inherent intractability of certain coding problems (corresp.). IEEE Trans. Inf. Theor. **24**(3), 384–386 (1978)
9. Bernstein, D.J., et al.: Classic McEliece: conservative code-based cryptography. NIST Submissions (2017)
10. Bertoni, G., Daemen, J., Peeters, M., Van Assche, G., Van Keer, R., Viguier, B.: KANGAROOTWELVE: fast hashing based on KECCAK-p. In: Preneel, B., Vercauteren, F. (eds.) ACNS 2018. LNCS, vol. 10892, pp. 400–418. Springer, Cham (2018). https://doi.org/10.1007/978-3-319-93387-0_21
11. Fabšič, T., Hromada, V., Stankovski, P., Zajac, P., Guo, Q., Johansson, T.: A reaction attack on the QC-LDPC McEliece cryptosystem. In: Lange, T., Takagi, T. (eds.) PQCrypto 2017. LNCS, vol. 10346, pp. 51–68. Springer, Cham (2017). https://doi.org/10.1007/978-3-319-59879-6_4
12. Faugere, J.C., Gauthier-Umana, V., Otmani, A., Perret, L., Tillich, J.P.: A distinguisher for high-rate McEliece cryptosystems. IEEE Trans. Inf. Theor. **59**(10), 6830–6844 (2013)
13. Goldwasser, S., Micali, S.: Probabilistic encryption. J. Comput. Syst. Sci. **28**(2), 270–299 (1984)
14. Guo, Q., Johansson, T., Stankovski, P.: A key recovery attack on MDPC with CCA security using decoding errors. In: Cheon, J.H., Takagi, T. (eds.) ASIACRYPT 2016. LNCS, vol. 10031, pp. 789–815. Springer, Heidelberg (2016). https://doi.org/10.1007/978-3-662-53887-6_29
15. Hofheinz, D., Hövelmanns, K., Kiltz, E.: A modular analysis of the Fujisaki-Okamoto transformation. In: Kalai, Y., Reyzin, L. (eds.) TCC 2017. LNCS, vol. 10677, pp. 341–371. Springer, Cham (2017). https://doi.org/10.1007/978-3-319-70500-2_12
16. MacWilliams, F.J., Sloane, N.J.A.: The theory of error-correcting codes, vol. 16. Elsevier (1977)
17. McEliece, R.J.: A public-key cryptosystem based on algebraic. Coding Thv **4244**, 114–116 (1978)
18. Nojima, R., Imai, H., Kobara, K., Morozov, K.: Semantic security for the McEliece cryptosystem without random oracles. Des. Codes Crypt. **49**(1–3), 289–305 (2008)
19. Rackoff, C., Simon, D.R.: Non-interactive zero-knowledge proof of knowledge and chosen ciphertext attack. In: Feigenbaum, J. (ed.) CRYPTO 1991. LNCS, vol. 576, pp. 433–444. Springer, Heidelberg (1992). https://doi.org/10.1007/3-540-46766-1_35
20. Sarwate, D.V.: On the complexity of decoding Goppa codes (corresp.). IEEE Trans. Inf. Theor. **23**(4), 515–516 (1977)
21. Shor, P.W.: Algorithms for quantum computation: discrete logarithms and factoring. In: Proceedings 35th Annual Symposium on Foundations of Computer Science, pp. 124–134. IEEE (1994)

Improvement of Binary and Non Binary Statistical Decoding Algorithm

Pierre-Louis Cayrel[1], Cheikh Thiécoumba Gueye[2], Junaid Ahmad Khan[3]([⊠]),
Jean Belo Klamti[2], and Edoardo Persichetti[4]

[1] Laboratoire Hubert Curien, UMR CNRS 5516,
Bâtiment F 18 rue du professeur Benoît Lauras,
42000 Saint-Etienne, France
pierre.louis.cayrel@univ-st-etienne.fr
[2] Université Cheikh Anta Diop, Faculté des Sciences et Techniques,
DMI, LACGAA, Dakar, Senegal
{cheikht.gueye,jeanbelo.klamti}@ucad.edu.sn
[3] Dongguk University, Seoul, South Korea
junaid@dongguk.edu
[4] Department of Mathematical Sciences, Florida Atlantic University,
Boca Raton, FL 33431, USA
epersichetti@fau.edu

Abstract. The security of McEliece's cryptosystem relies heavily on the hardness of decoding a random linear code. The best known generic decoding algorithms are derived from the Information-Set Decoding (ISD) algorithm. This was first proposed in 1962 by Prange and subsequently improved in 1989 by Stern and later in 1991 by Dumer. In 2001 Al Jabri introduced a new decoding algorithm for general linear block codes which does not belong to this family, called *Statistical Decoding* (SD). Since then, like for the Information Set Decoding algorithm, there have been numerous work done to improve and generalize the SD algorithm. In this paper, we improve the SD algorithm using the notion of bases lists in binary case. Then, we give a non binary version of this improvement. Finally, we have computed complexity analysis and have made a complexity comparison of our results with that of recent results on SD algorithm and complexity of classic ISD algorithm.

Keywords: Code-based cryptography · Statistical decoding ·
McEliece system · Linear block code · Base list · MO-fusion

1 Introduction

Code-based cryptography, introduced by McEliece [9] in 1978, is one of the most promising solutions for designing cryptosystems that are secure against quantum attacks. The McEliece public-key encryption scheme using binary Goppa codes, has so far successfully resisted all cryptanalysis efforts. Its security relies on the fact that the public key does not have any known structure.

© Springer Nature Switzerland AG 2020
J. H. Seo (Ed.): ICISC 2019, LNCS 11975, pp. 194–207, 2020.
https://doi.org/10.1007/978-3-030-40921-0_12

Therefore, an attacker is faced with the problem of decoding a random code. The primary method to achieve this is by using generic decoding algorithm like Information-Set Decoding (ISD), introduced by Prange in 1962 [14]. Since then, there have been numerous improvements in ISD: among others, we mention Peters in 2010 [13], May, Meurer and Thomae in 2011 [7], Becker, Joux, May and Meurer in 2012 [1], May and Ozerov in 2015 [8], Hirose in 2016 [5] and recently Gueye et al. in 2017 [4].

In 2001, Al Jabri [6] introduced a new decoding algorithm called Statistical Decoding (SD) for general linear block codes. The SD algorithm generates a direct estimate of the error locations based on exploiting the statistical information embedded in the classical syndrome decoding. This new algorithm is not efficient as the ISD for codes having large cardinal. Nevertheless, it remains effective for the codes of small cardinal. Overbeck [12] in 2006 made the first improvement of the SD algorithm introduced by Al Jabri. He showed how to compute parity-check equations using Stern's algorithm [15]. In his improvement he used iterative algorithm to produce a few parity-check equations of small weight.

In 2007, Fossorier et al. [3] proposed a new variant of the SD algorithm. Their version is iterative. It is a two-stage algorithm : during the first step they compute an exponentially large number of parity-check equations of the smallest possible weight w, and then from these parity-check equations they are able to recover the error by some kind of majority voting based on these parity-check equations. In 2011, Niebuhr [11] gave the first generalization of the SD algorithm. He found that the biases in the binary case is not same to the q-ary case. In his paper, he gives an application of the SD algorithm and an instance of SD algorithm using the automorphism group of the code. In 2017, ten years after Overbeck, Debris-Alazard and Tillich [2] introduced a new improvement of the SD algorithm for the binary case. In their paper they used the technique used to improve ISD algorithm. They calculated a lower bound of complexity of SD algorithm and compared their improvement with the ISD algorithm.

In this paper our main contributions are to improve Statistical Decoding algorithm for the binary case. In addition we also generalize this new improvement over a finite field $\mathbb{F}_q$, where q is an arbitrary prime power. The paper is organized as follows: we start in Sect. 2 by providing some definitions and notation on coding theory. In Sect. 3, we present our new algorithm. In Sect. 4 we give a generalization of our improvement. Finally, in Sect. 5 we give a complexity analysis and provide a numerical complexity table, then in Sect. 6 we compare our algorithm with the previous generalization. Section 7 consists of conclusion.

2   Coding Theory Background

2.1   Notations

We use the following notation conventions:

- $\mathsf{wt}(\boldsymbol{x}) = |\{i \ \ s.t \ \ x_i \neq 0\}|$ the Hamming weight of $\boldsymbol{x}$.
- $\mathcal{S}_w := \{\boldsymbol{x} \in \mathbb{F}_q^n : \mathsf{wt}(\boldsymbol{x}) = w\}$ is the set of all q-ary words of weight w.

- $S_{w,i} := \{x \in S_w : x_i \neq 0\}$ is the set of words whose i-th position is not zero.
- $\mathcal{H}_w := S_w \cap \mathcal{C}^\perp$ is the set of all codewords of weight w in the dual of $\mathcal{C}$.
- $\mathcal{H}_{w,i} := S_{w,i} \cap \mathcal{C}^\perp$ is the set of all codewords in the dual of $\mathcal{C}$ whose i-th position is not zero.
- $h \sim S_{w,i}$ means we pick h uniformly at random in $S_{w,i}$.
- $c_k = R = \frac{k}{n}$
- $c_t = \frac{t}{n}$
- $c_w = \frac{w}{n}$
- $c_d = \frac{d}{n}$

2.2   Definitions

Let $\mathbb{F}_q$ be a finite field ($q = p^m$, p is prime). A q-ary linear code $\mathcal{C}$ of length n and dimension k over $\mathbb{F}_q$ is a vector subspace of dimension k of the full vector space $\mathbb{F}_q^n$. The code can be specified by a full rank matrix $G \in \mathbb{F}_q^{k \times n}$ called *generator matrix* of $\mathcal{C}$ whose rows span the code. Namely, $\mathcal{C} = \{xG : x \in \mathbb{F}_q^k\}$. A linear code can be also defined by the right kernel of matrix H called *parity-check matrix* of $\mathcal{C}$ as follows:

$$\mathcal{C} = \{x \in \mathbb{F}_q^k : Hx^T = 0\}$$

The *Hamming distance* between two codewords x and y denoted by $d_H(x, y) = t$ is the number of positions (coordinates) where they differ. The minimal distance of a code is the minimum distance between any two codewords. The *Hamming weight* of a codeword $x \in \mathbb{F}_q^n$, denote by $\mathrm{wt}(x)$, is the number of its nonzero positions. Then the minimal weight of a code $\mathcal{C}$ is the minimum of the weights of all codewords. If a code $\mathcal{C}$ is linear, the minimal distance is equal to the minimal weight of the code.

Let $\mathcal{C}$ be a q-ary linear code of length n, dimension k and generator matrix $G = (g_0, g_1, \cdots, g_{n-1})$ with $g_i \in \mathbb{F}_q^k$ for all $i \in \{0, 1, \cdots, n-1\}$. Let $I \subset \{0, 1, \cdots, n-1\}$ with $|I| = k$. We call I an *Information Set* if and only if the matrix $G_I = (g_i)_{i \in I}$ is invertible.

For the rest of this paper, we denote the *redundancy set* by $J = \{0, 1, \ldots, n-1\} \setminus I$ with I an information set.

For all integers n, let $[n] = \{1, 2, \ldots, n\}$. If I is a subset of $[n]$, for all vector $x = (x_1, x_2, \ldots, x_n) \in \mathbb{F}_q^n$, let $x_I = (x_i)_{i \in I}$.

We denote θ, as a mapping defined by

$$\theta : \mathbb{F}_q \longrightarrow \mathbb{F}_2$$

$$x \longmapsto \begin{cases} 0 \ if \ x = 0 \\ 1 \ if \ x \neq 1 \end{cases}$$

For all $x = (x_1, ..., x_n)$, $y = (y_1, ..., y_n) \in \mathbb{F}_q^n$ we set $\langle x, y \rangle = xy^T = \sum_{i=1}^{n} x_i y_i$.

Finally, we recall here the usual definition of the q-ary *entropy* function [10] :

$$H_q(x) = x \log_q(q-1) - x \log_q(x) - (1-x) \log_q(1-x).$$

Also in the binary case, we use the notation :

$$H(x) = -x \log_2(x) - (1-x) \log_2(1-x).$$

3   Improvement of Statistical Decoding Algorithm

3.1   Statistical Decoding Algorithm

Before talking about the improvement of SD it is necessary to recall and analyze the basic idea underlying the algorithm.

The main idea of statistical decoding consists of two parts. First, one computes a large set $\mathcal{S} \subset \mathcal{H}_w$ of parity-check equations of weight w. Second, computes all scalar product for $h \in \mathcal{S}$. Let us denote the number of equations (optimal parity-check equations) necessary for the SD success by P_w. Below we present the original SD algorithm [2]:

Algorithm 1. Statistical Decoding Algorithm

Input: A generator matrix $G \in \mathbb{F}_2^{k \times n}$ of a linear code $\mathcal{C}$ of length n and dimension k, a nonzero integer w and a noisy codeword $y = mG + e \in \mathbb{F}_2^n$.
Output: The error vector $e \in \mathbb{F}_2^n$ such that $\mathrm{wt}(e) \leq w$

1. **Procedure:** SD(G, y, w)
2.   **For** $i = 1$ to n **do:**
3. $S_i \longleftarrow ParityCheckComputation_w(G, i)$
4. $V_i \longleftarrow 0$
5.   **For** $h \in \mathcal{S}_i$ **do:**
6. $V_i \longleftarrow V_i + \langle y, h \rangle$
7.   **If** $V_i < s \cdot P_w \frac{1+\varepsilon_1+\varepsilon_0}{2}$ **then:**
8. $e_i \longleftarrow 1$
9.   **Else**
10. $e_i \longleftarrow 0$
11.   **Return** e
12. **End Procedure**
        # Parity Check Computation$_w$ is an auxilary algorithm see Appendix

---

In Algorithm 1, ε_0 and ε_1 are biases and s is defined as signum function in [2]. We see that the complexity of the SD algorithm depends on the complexity of the parity-check computation. Thus, improvement of the parity-check computation will improve the SD algorithm.

By definition of statistical decoding, its complexity is always greater than $\tilde{\mathcal{O}}(P_w)$. To the expected weight distribution $w = \frac{Rn}{2}$ of random code $[n, Rn]$, which is the binomial distribution, we have the following inequality (upper bound of P_w) [2,12]

$$P_w \leq \frac{\binom{n}{w}}{2^{Rn}}$$

We have the following remark:

Remark 1.

- When parity-check equations are already computed and stored, the asymptotic complexity of the SD algorithm is given by: $\tilde{\mathcal{O}}(P_w)$
- When parity-check equations have to be computed, the asymptotic complexity of the SD algorithm is given by: $\tilde{\mathcal{O}}(P_w + C_w)$

  where C_w is the complexity of the parity-check computation algorithm.

According to this remark, let us denote:

- $c_w \triangleq \frac{w}{n}$; $c_t \triangleq \frac{t}{n}$;
- $\pi(c_w, c_t) = \lim\limits_{n \longrightarrow +\infty} \frac{1}{n} \log_2 P_w$ (the lower bound of SD)

- $\pi(c_w, c_t)^{complete} = \max \left(\lim\limits_{n \longrightarrow +\infty} \frac{1}{n} \log_2 P_w, \lim\limits_{n \longrightarrow +\infty} \frac{1}{n} \log_2 C_w \right)$

We have the following result from [2].

Theorem 1. *Asymptotic complexity of statistical decoding $\pi(c_w, c_t)$ is equal to*

1. $2H(c_w) + 2c_w \log_2(r) - 2c_t \log_2(1 - r) - 2(1 - c_t) \log_2(1 + r)$ *if* $c_t \in \left[0, \frac{1}{2} - \sqrt{c_w - c_w^2}\right]$ *where r is the smallest root of* $(1-c_w)X^2 - (1-2c_t)X + c_w$
2. $H(c_w) + H(c_t) - 1$ *if* $c_t \in \left[\frac{1}{2} - \sqrt{c_w - c_w^2}, \frac{1}{2}\right]$

3.2   Improvement

In this section we present our new algorithm named *MO-Fusion$_w$*. This algorithm allows us to improve the parity-check computation step of the SD algorithm. Like the algorithm *DumerFusion$_w$* introduced in [2], the algorithm *MO-Fusion$_w$* contributes to the improvement of the SD complexity. In this algorithm we use two auxiliary algorithms *2B_Lists* and *MO-NN* (see the Appendix for more details).

We use *2B_Lists* to compute the sets $\mathcal{L}$ and $\mathcal{R}$ of vectors $e \in \{0\}^{k-\ell} \times \mathbb{F}_2^{n-k+\ell}$ using Base Lists such that $\mathrm{wt}\,(e) = \frac{\ell}{2} + \epsilon_1$ verifying for all $(e_1, e_2) \in \mathcal{L} \times \mathcal{R}$ $\mathrm{wt}(e_1 - e_2) = \rho$.

Algorithm 2. MO-Fusion$_w$

Parameters: Integers ρ, ℓ, ℓ_2, ϵ_1 and ϵ_2 such that $0 \leq \rho \leq \min\{n - k + \ell, w\}$, $0 < \ell_2 < \ell \leq \min\{k - w + \rho, k\}$

Input: A integer w and a binary matrix $\mathbf{G} \in \mathbb{F}_2^{k \times n}$.

Output: $\mathcal{S} \subset \mathcal{H}_w$ where $\mathcal{H}_w = \{\boldsymbol{x} \in \mathbb{F}_2^n \text{ s.t } \mathsf{wt}(\boldsymbol{x}) = w \text{ and } \boldsymbol{x}\mathbf{G} = 0\}$

1. **Procedure:** MO-Fusion$_w$(n, k, w, $\mathbf{G}$)
2.   Choose parameters ρ, ϵ_1, ϵ_2, $0 < \ell_2 < \ell$.
3. $\mathbf{P} \longleftarrow$ A random $n \times n$ permutation matrix
4. $\mathbf{G}' \longleftarrow \mathbf{UGP} = \begin{pmatrix} \mathbf{I}_{Rn-\ell} & \mathbf{G}_1 \\ \mathbf{0} & \mathbf{G}_2 \end{pmatrix}$ with $\mathbf{U} \in \mathbb{F}_2^{Rn \times Rn}$ a non singular matrix
5. $(\mathcal{L}, \mathcal{R}) \longleftarrow 2B\_Lists(\mathbf{G}', n, k, \ell, \rho, \ell_2, \epsilon_1, \epsilon_2)$
6.   We keep in $\mathcal{L}$ and $\mathcal{R}$ only vectors $\boldsymbol{x}$ such that $\mathsf{wt}(\boldsymbol{x}) = \frac{\ell}{2} + \epsilon_1$
7. $\mathcal{V} \longleftarrow$ MO-NN$(\mathcal{L}, \mathcal{R}, \frac{w-\rho}{k-\ell})$
8. $\mathcal{S} \longleftarrow \left\{ ((\boldsymbol{u}|0) + (\boldsymbol{a} - \boldsymbol{b}))\mathbf{P}^{-1} \text{ s.t } \boldsymbol{u} \in \mathcal{V} \cap (\mathcal{L} \times \mathcal{R}), \ \left(\mathbf{G}'(\boldsymbol{a} - \boldsymbol{b})^T\right)_{[k-\ell]} = \boldsymbol{u} \right\}$
9.   Return $\mathcal{S}$.
10. **End Procedure**
    # $2B\_Lists$ is an auxiliary algorithm see Appendix Alg. 4
    # $MO\text{-}NN$ is an auxiliary algorithm

The complexity of the MO-Fusion$_w$ algorithm is given below.

Proposition 1. *Let w be an integer and $\mathcal{C}$ be a binary code with generator matrix $\mathbf{G} \in \mathbb{F}_2^{k \times n}$. For all $\varepsilon > 0$ the complexity of the MO-Fusion$_w$ algorithm is given by*

$$\mathcal{C}_1 = \tilde{O}\left(2^{n\tau} + 2^{2n\tau_2 - \ell_2} + 2^{4n\tau - \ell_2 - \ell} + 2^{\mu n} + 2^{(y+\varepsilon)(k-\ell)}\right)$$

with

$$\tau = \frac{n - k + \ell}{2n} H\left(\frac{\frac{\ell}{4} + \frac{\epsilon_1}{2} + \epsilon_2}{n - k + \ell}\right), \quad \ell = \rho + (n - k + \ell - \rho)H\left(\frac{\epsilon_1}{n - k + \ell - \rho}\right)$$

$$\gamma = \frac{w - \rho}{k - \ell}, \quad 0 < \ell_2 < \ell \leq \min\{n - k - w + \rho, k\}$$

$$\mu = \frac{n - k + \ell}{2n} H\left(\frac{\frac{\ell}{2} + \epsilon_1}{n - k + \ell}\right) \quad \text{and} \quad y = (1 - \gamma)\left(1 - H\left(\frac{H^{-1}\left(1 - \frac{\mu n}{k - \ell}\right) - \frac{\gamma}{2}}{1 - \gamma}\right)\right)$$

Proof. In Algorithm 2, we start by executing the algorithm $2B\_Lists$; the complexity of this auxiliary algorithm is given by

$$\tilde{O}\left(2^{n\tau} + 2^{2n\tau - \ell_2} + 2^{4n\tau - \ell_2 - \ell}\right)$$

(see Appendix).

Step 6 of the algorithm gives us the following upper bound on $|\mathcal{L}|$ and $|\mathcal{R}|$.

$$\tilde{O}\left(\frac{\binom{k+\ell}{\frac{\ell}{2}+\epsilon_1}}{2^\ell}\right) = \tilde{O}\left(2^{n\left(\frac{k+\ell}{n}H\left(\frac{\frac{\ell}{2}+\epsilon_1}{k+\ell}\right)-\frac{\ell}{n}\right)}\right) = \tilde{O}\left(2^{\mu n}\right).$$

Finally, we make a last filtering using May-Ozerov's Nearest Neighbor algorithm [8]. We have $|\mathcal{L}| = |\mathcal{R}| = 2^{\mu n}$. In this paper, the Nearest Neighbor algorithm is given for the instance of (m, γ, λ)-Nearest Neighbor problem with

$$m = k - \ell, \quad \gamma = \frac{\omega - \rho}{k - \ell} \quad \text{and} \quad \lambda = \frac{\mu n}{k - \ell}.$$

The cost of this filtering is given by:

$$\tilde{O}\left(2^{(y+\varepsilon)(k-\ell)}\right).$$

For more details and the proof see [8] Sect. 4. Therefore

$$C_1 = \tilde{O}\left(2^{n\tau} + 2^{2n\tau_2 - \ell_2} + 2^{4n\tau - \ell_2 - \ell} + 2^{\mu n} + 2^{(y+\varepsilon)(k-\ell)}\right)$$

4   Non Binary Version of the New Improvement of SD

In the SD algorithm there are two steps and in this paper the main idea is to use the base lists used in the paper by Gueye et al. [4] to improve the first step of the algorithm. We call the algorithm q-BaseList-fusion$_w$.

Algorithm 3. q-MO-Fusion$_w$

Parameters: Integers ρ, ℓ, ℓ_2, ϵ_1 and ϵ_2 such that $0 \le \rho \le \min\{k+\ell, w\}$, $0 < \ell_2 < \ell \le \min\{n - k - w + \rho, n - k\}$
Input: A integer w and a binary matrix $\mathbf{G} \in \mathbb{F}_q^{k \times n}$.
Output: $\mathcal{S} \subset \mathcal{H}_w$ where $\mathcal{H}_w = \{x \in \mathbb{F}_q^n \text{ s.t } \text{wt}(x) = w \text{ and } x\mathbf{G}\}$

1. **Procedure:** MO-Fusion$_w(n, k, w, \mathbf{G})$
2.   Choose parameters p, ϵ_1, ϵ_2, $0 < \ell_2 < \ell < n - k$.
3. $\mathbf{P} \longleftarrow$ A random $n \times n$ permutation matrix
4. $\mathbf{G}' \longleftarrow \mathbf{UGP} = \begin{pmatrix} \mathbf{I}_{Rn-\ell} & \mathbf{G}_1 \\ \mathbf{0} & \mathbf{G}_2 \end{pmatrix}$ with $\mathbf{U} \in \mathbb{F}_q^{Rn \times Rn}$ a non-singular matrix
5. $(\mathcal{L}, \mathcal{R}) \longleftarrow qB\_Lists(\mathbf{G}', n, k, \ell, \rho, \ell_2, \epsilon_1, \epsilon_2)$
6.   We keep in $\mathcal{L}$ and $\mathcal{R}$ only vectors x such that $\text{wt}(x) = \frac{\ell}{2} + \epsilon_1$
7. $\mathcal{V} \longleftarrow qMO\text{-}NN(\mathcal{L}, \mathcal{R}, \frac{w-p}{k-\ell})$
8. $\mathcal{S} \longleftarrow \left\{((u|0) + (a - b))\mathbf{P}^{-1} \text{ s.t } u \in \mathcal{V} \cap (\mathcal{L} \times \mathcal{R}) \text{ with } (\mathbf{G}'(a - b)^T)_{[k-\ell]} = u\right\}$
9.   Return $\mathcal{S}$.
10. **End Procedure**

The complexity of the q-MO-Fusion$_w$ algorithm is given by the following proposition(see [4]):

Proposition 2. *Let w be an integer and $\mathcal{C}$ be a binary code of generator matrix $\mathbf{G} \in \mathbb{F}_q^{k \times n}$ over a finite field $\mathbb{F}_q$. The complexity of the q-MO-Fusion$_w$ algorithm is given by*

$$\mathcal{C}omp_q = \tilde{\mathcal{O}}\left(q^{n\tau} + q^{2n\tau - \ell_2} + q^{4n\tau - \ell_2 - \ell} + q^{\mu n} + q^{(y+\varepsilon)(k-\ell)}\right)$$

where

$$\tau = \frac{n-k+\ell}{2n} H_q\left(\frac{\frac{\rho}{4} + \frac{\epsilon_1}{2} + \epsilon_2}{n-k+\ell}\right) \quad and \quad \mu = \frac{n-k+\ell}{n} H_q\left(\frac{\frac{\rho}{2} + \epsilon_1}{n-k+\ell}\right) - \frac{\ell}{n}$$

with

$$y = (1-\gamma)\left(H_q(\beta) - \frac{1}{q}H_q\left(\frac{qh_x - \gamma}{1-\gamma}\beta\right)\right), \quad \gamma = \frac{w-\rho}{k-\ell}, \quad 0 < \beta < 1,$$

$$\max\{0, w+k+\ell - n\} \le \rho \le \min\{k+\ell\}, \quad \sum_{x \in \mathbb{F}_q} h_x = 1$$

$$\frac{\gamma}{q} < h_x < \frac{\gamma}{q} + \frac{1-\gamma}{q\beta} \quad for \quad each \quad x \in \mathbb{F}_q$$

$$\ell = \rho \log_q 2 + (n-k+\ell - \rho) H_q\left(\frac{\epsilon_1}{n-k+\ell-\rho}\right) \quad and \quad \ell \le \min\{k - \ell - w + \rho, n - k\}$$

$$\ell_2 = \left(\frac{\rho}{2} - \epsilon_1\right)\log_q 2 + \left(n-k+\ell - \frac{\rho}{2} - \epsilon_1\right)H_q\left(\frac{\epsilon_2}{n-k+\ell - \frac{\rho}{2} - \epsilon_1}\right)$$

$$\lambda = \frac{n\mu}{k-\ell} \le H_q(\beta) - \frac{1}{q}\sum_{x \in \mathbb{F}_q} H_q(qh_x\beta).$$

Proof. In Algorithm 4 we start by executing the algorithm qB_Lists: the complexity of this auxiliary algorithm is given by

$$\tilde{\mathcal{O}}\left(q^{n\tau} + q^{2n\tau - \ell_2} + q^{4n\tau - \ell_2 - \ell}\right)$$

Line 6 only gives the upper bound on $|\mathcal{L}| = |\mathcal{R}|$.

$$\tilde{\mathcal{O}}\left(\frac{\binom{k+\ell}{\frac{\rho}{2}+\epsilon_1}(q-1)^{\frac{\rho}{2}+\epsilon_1}}{q^\ell}\right) = \tilde{\mathcal{O}}\left(q^{n\left(\frac{k+\ell}{n}H_q\left(\frac{\frac{\rho}{2}+\epsilon_1}{k+\ell}\right) - \frac{\ell}{n}\right)}\right) = \tilde{\mathcal{O}}(q^{\mu n}).$$

Finally, we make a last filtering using the q-ary May-Ozerov Nearest Neighbor algorithm: the cost of this filtering is given by

$$\tilde{\mathcal{O}}\left(q^{(y+\varepsilon)(k-\ell)}\right).$$

We have $|\mathcal{L}| = |\mathcal{R}| = q^{\mu n}$. Thus qMO-NN is given an instance of (m, γ, λ)-NN with:

$$m = k - \ell, \quad \gamma = \frac{w-\rho}{k-\ell} \quad and \quad \lambda = \frac{\mu n}{k-\ell}.$$

Proposition 3. *The complexity of SD algorithm generalized using MO-Fusion$_w$ over an arbitrary finite fiels $\mathbb{F}_q$ is given by*

$$Comp_q = \tilde{\mathcal{O}}\left(q^{n\left(2H_q(\omega)-2(1-\zeta)H_q\left(\frac{\omega}{1-\zeta}\right)\right)} + q^{n\tau} + q^{2n\tau-\ell_2} + q^{4n\tau-\ell_2-\ell} + q^{\mu n} + q^{(y+\varepsilon)(k-\ell)}\right)$$

5   Complexity Comparison of Binary SD

In this section we present a comparison of the complexity of the SD algorithm obtained by using the MO-Fusion$_w$ algorithm as opposed to the DumerFusion algorithm of [2]. For ease of notation, we denote with $c_k, c_\ell, c_{\ell_2}, c_d, c_{e_1}, c_{e_2}, c_\rho$ and c_w the values $\frac{k}{n}, \frac{\ell}{n}, \frac{\ell_2}{n}, \frac{d}{n}, \frac{e_1}{n}, \frac{e_2}{n}, \frac{\rho}{n}$ and $\frac{w}{n}$ respectively. In the following table we consider $c_d = H^{-1}(1 - c_k)$, $c_{e_1} = 0.001759$ and $c_w = \frac{c_k}{2}$.

Table 1. Exponent complexity of the New improvement of the SD algorithm.

New SD algorithm						
c_k	c_ℓ	c_{ℓ_2}	c_w	c_ρ	c_{e_2}	Exp. Complexity
0.1	0.02583	0.00235	0.05000	0.00350	0.007850	0.12699
0.2	0.04291	0.00390	0.10000	0.00989	0.012985	0.18576
0.3	0.02647	0.00132	0.15000	0.01598	0.013450	0.21528
0.4	0.04988	0.00278	0.20000	0.02518	0.014950	0.22586
0.5	0.07691	0.01923	0.25000	0.05774	0.01625	0.22952
0.6	0.12234	0.03058	0.30000	0.06950	0.017050	0.21989
0.7	0.13141	0.03285	0.03500	0.07150	0.018250	0.20003
0.8	0.17470	0.03882	0.40000	0.08350	0.01895	0.15801
0.9	0.17825	0.08913	0.45000	0.0935	0.01905	0.08678

According to the following figure we see that the SD algorithm with MO-Fusion$_w$ is faster than the SD algorithm with Dumer Fusion (Fig. 1 and Table 1).

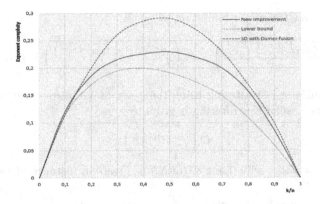

Fig. 1. Complexity comparison of SD algorithm

6   Complexity Comparison of Generalized SD

For the generalized version of the SD algorithm, it is important to note that in [11], the author mentions how generalized SD is more efficient than the generalized ISD algorithm introduced by Peters when the cardinality of the finite field satisfies $q \geq 233$. For the case $q = 3$, for a code of parameters $(64, 40)$ the author claims that the generalized SD algorithm needs $2^{20.2}$ operations, versus the $2^{13.2}$ operations required by generalized ISD. For a code with parameters $(128, 72)$ he obtained an estimate of $2^{22.2}$ operations versus $2^{18.3}$ operations for generalized ISD.

In this paper, when $q = 3$ we have $c_d = H^{-1}(1 - c_k)$, $c_w = \frac{c_k}{2}$, therefor we can see that

1. For a code of parameters $(128, 72)$ with $c_\ell = 0.01422$ and $c_\rho = 0.02813$ and for the SD algorithm using MO-Fusion$_w$ we have $2^{19.71}$ operations, where $c_{e_1} = 0.00402$, $c_{e_2} = 0.00254$, $c_{\ell_2} = 0.00129$, $beta = 0.21450$ and $h = 0.1881$
2. For a code of parameters $(64, 40)$ with $c_\ell = 0.01582$ and $c_\rho = 0.06250$ and for the SD algorithm using MO-Fusion$_w$ we have $2^{16.49}$ operations, where $c_{e_1} = 0.00702$, $c_{e_2} = 0.00254$, $c_{\ell_2} = 0.00144$, $beta = 0.21450$ and $h = 0.28810$

In the above, we chose the parameter h_x such that only one $x \in \mathbb{F}_q$ has a value of h_x such that $h_x = h$ and the others have the same value of h_x.

7   Conclusion

In this paper we presented an improvement of the SD algorithm using the MO-Fusion$_w$ algorithm based on the idea introduced by May and Ozerov [8] for improving the ISD algorithm. We then generalized this new version of the SD algorithm to the case of generic finite fields $\mathbb{F}_q$. We have shown that the SD algorithm using MO-Fusion$_w$ algorithm is more efficient than the previous version. This new SD version is closer to the lower bound given by the authors in [2]. Finally, it is possible to see that the generalization of the SD algorithm using MO-Fusion$_w$ and the version of SD algorithm using DumerFusion are faster than the generalization of the SD algorithm proposed by Niebuhr [11].

Appendix

$qB\_$Lists algorithm

The auxilary algorithm named $qB\_$Lists is given below.

Algorithm 4. $qB\_$Lists

Input: A matrix $\mathbf{G} \in \mathbb{F}_q^{k \times n}$, five nonzero and positive integers n, k, ℓ_2, ℓ, ϵ_1 and ϵ_2.
Output: Two lists $\mathcal{L}$ and $\mathcal{R}$

1. **Procedure:**
2.   Choose randomly $t_1, t_2 \in \mathbb{F}_q^\ell$ and $t_{\mathcal{L}_0}, t_{\mathcal{R}_0} \in \mathbb{F}_q^{\ell_2}$
3.   Compute $t_{\mathcal{L}} = t_1 - (t_2^{[\ell-\ell_2]}|0)$, $t_{\mathcal{L}} = t_2 - (t_1^{[\ell-\ell_2]}|0)$, $t_{\mathcal{L}_1} = t_{\mathcal{L}_0} + (t_1)_{[\ell_2]}$ and
       $t_{\mathcal{R}_1} = t_{\mathcal{R}_0} + (t_2)_{[\ell_2]}$.
4.   Compute base lists $\mathcal{B}_{i,1}^{\mathcal{L}_i}$, $\mathcal{B}_{i,2}^{\mathcal{L}_i}$, $\mathcal{B}_{i,1}^{\mathcal{R}_i}$ and $\mathcal{B}_{i,1}^{\mathcal{R}_i}$, with $i = 0, 1$
5. $\mathcal{L}_i \longleftarrow \left\{ u = a - b \ \ s.t \ \ a \in \mathcal{B}_{i,1}^{\mathcal{L}_i}, b \in \mathcal{B}_{i,2}^{\mathcal{L}_i}, \ \ \mathrm{wt}\,(u) = \frac{p}{4} + \frac{\epsilon_1}{2} + \epsilon_2, \right.$
       $\left. and \ \ (\mathbf{G}u^T)^{[\ell_2]} = t_{\mathcal{L}_i} \right\}$
6. $\mathcal{R}_i \longleftarrow \left\{ u = a - b \ \ s.t \ \ a \in \mathcal{B}_{i,1}^{\mathcal{R}_i}, b \in \mathcal{B}_{i,2}^{\mathcal{R}_i}, \ \ \mathrm{wt}\,(u) = \frac{p}{4} + \frac{\epsilon_1}{2} + \epsilon_2, \right.$
       $\left. and \ \ (\mathbf{G}u^T)^{[\ell_2]} = t_{\mathcal{R}_i} \right\}$
7. $\mathcal{L} \longleftarrow \left\{ (\mathbf{G}z^T)_{[k-\ell]} \ \ s.t \ \ z = u - v \ \ and \ \ (u, v) \in \mathcal{L}_0 \times \mathcal{L}_1 \right.$
       $\left. \text{with } \left(\tilde{\mathbf{G}}z^T \right)^{[\ell]} = t_{\mathcal{L}} \right\}$
8. $\mathcal{R} \longleftarrow \left\{ \left(\tilde{\mathbf{G}}z^T \right)_{[k-\ell]} \ \ s.t \ \ z = u - v \ \ and \ \ (u, v) \in \mathcal{R}_0 \times \mathcal{R}_1 \right.$
       $\left. \text{with } \left(\tilde{\mathbf{G}}z^T \right)^{[\ell]} = t_{\mathcal{R}} \right\}$
9.   Return $(\mathcal{L}, \mathcal{R})$
10. **End Procedure:**

In the qB_Lists we use base lists like in [1,7,8] but the construction and weight distribution vector in our construction is few different. The construction of Base Lists in the algorithm qB_Lists is over an arbitrary finite field $\mathbb{F}_q$.

For all $j = 0, 1$ we denote the base lists by $\mathcal{B}_{j,1}^{\mathcal{L}_j}$, $\mathcal{B}_{j,2}^{\mathcal{L}_j}$, $\mathcal{B}_{j,1}^{\mathcal{R}_j}$ and $\mathcal{B}_{j,2}^{\mathcal{R}_j}$. We define $\mathcal{B}_{j,1}^{\mathcal{L}_j}$ as follows:

Let $\mathcal{P}_{j,1}^{\mathcal{L}_j}$ and $\mathcal{P}_{j,2}^{\mathcal{L}_j}$ be be a partition of $[n - k + \ell] = \{n - k - \ell, 1, ..., n\}$ such that $\left| \mathcal{P}_{j,1}^{\mathcal{L}_j} \right| = \left| \mathcal{P}_{j,2}^{\mathcal{L}_j} \right| = \dfrac{n - k + \ell}{2}$ then

$$\mathcal{B}_{j,1}^{\mathcal{L}_j} = \left\{ x \in \left\{ 0^{k-\ell} \right\} \times \mathbb{F}_q^{n-k+\ell} \ \ s.t \ \ \mathrm{wt}\,(x) = \frac{\rho}{8} + \frac{\epsilon_1}{4} + \frac{\epsilon_2}{2} \ \ with \ \ x_{\mathcal{P}_{j,2}^{\mathcal{L}_j}} = (0, 0, ..., 0) \right\}$$

Where p, ϵ_1 and ϵ_2 are the parameters of the algorithm such that $0 \leq \rho < n - k + \ell$, $0 < \epsilon_1 < n - k + \ell - \rho$, $0 < \epsilon_2 < n - k + \ell - \dfrac{\rho}{2} - \epsilon_1$. The construction of $\mathcal{B}_{j,2}^{\mathcal{L}_j}$, $\mathcal{B}_{j,1}^{\mathcal{R}_j}$ and $\mathcal{B}_{j,2}^{\mathcal{R}_j}$ is similar.

We use these base lists to compute a vector $e \in \{0^{k-\ell}\} \times \mathbb{F}_q^{n-k+\ell}$ such that $\mathsf{wt}\left(e_{[n-k+\ell]}\right) = \rho$ and $e = e_1 - e_2$ with $e_1, e_2 \in \{0^{k-\ell}\} \times \mathbb{F}_q^{n-k+\ell}$ and $\mathsf{wt}(e_1) = \mathsf{wt}(e_2) = \dfrac{\rho}{2} + \epsilon_1$.

For all arbitrary finite field $\mathbb{F}_q$, the complexity of the algorithm qB_Lists is given by the following *Proposition*:

Proposition 4. *The complexity of qB_Lists is given by:*

$$Comp_q = \tilde{\mathcal{O}}\left(q^{n\tau} + q^{2n\tau - \ell_2} + q^{4n\tau - \ell_2 - \ell}\right)$$

with

$$\tau = \frac{n - k + \ell}{2n} H_q\left(\frac{\frac{\rho}{4} + \frac{\epsilon_1}{2} + \epsilon_2}{n - k + \ell}\right)$$

$$\ell = \rho \log_q 2 + (n - k + \ell - \rho) H_q\left(\frac{\epsilon_1}{n - k + \ell - \rho}\right) \quad and \quad \ell \le \min\{k - \ell - w + \rho, n - k\}$$

$$\ell_2 = \left(\frac{\rho}{2} - \epsilon_1\right) \log_q 2 + \left(n - k + \ell - \frac{\rho}{2} - \epsilon_1\right) H_q\left(\frac{\epsilon_2}{n - k + \ell - \frac{\rho}{2} - \epsilon_1}\right)$$

Proof. At line 4, we construct base lists and the cardinality of each Base List is given for all $i, j \in \{1, 2\}$ by:

$$|\mathcal{B}_{j,i}^{\mathcal{L}_j}| = |\mathcal{B}_{j,i}^{\mathcal{R}_j}| = \binom{\frac{n-k+\ell}{2}}{\frac{\rho}{8} + \frac{\epsilon_1}{4} + \frac{\epsilon_2}{2}} (q-1)^{\frac{\rho}{8} + \frac{\epsilon_1}{4} + \frac{\epsilon_2}{2}}.$$

Then by using the identity

$$\binom{n}{k}(q-1)^k = \tilde{\mathcal{O}}\left(q^{nH_q(\frac{k}{n})}\right),$$

the complexity to compute base lists is given by

$$\tilde{\mathcal{O}}\left(q^{n\left(\frac{n-k+\ell}{2n} H_q\left(\frac{\frac{\rho}{4} + \frac{\epsilon_1}{2} + \epsilon_2}{n-k+\ell}\right)\right)}\right) = \tilde{\mathcal{O}}\left(q^{n\tau}\right).$$

We use base lists to make a filtering to compute $\mathcal{L}_i$ and $\mathcal{R}_i$ for each $i = 1, 2$ and the cost of this filtering is given by:

$$\tilde{\mathcal{O}}\left(\frac{|\mathcal{B}_{i,1}^{\mathcal{L}_i}||\mathcal{B}_{i,2}^{\mathcal{L}_i}|}{q^{\ell_1}}\right) = \tilde{\mathcal{O}}\left(q^{2n\tau - \ell_1}\right).$$

Third we compute the lists $\mathcal{L}$ and $\mathcal{R}$ with a filtering and the cost of this filtering is given by

$$\tilde{\mathcal{O}}\left(\frac{|\mathcal{L}_1||\mathcal{L}_2|}{q^{\ell - r_1}}\right) = \tilde{\mathcal{O}}\left(q^{4n\tau - \ell_1 - \ell}\right).$$

7.1 q-$ParityCheckComputation_w$

Following we give the generalization of the algorithm $ParityCheckComputation_w$
given in [2]. We call it q-$ParityCheckComputation_w$

Algorithm 5. q-$ParityCheckComputation_w$

Input: A generator matrix $G \in \mathbb{F}_q^{k \times n}$ of a linear code $\mathcal{C}$ of length n and dimension k, an integer i.
Output: $\mathcal{S}_i$

1. **Procedure:** q-$ParityCheckComputation_w(G, i)$
2. $\mathcal{S}_i \longleftarrow [\,]$
3.   **While** $|\mathcal{S}_i| < w$ **do:**
4. $P \longleftarrow$ a random $n \times n$ permutation matrix
5. $[G'|\mathbf{I}_k] \longleftarrow GaussElim(GP)$
6. $H \longleftarrow [\mathbf{I}_{n-k}|G'^T]$
7.   **For** $j = 1$ to $n(1 - R)$ **do:**
8.   **If** $L_j(H)_i \neq 0$ and $\mathsf{wt}(L_j(H)) = w$ **then:**
9. $\mathcal{S}_i \longleftarrow \mathcal{S}_i \cup \{L_j(H)P^T\}$
10.   **Return** $\mathcal{S}_i$
11. **End Procedure**

References

1. Becker, A., Joux, A., May, A., Meurer, A.: Decoding random binary linear codes in $2^{n/20}$: How $1 + 1 = 0$ improves information set decoding. In: Eurocrypt 2012 (2012)
2. Debris-Alazard, T., Tillich, J.-P.: Statistical decoding (2017). CoRR, abs/1701.07416,
3. Fossorier, M.P.C., Kobara, K., Imai, H.: Modeling bit flipping decoding based on nonorthogonal check sums with application to iterative decoding attack of mceliece cryptosystem. IEEE Trans. Inf. Theory **53**(1), 402–411 (2007)
4. Gueye, C.T., Klamti, J.-B., Hirose, S.: Generalization of BJMM-ISD using may-ozerov nearest neighbor algorithm over an arbitrary finite field $\mathbb{F}_q$. In: El Hajji, S., Nitaj, A., Souidi, E.M. (eds.) Codes. Cryptology and Information Security: Second International Conference, C2SI 2017, Rabat, Morocco, April 10–12, 2017, Proceedings - In Honor of Claude Carlet, pp. 96–109. Springer International Publishing, Cham (2017). https://doi.org/10.1007/978-3-319-55589-8_7
5. Hirose, S.: May-ozerov algorithm for nearest-neighbor problem over $\mathbb{F}_q$ and its application to information set decoding. Cryptology ePrint Archive, Report 2016/237 (2016). http://eprint.iacr.org/
6. Jabri, A.A.: A statistical decoding algorithm for general linear block codes. In: Honary, B. (ed.) Cryptography and Coding 2001. LNCS, vol. 2260, pp. 1–8. Springer, Heidelberg (2001). https://doi.org/10.1007/3-540-45325-3_1

7. May, A., Meurer, A., Thomae, E.: Decoding random linear codes in $\tilde{\mathcal{O}}(2^{0.054n})$. In: Lee, D.H., Wang, X. (eds.) ASIACRYPT 2011. LNCS, vol. 7073, pp. 107–124. Springer, Heidelberg (2011). https://doi.org/10.1007/978-3-642-25385-0_6

8. May, A., Ozerov, I.: On computing nearest neighbors with applications to decoding of binary linear codes. In: Oswald, E., Fischlin, M. (eds.) EUROCRYPT 2015. LNCS, vol. 9056, pp. 203–228. Springer, Heidelberg (2015). https://doi.org/10.1007/978-3-662-46800-5_9

9. McEliece, R.J.: A public-key cryptosystem based on algebraic coding theory. DNS Progress Report, pp. 114–116 (1978)

10. Moon, T.K.: Error Correction Coding: Mathematical Methods and Algorithms. Wiley, New York (2005)

11. Niebuhr, R.: Statistical decoding of codes over $\mathbb{F}_q$. In: Yang, B.-Y. (ed.) PQCrypto 2011. LNCS, vol. 7071, pp. 217–227. Springer, Heidelberg (2011). https://doi.org/10.1007/978-3-642-25405-5_14

12. Overbeck, R.: Statistical decoding revisited. In: Batten, L.M., Safavi-Naini, R. (eds.) ACISP 2006. LNCS, vol. 4058, pp. 283–294. Springer, Heidelberg (2006). https://doi.org/10.1007/11780656_24

13. Peters, C.: Information-set decoding for linear codes over $\mathbb{F}_q$. In: Sendrier, N. (ed.) PQCrypto 2010. LNCS, vol. 6061, pp. 81–94. Springer, Heidelberg (2010). https://doi.org/10.1007/978-3-642-12929-2_7

14. Prange, E.: The use of information sets in decoding cyclic codes. IRE Trans. Inf. Theory **8**(5), 5–9 (1962)

15. Stern, J.: A method for finding codewords of small weight. In: Proceedings of Coding Theory and Applications, pp. 106–113 (1989)

LizarMong: Excellent Key Encapsulation Mechanism Based on RLWE and RLWR

Chi-Gon Jung[1(✉)], JongHyeok Lee[2], Youngjin Ju[3], Yong-Been Kwon[4], Seong-Woo Kim[1], and Yunheung Paek[5]

[1] Department of Engineering Practice, Seoul National University, Seoul, Korea
{cgjung,snwoo}@snu.ac.kr
[2] Department of Financial Information Security, Kookmin University, Seoul, Korea
n_seeu@kookmin.ac.kr
[3] Department of Mathematics, Hanyang University, Seoul, Korea
jyj9327kr@hanyang.ac.kr
[4] Department of IT Convergence, Hansung University, Seoul, Korea
vexyoung@gmail.com
[5] Department of Electrical and Computer Engineering, Seoul National University,
Seoul, Korea
ypaek@snu.ac.kr

Abstract. The RLWE family algorithms submitted to the NIST post-quantum cryptography standardization process have each merit in terms of security, correctness, performance, and bandwidth. However, there is no splendid algorithm in all respects. Besides, various recent studies have been published that affect security and correctness, such as side-channel attacks and error dependencies. To date, though, no algorithm has fully considered all the aspects. We propose a novel Key Encapsulation Mechanism scheme called LizarMong, which is based on RLizard. LizarMong combines the merit of each algorithm and state-of-the-art studies. As a result, it achieves up to 85% smaller bandwidth and 3.3 times faster performance compared to RLizard. Compared to the NIST's candidate algorithms with a similar security, the bandwidth is about 5–42% smaller, and the performance is about 1.2-4.1 times faster. Also, our scheme resists the known side-channel attacks.

Keywords: Lattice-based cryptography · Ring-LWE · Ring-LWR

1 Introduction

Among candidates for the National Institute of Standards and Technology (NIST) post-quantum cryptography standardization process [12], the Ring Learning With Error (RLWE) family[1] is the spotlight in Key Encapsulation Mechanism (KEM) because of its proven hardness, small bandwidth, and good performance.

---

[1] Ring-LWE (RLWE), Ring-Learning With Rounding (RLWR), Module-LWE (MLWE), Module-LWR (MLWR), Integer-MLWE (I-MLWE).

J. Lee, Y. Ju and Y.-B. Kwon—These authors contributed equally to this work.

© Springer Nature Switzerland AG 2020
J. H. Seo (Ed.): ICISC 2019, LNCS 11975, pp. 208–224, 2020.
https://doi.org/10.1007/978-3-030-40921-0_13

The design factors of the RLWE family algorithms consist of the underlying problems, the choice of ring, the dimensions of the lattice, the modulus, and the error rate determined by the ratio between the standard deviation of the error distribution and the modulus. These factors have trade-offs and determine security, correctness, performance, and bandwidth. Looking at NIST's candidate algorithms from a trade-off perspective, we can see some notable characteristics.

First, the choice of the underlying problems and the ring determines the innate temperament of the algorithm. The underlying problems are classified as RLWE, Ring Learning With Rounding (RLWR), Module-LWE (MLWE), and MLWR. RLWE has good performance and bandwidth. Also, RLWE has been well-studied for the most prolonged time among the underlying problems of lattice from algebraic structures and is used for other schemes such as homomorphic encryption. Thus, RLWE can claim that it is more conservative security than other underlying problems of the lattice from algebraic structures. MLWE can reduce bandwidth because they are small and flexible in dimension choice, but require more computation if into dimension the same as RLWE. RLWR and MLWR discard some Least Significant Bits (LSBs) instead of error sampling, resulting in better performance and bandwidth compare to RLWE and MLWE. The ring is commonly chosen as the cyclotomic polynomial $X^n + 1$ due to performance and security, where n is a power of two. Exceptionally, Round5 [8] uses the $X^{n+1} - 1$ cyclotomic polynomial. Since $n + 1$ is prime, this polynomial is less constrictive in n choosing. So, it can choose an optimized n for each security level. The required bandwidth can be reduced. However, $X^{n+1} - 1$ is more expensive computation to polynomial modular reduction operation than common polynomial. The algorithm with the smallest bandwidth among NIST's candidates is Round5, which based on RLWR and does not use $X^n + 1$ polynomial. Thus, it is important to choose the underlying problem and the ring.

Another notable characteristic is the modulus size. Modulus size is the main factor that affects the correctness, bandwidth, and performance of RLWE family schemes. Large modulus (2^{12-14}) like Newhope [5] reach security-level by adding relatively large error, but can maintain correctness because of a small error rate. Large modulus, however, increases computation and bandwidth. Thus, they use fast multiplication algorithms (e.g., NTT), public-key compression, and ciphertext compression to solve this problem. Conversely, small modulus (2^{8-12}) like LAC [24] can have relatively low bandwidth and good performance. However, if a large error such as the large modulus is used, the correctness decreases as the error rate increases. Thus, these are using tiny error and secret, and error correction code to improve correctness.

Meanwhile, NIST's standardization process has recently been making impressive results by promoting a study on the RLWE family. In particular, the study that disproves the independent assumptions about the failure of individual bits to calculate the overall failure rate [16], as well as various side-channel attack studies, is meaningful because of affecting most RLWE family algorithms. To date, however, many algorithms do not include most of those studies.

As mentioned above, each algorithm complements the trade-off with brilliant techniques. Unfortunately, however, choosing one excellent algorithm in all aspects (security, performance, bandwidth, and correctness) is a hard decision. Furthermore, considering the recent studies, it is almost infeasible to choose one.

In this paper, we propose a novel key encapsulation mechanism scheme called LizarMong that is excellent in all aspects. It combines each merit of NIST's candidate algorithms with state-of-the-art studies.

Contributions. The contributions of this study can be summarized as follow:

- To improve bandwidth and performance, we set small dimensions and modulus, and apply ciphertext and public-key compression.
- We adopt the error correction code called XE5 [8] to compensate for the reduced correctness due to small modulus.
- Resistance to known side-channel attacks, we devise a sparse polynomial multiplication with hiding. Also, we do not use the Cumulative Distribution Table (CDT) technique as the error sampler.
- We estimate the correctness more conservatively by calculating the decryption failure rate considering the dependency of each bit error.

2   Preliminaries

2.1   Notation

The log indicates the logarithm with base 2. For a positive integer q, we use $\mathbb{Z} \cap (-q/2, q/2]$ as a representative of $\mathbb{Z}_q$. We denote by R_q the ring $\mathbb{Z}_q[X]/(X^n + 1)$. Bold lower-case letters represent polynomials with coefficients in R_q. For a polynomial $\mathbf{a}$, we write $a(i)$ to denote it's the coefficient of order i. Multiplication in R_q is represented by $*$. $\lceil r \rfloor$ is the rounding to the nearest integer to real r, and $\lfloor \mathbf{a} \rceil$ is the rounding to the nearest integer for each coefficient in the polynomial $\mathbf{a}$. $\|x\|$ means the l_2 norm. $x \parallel y$ is the concatenation of x and y. There are two distributions used in this paper, $HWT_n(h)$ and ψ_{cb}. $HWT_n(h)$ is the uniform distribution over the subset of $\{-1, 0, 1\}^n$ whose elements contain $n - h$ number of zeros. ψ_{cb} is the centered binomial distribution with mean zero and standard deviation $\sqrt{cb/2}$. SHAKE256(m, len) is a hash function that receives m and outputs a byte-string of the length len. eccENC and eccDEC are functions for encoding and decoding using the error correction code.

2.2   RLizard

RLizard is the KEM and PKE based on RLWE and RLWR submitted to the NIST standardization process 1round. RLizard uses RLWE for key-generation, considering relatively conservative security, and RLWR for encryption and decryption to improve bandwidth and performance. Another effort to ensure robust security in key-generation is the adoption of CDT from Gaussian distribution as an error sampler. It is a high precision sampler that does not damage the original RLWE. The ring is chosen as the common form $X^n + 1$. RLizard uses a small modulus and sparse ternary secret, which improved correctness and performance. Moreover, for providing IND-CCA2 PKE and KEM, they use a variant of Fujisaki-Okamoto transformation [18]. As a result, RLizard supports IND-CCA2 PKE and KEM and enjoys fast encryption and decryption, robust security, and high correctness. However, the bandwidth is relatively large.

3 LizarMong

In this section, we detail our KEM scheme called LizarMong. Our goal is to satisfy both security and correctness while making excellent performance and bandwidth. To achieve the goal, LizarMong was designed by adequately combining the design elements of NIST's candidate algorithms and their superior techniques that are used to compensate for the trade-off. Our scheme also considered recent studies such as side-channel attacks and dependency error issues.

3.1 Design Element Selection

Choice of the Ring. We use $f(X) = X^n + 1$ in $R_q := \mathbb{Z}_q[X]/(f(X))$, where n is the power of two. It is the common choice used by most of NIST's candidate algorithms and RLizard. The common ring has the advantage in that the polynomial modular reduction operation is straightforward, and there have been no known attacks exploit it [23].

Modulus Selection. We select $q = 256$, which is small and to the power of two. Intuitively, this choice enjoys a small bandwidth and improved performance. It also provides very efficient modulo operation and memory usage and is suitable for single instruction multiple data (SIMD) implementations such as AVX2 and NEON. Even though the modulus is small, it can not affect the security since we maintain the error rate by selecting proper error distribution [24,27]. The modulus p used for RLWR and the modulus k used for ciphertext compression are also to the power of two. It improve performance by replacing $\lfloor (p/q) \cdot \mathbf{x} \rceil$ with ADD and AND operations [13].

Distribution. The RLWE family can sample secret polynomial $\mathbf{s}$ and error polynomial $\mathbf{e}$ using different *Seed* in the same distribution for efficient implementation. Also, this variant has proven to be equivalent to the original RLWE problem [6]. For the above reason, most of NIST's candidate algorithms use the same distribution for error and secret sampling. Recently, however, a fault-attack [29] attempted to analyze by manipulating the *Seed* to make $\mathbf{s}$ and $\mathbf{e}$ the same value. Therefore, we sample $\mathbf{e}$ and $\mathbf{s}$ from each distribution, like the original RLWE, to remove the fault-attack point [29].

- **Error Distribution.** We use the centered binomial distribution with the standard deviation $1/\sqrt{2}$, i.e. the range of the distribution is $\{-1, 0, 1\}$. Although the original RLWE is defined as a Gaussian distribution, switching to the centered binomial distribution is known to have a negligible impact on security [5]. Also, the best-known attacks against RLWE depend not on the type of the distribution but the standard deviation [5,9].

- **Secret Distribution.** We use a sparse ternary secret with a Hamming weight, such as RLizard. [13] and [8] proved the hardness of the sparse ternary secret variants LWE and LWR. Multiplication of sparse ternary secret polynomials can be replaced with addition (subtraction) to improve performance [1]. It also maintains correctness by preventing decryption errors from increasing.

Adopt Error Correction Code. Our analysis in Sect. 4.3 shows that 4–5 bits error correction capability is needed. Therefore, we adopted XE5 [8] that is specialized in the RLWE family. Since XE5 avoids table look-up and branch conditions, it resists timing attacks [8]. XE5 has a block size of 490 bits, of which 256 bits is the message, and 234 bits is parity check. Our scheme differs in message length from HILA5 [32] and Round5, which previously used XE5. δ, used in place of PKE messages in the IND-CCA2 KEM, has a significant impact on the security of the scheme. Thus, we match the length of the δ (messages) to the overall security level. The 512-bit δ (messages) in the Strong parameter seems to constrain the use of XE5, but we can solve it very simply. Divide the 512-bit δ (messages) in half, encode it with XE5, and concatenate it. Decoding is in reverse order. This process does not affect security and makes our calculation of correctness more conservative in our Strong parameters.

Compress Public-Key and Ciphertext. NIST's candidate algorithms commonly use compression techniques. RLizard can also use these techniques [23], although it does not include in the version submitted to NIST. Public-key compression means sending only the *Seed* instead of **a** in R_q, and the receiver recovers **a** using the hash function. This reduces the public-key size from $2n \log q$ to size-of-*Seed* + $n \log q$. Ciphertext compression is similar to the RLWR idea of discarding a few LSBs in $\mathbf{c_2}$. IND-CCA2 KEM also can do the same.

3.2 Algorithm Specifications

3.2.1 IND-CPA PKE

Algorithm 1. IND-CPA.KeyGen

Input: The set of public *parameters*
Output: Public key $pk = (Seed_a \parallel \mathbf{b})$, Private Key $sk = (\mathbf{s})$

1: $Seed_a \xleftarrow{\$} \{0,1\}^{256}$
2: $\mathbf{a} \leftarrow \texttt{SHAKE256}(Seed_a, n/8)$
3: $\mathbf{s} \xleftarrow{\$} HWT_n(h_s)$ and $\mathbf{e} \xleftarrow{\$} \psi_{cb}^n$
4: $\mathbf{b} \leftarrow -\mathbf{a} * \mathbf{s} + \mathbf{e}$
5: $pk \leftarrow (Seed_a \parallel \mathbf{b})$ and $sk \leftarrow \mathbf{s}$
6: **return** pk, sk

Algorithm 2. IND-CPA.Encryption

Input: pk, Message $\mathbf{M} \in \{0,1\}^d$
Output: Ciphertext $\mathbf{c} = (\mathbf{c_1} \parallel \mathbf{c_2})$
1: $\mathbf{r} \xleftarrow{\$} HWT_n(h_r)$ and $\mathbf{M'} \leftarrow \text{eccENC}(\mathbf{M})$
2: $Seed_a, \mathbf{b} \leftarrow \text{Parsing}(pk)$
3: $\mathbf{a} \leftarrow \text{SHAKE256}(Seed_a, n/8)$
4: $\mathbf{c_1} \leftarrow \lfloor (p/q) \cdot \mathbf{a} * \mathbf{r} \rceil$ and $\mathbf{c_2} \leftarrow \lfloor (k/q) \cdot ((q/2) \cdot \mathbf{M'} + \mathbf{b} * \mathbf{r}) \rceil$
5: $\mathbf{c} \leftarrow (\mathbf{c_1} \parallel \mathbf{c_2})$
6: **return c**

Algorithm 3. IND-CPA.Decryption

Input: sk, Ciphertext $\mathbf{c} = (\mathbf{c_1} \parallel \mathbf{c_2})$
Output: Message $\hat{\mathbf{M}}$
1: $\mathbf{c_1}, \mathbf{c_2} \leftarrow \text{Parsing}(\mathbf{c})$
2: $\hat{\mathbf{M}}' \leftarrow \lfloor (2/p) \cdot ((p/k) \cdot \mathbf{c_2} + \mathbf{c_1} * \mathbf{s}) \rceil$
3: **return** $\mathbf{M} \leftarrow \text{eccDEC}(\hat{\mathbf{M}}')$

3.2.2 IND-CCA2 KEM

We design IND-CCA KEM using the transformation technique by Jiang et al. [21]. We use a hash function $H : R_2 \rightarrow HWT_n(h)$, and a hash function $G : \{0,1\}^* \rightarrow \{0,1\}^n$ for Jiang's transformation technique.

Algorithm 4. IND-CCA2-KEM.KeyGen

Input: The set of public *parameters*
Output: Public Key $pk = (Seed_a \parallel \mathbf{b})$, Private Key $sk = (sk_{cpa} \parallel \mathbf{u})$
1: $pk, sk_{cpa} := \text{IND-CPA.KeyGen (Algorithm 1)}$
2: $\mathbf{u} \xleftarrow{\$} R_2$
3: **return** $pk, sk \leftarrow (sk_{cpa} \parallel \mathbf{u})$

Algorithm 5. IND-CCA2-KEM.Encapsulation

Input: pk
Output: Ciphertext $\mathbf{c} = (\mathbf{c_1} \parallel \mathbf{c_2})$, Shared Key $\mathbf{K}$
1: $\delta \xleftarrow{\$} \{0,1\}^{sd}$
2: $\mathbf{r} \leftarrow H(\delta)$
3: $\delta' \leftarrow \text{eccENC}(\delta)$
4: $\mathbf{c_1} \leftarrow \lfloor (p/q) \cdot \mathbf{a} * \mathbf{r} \rceil$
5: $\mathbf{c_2} \leftarrow \lfloor (k/q) \cdot ((q/2) \cdot \delta' + \mathbf{b} * \mathbf{r}) \rceil$
6: $\mathbf{c} \leftarrow (\mathbf{c_1} \parallel \mathbf{c_2})$
7: $\mathbf{K} \leftarrow G(\mathbf{c}, \delta')$
8: **return** $\mathbf{c}, \mathbf{K}$

Algorithm 6. IND-CCA2-KEM.Decapsulation

Input: pk, sk, Ciphertext $\mathbf{c}$
Output: Shared Key $\mathbf{K}$

1: $\mathbf{c_1}, \mathbf{c_2} \leftarrow$ Parsing($\mathbf{c}$)
2: $sk_{cpa}, \mathbf{u} \leftarrow$ Parsing(sk)
3: $\hat{\delta}' \leftarrow \lfloor (2/p) \cdot ((p/k) \cdot \mathbf{c_2} + \mathbf{c_1} * sk_{cpa}) \rceil$
4: $\hat{\delta} \leftarrow$ eccDEC($\hat{\delta}'$)
5: $\hat{\mathbf{r}} \leftarrow H(\hat{\delta})$
6: $\hat{\delta}'' \leftarrow$ eccENC($\hat{\delta}$)
7: $\hat{\mathbf{c}} \leftarrow \lfloor (p/q) \cdot \mathbf{a} * \hat{\mathbf{r}} \rceil \parallel \lfloor (k/q) \cdot ((q/2) \cdot \hat{\delta}'' + \mathbf{b} * \hat{\mathbf{r}}) \rceil$
8: **if** $\mathbf{c} \neq \hat{\mathbf{c}}$ **then** $\mathbf{K} \leftarrow G(\mathbf{c}, \mathbf{u})$ **else** $\mathbf{K} \leftarrow G(\mathbf{c}, \hat{\delta}'')$
9: **return** $\mathbf{K}$

3.3 Parameter Selection

We construct a Comfort version that satisfies category1 security level (128-bit) and a Strong version that satisfies category5 security level (256-bit) as required by the NIST standardization process. The assessment of the security level reflected the computational complexity of all known attacks described in Sect. 4.2. Table 1 shows the detailed parameters of each security level and the bandwidth according to each security level is summarized in Table 2.

n is the dimension of the lattice, q is the modulus of RLWE, p is the modulus of RLWR, k is the modulus used for ciphertext compression, h_s is the Hamming weight of the secret key, h_r is the Hamming weight of the ephemeral secret used to encapsulation. d is the length of the message, and sd is the length of δ used in the IND-CCA2 conversion. cb is a variable used for the centered binomial distribution.

Table 1. The detail parameters for each security level

Parameters	n	q	p	k	h_s	h_r	d	sd	cb
Comfort (128-bit)	512	256	64	16	128	128	256	256	1
Strong (256-bit)	1024	256	64	16	128	128	512	512	1

Table 2. Size of pk, sk, and ciphertext of LizarMong in bytes

Security level	Ciphertext	Public key	Secret key
Comfort	640	544	544(210)*
Strong	1280	1056	1088(290)*

*sk_{cpa} can be encoded by storing only non-zero indexes. Thus, optionally, sk can be compressed with $encoding(sk_{cpa})$, a flag of -1, and $\mathbf{u}$ (for IND-CCA2 KEM).

4 Security Analysis

4.1 Security Proofs of IND-CPA and IND-CCA2

We proved the IND-CPA security of the IND-CPA PKE version of LizarMong under the assumption of the IND-CPA security of RLizard.CPA [13].

Theorem 1. *The IND-CPA PKE version of LizarMong is IND-CPA secure under the hardness assumption of RLWE and RLWR problem for a given parameter, and the assumption that SHAKE256 is a random oracle model.*

Proof. Note that in this proof, we call the IND-CPA PKE version of LizarMong as LizarMong. An encryption of m can be generated from an encryption of zero by the homomorphic property of LizarMong. Hence, it is enough to show that the pair of public information pk and the encryption of zero is computationally indistinguishable from the uniform distribution. Let $LizarMong'$ be an algorithm that is the same as LizarMong except for the ciphertext compression.

Algorithm 7. KeyGen'

Input: The set of public parameters
Output: Public key $pk' = (\mathbf{a}, \mathbf{b})$
1: $pk = (Seed_a, \mathbf{b}) \leftarrow LizarMong.KeyGen$
2: $\mathbf{a} \leftarrow \mathsf{SHAKE256}(Seed_a, n)$
3: $pk' \leftarrow (\mathbf{a}, \mathbf{b})$
4: **return** pk'

First, we show that $LizarMong'$ is IND-CPA secure. Define $KeyGen'$ as Algorithm 7. Define distribution D_0, D_1, and D_2 as followings:

$$D_0 = \{(pk', C) : pk' \leftarrow KeyGen'(params),$$
$$C = (c_1, c_2) \leftarrow LizarMong.Enc_pk(0)\}$$
$$D_1 = \{(pk, C) : pk \leftarrow RLizard.KeyGen(params),$$
$$C = (c_1, c_2) \leftarrow RLizard.Enc_pk(ecc(0))\}$$
$$D_2 = \{(pk, C) : pk \leftarrow Ring,$$
$$C = (c_1, c_2) \leftarrow Ring\}$$

Since SHAKE is a random oracle model, distribution of pk' and pk are computationally indistinguishable. $C_{LizarMong'} \leftarrow LizarMong'.Enc_pk(0)$ for $pk = (Seed_a, b)$ and $C_{RLizard} \leftarrow RLizard.Enc_pk'(ecc(0))$ for $pk' = (\mathsf{SHAKE256}(Seed_a, n), b)$ are same by the definition of $RLizard$ and $LizarMong'$ (i.e. $C_{LizarMong} = C_{RLizard}$). Thus, D_0 and D_1 are computationally indistinguishable.

Lemma 1 (See [13]). *RLizard.CPA is IND-CPA secure under the hardness assumption of RLWE and RLWR problem for a given parameter.*

By Lemma 1, D_1 and D_2 are computationally indistinguishable. Therefore, D_0 and D_2 are computationally indistinguishable. In conclusion, $LizarMong'$ IND-CPA secure. Since ciphertext compression does not affect the security of LWE and LWR based public-key cryptography [24], $LizarMong$ is IND-CPA secure.   □

By Theorem 1, IND-CPA PKE version of LizarMong is IND-CPA secure PKE. We make IND-CCA2 KEM version of LizarMong by using Jiang et al. transformation [21]. Thus IND-CCA2 KEM version of LizarMong is IND-CCA2 secure.

4.2 Security Analysis Against Known Attacks

Our security analysis is based on the pessimistic approach of the BKZ lattice basis reduction algorithm [5]. Also, we use the attack complexity calculation and the online LWE estimator by Albrecht et al. [3,4]. Those are common methods used by most RLWE family algorithms. The BKZ algorithm proceeds by reducing a lattice basis using the SVP oracle repeatedly. There are several discussions about measuring the number of iterations. The core SVP method ignores repeated calls for SVP oracle, which is a pessimistic estimation from the defender point of view. We use the quantum sieve as the SVP oracle, which is also a pessimistic approach [5]. The computational complexity of the BKZ lattice basis reduction algorithm is 2^{cn}, where n is a dimension of lattice, and c is a constant value such that $c = 0.292$ in the classical environment and $c = 0.265$ in the quantum environment.

Table 3. Computational complexity of best RLWE and RLWR attacks

Parameters	Claim security	Attacks		Classical	Quantum
Comfort	NIST Category 1 (AES 128-bit)	Primal	RLWE	**133**	**121**
			RLWR	144	131
		Dual	RLWE	165	154
			RLWR	180	170
Strong	NIST Category 5 (AES 256-bit)	Primal	RLWE	**256**	**236**
			RLWR	269	249
		Dual	RLWE	304	275
			RLWR	328	301

We considered the attack on the RLWE family studied in [3] and the specific attack on the sparse ternary secret in [2]. The computational complexity for RLWR attacks is the same as RLWE attacks with the same dimensions, same RLWE modulus q, and error rates $p^{-1}\sqrt{\pi}/6$ [13]. Hence, the computational complexities for RLWR attacks are calculated similarly to the RLWE attacks. The online LWE estimator helped the complexity calculation for these attacks. The Python code for calculating computational complexity can be found at https://github.com/LizarMong.

We concluded that the primal attack [2] that uses the BKZ algorithm is the best. Table 3 shows the computational complexities of the best attacks. In summary, LizarMong.Comfort satisfies NIST's category1 security level (AES128), and Strong satisfies category5 security level (AES256).

In the Comfort parameters, our security is overshoots with the requirements of the security level. It is a security margin that we knowingly made. Attacks against RLWE and RLWR have not been enough studied yet, so the security margin prepares for unknown and vital attacks. In Strong parameters, on the other hand, it has no security margin. Since the 256-bit security level is very high, the NIST standardization process focuses on up to the 192-bit security level. So, the Strong parameter is robust in itself.

4.3   Correctness Analysis

The failure probability calculations of the RLWE family designed so far have been analyzed on the assumption that errors in each bit occur independently. However, D'Anvers et al. proved [16] theoretically and experimentally that the error between each bit does not occur independently. According to D'Anvers et al. [16], even if the probability of error occurrence between each bit is not independent, the calculation based on the independence assumption is valid when the error correction code is not used. However, it is inappropriate when the error correction code is used.

Since LizarMong uses the error correction code, we calculate the probability of failure under the assumption that the error of each bit occurs dependently [16]. Cheon et al. showed that RLizard decryption fails when $|e * r + s * f| \geq \frac{q}{4} - \frac{q}{2p}$ where $f = a * r - (q/p) \cdot c_1$ in [14]. Because of ciphertext compression, LizarMong has more errors than RLizard. That is the difference between $c_2 := \lfloor (k/q) \cdot ((q/2) \cdot M' + b * r) \rceil$ and $\hat{c}_2 := (p/k) \cdot c_2$. Hence, decryption failure of LizarMong occurs when $|e * r + s * f + g| \geq \frac{q}{4} - \frac{q}{2p}$ where $g = c_2 - \hat{c}_2$. We define $S = (s, e)^T$, $C = (f, r)^T$ to calculate the probability of decryption failure. On the assumption that the error of each bit occurs dependently, the probability of decryption failure is calculated according to the Eq. (1). Note that $\Pr[Fail]$ is the probability of decryption failure, $\Pr[F_i]$ is the probability that an error occurs in the ith bit, $Binom(k, n, p) = \sum_{i=0}^{k} \binom{n}{i} p^i (1-p)^{n-i}$, $p_b = \Pr[F_0 \mid \|S\|, \|C\|]$, l_m is the length of encoded message, and d is error correcting capability. Since we use XE5 as an error correction code, $d = 5$.

$$\Pr[Fail] \approx \sum_{\|S\|, \|C\|} (1 - Binom(d, l_m, p_b)) \cdot \Pr[\|S\|] \cdot \Pr[\|C\|] \qquad (1)$$

We can calculate $p_b = \Pr[F_0 \mid \|S\|, \|C\|]$ as Eq. (2) by [15].

$$p_b = \sum_{l} \sum_{g_0} (\Pr[|C^T S + g|_0 > q/4 - q/2p \mid |C^T Ss|_0 = l, g_0] \cdot$$
$$\Pr[|C^T S|_0 = l \mid \|S\|, \|C\|] \cdot \Pr[g_0]) \qquad (2)$$

The above calculation process is implemented in Python and can be found at https://github.com/LizarMong. According to our calculation, the decryption failure probability of LizarMong is 2^{-179} in the Comfort and 2^{-302} in the Strong.

4.4   Side-Channel Attacks

The strategy for making LizarMong resistant to known side-channel attacks is as follows. First, we ruled out the operations targeted by the known attacks at the design element selection stage, Sect. 3.1. Second, for unavoidable vulnerabilities, we added a strategy that internalizes efficient countermeasures.

Table 4. Known side-channel attacks and countermeasures of LizarMong

Attack methods	Attacks	Attack points	Countermeasures
Differential Attacks	[7]	Multiplication	hiding scheme
	[20]		
Template Attacks	[10]		
Fault Attacks	[17]	Error sampling	Loop index check

According to the first strategy, LizarMong resists known cache and timing attacks, as well as some differential and fault attacks. The timing attack of [26] performs the attack by using the time difference depending on whether the modulus is operating or not. This attack does not apply to LizarMong, however, because LizarMong uses all of the moduli to the power of two to replace the modulo operation with ADD and AND operations. Moreover, LizarMong does not use the CDT technique in order to resist the timing attack by Kim et al. [22] and the cache attack of [11], which exploits the CDT technique used by RLizard. The fault attack of [29], which attacks the situation of sampling s and e within the same distribution, does not apply to LizarMong, which is designed to sample s and e within each distribution. Also, the differential attack of [28] targeting NTT does not apply to LizarMong, which does not use NTT. Despite efforts to minimize attack points at the design element selection stage, some differential attacks and fault attacks are still applicable, as shown in Table 4. Therefore, according to the second strategy, we added countermeasures against the remaining attacks in our scheme.

Differential Attacks. [7] and [20] used polynomial multiplication between public and secret keys as the point of attack. Since the polynomial multiplication is necessary for the RLWE family algorithms, it is necessary to design additional countermeasures. Known countermeasures include masking [25,30,31] and hiding schemes [10]. Masking schemes include a general method of construction using random values and a decoder and a unique method of using a homomorphism under the addition of the RLWE family. Hiding schemes include shuffling the order of multiplication operations or adding dummy operations between real

Algorithm 8. Sparse Polynomial Multiplication with Hiding Countermeasure

Input: $\mathbf{a} = \sum_{i=0}^{n-1} a(i) \cdot x^i \in R_q$, $\mathbf{r} = \sum_{i=0}^{n-1} r(i) \cdot x^i \in HWT_n(h)$,
    $d = [i_0, \ldots, i_{g-1}, i_g, \ldots, i_{h-1}]$ with $d[k] = i_k$ such that $r(i_k) = 1$ for $k \in [0, g)$ and
    $r(i_k) = -1$ for $k \in [g, h)$
Output: $\mathbf{v} = \mathbf{a} * \mathbf{r} = \sum_{i=0}^{n-1} v(i) \cdot x^i \in R_q$
 1: initialize $\mathbf{v}$ to zero polynomial $\triangleright$ size of $\mathbf{v} = 2n$
 2: $m \xleftarrow{\$} \{0, 1, \ldots, h-1\}$ $\triangleright$ random starting index
 3: **for** $i \in \{0, \ldots, h-1\}, j \in \{0, \ldots, n-1\}$ **do**
 4:    **if** $m + i \pmod{h} < g$ **then**
 5:       $v(d[m + i \pmod{h}] + j) = v(d[m + i \pmod{h}] + j) + a(j)$
 6:    **else**
 7:       $v(d[m + i \pmod{h}] + j) = v(d[m + i \pmod{h}] + j) - a(j)$
 8: **for** $i \in \{0, \ldots, n-1\}$ **do**
 9:    $v(i) = v(i) - v(n + i)$
10: **return** $\mathbf{v}$

operations. In the RLWE family, masking methods such as masked decoders or additively homomorphic masking are relatively expensive. Thus, we devised the sparse polynomial multiplication with the hiding scheme, like Algorithm 8. It combines the fast sparse polynomial multiplication algorithm of [1] with the hiding scheme of [10]. This method has fewer overheads than shuffling tasks since that it uses only one random value.

Fault Attacks. Known fault attacks targeting the RLWE family exploit the process of generating $\mathbf{s}$ and $\mathbf{e}$. $\mathbf{s}$ and $\mathbf{e}$ are generated by loops after extracting random values. [17] frustrates the loop by injecting a fault and makes $\mathbf{s}$ and $\mathbf{e}$ the initial values of zero. LizarMong is vulnerable to this attack because it generates $\mathbf{s}$ and $\mathbf{e}$ using the above method. Therefore, our scheme resists the fault attack of [17] by applying statistical tests of [19]. The statistical test we use consists of a straightforward operation that compares the expected index with the final index after the loop statement is done, so there is negligible overhead.

5 Evaluation

We evaluate security (computational complexity), correctness (failure probability of decryption), bandwidth (size of ciphertext and public-key), and performance (CPU cycle of encryption, decryption, and key-generation) in comparison with NIST's candidate algorithms and RLizard.

Our comparison is based on the NIST official documents. The result of evaluation is shown in Table 5 and Fig. 1. In Table 5, the three rows for each algorithm correspond to 128, 192, and 256-bit security levels. (i.e., our scheme and NewHope do not support the 192-bit security level.)

Note that the performance evaluation used each optimization code, and the evaluation environment is Intel i7-9700K@3.2 GHz CPU, ubuntu 16.04.11, GCC 5.4.0 with option $-O3$, and the value is the average for 1000 iterations. Also, our implementation codes are available to https://github.com/LizarMong.

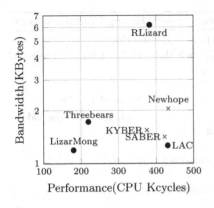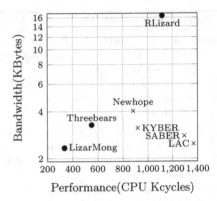

Fig. 1. Comparison of bandwidth and performance based on IND-CCA2 KEM. (left) 128-bit security level (right) 256-bit security level (Note: • are algorithms with security and correctness similar to each security level, and × are not.)

Security. The security of some algorithms seems to be slightly lacking to each security level (see Table 5). However, LizarMong.Comfort reaches 128-bit security level and LizarMong.Strong reaches 256-bit security level. In the Comfort, the security overshoots the requirements of the security level. It is a security margin that we knowingly made from a conservative perspective. Strong has no security margin because the 256-bit security level is regarded as very highly. Unfortunately, our scheme does not support the 192-bit security level, but Strong has a competitive bandwidth and performance compared with the 192-bit security level of other algorithms. Therefore, Strong can sufficiently replace the 192-bit security level of other algorithms.

Correctness. KYBER, SABER, LAC, and Round5 have smaller failure probability of decryption compared to the mapped security level. However, LizarMong has negligible failure probability such as 2^{-179} in Comfort and 2^{-302} in Strong. Also, our estimation is accurate than others because we consider dependency.

Bandwidth. Bandwidth is one of the significant determinants of algorithm practicality in resource-constrained devices and poor communication environments. In general, because the bandwidth of the RLWE family has a larger bandwidth than the current public-key cryptography such as RSA and ECC, the evaluation of bandwidth is a critical evaluation criterion. LizarMong is the best among the key encapsulation mechanisms supporting IND-CCA2. Comfort and Strong are smaller about 5% compared with LAC (which is ranked second in bandwidth).

Performance. LizarMong has the best performance among NIST's candidate algorithms and RLizard. Comfort and Strong faster 1.25 times and 1.65 times than ThreeBears that is ranked second in performance. The crucial point is that the recorded performance of LizarMong includes all countermeasures of the known side-channel attacks in Sect. 4.4.

Table 5. Comparison KEM with NIST candidate algorithms and RLizard

Algorithms	Security (log)	Correctness (log)	Bandwidth (Bytes)	Performance (K cycles)	
				Enc+Dec	KeyGen
LizarMong	133	−179	1184	137.5	42.4
	256	−302	2336	272.7	61.8
RLizard	147	−188	6176	217.8	165.3
	195	−246	8240	416.9	232.7
	318	−306	16448	737.3	382.7
NewHope	112	−213	2048	329.6	103.6
	257	−216	4032	673.5	209.2
KYBER	111	−178	1536	278.2	97.5
	181	−164	2272	463.6	174.3
	254	−174	3136	656.0	263.1
SABER	125	−120	1408	316.9	106.1
	203	−136	2080	587.6	213.6
	283	−165	2784	934.8	359.2
LAC	147	−116	1256	341.2	90.0
	286	−143	2244	840.1	235.6
	320	−122	2480	1101.6	266.6
Round5 (IND-CPA)	128	−88	994	384.4	114.6
	193	−117	1639	857.2	311.3
	256	−64	2035	1794.9	643.4
Threebears	154	−156	1721	167.8	52.1
	235	−206	2501	271.4	91.9
	314	−256	3281	402.5	148.2

6   Conclusion

Our scheme, called LizarMong, is the best of the RLWE family of key encapsulation algorithms to date. Our scheme achieves security levels 1 (128-bit) and
5 (256-bit), and compared with NIST's candidate algorithms, the bandwidth is
about 5–42% smaller, and the performance is about 1.2–4.1 times faster. Also,
it resists known side-channel attacks.

   We need to recall the goal of the NIST post-quantum cryptography standardization process. The purpose of this process is to design cryptography that
is compatible with current networks and protocols. Thus, there is a need for
algorithms that are excellent in all respects, such as RSA and ECC. The RLWE
family algorithms submitted to the NIST post-quantum cryptography standardization process have each merit in terms of security, correctness, performance,
and bandwidth. Thus, choosing one optimal algorithm satisfying all aspects is
challenging. Besides, various recent studies have been published that affect security and correctness, such as side-channel attacks and error dependencies. These
studies are meaningful because it affects most RLWE family algorithms. To date,
however, many algorithms do not include most of those studies.

   We consider to break down the barriers between candidate algorithms, merg-
ing unique strengths, and quickly reflecting the state-of-the-art studies, for excellent algorithm in all respects. LizarMong, based on the RLizard that was submitted to NIST 1round, muses each of the merit of NIST's candidate algorithms.

Specifically, we have inspired by a small modulus of LAC, the error correction code of Round5, and the centered binomial distribution of NewHope. We also included recent studies such as side-channel attacks and error dependencies.

In conclusion, our scheme is an excellent key encapsulation mechanism that combines each merit of NISTs candidate algorithms with state-of-the-art studies.

Acknowledgements. We would like to thank anonymous reviews of ICISC 2019 and Jung Hee Cheon for their helpful comments and suggestions. This work was supported as part of the Military Crypto Research Center (UD170109ED) funded by Defense the Acquisition Program Administration (DAPA) and the Agency for Defense Development (ADD).

References

1. Akleylek, S., Alkım, E., Tok, Z.Y.: Sparse polynomial multiplication for lattice-based cryptography with small complexity. J. Supercomput. **72**(2), 438–450 (2016)
2. Albrecht, M.R., Göpfert, F., Virdia, F., Wunderer, T.: Revisiting the expected cost of solving uSVP and applications to LWE. In: Takagi, T., Peyrin, T. (eds.) ASIACRYPT 2017. LNCS, vol. 10624, pp. 297–322. Springer, Cham (2017). https://doi.org/10.1007/978-3-319-70694-8_11
3. Albrecht, M.R., Player, R., Scott, S.: On the concrete hardness of learning with errors. J. Math. Cryptol. **9**(3), 169–203 (2015)
4. Albrecht, M.: A sage module for estimating the concrete security of learning with errors instances (2017)
5. Alkim, E., Ducas, L., Pöppelmann, T., Schwabe, P.: Post-quantum key exchange-a new hope. In: 25th {USENIX} Security Symposium ({USENIX} Security 16), pp. 327–343 (2016)
6. Applebaum, B., Cash, D., Peikert, C., Sahai, A.: Fast cryptographic primitives and circular-secure encryption based on hard learning problems. In: Halevi, S. (ed.) CRYPTO 2009. LNCS, vol. 5677, pp. 595–618. Springer, Heidelberg (2009). https://doi.org/10.1007/978-3-642-03356-8_35
7. Aysu, A., Tobah, Y., Tiwari, M., Gerstlauer, A., Orshansky, M.: Horizontal side-channel vulnerabilities of post-quantum key exchange protocols. In: 2018 IEEE International Symposium on Hardware Oriented Security and Trust (HOST), pp. 81–88. IEEE (2018)
8. Baan, H., et al.: Round5: Compact and fast post-quantum public-key encryption. IACR Cryptology ePrint Arch. 2019/90 (2019)
9. Bos, J., et al.: CRYSTALS-Kyber: a CCA-secure module-lattice-based KEM. In: 2018 IEEE European Symposium on Security and Privacy (EuroS&P), pp. 353–367. IEEE (2018)
10. Bos, J.W., Friedberger, S., Martinoli, M., Oswald, E., Stam, M.: Assessing the feasibility of single trace power analysis of Frodo. In: Cid, C., Jacobson, M. (eds.) SAC 2019. LNCS, vol. 11349, pp. 216–234. Springer, Cham (2019). https://doi.org/10.1007/978-3-030-10970-7_10
11. Groot Bruinderink, L., Hülsing, A., Lange, T., Yarom, Y.: Flush, gauss, and reload – a cache attack on the bliss lattice-based signature scheme. In: Gierlichs, B., Poschmann, A.Y. (eds.) CHES 2016. LNCS, vol. 9813, pp. 323–345. Springer, Heidelberg (2016). https://doi.org/10.1007/978-3-662-53140-2_16

12. Chen, L., et al.: Report on post-quantum cryptography. US Department of Commerce, National Institute of Standards and Technology (2016)
13. Cheon, J.H., Kim, D., Lee, J., Song, Y.: Lizard: cut off the tail! Practical post-quantum public-key encryption from LWE and LWR. Cryptology ePrint Archive, Report 2016/1126 (2016). https://eprint.iacr.org/2016/1126
14. Cheon, J.H., Kim, D., Lee, J., Song, Y.: Lizard public key encryption. Technical report, National Institute of Standards and Technology, 2017 (2018)
15. D'Anvers, J.P., Vercauteren, F., Verbauwhede, I.: On the impact of decryption failures on the security of LWE/LWR based schemes. Cryptology ePrint Archive, Report 2018/1089 (2018). https://eprint.iacr.org/2018/1089
16. D'Anvers, J.-P., Vercauteren, F., Verbauwhede, I.: The impact of error dependencies on Ring/Mod-LWE/LWR based schemes. In: Ding, J., Steinwandt, R. (eds.) PQCrypto 2019. LNCS, vol. 11505, pp. 103–115. Springer, Cham (2019). https://doi.org/10.1007/978-3-030-25510-7_6
17. Espitau, T., Fouque, P.A., Gerard, B., Tibouchi, M.: Loop-abort faults on lattice-based signature schemes and key exchange protocols. IEEE Trans. Comput. 67(11), 1535–1549 (2018)
18. Hofheinz, D., Hövelmanns, K., Kiltz, E.: A modular analysis of the Fujisaki-Okamoto transformation. In: Kalai, Y., Reyzin, L. (eds.) TCC 2017. LNCS, vol. 10677, pp. 341–371. Springer, Cham (2017). https://doi.org/10.1007/978-3-319-70500-2_12
19. Howe, J., Khalid, A., Martinoli, M., Regazzoni, F., Oswald, E.: Fault attack countermeasures for error samplers in lattice-based cryptography. In: 2019 IEEE International Symposium on Circuits and Systems (ISCAS), pp. 1–5. IEEE (2019)
20. Huang, W.L., Chen, J.P., Yang, B.Y.: Correlation power analysis on NTRU prime and related countermeasures. IACR Cryptology ePrint Archive 2019/100 (2019)
21. Jiang, H., Zhang, Z., Chen, L., Wang, H., Ma, Z.: IND-CCA-secure key encapsulation mechanism in the quantum random oracle model, revisited. In: Shacham, H., Boldyreva, A. (eds.) CRYPTO 2018. LNCS, vol. 10993, pp. 96–125. Springer, Cham (2018). https://doi.org/10.1007/978-3-319-96878-0_4
22. Kim, S., Hong, S.: Single trace analysis on constant time CDT sampler and its countermeasure. Appl. Sci. 8(10), 1809 (2018)
23. Lee, J., Kim, D., Lee, H., Lee, Y., Cheon, J.H.: RLizard: post-quantum key encapsulation mechanism for IoT devices. IEEE Access 7, 2080–2091 (2018)
24. Lu, X., et al.: LAC: practical ring-LWE based public-key encryption with byte-level modulus. IACR Cryptology ePrint Archive 2018/1009 (2018)
25. Oder, T., Schneider, T., Pöppelmann, T., Güneysu, T.: Practical CCA2-secure and masked ring-LWE implementation. IACR Trans. Crypt. Hardware Embed. Syst. 142–174 (2018)
26. Park, A., Han, D.G.: Chosen ciphertext simple power analysis on software 8-bit implementation of ring-LWE encryption. In: 2016 IEEE Asian Hardware-Oriented Security and Trust (AsianHOST), pp. 1–6. IEEE (2016)
27. Peikert, C., Regev, O., Stephens-Davidowitz, N.: Pseudorandomness of ring-LWE for any ring and modulus. In: Proceedings of the 49th Annual ACM SIGACT Symposium on Theory of Computing, pp. 461–473. ACM (2017)
28. Primas, R., Pessl, P., Mangard, S.: Single-trace side-channel attacks on masked lattice-based encryption. In: Fischer, W., Homma, N. (eds.) CHES 2017. LNCS, vol. 10529, pp. 513–533. Springer, Cham (2017). https://doi.org/10.1007/978-3-319-66787-4_25

29. Ravi, P., Roy, D.B., Bhasin, S., Chattopadhyay, A., Mukhopadhyay, D.: Number "not used" once - practical fault attack on *pqm4* implementations of NIST candidates. In: Polian, I., Stöttinger, M. (eds.) COSADE 2019. LNCS, vol. 11421, pp. 232–250. Springer, Cham (2019). https://doi.org/10.1007/978-3-030-16350-1_13

30. Reparaz, O., de Clercq, R., Roy, S.S., Vercauteren, F., Verbauwhede, I.: Additively homomorphic ring-LWE masking. In: Takagi, T. (ed.) PQCrypto 2016. LNCS, vol. 9606, pp. 233–244. Springer, Cham (2016). https://doi.org/10.1007/978-3-319-29360-8_15

31. Reparaz, O., Sinha Roy, S., Vercauteren, F., Verbauwhede, I.: A masked ring-LWE implementation. In: Güneysu, T., Handschuh, H. (eds.) CHES 2015. LNCS, vol. 9293, pp. 683–702. Springer, Heidelberg (2015). https://doi.org/10.1007/978-3-662-48324-4_34

32. Saarinen, M.J.O.: HILA5: on reliability, reconciliation, and error correction for ring-LWE encryption. Cryptology ePrint Archive, Report 2017/424 (2017). https://eprint.iacr.org/2017/424

Efficient Identity-Based Encryption from LWR

Jung Hee Cheon[1], Haejin Cho[2], Jaewook Jung[2], Joohee Lee[1(✉)], and Keewoo Lee[1]

[1] Seoul National University, Seoul, Republic of Korea
{jhcheon,skfro6360,activecondor}@snu.ac.kr
[2] LG Electronics Seocho R&D Campus, Seoul, Republic of Korea
{haejin.cho,jaewook.jung}@lge.com

Abstract. The Learning with Rounding (LWR) problem is a deterministic variant of the classical Learning with Errors (LWE) problem, for which sampling an instance does not involve discrete Gaussian sampling. We propose the first probabilistic Identity-Based Encryption (IBE) from the LWR problem which is secure in the standard model. The encryption of our IBE scheme does not require discrete Gaussian sampling as it is based on the LWR problem, and hence it is simpler and faster than that of LWE-based IBEs such as ABB scheme. We also present an efficient instantiation employing algebraic ring structure and MP12 trapdoor sampling algorithms with an implementation result. With our proposed parameter sets, the ciphertext sizes can be reduced in a large extent compared to the ABB scheme with the same security level.

Keywords: Lattice · Identity-Based Encryption · Learning with Rounding

1 Introduction

Identity-Based Encryption. In 1985, Shamir [Sha85] first introduced the concept of Identity-Based Encryption (IBE). The underlying idea is to use an arbitrary string, e.g., e-mail address, as a public key for an encryption scheme, for easier certification of users. Since Boneh and Franklin [BF01] proposed a first practical IBE scheme using groups with bilinear pairings, various attempts have been made to construct an efficient IBE scheme. Gentry et al. [GPV08] marked the beginning of lattice-based, thus possibly quantum secure IBE scheme. The security of their scheme is proved in the random oracle model, and is based on the hardness of the Small Integer Solution (SIS) problem and Learning with Errors (LWE) problem. Agrawal et al. [ABB10], say ABB scheme, constructed an IBE from SIS and LWE in the standard model of which performance is comparable to the previous one secure in the random oracle model. Until recently,

This work was supported by the LG Electronics (LGE) grant.

J. H. Seo (Ed.): ICISC 2019, LNCS 11975, pp. 225–241, 2020.
https://doi.org/10.1007/978-3-030-40921-0_14

the ABB scheme is the state-of-the-art of the IBE structure based on the lattice problems. Recently, some works suggested ring-based efficient instantiations for the ABB scheme [AFL16, BFRLS18].

Learning with Rounding. Learning with Rounding (LWR) [BPR12] is a modified version of Learning with Errors (LWE) [Reg05] with *deterministic* errors. It is a definite advantage of LWR and RLWR (ring-LWR) that selecting random errors in a certain distribution (e.g. discrete Gaussian distribution) is unnecessary. [BPR12] showed the reduction from LWE and RLWE to LWR and RLWR, so that LWR is at least as hard as LWE where q/p is superpolynomial. In 2016, Bogdanov et al. [BGM+16] proved that LWR with small modulus but bounded number of samples is still hard under the LWE assumption. Due to its efficiency and deterministic flavor, the LWR problem has been exploited in some of the lattice-based cryptosystems: Psuedorandom functions [BPR12]; deterministic encryption, lossy trapdoor function, and reusable extractor [AKPW13]; key encapsulation mechanism and public key encryption [CKLS18, LKL+18, BBF+19]; *deterministic* hierarchical IBE [FLL+16]; somewhat homomorphic encryption [CS17].

Our Contribution. We propose the first IBE scheme based on SIS and LWR. The main difference with existing IBE schemes based on SIS and LWE is that we replace Gaussian errors with rounding errors in the encryption algorithm. In particular, our encryption algorithm does not require discrete Gaussian sampling step, which leads to a simpler and faster encryption algorithm. Moreover, the modulus of the ciphertext space of our scheme is the rounding modulus prime p instead of the large modulus prime q as other LWE based IBE schemes. In this sense, our scheme enjoys small ciphertext sizes. For example, compared to an LWE based IBE scheme of a recent paper [BFRLS18], our IBE scheme reduces ciphertext size about 73% (*resp.* 72%) for 190-bit (*resp.* 80-bit) security.

We also present an efficient instantiation with a proof-of-concept implementation result of the ring variant of our scheme with efficient trapdoor sampling algorithms [MP12] and working parameters for moderate security.

Organization. The rest of the paper is organized as follows. In Sect. 2, we summarize some notations used in this paper, and introduce lattice related concepts and cryptographic primitives including IBE, LWR, and lattice trapdoor. We describe our LWR based IBE scheme with correctness and security proofs in Sect. 3. We also provide its efficient ring variant and extensions to adaptive security version and HIBE. In Sect. 4, we suggest an efficient instantiation of our scheme with efficient trapdoor proposed in [MP12] and working parameters. We also present a proof-of-concept implementation results.

2   Preliminaries

2.1   Notation

All logarithms are base 2 unless otherwise indicated. For a positive integer q, we use $\mathbb{Z} \cap (-q/2, q/2]$ as a representative of $\mathbb{Z}_q$. For a real number r, $\lfloor r \rceil$ denotes the nearest integer to r, rounding upwards in case of a tie. Also, $\lfloor r \rfloor$, and $\lceil r \rceil$ are rounding down and up to the nearest integers, respectively. We denote vectors in bold, $e.g.$ $\mathbf{a}$, and every vector in this paper is a column vector. The norm $\|\cdot\|$ is always 2-norm in this paper. We denote by $\langle \cdot, \cdot \rangle$ the usual dot product of two vectors. We use $x \leftarrow D$ to denote the sampling x according to the distribution D. It denotes the uniform sampling when D is a finite set. For an integer $n \geq 1$, D^n denotes the product of i.i.d. random variables $D_i \sim D$. We let λ denote the security parameter throughout the paper: all known valid attacks against the cryptographic scheme under scope should take $\Omega(2^\lambda)$ bit operations. A function $\mathsf{negl} : \mathbb{N} \rightarrow \mathbb{R}^+$ is negligible if for every positive polynomial $p(\lambda)$ there exists $\lambda_0 \in \mathbb{N}$ such that $\mathsf{negl}(\lambda) < 1/p(\lambda)$ for all $\lambda > \lambda_0$. For two matrices A and B with the same number of rows, $(A\|B)$ denotes their row concatenation, $i.e.$, for $A \in \mathbb{Z}^{m \times n_1}$ and $B \in \mathbb{Z}^{m \times n_2}$, the $m \times (n_1 + n_2)$ matrix $C = (A \| B)$ is defined as $c_{ij} = \begin{cases} a_{i,j} & 1 \leq j \leq n_1 \\ b_{i,(j-n_1)} & n_1 < j \leq n_1 + n_2 \end{cases}$. The Gadget matrix G which will be used in the construction of functional encryptions is defined by $G = (1, 2, 4, \cdots, 2^{\lfloor \log q \rfloor - 1})^t \otimes I_n \in \mathbb{Z}_q^{n \times n\ell}$. For an ordered set $A = \{\mathbf{a}_1, \mathbf{a}_2, \cdots \mathbf{a}_m\} \in \mathbb{R}^n$, $Gram\text{-}Schmidt$ $norm$ of A is defined by $\|\tilde{A}\| = \max_{1 \leq i \leq m} \|\tilde{\mathbf{a}}_i\|$, where $\tilde{A} = \{\tilde{\mathbf{a}}_1, \tilde{\mathbf{a}}_2, \cdots \tilde{\mathbf{a}}_m\}$ is the $Gram\text{-}Schmidt$ $orthogonalization$ of A. We denote $\mathcal{R}$ the cyclotomic polynomial ring $\mathcal{R} = \mathbb{Z}[x]/(x^n + 1)$ for n with a power of 2; for any integer modulus q, define the quotient ring $\mathcal{R}_q = \mathcal{R}/q\mathcal{R}$.

2.2 Lattice

Let $B = \{\mathbf{b}_1, \mathbf{b}_2, \cdots \mathbf{b}_m\}$ be a subset of $\mathbb{R}^n$ with m linearly independent vectors. The m dimensional $lattice$ generated by the $basis$ B is the set,

$$\Lambda = \mathcal{L}(B) = \{\mathbf{y} \in \mathbb{R}^n : \exists \mathbf{x} = (x_1, \cdots, x_m) \in \mathbb{Z}^m \text{ s.t. } \mathbf{y} = B\mathbf{x} = \sum_{i=1}^{m} x_i \mathbf{b}_i\}$$

The $determinant$ of $\Lambda = \mathcal{L}(B)$ is defined as $det(\Lambda) = \sqrt{det(B^T B)}$. Throughout this paper, we consider certain families of integer lattices in [Ajt96]:

Definition 1 ([Ajt96]). *Let q be a prime, $A = \{\mathbf{a}_1, \mathbf{a}_2, \cdots \mathbf{a}_m\} \in \mathbb{Z}^{n \times m}$, and $\mathbf{u} \in \mathbb{Z}_q^n$.*

- $\Lambda_q(A) := \{\mathbf{y} \in \mathbb{Z}^m : \exists \mathbf{x} \in \mathbb{Z}_q^n \text{ s.t. } A^T \mathbf{x} = \mathbf{y}\} \subseteq \mathbb{Z}^m$
- $\Lambda_q^\perp(A) := \{\mathbf{y} \in \mathbb{Z}^m : A\mathbf{y} = \sum_{i=1}^{m} y_i \mathbf{a}_i = \mathbf{0} \in \mathbb{Z}_q^n\} \subseteq \mathbb{Z}^m$
- $\Lambda_q^{\mathbf{u}}(A) := \{\mathbf{y} \in \mathbb{Z}^m : A\mathbf{y} = \sum_{i=1}^{m} y_i \mathbf{a}_i = \mathbf{u}\} \subseteq \mathbb{Z}^m$

Given a basis of m dimensional lattice Λ, a $lattice$ $reduction$ $algorithm$ outputs a short and nearly orthogonal basis. We define the $root$ $Hermite$ $factor$ δ of the lattice reduction algorithm as $\|b_1\|/det(\Lambda)^{1/m}$, where b_1 is the shortest vector in the output basis. In the aspect of cryptanalysis, the root Hermite factor is usually regarded as the dominant parameter for the runtime of the lattice basis reduction algorithms and quality of the reduced bases.

2.3   Discrete Gaussian Distribution

For $\mathbf{c} \in \mathbb{R}^m$ and $\sigma > 0$, the Gaussian distribution on $\mathbb{R}^m$ is defined as $\rho_{\sigma,\mathbf{c}}(\mathbf{x}) = \exp\left(-\pi \dfrac{\|\mathbf{x} - \mathbf{c}\|^2}{\sigma^2}\right)$.

Definition 2. *For a countable set $S \subset \mathbb{Z}^m$, define $\rho_{\sigma,\mathbf{c}}(S) = \sum_{\mathbf{x} \in S} \rho_{\sigma,\mathbf{c}}(\mathbf{x})$. Then, the discrete Gaussian distribution over S is defined as follows:*

$$\forall \mathbf{x} \in S, \mathcal{D}_{S,\sigma,\mathbf{c}}(\mathbf{x}) = \frac{\rho_{\sigma,\mathbf{c}}(\mathbf{x})}{\rho_{\sigma,\mathbf{c}}(S)}$$

When $\mathbf{c} = \mathbf{0}$, we may use the notation ρ_σ and $\mathcal{D}_{S,\sigma}$. Also, we may write $\mathcal{D}_\sigma$ for a discrete Gaussian distribution over $\mathbb{Z}$.

2.4   Lattice Trapdoor

We review the algorithms related to lattice trapdoors in [GPV08, ABB10, MP12].

TrapGen. TrapGen(q, n) is an algorithm that outputs a full-rank pseudorandom matrix $A \in \mathbb{Z}_q^{n \times m}$ and short orthogonal basis (trapdoor) $T_A \in \mathbb{Z}^{m \times m}$ for $\Lambda_q^\perp(A)$, where $m = \Theta(n \log q)$. The output A is $\mathsf{negl}(n)$ close to uniform and the Gram-Schmidt norm $\left\|\tilde{T}_A\right\| = O(\sqrt{n \log q})$ with all but $\mathsf{negl}(\lambda)$ probability.

[Ajt99] proposed how to generate a lattice with a short basis, and [AP11] and [MP12] refine the algorithm. [MP12] proposed two types of TrapGen. The first type outputs statistically near-uniform A. The second type outputs *computationally* pseudorandom A with $m = 2n$, based on LWE assumption.

[ABB10] suggested LWE-based IBE, using the TrapGen algorithm in [AP11]. As [MP12] suggested a more efficient algorithm than that in [AP11], and briefly explained the concept of its extension to ring setting, [EBB13] presented an implementation of [MP12] in both matrix and ring version. [GPR+18] implemented the result of [MP12] and [EBB13] in PALISADE library. [BFRLS18] also made a ring version implementation of [ABB10] and [MP12].

SampleLeft. SampleLeft$(A, B, T_A, \mathbf{u}, \sigma)$ is an algorithm that takes input $A \in \mathbb{Z}_q^{n \times m}$, $B \in \mathbb{Z}_q^{n \times m_1}$, trapdoor T_A of $\Lambda_q^\perp(A)$, a vector $\mathbf{u} \in \mathbb{Z}_q^n$, and a Gaussian parameter $\sigma > \left\|\tilde{T}_A\right\| \cdot \omega(\sqrt{\log n})$, then outputs a "short" vector $\mathbf{e}$ from a distribution statistically close to $\mathcal{D}_{\Lambda_q^{\mathbf{u}}(F),\sigma}$ where $F = [A|B]$.

SampleLeft requires another algorithm called SamplePre as its building block, and [MP12] described SamplePre algorithm in $\mathbb{Z}_q$. [ABB10] constructed SampleLeft algorithm in $\mathbb{Z}_q$, and [BFRLS18] and [GPR+18] clearly expressed ring version of SampleLeft. In particular, [GPR+18] use the result of [GM18] which improved [MP12].

SampleRight. SampleRight$(A, H, R, \mathbf{u}, \sigma)$ is an algorithm that inputs matrices $A \in \mathbb{Z}_q^{n \times m}$ and $H \in \mathbb{Z}_q^{n \times n}$, a uniform random matrix $R \in \{0, 1\}^{m \times m}$, a vector $\mathbf{u} \in \mathbb{Z}_q^n$, and a parameter σ, outputs a vector $\mathbf{e} \in \mathbb{Z}_q^{2m}$ sampled from a distribution statistically close to $\mathcal{D}_{\Lambda_q^{\mathbf{u}}(F),\sigma}$, where $F = [A|AR + HG] \in \mathbb{Z}_q^{n \times 2m}$. We recommend to see [ABB10, MP12] for details.

2.5   LWE, LWR, and RLWR

The learning with errors (LWE) problem was first introduced by Regev [Reg05], and its ring variant version, ring-LWE (RLWE), was introduced in [LPR10]. For positive integers n and q and a distribution χ over $\mathbb{Z}_q$, the (decision) $\mathsf{LWE}_{n,q,\chi}(\mathbf{s})$ problem for $\mathbf{s} \leftarrow \mathbb{Z}_q^n$ aims to distinguish the distribution of $(\mathbf{a}, \langle \mathbf{a}, \mathbf{s}\rangle + e) \in \mathbb{Z}_q^n \times \mathbb{Z}_q$ where $\mathbf{a} \leftarrow \mathbb{Z}_q^n$ are uniformly chosen and e is sampled from a certain error distribution χ (e.g., discrete Gaussian distribution) from the uniform distribution over $\mathbb{Z}_q^n \times \mathbb{Z}_q$. It was proved that for certain choice of parameter, a solution for LWE implies a *quantum* solution to worst-case lattice problems in [Reg09].

More recently, a "derandomized" variant of LWE is proposed [BPR12] to construct a lattice-based pseudorandom function, called *learning with rounding* (LWR). They use a rounding function $\lfloor \cdot \rceil_p : \mathbb{Z}_q \to \mathbb{Z}_p$ that is defined by $\lfloor x \rceil_p = \lfloor (p/q) \cdot x \rceil \in \mathbb{Z}_p$ to generate deterministic errors in the LWR instance. The LWR and its ring variant ring-LWR (RLWR) problems are defined as follows:

Definition 3. *(Decision version, Definition 3.1 in [BPR12]). Let $n \geq 1$ be the main security parameter and moduli $q \geq p \geq 2$ be integers.*

- *For a vector $\mathbf{s} \in \mathbb{Z}_q^n$, define the LWR distribution L_s to be the distribution over $\mathbb{Z}_q^n \times \mathbb{Z}_p$ obtained by choosing a vector $\mathbf{a} \leftarrow \mathbb{Z}_q^n$ uniformly at random, and outputting $(\mathbf{a}, b = \lfloor \langle \mathbf{a}, \mathbf{s}\rangle \rceil_p)$.*
- *For $s \in \mathcal{R}_q$, define the RLWR distribution L_s to be the distribution over $\mathcal{R}_q \times \mathcal{R}_p$ obtained by choosing $a \leftarrow \mathcal{R}_q$ uniformly at random and outputting $(a, b = \lfloor a \cdot s \rceil_p)$.*
- *For a given distribution over $\mathbf{s} \in \mathbb{Z}_q^n$, the LWR problem is to distinguish (with advantage non-negligible in n) between any desired number of independent samples $(\mathbf{a}_i, b_i) \leftarrow L_s$, and the same number of samples drawn uniformly and independently from $\mathbb{Z}_q^n \times \mathbb{Z}_p$. The RLWR problem is defined analogously. These two problems with previously explained parameter are denoted by $\mathsf{LWR}_{n,q,p}$ and $\mathsf{RLWR}_{n,q,p}$.*

We defer the explanation for cryptanalytic hardness of the LWR problem to Appendix A.

2.6   Identity-Based Encryption

Identity-Based Encryption (IBE) was firstly introduced by Shamir [Sha85] and constructed in [BF01], which allows to manage certificates in traditional public-key encryption in a simple and intuitive way. Recall that IBE consists of four algorithms: $\Pi = \{\text{SETUP}, \text{EXTRACT}, \text{ENCRYPT}, \text{DECRYPT}\}$.

- SETUP$(\lambda) \to (\mathsf{PP}, \mathsf{MK})$: receives a security parameter λ as input. It outputs public parameters PP and master secret key MK.
- EXTRACT$(\mathsf{PP}, \mathsf{MK}, \mathsf{id}) \to \mathsf{SK}_{\mathsf{id}}$: receives PP, MK, and an identity id. It outputs a secret key $\mathsf{SK}_{\mathsf{id}}$ corresponding to id.
- ENCRYPT$(\mathsf{PP}, \mathsf{id}, \mu) \to \mathsf{CT}$: receives PP, id and a message μ. It outputs the ciphetext CT, the encryption of μ.

- DECRYPT(PP, SK$_{id}$, CT) → μ: receives PP, SK$_{id}$, CT and outputs the message μ.

Correctness. An IBE scheme Π is correct if DECRYPT(PP, SK$_{id}$, CT) $= \mu$ where SETUP(λ) → (PP, MK), EXTRACT(PP, MK, id) → SK$_{id}$, and CT $=$ ENCRYPT(PP, id, μ) with an overwhelming probability in the security parameter λ.

Security. We define the selective security of IBE by the following game.

- Init: The adversary $\mathcal{A}$ outputs a target identity id*.
- Setup: The challenger $\mathcal{C}$ runs Setup(1^λ) → (PP, MK) and sends the public parameters PP to $\mathcal{A}$. $\mathcal{C}$ keeps the master secret key MK.
- Phase 1: $\mathcal{A}$ sends queries id$_1, \cdots,$ id$_{Q_1}$ where id$_i$ is not id* for $i = 1, \cdots, Q_1$. $\mathcal{C}$ runs Extract(MK, id$_i$) → sk_i and sends sk_i back to $\mathcal{A}$.
- Challenge: $\mathcal{A}$ outputs a plaintext challenge $\mu \in \mathcal{M}$. $\mathcal{C}$ choose $b \leftarrow \{0,1\}$, and a random ciphertext $c \in \mathcal{CT}$. If $b = 0$, $\mathcal{C}$ sets the challenge ciphertext as $c^* \leftarrow$ Encrypt(PP, id*, μ). Otherwise, it sets the challenge ciphertext to $c^* \leftarrow c$. It sends c^* to $\mathcal{A}$.
- Phase 2: $\mathcal{A}$ issues queries id$_{Q_1+1}, \cdots,$ id$_{Q_2}$, where id$_i \neq$ id*. $\mathcal{C}$ does the same as in the Phase 1.
- Guess: $\mathcal{A}$ outputs a bit $b' \in \{0,1\}$.

We refer to an adversary $\mathcal{A}$ defined above as an INDr–sID-CPA adversary.

Definition 4. *An IBE system Π is INDr-sID-CPA secure if, for all INDr-sID-CPA PPT adversaries $\mathcal{A}$,*

$$\mathsf{Adv}_{\mathcal{A}}^{\mathsf{IBE}} = |Pr[b = b'] - 1/2| < \mathsf{negl}(\lambda),$$

where the probability is over the random bits used by $\mathcal{A}$ and the challenger.

3   Our Identity-Based Encryption Scheme

In this section, we present our IBE scheme from LWR which has a similar structure with the LWE-based IBE in [ABB10] equipped with the trapdoor in [MP12]. To encode identities which are binary strings, we use a hash function satisfying certain conditions defined in [ABB10] which is referred as an FRD hash function in this section. The definition of FRD hash function is the following:

Definition 5. *(Encoding with Full-Rank Differences (FRD) [ABB10]). Let q and n be positive integers. A hash function $H : \mathbb{Z}^n \to \mathbb{Z}_q^{n \times n}$ is an encoding with full-rank differences (FRD) if*

1. *for all distinct x and y, $H(x) - H(y)$ in $\mathbb{Z}_q^{n \times n}$ is of full rank, and*
2. *H is efficiently computable, i.e., H is computable in polynomial time in $(n \log q)$.*

3.1   Construction

- IBE.Setup(λ): On input a security parameter λ, set the parameters q, p, n, m, s as specified in Sect. 4.1. Next do:
  - Use TrapGen(q, n) to generate a uniformly random $n \times m$-matrix $A \in \mathbb{Z}_q^{n \times m}$ with a basis T_A for $\Lambda_q^{\perp}(A)$ of which entries are independently sampled from a discrete Gaussian distribution $\mathcal{D}_\sigma$.
  - Generate a uniformly random $n \times m$ matrix $B \in \mathbb{Z}_q^{n \times m}$.
  - Select a uniformly random n-vector $\mathbf{u} \in \mathbb{Z}_q^n$.
  - Output the public parameters and master secret key,

$$\mathsf{PP} = (A, B, \mathbf{u}), \qquad \mathsf{MK} = (T_A)$$

- IBE.Extract($\mathsf{PP}, \mathsf{MK}, \mathsf{id}$): On input public parameters PP, a master secret key MK, and an identity id, do:
  - Sample $\mathbf{e} \in \mathbb{Z}^{2m}$ as $\mathbf{e} \leftarrow \mathsf{SampleLeft}(A, B + H(\mathsf{id})G, T_A, \mathbf{u}, s)$ where H is an FRD hash function in Definition 5.
  - Output $\mathsf{SK}_{\mathsf{id}} := \mathbf{e}$.
- IBE.Encrypt($\mathsf{PP}, \mathsf{id}, b$): On input public parameter PP, an identity id, and a message $b \in \{0, 1\}$, do:
  - Sample a uniform random vector $\mathbf{s} \leftarrow \mathbb{Z}_q^n$.
  - $c_{out} \leftarrow \left\lfloor \frac{p}{q} \cdot \mathbf{u}^T \cdot \mathbf{s} \right\rceil + b \cdot \left\lfloor \frac{p}{2} \right\rfloor$.
  - $\mathbf{c}_{in} \leftarrow \left\lfloor \frac{p}{q}(A^T \cdot \mathbf{s}) \right\rceil \in \mathbb{Z}_p^m$, and let $\mathbf{f}_A := A^T \cdot \mathbf{s} - \frac{q}{p}\left\lfloor \frac{p}{q}(A^T \cdot \mathbf{s}) \right\rceil$.
  - $R \leftarrow \{-1, 1\}^{m \times m}$, and let $\mathbf{f}_B \leftarrow R^T \cdot \mathbf{f}_A$.
  - $\mathbf{c}_{\mathsf{id}} \leftarrow \left\lfloor \frac{p}{q} \cdot \left((B + H(\mathsf{id})G)^T \cdot \mathbf{s} - \mathbf{f}_B\right) \right\rceil$.
  - Output the ciphertext $\mathsf{CT} := (\mathbf{c}_{in}, \mathbf{c}_{\mathsf{id}}, c_{out}) \in \mathbb{Z}_p^m \times \mathbb{Z}_p^m \times \mathbb{Z}_p$.
- IBE.Decrypt($\mathsf{PP}, \mathsf{SK}_{\mathsf{id}}, \mathsf{CT}$): On input public parameters PP, a private key $\mathsf{SK}_{\mathsf{id}} := \mathbf{e} \in \mathbb{Z}^{2m}$, and a ciphertext $\mathsf{CT} := (\mathbf{c}_{in}, \mathbf{c}_{\mathsf{id}}, c_{out})$, do:
  - Compute $w \leftarrow c_{out} - \mathbf{e}^T \cdot (\mathbf{c}_{in}^T | \mathbf{c}_{\mathsf{id}}^T)^T$.
  - Compare w and $\lfloor p/2 \rfloor$ treating them as integers in $\mathbb{Z}$. If $|w - \lfloor p/2 \rfloor| < \lfloor p/4 \rfloor$ in $\mathbb{Z}$, output 1, otherwise, output 0.

Remark 1. We remark that

$$\mathbf{c}_{\mathsf{id}} = \left\lfloor \frac{p}{q} \cdot \left((B + H(\mathsf{id})G)^T \cdot \mathbf{s} - \mathbf{f}_B\right) \right\rceil$$

$$= \left\lfloor \frac{p}{q} \cdot \left((B + H(\mathsf{id})G)^T \cdot \mathbf{s} - R^T A^T \cdot \mathbf{s} + \frac{q}{p}R^T \left\lfloor \frac{p}{q}(A^T \cdot \mathbf{s}) \right\rceil\right) \right\rceil$$

$$= \left\lfloor \frac{p}{q} \cdot \left((B + H(\mathsf{id})G)^T \cdot \mathbf{s} - (AR)^T \cdot \mathbf{s}\right) \right\rceil + R^T \left\lfloor \frac{p}{q}(A^T \cdot \mathbf{s}) \right\rceil,$$

so that $\mathbf{c}_{\mathsf{id}}$ is alternatively defined as $\left\lfloor \frac{p}{q} \cdot \left((B + H(\mathsf{id})G)^T \cdot \mathbf{s} - (AR)^T \cdot \mathbf{s}\right) \right\rceil +$

$R^T \left\lfloor \frac{p}{q}(A^T \cdot \mathbf{s}) \right\rceil$ when appropriate (for example, to a certain parameter set that p does not divide q).

3.2   Correctness

In this section, we present a correctness condition of the presented IBE scheme.

Lemma 1 (Correctness). *The IBE scheme works correctly as long as the following inequality holds for the security parameter λ:*

$$\Pr[|\langle \mathbf{e}_A, \mathbf{f}_A \rangle + \langle \mathbf{e}_B, \mathbf{f}_B - R^T \mathbf{f}_A \rangle| \geq \frac{q}{4} - \frac{q}{2p} :$$

$$\mathbf{e}_A, \mathbf{e}_B \leftarrow \mathcal{D}_\sigma^m, \mathbf{f}_A, \mathbf{f}_B \leftarrow \mathbb{Z}_{q/p}^m, R \leftarrow \{-1, 1\}^{m \times m}] < \mathsf{negl}(\lambda).$$

Proof. Let $\mathbf{e} = (\mathbf{e}_A^T | \mathbf{e}_B^T)^T$, for $\mathbf{e}_A, \mathbf{e}_B \in \mathbb{Z}_q^m$, and $f \leftarrow \mathbf{u}^T \cdot \mathbf{s} - \frac{q}{p} \left\lfloor \frac{p}{q} \mathbf{u}^T \cdot \mathbf{s} \right\rceil$. Setting

$$\mathbf{f}_A \leftarrow A^T \cdot \mathbf{s} - \frac{q}{p} \left\lfloor \frac{p}{q} A^T \cdot \mathbf{s} \right\rceil, \text{ and}$$

$$\mathbf{f}_B \leftarrow (B + H(\mathsf{id})G)^T \cdot \mathbf{s} - R^T \mathbf{f}_A - \frac{q}{p} \left\lfloor \frac{p}{q} \cdot ((B + H(\mathsf{id})G)^T \cdot \mathbf{s} - R^T \mathbf{f}_A) \right\rceil,$$

It holds that

$$c_{out} - \mathbf{e}^T \cdot (\mathbf{c}_{in}^T | \mathbf{c}_{\mathsf{id}}^T)^T = \lfloor p/2 \rfloor \cdot b + (p/q) \cdot (\langle \mathbf{e}_A, \mathbf{f}_A \rangle + \langle \mathbf{e}_B, \mathbf{f}_B + R^T \mathbf{f}_A \rangle - f).$$

Hence, the scheme works correctly if

$$(p/q) \cdot |(\langle \mathbf{e}_A, \mathbf{f}_A \rangle + \langle \mathbf{e}_B, \mathbf{f}_B + R^T \mathbf{f}_A \rangle)| + (p/q) \cdot |f| \leq p/4$$

The correctness condition follows directly because $|f| \leq q/2p$.

3.3   Security

Theorem 1. *The IBE system with parameters (q, p, n, m, σ) is INDr–sID–CPA secure provided that the $\mathsf{LWR}_{n,q,p}$ assumption holds.*

Proof. Let Game 0 denote the original INDr-sID-CPA game from Definition 4 against our scheme between an adversary $\mathcal{A}$ and a challenger $\mathcal{C}$.

Game 1. Recall that, in Game 0, the challenger $\mathcal{C}$ runs IBE.Setup algorithm to generate random $(A, B, \mathbf{u}) \in \mathbb{Z}_q^{n \times m} \times \mathbb{Z}_q^{n \times m} \times \mathbb{Z}_q^n$ as public parameters with a master secret key T_A, a short orthogonal basis for A. In Game 1, $\mathcal{C}$ sets $B \leftarrow AR^* - H(\mathsf{id}^*)G$ instead, where $R^* \leftarrow \{-1, 1\}^{m \times m}$ and id^* is committed by the adversary $\mathcal{A}$ at the beginning. In the challenge phase, $\mathcal{C}$ sets $R^* \in \{-1, 1\}^{m \times m}$ as a random matrix generated in the encryption phase. By the generalized leftover hash lemma, $(A, AR^*, \mathbf{f}_B = (R^*)^T \cdot \mathbf{f}_A)$ is statistically close to $(A, B, \mathbf{f}_B)$ where $B \leftarrow \mathbb{Z}_q^{n \times m}$ is uniform random so that Game 0 and Game 1 are indistinguishable for $\mathcal{A}$.

Game 2. The only change in Game 2 compared to Game 1 is that $\mathcal{C}$ responds a key extraction query for id with $\mathbf{e} \leftarrow \mathsf{SampleRight}(A, (H(\mathsf{id}) - H(\mathsf{id}^*)), R^*, \mathbf{u}, s)$, where $(A|AR^* + (H(\text{id}) - H(\text{id}^*))G)\mathbf{e} = \mathbf{u}$. The distribution of answers for the key extraction queries is statistically close to that in Game 1.

Game 3. The challenge ciphertext is chosen as a random independent element in $\mathbb{Z}_q^m \times \mathbb{Z}_q^m \times \mathbb{Z}_q$.

Indistinguishability Between Game 2 and Game 3. Suppose there exists a polynomial time adversary $\mathcal{A}$ who distinguishes Game 2 and Game 3 with non-negligible advantage. We construct an LWR adversary $\mathcal{B}$ using $\mathcal{A}$.

Let $\mathcal{O}$ be a sampling oracle for the LWR problem which is either a truly random $\mathcal{O}_\$$ or a rounded pseudo-random $\mathcal{O}_\mathbf{s}$ for some fixed $\mathbf{s}$. $\mathcal{B}$ requests from $\mathcal{O}$ and receives $(m+1)$ samples $\{(\mathbf{a}_i, v_i)\}_{i=0}^m$. After $\mathcal{A}$ announce id^*, $\mathcal{B}$ does the following:

- Construct a matrix $A \in \mathbb{Z}_q^{n \times m}$ as a matrix of which i-th column is $\mathbf{a}_i$ for $i = 1, \cdots, m$.
- Set $\mathbf{u} = \mathbf{a}_0$.
- Set $B \in \mathbb{Z}_q^{n \times m}$ as in the Game 2 using R^* and id^*.
- Send $\mathsf{PP} = (A, B, \mathbf{u})$ to $\mathcal{A}$.

Receiving private-key queries from $\mathcal{A}$, $\mathcal{B}$ answers them as in Game 2. For the challenge phase, upon receiving a message bit b^* from $\mathcal{A}$, $\mathcal{B}$ does the following.

- $c_{out}^* \leftarrow v_0 + b^* \lfloor p/2 \rfloor$.
- Set $\mathbf{v}^* = (v_1, v_2, \cdots, v_m) \in \mathbb{Z}_q^m$.
- Let $\mathbf{c}_{in}^* = \mathbf{v}^*$, and $\mathbf{c}_{id}^* = (R^*)^T \mathbf{v}^*$.
- Set $\mathsf{CT}^* = (\mathbf{c}_{in}, \mathbf{c}_{id}, c_{out})$ and send it to $\mathcal{A}$.

Claim 1: If $\mathcal{O} = \mathcal{O}_\mathbf{s}$, then the distribution of CT^* is the same as in Game 2.

It suffices to show that, for a challenge ciphertext $\mathsf{CT} = (\mathbf{c}_{in}, \mathbf{c}_{id}, c_{out})$ in Game 2, $\mathbf{c}_{id} = (R^*)^T \mathbf{c}_{in}$. In Game 2,

$$\mathbf{c}_{in} = \lfloor (p/q) \cdot A^T \mathbf{s} \rceil \text{ and } \mathbf{c}_{id} = \lfloor (p/q) \cdot ((AR^*)^T \mathbf{s} - (R^*)^T \mathbf{f}_A) \rceil,$$

where $\mathbf{f}_A = A^T \mathbf{s} - (q/p) \cdot \lfloor (p/q) \cdot A^T \mathbf{s} \rceil$. It follows that

$$\begin{aligned}
\mathbf{c}_{id} &= \lfloor (p/q) \cdot ((AR^*)^T \mathbf{s} - (R^*)^T \mathbf{f}_A) \rceil \\
&= \lfloor (p/q) \cdot ((AR^*)^T \mathbf{s} + (R^*)^T ((q/p) \cdot \lfloor (p/q) \cdot A^T \mathbf{s} \rceil - A^T \mathbf{s})) \rceil \\
&= (R^*)^T \lfloor (p/q) \cdot A^T \mathbf{s} \rceil \\
&= (R^*)^T \mathbf{c}_{in}.
\end{aligned}$$

Claim 2: If $\mathcal{O} = \mathcal{O}_\$$, then the distribution of CT^* is the same as in Game 3.

It suffices to show that CT^* is uniform as in Game 3. By the left over hash lemma where the hash function is defined by $(A^T|\mathbf{v}^*)$, $(AR^*, (R^*)^T \mathbf{v}^*)$ is uniformly random in $\mathbb{Z}_q^{n \times m} \times \mathbb{Z}_p^m$. Hence, CT^* is uniform in $\mathbb{Z}_p^m \times \mathbb{Z}_p^m \times \mathbb{Z}_p$.

3.4   Ring Version

In the ring version, we consider the gadget vector $\mathbf{g} = (1, 2, \cdots, 2^{\lceil \log q \rceil - 1}, 0, 0) \in \mathcal{R}_q^m$ of which entries are in $\mathcal{R}_q$, and the FRD hash function $H : \mathbb{Z}^n \to \mathcal{R}_q$ which satisfies that for any distinct $\mathbf{u}$ and $\mathbf{v}$ in $\mathbb{Z}^n$, the difference $H(\mathbf{u}) - H(\mathbf{v}) \in \mathcal{R}_q$ is invertible and is computable in polynomial time in $(n \log q)$.

- IBE.Ring.Setup(λ): On input a security parameter λ, set the parameters q, p, n, σ as specified in Sect. 4.1. Let $k = \lceil \log q \rceil$ and $m = k + 2$. Next do:
  - Use TrapGen(q, n) to generate a vector $\mathbf{a} \in \mathcal{R}_q^m$ together with a basis $T_\mathbf{a} \in \mathcal{R}_q^{(m-k) \times k}$ for $\Lambda_q^\perp(\mathbf{a})$ of which entries are independently sampled from discrete Gaussian distribution $\mathcal{D}_\sigma$.
  - Generate a uniformly random vector $\mathbf{b} \in \mathcal{R}_q^m$.
  - Select a uniformly random $u \in \mathcal{R}_q$.
  - Output the public parameters and master secret key,

$$\mathsf{PP} = (\mathbf{a}, \mathbf{b}, u), \qquad \mathsf{MK} = (T_\mathbf{a})$$

- IBE.Ring.Extract($\mathsf{PP}, \mathsf{MK}, \mathsf{id}$): On input public parameters PP, a master secret key MK, and an identity id, do:
  - Sample $\mathbf{e} \in \mathcal{R}^{2m}$ as $\mathbf{e} \leftarrow \mathsf{SampleLeft}(\mathbf{a}, \mathbf{b} + H(\mathsf{id}) \cdot \mathbf{g}, T_\mathbf{a}, u, \sigma)$.
  - Output $\mathsf{SK}_{\mathsf{id}} := \mathbf{e}$.
- IBE.Ring.Encrypt($\mathsf{PP}, \mathsf{id}, \mu$): On input public parameter PP, an identity id, and a message $\mu \in \mathcal{R}_2$, do:
  - Sample a uniform random element $s \leftarrow \mathcal{R}_q$.
  - $c_{out} \leftarrow \left\lfloor \frac{p}{q} \cdot u \cdot s \right\rceil + \mu \cdot \left\lfloor \frac{p}{2} \right\rfloor$.
  - $\mathbf{c}_{in} \leftarrow \left\lfloor \frac{p}{q}(\mathbf{a} \cdot s) \right\rceil \in \mathcal{R}_p^m$, and let $\mathbf{f}_A := \mathbf{a} \cdot s - \frac{q}{p} \left\lfloor \frac{p}{q}(\mathbf{a} \cdot s) \right\rceil$.
  - $R \leftarrow \{-1, 1\}^{m \times m}$, and let $\mathbf{f}_B \leftarrow R \cdot \mathbf{f}_A$.
  - $\mathbf{c}_{\mathsf{id}} \leftarrow \left\lfloor \frac{p}{q} \cdot ((\mathbf{b} + H(\mathsf{id}) \cdot \mathbf{g}) \cdot s - \mathbf{f}_B) \right\rceil$.
  - Output the ciphertext $\mathsf{CT} := (\mathbf{c}_{in}, \mathbf{c}_{\mathsf{id}}, c_{out}) \in \mathcal{R}_p^m \times \mathcal{R}_p^m \times \mathcal{R}_p$.
- IBE.Ring.Decrypt($\mathsf{PP}, \mathsf{SK}_{\mathsf{id}}, \mathsf{CT}$): On input public parameters PP, a private key $\mathsf{SK}_{\mathsf{id}} := \mathbf{e} \in \mathcal{R}^{2m}$, and a ciphertext $\mathsf{CT} := (c_{in}, \mathbf{c}_{\mathsf{id}}, c_{out})$, do:
  - Output $\mu' \leftarrow \left\lfloor \frac{2}{p} \cdot (c_{out} - \mathbf{e}^T \cdot (\mathbf{c}_{in}^T | \mathbf{c}_{\mathsf{id}}^T)^T) \right\rceil$.

Correctness. The correctness lemma as below shows when the ring version of our IBE scheme is correct.

Lemma 2 (Correctness). *The ring version IBE scheme works correctly as long as the following inequality holds for the security parameter λ:*

$$\Pr[|\langle \mathbf{e}_A, \mathbf{f}_A \rangle + \langle \mathbf{e}_B, \mathbf{f}_B - R^T \mathbf{f}_A \rangle| \geq \frac{q}{4} - \frac{q}{2p} :$$

$$\mathbf{e}_A, \mathbf{e}_B \leftarrow \mathcal{D}_\sigma^m, \mathbf{f}_A, \mathbf{f}_B \leftarrow \mathcal{R}_{q/p}^m, R \leftarrow \{-1, 1\}^{m \times m}] < \mathsf{negl}(\lambda).$$

Proof. The proof is the same as in Lemma 2.

Security. The ring version of our IBE scheme is secure under the hardness assumption of ring-LWR in the standard model.

Theorem 2. *The ring version IBE system with parameters (q, p, n, σ) is INDr–sID-CPA secure provided that the ring-$\mathsf{LWR}_{n,q,p}$ assumption holds.*

Proof. The security proof is the same with that of Theorem 1.

3.5   Extensions

Our IBE construction is an analogue of the LWE-based IBE scheme in [ABB10] alternating the discrete Gaussian errors generated in the encryption phase with deterministic rounding errors. The ideas and security proofs in [ABB10] to convert a selectively-secure IBE scheme into an adaptively-secure scheme or Hierarchical IBE (HIBE) scheme can be easily adapted to our scheme.

- **Adaptively-Secure IBE:** Let id is a ℓ-bit string $\mathsf{id} = (d_1, \cdots, d_\ell) \in \{0,1\}^\ell$. Public key contains uniform random matrices $A_0, \cdots, A_\ell$ instead of A in the selectively-secure scheme, and for an encryption procedure, the matrix $(A\|B + H(\mathsf{id})G)$ is replaced with

$$\left(A_0 \middle\| B + \sum_{i=1}^{\ell} d_i \cdot A_i \right)$$

  to calculate the ciphertext. The resulting scheme is adaptively-secure.
- **HIBE:** For d, a maximum depth, public key contains uniform random matrices $A_0, \cdots, A_d$ instead of A. Let $\mathsf{id} = (\mathsf{id}_1, \cdots, \mathsf{id}_\ell)$ be an identity sequence of length $\ell < d$. To encrypt, instead of the matrix $(A\|B + H(\mathsf{id})G)$,

$$(A_0\|B + H(\mathsf{id}_1)A_1\| \cdots \|B + H(\mathsf{id}_\ell)A_\ell)$$

  is used.

4   Efficient Instantiation

We present efficient instantiation for the proposed ring-LWR based IBE scheme, using the trapdoor proposed in [MP12].

4.1   Proposed Parameters

- σ for the trapdoor sampling is $\sigma > \sqrt{(ln(2n/(1 + 1/\epsilon)))/\pi}$ [MP12], where ϵ is the bound on the statistical error introduced by each randomized-rounding operation. For $n \leq 2^{14}$ and $\epsilon \geq 2^{-80}$, $\sigma > 4.554$.

- The spectral norm (trapdoor quality) s is $s > C\sigma^2(\sqrt{m} + \sqrt{2n} + t')$ except for the probability $2 \cdot \exp(-\pi(t')^2)$, where C is experimentally chosen as $C \approx 1.8$ [GPR+18].
- By the central limit theorem, to satisfy the correctness condition, the modulus q and p are required to satisfy

$$\frac{q}{4} - \frac{q}{2p} > \sqrt{mn}\Delta_{\mathbf{e}}(\Delta_{func} + \Delta_p),$$

where
  - $\Delta_{\mathbf{e}}$ and Δ_p are the upper bounds for the infinite norm of $\mathbf{e}$ and the coefficient-wise rounding error induced by the operation $\left\lfloor \frac{p}{q} \cdot \right\rceil$, respectively. $\Delta_{\mathbf{e}} \approx \omega(\sqrt{\lambda}) \cdot s$ and $\Delta_p = \omega(\sqrt{\lambda}) \cdot q/\sqrt{12}p$.
  - Δ_{func} is an upper bound for the summation of the $(m+1)$ independent random variables in $[\lfloor -q/2p \rfloor, \lfloor q/2p \rfloor] \cap \mathbb{Z}$. Hence, $\Delta_{func} \approx \omega(\sqrt{\lambda})\sqrt{m+1} \cdot (q/\sqrt{12}p)$.
- n is the LWR dimension, and is set to satisfy that $\mathsf{LWR}_{n,q,p}$ is secure against the attacks in Sect. A.
- m in the *non-ring* version of our scheme is set to either $n(1 + \log q)$ to make A of public key statistically close to uniform, or $2 \log q$ to sample a computationally pseudorandom A as mentioned in [MP12].

Based on the analyses as above, we can set the parameters for the ring versions of our IBE as follows (Table 1):

Table 1. Suggested parameter set for IBE; $\delta = 1.0075$ for Parameter I and $\delta = 1.005$ for Parameter II which provide 80-bit and 190-bit of security according to Albrecht's LWE estimator [APS15], respectively.

Parameter	n	$\log q$	$\log p$	$\log s$
I	512	29	24	10.61
II	1024	35	30	12.80

4.2 Proof-of-Concept Implementation

As a proof of concept, we implemented ring version of our LWR-based IBE scheme using lattice cryptography library PALISADE [PRR] with its NativePoly class. All experiments were tested on Intel(R) Xeon(R) CPU E5-2620 v4 @ 2.10 GHz processor (Table 2).

Although our code use TrapGen, SamplePre, and ring operations as blackboxes, we carried out some high-level optimizations like minimizing NTT and iNTT operations. For example, we replaced the matrix-vector multiplication $R \cdot \mathbf{f}_A$ in the encryption algorithm as a linear sum of elements. This can be done since R is a random matrix from $\{-1,1\}^{m \times m}$ which is not needed after this step.

This can speed up the step remarkably: we can keep $m \times m$ polynomial multiplications. We note that the performance can be largely improved by applying further optimization methods. For example, the performance can be improved by multi-threading, precomputing NTT (Number-Theoretic Transform)-related variables for faster polynomial multiplications, or using primes of special form to speed up modular multiplications by replacing some integer multiplications with shift operators.

Table 2. Proof of concept implementation timing results

Parameter	Setup	Extract	Encrypt	Decrypt
I	6.9 ms	29.6 ms	8.0 ms	0.5 ms
II	17 ms	65 ms	19 ms	1 ms

Our scheme has strength in ciphertext size since our ciphertext size depends on $\log p$ instead of $\log q$. Recent paper [BFRLS18] implemented a ring version of ABB IBE scheme and suggested concrete parameters. Among their parameter sets, the set of $n = 1024$ and $n = 2048$ correspond to $\delta = 1.0079$ and $\delta = 1.005$ (about 80-bit and 190-bit of security according to Albrecht's LWE estimator [APS15]), respectively. Compared to their scheme, our IBE scheme reduces ciphertext size about 72–73% for the same security. For 190-bit security (*resp.* 80-bit security), their ciphertext size is about 1 MB (*resp.* 0.35 MB), while our ciphertext size is about 0.27 MB (*resp.* 0.1 MB).

A   Cryptanalytic Hardness of the LWR Problem

In this section, we analyze the attack complexity for an LWR instance using lattice basis reduction algorithms, e.g., the BKZ algorithm [CN11,SE94]. We remark that the attack strategy to analyze the LWR problem shares the essence of the LWE attacks which has been studied in the recent papers [Alb17, CHK+16, AGVW17]. Actually, we surveyed all the LWE attacks and concluded that the primal and dual attack strategies are the most powerful in our usage. We focus on how to apply the primal attack strategy to analyze LWR, and for dual attack strategy applied to LWR, we recommend to see the analysis in [CKKS17].

The conclusion of this section is as follows.

Remark 2. the attack complexity of the LWR problem of dimension n, modulus q, and the rounding modulus p is equal to that of the LWE problem of the same dimension n, the same modulus q, and an error rate $\alpha = p^{-1} \cdot \sqrt{\pi/6}$.

This agrees with the view that an LWR sample $(\mathbf{a}, b = \lfloor (p/q) \cdot \langle \mathbf{a}, \mathbf{r} \rangle \rceil) \in \mathbb{Z}_q^n \times \mathbb{Z}_p$ can be naturally seen as a kind of an LWE sample by sending back the value b to an element of $\mathbb{Z}_q$, i.e., $b' = (q/p) \cdot b \in \mathbb{Z}_q$ satisfies $b' = \langle \mathbf{a}, \mathbf{r} \rangle + f$ (mod q) for a small error $f = -\langle \mathbf{a}, \mathbf{r} \rangle$ (mod q/p). Note that, in this view, the inserted error is deterministically chosen by random part $\mathbf{a}$ and secret $\mathbf{r}$, but it does not affect on the attack complexity.

A.1   Primal Attack for LWR

The key idea of the primal attack is the reduction from LWR to unique-SVP over a special lattice generated by an LWR instance. As described in [ADPS16] and [AGVW17], we use geometric series assumption (GSA) on the BKZ-reduced basis, and detect the shortest vector in the projected lattice.

Let Λ be a d-dimensional lattice. GSA asserts that the norms of Gram-Schmidt vectors of the lattice basis after lattice reduction forms a geometric series as follows.

Definition 6 (Geometric Series Assumption [Sch03]). *For a lattice $\Lambda = \mathbb{Z} \cdot \mathbf{b}_1 + \cdots \mathbb{Z} \cdot \mathbf{b}_d$ of dimension d, the norm of the Gram-Schmidt vectors after lattice reduction satisfy*

$$\|\mathbf{b}_i^*\| = \alpha^{i-1} \cdot \|\mathbf{b}_1\|,$$

for some $0 < \alpha < 1$.

Since $\|\mathbf{b}_1\| = \delta^d \cdot Vol(\Lambda)$ where δ is a root Hermite factor and $Vol(\Lambda) = \prod_{i=1}^d \|\mathbf{b}_i^*\|$ by definition, $\alpha \approx \delta^{-2}$.

Suppose there exists a vector $\mathbf{v} \in \Lambda$ of small norm such that

$$\sqrt{b/d} \cdot \|\mathbf{v}\| \leq \delta^{2b-d} Vol(\Lambda)^{1/d}. \tag{1}$$

Then, running the BKZ algorithm, when the SVP oracle is called on the last full projected block of size b, the projection $\pi_{d-b+1}(\mathbf{v})$ of $\mathbf{v}$ is contained in the lattice

$$\Lambda_{d-b+1} := \mathbb{Z} \cdot \pi_{d-b+1}(\mathbf{b}_{d-b+1}) + \cdots + \mathbb{Z} \cdot \pi_{d-b+1}(\mathbf{b}_d).$$

Note that, based on the following analysis, $\pi_{d-b+1}(\mathbf{v})$ is unusually short so that SVP oracle finds $\pi_{d-b+1}(\mathbf{v})$ in Λ_{d-b+1}.

- $\|\pi_{d-b+1}(\mathbf{v})\| \approx \sqrt{b/d}\|\mathbf{v}\| \leq \delta^{2b-d} Vol(\Lambda)^{1/d}$.
- We remark that $\mathbf{b}_{d-b+1}^* \leq \lambda_1(\Lambda_{d-b+1})$. By GSA, $\mathbf{b}_{d-b+1}^* = (\delta^{-2})^{d-b} \cdot \lambda_1(\Lambda) = \delta^{-2(d-b)+d} \cdot Vol(\Lambda)^{1/d}$.

Hence, we can conclude that if there exists $\mathbf{v}$ of norm $\delta^{2b-d} Vol(\Lambda)^{1/d}$, then an attacker can detect it running BKZ algorithm. Now we describe the lattices induced from an LWR instance in which an unusually short vector exists using the two embedding strategies in [Kan87, BG14].

Kannan's Embedding for LWR. Let $\left(A, \mathbf{b} = \left\lfloor \frac{p}{q} \cdot A\mathbf{r} \right\rceil\right) \in \mathbb{Z}_q^{m \times n} \times \mathbb{Z}_p^m$ be a given $\text{LWR}_{n,m,q,p}(\mathcal{D}_r)$ instance. For a reduced row echelon form $[I_n|A']$ for A, consider the $(m+1)$ dimensional lattice

$$\Lambda = \mathbb{Z}^{m+1} \cdot \begin{pmatrix} I_n & A' & 0 \\ 0 & qI_{m-n} & 0 \\ (q/p) \cdot \mathbf{b}^T & & 1 \end{pmatrix},$$

which is an LWR version of the Kannan's embedding [Kan87] when the embedding factor is 1. The lattice contains a vector of norm $\|(\mathbf{f}^T|1)\|$, where $\mathbf{f} = (q/p)\lfloor (p/q)\cdot A\mathbf{r} \rceil - A\mathbf{r}$. The lattice Λ has dimension $(m+1)$ and volume q^{m-n}. Hence, the attack is successful if

$$\sqrt{b}\cdot (q/p\cdot\sqrt{\pi/6}) \leq \delta^{2b-m-1}q^{(m-n)/m+1},$$

by (1).

Bai-Galbraith's Embedding for LWR. For a given $\mathsf{LWR}_{n,m,q,p}(\mathcal{D}_r)$ instance $\left(A,\ \mathbf{b} = \left\lfloor \frac{p}{q}\cdot A\mathbf{r}\right\rceil\right) \in \mathbb{Z}_q^{m\times n}\times\mathbb{Z}_p^m$, construct the lattice

$$\Lambda = \{\mathbf{v}\in\mathbb{Z}^{n+m+1} : (A\|I_m\| - (q/p)\cdot\mathbf{b})\,\mathbf{v} = 0\pmod{q}\}.$$

with the unique shortest vector $(\mathbf{r},\mathbf{f},1)$. Similarly to the case of dual attack, we consider the weighted lattice

$$\Lambda' = \{(\mathbf{x},\mathbf{y},z)\in\mathbb{Z}^n\times(w^{-1}\mathbb{Z})^m\times\mathbb{Z} : (\mathbf{x},w\cdot\mathbf{y},z)\in\Lambda\}.$$

for the constant $w = (q/\sqrt{12}p)\cdot\sigma_r^{-1}$ where σ_r^2 is the variance of component of secret vector $\mathbf{r}$. which contains the short vector $\mathbf{v} = (\mathbf{r},w^{-1}\cdot\mathbf{f},1)$. Let $\hat{q} = q/w = \sqrt{12}p/\sigma_r$, then the dimension and the volume of Λ' are $(n+m+1)$ and $\hat{q}^m$ respectively.

Therefore, the attack is successful if

$$\sqrt{b/(m+n+1)}\|(\mathbf{r},w^{-1}\cdot\mathbf{f},1)\| \approx \sqrt{b}\cdot\sigma_r \leq \delta^{2b-m-n-1}\hat{q}^{m/(m+n+1)},$$

by (1). In other words,

$$\sqrt{b}\cdot\sigma_r^{(n+1)/(m+n+1)} \leq \delta^{2b-m-n-1}(\sqrt{12}p)^{m/(m+n+1)}.$$

References

[ABB10] Agrawal, S., Boneh, D., Boyen, X.: Efficient lattice (H)IBE in the standard model. In: Gilbert, H. (ed.) EUROCRYPT 2010. LNCS, vol. 6110, pp. 553–572. Springer, Heidelberg (2010). https://doi.org/10.1007/978-3-642-13190-5_28

[ADPS16] Alkim, E., Ducas, L., Pöppelmann, T., Schwabe, P.: Post-quantum key exchange—a new hope. In: 25th USENIX Security Symposium (USENIX Security 16), pp. 327–343. USENIX Association, Austin, August 2016

[AFL16] Apon, D., Fan, X., Liu, F.: Compact identity based encryption from LWE. Cryptology ePrint Archive 2016 (2016)

[AGVW17] Albrecht, M.R., Göpfert, F., Virdia, F., Wunderer, T.: Revisiting the expected cost of solving uSVP and applications to LWE. In: Takagi, T., Peyrin, T. (eds.) ASIACRYPT 2017. LNCS, vol. 10624, pp. 297–322. Springer, Cham (2017). https://doi.org/10.1007/978-3-319-70694-8_11

[Ajt96] Ajtai, M.: Generating hard instances of lattice problems. In: Proceedings of the Twenty-eighth Annual ACM Symposium on Theory of Computing, pp. 99–108. ACM (1996)

[Ajt99] Ajtai, M.: Generating hard instances of the short basis problem. In: Wiedermann, J., van Emde Boas, P., Nielsen, M. (eds.) ICALP 1999. LNCS, vol. 1644, pp. 1–9. Springer, Heidelberg (1999). https://doi.org/10.1007/3-540-48523-6_1

[AKPW13] Alwen, J., Krenn, S., Pietrzak, K., Wichs, D.: Learning with rounding, revisited. In: Canetti, R., Garay, J.A. (eds.) CRYPTO 2013. LNCS, vol. 8042, pp. 57–74. Springer, Heidelberg (2013). https://doi.org/10.1007/978-3-642-40041-4_4

[Alb17] Albrecht, M.R.: On dual lattice attacks against small-secret LWE and parameter choices in HElib and SEAL. IACR Cryptology ePrint Archive 2017:047 (2017)

[AP11] Alwen, J., Peikert, C.: Generating shorter bases for hard random lattices. Theory Comput. Syst. **48**(3), 535–553 (2011)

[APS15] Albrecht, M.R., Player, R., Scott, S.: On the concrete hardness of learning with errors. J. Math. Cryptol. **9**(3), 169–203 (2015)

[BBF+19] Baan, H., et al.: Round5: KEM and PKE based on (ring) learning with rounding (2019). https://csrc.nist.gov/projects/post-quantum-cryptography/round-2-submissions

[BF01] Boneh, D., Franklin, M.: Identity-based encryption from the weil pairing. In: Kilian, J. (ed.) CRYPTO 2001. LNCS, vol. 2139, pp. 213–229. Springer, Heidelberg (2001). https://doi.org/10.1007/3-540-44647-8_13

[BFRLS18] Bert, P., Fouque, P.-A., Roux-Langlois, A., Sabt, M.: Practical implementation of ring-SIS/LWE based signature and IBE. In: Lange, T., Steinwandt, R. (eds.) PQCrypto 2018. LNCS, vol. 10786, pp. 271–291. Springer, Cham (2018). https://doi.org/10.1007/978-3-319-79063-3_13

[BG14] Bai, S., Galbraith, S.D.: Lattice decoding attacks on binary LWE. In: Susilo, W., Mu, Y. (eds.) ACISP 2014. LNCS, vol. 8544, pp. 322–337. Springer, Cham (2014). https://doi.org/10.1007/978-3-319-08344-5_21

[BGM+16] Bogdanov, A., Guo, S., Masny, D., Richelson, S., Rosen, A.: On the hardness of learning with rounding over small modulus. In: Kushilevitz, E., Malkin, T. (eds.) TCC 2016. LNCS, vol. 9562, pp. 209–224. Springer, Heidelberg (2016). https://doi.org/10.1007/978-3-662-49096-9_9

[BPR12] Banerjee, A., Peikert, C., Rosen, A.: Pseudorandom functions and lattices. In: Pointcheval, D., Johansson, T. (eds.) EUROCRYPT 2012. LNCS, vol. 7237, pp. 719–737. Springer, Heidelberg (2012). https://doi.org/10.1007/978-3-642-29011-4_42

[CHK+16] Cheon, J.H., Han, K., Kim, J., Lee, C., Son, Y.: A practical post-quantum public-key cryptosystem based on spLWE. In: Hong, S., Park, J.H. (eds.) ICISC 2016. LNCS, vol. 10157, pp. 51–74. Springer, Cham (2017). https://doi.org/10.1007/978-3-319-53177-9_3. https://eprint.iacr.org

[CKKS17] Cheon, J.H., Kim, A., Kim, M., Song, Y.: Homomorphic encryption for arithmetic of approximate numbers. In: Takagi, T., Peyrin, T. (eds.) ASIACRYPT 2017. LNCS, vol. 10624, pp. 409–437. Springer, Cham (2017). https://doi.org/10.1007/978-3-319-70694-8_15

[CKLS18] Cheon, J.H., Kim, D., Lee, J., Song, Y.: Lizard: cut off the tail! a practical post-quantum public-key encryption from LWE and LWR. In: Catalano, D., De Prisco, R. (eds.) SCN 2018. LNCS, vol. 11035, pp. 160–177. Springer, Cham (2018). https://doi.org/10.1007/978-3-319-98113-0_9

[CN11] Chen, Y., Nguyen, P.Q.: BKZ 2.0: better lattice security estimates. In: Lee, D.H., Wang, X. (eds.) ASIACRYPT 2011. LNCS, vol. 7073, pp. 1–20. Springer, Heidelberg (2011). https://doi.org/10.1007/978-3-642-25385-0_1

[CS17] Costache, A., Smart, N.P.: Homomorphic encryption without gaussian noise. IACR Cryptology ePrint Archive 2017:163 (2017)

[EBB13] El Bansarkhani, R., Buchmann, J.: Improvement and efficient implementation of a lattice-based signature scheme. In: Lange, T., Lauter, K., Lisoněk, P. (eds.) SAC 2013. LNCS, vol. 8282, pp. 48–67. Springer, Heidelberg (2014). https://doi.org/10.1007/978-3-662-43414-7_3

[FLL+16] Fang, F., Li, B., Lu, X., Liu, Y., Jia, D., Xue, H.: (Deterministic) hierarchical identity-based encryption from learning with rounding over small modulus. In: Proceedings of the 11th ACM on Asia Conference on Computer and Communications Security, pp. 907–912. ACM (2016)

[GM18] Genise, N., Micciancio, D.: Faster gaussian sampling for trapdoor lattices with arbitrary modulus. In: Nielsen, J.B., Rijmen, V. (eds.) EUROCRYPT 2018. LNCS, vol. 10820, pp. 174–203. Springer, Cham (2018). https://doi.org/10.1007/978-3-319-78381-9_7

[GPR+18] Gür, K.D., Polyakov, Y., Rohloff, K., Ryan, G.W., Savas, E.: Implementation and evaluation of improved gaussian sampling for lattice trapdoors. In: Proceedings of the 6th Workshop on Encrypted Computing & Applied Homomorphic Cryptography, pp. 61–71. ACM (2018)

[GPV08] Gentry, C., Peikert, C., Vaikuntanathan, V.: Trapdoors for hard lattices and new cryptographic constructions. In: Proceedings of the Fortieth Annual ACM Symposium on Theory of Computing, pp. 197–206. ACM (2008)

[Kan87] Kannan, R.: Minkowski's convex body theorem and integer programming. Math. Oper. Res. 12(3), 415–440 (1987)

[LKL+18] Lee, J., Kim, D., Lee, H., Lee, Y., Cheon, J.H.: Rlizard: post-quantum key encapsulation mechanism for IoT devices. IEEE Access 7, 2080–2091 (2018)

[LPR10] Lyubashevsky, V., Peikert, C., Regev, O.: On ideal lattices and learning with errors over rings. In: Gilbert, H. (ed.) EUROCRYPT 2010. LNCS, vol. 6110, pp. 1–23. Springer, Heidelberg (2010). https://doi.org/10.1007/978-3-642-13190-5_1

[MP12] Micciancio, D., Peikert, C.: Trapdoors for lattices: simpler, tighter, faster, smaller. In: Pointcheval, D., Johansson, T. (eds.) EUROCRYPT 2012. LNCS, vol. 7237. Springer, Berlin (2012). https://doi.org/10.1007/978-3-642-29011-4_41

[PRR] Polyakov, Y., Rohloff, K., Ryan, G.: Palisade lattice cryptography library. https://palisade-crypto.org/. Accessed 2019 Sept 04

[Reg05] Regev, O.: On lattices, learning with errors, random linear codes, and cryptography. In: Proceedings of the Thirty-Seventh Annual ACM Symposium on Theory of Computing, STOC 2005, pp. 84–93. ACM, New York (2005)

[Reg09] Regev, O.: On lattices, learning with errors, random linear codes, and cryptography. J. ACM (JACM) 56(6), 34 (2009)

[Sch03] Schnorr, C.P.: Lattice reduction by random sampling and birthday methods. In: Alt, H., Habib, M. (eds.) STACS 2003. LNCS, vol. 2607, pp. 145–156. Springer, Heidelberg (2003). https://doi.org/10.1007/3-540-36494-3_14

[SE94] Schnorr, C.-P., Euchner, M.: Lattice basis reduction: improved practical algorithms and solving subset sum problems. Math. Program. 66(1–3), 181–199 (1994)

[Sha85] Shamir, A.: Identity-based cryptosystems and signature schemes. In: Blakley, G.R., Chaum, D. (eds.) CRYPTO 1984. LNCS, vol. 196, pp. 47–53. Springer, Heidelberg (1985). https://doi.org/10.1007/3-540-39568-7_5

Faster Bootstrapping of FHE
over the Integers

Jung Hee Cheon[1(✉)], Kyoohyung Han[2], and Duhyeong Kim[1]

[1] Seoul National University (SNU), Seoul, Republic of Korea
{jhcheon,doodoo1204}@snu.ac.kr
[2] Coinplug Inc., Seongnam-si, Republic of Korea
kyoohyunghan@coinplug.com

Abstract. In FHE over the integers, decryption function is simplified by sparse subset subset sum problem (SSSP) assumption, which is introduced by Dijk et al. (Eurocrypt 2010), so that bootstrapping can be achieved successfully. Later, Nuida and Kurowasa (Eurocrypt 2015) proposed an advanced method of which the degree is very low and the message space is non-binary. These previous methods require low degree but more than $O(\lambda^4)$ homomorphic multiplications which make them very slow. For a general bootstrapping method in FHE over the integers, the number of homomorphic multiplications and the degree of decryption function are important factors for the efficiency of bootstrapping procedure.

In this paper, we propose a new bootstrapping method for FHE over the integers requiring only $O(\log^2 \lambda)$ homomorphic multiplications which is significantly lower than previous methods. Implementing our bootstrapping method on the scale-invariant FHE over the integers called CLT scheme, it takes 6 s for 500-bit message space and 80-bit security on a desktop. We also apply our bootstrapping method to the homomorphic evaluation of AES-128 circuit: It takes about 8 s per 128-bit block and is faster than the previous results of homomorphic AES evaluation using FHEs over the integers without bootstrapping.

Keywords: Bootstrapping · Fully Homomorphic Encryption · Squashing technique · Approximate GCD

1 Introduction

Following Gentry's blueprint [9], the essential step from Somewhat Homomorphic Encryption (SHE) to Fully Homomorphic Encryption (FHE) is a homomorphic evaluation of decryption circuit, which is called *bootstrapping*. After Gentry proposed the first FHE, various FHEs have been proposed and they can be classified into two categories: lattice-based FHEs and integer-based FHEs. In

K. Han—This work is done when the second author is in Seoul National University (SNU).

case of integer-based FHEs, it is harder to construct bootstrapping method than lattice-based FHEs since they need additional assumption to simplify a decryption circuit. Until Nuida and Kurosawa [13] suggested improved bootstrapping method, similar methods to [14] had been used in integer-based FHEs. In [13], they proposed new bootstrapping method which can be applied for integer-based FHEs supporting non-binary message space, and lower the degree of squashed decryption circuit. However, their method needs too many homomorphic multiplications while bootstrapping and this yields slow speed of bootstrapping procedure.

In this paper, we propose new bootstrapping method for integer-based FHEs [5,6,14], which is more efficient than previous works [13,14]. In [13], they adapted their method only to the scheme of [14] (ciphertext with the form $pq + 2r + m$), but actually their method can be adapted to all integers-based FHEs because their method works well regardless of which homomorphic encryption schemes the method is applied for. Our new bootstrapping method also contains such generality of the method in [13] so that it can be applied to all integer-based FHEs. The main advantages of our method are following:

- First, our bootstrapping method is significantly more efficient (and faster) than previous methods [13,14]. The number of homomorphic multiplications in our bootstrapping method is much smaller than previous methods ; reduced from $O(\lambda^4 \log^6 \lambda)$ to $O(\log^2 \lambda)$.
- Second, we apply our method to scale-invariant FHE over the integers (CLT scheme [6]) with non-binary message space. Error growth while bootstrapping in this scheme is $O(n \log \Theta)$ and the bootstrapping procedure takes about 6 s for depth 8 and 80-bit security.
- Third, homomorphic Advanced Encryption Standard (AES) evaluation in low depth using our efficient bootstrapping method with CLT scheme is faster than previous AES evaluation in large depth without bootstrapping [6].

1.1   Previous Work and Problems

There were two kinds of bootstrapping methods in FHE over the integers, which were proposed in [14] and [13]. In [13,14], the decryption circuit was simplified into following equation with sparse subset sum problem (SSSP) assumption for given ciphertext c:

$$m = \left\lfloor \sum_{i=1}^{\Theta} s_i \cdot \frac{w_i}{t^n} \right\rceil \bmod t \text{ or } c - \left\lfloor \sum_{i=1}^{\Theta} s_i \cdot \frac{w_i}{t^n} \right\rceil \bmod t.$$

Here s_i is a secret chosen from $\{0, 1\}$, $w_i = \lfloor c \cdot u_i/t^{\kappa-n} \rceil \bmod t^{n+1}$ for public rational number u_i and prime t, where $n \approx \log_t \lambda$ and $\kappa \approx \log |c| + \lambda$. In [14], they achieved bootstrapping by homomorphically evaluating this circuit, and this method was generalized to non-binary message space in [13]. The method use a bit-wise approach: namely, each s_i is encrypted as a ciphertext of message space $\mathbb{Z}_2$ ($\mathbb{Z}_t$ in [13]). By using bit-wise approach, output of addition part is ciphertext of each bit of $\sum s_i w_i$ so that the rounding part becomes just one XOR circuit. The complexity of addition part depends on Θ and n. Also Θ is larger than $O(\lambda^4)$, so it becomes bottleneck in efficiency of bootstrapping for FHE over the integers.

1.2 Our Contribution

Efficient Bootstrapping Method. To overcome the bottleneck, we propose new bootstrapping method whose addition part is much simpler than [13] and rounding part is more complicated than that. The important point is that complexity of rounding part depends only on small parameter n, and this point makes our method reasonable. Contrary to [13], we expand the message space to $\mathbb{Z}_{t^{n+1}}$ so that the addition part exactly consists of homomorphic additions. As the message space becomes larger, rounding part can be regarded as an extracting significant bit of $(\sum s_i z_i)$. In [10] (resp. [12]), homomorphic bit (resp. digit) extraction is proposed, and we apply it to the integer-based FHE [6] successfully (Table 1).

Table 1. Comparison with [NK15] method.

	[13]	Our method
Degree	$O(\lambda)$	$O(\lambda^{1+\epsilon})$
The number of Hommult	$O(\lambda^4 \log^6 \lambda)$	$O(\log^2 \lambda)$

Even though the degree of rounding part increases exponentially in n, parameter n is as small as $\log \lambda$ and only n^2 number of multiplications are needed in the part. The small constant ϵ part above is due to using large message space $\mathbb{Z}_{t^{n+1}}$.

Applying Our Bootstrapping Method on CLT Scheme. We apply our method on scale-invariant FHE over the integers, CLT scheme introduced by Coron, Lepoint, and Tibushi [6]. The ciphertext form of CLT scheme is appropriate to apply our method since the form allows trivial transition of various message spaces. Also, the noise growth during homomorphic multiplication in CLT scheme is linear. Applying our method on CLT scheme, we produce precise noise analysis of the bootstrapping procedure and its implementation result, 6 s for 500-bit message space. This result is far superior comparing with previous result in [4], 13 min for 500-bit message space.

We also implement a homomorphic evaluation of AES-128 encryption circuit. In our implementation, the evaluation takes 8 s per block and this result is better than 26 s per block [6], which is the result under large depth without bootstrapping.

1.3   Notation

- $[n] = \{0, 1, \cdots, n-1\}$, and $\mathbb{Z}_n$ is treated as $[n]$ in this paper.
- $a \bmod p$ for $a \in \mathbb{R}$ is an unique number $\in [0, p)$ such that $a - (a \bmod p)$ is an integer and a multiple of p.
- $[a]_p$ is an unique integer in $(-p/2, p/2]$ such that $a - [a]_p$ is a multiple of p.
- $a\langle k \rangle_t := a_k$ for a non-negative integer $a = \sum a_i t^i$ and $a_i \in [t]$. When $t = 2$, we omit the subscript t.

2   Preliminaries

In this section, we introduce squashing technique of FHEs over the integers and digit extraction techniques in detail, which will be applied for our bootstrapping method.

2.1   Squashed Decryption Circuit

The original decryption functions of integer-based FHE schemes [5,6,14] have form of $\lfloor tc/p \rceil \bmod t$ or $c - \lfloor c/p \rceil \bmod t$ for secret integer p, and these functions should be homomorphically evaluated for bootstrapping. Since division is not suitable for homomorphic evaluation, decryption functions of integer-based FHEs are *squashed* for efficient bootstrapping. *Squashing* is the procedure of expressing secret value $1/p$ as the subset sum of public numbers within very small error, which enable to bootstrap efficiently.

Squashed scheme was first introduced in [14], and generalized in [13]. Let κ', Θ', and θ' be additional parameters satisfying $\kappa' > (\gamma + \lambda)/\log t$. The concrete parameter settings of Θ' and θ' are discussed in Sect. 4.5. The method of squashing is identical to that in [13].

- KeyGen. Generate $\mathsf{sk}^* = p$ and pk as before. Set $x_p = \lfloor t^{\kappa'+1}/p \rceil$, choose a random Θ'-bit vector s with Hamming weight θ', and let $S = \{i : s_i = 1\}$. Choose random integer $u_i \in [0, t^{\kappa'+1})$ such that $\sum_{i \in S} u_i = x_p$. Output secret key $\mathsf{sk} = s$ and $\mathsf{pk} = (\mathsf{pk}^*, u)$.
- Encrypt. c^* is a ciphertext of given integer-based FHE. For $1 \leq i \leq \Theta'$, let w_i given by an integer nearest to the value of $c^* \cdot u_i / t^{\kappa'-n}$ where $n = \lceil \log_t \theta' \rceil + 3$. Output both c^* and w.
- Decrypt. Output $m' \leftarrow \lfloor \sum s_i w_i / t^n \rceil \bmod t$.

Remark 1. The squashing technique can be applied not only to the original scheme in [6], but also to the batch version of the scheme by squashing for each p_j as in [13].

2.2 Extraction Technique

In [10], Gentry et al. introduced a method of homomorphically evaluating decryption circuit through bit extraction. For an integer x, we can easily check the following equation holds inductively:

$$x^{2^k} \bmod 2^{k+1} = x \bmod 2 \quad \forall k \in \mathbb{N}.$$

With this property, we can extract $x\langle r \rangle$ for any non-negative integer x and r as a polynomial. Namely, when we define $x_r = [x_0 - \sum_{j=0}^{r-1} 2^j x_j^{2^{r-j}}]_{2^{r+1}}/2^r$, then the equality $x_r = x\langle r \rangle$ holds. With similar manner, this algorithm can be extended to non-binary case.

Digit Extraction Technique $(t > 2)$. Let $F^k(X) = F(F(\cdots(F(X))))$, a k-time evaluation of the function F. In general, $F(X) = X^t$ does not satisfy following property when $t > 2$:

$$F^k(x) \bmod t^{k+1} = x \bmod t \quad \forall k \in \mathbb{N}.$$

In [12], for prime t and positive integer e, they constructed the polynomial $F_{t,e}(X)$ satisfying the above equation for any $k \le e$. With this polynomial, we can extract $a\langle e' \rangle_t$ for $1 \le e' \le e$ using similar method in [10]. Following lemmas are about existence and construction of the polynomial $F_{t,e}(X)$, which is introduced in [12].

Lemma 1. *(Corollary 5.4 in [12])* *For every prime t, there exists a sequence of integer polynomial $f_1, f_2, \cdots$, all of degree $\le t - 1$, such that for every exponent $e \ge 1$ and every integer $z = z_0 + t^e z_1$ $(z_0 \in [t], z_1 \in \mathbb{Z})$, we have*

$$z^t \equiv z_0 + \sum_{i=1}^{e} f_i(z_0) t^i \pmod{t^{e+1}}.$$

Lemma 2. *(Corollary 5.5 in [12])* *For every prime t and every $e \ge 1$, there exists a polynomial $F_{t,e}$ of degree p such that the equality $F_{t,e}(z_0 + t^{e'} z_1) \equiv z_0$ (mod $t^{e'+1}$) holds for every integer z_0, z_1 with $z_0 \in [t]$ and every $1 \le e' \le e$.*

Using a special polynomial $F_{t,r}$, we can extract $x\langle r \rangle_t$ from x, through a polynomial circuit for any non-negative integer x and r, by Algorithm 1. Note that the equality in Lemma 2 implies that recursively defined x_is are integers.

Remark 2. Instead of using Algorithm 1, we can apply lower digit extraction algorithm [2] for extract digit. The method gives algorithm with lower depth and complexity, but the difference in our parameter setting is not big.

3 Our Bootstrapping Method

The rounding function in the squashed decryption circuit can be expressed as following :

$$\lceil a \rfloor \bmod t = \lfloor a + 0.5 \rfloor \bmod t = (a \cdot t^n + \lfloor t^n/2 \rfloor)\langle n \rangle_t.$$

Algorithm 1. Digit Extraction Algorithm

Require: $x, r \in \mathbb{N}$

Ensure: x_r such that $x_r \pmod{t} = x\langle r\rangle_t$

1: $x_0 \leftarrow x$

2: **for** $i \leftarrow 1$ to r **do**

3: $\quad x_i \leftarrow \dfrac{[x - F_{t,r}^i(x) - \sum_{j=1}^{i-1} t^j F_{t,r}^{i-j}(x_j)]_{t^{r+1}}}{t^i} \in \mathbb{Z}_{t^{r-i+1}}$

4: **end for**

5: **return** x_r

Thus, squashed decryption could be expressed as addition and digit-extraction. The problem is how to homomorphically evaluate the circuit $(\sum s_i w_i + \lfloor t^n/2 \rfloor)\langle n\rangle_t$ where w_is are defined in Sect. 2.

Let t be a prime integer, n be a positive integer less than $\log \lambda$, and $\mathcal{M}$ be a message space. For a given homomorphic encryption scheme, we can define $\mathcal{E}_k(m)$ as a set of ciphertext with message $m \in \mathcal{M} = \mathbb{Z}_{t^k}$. We follow notations in Sect. 2.1 about squashing. In this section, we suggest a new bootstrapping method. It works on homomorphic encryption (HE) scheme which satisfies following conditions:

1. Form of decrypt function is $\lfloor \sum s_i w_i/t^n \rceil \bmod t$ or $c - \lfloor \sum s_i w_i/t^n \rceil \bmod t$ where w_i can be computed by public values c and u_i.
2. It supports homomorphic operations with $\mathcal{M} = \mathbb{Z}_{t^i}$ for $1 \leq i \leq n+1$.
3. There exists polynomial time algorithm HomExt, a function from $\mathcal{E}_{n+1}(m)$ to $\mathcal{E}_1(m\langle n\rangle_t)$, which is a homomorphic evaluation of digit-extraction algorithm in Fig. 1.

Supposing the given homomorphic encryption scheme satisfies conditions above, the overview of our bootstrapping method is in Fig. 1. New parameters $s_0 = 1$ and $w_0 = \lfloor t^n/2 \rceil$ are included in the summation.

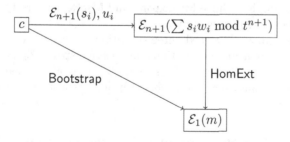

Fig. 1. Overview of our bootstrapping.

Actually, all integer-based schemes satisfy above conditions, which means our method can be applied to all integers-based HEs. In the diagram, our bootstrapping method consists of two steps: addition and extraction. Since w_i can be computed by public values and the set $\{\mathcal{E}_{n+1}(s_i)\}$ is given as bootstrapping key, addition step in this diagram is composed of homomorphic additions on $\mathcal{M} = \mathbb{Z}_{t^{n+1}}$ and modulus operation. Note that modulus operation mod t^{n+1} is actually very trivial step since message space is given by $\mathcal{M} = \mathbb{Z}_{t^{n+1}}$.

As a result, HomExt is the most important part and this part takes the most of running time in bootstrapping procedure. HomExt is a homomorphic evaluation of digit-extraction algorithm. The algorithm consists of operations on $\mathbb{Z}_{t^i}$, multiplication & division by t, and modulus operation mod t^i for $1 \leq i \leq n$. In $(j+1)$-th stage of **Compute** in digit extraction algorithm (in Algorithm 1), operations on $\mathbb{Z}_{t^k}$ become operations on $\mathbb{Z}_{t^{k-j}}$ after divided by t^j since the numerator is multiple of t^j. Furthermore, operations on $\mathbb{Z}_{t^k}$ can be regarded as operations on $\mathbb{Z}_{t^{k+j}}$ after multiplied by t^j. Therefore, we can absolutely evaluate digit-extraction with following *message space switching* functions: MsgExpand : $\mathcal{E}_k(m) \rightarrow \mathcal{E}_{k+1}(tm)$ and MsgReduce : $\mathcal{E}_k(tm) \rightarrow \mathcal{E}_{k-1}(m)$. Those functions can be constructed easily or trivially in all integer-based HE schemes.

As mentioned in Sect. 2.2, the algorithm can be seen as a polynomial of degree t^n with $n(n+1)/2$ times evaluation of $F_{n,t}$. Since n is an integer less than $\log_t \lambda$, the number of homomorphic multiplications in HomExt is $O(\log^2 \lambda)$. Actually the degree of the algorithm is $t^n \approx \lambda$; however, we use large message space $\mathbb{Z}_{t^{n+1}}$ in the procedure. Therefore, we write the degree as $O(\lambda^{1+\epsilon})$ and ϵ depends on which scheme is used for our bootstrapping method. We will analyze the degree and error growth of our method applying to integer-based scale-invariant homomorphic encryption scheme, CLT scheme [6], in Sect. 4.

4   Our Method on Scale-Invariant Homomorphic Encryption Scheme

We apply our method on scale-invariant homomorphic encryption scheme in [6], CLT scheme, since error growth during homomorphic evaluation is linear so that it is suitable to choose low depth parameter for implementation. Furthermore, as mentioned in Example 1, since MsgExpand and MsgReduce are trivial mapping, description of HomExt is very simple.

As mentioned above, we need three conditions: squashed decryption circuit with $\mathcal{M} = \mathbb{Z}_t$, homomorphic operations on message spaces $\mathbb{Z}_{t^a}$, and homomorphic digit extraction technique. The scheme below is almost same with scale-invariant homomorphic encryption scheme in [6], we just extend it to message space $\mathbb{Z}_t$ for prime t.

4.1   Scale-Invariant Homomorphic Encryption Scheme with $\mathcal{M} = \mathbb{Z}_t$

In this section, we follow the notation in [6]. The scheme below is on the message space $\mathbb{Z}_t$ for prime t. For an η-bit odd integer p and integer q_0 in $[0, 2^\gamma/p^2)$, we define the set

$$\mathcal{D}_{p,q_0}^\rho = \{p^2 \cdot q + r : \text{Choose } q \leftarrow [0, q_0), r \leftarrow (-2^\rho, 2^\rho)\}.$$

- SIDGHV.$\text{KeyGen}_t(1^\lambda)$. Generate an odd η-bit integer p and a γ-bit integer $x_0 = q_0 \cdot p^2 + r_0$ with $r_0 \leftarrow (-2^\rho, 2^\rho) \cap \mathbb{Z}$ and $q_0 \leftarrow [0, 2^\gamma/p^2) \cap \mathbb{Z}$. Let $x_i \leftarrow \mathcal{D}^\rho_{p,q_0}$ for $1 \leq i \leq \tau$, $y' \leftarrow \mathcal{D}^\rho_{p,q_0}$, and $y = y' + \lfloor p/t \rfloor$, which is the encryption of 1. Let z be a vector of length Θ, the components of which have $\kappa = 2\gamma + 2$ bits of precision following the binary point. Let $s \in \{0,1\}^\Theta$ such that

$$\frac{t \cdot 2^\eta}{p^2} = \langle s, z \rangle + \epsilon \mod (t \cdot 2^\eta),$$

  with $|\epsilon| \leq 2^{-\kappa}$. Now define

$$\sigma = q \cdot p^2 + r + \left\lfloor \mathsf{PowersofTwo}_\eta(s) \cdot \frac{p}{2^{\eta+1}} \right\rceil,$$

  where the components of q are randomly chosen from $[0, q_0) \cap \mathbb{Z}$ and those of r from $(-2^\rho, 2^\rho) \cap \mathbb{Z}$. The secret key is $\mathsf{sk} = \{p\}$ and the public key is $\mathsf{pk} = \{x_0, x_1, \cdots, x_\tau, y, \sigma, z\}$.
- SIDGHV.$\text{Encrypt}_t(\mathsf{pk}, m \in [t])$. Choose a random subset $S \subset \{1, \cdots, \tau\}$ and output

$$c \leftarrow [m \cdot y + \sum_{i \in S} x_i]_{x_0}.$$

- SIDGHV.$\text{Decrypt}_t(\mathsf{sk}, c)$. Output $m \leftarrow \left\lfloor t \cdot \frac{c}{p} \right\rceil \mod t$.
- SIDGHV.$\text{Add}_t(\mathsf{pk}, c_1, c_2)$. Output $c' \leftarrow c_1 + c_2 \mod x_0$.
- SIDGHV.$\text{Convert}_t(\mathsf{pk}, c)$. Output $c' \leftarrow 2 \cdot \langle \sigma, \mathsf{BitDecomp}_\eta(c) \rangle$, where $c = (\lfloor c \cdot z_i \rceil \mod 2^\eta)_{1 \leq i \leq \Theta}$.

- SIDGHV.$\text{Mult}_t(\mathsf{pk}, c_1, c_2)$. Output $c' \leftarrow [\text{SIDGHV.Convert}(\mathsf{pk}, c_1 \cdot c_2)]_{x_0}$.

Remark 3. In the original SIDGHV.Mult procedure need message space parameter t and this makes simultaneous multiplication impossible when the message space is $\mathbb{Z}_M$ where $M = \prod t_i^{k_i}$. So we described the variant form of original SIDGHV.Convert algorithm in [6].

Semantic Security. Security for this scheme is from same problem introduced in [6]. The only difference is change of message space from $\mathbb{Z}_2$ to $\mathbb{Z}_t$, so we omit this part.

Conditions on the Parameters. The parameters must satisfy the following conditions for security parameter λ and message space $\mathbb{Z}_t$:

- $\rho = \Omega(\lambda)$ to avoid brute force attacks on noise [3,8],
- $\eta \geq \rho + O(L(\log \lambda + \log t))$, where L is the depth of multiplication of the circuits to be evaluated,
- $\gamma \geq \omega((2\eta - \rho)^2 \cdot \log \lambda)$ to avoid lattice-based attacks [7,14],
- $\Theta^2 \geq \gamma \cdot \omega(\log \lambda)$ to avoid lattice attacks on the subset sum problem [7],
- $\tau \geq \gamma + 2\lambda$ to apply the leftover hash lemma.

4.2 Homomorphic Operations with $\mathcal{M} = \mathbb{Z}_{t^a}$

During bootstrapping, we use homomorphic addition and multiplication between ciphertexts on the message space $\mathcal{M} = \mathbb{Z}_{t^a}$ for $1 \leq a \leq \log_t \lambda$. Homomorphic addition and multiplication are described below. Note that x_0 is defined in the same manner as in the previous section, and the definition of SIDGHV.Eval is heuristic because method of evaluation depend on formation of given polynomial.

- SIDGHV.Add$_t^a$(pk, c_1, c_2) Output $c_1 + c_2 \bmod x_0$.
- SIDGHV.Mult$_t^a$(pk, c_1, c_2). Output SIDGHV.Convert(pk, $t^{a-1} \cdot c_1 \cdot c_2$)
- SIDGHV.Eval$_t^a$(pk, f, c). Output homomorphic evaluation of ciphertext c with polynomial f by operations defined as above.

A ciphertext $c = q \cdot p^2 + (t^a r^* + m) \cdot \lfloor p/t^a \rfloor + r$ has two kinds of errors, r and r^*. We call c a ciphertext with noise (ρ, ρ^*) if $|r| < 2^\rho$ and $|r^*| < 2^{\rho^*}$. Lemma 3 shows the correctness of SIDGHV.Add$_t^a$ and SIDGHV.Mult$_t^a$ as well as analysis on noise growth during the homomorphic operations.

Lemma 3 (Noise growth analysis). *Let c_1 and c_2 be ciphertexts with noise (ρ_1, ρ_1^*) and (ρ_2, ρ_2^*), respectively. Then,*

- *SIDGHV.Add$_t^a$(pk, c_1, c_2) is a ciphertext with noise $(\rho + 2, \rho^* + 1)$*
- *SIDGHV.Mult$_t^a$(pk, c_1, c_2) is a ciphertext with noise $(\rho + \rho^* + a \log t + 8, \log \Theta)$*

Here, $\rho = \max(\rho_1, \rho_2)$ and $\rho^* = \max(\rho_1^*, \rho_2^*)$.

Proof. In Appendix.   □

4.3 Homomorphic Digit Extraction for Scale-Invariant SHE over the Integers

During homomorphic digit extraction, we use various message spaces from $\mathbb{Z}_t$ to $\mathbb{Z}_{t^{n+1}}$. Let $\mathcal{E}_k(m)$ be a ciphertext of m with message space $\mathbb{Z}_{t^k}$ in the form of $q \cdot p^2 + \lfloor p/t^k \rfloor \cdot (m + t^k \cdot r^*) + r$. The polynomial $F_{t,n}$ is from Sect. 2.2. The following algorithm represents homomorphic digit extraction with scale-invariant FHE over the integers:

- HomExt(c). Input ciphertext c of message space $\mathbb{Z}_{t^{n+1}}$.
  Let $c_{0,0} \leftarrow c$.

$$c_{i,j+1} \leftarrow \text{SIDGHV.Eval}_t^{n-i+1}(\text{pk}, F_{t,n}, c_{i,j}) \text{ for } 0 \leq i < n, \ 0 \leq j < n - i,$$

$$c_{i,0} \leftarrow c_{0,0} - c_{0,i} - c_{1,i-1} - \cdots - c_{i-1,1} \text{ for } 1 \leq i \leq n,$$

and output $c_{n,0}$.

To understand the above algorithm, we need to check when we can change the message space for a fixed ciphertext. In scale invarient FHE over the integer, $\mathcal{E}_k(m)$ can be treated as $\mathcal{E}_{k'}(t^{k'-k}m)$ for $k < k'$. Conversely, if m is a multiple of $t^{k'-k}$, $\mathcal{E}_{k'}(m)$ can be treated as $\mathcal{E}_k(m/t^{k'-k})$.

The following lemma shows the correctness of the proposed homomorphic digit extraction algorithm.

Lemma 4 (Correctness of HomExt). *For given $m = b_{0,0}$, define $b_{i,j}$:*

$$b_{i,0} = (b_{0,0} - \sum_{j=0}^{i-1} t^j \cdot b_{j,i-j} \bmod t^{n+1})/t^i \text{ for } 1 \leq i \leq n,$$

$$b_{i,j+1} = F_{t,n}(b_{i,j}) \text{ for } 0 \leq i < n, \ 0 \leq j \leq n - i.$$

If $c_0 = \mathcal{E}_{n+1}(b_{0,0})$, and

$$c_{i,0} = c_{0,0} - \sum_{j=0}^{i-1} c_{j,i-j} \text{ for } 1 \leq i \leq n,$$

$$c_{i,j+1} = SIDGHV.Eval_t^{n-i+1}(pk, F_{t,n}, c_{i,j}) \text{ for } 0 \leq i < n, \ 0 \leq j \leq n - i.$$

Then, $c_{i,0} = \mathcal{E}_{n-i+1}(b_{i,0}) = \mathcal{E}_1(m\langle n \rangle_t)$ for $0 \leq i \leq n$.

Proof. In Appendix. ◻

Now we can homomorphically evaluate digit-extraction, and this scheme satisfies all conditions in Sect. 3. Our method can be adapted to this scheme.

4.4 Our Method on CLT Scheme

For an η-bit odd integer p and integer q_0 in $[0, 2^\gamma/p^2)$, we define the set

$$\mathcal{D}_{p,q_0}^\rho = \{\text{Choose } q \leftarrow [0, q_0), r \leftarrow (-2^\rho, 2^\rho) : \text{Output } p^2 \cdot q + r\}.$$

- KeyGen(1^λ). Generate $pk = \{x_0, x_1, \cdots, x_\tau, \boldsymbol{\sigma}, \boldsymbol{z}\}$ as in Sect. 4.1. Set $x_p = \lfloor t^{\kappa+1}/p \rceil$, choose a random a Θ'-bit vector $\boldsymbol{s}'$ with Hamming weight θ', and let $S' = \{i : s_i' = 1\}$. Choose a random integer $u_i \in [0, t^{\kappa+1})$ such that $\sum_{i \in S'} u_i = x_p$. For $n = \lceil \log_t \theta' \rceil + 3$, generate

$$v_i = q_i \cdot p^2 + \left\lfloor \frac{p}{t^{n+1}} \right\rfloor \cdot s_i' + r_i$$

and $v_0 = q \cdot p^2 + \left\lfloor \frac{p}{t^{n+1}} \right\rfloor \cdot \frac{t^n}{2} + r$, with $q, q_i \in [0, q_0)$ and $r, r_i \in (-2^\rho, 2^\rho)$ for $1 \leq i \leq \Theta'$. The secret key is $sk = \{p\}$ and the public key is $pk^* = \{pk, \boldsymbol{u}, \boldsymbol{v}\}$.
- HomSum($c, \boldsymbol{u}, \boldsymbol{v}$). Generate $w_0 = 1$, $w_i = \lfloor c \cdot u_i/t^{\kappa-n} \rceil \bmod t^{n+1}$ for $n = \lceil \log_t \theta' \rceil + 3$, and output

$$c' \leftarrow \sum_{i=0}^{\Theta'} v_i \cdot w_i \bmod x_0.$$

- HomExt(c). Let $c_{0,0} \leftarrow c$.

$$c_{i,j+1} \leftarrow \texttt{SIDGHV.Eval}_t^{n-i+1}(\texttt{pk}, F_{t,n}, c_{i,j}) \text{ for } j = 0 \text{ to } j = n - i,$$

$$c_{i,0} \leftarrow c_{0,0} - c_{0,i} - c_{1,i-1} - \cdots - c_{i-1,1},$$

for $i = 0$ to $i = n$ and output $c_{n,0}$.
- Bootstrap$(c, \boldsymbol{u}, \boldsymbol{v})$. Output $c^* \leftarrow \texttt{HomExt}(\texttt{HomSum}(c, \boldsymbol{u}, \boldsymbol{v}))$.

Remark 4. If the scheme in Sect. 4.1 becomes batch version, bootstrapping procedure above also becomes batch version.

4.5   Conditions on the Parameters

The security of the squashed scheme has been studied in [7,8,14]. Here, λ is a security parameter, and γ is as in the previous section.

- $n = \lceil \log_t \theta \rceil + 3$ for the correctness of squashed decryption circuit,
- $\kappa' > (\gamma + \lambda)/\log t$ for the correctness of squashed decryption circuit,
- $\Theta'^2 \geq \gamma \cdot \omega(\log \lambda)$ to avoid a lattice-based attack on the subset sum problem [7,8],
- $\binom{\Theta'}{\theta'/2} \geq 2^\lambda$ to avoid an attack on the sparse subset sum problem [1].

Remark 5. n can be a bit smaller than $\lceil \log_t \theta \rceil + 3$. For example, with security parameter $\lambda = 72$, we set $t = 2$, $n = 4$, $\Theta' = 8000$, and $\theta' = 15$.

5   Analysis of Proposed Bootstrapping Method

Our analysis can be more tight for binary message space, but various form of polynomial $F_{t,n}(X)$ makes it very hard. In this section, we first check the correctness of our bootstrapping method and analyze the noise growth during bootstrapping procedure. Also, we compute the number of homomorphic multiplications in our method, which directly implies the efficiency of our method.

Theorem 1 (Correctness and Noise analysis). $c^* \leftarrow Bootstrap(pk, c)$, *then* c^* *is ciphertext with noise:* $(\rho_2, \rho_2^*) = (\rho + (n + 1)\log t + \log(\Theta' + 1) + n\log t(\log t + \log \Theta + 8) \cdot (1 + \epsilon), \log \Theta + n)$ *for* $\epsilon = \left(\frac{n+1}{2} \cdot \log t + t + \frac{n+2}{\log t} \right)/(\log t + \log \Theta + 8)$ *and two ciphertext* c, c^* *with same messages.*

Proof. In Appendix. $\square$

Since the first noise grows approximately $(\log t + \log \Theta + 8)$ per each multiplication, we can think of the degree of Bootstrap circuit is

$$2^{n \log t(1+\epsilon)+\epsilon_1} = O(\lambda^{1+\epsilon+\frac{\epsilon_1}{n \log t}}) = O(\lambda^{1+\epsilon_2})$$

where $\epsilon_1 = \{(n + 1)\log t + \log(\Theta' + 1)\}/(\log t + \log \Theta + 8)$.

Theorem 2. *The number of multiplication operations in our bootstrapping algorithm is $O(n(n+1)/2) = O(\log^2 \lambda)$.*

Proof. We will treat t as a constant, so the number of multiplication while evaluating polynomial $F_{t,n}$ is constant. The number of evaluation k is equal to $1 + 2 + \cdots + n = n(n+1)/2$; thus, the number of multiplication operations is $O(n(n+1)/2)$. $\qquad\square$

As a result, in our bootstrapping method, the number of homomorphic multiplications is $O(\log^2 \lambda)$ and multiplicative degree is $O(\lambda^{1+\epsilon})$. Comparing to the previous methods including the result in [13], $O(\lambda^4 \log^6 \lambda)$ multiplications, our method shows significantly improved result within the framework of efficiency. In addition to theoretical analysis, we will explain the implementation result of our bootstrapping method applying to CLT scheme in next section.

6 Implementation

While implementing our bootstrapping method, we used word decomposition and the powers of word instead of BitDecomp and PowersofTwo with word size $w = 32$. Moreover, in order to use a public key of reasonable size, we compressed the ciphertext using the same method as in [7]. We implemented our bootstrapping method and checked the running time of Bootstrap. Furthermore, for precise comparison with other FHE, we implemented the homomorphic evaluation of the AES-128 circuit, which has emerged lately as a standard homomorphic evaluation circuit.

Parameters ($\ell = 500, \lambda = 72$)

> AGCD parameters: $\eta = 192$, $\gamma = 3.8 \times 10^5$, $\rho = 52$
> Convert parameters: $\Theta = 1500$, $\theta = 100$
> Bootstrap parameters: $\Theta' = 8000$, $\theta' = 15$

Efficiency

> The number of Add: $8000 + 10$
> The number of Mult: 8
> Error size after bootstrapping: 122

AES evaluation

> Bootstrap Time: $6.7 \times 128\,\text{s}$ (for 128 number of ciphertexts)
> SubByte Time: $128\,\text{s}$
> **Total AES** Time: $4020\,\text{s}$
> **Relative** Time: $8\,\text{s}$

Remark 6. Implementations of our bootstrapping method and homomorphic AES evaluation on a desktop with eight core Intel(R) Core(TM) i7-2600 CPU @ 3.40 GHz processors and 16 GB RAM using C++ and GMP 6.0.0 [11].

Our bootstrapping procedure for one ciphertext takes about $6\,\mathrm{s}$. This result is faster than results in FHE over the integers [4,7,14], and also compatable with the result in [12], $320\,\mathrm{s}$ for 16000-bit message space. Comparing to the results of homomorphic AES evaluation in [4,6], $13\,\mathrm{min}$ and $23\,\mathrm{s}$ per block at security level $\lambda = 72$, homomorphic AES evaluation applying our bootstrapping method takes $8\,\mathrm{s}$ per block on a 8-core machine at $3.4\,\mathrm{GHz}$ for same security level.

Acknowledgements. This work was supported by National Research Foundation of Korea under both contract number NRF-2013H1A2A1033939 and contract number NRF-2016H1A2A1906584. We would like to thank Jinsu Kim and Jiseung Kim for their valuable comments.

A   Proof of Theorem and Lemmas

Lemma 3 (Noise growth analysis). *Let c_1, c_2 are ciphertext with noise (ρ_1, ρ_1^*) and (ρ_2, ρ_2^*), then*

- *SIDGHV.$Add_t^a(pk, c_1, c_2)$ is ciphertext with noise $(\rho + 2, \rho^* + 1)$*
- *SIDGHV.$Mult_t^a(pk, c_1, c_2)$ is ciphertext with noise $(\rho + \rho^* + a\log t + 8, \log \Theta)$*

Here $\rho = max(\rho_1, \rho_2)$ and $\rho^* = max(\rho_1^*, \rho_2^*)$.

Proof. First, lets prove about SIDGHV.Add part. Let c_1, c_2 as below.

$$c_1 = q_1 \cdot p^2 + \lfloor p/t^a \rfloor \cdot (m_1 + t^a r_1^*) + r_1,$$

$$c_2 = q_2 \cdot p^2 + \lfloor p/t^a \rfloor \cdot (m_2 + t^a r_2^*) + r_2.$$

Then addition of c_1 and c_2 is

$$c_1 + c_2 = (q_1 + q_2) \cdot p^2 + \lfloor p/t^a \rfloor \cdot ([m_1 + m_2]_{t^a} + t^a(r_1^* + r_2^* + 1/0)) + r_1 + r_2$$
$$= q_3 \cdot p^2 + \lfloor p/t^a \rfloor \cdot (m_3 + t^a r_3^*) + r_3$$

for $r_3^* < 2^{\rho_1^*} + 2^{\rho_2^*} + 1$ and $r_3 < 2^{\rho_1} + 2^{\rho_2}$. The ciphertext of $[m_1 + m_2]_{2^a}$ is $c_3 = [c_1 + c_2]_{x_0} = c_1 + c_2 - k \cdot x_0$ for $k \in \{0, 1\}$ since $c_1, c_2 < x_0$. Therefore, $c_3 \leftarrow$ SIDGHV.$Add^a(pk, c_1, c_2)$ is a ciphertext $c_3 = q \cdot p^2 + \lfloor p/t^a \rfloor (m + t^a r^*) + r$ satisfying $r^* < 2^{\rho_1^*} + 2^{\rho_2^*} + 1$ and $r < 2^{\rho_1} + 2^{\rho_2} + 2^{\rho_0}$.

Second part is about SIDGHV.Mult algorithm. Let c_1, c_2 as defined above, and k, l be integers such that $\lfloor p/t^a \rfloor = (p - k)/t^a$ and $\lfloor p^2/t^a \rfloor = (p^2 - l)/t^a$. Then following equation holds,

$$c_3 = t^a \cdot c_1 \cdot c_2 = q_3 \cdot p^2 + ((p - k)^2/t^a) \cdot (m_1 + t^a r_1^*)(m_2 + t^a r_2^*) + R$$
$$= q_3 \cdot p^2 + ((p^2 - l)/t^a) \cdot (m_1 m_2 \bmod t^a) + R + R'$$
$$= q_3 \cdot p^2 + \lfloor p^2/t^a \rfloor \cdot (m_1 m_2 \bmod t^a) + r_3$$

where $|R| < 3 \cdot 2^\eta \cdot t^a \cdot 2^{\rho^* + \rho}$ and $|R'| < 2 \cdot 2^\eta \cdot t^{2a} \cdot 2^{2\rho^*} + t^{2a} \cdot 2^{2\rho^*} < 3 \cdot 2^\eta \cdot t^{2a} \cdot 2^{2\rho^*}$. Therefore, the inequality $|r_3| < 6 \cdot 2^{\eta + a\log t + \rho + \rho^*}$ holds when assuming $a\log t + \rho^* < \rho$.

Now we will analyze the error of ciphertext after processing **Convert** procedure. We followed the proof of lemma 1 in [6]. Let $\lceil \log r_3 \rceil = \rho_3 < \eta + 2a \log t + \rho + \rho^* + 3$ and $c \leftarrow$ **Convert**(c_3/t), then from the following equation:

$$\sigma = p^2 \cdot q + r + \lfloor s' \cdot \frac{p}{2^{\eta+1}} \rceil.$$

Let $c' = \mathsf{BitDecomp}_\eta(c)$, then we have:

$$c = 2\langle \sigma, c' \rangle = 2p^2 \cdot \langle q, c' \rangle + 2\langle r, c' \rangle + 2\langle \lfloor s' \cdot \frac{p}{2^{\eta+1}} \rceil, c' \rangle.$$

Since the components of c' are bits,

$$2\langle \lfloor s' \cdot \frac{p}{2^{\eta+1}} \rceil, c' \rangle = \langle \frac{p}{2^\eta} \cdot s', c' \rangle + \nu_2 = \frac{p}{2^\eta} \langle s', c' \rangle + \nu_2,$$

where $|\nu_2| < \Theta \cdot \eta$. From the definition of BitDecomp and PowersofTwo, we have $\langle s', c' \rangle = \langle s, c \rangle \bmod 2^\eta = \langle s, c \rangle + q_2 \cdot 2^\eta$. Moreover

$$\langle s, c \rangle = \sum s_i \left\lfloor \frac{c_3}{t} \cdot z_i \right\rceil + \Delta \cdot 2^\eta = \sum \frac{s_i \cdot c_3 \cdot z_i}{t} + \delta_1 + \Delta \cdot 2^\eta = \frac{c_3}{t} \cdot \langle s, z \rangle + \delta_1 + \Delta \cdot 2^\eta,$$

for some $\Delta \in \mathbb{Z}$ and $|\delta_1| \leq \Theta/2$. Using $\langle s, z \rangle = 2^\eta \cdot t/p^2 - \epsilon - \mu \cdot 2^\eta \cdot t$ for some $\mu \in \mathbb{Z}$, and $c_3 = r_3 + \lfloor p^2/t^a \rfloor \cdot m + q_3 \cdot p^2$, this gives following equation:

$$\langle s, c \rangle = q_3 \cdot 2^\eta + \frac{2^\eta}{t^a} \cdot m - \frac{2^\eta \cdot \ell}{p^2 t^a} \cdot m + r_3 \cdot \frac{2^\eta}{p^2} - \frac{c_3}{t} \cdot \epsilon + \delta_1 + (\Delta - c_3 \cdot \mu) \cdot 2^\eta.$$

Therefore we can write

$$\langle s, c \rangle = q_1 \cdot 2^\eta + m \cdot \frac{2^\eta}{t^a} + r^*$$

for some $r^* \in \mathbb{Z}$, with $|r^*| \leq 2^{\rho_3 - \eta + 3}$. Now we get an equation below:

$$2\langle \lfloor \frac{p}{2^{\eta+1}} \cdot s' \rceil, c' \rangle = q_4 \cdot p + m \cdot \frac{p}{t^a} + r^* \cdot \frac{p}{2^\eta} + \nu_2$$

with $|q_4| \leq \Theta$; namely the components of $(p/2^{\eta+1}) \cdot s'$ are smaller than p and c' is a binary vector. This gives

$$2\langle \lfloor \frac{p}{2^{\eta+1}} \cdot s' \rceil, c' \rangle = (t^a q_4 + m) \cdot \lfloor \frac{p}{t^a} \rfloor + r_2^*$$

with $|r_2^*| \leq 2^{\rho_3 - \eta + 4}$. Then we obtain:

$$c = 2p^2 \cdot \langle q, c' \rangle + 2\langle r, c' \rangle + (t^a q_4 + m) \cdot \lfloor \frac{p}{t^a} \rfloor + r_2^*$$

$$c = 2q'' \cdot p^2 + (t^a q_4 + m) \cdot \lfloor \frac{p}{t^a} \rfloor + r'$$

where $|r'| \leq |r_2^*| + \eta \cdot \Theta \cdot 2^{\rho+1} \leq 2^{\rho_3 - \eta + 4} + \eta \cdot \Theta \cdot 2^{\rho+1} < 2^{a \log t + \rho + \rho^* + 7} + \eta \cdot \Theta \cdot 2^{\lambda+1}$. Therefore, the return ciphertext c has following noise:

$$(\rho + \rho^* + a \log t + 8, \log \Theta) \text{ if } a \log t + \rho + \rho^* + 5 > \log \eta + \log \Theta + \lambda.$$

Above equation prove the second part of this lemman. □

Lemma 4 (Correctness of HomMsb). *For given* $m = b_{0,0}$, *define* $b_{i,j}$:

$$b_{i,0} = \left(b_{0,0} - \sum_{j=0}^{i-1} t^j \cdot b_{j,i-j} \bmod t^{n+1}\right)/t^i \ \text{for } 1 \le i \le n$$

and $b_{i,j+1} = F_{t,n}(b_{i,j})$ *for* $0 \le i < n,\ 0 \le j \le n-i$.

If $c_0 = \mathcal{E}_{n+1}(b_{0,0})$, *and*

$$c_{i,0} = c_{0,0} - \sum_{j=0}^{i-1} c_{j,i-j} \ \text{for } 1 \le i \le n$$

& $c_{i,j+1} = SIDGHV.Eval_t^{n-i+1}(pk, F_{t,n}, c_{i,j})$ *for* $0 \le i < n,\ 0 \le j \le n-i$.

Then, $c_{i,0} = \mathcal{E}_{n-i+1}(b_{i,0})$ *for* $0 \le i \le n$.

Proof. We use induction on i. The statement is clear when $i = 0$. Suppose the proposition is true for $i < m$. Then we have

$$\begin{aligned}
c_{m,0} &= c_{0,0} - \sum_{j=0}^{m-1} c_{j,m-j} \\
&= c_0 - \sum_{j=0}^{m-1} \mathcal{E}_{n-j+1}\left(F_{t,n}^{m-j}(b_{j,0})\right) \\
&= c_0 - \sum_{j=0}^{m-1} \mathcal{E}_{n+1}\left(t^j F_{t,n}^{m-j}(b_{j,0})\right) \\
&= \mathcal{E}_{n+1}\left(b_{0,0} - \sum_{j=0}^{m-1} t^j F_{t,n}^{m-j}(b_{j,0})\right) \\
&= \mathcal{E}_{n+1}\left(b_{0,0} - \sum_{j=0}^{m-1} t^j b_{j,m-j} \bmod t^{n+1}\right). \\
&= \mathcal{E}_{n+1}\left(t^m b_{m,0}\right) = \mathcal{E}_{n+1-m}(b_{m,0}).
\end{aligned}$$

Then we can see that this lemma holds for any positive $i \le n$. And this means $c_{n,0} = \mathcal{E}_1(b_{n,0}) = \mathcal{E}_1(m\langle n\rangle_t)$, so this lemma shows the correctness of our bootstrapping procedure. □

Theorem 1 (Correctness and Noise analysis of Bootstrap). $c^* \leftarrow$ Bootstrap(pk, c), *then* c^* *is ciphertext with noise*

$$(\rho_2, \rho_2^*) = (\rho + (n+1)\log t + \log(\Theta' + 1) + n\log t(\log t + \log\Theta + 8) \cdot (1 + \epsilon),\ \log\Theta + n)$$

for $\epsilon = \left(\frac{n+1}{2} \cdot \log t + t + \frac{n+2}{\log t}\right)/(\log t + \log\Theta + 8)$ *and two ciphertext* c, c^* *with same messages.*

Proof.

1. *Expand*

$$v_i = q_i \cdot p^2 + \left\lfloor \frac{p}{t^{n+1}} \right\rfloor \cdot s_i + r_i \text{ and } v_0 = q \cdot p^2 + \left\lfloor \frac{p}{t^{n+1}} \right\rfloor \cdot \left\lfloor \frac{t^n}{2} \right\rfloor + r \text{ with } q, \ q_i \in [0, q_0)$$

and r, $r_i \in (-2^\rho, 2^\rho)$ for $1 \leq i \leq \Theta'$. So if $c_{0,0} \leftarrow \text{Expand}(c, \boldsymbol{y})$, then

$$c_{0,0} = q' \cdot p^2 + \left\lfloor \frac{p}{t^{n+1}} \right\rfloor \cdot \left(\left(\sum s_i w_i + \left\lfloor \frac{t^n}{2} \right\rfloor \right) \bmod t^{n+1} + r^* t^{n+1} \right) + r'$$

for $|r'| = |\sum_{i=1}^{\Theta'} w_i r_i + r| < (\Theta' + 1)2^{\rho + (n+1)\log t}$ and $|r^*| \leq \Theta'$. Therefore, $c_{0,0}$ is a ciphertext with noise $(\rho_1, \rho_1^*) = (\rho + (n+1)\log t + \log(\Theta'+1), \ \log \Theta')$ whose message space is $\mathbb{Z}_{t^{n+1}}$.

2. *HomMsb*

   Let $c_{i,j}$ is a ciphertext with noise $(\rho_{i,j}, \rho_{i,j}^*)$, then the equations $\rho_{0,0} = \rho + (n+1)\log t + \log(\Theta'+1)$ and $\rho_{0,0}^* = \log \Theta'$ holds by above *Expand* procedure. By applying Lemma 3, we can set

$$\rho_{i,0} = \max\{\rho_{0,i}, \cdots, \rho_{i-1,1}\} + 2i, \ \rho_{i,0}^* = \log \Theta + i \log t$$

for $1 \leq i \leq n$.

First, we will show the equality

$$\max\{\rho_{0,i+1}, \cdots, \rho_{i,1}\} = \rho_{i,1}$$

holds for $0 \leq i \leq n - 1$. Since $c_{j,i-j+1} = \text{SIDGHV.Eval}_t^{n-j+1}(\text{pk}, F_{t,n}, c_{j,i-j})$ for $0 \leq j \leq i$, it is sufficient to compare noise increase of $c_{j,i-j}$ after SIDGHV.Mult_t^a. For $1 \leq j \leq i - 1$, the increase of first noise of $c_{j,i-j}$ is less than or equal to $\log \Theta + (n+1)\log t + 8$, and the increase of noise of $c_{i,0}$ is $\rho_{i,0}^* + (n-i+1)\log t + 8 = \log \Theta + (n+1)\log t + 8$. Therefore, the equality $\max\{\rho_{0,i+1}, \cdots, \rho_{i,1}\} = \rho_{i,1}$ holds and we can get

$$\rho_{i,0} = \rho_{i-1,1} + 2i.$$

Second, we will analyze the noise increase in while evaluating $F_{t,n}$. $F_{t,n}$ is a polynomial of degree t and its coefficients are bounded by t^{n+1}. Then, we can regard each term of $F_{t,n}$ is contained by at most t times of multiplications, so we get $\rho_{i-1,1} = \rho_{i-1,0} + \lceil \log t \rceil \cdot (\log t \cdot (n-i+2) + \log \Theta + 8) + t \lceil \log t \rceil$. Now, we obtain a recursion formula :

$$\rho_{i,0} = \rho_{i-1,0} + \lceil \log t \rceil \cdot (\log t \cdot (n-i+2) + \log \Theta + 8) + t \lceil \log t \rceil + 2i.$$

The consequence of the recursion formula is

$$\rho_{n,0} = \rho_{0,0} + \log^2 t \cdot \frac{n^2 + 3n}{2} + n \log t(\log \Theta + 8) + nt \log t + n^2 + 2n$$

$$= \rho_{0,0} + n \log t(\log t + \log \Theta + 8)(1 + \epsilon)$$

for $\epsilon = \left(\frac{n+1}{2} \cdot \log t + t + \frac{n+2}{\log t} \right) / (\log t + \log \Theta + 8)$.

3. Correctness

$$CTX_t^{\rho,\log\Theta}(m,1) \xrightarrow{\text{Expand}} CTX_t^{\rho_1,\rho_1^*}(\sum s_i w_i + \lfloor t^n/2 \rceil \bmod t^{n+1}, n+1)$$

$$\| \quad\quad\quad\quad\quad\quad\quad\quad\quad\quad\quad\quad\quad\quad\quad\quad\quad\quad\quad\quad$$

$$\text{Bootstrap} \downarrow \quad\quad\quad\quad\quad\quad\quad\quad\quad\quad\quad\quad\quad \text{HomMsb} \downarrow$$

$$CTX_t^{\rho_2,\rho_2^*}(m,1) =\!=\!=\!=\! CTX_t^{\rho_2,\rho_2^*}((\sum s_i w_i + \lfloor t^n/2 \rceil \bmod t^{n+1})\langle n \rangle_t, 1)$$

Top side of the diagram was proved in 1. Expand. Also, Lemma 4 and 2. HomMsb exactly signify the right side of the diagram, and the discussion in Sect. 4.3 shows the equality $m = (\sum s_i w_i + \lfloor t^n/2 \rceil \bmod t^{n+1})\langle n \rangle_t$ holds so that bottom side of the diagram is proved. □

References

1. Bhattacharyya, A., Indyk, P., Woodruff, D.P., Xie, N.: The complexity of linear dependence problems in vector spaces. In: ICS, pp. 496–508 (2011)

2. Chen, H., Han, K.: Homomorphic lower digits removal and improved FHE bootstrapping. In: Nielsen, J.B., Rijmen, V. (eds.) EUROCRYPT 2018. LNCS, vol. 10820, pp. 315–337. Springer, Cham (2018). https://doi.org/10.1007/978-3-319-78381-9_12

3. Chen, Y., Nguyen, P.Q.: Faster algorithms for approximate common divisors: breaking fully-homomorphic-encryption challenges over the integers. In: Pointcheval, D., Johansson, T. (eds.) EUROCRYPT 2012. LNCS, vol. 7237, pp. 502–519. Springer, Heidelberg (2012). https://doi.org/10.1007/978-3-642-29011-4_30

4. Cheon, J.H., et al.: Batch fully homomorphic encryption over the integers. In: Johansson, T., Nguyen, P.Q. (eds.) EUROCRYPT 2013. LNCS, vol. 7881, pp. 315–335. Springer, Heidelberg (2013). https://doi.org/10.1007/978-3-642-38348-9_20

5. Cheon, J.H., Stehlé, D.: Fully homomophic encryption over the integers revisited. In: Oswald, E., Fischlin, M. (eds.) EUROCRYPT 2015. LNCS, vol. 9056, pp. 513–536. Springer, Heidelberg (2015). https://doi.org/10.1007/978-3-662-46800-5_20

6. Coron, J.-S., Lepoint, T., Tibouchi, M.: Scale-invariant fully homomorphic encryption over the integers. In: Krawczyk, H. (ed.) PKC 2014. LNCS, vol. 8383, pp. 311–328. Springer, Heidelberg (2014). https://doi.org/10.1007/978-3-642-54631-0_18

7. Coron, J.-S., Mandal, A., Naccache, D., Tibouchi, M.: Fully homomorphic encryption over the integers with shorter public keys. In: Rogaway, P. (ed.) CRYPTO 2011. LNCS, vol. 6841, pp. 487–504. Springer, Heidelberg (2011). https://doi.org/10.1007/978-3-642-22792-9_28

8. Coron, J.-S., Naccache, D., Tibouchi, M.: Public key compression and modulus switching for fully homomorphic encryption over the integers. In: Pointcheval, D., Johansson, T. (eds.) EUROCRYPT 2012. LNCS, vol. 7237, pp. 446–464. Springer, Heidelberg (2012). https://doi.org/10.1007/978-3-642-29011-4_27

9. Gentry, C.: Fully homomorphic encryption using ideal lattices. In: STOC, vol. 9, pp. 169–178 (2009)

10. Gentry, C., Halevi, S., Smart, N.P.: Better bootstrapping in fully homomorphic encryption. In: Fischlin, M., Buchmann, J., Manulis, M. (eds.) PKC 2012. LNCS, vol. 7293, pp. 1–16. Springer, Heidelberg (2012). https://doi.org/10.1007/978-3-642-30057-8_1

11. Granlund, T., et al.: The GNU Multiple Precision Arithmetic Library. TMG Datakonsult, Boston, MA, USA, vol. 2, no. 2 (1996)

12. Halevi, S., Shoup, V.: Bootstrapping for HElib. In: Oswald, E., Fischlin, M. (eds.) EUROCRYPT 2015. LNCS, vol. 9056, pp. 641–670. Springer, Heidelberg (2015). https://doi.org/10.1007/978-3-662-46800-5_25

13. Nuida, K., Kurosawa, K.: (Batch) fully homomorphic encryption over integers for non-binary message spaces. In: Oswald, E., Fischlin, M. (eds.) EUROCRYPT 2015. LNCS, vol. 9056, pp. 537–555. Springer, Heidelberg (2015). https://doi.org/10.1007/978-3-662-46800-5_21

14. van Dijk, M., Gentry, C., Halevi, S., Vaikuntanathan, V.: Fully homomorphic encryption over the integers. In: Gilbert, H. (ed.) EUROCRYPT 2010. LNCS, vol. 6110, pp. 24–43. Springer, Heidelberg (2010). https://doi.org/10.1007/978-3-642-13190-5_2

Complete Addition Law for Montgomery Curves

Jaeheon Kim[1], Je Hong Park[1], Dong-Chan Kim[2(✉)], and Woo-Hwan Kim[1]

[1] The Affiliated Institute of ETRI, Daejeon, Korea
{jaeheon,jhpark,whkim5}@nsr.re.kr
[2] Kookmin University, Seoul, Korea
dckim@kookmin.ac.kr

Abstract. Montgomery curves allow efficient and side-channel resistant computation of ECDH using the Montgomery ladder. But the addition law of a Montgomery curve derived from the chord-tangent method is less efficient than other curve models such as a short Weierstrass curve and an Edwards curve. So, the usage of a Montgomery curve is strictly limited to ECDH only, such as X25519 and X448 functions in IETF RFC 7748. For other operations including fixed-base and multiple scalar multiplications, their birationally-equivalent (twisted) Edwards curves are recommended for use since the conversions between Montgomery curves and their Edwards equivalents are simple. This conversion enables the use of the efficient complete addition law of the Edwards curve that works for all pairs of input points with no exceptional cases. As a result, the combination allows secure and exception-free implementations, but at the expense of additional storage for the two curve parameters and for the conversion between them. However, smart devices in IoT environments that mainly operate ECDH (for example, RawPublicKey mode of IETF RFC 7250) do not need to implement such a conversion if a complete addition law does exist for the Montgomery curves.

To make such implementations possible, we provide a complete addition law on Montgomery curves. The explicit formulas for the complete addition law are not as efficient as those of Edwards curves, but they can make the Montgomery curve addition operation more efficient compared to using the conversion to the (twisted) Edwards equivalent. We also confirmed the validity of the comparison by implementing such two methods of realizing the addition operation on Curve25519.

Keywords: Elliptic curves · Montgomery curve · Complete addition law

1 Introduction

In [16], Montgomery considered an elliptic curve model over a non-binary field, which is now generally referred to as a Montgomery curve. Montgomery curves support optimal efficiency for computing scalar multiples of points through an

© Springer Nature Switzerland AG 2020
J. H. Seo (Ed.): ICISC 2019, LNCS 11975, pp. 260–277, 2020.
https://doi.org/10.1007/978-3-030-40921-0_16

algorithm called the Montgomery ladder [16]. In particular, the Montgomery ladder is considered one of the best scalar multiplication techniques to cope with side-channel attacks due to the inherent constant-time behavior. We refer the reader to [9] for brief history of the developments of Montgomery curve arithmetic.

Recently, IKEv2 and TLS have added two Montgomery curve parameters, Curve25519 [2] and Curve448 [13] for ephemeral key agreement [17,18,20]. Both protocols adopted the Montgomery ladder-based scalar multiplication functions X25519 and X448 described in RFC 7748 [15] to enhance efficiency as well as the prevention of side-channel attacks. However, the usage of Montgomery curves is limited to ephemeral DH key agreement. Either directly or indirectly, other models of elliptic curves, especially birationally-equivalent (twisted) Edwards curves are recommended to be used for other operations such as fixed-base and multiple scalar multiplications [7,15]. One of the reasons is that Edwards curves have an efficient *complete addition law*. An elliptic curve addition law is said to be *complete* if it correctly computes the sum of *any* two points in the elliptic curve group. Note that, although complete addition laws are typically less efficient compared to the traditional chord-tangent addition laws, it allows much simpler and exception-free code.

Though IKEv2 and TLS are general-purpose security protocols for the Internet domain, the range of their usage has been extended to Internet-of-Thing (IoT) environments [12]. For example, CoAP (Constrained Application Protocol) [21] which is a communication protocol for resource-constrained networks of smart devices is protected by DTLS. To bind DTLS for CoAP, RawPublicKey mode [21,23], where smart devices have public/private key pairs but no certificates to verify the ownership is recommended. In this case, the simplest approach for lightweight, easy and secure elliptic curve implementations is to only use the Montgomery curve with the ladder technique. However, the addition operation is required if other elliptic curve arithmetic is less frequent but may be necessary. To avoid implementing arithmetic for (twisted) Edwards equivalent in consideration of the storage of smart devices running RawPublicKey mode of CoAP, a complete addition law on the Montgomery curves is required, but not known yet.

To solve this problem, we present a complete addition law for Montgomery curves. Similar to the case of short Weierstrass curves [19], the complete addition law we provide in this paper is derived from the formulas given by Bosma and Lenstra for the elliptic curve with Weierstrass form [8]. We optimize the explicit computation of the formulas for Montgomery curves and compare it with those for other curve models. The cost of our complete addition law is $15\mathbf{M} + 2\mathbf{M}_c + (3s + 17)\mathbf{A}$, where s is the positive integer such that $X^3 + AX^2 + X - s^2$ is irreducible over k and A is the Montgomery curve coefficient. For example, the smallest s for Curve25519 and Curve448 are 1 and 3, respectively. Here $\mathbf{M}$, $\mathbf{M}_c$ and $\mathbf{A}$ are multiplication, constant multiplication and addition operations, all in the base field. Unlike other curve models, the computational cost of evaluating Montgomery curve complete addition law varies with s; the lower the value of

Table 1. Montgomery curves that have k-complete addition law

Curve	A	p	$s^{\dagger}$	Ref.
Curve25519	486,662	$2^{255} - 19$	1	[2]
Curve448	156,326	$2^{448} - 2^{224} - 1$	3	[13]
Curve383187	229,969	$2^{383} - 187$	6	[1]
M-221	117,050	$2^{221} - 3$	6	
M-383	2,065,150	$2^{383} - 187$	3	
M-511	530,438	$2^{511} - 187$	5	
ed-256-mont	$-54,314$	$2^{240}(2^{16} - 88) - 1$	5	[7]
ed-254-mont	$-55,790$	$2^{240}(2^{14} - 127) - 1$	5	
ed-256-mers	$-61,370$	$2^{256} - 189$	1	
ed-255-mers	$-240,222$	$2^{255} - 765$	2	
ed-384-mont	$-113,758$	$2^{376}(2^{8} - 79) - 1$	1	
ed-382-mont	$-2,870,790$	$2^{368}(2^{14} - 5) - 1$	1	
ed-384-mers	$-1,332,778$	$2^{384} - 317$	4	
ed-383-mers	$-2,095,962$	$2^{383} - 421$	1	
ed-512-mont	$-305,778$	$2^{496}(2^{16} - 491) - 1$	2	
ed-510-mont	$-2,320,506$	$2^{496}(2^{14} - 290) - 1$	8	
ed-512-mers	$-2,550,434$	$2^{512} - 569$	6	
ed-512-mers	$-4,390,390$	$2^{511} - 481$	2	

$^{\dagger}s$ is the smallest integers such that Eq. (3) is irreducible over k.

s, the better. Table 1 shows some known Montgomery curve parameters and the corresponding smallest s. We also derive formulas for mixed complete addition and doubling operations from our complete addition formulas.

The complete addition law presented in this paper itself is less efficient than those of other curve models. Previous studies have shown that the costs of complete addition laws of Edwards and short Weierstrass curves are $10\mathbf{M} + 1\mathbf{S} + 1\mathbf{M}_c + 7\mathbf{A}$ and $12\mathbf{M} + 2\mathbf{M}_c + 29\mathbf{A}$, respectively [5,19]. Here $\mathbf{S}$ is squaring in the base field. But it may not significantly increase overall complexity considering the proportion of general addition operations used in several protocols. In particular, the case of smart devices mainly running RawPublicKey mode of CoAP, implementing only specific Montgomery curve parameter such as Curve25519 may not be a bad choice. Note that, to use the complete addition law of the (twisted) Edwards equivalent for a given Montgomery curve, we should consider the conversions between both curves.

$$\underset{\text{Montgomery}}{P, Q} \xrightarrow{\text{conv.}} \underset{\text{(twisted) Edwards}}{P', Q'} \longrightarrow \underset{\text{(twisted) Edwards}}{R'(\leftarrow P' + Q')} \xrightarrow{\text{conv.}} \underset{\text{Montgomery}}{R}$$

The forward and backward conversions [3,9] which requires 3**M** for each (see Sect. 4), are simple and efficient in terms of scalar multiplications, but have a weight that cannot be ignored when only considering the addition operation itself of Montgomery curves. By comparing the number of base field operations and confirming the implementation results, we can see that using the complete addition law proposed in this paper is more efficient than the case based on the addition operation of (twisted) Edwards equivalent via conversions.

This paper is organized as follows. Section 2 gives preliminaries for the definitions and theories used throughout this paper. Section 3 introduces complete addition formulas for Montgomery curves and Sect. 4 gives an implementation result of the addition operation with the complete addition law on Curve25519 and shows the performance comparison with the case using the conversion to the (twisted) Edwards equivalent.

2 Preliminaries and Related Works

In this section, we provide the required background that will be used throughout the paper and a brief introduction to previous results for other curve models. Note that we follow the notations and definitions of Bosma and Lenstra [8] and Renes et al. [19] with some modifications.

2.1 Elliptic Curves and the Group Law

Let k be a field of characteristic not 2 or 3 and let $\mathbb{P}^2(k)$ be the homogeneous projective plane of dimension 2. In $\mathbb{P}^2(k)$, two points $(x_1 : y_1 : z_1)$ and $(x_2 : y_2 : z_2)$ are equal if there exists $\lambda \in k \setminus \{0\}$ such that $(x_1, y_1, z_1) = (\lambda x_2, \lambda y_2, \lambda z_2)$.

An elliptic curve E/k is a smooth algebraic curve with genus 1 defined in projective plane $\mathbb{P}^2(k)$. In general, an elliptic curve can be expressed by the Weierstrass equation

$$E : Y^2 Z + a_1 XYZ + a_3 YZ^2 = X^3 + a_2 X^2 Z + a_4 XZ^2 + a_6 Z^3,$$

where coefficients $a_j \in k$ ($j \in \{1, 2, 3, 4, 6\}$). The set $E(k)$ of all k-rational points of E is an additive abelian group with the identity $\mathcal{O} = (0 : 1 : 0)$. For any two points P and Q in $E(k)$, the addition $P + Q$ is defined by the chord-tangent method [22]. The inverse $-P$ of $P = (x : y : z) \in E(k)$ is $(x : -y - a_1 x - a_3 z : z)$.

Note that the case $P = Q$ and the other case $P \neq Q$ have different addition formulas under the chord-tangent method. Therefore, the case $P = Q$ is called *doubling*, and it is usual to distinguish it from the case of $P \neq Q$. When implementing the elliptic curve addition simply and intuitively, however, it is necessary to divide the branches into even more cases as follows:

(1) If $P = \mathcal{O}$ (i.e., $x_1 = z_1 = 0$), return Q.
(2) If $Q = \mathcal{O}$ (i.e., $x_2 = z_2 = 0$), return P.
(3) If $Q = -P$ (i.e., $x_1 z_2 = x_2 z_1$ and $(-y_1 - a_1 x_1 - a_3 z_1)z_2 = y_2 z_1$), return $\mathcal{O}$.

(4) If $P = Q$ (i.e., $x_1 z_2 = x_2 z_1$ and $y_1 z_2 = y_2 z_1$), return doubling(P).
(5) Otherwise, return addition(P, Q).

This shows that for the exception-free addition on elliptic curves using traditional doubling and addition formulas, five addition laws corresponding to each case should be reflected. However, a code with these conditional branches can cause performance overhead because the case-check routine must run whenever points are given. In addition, the difference of the number of base field operations between traditional doubling and addition formulas can be a factor that allows side-channel attacks. Therefore, a lot of research on how to unify such conditions has been considered in terms of implementation. One approach is to design *unified* addition formulas that can be used for doubling. Such unified addition formulas eliminate the need to check for equal inputs, but do not eliminate other exceptional cases.

Theoretically, it was shown by Bosma and Lenstra [8] that an elliptic curve has a complete system with only two addition laws in $E(\overline{k})$ where $\overline{k}$ is the algebraic closure of a field k. This means that, over the algebraic closure of k, at least two elliptic curve addition laws are required to work any pair of points. But, Edwards [10] proposed the first normal form for elliptic curves

$$X^2 Z^2 + Y^2 Z^2 = Z^4 + d X^2 Y^2 \quad (d \in k \setminus \{0, 1\} \text{ is not square}), \qquad (1)$$

that has a complete addition law that working on all pairs of k-rational points, referred as k-*complete addition law*. This work is generalized and optimized by Bernstein et al. [3,5,6]. In 2010, Farashahi and Joy [11] introduced a k-complete addition law of the Hessian form of elliptic curves

$$X^3 + Y^3 + Z^3 = d X Y Z \quad (d \in k \text{ and } d^3 \neq 27),$$

and in 2016, Renes et al. [19] presented a k-complete addition law of short Weierstrass curves

$$Y^2 Z = X^3 - 3 X Z^2 + b Z^3 \quad (b \in k). \qquad (2)$$

2.2   Montgomery Curve

A *Montgomery curve* over k is an elliptic curve in $\mathbb{P}^2(k)$ defined by the equation

$$E : B Y^2 Z = X^3 + A X^2 Z + X Z^2,$$

where $A, B \in k$ satisfy $B(A^2 - 4) \neq 0$. For any $P = (x_1 : y_1 : z_1)$ and $Q = (x_2 : y_2 : z_2)$ over E such that both are not $\mathcal{O}$, the point $P + Q = (x_3 : y_3 : z_3)$ is computed as follows:

$$x_3 = B u^2 v z_1 z_2 - (A z_1 z_2 + x_1 z_2 + x_2 z_1) v^3,$$
$$y_3 = -B u^3 z_1 z_2 + (A z_1 z_2 + 2 x_1 z_2 + x_2 z_1) u v^2 - y_1 z_2 v^3,$$
$$z_3 = v^3 z_1 z_2,$$

where $(u, v) := (y_2 z_1 - y_1 z_2, x_2 z_1 - x_1 z_2)$ if $P \neq Q$, and $(u, v) := (3x_1^2 + 2Ax_1 z_1 + z_1^2, 2By_1 z_1)$ if $P = Q$. When $B = 1$, the computational costs of traditional chord-tangent addition and doubling are $13\mathbf{M} + 2\mathbf{S} + \mathbf{M}_c + 7\mathbf{A}$ and $11\mathbf{M} + 3\mathbf{S} + 2\mathbf{M}_c + 11\mathbf{A}$, respectively. See Appendix A for more details.

2.3 Other Views of the Group Law

Let $f(X, Y, Z)$ be the homogeneous polynomial $Y^2 Z + a_1 XYZ + a_3 YZ^2 - X^3 - a_2 X^2 Z - a_4 XZ^2 - a_6 Z^3$ representing a Weierstrass elliptic curve E defined in $\mathbb{P}^2(k)$. For two points $P = (x_1 : y_1 : z_1)$ and $Q = (x_2 : y_2 : z_2)$ in $E(k)$, the *addition law* for the pair (P, Q) is a triple $(\mathcal{X}, \mathcal{Y}, \mathcal{Z})$ of polynomials

$$\mathcal{X}, \mathcal{Y}, \mathcal{Z} \in k[X_1, Y_1, Z_1, X_2, Y_2, Z_2]/(f(X_1, Y_1, Z_1), f(X_2, Y_2, Z_2))$$

such that the evaluation of $\mathcal{X}, \mathcal{Y}$ and $\mathcal{Z}$ at P and Q equals the group addition $P + Q = (x_3 : y_3 : z_3) \in E(k)$, i.e.,

$$x_3 = \mathcal{X}(x_1, y_1, z_1, x_2, y_2, z_2),$$
$$y_3 = \mathcal{Y}(x_1, y_1, z_1, x_2, y_2, z_2),$$
$$z_3 = \mathcal{Z}(x_1, y_1, z_1, x_2, y_2, z_2).$$

We define the equivalence classes $(\mathcal{X} : \mathcal{Y} : \mathcal{Z}) := (\mathcal{X}, \mathcal{Y}, \mathcal{Z})/\sim$ by $(\mathcal{X}, \mathcal{Y}, \mathcal{Z}) \sim (\mathcal{X}', \mathcal{Y}', \mathcal{Z}')$ if there exists $\lambda \in k \setminus \{0\}$ such that $(\mathcal{X}, \mathcal{Y}, \mathcal{Z}) = (\lambda \mathcal{X}', \lambda \mathcal{Y}', \lambda \mathcal{Z}')$. From now on, we consider an addition law as an equivalence class $(\mathcal{X} : \mathcal{Y} : \mathcal{Z})$.

The above addition law $(\mathcal{X} : \mathcal{Y} : \mathcal{Z})$ is for the pair (P, Q) and all evaluations of $\mathcal{X}, \mathcal{Y}$, and $\mathcal{Z}$ at some P' and Q' could be zero. Such a pair (P', Q') is called *exceptional* of $(\mathcal{X} : \mathcal{Y} : \mathcal{Z})$. The set of all addition laws for any two k-rational points, $S = \{(\mathcal{X} : \mathcal{Y} : \mathcal{Z})_{P,Q} : P, Q \in E(k)\}$, is called a *$k$-complete system*. If an addition law $(\mathcal{X} : \mathcal{Y} : \mathcal{Z})$ does not have any exceptional points, i.e., $|S| = 1$, then we call $(\mathcal{X} : \mathcal{Y} : \mathcal{Z})$ *k-complete*. The minimum number of addition laws for K-complete system equals 2, and the two addition laws forming K-complete systems have bidegree $(2, 2)$ such that $\mathcal{X}, \mathcal{Y}$ and $\mathcal{Z}$ are homogeneous of degree 2 in X_1, Y_1 and Z_1, and are homogeneous of degree 2 in X_2, Y_2 and Z_2 [8, Thm. 1].

Bosma and Lenstra also showed that there exists a one-to-one correspondence between $(a : b : c) \in \mathbb{P}^2(k)$ and addition laws $(\mathcal{X} : \mathcal{Y} : \mathcal{Z})$ of bidegree $(2, 2)$ on E. Let K be some extension field of k. The pair $(P, Q) \in (E \times E)(K)$ is exceptional for the addition law corresponding to $(a : b : c)$ if and only if $P - Q$ lies on the line $aX + bY + cZ = 0$ in $\mathbb{P}^2(K)$ [8, Thm. 2]. They presented three addition laws $(\mathcal{X}^{(1)} : \mathcal{Y}^{(1)} : \mathcal{Z}^{(1)})$, $(\mathcal{X}^{(2)} : \mathcal{Y}^{(2)} : \mathcal{Z}^{(2)})$ and $(\mathcal{X}^{(3)} : \mathcal{Y}^{(3)} : \mathcal{Z}^{(3)})$ which corresponds to $(0 : 0 : 1)$, $(0 : 1 : 0)$ and $(1 : 0 : 0)$, respectively. The bijection in [8, Thm. 2] sends $(a : b : c) \in \mathbb{P}^2(K)$ to the addition law corresponding to $(a\mathcal{X}^{(3)} + b\mathcal{X}^{(2)} + c\mathcal{X}^{(1)} : a\mathcal{Y}^{(3)} + b\mathcal{Y}^{(2)} + c\mathcal{Y}^{(1)} : a\mathcal{Z}^{(3)} + b\mathcal{Z}^{(2)} + c\mathcal{Z}^{(1)})$.

3 Complete Addition Law of Montgomery Curves

Let p be a prime greater than 3. Let k be a finite field that has p elements, i.e., $k = \mathbb{F}_p$, and K be some extension field of k. In this section, we present a k-complete addition law for the Montgomery curves with $B = 1$.

3.1 Our Complete Addition Law

To use the bijection of Bosma-Lenstra, we first simplifies the addition laws $(\mathcal{X}^{(1)} : \mathcal{Y}^{(1)} : \mathcal{Z}^{(1)})$, $(\mathcal{X}^{(2)} : \mathcal{Y}^{(2)} : \mathcal{Z}^{(2)})$ and $(\mathcal{X}^{(3)} : \mathcal{Y}^{(3)} : \mathcal{Z}^{(3)})$ for Montgomery curves. These formulas are obtained by negating all terms in [8] and following the revision summarized in [6, Fig. 1.2].

$$
\begin{aligned}
\mathcal{X}^{(1)} =\ & (X_1Z_2 - X_2Z_1)((X_1Z_2 + X_2Z_1) + AX_1X_2 - Y_1Y_2) \\
& - (X_1Y_2 - X_2Y_1)(Y_1Z_2 + Y_2Z_1), \\
\mathcal{Y}^{(1)} =\ & (3X_1X_2 + Z_1Z_2)(X_1Y_2 - X_2Y_1) + A(X_1Y_2 + X_2Y_1)(X_1Z_2 - X_2Z_1) \\
& - ((X_1Z_2 + X_2Z_1) + 3AX_1X_2 - Y_1Y_2)(Y_1Z_2 - Y_2Z_1), \\
\mathcal{Z}^{(1)} =\ & (Y_1Z_2 - Y_2Z_1)(Y_1Z_2 + Y_2Z_1) \\
& - (X_1Z_2 - X_2Z_1)(A(X_1Z_2 + X_2Z_1) + 3X_1X_2 + Z_1Z_2), \\
\mathcal{X}^{(2)} =\ & (X_1X_2 - Z_1Z_2)(Y_1Z_2 + Y_2Z_1) \\
& + (X_1Y_2 + X_2Y_1)((X_1Z_2 + X_2Z_1) + AX_1X_2 - Y_1Y_2), \\
\mathcal{Y}^{(2)} =\ & X_1Z_2(X_1Z_2 + 2X_2Z_1) + X_2Z_1(2X_1Z_2 + X_2Z_1) + (Z_1Z_2)^2 - (Y_1Y_2)^2 \\
& + A(X_1X_2 + Z_1Z_2)(X_1Z_2 + X_2Z_1) + (A^2 - 3)(X_1X_2)^2, \\
\mathcal{Z}^{(2)} =\ & - ((X_1Z_2 + X_2Z_1) + AX_1X_2 + Y_1Y_2)(Y_1Z_2 + Y_2Z_1) \\
& - (X_1Y_2 + X_2Y_1)(A(X_1Z_2 + X_2Z_1) + 3X_1X_2 + Z_1Z_2), \\
\mathcal{X}^{(3)} =\ & (X_1Y_2 + X_2Y_1)(X_1Y_2 - X_2Y_1) + X_1X_2(X_1Z_2 - X_2Z_1), \\
\mathcal{Y}^{(3)} =\ & (AX_1X_2 + Y_1Y_2)(X_1Y_2 - X_2Y_1) - (3X_1X_2 - Z_1Z_2)(Y_1Z_2 - Y_2Z_1) \\
& + (X_1Y_2 + X_2Y_1)(X_1Z_2 - X_2Z_1), \\
\mathcal{Z}^{(3)} =\ & - (X_1Y_2 + X_2Y_1)(Y_1Z_2 - Y_2Z_1) - (X_1Z_2 - X_2Z_1)(AX_1X_2 + Y_1Y_2) \\
& - (X_1Z_2 + X_2Z_1)(X_1Z_2 - X_2Z_1).
\end{aligned}
$$

Now we try to find a line $aX + bY + cZ = 0$ $(a, b, c \in k)$ which does not intersect with $E(K)$. The lines $X = 0$, $Y = 0$, $Z = 0$ and any lines of the form $aX + bY = 0$ or $aX + cZ = 0$ in $\mathbb{P}^2(K)$ have an intersection with $E(K)$, which means the addition laws corresponding to $(1 : 0 : 0)$, $(0 : 1 : 0)$, $(0 : 0 : 1)$, $(a : b : 0)$ and $(a : 0 : c)$ are not K-complete. Therefore, we can narrow it down to two cases $(0 : b : c)$ and $(a : b : c)$. However, in order to get a good K-complete addition law in terms of field operation performance, we only consider the addition laws corresponding to $(0 : b : c)$. If $a, b, c \in k \setminus \{0\}$, it is difficult to simplify the addition formulas by canceling terms. After all, even if there is a k-complete addition law corresponding to $(a : b : c)$, it is difficult to expect practical use.

Let $s := -cb^{-1}$. Since $(0, b, c) \sim (0, 1, -s)$, we check the intersection between $Y - sZ = 0$ and $Y^2Z = X^3 + AX^2Z + XZ^2$. By substituting $Y = sZ$ to E, we obtain $s^2Z^3 = X^3 + AX^2Z + XZ^2$. If $Z = 0$, then $X = Y = 0$, so Z should not be zero. If we set $Z = 1$ we obtain Eq. (3).

$$X^3 + AX^2 + X - s^2 = 0. \tag{3}$$

If Eq. (3) is irreducible over k, then there exists no intersection between the line and the curve E over k. It means that the addition law corresponding to $(0 : 1 : -s)$ is k-complete. The bijection in [8, Thm. 2] sends $(0 : 1 : -s)$ to the addition law

$$(\mathcal{X}^{(2)} - s\mathcal{X}^{(1)} : \mathcal{Y}^{(2)} - s\mathcal{Y}^{(1)} : \mathcal{Z}^{(2)} - s\mathcal{Z}^{(1)}). \tag{4}$$

From the above, we have the following theorem.

Theorem 1. *Let $X^3 + AX^2 + X - s^2$ be irreducible over k where $s \in k \setminus \{0\}$. Then the following addition law $(\mathcal{X} : \mathcal{Y} : \mathcal{Z})$ is k-complete.*

$$\mathcal{X} = \mathcal{RS} - \mathcal{TU}, \quad \mathcal{Y} = \mathcal{TW} - \mathcal{VS}, \quad \mathcal{Z} = \mathcal{VU} - \mathcal{RW},$$

where

$$
\begin{aligned}
\mathcal{R} &:= Y_1 Z_2 + Y_2 Z_1, \\
\mathcal{S} &:= s(X_1 Y_2 - X_2 Y_1) + X_1 X_2 - Z_1 Z_2, \\
\mathcal{T} &:= (X_1 Z_2 + X_2 Z_1) + A X_1 X_2 - Y_1 Y_2, \\
\mathcal{U} &:= s(X_1 Z_2 - X_2 Z_1) - (X_1 Y_2 + X_2 Y_1), \\
\mathcal{W} &:= s(Y_1 Z_2 - Y_2 Z_1) + (X_1 Z_2 + X_2 Z_1) + A X_1 X_2 + Y_1 Y_2, \\
\mathcal{V} &:= A(X_1 Z_2 + X_2 Z_1) + 3 X_1 X_2 + Z_1 Z_2.
\end{aligned}
$$

Proof. As stated above, the addition law $(\mathcal{X} : \mathcal{Y} : \mathcal{Z})$ corresponding to $(0 : 1 : -s) \in \mathbb{P}^2(K)$ can be obtained by Eq. (4), i.e.,

$$\mathcal{X} = \mathcal{X}^{(2)} - s\mathcal{X}^{(1)}, \quad \mathcal{Y} = \mathcal{Y}^{(2)} - s\mathcal{Y}^{(1)}, \quad \mathcal{Z} = \mathcal{Z}^{(2)} - s\mathcal{Z}^{(1)}.$$

First, $\mathcal{X}$ and $\mathcal{Z}$ can be obtained easily:

$$
\begin{aligned}
\mathcal{X} =& \mathcal{X}^{(2)} - s\mathcal{X}^{(1)} \\
=& (Y_1 Z_2 + Y_2 Z_1)(s(X_1 Y_2 - X_2 Y_1) + X_1 X_2 - Z_1 Z_2) \\
&- ((X_1 Z_2 + X_2 Z_1) + A X_1 X_2 - Y_1 Y_2)(s(X_1 Z_2 - X_2 Z_1) - (X_1 Y_2 + X_2 Y_1)), \\
\mathcal{Z} =& \mathcal{Z}^{(2)} - s\mathcal{Z}^{(1)} \\
=& (A(X_1 Z_2 + X_2 Z_1) + 3 X_1 X_2 + Z_1 Z_2)(s(X_1 Z_2 - X_2 Z_1) - (X_1 Y_2 + X_2 Y_1)) \\
&- (Y_1 Z_2 + Y_2 Z_1)((X_1 Z_2 + X_2 Z_1) + s(Y_1 Z_2 - Y_2 Z_1) + A X_1 X_2 + Y_1 Y_2).
\end{aligned}
$$

Prior to computing $\mathcal{Y}$, we obtain new formulas of $\mathcal{Y}^{(1)}$ and $\mathcal{Y}^{(2)}$ as follows:

$$
\begin{aligned}
\mathcal{Y}^{(1)} =& (A(X_1 Z_2 + X_2 Z_1) + 3 X_1 X_2 + Z_1 Z_2)(X_1 Y_2 - X_2 Y_1), \\
&- ((X_1 Z_2 + X_2 Z_1) + A X_1 X_2 - Y_1 Y_2)(Y_1 Z_2 - Y_2 Z_1) \\
\mathcal{Y}^{(2)} =& ((X_1 Z_2 + X_2 Z_1) + A X_1 X_2 - Y_1 Y_2)((X_1 Z_2 + X_2 Z_1) + A X_1 X_2 + Y_1 Y_2) \\
&- (A(X_1 Z_2 + X_2 Z_1) + 3 X_1 X_2 + Z_1 Z_2)(X_1 X_2 - Z_1 Z_2).
\end{aligned}
$$

Here $\mathcal{Y}^{(2)}$ is transformed as follows.

$$
\begin{aligned}
\mathcal{Y}^{(2)} = {} & (X_1X_2 + Z_1Z_2)(X_1Z_2 + X_2Z_1) + (X_1Z_2 + X_2Z_1)(X_1Z_2 + X_2Z_1) \\
& - Y_1^2Y_2^2 + A^2X_1^2X_2^2 - 3X_1^2X_2^2 + 2X_1X_2Z_1Z_2 + Z_1^2Z_2^2 \\
= {} & A(X_1X_2 + Z_1Z_2)(X_1Z_2 + X_2Z_1) \\
& + (X_1Z_2 + X_2Z_1 + Y_1Y_2)(X_1Z_2 + X_2Z_1 - Y_1Y_2) \\
& + A^2X_1^2X_2^2 - (3X_1X_2 + Z_1Z_2)(X_1X_2 - Z_1Z_2) \\
= {} & - A(X_1X_2 - Z_1Z_2)(X_1Z_2 + X_2Z_1) + 2AX_1X_2(X_1Z_2 + X_2Z_1) \\
& - (3X_1X_2 + Z_1Z_2)(X_1X_2 - Z_1Z_2) \\
& + A^2X_1^2X_2^2 + (X_1Z_2 + X_2Z_1 + Y_1Y_2)(X_1Z_2 + X_2Z_1 - Y_1Y_2) \\
= {} & - (3X_1X_2 + Z_1Z_2 + A(X_1Z_2 + X_2Z_1))(X_1X_2 - Z_1Z_2) \\
& + AX_1X_2(X_1Z_2 + X_2Z_1) + AX_1X_2(AX_1X_2 - Y_1Y_2) \\
& + (X_1Z_2 + X_2Z_1 + Y_1Y_2)(X_1Z_2 + X_2Z_1 + AX_1X_2 - Y_1Y_2) \\
= {} & - (3X_1X_2 + Z_1Z_2 + A(X_1Z_2 + X_2Z_1))(X_1X_2 - Z_1Z_2) \\
& + AX_1X_2(X_1Z_2 + X_2Z_1 + AX_1X_2 - Y_1Y_2) \\
& + (X_1Z_2 + X_2Z_1 + Y_1Y_2)(X_1Z_2 + X_2Z_1 + AX_1X_2 - Y_1Y_2) \\
= {} & - (3X_1X_2 + Z_1Z_2 + A(X_1Z_2 + X_2Z_1))(X_1X_2 - Z_1Z_2) \\
& + (X_1Z_2 + X_2Z_1 + AX_1X_2 - Y_1Y_2)(X_1Z_2 + X_2Z_1 + AX_1X_2 + Y_1Y_2).
\end{aligned}
$$

Using the new forms $\mathcal{Y}^{(1)}$ and $\mathcal{Y}^{(2)}$, we obtain $\mathcal{Y}$:

$$
\begin{aligned}
\mathcal{Y} = {} & \mathcal{Y}^{(2)} - s\mathcal{Y}^{(1)} \\
= {} & ((X_1Z_2 + X_2Z_1) + AX_1X_2 - Y_1Y_2) \\
& ((X_1Z_2 + X_2Z_1) + s(Y_1Z_2 - Y_2Z_1) + AX_1X_2 + Y_1Y_2) \\
& - (A(X_1Z_2 + X_2Z_1) + 3X_1X_2 + Z_1Z_2)(s(X_1Y_2 - X_2Y_1) + X_1X_2 - Z_1Z_2).
\end{aligned}
$$

$\square$

3.2   Counting Field Operations

For performance comparison of complete addition laws for several curve models, we use the field operation counts in the base field k. Multiplication, squaring, multiplication by a constant A, and addition in k are expressed by $\mathbf{M}$, $\mathbf{S}$, $\mathbf{M_c}$, and $\mathbf{A}$, respectively.

General Counting. In Theorem 1, the s is an element of a prime field k, but we can consider the s to be a non-negative integer less than p. If s is very small (as Table 1), multiplication by s can be done by $(s-1)\mathbf{A}$. For example, $3X_1X_2$ can be computed by $X_1X_2 + X_1X_2 + X_1X_2$, just $2\mathbf{A}$ that may be faster than $\mathbf{M_c}$. In this paper, we count the number of field operations using this approach. Note, however, that this calculation can be faster if s has a special form such as power of 2.

Algorithm 1 shows the computation of $(\mathcal{X} : \mathcal{Y} : \mathcal{Z})$. This k-complete addition law can be computed using $15\mathbf{M} + 2\mathbf{M}_c + (3s + 17)\mathbf{A}$. (We compute the multiplication by 3 as $2\mathbf{A}$.) For example, the computational cost of evaluating the addition of Curve25519 using the complete addition law is $15\mathbf{M} + 2\mathbf{M}_c + 20\mathbf{A}$. The sage verification code of Algorithm 1 is given in Appendix B.

Algorithm 1. k-complete addition for Montgomery curves

Input: $P = (X_1 : Y_1 : Z_1)$, $Q = (X_2 : Y_2 : Z_2)$ on E
Output: $P + Q \leftarrow (\mathcal{X} : \mathcal{Y} : \mathcal{Z})$

1: $T_0 \leftarrow X_1 X_2$ // $\mathbf{M}$	11: $T_{10} \leftarrow T_9 + A T_0$ // $\mathbf{A} + \mathbf{M}_c$
2: $T_1 \leftarrow Y_1 Y_2$ // $\mathbf{M}$	12: $\mathcal{R} \leftarrow T_5 + T_6$ // $\mathbf{A}$
3: $T_2 \leftarrow Z_1 Z_2$ // $\mathbf{M}$	13: $\mathcal{T} \leftarrow T_{10} - T_1$ // $\mathbf{A}$
4: $T_3 \leftarrow X_1 Y_2$ // $\mathbf{M}$	14: $\mathcal{V} \leftarrow A T_9 + 3 T_0 + T_2$ // $4\mathbf{A} + \mathbf{M}_c$
5: $T_4 \leftarrow X_2 Y_1$ // $\mathbf{M}$	15: $\mathcal{S} \leftarrow s(T_3 - T_4) + T_0 - T_2$ // $(s+2)\mathbf{A}$
6: $T_5 \leftarrow Y_1 Z_2$ // $\mathbf{M}$	16: $\mathcal{U} \leftarrow s(T_7 - T_8) - T_3 - T_4$ // $(s+2)\mathbf{A}$
7: $T_6 \leftarrow Y_2 Z_1$ // $\mathbf{M}$	17: $\mathcal{W} \leftarrow s(T_5 - T_6) + T_{10} + T_1$ // $(s+2)\mathbf{A}$
8: $T_7 \leftarrow X_1 Z_2$ // $\mathbf{M}$	18: $\mathcal{X} \leftarrow \mathcal{R}\mathcal{S} - \mathcal{T}\mathcal{U}$ // $\mathbf{A} + 2\mathbf{M}$
9: $T_8 \leftarrow X_2 Z_1$ // $\mathbf{M}$	19: $\mathcal{Y} \leftarrow \mathcal{T}\mathcal{W} - \mathcal{V}\mathcal{S}$ // $\mathbf{A} + 2\mathbf{M}$
10: $T_9 \leftarrow T_7 + T_8$ // $\mathbf{A}$	20: $\mathcal{Z} \leftarrow \mathcal{V}\mathcal{U} - \mathcal{R}\mathcal{W}$ // $\mathbf{A} + 2\mathbf{M}$

Trade-Off Technique. The cost for computing $\mathcal{R}, \mathcal{S}, \mathcal{T}, \mathcal{U}, \mathcal{W}$ and $\mathcal{V}$ in Theorem 1 is $9\mathbf{M} + 2\mathbf{M}_c + (3s + 14)\mathbf{A}$. Consider the final steps for getting $\mathcal{X}, \mathcal{Y}, \mathcal{Z}$ using $\mathcal{R}, \mathcal{S}, \mathcal{T}, \mathcal{U}, \mathcal{W}$ and $\mathcal{V}$. Since $\mathrm{char}(k) \neq 2$ and $(\mathcal{X} : \mathcal{Y} : \mathcal{Z}) = (2\mathcal{X} : 2\mathcal{Y} : 2\mathcal{Z})$, those steps can be done by $5\mathbf{M} + 17\mathbf{A}$ using the technique presented in [4, Sec.6] as follows:

$$\mathcal{X} = \mathcal{C} + \mathcal{D}, \quad \mathcal{Y} = \mathcal{E} + \mathcal{F}, \quad \mathcal{Z} = 2(\mathcal{U} - \mathcal{W})(\mathcal{R} + \mathcal{V}) + \mathcal{C} - \mathcal{D} + \mathcal{E} - \mathcal{F},$$

where

$$\mathcal{C} := (\mathcal{R} + \mathcal{T})(\mathcal{S} - \mathcal{U}), \quad \mathcal{D} := (\mathcal{R} - \mathcal{T})(\mathcal{S} + \mathcal{U}),$$
$$\mathcal{E} := (\mathcal{T} + \mathcal{V})(\mathcal{W} - \mathcal{S}), \quad \mathcal{F} := (\mathcal{T} - \mathcal{V})(\mathcal{W} + \mathcal{S}).$$

Therefore, in this case, addition needs $14\mathbf{M} + 2\mathbf{M}_c + (3s + 31)\mathbf{A}$.

Mixed Addition. Mixed addition means the addition of a projective coordinated point $P = (x_1 : y_1 : z_1)$ and an affine coordinated point $Q = (x_2, y_2)$. This can be considered as the addition of $P = (x_1 : y_1 : z_1)$ and $Q = (x_2 : y_2 : 1)$. Algorithm 2 shows the complete mixed addition of Montgomery curves. It costs $12\mathbf{M} + 2\mathbf{M}_c + (3s + 17)\mathbf{A}$ and can be computed with $11\mathbf{M} + 2\mathbf{M}_c + (3s + 31)\mathbf{A}$ when applying the trade-off technique.

Algorithm 2. k-complete mixed addition for Montgomery curves

Input: $P = (X_1 : Y_1 : Z_1), Q = (X_2 : Y_2 : 1)$ on E
Output: $P + Q \leftarrow (\mathcal{X} : \mathcal{Y} : \mathcal{Z})$

1: $T_0 \leftarrow X_1 X_2$ // **M**
2: $T_1 \leftarrow Y_1 Y_2$ // **M**
3: $T_2 \leftarrow Z_1$
4: $T_3 \leftarrow X_1 Y_2$ // **M**
5: $T_4 \leftarrow X_2 Y_1$ // **M**
6: $T_5 \leftarrow Y_1 Z_2$ // **M**
7: $T_6 \leftarrow Y_2$
8: $T_7 \leftarrow X_1 Z_2$ // **M**
9: $T_8 \leftarrow X_2$
10: $T_9 \leftarrow T_7 + T_8$ // **A**

11: $T_{10} \leftarrow T_9 + AT_0$ // $\mathbf{A + M_c}$
12: $\mathcal{R} \leftarrow T_5 + T_6$ // **A**
13: $\mathcal{T} \leftarrow T_{10} - T_1$ // **A**
14: $\mathcal{V} \leftarrow AT_9 + 3T_0 + T_2$ // $\mathbf{4A + M_c}$
15: $\mathcal{S} \leftarrow s(T_3 - T_4) + T_0 - T_2$ // $(s+2)\mathbf{A}$
16: $\mathcal{U} \leftarrow s(T_7 - T_8) - T_3 - T_4$ // $(s+2)\mathbf{A}$
17: $\mathcal{W} \leftarrow s(T_5 - T_6) + T_{10} + T_1$ // $(s+2)\mathbf{A}$
18: $\mathcal{X} \leftarrow \mathcal{R}\mathcal{S} - \mathcal{T}\mathcal{U}$ // $\mathbf{A + 2M}$
19: $\mathcal{Y} \leftarrow \mathcal{T}\mathcal{W} - \mathcal{V}\mathcal{S}$ // $\mathbf{A + 2M}$
20: $\mathcal{Z} \leftarrow \mathcal{V}\mathcal{U} - \mathcal{R}\mathcal{W}$ // $\mathbf{A + 2M}$

Doubling. If two inputs are same, the cost of *exception-free* doubling is unaffected by the s because of $X_1 Y_2 - X_2 Y_1 = X_1 Z_2 - X_2 Z_1 = Y_1 Z_2 - Y_2 Z_1 = 0$. In the case of point doubling, we can save several multiplications by rewriting $2XY = (X + Y)^2 - X^2 - Y^2$ and by exploiting common subexpressions.

$$\mathcal{S} := X^2 - Z^2, \quad \mathcal{R} := 2YZ = (Y + Z)^2 - (Y^2 + Z^2),$$
$$\mathcal{U} := -2XY = (X^2 + Y^2) - (X + Y)^2,$$
$$\mathcal{V} := 2AXZ + 3X^2 + Z^2 = A((X + Z)^2 - (X^2 + Z^2)) + (X^2 + Z^2) + 2X^2,$$
$$\mathcal{T} := 2XZ + AX^2 - Y^2 = ((X + Z)^2 - (X^2 + Z^2) + AX^2) - Y^2,$$
$$\mathcal{W} := 2XZ + AX^2 + Y^2 = ((X + Z)^2 - (X^2 + Z^2) + AX^2) + Y^2.$$

This simple approach costs $6\mathbf{M} + 6\mathbf{S} + 2\mathbf{M_c} + 19\mathbf{A}$. If we use the trade-off technique, the total cost is $5\mathbf{M} + 6\mathbf{S} + 2\mathbf{M_c} + 34\mathbf{A}$. However, we can directly use the technique in [4] to save two field additions as follows:

$$\mathcal{S} - \mathcal{U} = (X + Y)^2 - (Y^2 + Z^2), \quad \mathcal{S} + \mathcal{U} = -(\mathcal{S} - \mathcal{U}) + 2(X^2 - Z^2)$$
$$\mathcal{R} - \mathcal{T} = (Y + Z)^2 - (X + Z)^2 - (A - 1)X^2$$
$$\mathcal{R} + \mathcal{T} = (Y + Z)^2 - 2(Y^2 + Z^2) + (X + Z)^2 + (A - 1)X^2$$
$$\mathcal{W} - \mathcal{S} = (X + Z)^2 + (A - 1)X^2 - (X^2 - Y^2)$$
$$\mathcal{W} + \mathcal{S} = (\mathcal{W} - \mathcal{S}) + 2(X^2 - Z^2)$$
$$\mathcal{T} - \mathcal{V} = (X + Z)^2 + (A - 1)X^2 - (A((X + Z)^2 - Z^2) + (X^2 - Y^2) + X^2)$$
$$+ (A - 1)X^2 - 2(Y^2 + Z^2)$$
$$\mathcal{T} + \mathcal{V} = (X + Z)^2 + (A((X + Z)^2 - Z^2) + (X^2 - Y^2) + X^2)$$
$$\mathcal{U} - \mathcal{W} = (\mathcal{S} + \mathcal{U}) - (\mathcal{W} + \mathcal{S}), \quad \mathcal{R} + \mathcal{V} = (\mathcal{R} - \mathcal{T}) + (\mathcal{T} + \mathcal{V})$$

This can be computed using $5\mathbf{M} + 6\mathbf{S} + 2\mathbf{M_c} + 32\mathbf{A}$. Algorithm 3 shows the computation.

Algorithm 3. Exception-free doubling for Montgomery curves

Input: $P = (X : Y : Z)$ on E
Output: $[2]P \leftarrow (\mathcal{X} : \mathcal{Y} : \mathcal{Z})$

1: $T_0 \leftarrow X^2, T_1 \leftarrow Y^2, T_2 \leftarrow Z^2$ // 3S
2: $T_3 \leftarrow (X+Y)^2$ // $\mathbf{A+S}$
3: $T_4 \leftarrow (Y+Z)^2$ // $\mathbf{A+S}$
4: $T_5 \leftarrow (X+Z)^2$ // $\mathbf{A+S}$
5: $T_6 \leftarrow T_1 + T_2$ // $\mathbf{A}$
6: $T_7 \leftarrow 2(T_0 - T_2)$ // $\mathbf{2A}$
7: $T_8 \leftarrow (A-1)T_0$ // $\mathbf{A+M_c}$
8: $T_9 \leftarrow T_0 - T_1$ // $\mathbf{A}$
9: $T_{10} \leftarrow A(T_5 - T_2) + T_0 + T_9$ // $\mathbf{3A+M_c}$
10: $T_{11} \leftarrow T_5 + T_8$ // $\mathbf{A}$
11: $T_{12} \leftarrow T_{10} - 2T_6$ // $\mathbf{2A}$
12: $\mathcal{SU}^- \leftarrow T_3 - T_6$ // $\mathbf{A}$
13: $\mathcal{SU}^+ \leftarrow -\mathcal{SU}^- + T_7$ // $\mathbf{A}$
14: $\mathcal{RT}^- \leftarrow T_4 - T_{11}$ // $\mathbf{A}$
15: $\mathcal{RT}^+ \leftarrow T_4 + T_{12}$ // $\mathbf{A}$
16: $\mathcal{WS}^- \leftarrow T_{11} - T_9$ // $\mathbf{A}$
17: $\mathcal{WS}^+ \leftarrow \mathcal{WS}^- + T_7$ // $\mathbf{A}$
18: $\mathcal{TV}^- \leftarrow T_{12} - T_{10} + T_8$ // $\mathbf{2A}$
19: $\mathcal{TV}^+ \leftarrow T_5 + T_{10}$ // $\mathbf{A}$
20: $\mathcal{UW}^- \leftarrow \mathcal{SU}^+ - \mathcal{WS}^+$ // $\mathbf{A}$
21: $\mathcal{RV}^+ \leftarrow \mathcal{RT}^- + \mathcal{TV}^+$ // $\mathbf{A}$
22: $\mathcal{C} \leftarrow \mathcal{RT}^+\mathcal{SU}^-$ // $\mathbf{M}$
23: $\mathcal{D} \leftarrow \mathcal{RT}^-\mathcal{SU}^+$ // $\mathbf{M}$
24: $\mathcal{E} \leftarrow \mathcal{TV}^+\mathcal{WS}^-$ // $\mathbf{M}$
25: $\mathcal{F} \leftarrow \mathcal{TV}^-\mathcal{WS}^+$ // $\mathbf{M}$
26: $\mathcal{X} \leftarrow \mathcal{C} + \mathcal{D}$ // $\mathbf{A}$
27: $\mathcal{Y} \leftarrow \mathcal{E} + \mathcal{F}$ // $\mathbf{A}$
28: $\mathcal{Z} \leftarrow 2\mathcal{UW}^-\mathcal{RV}^+ + \mathcal{C} - \mathcal{D} + \mathcal{E} - \mathcal{F}$
     // $\mathbf{5A+M}$

4 Performance

First, Table 2 shows the number of base field operations of complete addition laws among three models of elliptic curves: short Weierstrass, Edwards, and Montgomery.

Table 2. Performance comparison of complete addition of several curves

Curve	Type	M	S	M_c	A	Ref.
Edwards	Compl. Add.	10	1	1	7	[5]
(Eq. (1))	Doubling	3	4	3	6	[5]
Short	Compl. Add.	12	0	2	29	[19]
Weierstrass	Compl. Add.	11	0	2	43	Appendix C
(Eq. (2))	Doubling	8	3	2	21	[19]
Montgomery	Compl. Add.	15	0	2	$(3s+17)$	Section 3
with $B = 1$		14	0	2	$(3s+31)$	
	Compl. Mixed Add.	12	0	2	$(3s+17)$	
		11	0	2	$(3s+31)$	
	Doubling	5	6	2	32	

As a remark, we applied the technique in [4] to the complete addition law on the short Weierstrass curves [19] and saved 1**M** at the cost of 17**A**. See Appendix C for detail.

Next, we compare two implementation methods of Montgomery curve addition. One is to use the complete addition law provided in this paper and the other is to use the addition of the corresponding (twisted) Edwards equivalent. The explicit transformation from a Montgomery curve to a twisted Edwards curve is defined as follows.

$$BY^2Z = X^3 + AX^2Z + XZ^2 \implies$$
$$\left(\frac{A+2}{B}\right)X^2Z^2 + Y^2Z^2 = Z^4 + \left(\frac{A-2}{B}\right)X^2Y^2,$$

$$\begin{aligned}
(x:y:z) &\longmapsto (x(x+z):y(x-z):y(x+z)), \\
(0:0:1) &\longmapsto (0:-1:1), \\
(0:1:0) &\longmapsto (0:1:1).
\end{aligned}$$

Since this transformation is an isomorphism, we can use the following inverse relation:

$$aX^2Z^2 + Y^2Z^2 = Z^4 + dX^2Y^2 \implies$$
$$\left(\frac{4}{a-d}\right)Y^2Z = X^3 + \left(\frac{2(a+d)}{a-d}\right)X^2Z + XZ^2,$$

$$\begin{aligned}
(x:y:z) &\longmapsto (x(z+y):z(z+y):x(z-y)), \\
(0:1:1) &\longmapsto (0:1:0), \\
(0:-1:1) &\longmapsto (0:0:1).
\end{aligned}$$

Such forward and backward conversions require 6**M** for each, and so in total 16**M** are needed in the latter case. Considering the difference of one multiplication and other base field operations, we can expect that the proposed complete addition law will be more efficient. Note that the efficiency of conversions may be lower than the formulas stated above, in order to use the optimized complete addition of the Edwards equivalent.

We confirmed this expectation through implementation of Curve25519. We wrote code in C with FLINT library [14] and complied with GCC 4.2.1. All our experiments were performed on a MacBook Pro with a single Intel Core i5 2 GHz CPU, 8 GB RAM running Mac OS (Mojave, ver. 10.14.6) (Table 3).

Table 3. Algorithm 1 vs. Conversion to twisted Edwards for Curve25519

Algorithm	Cycles	Millisecond
Algorithm 1	6.844	0.007
Conversion to twisted Edwards	7.295	0.007

For comparison with the case using the addition operation of the Edwards equivalent, we chose a complete addition law without applying the trade-off technique (See Algorithm 1). As a remark, the complete addition law reflecting the trade-off technique was performed in 8.306 cycles, slower than Algorithm 1.

Acknowledgement. We are grateful to the anonymous reviewers for their help in improving the quality of the paper. This work was supported by Institute for Information & Communications Technology Planning & Evaluation (IITP) grant funded by the Korean government (MSIT) (No.2017-0-00267).

A   Addition and doubling in Montgomery curve (when $B = 1$)

For $P = (x_1 : y_1 : z_1)$ and $Q = (x_2 : y_2 : z_2)$ such that both are not $\mathcal{O}$, Algorithm 4 shows that the addition $P + Q = (x_3 : y_3 : z_3)$ can be computed using $13\mathbf{M} + 2\mathbf{S} + \mathbf{M}_c + 7\mathbf{A}$. For $P = (x : y : z) \neq \mathcal{O}$, Algorithm 5 shows that the doubling $[2]P = (x_3 : y_3 : z_3)$ can be computed using $11\mathbf{M} + 3\mathbf{S} + 2\mathbf{M}_c + 11\mathbf{A}$.

B   Sage code for verification (Algorithm 1)

Algorithm 4. Addition for Montgomery curves $E : Y^2 Z = X^3 + AX^2 Z + XZ^2$

Input: $P = (x_1 : y_1 : z_1)$, $Q = (x_2 : y_2 : z_2)$ on E $(P, Q \neq \mathcal{O}, P + Q \neq \mathcal{O})$
Output: $P + Q \leftarrow (x_3 : y_3 : z_3)$

1: $T_1 \leftarrow x_1 z_2$ $\quad$ // $\mathbf{M}$	9: $v \leftarrow T_2 - T_1$ $\quad$ // $\mathbf{A}$
2: $T_2 \leftarrow x_2 z_1$ $\quad$ // $\mathbf{M}$	10: $T_8 \leftarrow u^2$ $\quad$ // $\mathbf{S}$
3: $T_3 \leftarrow y_1 z_2$ $\quad$ // $\mathbf{M}$	11: $T_9 \leftarrow v^2$ $\quad$ // $\mathbf{S}$
4: $T_4 \leftarrow y_2 z_1$ $\quad$ // $\mathbf{M}$	12: $T \leftarrow T_8 - (AT_5 + T_1 + T_2)T_9$ $\quad$ // $\mathbf{M} + \mathbf{M}_c + 3\mathbf{A}$
5: $T_5 \leftarrow z_1 z_2$ $\quad$ // $\mathbf{M}$	13: $T_8 \leftarrow T_5 T_9$ $\quad$ // $\mathbf{M}$
6: $T_6 \leftarrow x_1 y_2$ $\quad$ // $\mathbf{M}$	14: $x_3 \leftarrow vT$ $\quad$ // $\mathbf{M}$
7: $T_7 \leftarrow x_2 y_1$ $\quad$ // $\mathbf{M}$	15: $y_3 \leftarrow T_8(T_6 - T_7) - uT$ $\quad$ // $2\mathbf{M} + 2\mathbf{A}$
8: $u \leftarrow T_4 - T_3$ $\quad$ // $\mathbf{A}$	16: $z_3 \leftarrow vT_8$ $\quad$ // $\mathbf{M}$

Algorithm 5. Doubling for Montgomery curves $E : Y^2 Z = X^3 + AX^2 Z + XZ^2$

Input: $P = (x : y : z) \neq \mathcal{O}$ on E
Output: $[2]P \leftarrow (x_3 : y_3 : z_3)$

1: $T_1 \leftarrow xz$ $\quad$ // $\mathbf{M}$	8: $T_6 \leftarrow zv$ $\quad$ // $\mathbf{M}$
2: $T_2 \leftarrow yz$ $\quad$ // $\mathbf{M}$	9: $T_7 \leftarrow vT_6$ $\quad$ // $\mathbf{M}$
3: $T_3 \leftarrow x^2$ $\quad$ // $\mathbf{S}$	10: $T \leftarrow T_5 - (AT_4 + 2x)T_7$ $\quad$ // $\mathbf{M} + \mathbf{M}_c + 3\mathbf{A}$
4: $T_4 \leftarrow z^2$ $\quad$ // $\mathbf{S}$	11: $x_3 \leftarrow vT$ $\quad$ // $\mathbf{M}$
5: $u \leftarrow 3T_3 + 2AT_1 + T_4$ $\quad$ // $\mathbf{M}_c + 5\mathbf{A}$	12: $y_3 \leftarrow (xu - yv)T_7 - uT$ $\quad$ // $4\mathbf{M} + 2\mathbf{A}$
6: $v \leftarrow 2T_2$ $\quad$ // $\mathbf{A}$	13: $z_3 \leftarrow T_6 T_7$ $\quad$ // $\mathbf{M}$
7: $T_5 \leftarrow u^2$ $\quad$ // $\mathbf{S}$	

––––––––––––––––––––––– Sage code –––––––––––––––––––––––

```
CURVE25519 = [
    2^(255) - 19, # p mod 4 = 1
    0x76d06,
    1,
    9,
    0x20ae19a1b8a086b4e01edd2c7748d14c923d4d7e6d7c61b229e9c5a27eced3d9,
    0x1000000000000000000000000000000014def9dea2f79cd65812631a5cf5d3ed,
    8,
    1
]


E = CURVE25519
p, A, B, Px, Py, n, h, s = E[0], E[1], E[2], E[3], E[4], E[5], E[6], E[7]

F = GF(p)
PS.<X,Y,Z> = ProjectiveSpace(F, 2)
R.<X> = PolynomialRing(F)

A, B, Px, Py = F(A), F(B), F(Px), F(Py)
E = EllipticCurve([0,A,0,F(1),0]) # assume B = 1

def CompleteADD(P1, P2):
    x1, y1, z1 = P1[0], P1[1], P1[2]
    x2, y2, z2 = P2[0], P2[1], P2[2]
    t0, t1, t2 = x1*x2, y1*y2, z1*z2     # 3M
    t3, t4 = x1*y2, x2*y1                # 2M
    t5, t6 = y1*z2, y2*z1                # 2M
    t7, t8 = x1*z2, x2*z1                # 2M
    t9 = t7 + t8                         # 1A
    t10 = t9 + A*t0                      # 1A + Mc
    R = t5 + t6                          # 1A
    T = t10 - t1                         # 1A
    V = A*t9 + F(3)*t0 + t2              # 4A + Mc
    S = s*(t3 - t4) + t0 - t2            # (s+2)A
    U = s*(t7 - t8) - t3 - t4            # (s+2)A
    W = s*(t5 - t6) + t10 + t1           # (s+2)A
    x3 = R*S - T*U                       # 1A + 2M
    y3 = T*W - V*S                       # 1A + 2M
    z3 = V*U - R*W                       # 1A + 2M
    return PS([x3, y3, z3])

P1, P2 = E(PS([0,1,0])), E(PS([0,1,0]))
P3 = P1 + P2
P4 = CompleteADD(P1, P2)
print PS(P3) == PS(P4)

P1, P2 = E.random_point(), E(PS([0,1,0]))
P3 = P1 + P2
P4 = CompleteADD(P1, P2)
```

```
print PS(P3) == PS(P4)

P1, P2 = E(PS([0,1,0])), E.random_point()
P3 = P1 + P2
P4 = CompleteADD(P1, P2)
print PS(P3) == PS(P4)

P1 = E.random_point()
P2 = -P1
P3 = P1 + P2
P4 = CompleteADD(P1, P2)
print PS(P3) == PS(P4)

P1 = E.random_point()
P2 = P1
P3 = P1 + P2
P4 = CompleteADD(P1, P2)
print PS(P3) == PS(P4)

P1, P2 = E.random_point(), E.random_point()
P3 = P1 + P2
P4 = CompleteADD(P1, P2)
print PS(P3) == PS(P4)
```

C   Complete addition law of short Weierstrass curves applying the trade-off technique

Let E be an elliptic curve in $\mathbb{P}^2(k)$ as a short Weierstrass equation

$$E : Y^2 Z = X^3 - 3XZ^2 + bZ^3, \ (b \in k).$$

Using the same notation, the complete addition law in [19] can be written as

$$\mathcal{X} = \mathcal{R}\mathcal{S} - \mathcal{T}\mathcal{U}, \quad \mathcal{Y} = \mathcal{U}\mathcal{V} - \mathcal{S}\mathcal{W}, \quad \mathcal{Z} = \mathcal{T}\mathcal{W} - \mathcal{R}\mathcal{V},$$

where

$$\begin{aligned}
\mathcal{R} &= X_1 Y_1 + X_2 Y_2, & \mathcal{S} &= Y_1 Y_2 + 3(X_1 Z_2 + X_2 Z_1 - bZ_1 Z_2), \\
\mathcal{T} &= Y_1 Z_2 + Y_2 Z_1, & \mathcal{U} &= 3(b(X_1 Z_2 + X_2 Z_1) - X_1 X_2 - 3Z_1 Z_2), \\
\mathcal{V} &= 3X_1 X_2 - 3Z_1 Z_2, & \mathcal{W} &= Y_1 Y_2 - 3(X_1 Z_2 + X_2 Z_1 - bZ_1 Z_2).
\end{aligned}$$

Then we can rewrite the above formulas as

$$\mathcal{X} = \mathcal{C} + \mathcal{D}, \quad \mathcal{Y} = \mathcal{E} + \mathcal{F}, \quad \mathcal{Z} = 2(\mathcal{T} - \mathcal{V})(\mathcal{V} - \mathcal{S}) + \mathcal{C} - \mathcal{D} + \mathcal{E} - \mathcal{F},$$

where

$$\begin{aligned}
\mathcal{C} &= (\mathcal{R} + \mathcal{U})(\mathcal{S} - \mathcal{T}), & \mathcal{D} &= (\mathcal{R} - \mathcal{U})(\mathcal{S} + \mathcal{T}), \\
\mathcal{E} &= (\mathcal{U} + \mathcal{W})(\mathcal{V} - \mathcal{S}), & \mathcal{F} &= (\mathcal{U} - \mathcal{W})(\mathcal{V} + \mathcal{S}).
\end{aligned}$$

Since $\mathcal{R}, \mathcal{S}, \mathcal{T}, \mathcal{U}, \mathcal{V}, \mathcal{W}$ can be computed using $6\mathbf{M} + 2\mathbf{M}_c + 26\mathbf{A}$ [19, Algorithm 4], total computational cost is $11\mathbf{M} + 2\mathbf{M}_c + 43\mathbf{A}$.

References

1. Aranha, D.F., Barreto, P.S., Pereira, G.C., Ricardini, J.E.: A note on high-security general-purpose elliptic curves. Cryptology ePrint Archive, Report 2013/647 (2013). http://eprint.iacr.org/2013/647.pdf
2. Bernstein, D.J.: Curve25519: new Diffie-Hellman speed records. In: Yung, M., Dodis, Y., Kiayias, A., Malkin, T. (eds.) PKC 2006. LNCS, vol. 3958, pp. 207–228. Springer, Heidelberg (2006). https://doi.org/10.1007/11745853_14
3. Bernstein, D.J., Birkner, P., Joye, M., Lange, T., Peters, C.: Twisted Edwards curves. In: Vaudenay, S. (ed.) AFRICACRYPT 2008. LNCS, vol. 5023, pp. 389–405. Springer, Heidelberg (2008). https://doi.org/10.1007/978-3-540-68164-9_26
4. Bernstein, D.J., Chuengsatiansup, C., Kohel, D., Lange, T.: Twisted Hessian curves. In: Lauter, K., Rodríguez-Henríquez, F. (eds.) LATINCRYPT 2015. LNCS, vol. 9230, pp. 269–294. Springer, Cham (2015). https://doi.org/10.1007/978-3-319-22174-8_15
5. Bernstein, D.J., Lange, T.: Faster addition and doubling on elliptic curves. In: Kurosawa, K. (ed.) ASIACRYPT 2007. LNCS, vol. 4833, pp. 29–50. Springer, Heidelberg (2007). https://doi.org/10.1007/978-3-540-76900-2_3
6. Bernstein, D.J., Lange, T.: A complete set of addition laws for incomplete Edwards curves. J. Number Theory 131(5), 858–872 (2011). https://doi.org/10.1016/j.jnt.2010.06.015
7. Bos, J.W., Costello, C., Longa, P., et al.: Selecting elliptic curves for cryptography: an efficiency and security analysis. J. Cryptogr. Eng. 6, 259 (2016). https://doi.org/10.1007/s13389-015-0097-y
8. Bosma, W., Lenstra, H.: Complete systems of two addition laws for elliptic curves. J. Number Theory 53(2), 229–240 (1995). https://doi.org/10.1006/jnth.1995.1088
9. Costello, C., Smith, B.: Montgomery curves and their arithmetic. J. Cryptogr. Eng. 8, 227 (2018). https://doi.org/10.1007/s13389-017-0157-6
10. Edwards, H.M.: A normal form for elliptic curves. Bull. Am. Math. Soc. 44(3), 393–422 (2007). https://doi.org/10.1090/S0273-0979-07-01153-6
11. Farashahi, R.R., Joye, M.: Efficient arithmetic on Hessian curves. In: Nguyen, P.Q., Pointcheval, D. (eds.) PKC 2010. LNCS, vol. 6056, pp. 243–260. Springer, Heidelberg (2010). https://doi.org/10.1007/978-3-642-13013-7_15
12. Garcia-Morchon, O., Kumar, S., Sethi, M.: Internet of Things (IoT) Security: State of the Art and Challenges. IETF RFC 8576 (2019). https://doi.org/10.17487/RFC8576
13. Hamburg, M.: Ed448-Goldilocks, a new elliptic curve. Cryptology ePrint Archive, Report 2015/625 (2015). http://eprint.iacr.org/2015/625
14. Hart, W.: FLINT: Fast Library for Number Theory (2016). http://www.flintlib.org
15. Langley, A., Hamburg, M., Turner, S.: Elliptic Curves for Security. IETF RFC 7748 (2016). https://doi.org/10.17487/RFC7748
16. Montgomery, P.L.: Speeding the Pollard and elliptic curve methods of factorization. Math. Comput. 48(177), 243–264 (1987). https://doi.org/10.1090/S0025-5718-1987-0866113-7
17. Nir, Y., Josefsson, S.: Curve25519 and Curve448 for the Internet Key Exchange Protocol Version 2 (IKEv2) Key Agreement. IETF RFC 8031 (2016). https://doi.org/10.17487/RFC8031
18. Nir, Y., Josefsson, S., Pégourié-Gonnard, M.: Elliptic Curve Cryptography (ECC) Cipher Suites for Transport Layer Security (TLS) Versions 1.2 and Earlier. IETF RFC 8422 (2018). https://doi.org/10.17487/RFC8422

19. Renes, J., Costello, C., Batina, L.: Complete addition formulas for prime order elliptic curves. In: Fischlin, M., Coron, J.-S. (eds.) EUROCRYPT 2016. LNCS, vol. 9665, pp. 403–428. Springer, Heidelberg (2016). https://doi.org/10.1007/978-3-662-49890-3_16
20. Rescorla, E.: The Transport Layer Security (TLS) Protocol Version 1.3. IETF RFC 8446 (2018). https://doi.org/10.17487/RFC8446
21. Shelby, Z., Hartke, K., Bormann, C.: The Constrained Application Protocol (CoAP). IETF RFC 7252 (2014). https://doi.org/10.17487/RFC7252
22. Silverman, J.H.: The Arithmetic of Elliptic Curves. Graduate Texts in Mathematics, vol. 186, 2nd edn. Springer, New York (2009). https://doi.org/10.1007/978-1-4757-1920-8
23. Wouters, P., Tschofenig, H., Gilmore, J., Weiler, S., Kivinen, T.: Using Raw Public Keys in Transport Layer Security (TLS) and Datagram Transport Layer Security (DTLS). IETF RFC 7250 (2014). https://doi.org/10.17487/RFC7250

Improved CRT-RSA Secret Key Recovery Method from Sliding Window Leakage

Kento Oonishi[1]([✉]), Xiaoxuan Huang[1], and Noboru Kunihiro[2]([✉])

[1] The University of Tokyo, Tokyo, Japan
kento_oonishi@mist.i.u-tokyo.ac.jp
[2] University of Tsukuba, Tsukuba, Japan
kunihiro@cs.tsukuba.ac.jp

Abstract. In this paper, we discuss side-channel attacks on the CRT-RSA scheme (RSA scheme with Chinese Remainder Theorem) implemented by the left-to-right sliding window method. This method calculates exponentiations by repeating squaring and multiplication. In CHES 2017, Bernstein et al. proposed side-channel attacks on the CRT-RSA signature scheme implemented by the left-to-right sliding window method. We can obtain square-and-multiply sequences by their side-channel attacks, but cannot calculate CRT-RSA secret keys because there are multiple candidates of multiplications. Then, Bernstein et al. calculated CRT-RSA secret keys by using two methods. First, they recovered CRT-RSA secret keys partially and calculated all secret key bits by using the Heninger–Shacham method. Second, they applied the Heninger–Shacham method to square-and-multiply sequences directly. They showed that we can calculate CRT-RSA secret keys more efficiently when we use square-and-multiply sequences directly. They also showed that we can recover CRT-RSA secret keys in polynomial time when $w \leq 4$. Moreover, they experimentally showed that we can recover secret keys of 2048-bit CRT-RSA scheme when $w = 5$. However, their latter method is simple and has room for improvement. Here, we study bit recovery more profoundly to improve their method. First, we calculate the exact rate of all knowable bits. Next, we propose a new method for calculating the proportion of each bit **0** or **1** in each nonrecovery bit. Finally, we propose a new method for calculating CRT-RSA secret key using this bit information. In our proposed algorithm, we extend Bernstein et al.'s method in combination with Kunihiro et al.'s method. We calculate more secret keys when $w = 5$ by our proposed method compared to Bernstein et al.'s method.

Keywords: Side-channel attacks · Sliding window method · CRT-RSA scheme · Secret key recovery

© Springer Nature Switzerland AG 2020
J. H. Seo (Ed.): ICISC 2019, LNCS 11975, pp. 278–296, 2020.
https://doi.org/10.1007/978-3-030-40921-0_17

1   Introduction

1.1   Background

Side-channel attacks [8] are major threats when using cryptography in systems. For example, when we decrypt messages, secret keys can be obtained from different types of physical information such as decryption time [8], power [6,9], sound [3], accessing cache [1,7,14,18,19], and so on. Even if we prove the security of cryptography strictly, we can somehow extract the full or partial secret information by observing this physical information. In this paper, we focus on the CRT-RSA (RSA scheme [15] with Chinese Remainder Theorem) encryption or signature scheme [12] implemented using the left-to-right sliding window method.

In side-channel attacks on the CRT-RSA scheme, there are two directions: reading all secret key bits from DRAM data remanence (cold boot attack [4]) or attacking two modular exponentiations using secret keys. In the former attack, we read DRAM data remanence on the target device, so we need the target device. However, this situation is not realistic, and therefore, we focus on the latter, side-channel attacks on two modular exponentiations.

Modular exponentiations in the CRT-RSA scheme are implemented using the binary method, fixed window method, or sliding window method. These methods are implemented by repeating squaring and multiplication. In the binary method, we use only one multiplier. In the other methods, we use many multipliers, which are defined by window size w. When we use a larger w, we can calculate exponentiations faster by reducing the number of multiplications, instead of using more memory, because of saving more multipliers.

When we conduct side-channel attacks on modular exponentiation, we obtain a square-and-multiply sequence from the physical information. If we obtain the multiplier of each multiplication [2,6,7], we can calculate CRT-RSA secret keys immediately. However, if we fail to do so, we cannot calculate CRT-RSA secret keys immediately because there are many candidates in each multiplication. To address this issue, Bernstein et al. [1] discussed how to calculate CRT-RSA secret keys from square-and-multiply sequences without a multiplier on sliding window method. They calculated CRT-RSA secret keys by using two methods. First, they recovered CRT-RSA secret keys partially, and thereafter, recovered all secret key bits. Second, they calculated CRT-RSA secret keys from square-and-multiply sequences directly. Both these methods use the Heninger–Shacham method [5] to calculate the CRT-RSA secret keys.

First, Bernstein et al. [1] researched how to recover CRT-RSA secret keys partially from square-and-multiply sequences. They proposed the method of recovering bits of partial CRT-RSA secret keys, especially in the left-to-right sliding window method. Based on this method, they showed that we can recover more bits in the left-to-right sliding window method than in the right-to-left sliding window method. Moreover, they succeeded in calculating secret keys of 1024-bit CRT-RSA scheme when $w = 4$, by applying the Heninger–Shacham method [5] to the recovered bits.

Next, Bernstein et al. [1] calculated the CRT-RSA secret keys directly from square-and-multiply sequences in the left-to-right sliding window method. They proved that their algorithm works in polynomial time when $w \leq 4$. Moreover, they succeeded in calculating secret keys of 2048-bit CRT-RSA scheme when $w = 5$. Their result indicated that it is better to calculate CRT-RSA secret keys directly from square-and-multiply sequences.

However, their method of calculating CRT-RSA secret keys directly from square-and-multiply sequences is simple. Therefore, there is an opportunity of calculating more CRT-RSA secret keys by extending their method.

To improve their algorithm, we should research why we can calculate more CRT-RSA secret keys directly from square-and-multiply sequences than partially recovering bits. Especially, we need to conduct more research on bit information of a square-and-multiply sequence. However, this requires more in-depth research [1]. First, Bernstein et al. did not analyze the exact behavior of the method of recovering bits of partial CRT-RSA secret keys. Although they showed that they can recover more bits when applying the method repeatedly, they discarded this situation because of a rare occurrence. Second, they did not completely discuss the difference between the two methods.

Van Vredendaal [17] addressed these problems. First, he proposed the optimal bit recovery method, which can recover all knowable bits. According to his rules, we can recover all knowable bits that are common in all candidates corresponding to a given square-and-multiply sequence. Second, he proposed a method to calculate the number of input candidates corresponding to a given square-and-multiply sequence. Using these two results, he researched more about the bit recovery method. However, this result also needs to be further researched to connect with improving Bernstein et al.'s method.

1.2 Our Contribution

In this paper, we obtain three results. First, we calculate the exact rate of all knowable bits. For this purpose, we use the renewal reward theorem (RRT) [16]. Bernstein et al. [1] also tried to calculate the bit recovery rate by using RRT. However, they only calculate the upper bound and the lower bound of the rate of recovering bits using their bit recovery rules. We revisit their analysis and calculate the exact rate of all knowable bits.

Second, we extract embedding information from the nonrecovery bits by proposing a new method of calculating the proportion of each bit value **0** or **1** in each nonrecovery bit. To calculate this proportion, we develop a random sampling method of bit sequences not to contradict a square-and-multiply sequence. We develop our method based on Vredendaal's method [17] to calculate the number of input candidates corresponding to a given square-and-multiply sequence. The result of this calculation indicates that there is a difference between the proportion of each bit value in each nonrecovery bit.

Finally, we propose a new CRT-RSA secret key recovery algorithm using the proportion of each bit value as additional information. In our proposed method, we apply Kunihiro et al.'s algorithm [10] on the obtained proportion of each bit value. We extend Bernstein et al.'s method based on square-and-multiply sequences directly in combination with Kunihiro et al.'s algorithm. Using our new algorithm, we can calculate 21% CRT-RSA secret keys when $w = 5$. This is a significant improvement compared to 13% in the original Bernstein et al.'s method.

2   Preliminary

In this section, we introduce CRT-RSA scheme [12], and the left-to-right sliding window method [11]. In addition, we introduce the method of recovering CRT-RSA secret keys partially [1], and the method of recovering all knowable bits from square-and-multiply sequences [17]. Moreover, we introduce previous methods of calculating CRT-RSA secret keys [1,5,10].

2.1   CRT-RSA Scheme

Before introducing the CRT-RSA encryption and signature scheme, we introduce the standard RSA scheme [15]. This scheme comprises public keys (N, e) and a secret key (p, q, d). p and q are $n/2$ bit prime numbers; public keys (N, e) and a secret key d satisfy $N = pq$ and $ed \equiv 1 \bmod (p-1)(q-1)$. In the standard RSA encryption scheme, we encrypt a plaintext m by calculating $C = m^e \bmod N$, and decrypt ciphertext C by calculating $m = C^d \bmod N$. In the standard RSA signature scheme, we generate a signature on m by calculating $\sigma = h(m)^d \bmod N$, and verify the signature σ by checking $h(m) = \sigma^e \bmod N$. In this signature scheme, h is a secure hash function. These two RSA schemes are composed of two modular exponentiations: $x^e \bmod N$, using a public key e, and $x^d \bmod N$, using a secret key d. While we use a small public key e, such as $2^{16} + 1 = 65537$, we use a larger key d. Therefore, the implementation time may be longer in decryption or signature generation than in encryption or verification.

The CRT-RSA scheme realizes faster decryption and signature generation by applying the Chinese remainder theorem (CRT) decomposition on a secret key d. We add secret keys $d_p := d \bmod p-1$, $d_q := d \bmod q-1$ and $q_p := q^{-1} \bmod p$. Encryption is the same as that of the standard RSA scheme. In decryption or signature generation, we calculate two modular exponentiations, $x^{d_p} \bmod p$ and $x^{d_q} \bmod q$, using secret keys, and calculate $x^d \bmod N$ by applying CRT on these two values. Calculating $x^d \bmod N$ is about four times faster in the CRT-RSA scheme compared to the standard RSA scheme because we deal with half bits in modular exponentiations.

2.2   Left-to-Right Sliding Window Method

Exponentiation using left-to-right sliding window method is calculated using Algorithm 1. During the calculation, we read bits from the MSB side to the LSB side. We calculate the left-to-right sliding window method by repeating squaring (**S**) and multiplication (**M**), as in Algorithm 1. Multiplication is conducted in

---

Algorithm 1. Left-to-Right Sliding Window Method [11]

Input: $c, d = (d_t, d_{t-1}, \cdots, d_0)_2$, the window size $w \geq 1$
Output: c^d
Precomputation
   $c_1 = c, c_2 = c^2$
   for $i = 1$ **to** $2^{w-1} - 1$
      $c_{2i+1} = c_{2i-1} \cdot c_2$
   end for
Exponentiation
   $A = 1, i = t$
   while $i \geq 0$
      if $d_i = 0$
         1: $A = A^2$ (Squaring)
         2: $i = i - 1$
      else
         1: Find the longest bit-string $d_i d_{i-1} \cdots d_l$ such that $i - l + 1 \leq w$ and
            $d_l = 1$.
         2: $A = A^{2(i-l+1)} \cdot c_{\left(d_i d_{i-1} \cdots d_l\right)_2}$ (Squaring and Multiplication)
         3: $i = l - 1$
      end if
   end while
   return A

---

w-bits with leading one. In this paper, we call the w-bits led by one as a window. Note that when we use a larger w, we can calculate exponentiations faster by reducing the number of multiplications, instead of using more memory.

2.3 Extract CRT-RSA Secret Key Bits from Side-Channel Information

As mentioned in the previous subsection, we calculate exponentiations by repeating squaring (**S**) and multiplication (**M**) in the sliding window method. In the CRT-RSA scheme, we can obtain square-and-multiply sequences of two exponentiations, $x^{d_p} \bmod p$ and $x^{d_q} \bmod q$, by side-channel attacks [1]. However, because there are many candidates in each multiplication (**M**), we cannot determine CRT-RSA secret keys from square-and-multiply sequences immediately.

Bernstein et al. [1] proposed the method of recovering bits of partial CRT-RSA secret keys. Their method comprised four rules, Rule 0–3. We explain these rules by using an example for $w = 4$, as follows.

SSSMSSSSSSMSSSMSSSSSMSMSSSSSSMSSSSSSM

Before applying the optimal bit recovery rules, we convert square-and-multiply sequences into **x** and **x̲** sequences by converting **SM** into **x̲** and the remaining **S** into **x**. This **x** and **x̲** sequence is a bit sequence with a value of **0** or **1**. By applying this conversion, our example is converted to the following.

$$\text{xx}\underline{\text{xxxxxx}}\text{xx}\underline{\text{xxxxxxx}}\underline{\text{xx}}\text{xxxxxx}\underline{\text{x}}\text{xxxxxx}$$

They apply following Rule 0–3 to the given sequences:

- **Rule 0**: $\underline{\text{x}} \rightarrow \underline{1}$.
- **Rule 1**: $\underline{1}\text{x}^i\underline{1}\text{x}^{w-1-i} \rightarrow \underline{1}\text{x}^i\underline{10}^{w-1-i}$ for $0 \leq i \leq w - 2$.
- **Rule 2**: $\text{x}^{w-1}\underline{11} \rightarrow 1\text{x}^{w-2}\underline{11}$.
- **Rule 3**: $\underline{1}\text{x}^i\text{x}^{w-1}\underline{1} \rightarrow \underline{10}^i\text{x}^{w-1}\underline{1}$ for $i > 0$.

In each rules, they recover multiplication bits in Rule 0, trailing zeros in Rule 1, leading one in Rule 2, and, leading zeros in Rule 3. Note that they actually recovered more bits by applying more extended situation in Rule 1 [1]. In their widen Rule 1, they search $\underline{1}$ from the MSB to the LSB. In the highest-order $\underline{1}$, if $\underline{1}$ satisfies $\text{x}^i\underline{1}\text{x}^{w-1-i}$ for $0 \leq i \leq w - 2$, they recover x after $\underline{1}$ as $\mathbf{0}$, namely,

$$\text{x}^i\underline{1}\text{x}^{w-1-i} \rightarrow \text{x}^i\underline{10}^{w-1-i}.$$

In other $\underline{1}$s, if $\underline{1}$ satisfies $(\mathbf{0} \text{ or } \underline{1})\text{x}^i\underline{1}\text{x}^{w-1-i}$ for $0 \leq i \leq w - 2$, they recover x after the latter $\underline{1}$ as $\mathbf{0}$, namely,

$$(\mathbf{0} \text{ or } \underline{1})\text{x}^i\underline{1}\text{x}^{w-1-i} \rightarrow (\mathbf{0} \text{ or } \underline{1})\text{x}^i\underline{10}^{w-1-i}.$$

By applying these Rule 0–3 in this order, the recovery bits are given as

Applying Rule 0: xx$\underline{1}$xxxxx$\underline{1}$xx$\underline{1}$xxxx$\underline{11}$xxxxx$\underline{1}$xxxxx$\underline{1}$,

Applying Rule 1: xx$\underline{1}$0xxxx$\underline{1}$xx$\underline{1}$0xxx$\underline{11}$000xx$\underline{1}$0xxxx$\underline{1}$,

Applying Rule 2: xx$\underline{1}$0xxxx$\underline{1}$xx$\underline{1}$01xx$\underline{11}$000xx$\underline{1}$0xxxx$\underline{1}$,

Applying Rule 3: xx$\underline{1}$00xxx$\underline{1}$xx$\underline{1}$01xx$\underline{11}$000xx$\underline{1}$00xxx$\underline{1}$.

They remarked that they recover more bits by repeating their rules. For example, if we apply their bit recovery rules on our example twice, the recovery bits are given as

Applying once: xx$\underline{1}$00xxx$\underline{11}$x$\underline{1}$01xx$\underline{11}$000xx$\underline{1}$00xxx$\underline{1}$,

Applying twice: xx$\underline{1}$001xx$\underline{11}$x$\underline{1}$01xx$\underline{11}$000xx$\underline{1}$00xxx$\underline{1}$.

In above example, they recover the leading one by extending their Rule 2. If there is $\underline{1}$ satisfies $\text{x}^{w-1-i}\underline{10}^i$ ($\mathbf{1}$ or $\underline{1}$) for $0 \leq i \leq w - 2$ and $\mathbf{0}$s are recovered in Rule 1, they recover as

$$\text{x}^{w-1-i}\underline{10}^j(\mathbf{1} \text{ or } \underline{1}) \rightarrow 1\text{x}^{w-2-i}\underline{10}^j(\mathbf{1} \text{ or } \underline{1}).$$

They discarded this situation because of a rare occurrence and they did not study more about additional recovery bits. Therefore, their method does not recover all bits we can recover.

Van Vredendaal [17] tackled this problem more rigorously, and he proposed the new method recovering all knowable bits. From now on, we explain all knowable bits by the toy example. We consider **SSMSSM** in $w = 2$. Bit sequences **0101**, **1101**, and **1111** do not contradict with **SSMSSM**. Common bits are the second one and fourth one; thus, all knowable bits are **x1x1**. In this sense, Vredendaal's bit recovery method has optimality in bit recovery.

From now on, we explain Vredendaal's method briefly. In Van Vredendaal's method, he indexes the original number b converted into square-and-multiply sequence as $b_{n-1}b_{n-2}\ldots b_0$. After that, he defines the set of indexes of multiplication bits as $M = \{k_0, k_1, \ldots, k_l\}$ with $k_0 > k_1 > \cdots > k_l$. In each multiplication bits k_j, he defines the multiplier width m_{k_j} as the number of bits used in determining multiplier. For, example if multiplier is $5 = 101_2$, the multiplier width is 3. Next, he calculates $m_{k_j}^+ := \max m_{k_j}$ in each window from MSB sides, by greedy algorithm determining each window as near as MSB sides. As similarly, he calculates $m_{k_j}^- := \min m_{k_j}$ in each window from LSB sides. For example, we consider our example,

$$\text{xx}\underline{1}\text{xxxxx}\underline{1}\text{xx}\underline{1}\text{xxxx}\underline{11}\text{xxxxx}\underline{1}\text{xxxx}\underline{1}.$$

We calculate $m_{k_j}^+$ by dividing as

$$\text{xx}\underline{1}\text{x x xxx}\underline{1}\text{ xx}\underline{1}\text{x xxx}\underline{1}\text{ }\underline{1}\text{xxx xx}\underline{1}\text{x x xxx}\underline{1},$$

and $m_{k_0}^+ = 3, m_{k_1}^+ = 4, m_{k_2}^+ = 3, m_{k_3}^+ = 4, m_{k_4}^+ = 1, m_{k_5}^+ = 3, m_{k_6}^+ = 4$. Similarly, we calculate $m_{k_j}^-$ by dividing as

$$\text{x x}\underline{1}\text{xx xxx}\underline{1}\text{ xx}\underline{1}\text{x xxx}\underline{1}\text{ }\underline{1}\text{xxx xx }\underline{1}\text{xxx xx }\underline{1}.$$

and $m_{k_0}^- = 2, m_{k_1}^- = 4, m_{k_2}^- = 3, m_{k_3}^- = 4, m_{k_4}^- = 1, m_{k_5}^- = 1, m_{k_6}^- = 1$.

After calculating $m_{k_j}^+$ and $m_{k_j}^-$, he recovers bits as

$$b_i = \begin{cases} 1 & \text{if } i \in M \\ 1 & \text{else if } j + m_{k_j}^- - 1 = i = j + m_{k_j}^+ - 1 \text{ for some } j \in M \\ \text{x} & \text{else if } j + m_{k_j}^- - 1 \leq i \leq j + m_{k_j}^+ - 1 \text{ for some } j \in M \\ 0 & \text{otherwise} \end{cases}$$

and all knowable bits by Van Vredendaal's method are given as

$$\text{xx}\underline{1}\text{001xx}\underline{11}\text{x}\underline{1}\text{01xx}\underline{11}\text{000xx}\underline{1}\text{00xxx}\underline{1}.$$

He remarked that the second **1** corresponds to Rule 2 in [1] and last **0** corresponds to Rule 1 and 3 in [1].

By considering Vredendaal's method more detail, the same bit recovery can be realized by a small modification of Bernstein et al.'s method [1]. Especially, we can recover some bits when we calculate $m_{k_j}^+$ and $m_{k_j}^-$. First, the calculation of $m_{k_j}^+$ corresponds to Rule 1 in the extending Bernstein et al.'s rules. Second, the calculation of $m_{\overline{k}_j}$ corresponds to Rule 2 in the extending Bernstein et al.'s rules. After calculating $m^{+}_{k_j}$ and $m^{-}_{k_j}$, we can recover $\mathbf{0}$ in the original Bernstein et al.'s rules. Therefore, all knowable bits can be recovered by a small modification of Bernstein et al.'s method [1]. Hereinafter, we refer to this method as the optimal bit recovery rules.

From now on, we explain the optimal bit recovery rules. Rule 0 and Rule 1 are the same as [1]. In Rule 2, we search $\underline{1}$ from the LSB to the MSB. If $\underline{1}$ satisfies $\mathbf{x}^{w-1-i}\underline{1}0^i(1$ or $\underline{1})$ for $0 \leq i \leq w - 2$, we recover as

$$\mathbf{x}^{w-1-i}\underline{1}0^i(1 \text{ or } \underline{1}) \rightarrow 1\mathbf{x}^{w-2-i}\underline{1}0^i(1 \text{ or } \underline{1})$$

Note that Bernstrin et al. only dealt with $i = 0$ because another event rarely occurred [1]. Because Rule 2 is modified, we modify Rule 3 corresponding to Rule 2. In Rule 3, where we search $\underline{1}$ from the MSB to the LSB. In the highest-order $\underline{1}$, if $\underline{1}$ satisfies $\mathbf{x}^i1\mathbf{x}^k\underline{1}$ or $\mathbf{x}^i\mathbf{x}^{w-1}\underline{1}$ for $i \geq 0$, we recover as following.

$$\mathbf{x}^i1\mathbf{x}^k\underline{1} \text{ or } \mathbf{x}^i\mathbf{x}^{w-1}\underline{1} \rightarrow 0^i1\mathbf{x}^k\underline{1} \text{ or } 0^i\mathbf{x}^{w-1}\underline{1}.$$

In other $\underline{1}$s, if $\underline{1}$ satisfies $(\mathbf{0}$ or $\underline{1})\mathbf{x}^j1\mathbf{x}^k\underline{1}$ or $(\mathbf{0}$ or $\underline{1})\mathbf{x}^j\mathbf{x}^{w-1}\underline{1}$, we recover as

$$(\mathbf{0} \text{ or } \underline{1})\mathbf{x}^j1\mathbf{x}^k\underline{1} \rightarrow (\mathbf{0} \text{ or } \underline{1})0^j1\mathbf{x}^k\underline{1},$$

$$(\mathbf{0} \text{ or } \underline{1})\mathbf{x}^j\mathbf{x}^{w-1}\underline{1} \rightarrow (\mathbf{0} \text{ or } \underline{1})0^j\mathbf{x}^{w-1}\underline{1}.$$

Note that there is no overlap in recovered bit in each Rule in the optimal bit recovery rules, while there are overlaps in Rule 1 and 3 in the original Bernstein et al.'s rules. By applying modified Rule 2 and 3, our example is recovered as

Applying Rule 1: xx$\underline{1}$0xxxx$\underline{1}$xx$\underline{1}$0xxx$\underline{11}$000xx$\underline{1}$0xxxx$\underline{1}$,

Applying Modified Rule 2: xx$\underline{1}$0x1xx$\underline{11}$x$\underline{1}$01xx$\underline{11}$000xx$\underline{1}$0xxxx$\underline{1}$,

Applying Modified Rule 3: xx$\underline{1}$001xx$\underline{11}$x$\underline{1}$01xx$\underline{11}$000xx$\underline{1}$00xxx$\underline{1}$.

2.4 Previous Method of Calculating CRT-RSA Secret Keys

In this subsection, we explain previous methods of calculating CRT-RSA secret keys used in our new proposed algorithm. First, we explain Heninger–Shacham method [5], the basis of calculating CRT-RSA secret keys. Next, we explain Bernstein et al.'s method [1] and Kunihiro et al.'s method [10].

Heninger–Shacham Method [5]. Heninger and Shacham proposed the method constructing the CRT-RSA key candidate tree. They construct the CRT-RSA key candidate tree when the public keys (N, e) and parameters $(k_p, k_q) \in \mathbb{Z}^2$ satisfying $ed_p = 1 + k_p(p - 1)$ and $ed_q = 1 + k_q(q - 1)$ are given. (k_p, k_q) are initially unknown. However, these value satisfies $0 < k_p, k_q < e$. Moreover, k_p and k_q satisfy $(k_p - 1)(k_q - 1) \equiv k_p k_q N \bmod e$ [7,19]. Therefore, the number of candidates of (k_p, k_q) is at most $e - 1$.

They define $\tau(x) = \max_{m \in \mathbb{Z}} 2^m | x$ in order to explain the CRT-RSA key candidate tree. At i-th depth of the CRT-RSA key candidate tree, they have leaves containing $(i+1)$-bit number p', q', $(i+1+\tau(k_p))$-bit number d'_p, and $(i+1+\tau(k_q))$-bit number d'_q satisfying

$$p'q' \equiv N \bmod 2^{i+1},$$
$$ed'_p \equiv 1 + k_p(p'-1) \bmod 2^{i+1+\tau(k_p)},$$
$$ed'_q \equiv 1 + k_q(q'-1) \bmod 2^{i+1+\tau(k_q)}.$$

From the root, they adopt branch and bound algorithm by saving leaves satisfying above. Then, CRT-RSA key candidate tree becomes the binary tree. At last, they have $2^{n/2}$ candidates. However, finding the correct secret keys consumes tremendous time. Therefore, we adopt more pruning using side-channel information in previous works [1, 10].

Bernstein et al.'s Method [1]. Bernstein et al. [1] calculated the CRT-RSA secret keys from square-and-multiply sequences in two ways: from via recovery bits and from square-and-multiply sequences directly. In the former method, they calculate CRT-RSA secret keys by discarding leaves that do not match with the partial recovery bits. From now on, we explain the latter method mainly. In the latter method, they focus on the fact that the number of bits and the number of **S** in a square-and-multiply sequence are the same. They define the index of **S** focusing only on **S** in a square-and-multiply sequence from LSB side. After that, they define the set S as the indexes of **S** that is the next of **M** or the beginning of w **S** in d_p, d_q. The set S directly corresponds to the position of bits in d_p, d_q. Their method repeats branch and bound based on the set S. First, they calculate bits of d_p, d_q. When they calculate bits in S, they only convert d_p or d_q calculating bits in S into a square-and-multiply sequence, and they discard a leaf if there are mismatches with the given sequence. By repeating these, they calculate CRT-RSA secret keys from square-and-multiply sequences.

Kunihiro et al.'s Method [10]. Kunihiro et al.'s method [10] recovers CRT-RSA secret keys when there are erasures and errors in secret keys. Their method repeats branch and bound. First, they calculate t-revealed d_p, d_q bits by skipping the erasure bits. Second, they discard a leaf if there are more than c mismatches between the calculated and given t bits. By repeating these, they recover CRT-RSA secret keys with erasures and errors.

3 Rate of All Knowable Bits

3.1 Theoretical Analysis of the Exact Rate of All Knowable Bits

Hereinafter, we provide a theoretical analysis of the exact rate of all knowable bits, which is given by Theorem 1.

Theorem 1. Suppose that we generate bits randomly. If $w \geq 2$, the average rate of all knowable bits is given by

$$\frac{2}{w+1} + \frac{\displaystyle\sum_{k=0}^{w-2} f_w(k)g(k)}{2(w+1)} + \frac{2^w - 1}{2^{w-1}(2^{w-1}+1)}\frac{1}{3(w+1)}$$

where

$$f_w(k) = \frac{2}{3 \cdot 2^k}\left(1 - \frac{1}{2^{w-k}}\right)\left(1 - \frac{2}{2^{w-k}}\right), g(k) = 2\left(1 - \frac{2^k}{2^{k+2}-1}\right)\prod_{j=1}^{k}\frac{2^{j-1}}{2^{j+1}-1}.$$

To prove Theorem 1, we analyze the optimal bit recovery rules. The first term $2/(w+1)$ corresponds to Rule 0 and Rule 3, the second term corresponds to Rule 1, and the third term corresponds to Rule 2.

To prove Theorem 1, we use the renewal reward theorem [16]. This theorem is given as Theorem 2 with notation in [1].

Theorem 2 [16]. We are given i.i.d. probability distribution (X_i, Y_i) $(i \in \mathbb{N})$. We define $S_n = \displaystyle\sum_{i=1}^{n} X_i$ $(n \in \mathbb{N})$, $N_t = \displaystyle\sum_{n=1}^{\infty} 1\,(S_n \leq t)$ $(t \in \mathbb{R}^+)$, and $R_t = \displaystyle\sum_{i=1}^{N_t} Y_i$ $(t \in \mathbb{R}^+)$. If $E[X_1] < \infty$, $E[Y_1] < \infty$, then $\displaystyle\lim_{t \to \infty} \frac{R_t}{t} = \frac{E[Y_1]}{E[X_1]}$.

In the renewal reward theorem, we define the time that satisfies some condition as renewal. In Theorem 2, we can regard X_i as inter-arrival times, S_n as the arrival time of n-th elements, and N_t as the number of arrivals in time t. Renewal occurs in each X_i. Moreover, we define the reward in each renewal. In Theorem 2, we regard Y_i as the reward in each inter-arrival time X_i. Then, we can regard R_t as the reward in time t. We regard the length of CRT-RSA secret keys (d_p, d_q) as time t and that of the recovering bits as reward R_t. Bernstein et al. [1] attempted to calculate the bit recovery rate by using the renewal reward theorem [16] under the same settings. However, they only calculate the upper bound and the lower bound of the rate of recovering bits using their bit recovery rules. Thus, they failed to calculate the exact bit recovery rate.

We define i.i.d. (X_i, Y_i) in the analysis of each Rule j as follows:

- X_i: The length of bit sequences until the designated bit pattern in Rule j occurs,
- Y_i: The number of recovered bits in X_i.

To define (X_i, Y_i) as i.i.d., we determine the definition of X_i in each rule, while Bernstein et al. only considered one window. This is because we consider $m_{k_j}^+$ or $m_{k_j}^-$ in each rule, not the actual m_{k_j}. Therefore, we must consider how we make $m_{k_j}^+$ or $m_{k_j}^-$ constant. From now on, we explain (X_i, Y_i) in each Rule 0–3.

Table 1. Bit recovery rate in each rule

w	Rule 0 (%)	Rule 1 (%)	Rule 2 (%)	Rule 3 (%)	all (%)
3 (Experimental)	25.01	8.06	2.93	24.96	60.97
3 (Theoretical)	25.00	8.04	2.92	25.00	60.95
4 (Experimental)	20.00	8.41	1.38	19.99	49.78
4 (Theoretical)	20.00	8.42	1.39	20.00	49.81
5 (Experimental)	16.67	7.94	0.63	16.67	41.90
5 (Theoretical)	16.67	7.95	0.63	16.67	41.92
6 (Experimental)	14.29	7.24	0.28	14.29	36.09
6 (Theoretical)	14.29	7.24	0.28	14.29	36.09
7 (Experimental)	12.50	6.49	0.13	12.53	31.65
7 (Theoretical)	12.50	6.52	0.13	12.50	31.65

At first, we explain (X_i, Y_i) in Rule 0. In Rule 0, we recover a multiplication bit in each window. Thus, the number of recovery bits is independent between each window. Therefore, we simply define X_i as the number of bits until we hit a window.

Next, we explain (X_i, Y_i) in Rule 1. In Rule 1, we recover trailing zeros by greedy algorithm as calculating $m_{k_j}^+$. If we focus on one window, the value of $m_{k_j}^+$ depends on the difference between $m_{k_{j-1}}^+$ and the actual $m_{k_{j-1}}$. Thus, there is dependency on Y_{j-1} and Y_j. Now, we recall the definition of $m_{k_j}^+ := \max m_{k_j}$. When we hit the window whose $m_{k_j} = w$, then we consider the same window in Rule 1 as actual. Thus, we define X_i as the number of bits until we hit window $\mathbf{1x} \ldots \mathbf{x\underline{1}}$, whose $m_{k_j} = w$.

The same X_i as Rule 1 is used in Rule 3, recovering leading zeros. This is because the difference between $m_{k_{j-1}}^+$ and the actual $m_{k_{j-1}}$ causes more recovering bits in Rule 3. This means that the recovered bits in Rule 3 have dependency with $m_{k_{j-1}}$. Therefore, we use the same X_i in Rule 3 as Rule 1, because of the same reason.

Finally, we explain (X_i, Y_i) in Rule 2. In Rule 2, we recover leading one when $m_{k_j}^+ = m_{k_j}^-$ during the calculation of $m_{k_j}^-$. Thus, if we assure $m_{k_{j+1}}^+ \neq m_{k_{j+1}}^-$, there is no dependency between Y_j and Y_{j+1}. Especially, if we we assure $m_{k_{j+1}}^+ \neq m_{k_{j+1}}$, there is no dependency between Y_j and Y_{j+1}. Therefore, we define X_i as the number of bits until we hit window that moves certainly, and calculate the bit recovery rate.

The proof of Theorem 1 is given in the full version of this paper.

3.2 Numerical Experiment: Calculating the Exact Rate of All Knowable Bits

To check the validity of our analysis, we generate 10000 bits randomly, convert them into square-and-multiply sequences, and apply the optimal bit recovery

Table 2. All knowable bit rates in 2048-bit CRT-RSA scheme

w	3	4	5	6	7
CRT-RSA (%)	60.80	49.96	41.84	36.19	31.76
Random Bits (%)	60.97	49.80	41.89	35.98	31.65

rules. We conduct experiment 1000 times and calculate the average rate in each rule and the average rate of all knowable bits. Table 1 shows the results of this experiment. Table 1 shows that our analysis matches the experimental result.

3.3 Numerical Experiment: Applying to the CRT-RSA Scheme

Now, we apply the optimal bit recovery rules on CRT-RSA secret keys d_p and d_q. In this experiments, we check if the rates of recovered bits are similar between CRT-RSA secret keys and random bits. We generate secret keys on 2048-bit CRT-RSA scheme, and generate square-and-multiply sequences. In each CRT-RSA secret key, we generate square-and-multiply sequences on (d_p, d_q), and therefore, obtain two square-and-multiply sequences. We apply the optimal bit recovery rules on these two square-and-multiply sequences, and calculate all knowable bit rates. We repeat the above for 100 CRT-RSA secret keys generated randomly. After that, we average all knowable bit rates over 100 times results. Moreover, we generate 1024 bits randomly 200 times, generate square-and-multiply sequences, apply the optimal bit recovery rules, and average all knowable bit rates over 200 times results.

Table 2 shows our experimental results. The bit recovery rates in CRT-RSA secret keys and random bits are almost the same. Therefore, the rates of recovered bits are similar between CRT-RSA secret keys and random bits.

4 Obtaining More Information on Bits

In the previous section, we gave the exact rate of all knowable bits. However, when we only use all knowable bits, we cannot recover CRT-RSA secret keys in polynomial time when $w = 4$ because the exact rate of all knowable bits is less than 50% [13]. This contradicts with Bernstein et al.'s result, according to which we can recover CRT-RSA secret keys in polynomial time when $w = 4$ [1].

From now on, we focus on nonrecovered bits. The additional information is embedded in nonrecovered bits, as dictated in [1,17]. We capture this additional information by calculating the proportion of each bit value **0** or **1** in nonrecovered bits. For example, we consider **SSMSSM** in $w = 2$ again. Bit sequences **0101**, **1101**, and **1111** do not contradict with **SSMSSM**. Common bits are the second one and fourth one; thus, all knowable bits are **x1x1**. If there is no information on the nonrecovered bits, the first and third bits, we have $2^2 = 4$ candidates.

Algorithm 2. Random Sampling

Input: the window size w, a square-and-multiply sequence

Output: An input candidate that does not contradict to a given square-and-multiply sequence

Step 1: Calculate the Number of Candidates

from The lowest-order window **to** The highest-order window

    for all possible windows

        1. Sum of number of candidates of the neighboring lower-order windows that do not have common bits with the current window (A).

        2. Calculate the number of candidates of the current window (B).

        3. Calculate A times B and store in the current candidate window.

    end for

Step 2: Sampling a Bit Sequence

from The highest-order window **to** The lowest-order window

    1. Define $X_1, X_2, \ldots, X_k$ as the number of candidates for all possible current windows that do not overlap with the neighboring higher-order window.

    2. Choose a window with probability $X_i / \left(\sum_{j=1}^k X_j \right)$.

    3. Set 0 between the current window and the neighboring higher-order window.

    4. In the current window,

        a. Set MSB bit as **1**.

        b. Set lower-order bits of **1** as **0**.

        c. Set nondetermined bits as **0** or **1** randomly.

However, there are actually 3 candidates. When we focus on the nonrecovered bits, the proportions of each bit value are not the same. Therefore, additional information on nonrecovered bits is embedded in the proportion of each bit value.

In this section, we propose the method for obtaining the proportion of each bit value in each nonrecovered bit. For this purpose, we adopt the Monte-Carlo approach. First, we choose many input sequences uniformly that do not contradict with a given square-and-multiply sequence. However, the method of choosing the input sequences uniformly is not trivial. To construct this random sampling method, we construct our method based on van Vredendaal's method [17] to calculate the number of input candidates corresponding to the given square-and-multiply sequences. Vredendaal's method is a straightforward dynamic programming approach that calculates the number of candidates in each window. We use this information, the number of candidates, in our method for obtaining the proportion of each bit value in each nonrecovered bit.

Now, we propose the random sampling method to choose an input candidate uniformly that does not contradict with a given square-and-multiply sequence. Then, we show the result of numerical experiments conducted for calculating the proportion of each bit value.

4.1 Random Sampling Method Based on a Given Square-and-Multiply Sequence

Here, we propose a random sampling method of input candidates that do not contradict with a given square-and-multiply sequence. Our random sampling method is given as Algorithm 2. When we sample many outputs corresponding to the input, we run Step 1 once and Step 2 many times.

Step 1 of Algorithm 2 corresponds to van Vredendaal's method [17] for calculating the number of input candidates corresponding to a given square-and-multiply sequence. Step 1 calculates the number of candidates in each possible position of windows from low-order windows. The value A summarizes the information of low-order windows. The value B calculates the number of candidates of the current window as the b th of 2, when b is the number of non-determined bits in the current window. By storing A times B in each window, we preserve the number of candidates in each possible position of windows, including the information of low-order windows. When we finish Step 1, we obtain the number of input candidates corresponding to the given square-and-multiply sequence.

In Step 2, we sample an input candidate uniformly corresponding to the given square-and-multiply sequence. We determine the position of the window from higher windows. When the position of some windows is determined, we choose the neighboring low-order windows based on the number of candidates of each window in step 1. This selection method realizes sampling uniformly corresponding to the given square-and-multiply sequence. When the position of a window is determined, we set **0** between the current window and the neighboring higher-order window (leading zeros), set the MSB bit as **1** (leading one), and the lower-order bits of $\underline{1}$ as **0** (trailing zeros). Moreover, we set the nondetermined bits as **0** or **1** randomly because these bits are flat when the position of the window is determined. When we finish Step 2, we sample the input candidates that do not contradict with the square-and-multiply sequence, uniformly.

4.2 Numerical Experiment: Calculating the Proportion of Each Bit Value in Each Nonrecovered Bit

Here, we calculate the proportion of each bit in CRT-RSA secret keys using Algorithm 2. We conduct a numerical experiment on $w = 3$–7. In each w, we generate 2048-bit CRT-RSA secret keys 100 times randomly. In each CRT-RSA secret key, we generate square-and-multiply sequences on (d_p, d_q), and therefore, obtain two square-and-multiply sequences. Therefore, we generate 200 square-and-multiply sequences corresponding to 1024-bit number. In each square-and-multiply sequence, we obtain 1000 samples using Algorithm 2 and calculate the proportion of **1**. Moreover, we calculate the number of input candidates and that of bits that are not the same in 1000 samples. Finally, we average the above information over 200 square-and-multiply sequences and calculate the proportion of one bit, the average of unknown bits, and the average of $\log_2$(the average of #Candidate). The result is given in Table 3. Note that we drop fractions in the unknown bits and $\log_2$(the average of #Candidate) in Table 3.

Table 3. Distribution of proportion of **1** in 2048-bit CRT-RSA scheme

w	3	4	5	6	7
All 0	0.328	0.285	0.248	0.212	0.189
All 1	0.280	0.214	0.174	0.147	0.127
0–10%	0	0	0	0	0
10–20%	3.38×10^{-4}	3.91×10^{-5}	4.89×10^{-6}	0	0
20–30%	1.02×10^{-2}	5.17×10^{-3}	2.52×10^{-3}	1.41×10^{-3}	9.00×10^{-4}
30–40%	3.27×10^{-2}	2.45×10^{-2}	1.93×10^{-2}	1.55×10^{-2}	1.30×10^{-2}
40–50%	7.99×10^{-2}	0.104	0.133	0.168	0.199
50–60%	0.143	0.230	0.295	0.338	0.363
60–70%	5.90×10^{-2}	6.42×10^{-2}	5.86×10^{-2}	5.23×10^{-2}	4.74×10^{-2}
70–80%	3.20×10^{-2}	3.13×10^{-2}	2.73×10^{-2}	2.55×10^{-2}	2.23×10^{-2}
80–90%	2.31×10^{-2}	2.39×10^{-2}	2.29×10^{-2}	2.02×10^{-2}	1.84×10^{-2}
90–100%	1.22×10^{-2}	1.80×10^{-2}	2.00×10^{-2}	2.04×10^{-2}	1.90×10^{-2}
Unknown bits	400	512	591	655	699
$\log_2(\#\text{Candidate})$	350	448	534	608	660

From Table 3, the values of unknown bits and $\log_2(\#\text{Candidate})$ are larger in larger w, which agrees with our intuition that it is more difficult to calculate CRT-RSA secret keys in a larger w. Moreover, the proportion of **1** gathers at 40-60% when w is larger. This is the reason why it is more difficult to calculate CRT-RSA secret keys in a larger w.

From now on, we focus on $w = 4, 5$, because there is a gap between $w = 4, 5$ as we can recover CRT-RSA secret keys when $w = 4$ and cannot recover when $w = 5$ in polynomial time.

When $w = 4$, the number of unknown bits is 512 and $\log_2(\#\text{Candidate})$ is 448. The number of unknown bits is almost the same as $1024/2 = 512$ and $\log_2(\#\text{Candidate})$ is smaller than $1024/2 = 512$. Therefore, this corresponds to the fact that we can recover CRT-RSA secret keys when $w = 4$ in Bernstein et al.'s analysis [1].

When $w = 5$, the number of unknown bits is 591 and $\log_2(\#\text{Candidate})$ is 534. Both of the number of unknown bits and $\log_2(\#\text{Candidate})$ are larger than $1024/2 = 512$. Therefore, it is difficult to recover CRT-RSA secret keys when $w = 5$ in polynomial time. However, there are about 2% bits, that are **1** with high probability. This information corresponds to about 20 bits. In the next section, we use this information for calculating CRT-RSA secret keys.

5   New Method for Calculating CRT-RSA Secret Keys

Here, we propose a new method for calculating CRT-RSA secret keys. Our method is a combination Bernstein et al.'s method [1] and Kunihiro et al.'s method [10].

From now on, we explain our proposed method. First, we collect the information of d_p, d_q. At first, we recover all knowable bits using the optimal bit recovery rules and define the set of the position of these bits as R. Next, we calculate set

Table 4. Result of our proposed method in 2048-bit CRT-RSA scheme when $w = 5$

	ε	0	0.01	0.02	0.03	0.04	0.05	0.06	0.07	0.08	0.09	0.1
	t	1	100	50	33	25	20	16	14	12	11	10
$l = 1,000,000$	Time (s)	8.37	7.71	8.27	7.12	7.23	16.6	8.70	11.3	19.1	14.2	32.9
	Success Rate (%)	11	12	11	17	12	14	12	16	9	11	8
	Too Many (%)	89	88	89	83	88	86	83	78	86	74	75
	Pruning (%)	0	0	0	0	0	0	5	6	5	15	17
$l = 2,000,000$	Time (s)	12.1	11.2	15.9	17.0	14.0	27.8	8.50	12.6	20.4	17.5	12.6
	Success Rate (%)	19	16	14	16	19	17	20	21	11	15	10
	Too Many (%)	81	84	86	84	80	83	79	74	78	76	73
	Pruning (%)	0	0	0	0	1	0	1	5	11	9	17

S similar to [1]. Moreover, we run our random sampling algorithm r times on each d_p and d_q. In each d_p and d_q we recover bits as **0** when the proportion of **1** is less than ε, and **1** when the proportion is more than $1 - \varepsilon$. We define the set of the position of these bits as P.

Second, we calculate CRT-RSA secret keys using modification version of Kunihiro et al.'s method [10]. We basically apply Kunihiro et al.'s method on bits at the position in P. In Kunihiro et al.'s method, we must set the number of expanding bits t and threshold of mismatches c. These values are set in two points; $\varepsilon \leq c/t$ and t is as small as possible. The former condition is set not to discard the correct leaf. The latter condition is set to decrease the interval of pruning. Therefore, we basically set $c = 1$ and t as the smallest value such that $1/t \geq \varepsilon$, with the exception that $c = 0$ and $t = 1$ when $\varepsilon = 0$. After we set (t, c), we conduct branch and bound method by repeating

- we calculate t-revealed d_p, d_q bits at the position in P.
- we discard a leaf if there are more than c mismatches between the calculated and given t bits.

Additional to this pruning strategy, we adopt exception handling on the bits at the position in R or S. First, if we calculate the bits in R, we discard a leaf if there is mismatch with the information of all knowable bits. Next, if we calculate the bits in S, we convert calculated bits hitting S to a square-and-multiply sequence and we discard a leaf if there are mismatches with the given square-and-multiply sequence. By doing these, we recover CRT-RSA secret keys from square-and-multiply sequences.

Here, we compare our proposed method to the original Bernstein et al.'s method [1]. Our method conducts more pruning using the proportion of each bit value as additional information than the original method using only information of S. Thus, our proposed method generates less leaves while there are possibility of discarding the correct leaf. Therefore, when $w = 5$, we assume that our method recovers more CRT-RSA secret keys because we search less leaves than the original method.

Here, we calculate CRT-RSA secret keys using our proposed method and verify our assumption. We run our algorithm on $w = 5$ and set the number of random sampling as $r = 1000$. In our experiment, we implement our algorithm in depth first search and abort if we search l leaves similar to [1]. In each parameters, we make secret keys of 2048-bit CRT-RSA scheme 100 times randomly. We measure average time in successful trials and success rate when we are given the correct k_p, k_q.

Moreover, we record why our proposed method failed. There are two reasons of failure:

- We search more than l leaves.
- We prune the correct leaf.

In the original Bernstein et al.'s method, the reason of failure is only the former. However, stated above, our proposed method may discard the correct leave, and then, our method fails. Thus, we record the reason of failure.

The result is given in Table 4. In Table 4, "Too Many" means the failure because of searching more than l leaves and "Pruning" means the failure because of pruning the correct leaf.

When $l = 1,000,000$, we calculate 17% CRT-RSA secret keys when $(\varepsilon, t) = (0.03, 33)$, while the original Bernstein et al.'s method [1] calculates 8.6% CRT-RSA secret keys. When $l = 2,000,000$, we calculate 21% CRT-RSA secret keys when $(\varepsilon, t) = (0.07, 14)$, while the original method calculates 13% CRT-RSA secret keys. In almost all parameters, our method calculates more CRT-RSA secret keys than the original method. Therefore, our method calculates more secret keys compared to Bernstein et al.'s method when $w = 5$.

From now on, we focus on the reason of failure. The failure probability because of too many leaves is 70–90% in Table 4, that is much higher than the failure probability because of pruning the correct leaf. This is because we have small chance to hit the correct leaf because of too many leaves originally. In larger ε, the failure probability of too many leaves decreases, especially $\varepsilon \geq 0.09$ when $l = 1,000,000$, and $\varepsilon \geq 0.06$ when $l = 2,000,000$. This matches our intuition that our proposed method generate less leaves in larger ε. Moreover, in larger ε, the failure probability of pruning the correct leaf increases, especially $\varepsilon \geq 0.06$ in both l. This matches our intuition that our proposed method tends to discard the correct leaf in larger ε. Especially, when we set $\varepsilon \leq 0.05$, there is almost no failure because of pruning the correct leaf. However, when we set $\varepsilon \geq 0.08$, our method prunes the correct leaf with high probability. Therefore, the appropriate parameter of our method exists in $0.05 < \varepsilon < 0.08$.

6 Conclusion

Here, we improve Bernstein et al.'s method [1] when $w = 5$ by studying the bit recovery method more profoundly. First, we calculate the exact rate of all knowable bits. Next, we extract the information embedded in nonrecovery bits by proposing a method for calculating the proportion of each bit value in each nonrecovery bit. Finally, we propose a new method of calculating CRT-RSA secret key using the proportion of each bit value and improve Bernstein et al.'s method when $w = 5$. In the future, we should determine appropriate parameters in our proposed method.

Acknowledgements. This research was partially supported by JST CREST Grant Number JPMJCR14D6, Japan and JSPS KAKENHI Grant Number JP16H02780.

References

1. Bernstein, D.J., et al.: Sliding right into disaster: left-to-right sliding windows leak. In: Fischer, W., Homma, N. (eds.) CHES 2017. LNCS, vol. 10529, pp. 555–576. Springer, Cham (2017). https://doi.org/10.1007/978-3-319-66787-4_27
2. Genkin, D., Pachmanov, L., Pipman, I., Tromer, E.: Stealing keys from PCs using a radio: cheap electromagnetic attacks on windowed exponentiation. In: Güneysu, T., Handschuh, H. (eds.) CHES 2015. LNCS, vol. 9293, pp. 207–228. Springer, Heidelberg (2015). https://doi.org/10.1007/978-3-662-48324-4_11
3. Genkin, D., Shamir, A., Tromer, E.: RSA key extraction via low-bandwidth acoustic cryptanalysis. In: Garay, J.A., Gennaro, R. (eds.) CRYPTO 2014. LNCS, vol. 8616, pp. 444–461. Springer, Heidelberg (2014). https://doi.org/10.1007/978-3-662-44371-2_25
4. Halderman, J.A., et al.: Lest we remember: cold-boot attacks on encryption keys. Commun. ACM **52**, 91–98 (2009). https://doi.org/10.1145/1506409.1506429
5. Heninger, N., Shacham, H.: Reconstructing RSA private keys from random key bits. In: Halevi, S. (ed.) CRYPTO 2009. LNCS, vol. 5677, pp. 1–17. Springer, Heidelberg (2009). https://doi.org/10.1007/978-3-642-03356-8_1
6. Homma, N., Miyamoto, A., Aoki, T., Satoh, A., Shamir, A.: Comparative power analysis of modular exponentiation algorithms. IEEE Trans. Comput. **59**, 795–807 (2010). https://doi.org/10.1109/TC.2009.176
7. Inci, M.S., Gulmezoglu, B., Irazoqui, G., Eisenbarth, T., Sunar, B.: Cache attacks enable bulk key recovery on the cloud. In: Gierlichs, B., Poschmann, A.Y. (eds.) CHES 2016. LNCS, vol. 9813, pp. 368–388. Springer, Heidelberg (2016). https://doi.org/10.1007/978-3-662-53140-2_18
8. Kocher, P.C.: Timing attacks on implementations of Diffie-Hellman, RSA, DSS, and other systems. In: Koblitz, N. (ed.) CRYPTO 1996. LNCS, vol. 1109, pp. 104–113. Springer, Heidelberg (1996). https://doi.org/10.1007/3-540-68697-5_9
9. Kocher, P., Jaffe, J., Jun, B.: Differential power analysis. In: Wiener, M. (ed.) CRYPTO 1999. LNCS, vol. 1666, pp. 388–397. Springer, Heidelberg (1999). https://doi.org/10.1007/3-540-48405-1_25
10. Kunihiro, N., Shinohara, N., Izu, T.: Recovering RSA secret keys from noisy key bits with erasures and errors. IEICE Trans. Fundam. **E97-A**, 1273–1284 (2014). https://doi.org/10.1587/transfun.E97.A.1273
11. Menezes, A.J., van Oorschot, P.C., Vanstone, S.A.: Handbook of Applied Cryptography. CRC Press, Boca Raton (1996)
12. Moriarty, K., Kaliski, B., Jonsson, J., Rusch, A.: PKCS #1: RSA cryptography specifications version 2.2 (2016). https://tools.ietf.org/html/rfc8017
13. Paterson, K.G., Polychroniadou, A., Sibborn, D.L.: A coding-theoretic approach to recovering noisy RSA keys. In: Wang, X., Sako, K. (eds.) ASIACRYPT 2012. LNCS, vol. 7658, pp. 386–403. Springer, Heidelberg (2012). https://doi.org/10.1007/978-3-642-34961-4_24
14. Percival, C.: Cache missing for fun and profit (2005). http://www.daemonology.net/papers/htt.pdf
15. Rivest, R.L., Shamir, A., Adleman, L.: A method for obtaining digital signatures and public-key cryptosystems. Commun. ACM **21**, 120–126 (1978). https://doi.org/10.1145/359340.359342

16. Smith, W.L.: Renewal theory and its ramifications. J. Roy. Stat. Soc. **20**, 243–302 (1958). https://doi.org/10.1111/j.2517-6161.1958.tb00294.x
17. van Vredendaal, C.: Exploiting Mathematical Structures in Cryptography. Technische Universiteit Eindhoven, Eindhoven (2018)
18. Yarom, Y., Falkner, K.: FLUSH+RELOAD: a high resolution, low noise, L3 cache side-channel attack. In: USENIX 2014, pp. 719–732 (2014)
19. Yarom, Y., Genkin, D., Heninger, N.: CacheBleed: a timing attack on OpenSSL constant time RSA. In: Gierlichs, B., Poschmann, A.Y. (eds.) CHES 2016. LNCS, vol. 9813, pp. 346–367. Springer, Heidelberg (2016). https://doi.org/10.1007/978-3-662-53140-2_17

Differential Random Fault Attacks
on Certain CAESAR Stream Ciphers

Kenneth Koon-Ho Wong[(✉)] [iD], Harry Bartlett[(✉)] [iD], Leonie Simpson[(✉)] [iD],
and Ed Dawson[(✉)] [iD]

Queensland University of Technology, Brisbane, Australia
{kk.wong,h.bartlett,lr.simpson,e.dawson}@qut.edu.au

Abstract. We show that a particular class of stream ciphers – namely those in which the output function contains a bitwise AND operation – are susceptible to a differential fault attack using random faults. Several finalists and other candidates from the recent CAESAR competition fall into this category, including the AEGIS variants, Tiaoxin and the MORUS family. Attack outcomes range from key or full state recovery for Tiaoxin, to full state recovery for the AEGIS family and partial state recovery for MORUS. We present attack requirements and success probabilities on these ciphers, along with design considerations to mitigate against this attack.

Keywords: Fault attack · Differential fault attack · Random faults · Stream ciphers · CAESAR competition · Tiaoxin · AEGIS · Side-channel attack

1 Introduction

Given an implementation of a cryptographic algorithm, a fault occurring during its operation will result in an erroneous output. Differential fault attacks exploit this by comparing the output of the fault-free operation of the algorithm with the faulty output after an error is induced during the operation [1]. The difference between fault-free and faulty outputs reveals information about the encryption, which may lead to the recovery of internal state or even secret key values. Note that this implies a nonce-reuse scenario, as the same nonce must be used to generate the fault-free and faulty outputs. In 1997, Boneh et al. [1] used fault attacks against an implementation of RSA. Since then, fault attacks have been widely used against many encryption algorithms, including DES [2] and AES [3]. Fault attacks can be very powerful, such that an entire AES key can be retrieved using only a single fault injection [4].

When applying a fault attack on the implementation of a cryptographic algorithm, there are a number of aspects to consider. These include:

Electronic supplementary material The online version of this chapter (https:// doi.org/10.1007/978-3-030-40921-0_18) contains supplementary material, which is available to authorized users.

© Springer Nature Switzerland AG 2020
J. H. Seo (Ed.): ICISC 2019, LNCS 11975, pp. 297–315, 2020.
https://doi.org/10.1007/978-3-030-40921-0_18

– Number of bits to be faulted: One bit, a few bits, one byte or multiple bytes;
– Modification type: Whether the faulted bits are stuck-at-zero, stuck-at-one, bit-flipped or affected randomly;
– Fault precision: How tightly the location and/or timing of the fault can be controlled;
– Fault duration: Whether the fault will be transient or permanent.

Combinations of these parameters determine the feasibility of a fault attack. For example, an attack performed under the assumption that a fault results in flipping every bit in a targeted variable implies a very strong adversary. This bit-flipping approach is considered unrealistic in practice [5]. A random fault model, in which a fault is injected but the adversary does not know in advance the effect of the fault on a variable value, is considered more realistic since less precise control of the fault outcome by the attacker is required [5].

The fault attack described in this paper is a differential random fault attack on one targeted word at a time. Note that we have not implemented the attack, but instead we present a theoretical analysis on its feasibility and success rate, and rely on the fact that the practicality of applying such attacks has previously been demonstrated in other literature such as [5,6]. The attack we describe can be applied to stream ciphers where the keystream output function includes at least one bitwise AND operation. Several stream ciphers from the Competition for Authenticated Encryption: Security, Applicability and Robustness (CAE-SAR) have output functions of this form. These include Tiaoxin [7], the AEGIS family of stream ciphers [8] and the MORUS family of stream ciphers [9].

This paper extends on several previous fault attacks. Firstly, the bit-flipping fault attack on Tiaoxin and AEGIS in [10] used a similar approach, but assumed that the attacker could induce bit-flipping faults. For Tiaoxin, bit-flip faults on three words were required to recover the 128-bit secret key in a known plaintext scenario. For AEGIS-128, AEGIS-256 and AEGIS-128L, the internal state could be recovered using bit-flip faults on 3, 4 and 4 words, respectively (also in a known plaintext scenario). Secondly, the random fault attack applied to Tiaoxin and AEGIS-128L in [11] demonstrated that a similar attack using random faults rather than bit-flips could be applied to recover the Tiaoxin key or the AEGIS-128L internal state. A requirement for both attacks from [10,11] is that the output function includes the bitwise AND of two state words. However, [11] has an additional requirement that the cipher must have two separate output functions, and at least one output function included the bitwise XOR of one of the state words that was used in the AND operation of the other ciphertext word. This additional structure allowed the values of the random faults to be determined. Hence, the attack in [11] requires less control of the induced faults compared to [10], but is more restrictive on the required cipher structure.

The attack presented in this paper is a random fault attack which requires only that the output function includes the bitwise AND of two state words. Unlike the attacks of [11], it does not require two ciphertext words to be produced by separate output functions at each time step, and the attacker does not need to know the values of the random faults. In fact, we show that all ciphers attacked in [10] can also be attacked with random faults, in place of the less realistic bit-flipping faults that were used. Our attack also provides partial state information in the case of other CAESAR candidates, for example the MORUS family. The applicability of our attack on these ciphers highlights the importance of preventing nonce-reuse with ciphers of this type.

The remainder of this paper is organised as follows. Section 2 introduces the notation used and presents the attack algorithm. Section 3 provides an analysis on the probabilities for successful recovery of underlying state bits. Section 4 presents the results on the application of this random fault attack to several CAESAR candidates, namely the AEGIS family and Tiaoxin, where full key or state recovery can be achieved. Section 5 provides a summary of the results, including a discussion on a possible partial state recovery attack on MORUS. Section 6 concludes the paper and provides suggestions for future work.

2   Random Fault Attacks

In this section, we first introduce the notation used, and then present our random fault attack in a general form. Theoretical details of the attack and an attack algorithm then follows.

2.1   Notation

The following notation will be used throughout the paper unless otherwise stated. Let P, C, and S be the plaintext, ciphertext and internal state of the stream cipher, respectively. At each timestep t, these values are denoted by P^t, C^t, and S^t. Where multiple words are present, the i-th word of these values are shown as $P^t[i]$, $C^t[i]$ and $S^t[i]$. We also use the common notations $\oplus$ and $\otimes$ to denote the bitwise XOR and bitwise AND operations respectively.

Some ciphers in this paper use the AES round function in their state updates. The function R is used to refer to the standard AES round function [12] without the AddSubKey operation i.e.

$$R(x) = \mathsf{MixColumns}(\mathsf{ShiftRows}(\mathsf{SubBytes}(x))) \tag{1}$$

Note that this transformation is invertible. This is an important property for state recovery, and in some cases, key recovery using this random fault attack, as it allows the internal state to be clocked backwards.

2.2   Attack Outline

As stated previously, the attack presented in this paper is a differential attack. That is, the plaintext is first encrypted without error and the ciphertext output noted. The encryption is then repeated with a random fault injected into a chosen state word. A comparison of the fault free and faulty ciphertexts reveals information about the underlying state value, which in some cases may lead to recovery of key bits. Repeating the encryption with the same key and initialisation vector is referred to as nonce reuse or misuse.

Suppose a keystream generator has a ciphertext output function of the form

$$C^t = f(S^t) \oplus (g(S^t) \otimes S^t[u]) \tag{2}$$

where $f(S^t)$ and $g(S^t)$ are functions in S^t that do not depend on $S^t[u]$. Let e be a randomly generated word unknown to the attacker. This random fault e is injected into the state word $S^t[u]$ such that its contents become faulty. The relationship between the fault-free state word $S^t[u]$ and the faulty state word, denoted as $\tilde{S}^t[u]$, is given by:

$$\tilde{S}^t[u] = S^t[u] \oplus e$$

The difference between the fault-free ciphertext C^t and faulty ciphertext, denoted as $\tilde{C}^t$, is then given by:

$$C^t \oplus \tilde{C}^t = f(S^t) \oplus (g(S^t) \otimes S^t[u]) \oplus f(S^t) \oplus (g(S^t) \otimes \tilde{S}^t[u])$$
$$C^t \oplus \tilde{C}^t = g(S^t) \otimes (S^t[u] \oplus S^t[u] \oplus e)$$
$$C^t \oplus \tilde{C}^t = g(S^t) \otimes e \tag{3}$$

From Eq. 3, it can be observed that for all bits in $C^t \oplus \tilde{C}^t$ that are equal to one, those bits in $g(S^t)$ in the corresponding positions must also be one. Thus, the difference in the ciphertexts reveals information about the underlying state words that appear in $g(S^t)$.

Unlike the attacks in [10,11], the full effect of these faults are unknown to the attacker. In fact, the attacker can only determine that a given bit of e equals one if the corresponding bit value of $g(S^t)$ is also one. Apart from this, the attacker does not know whether the remaining bits of e are one or zero. Therefore, the success of this attack in recovering all bits of $g(S^t)$ depends on repeating the random fault injection multiple times, so that every bit in e is one for at least one of these faults with high probability, thus revealing all non-zero bits of $g(S^t)$. Algorithm 1 outlines the random fault attack procedure.

Algorithm 1. Random fault attack

1: Load key and initialisation vector and perform the initialisation phase.
2: Obtain the fault free ciphertext C^t.
3: Repeat Steps 1 and 2 but inject a random multi-byte fault e into the state word $S^t[u]$ to obtain the faulty ciphertext $\tilde{C}^t$.
4: Compute $C^t \oplus \tilde{C}^t$.
5: Record all bits of $C^t \oplus \tilde{C}^t$ that are equal to one, which implies that the corresponding bits in $g(S^t)$ are also ones.
6: Repeat Steps 3 to 5 until all of the bits that equal one in $g(S^t)$ are likely to have been observed. The remaining bits are assumed to be zero with high probability.

As discussed in Sect. 1, random faults are considered easier to implement than bit flips and thus the attacks we present are more practical than the bit-flipping attacks in [10]. The tradeoff is that random fault attacks are probabilistic, whereas the bit-flipping fault attacks are deterministic. However, as we will show in Sect. 3, very high success rates can be achieved with a feasible number of repeated random faults.

3   Probability Calculations

In this section, we consider the probability of determining the contents of $g(S^t)$ after applying various numbers of random faults. In doing this, we focus on the scenario discussed above, in which the attacker has only limited knowledge of the values of the faulted bits in e. In this scenario, the attacker learns that a bit of $g(S^t)$ is equal to one when the corresponding fault bit equals one, but cannot know for sure when a bit of $g(S^t)$ is zero. Note that the zero bits in $C^t \oplus \tilde{C}^t$ do not reveal zeros in $g(S^t)$ deterministically, as the attacker does not know whether this is due to a zero value in the corresponding bit of $g(S^t)$ or a zero value in the relevant bit of the error word e.

The attacker's aim is to find the value of $g(S^t)$, which can be achieved by correctly locating all of the ones in $g(S^t)$. However, the attacker does not know how many of the bits in $g(S^t)$ are actually ones. We define success for the attacker to be the event that the value of $g(S^t)$ has been correctly determined, and our analysis of the probability of success must take into account that the number of ones in $g(S^t)$ is unknown by conditioning on this random variable.

We assume initially that $g(S^t)$ is a single state word of length w bits, and also note the following assumptions:

I.   Since the fault e is assumed to be random, we assume that the probability that a given bit of e is equal to one is exactly 0.5, independently of the values of all other bits.
II. Assuming that the attacker has no prior knowledge of the state contents, we may also assume that each bit in the state is equally likely to be a one or a zero, independently of all other bits in the state.

From these assumptions, we argue as follows:

1. Consider first a single bit in $g(S^t)$. If the value of this bit is zero, then (as discussed above) we cannot detect this directly. However, if the value of this bit is one, then the probability $p_{b,1}(s)$ that the value of this bit has not been determined after applying s faults is simply the probability that this bit is equal to zero in all s instances of e, namely $p_{b,1}(s) = 0.5^s$.
2. Now consider the entire word $g(S^t)$ containing w independent bits and suppose that the number of ones in this word happens to be N (with $0 \leq N \leq w$). Then:
    (a) The probability $p_N(k;s)$ that exactly k ones in this word have not yet been recovered after applying s random (multi-byte) faults is given by the binomial distribution $\text{Bi}(N, p_{b,1}(s))$; specifically, $p_N(k;s) = \binom{N}{k} p_{b,1}(s)^k (1 - p_{b,1}(s))^{N-k} = \binom{N}{k} 0.5^{sk} (1 - 0.5^s)^{N-k}$.

Table 1. Success rate $P_S(s; w)$ for $w = 128$ with different numbers of faults

Number of faults (s)	6	8	10	12	14	16
Success rate $P_S(s; 128)$	36.64%	77.86%	93.94%	98.45%	99.61%	99.90%

Table 2. Success rate for full recovery of 128-bit words using attacks from [11]

Number of faults	6	8	10	12	14
Calculated success rate	13.32%	60.59%	88.24%	96.92%	99.22%
Simulated results: Tiaoxin [11, Table 2]	12.81%	61.72%	87.64%	96.78%	99.16%
Simulated results: AEGIS-128L [11, Table 5]	13.18%	59.58%	88.35%	96.70%	99.07%

(b) The probability of recovering at least m ones out of N after applying s random (multi-byte) faults is equal to the probability that $N - m$ or fewer ones remain undiscovered after applying this number of faults. We denote this probability as $P_N(m; s)$; it can be calculated by using the cumulative form of the binomial distribution described above, namely as $P_N(m; s) = \sum_{k=0}^{N-m} p_N(k; s)$.

(c) The probability of discovering all N ones in a w-bit word after s (or fewer) multi-byte faults is then equal to $P_N(N; s) = p_N(0; s) = (1 - 0.5^s)^N$.

3. It follows from Assumption II that the number of ones (N) in the state word of Step 2 has a binomial distribution $\mathrm{Bi}(w, 0.5)$ with $\Pr(N = n) = \binom{w}{n} 0.5^n 0.5^{w-n} = \binom{w}{n} 0.5^w$.

4. Finally, let $P_S(s; w)$ denote the probability that the attacker has discovered all the ones in a w-bit state word after applying s random (multi-byte) faults (and without knowing how many ones there are to find). This probability is given by the following expression (conditioning on the value of N):

$$
\begin{aligned}
P_S(s; w) &= \sum_{n=0}^{w} P_N(N; s | N = n) \Pr(N = n) \\
&= \sum_{n=0}^{w} p_n(0; s) \Pr(N = n) \\
&= \sum_{n=0}^{w} \binom{w}{n} 0.5^{w-n} 0.5^n (1 - 0.5^s)^n \qquad (4) \\
&= \sum_{n=0}^{w} \binom{w}{n} 0.5^{w-n} (0.5 - 0.5^{s+1})^n = (1 - 0.5^{s+1})^w
\end{aligned}
$$

Table 1 presents some calculated values of $P_S(s; w)$ for the case $w = 128$ and various values of s. Note that the success rate exceeds 99% for 14 or more faults. To verify the applicability of our theoretical analysis, we applied a similar process to determine the theoretical probabilities of the attacks from [11]. Table 2 shows that our calculated success rates agree closely with the simulation results reported in [11].

We now relax the assumption that $g(S^t)$ is a single state word. Assuming that the attacker has no prior knowledge of the state contents S^t, Assumption II still holds for any state word. Provided that $g(S^t)$ contains only bitwise operations, the contents of each bit of $g(S^t)$ are then statistically independent of one another. Now suppose that the probability that a particular bit in $g(S^t)$ equals one (independently of all other bits) is $p_{b,1}^{(g)}$. The distribution of N in step 3 then becomes $\mathrm{Bi}(w, p_{b,1}^{(g)})$ with $\Pr(N = n) = \binom{w}{n}(p_{b,1}^{(g)})^n (1 - p_{b,1}^{(g)})^{w-n}$ and Eq. 4 becomes:

$$P_S(s; w) = \sum_{n=0}^{w} \binom{w}{n}(1 - p_{b,1}^{(g)})^{w-n} (p_{b,1}^{(g)})^n (1 - 0.5^s)^n$$

$$= \sum_{n=0}^{w} \binom{w}{n}(1 - p_{b,1}^{(g)})^{w-n} (p_{b,1}^{(g)} - p_{b,1}^{(g)} \times 0.5^s)^n$$

$$= (1 - p_{b,1}^{(g)} \times 0.5^s)^w$$

Now, provided that $g(S^t)$ contains at least one linear term, we may assume from II that $p_{b,1}^{(g)} = 0.5$ and the same result is obtained as before. On the other hand, if $g(S^t)$ is purely quadratic, then $p_{b,1}^{(g)} = 0.25$ and $P_S(s; w)$ becomes $P_S(s; w) = (1 - 0.25 \times 0.5^s)^w = (1 - 0.5^{s+2})^w$. Similar analyses can also be given for other forms of $g(S^t)$.

4   Key and State Recovery Attacks

In this section, we describe key recovery and full state recovery attacks on two CAESAR competition candidates using random fault injections. These are the AEGIS family of stream ciphers [8] and Tiaoxin [7]. Within the AEGIS family, AEGIS-128 (version 1.1) is in the final portfolio of the CAESAR competition for Use Case 2 (High-performance applications), whereas AEGIS-256 and AEGIS-128L are finalists for the same use case. Tiaoxin (version 2) is a third round candidate. In the cases of AEGIS-128L and Tiaoxin, ciphertext-only attacks are possible. Our cipher descriptions mostly focus on the encryption phase, which is where the random faults are injected. For details of the other phases, such as initialisation, associated data processing finalisation and tag generation, please refer to the respective cipher specification documents.

4.1   AEGIS-128

AEGIS-128 has an internal state with five 128-bit register stages $S^t[0], S^t[1], \ldots, S^t[4]$, and thus has a total state size of $5 \times 128 = 640$ bits. The internal state is updated at each timestep using a nonlinear state update function defined as follows.

$$S^{t+1}[i] = \begin{cases} R(S^t[4]) \oplus S^t[0] \oplus M^t & \text{for } i = 0 \\ R(S^t[i-1]) \oplus S^t[i] & \text{for } 1 \leq i \leq 4 \end{cases} \tag{5}$$

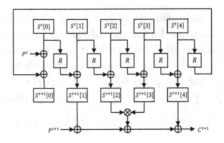

Fig. 1. AEGIS-128 state update and output

This update function has one external input, M^t, and nonlinearity is provided by applying the transformation R to the contents of each register stage, as shown in Fig. 1. During the encryption phase, each 128-bit plaintext block P^t is encrypted to obtain the corresponding ciphertext block C^t as per the AEGIS-128 output function:

$$C^t = P^t \oplus S^t[1] \oplus S^t[4] \oplus S^t[2]S^t[3] \tag{6}$$

This function is of the form identified in Eq. 2, which means that the random fault attack described in Sect. 2.2 can be applied to this cipher.

Attack Procedure. Comparing with the generic form in Eq. 2, we can obtain the following parameter sets:

$$(f(S^t), g(S^t), S^t[u]) = (P^t \oplus S^t[1] \oplus S^t[4], S^t[2], S^t[3]) \tag{7}$$
$$(f(S^t), g(S^t), S^t[u]) = (P^t \oplus S^t[1] \oplus S^t[4], S^t[3], S^t[2]) \tag{8}$$

Therefore, using the parameter set given in Eq. 7, the attacker can apply random faults on $S^t[3]$ to recover the contents of $S^t[2]$ as per the analysis presented in Sect. 2.2. Alternatively, using Eq. 8, random faults can be applied on $S^t[2]$ to recover $S^t[3]$ in a similar manner.

State Recovery. To extend the recovery of single stages to the entire internal state, observe from Eq. 5 that

$$S^t[2] = R(S^{t-1}[1]) \oplus S^{t-1}[2])$$
$$S^{t-1}[1] = R^{-1}(S^t[2] \oplus S^{t-1}[2])$$

Therefore, recovering of $S[2]$ over two consecutive timesteps permits the recovery of $S[1]$ on the earlier timestep. The process continues into $S^{t-2}[0]$ as follows.

$$S^{t-1}[1] = R(S^{t-2}[0]) \oplus S^{t-2}[1])$$
$$S^{t-2}[0] = R^{-1}(S^{t-1}[1] \oplus S^{t-2}[1])$$
$$= R^{-1}(R^{-1}(S^t[2] \oplus S^{t-1}[2]) \oplus R^{-1}(S^{t-1}[2] \oplus S^{t-2}[2]))$$

In summary, applying random faults on $S^t[2]$ with Eq. 7 on three consecutive timesteps $t, t-1, t-2$ allows recovery of the stages $S^{t-2}[0]$, $S^{t-2}[1]$, $S^{t-2}[2]$ at timestep $t-2$. Additionally, applying the attack with Eq. 8 allows recovery of $S^{t-2}[3]$.

To complete the full state recovery, the value $S^{t-3}[4]$ needs to be computed. Using one known plaintext block P^{t-2} and Eq. 6 gives

$$S^{t-2}[4] = P^{t-2} \oplus C^{t-2} \oplus S^{t-2}[1] \oplus S^{t-2}[2]S^{t-2}[3] \tag{9}$$

Once the entire internal state is known at a certain timestep t, the cipher can be clocked forwards to recover all subsequent plaintext using known ciphertext and state contents. This attack strategy improves on the requirement of two known plaintext blocks in [10], at the expense of injecting faults across three rounds instead of two.

Success Rate. For the above attack strategy, we require four targets stages, namely $S^t[2], S^{t-1}[2], S^{t-2}[2], S^{t-2}[3]$, to recover the entire AEGIS-128 internal state. From the analysis in Sect. 3, assuming that we require a 99.9% probability of correctly recovering the contents of each target state, 16 random faults would be injected for each target state, so a total of 64 random faults would be carried out. The success probability of the full state recovery attack is about $0.999^4 \approx 0.996$. Higher probabilities can be achieved if more random faults are made on each target stage.

4.2   AEGIS-256

AEGIS-256 has an internal state with six 128-bit register stages $S^t[0], S^t[1], \ldots, S^t[5]$, and thus has a total state size of $6 \times 128 = 768$ bits. The internal state is updated at each timestep using a nonlinear state update function defined as follows.

$$S^{t+1}[i] = \begin{cases} R(S^t[5]) \oplus S^t[0] \oplus M^t & \text{for } i = 0 \\ R(S^t[i-1]) \oplus S^t[i] & \text{for } 1 \leq i \leq 5 \end{cases} \tag{10}$$

This update function has one external input M^t, and nonlinearity is provided by applying the AES round function R to the contents of each register stage, as shown in Fig. 2. During the encryption phase, each 128-bit plaintext block P^t is encrypted to obtain the corresponding ciphertext block C^t as per the AEGIS-256 output function:

$$C^t = P^t \oplus S^t[1] \oplus S^t[4] \oplus S^t[5] \oplus S^t[2]S^t[3] \tag{11}$$

This function is of the form identified in Eq. 2, which means that the random fault attack described in Sect. 2.2 can be applied to this cipher.

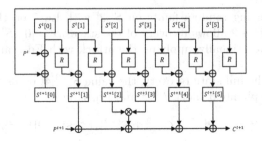

Fig. 2. AEGIS-256 state update and output

Attack Procedure. The AEGIS-256 output function differs from the AEGIS-128 output function by only a linear term $S^t[5]$, so the same random fault attack strategy applies. Comparing with the generic form in Eq. 2, we can obtain:

$$(f(S^t), g(S^t), S^t[u]) = (P^t \oplus S^t[1] \oplus S^t[4] \oplus S^t[5], S^t[2], S^t[3]) \qquad (12)$$

$$(f(S^t), g(S^t), S^t[u]) = (P^t \oplus S^t[1] \oplus S^t[4] \oplus S^t[5], S^t[3], S^t[2]) \qquad (13)$$

Therefore, applying random faults on $S^t[3]$ allows an attacker to recover the contents of $S^t[2]$ as per the analysis presented in Sect. 2.2. Alternatively, random faults can be applied on $S^t[2]$ to recover $S^t[3]$ in a similar manner.

State Recovery. The process for full state recovery is also similar to that for AEGIS-128 as we also have, for $1 \leq i \leq 2$:

$$S^{t-i}[2-i] = R^{-1}\left(\bigoplus_{k=0}^{i} R^{-1}(S^{t-k}[2] \oplus S^{t-k-1}[2])\right) \qquad (14)$$

This means that applying the random fault attack on three consecutive timesteps $t, t-1, t-2$ allows recovery of the stages $S^{t-2}[0], S^{t-2}[1], S^{t-2}[2]$ at timestep $t-2$. Additionally, applying the attack with Eq. 13 allows recovery of $S^{t-2}[3]$. In total, the attack is applied four times.

To complete the full state recovery, the values of $S^{t-2}[4], S^{t-2}[5]$ need to be computed. Using one known plaintext block P^{t-2} gives

$$S^{t-2}[4] \oplus S^{t-2}[5] = P^{t-2} \oplus C^{t-2} \oplus S^{t-2}[1] \oplus S^{t-2}[2]S^{t-2}[3] \qquad (15)$$

This cannot uniquely determine $S^{t-3}[4]$ and $S^{t-3}[5]$. However, from the state update function it is also known that

$$S^{t-1}[0] = R(S^{t-2}[5]) \oplus S^{t-2}[0] \oplus P^{t-2} \qquad (16)$$

Therefore, it is possible to calculate $S^{t-2}[5]$ if an extra fault attack is carried out at time $t+1$ to recover $S^{t+1}[2]$, so that $S^{t-1}[0]$ can be computed from Eq. 14. Once $S^{t-2}[5]$ is known, $S^{t-2}[4]$ can be readily computed via Eq. 15.

Similar to AEGIS-128, once the entire state is known at a certain timestep t, the cipher can be clocked forwards to recover all subsequent plaintext using known ciphertext and state contents. This attack strategy requires only one known plaintext block, which improves on the requirement of three known plaintext blocks in [10], at the expense of injecting faults across four rounds instead of three.

Success Rate. For the above attack strategy, we require five targets stages, namely $S^{t+1}[2]$, $S^t[2]$, $S^{t-1}[2]$, $S^{t-2}[2]$, $S^{t-2}[3]$, to recover the entire AEGIS-128 internal state. From the analysis in Sect. 3, assuming that we require a 99.9% probability of correctly recovering the contents of each target stage, 16 random faults would be injected for each target state, so a total of 80 random faults would be carried out. The success probability of the full state recovery attack is about $0.999^5 \approx 0.995$. Higher probabilities can be achieved if more random faults are made on each target stage.

4.3 AEGIS-128L

AEGIS-128L has an internal state with eight 128-bit register stages $S^t[0], S^t[1], \ldots, S^t[7]$, and thus has a total state size of $8 \times 128 = 1024$ bits. The internal state is updated at each time instant using a nonlinear state update function StateUpdate128L(S^t, M_0^t, M_1^t). This update function has two external inputs, M_0^t and M_1^t, and nonlinearity is provided by applying the transformation function R to the contents of each register stage, as shown in Fig. 3. Under this update function, the state of AEGIS-128L at time $t+1$ is defined as:

$$S^{t+1}[i] = \begin{cases} R(S^t[7]) \oplus S^t[0] \oplus M_0^t & \text{for } i = 0 \\ R(S^t[3]) \oplus S^t[4] \oplus M_1^t & \text{for } i = 4 \\ R(S^t[i-1]) \oplus S^t[i] & \text{for } i \in \{1,2,3,5,6,7\} \end{cases} \quad (17)$$

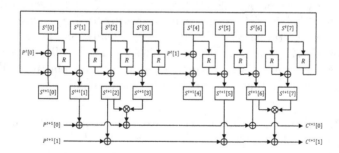

Fig. 3. AEGIS-128L state update and output

In contrast with AEGIS-128 and AEGIS-256, during the encryption phase each 256-bit plaintext block is split into two words: $P^t = P^t[0]||P^t[1]$, which are encrypted separately and then combined to obtain the corresponding ciphertext block $C^t = C^t[0]||C^t[1]$.

The output functions of AEGIS-128L for the two words in each block are

$$C^t[0] = P^t[0] \oplus S^t[1] \oplus S^t[6] \oplus S^t[2]S^t[3] \tag{18}$$

$$C^t[1] = P^t[1] \oplus S^t[2] \oplus S^t[5] \oplus S^t[6]S^t[7] \tag{19}$$

These function are of the form identified in Eq. 2, which means that the random fault attack described in Sect. 2.2 can be applied to this cipher.

Attack Procedure. Comparing with the generic form in Eq. 2, we can obtain four sets of attack parameters from the two output functions. From Eq. 18, the parameters corresponding to the first output function are:

$$(f_0(S^t), g_0(S^t), S^t[u]) = (P^t[0] \oplus S^t[1] \oplus S^t[6], S^t[2], S^t[3]) \tag{20}$$

$$(f_0(S^t), g_0(S^t), S^t[u]) = (P^t[0] \oplus S^t[1] \oplus S^t[6], S^t[3], S^t[2]) \tag{21}$$

From Eq. 19, the parameters corresponding to the second output function are:

$$(f_1(S^t), g_1(S^t), S^t[u]) = (P^t[1] \oplus S^t[2] \oplus S^t[5], S^t[6], S^t[7]) \tag{22}$$

$$(f_1(S^t), g_1(S^t), S^t[u]) = (P^t[1] \oplus S^t[2] \oplus S^t[5], S^t[7], S^t[6]) \tag{23}$$

Therefore, for example, at each timestep we can apply random faults to states $S^t[3], S^t[7]$ to recover the contents of $S^t[2], S^t[6]$ respectively. Alternatively, applying random faults to states $S^t[2], S^t[6]$ allows recovery of $S^t[3], S^t[7]$ respectively.

State Recovery. If the plaintext words $P^t[0]$, $P^t[1]$, $P^{t+1}[0]$ and $P^{t+1}[1]$ are also known, then the process used in [10] can be followed to obtain the whole state content at time t. However, our attack can also be modified to recover the entire state even when the attacker does not have access to the plaintext, by following a similar process to that used for AEGIS-128 and AEGIS-256. By recovering the values of $S^t[6], S^{t-1}[6], S^{t-2}[6]$ using Eq. 22, one can determine the values of $S^{t-2}[5], S^{t-2}[4]$. Likewise, by recovering $S^t[2], S^{t-1}[2], S^{t-2}[2]$ using Eq. 20, one can determine $S^{t-2}[1]$ and $S^{t-2}[0]$. Finally, $S^{t-2}[3], S^{t-2}[7]$ can be recovered by Eqs. 21 and 23 respectively. This means the all state contents at time $t - 2$ are known without having to use any known plaintext. Thus, this attack is stronger than that reported in [10], being a ciphertext-only attack.

Success Rate. For the above attack strategy, we require eight target stages, namely $S^t[2], S^{t-1}[2], S^{t-2}[2], S^{t-2}[3], S^t[6], S^{t-1}[6], S^{t-2}[6], S^{t-2}[7]$. From the analysis in Sect. 3, assuming that we require a 99.9% probability of correctly recovering the contents of each target state, 16 random faults would be injected for each target state, so a total of 128 random faults would be carried out. The success probability of the full state recovery attack is about $0.999^8 \approx 0.992$. Higher probabilities can be achieved if more random faults are made on each target stage.

4.4   Tiaoxin

Tiaoxin has an internal state consisting of three components T_3, T_4 and T_6 with three, four and six 128-bit stages respectively, and thus has a total state size of $13 \times 128 = 1664$ bits. Tiaoxin uses a 128-bit key K and a 128-bit initialisation vector IV. The state update of Tiaoxin is defined as

$$T_s^{t+1}[i] = \begin{cases} R(T_s^t[s-1]) \oplus T_s^t[0] \oplus M_s^t & \text{for } i = 0 \\ R(T_s^t[0]) \oplus Z_0 & \text{for } i = 1 \\ T_s^t[i-1] & 0 \le i \le s-1 \end{cases} \tag{24}$$

where $s \in \{3, 4, 6\}$, and M_3^t, M_4^t and M_6^t are the external inputs to T_3, T_4 and T_6, respectively. Therefore, all stages except for the first two stages in each component are updated by shifting, while the first two stages of each component are updated nonlinearly using the transformation function R defined in Sect. 2.1. Figure 4 shows the initialisation and encryption process of Tiaoxin. As shown in the figure, the plaintext P is divided into two blocks $P^t = P^t[0] \| P^t[1]$, which are successively loaded into the internal state of each component. Each ciphertext block C^t is then computed after loading the corresponding plaintext block. At the start of the initialisation phase, the state is loaded as

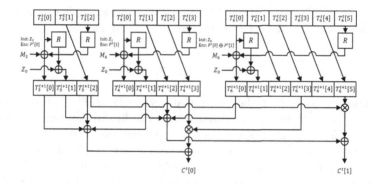

Fig. 4. Tiaoxin-346 state update and output

$$T_3 = (K, K, IV) \qquad T_4 = (K, K, IV, Z_0) \qquad T_6 = (K, K, IV, Z_1, 0, 0)$$

where K is the key, IV is the initialisation vector, and Z_0, Z_1 are known public constants. The state is then updated 15 times using the external inputs $(M_3^t, M_4^t, M_6^t) = (Z_0, Z_1, Z_0)$ to obtain the initial state.

Once the initial state is obtained, the encryption phase begins. At each timestep, the external inputs are composed from plaintext blocks, namely $(M_3^t, M_4^t, M_6^t) = (P^t[0], P^t[1], P^t[0] \oplus P^t[1])$. The output functions of Tiaoxin for the two blocks are

$$C^t[0] = T_3^{t+1}[0] \oplus T_3^{t+1}[2] \oplus T_4^{t+1}[1] \oplus T_6^{t+1}[3]T_4^{t+1}[3] \tag{25}$$

$$C^t[1] = T_6^{t+1}[0] \oplus T_4^{t+1}[2] \oplus T_3^{t+1}[1] \oplus T_6^{t+1}[5]T_3^{t+1}[2] \tag{26}$$

These functions are of the form identified in Eq. 2, which means that the random fault attack described in Sect. 2.2 can be applied to this cipher.

Attack Procedure. Comparing with the generic form in Eq. 2, we can obtain four sets of attack parameters from the two output functions. From Eq. 25, the parameters are:

$$(f_0(S^t), g_0(S^t), S^t[u]) = (T_3^t[0] \oplus T_3^t[2] \oplus T_4^t[1], T_6^t[3], T_4^t[3]) \tag{27}$$

$$(f_0(S^t), g_0(S^t), S^t[u]) = (T_3^t[0] \oplus T_3^t[2] \oplus T_4^t[1], T_4^t[3], T_6^t[3]) \tag{28}$$

From Eq. 26, the parameters are:

$$(f_1(S^t), g_1(S^t), S^t[u]) = (T_6^t[0] \oplus T_4^t[2] \oplus T_3^t[1], T_3^t[2], T_6^t[5]) \tag{29}$$

$$(f_1(S^t), g_1(S^t), S^t[u]) = (T_6^t[0] \oplus T_4^t[2] \oplus T_3^t[1], T_6^t[5], T_3^t[2]) \tag{30}$$

Since the state updates of T_3, T_4, T_6 are independent, it makes sense to target the shortest register, which is T_3. One set of parameters allows recovery of a stage in T_3, namely Eq. 29, through which $T^t[2]$ is recovered.

Key Recovery. Similar to the AEGIS family of stream ciphers, the following recurrence relations hold for the state update of T_3 in Tiaoxin:

$$T_3^{t-1}[i] = \begin{cases} T_3^t[i-1] & 1 \leq i \leq 2 \\ R^{-1}(T_3^t[1] \oplus Z_0) & i = 0 \end{cases} \tag{31}$$

This enables us to recover the entire state contents of T_3^{t-2} after recovering $T_3^t[2], T_3^{t-1}[2], T_3^{t-2}[2]$ using the parameters in Eq. 30 through random faults on $T_6^t[5], T_6^{t-1}[5], T_6^{t-2}[5]$. It is also possible to recover the secret key for Tiaoxin by extending the attack into the initialisation phase provided that the single plaintext block $P^0[0]$ is known. First, apply the above attack to recover the state contents of T_3^1. Then, use the process shown in Fig. 5 to recover T_3^0 and subsequently the key. Note that the external input Z_0 used during initialisation is public, so the updates of state component T_3 can be reversed from T_3^0 all the way to the beginning of the initialisation phase, which is T_3^{-15}. The key can then be readily obtained from the initial contents of $T_3^{-15}[0]$ from the loaded state. From this point, all components in the state of Tiaoxin-346 can be initialised with the known key K and initialisation vector IV, and the cipher can then be clocked forwards to encrypt and verify any message chosen by the attacker.

In light of the above comments, the security of this cipher against our key recovery attack depends entirely on maintaining the secrecy of the initial plaintext block. In cases where the message format requires particular header information to be included at the start of the message, this may be problematic.

State Recovery. If the initial plaintext block is not known, a state recovery attack is still possible. Using the attack parameters in Eqs. 29, 28, 30 allows

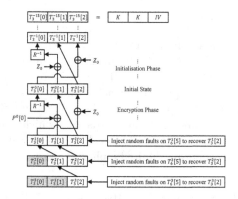

Fig. 5. Tiaoxin key recovery via random fault attack on T_3

recovery of $T_3[2], T_4[3], T_6[5]$ respectively. Observe that recurrence relations similar to T_3 shown in Eq. 31 also holds for T_4, T_6, namely:

$$T_4^{t-1}[i] = \begin{cases} T_4^t[i-1] & 1 \leq i \leq 3 \\ R^{-1}(T_3^t[1] \oplus Z_0) & i = 0 \end{cases}$$

$$T_6^{t-1}[i] = \begin{cases} T_6^t[i-1] & 1 \leq i \leq 5 \\ R^{-1}(T_3^t[1] \oplus Z_0) & i = 0 \end{cases}$$

Therefore, by recovering stages $T_3^{t-3}[2]$, $T_3^{t-4}[2]$, $T_3^{t-5}[2]$ using Eq. 29, $T_4^{t-2}[2]$, $T_4^{t-3}[3]$, $T_4^{t-4}[3]$, $T_4^{t-5}[3]$ using Eqs. 27 or 28, and $T_6^t[5]$, $T_6^{t-1}[5]$, $T_6^{t-2}[5]$, $T_6^{t-3}[5]$, $T_6^{t-4}[5]$, $T_6^{t-5}[5]$ using Eq. 30, we can recover the entire state $(T_3^{t-5}, T_4^{t-5}, T_6^{t-5})$ at time $t-5$ without the need of any known plaintext.

Success Rates. For the key recovery attack, we require three target stages. From the analysis in Sect. 3, assuming that we require a 99.9% probability of correctly recovering the contents of each target stage, 16 random faults would be injected for each target state, so a total of 48 random faults would be carried out. It can then be deduced that the success probability of the full key recovery attack is about $0.999^3 \approx 0.997$. For the state recovery attack, there are 13 target stages and hence 208 random fault injections. The gives a success probability of about $0.999^{13} \approx 0.987$ if the same attack parameters as the key recovery attack are chosen. Higher probabilities can be achieved if more random faults are made on each target stage.

5 Results

In this section, we summarise the results of our successful attacks on AEGIS and Tiaoxin presented in Sect. 4, and also discuss a further application of our attack on another CAESAR cipher, MORUS, where we achieve partial success.

5.1   Successful Attacks

We first compare the random fault attacks presented in this paper on the AEGIS family of ciphers and Tiaoxin with the bit-flipping fault attacks presented in [10] and the random fault attacks of [11]. Table 3 summarises the attack outcomes achieved and the corresponding attack requirements. In the table, "P'txt" denotes the number of known plaintext blocks required for the attack, whereas "Targets" denotes the number of state words into which random faults are to be injected to implement the attack. For each targeted state word, each of the attacks requires a corresponding faulted ciphertext word to be observed.

Table 3. Comparison of fault attacks on CAESAR candidates

Cipher	Recovery type	Bit-flipping attack [10]		Random fault attack [11]		Random fault attack (this work)	
		P'txt	Targets	P'txt	Targets	P'txt	Targets
AEGIS-128	State	2	3	N/A		1	4
AEGIS-256	State	2	4	N/A		1	5
AEGIS-128L	State	4	4	0	8	0	8
Tiaoxin	Key	1	3	2	6	1	3
Tiaoxin	State	N/A		N/A		0	13

The attack in [10] differs from the attack presented in this paper as it requires bit-flipping faults rather than the more practical random faults. There are also differences in the amount of plaintext required, with our attacks requiring fewer known plaintext blocks. The attack presented in the current paper also requires less plaintext than the attack of [11] while being applicable to a greater number of ciphers, since our attack requires fewer conditions on the cipher's structure. In addition, in the cases of AEGIS-128L and Tiaoxin state recovery, our attack is a ciphertext-only attack, requiring no knowledge of the plaintext.

5.2   Partially Successful Attacks

We now discuss briefly the potential application of this attack to the MORUS cipher family [9], which was a third-round candidate in the CAESAR competition. The ciphertext output function for each of the ciphers in this family has the form described in Eq. 2 so it is possible to obtain partial state information from these ciphers by applying the attack of Sect. 2. However, the overall structure of these ciphers prevents the attack from being extended to a full state recovery or key recovery attack.

Each cipher in the MORUS family has a state comprising five state words, and the ciphertext output function for each of these ciphers operates at the word level. In each case, our basic attack can be applied to obtain the contents of two of the five state words at any time step during the encryption phase. If the attack is performed at two adjacent time steps, it is also possible to determine the values of these two words through all the intermediate updates between these time steps. However, there does not appear to be a straightforward way to determine the contents of the remaining three state words from this known information, due to the use of AND operations between state words during the update process introduces nonlinearity and prevents recovery of those unknown state words.

For a full description on our attack on MORUS, the reader is referred to our supplementary material [13] on the IACR Cryptology ePrint Archive.

6 Discussion and Conclusion

This paper shows that attacks based on random faults are possible, under the nonce reuse scenario, on ciphers where the output function includes a bitwise AND operation. When using any such cipher, care must therefore be taken to avoid nonce reuse so that an attacker cannot obtain multiple encryptions using the same parameters. We demonstrated successful application of this random fault attack to several CAESAR finalists and other candidates. In particular, ciphertext-only attacks resulting in state recovery are possible for AEGIS-128L and Tiaoxin whereas a single plaintext block allows key recovery in Tiaoxin and state recovery in AEGIS-128 and AEGIS-256.

This paper has demonstrated that our random fault attack strategy is particularly applicable to ciphers where the following conditions are satisfied.

- The ciphertext output functions contains one quadratic term and is otherwise linear.
- The internal state transitions contain linear paths across different stages and do not have external input.

Our attack was less successful on ciphers in the MORUS family, which also have the form required for implementing the random fault attack. From our examination of these ciphers, we observe that a cipher's overall susceptibility to this random fault attack can be reduced by ensuring that the state update function provides nonlinear mixing of state words when moving from one time step to the next. Akin to this, it should not be possible to use the state update function to determine the value of any state word that is not in an AND term in the output function purely from the knowledge (at one or more time steps) of state words that do appear in an AND term in the output function. Other potentially useful strategies for preventing partial recovery of state information from leading to full state recovery or key recovery include the following:

- Any state word which appears within an AND term in the output function should occur in several such terms.
- State words which appear within AND terms in the output function should be as close as possible to structural features (e.g. external input) which prevent them being clocked back to reveal information at the previous time step. (For example, changing the non-linear term in the output function for AEGIS-128 to $S^t[0]S^t[1]$ would prevent the attacker from obtaining any of $S^t[2]$, $S^t[3]$ or $S^t[4]$ without knowledge of additional plaintext blocks.)

- The state update function during the initialisation phase of the cipher should not be reversible without knowledge of the secret key.

The first strategy restricts an attacker to obtaining the value of some combination of state words from each run of the attack, rather than obtaining a single state word directly. The second strategy limits the amount of state that can be recovered from repeated applications of the attack at successive times steps, and the third prevents the attacker from turning state recovery into key recovery.

This paper leaves several areas for future investigation. Firstly, further analysis is required to determine whether the existing attacks on MORUS can be extended to retrieve further information, such as a full state recovery. Secondly, we have only analysed the application of this attack to three CAESAR candidates. There may be more ciphers with similar output functions that are therefore susceptible to this attack. Finally, work is required to determine whether the mitigation strategies mentioned above introduce other vulnerabilities that could be exploited by alternative attacks.

References

1. Boneh, D., DeMillo, R.A., Lipton, R.J.: On the importance of checking cryptographic protocols for faults. In: Fumy, W. (ed.) EUROCRYPT 1997. LNCS, vol. 1233, pp. 37–51. Springer, Heidelberg (1997). https://doi.org/10.1007/3-540-69053-0_4

2. Biham, E., Shamir, A.: Differential fault analysis of secret key cryptosystems. In: Kaliski, B.S. (ed.) CRYPTO 1997. LNCS, vol. 1294, pp. 513–525. Springer, Heidelberg (1997). https://doi.org/10.1007/BFb0052259

3. Blömer, J., Seifert, J.-P.: Fault based cryptanalysis of the advanced encryption standard (AES). In: Wright, R.N. (ed.) FC 2003. LNCS, vol. 2742, pp. 162–181. Springer, Heidelberg (2003). https://doi.org/10.1007/978-3-540-45126-6_12

4. Tunstall, M., Mukhopadhyay, D., Ali, S.: Differential fault analysis of the advanced encryption standard using a single fault. In: Ardagna, C.A., Zhou, J. (eds.) WISTP 2011. LNCS, vol. 6633, pp. 224–233. Springer, Heidelberg (2011). https://doi.org/10.1007/978-3-642-21040-2_15

5. Barenghi, A., Breveglieri, L., Koren, I., Naccache, D.: Fault injection attacks on cryptographic devices: theory, practice, and countermeasures. Proc. IEEE 100(11), 3056–3076 (2012)

6. Skorobogatov, S.P., Anderson, R.J.: Optical fault induction attacks. In: Kaliski, B.S., Koç, K., Paar, C. (eds.) CHES 2002. LNCS, vol. 2523, pp. 2–12. Springer, Heidelberg (2003). https://doi.org/10.1007/3-540-36400-5_2

7. Nikolic, I.: Tiaoxin-346 (version 2.1). CAESAR competition. https://competitions.cr.yp.to/round3/tiaoxinv21.pdf

8. Wu, H., Preneel, B.: AEGIS: a fast authenticated encryption algorithm (v1.1) CAESAR competition. https://competitions.cr.yp.to/round3/aegisv11.pdf

9. Wu, H., Huang, T.: The authenticated cipher MORUS (version 2). CAESAR competition. https://competitions.cr.yp.to/round3/morusv2.pdf

10. Dey, P., Rohit, R.S., Sarkar, S., Adhikari, A.: Differential fault analysis on tiaoxin and aegis family of ciphers. In: Mueller, P., Thampi, S.M., Alam Bhuiyan, M.Z., Ko, R., Doss, R., Alcaraz Calero, J.M. (eds.) SSCC 2016. CCIS, vol. 625, pp. 74–86. Springer, Singapore (2016). https://doi.org/10.1007/978-981-10-2738-3_7

11. Bartlett, H., Dawson, E., Qahur Al Mahri, H., Salam, M.I., Simpson, L., Wong, K.K.-H.: Random fault attacks on a class of stream ciphers. Secur. Commun. Netw. **2019**, Article ID 1680263 (2019). https://doi.org/10.1155/2019/1680263
12. Daemen, J., Rijmen, V.: The Design of Rijndael. Springer, Berlin (2002). https://doi.org/10.1007/978-3-662-04722-4
13. Wong, K.K.-H., Bartlett, H., Simpson, L., Dawson, E.: Differential Random Fault Attacks on Certain CAESAR Stream Ciphers (Supplementary Material). Cryptology ePrint Archive, Report 2020/022 (2020). https://eprint.iacr.org/2020/022

Author Index

Printed in the United States
By Bookmasters